Motor Control and Motor Learning in Rehabilitation

Carolyn A. Crutchfield. Ed.D., P.T.

Professor
Department of Physical Therapy
Georgia State University
Atlanta, Georgia

Marylou R. Barnes Ed.D., P.T.

Professor
Department of Physical Therapy
Georgia State University
Atlanta, Georgia

Consulting Author
Special contributions in concept and content,
 including Chapters 5,6,7, and 10 by
Carolyn B. Heriza Ed.D., P.T.
Research Director and Associate Professor
Physical Therapy Program
University of Colorado
Denver, Colorado

Contributors:

Chapter 13 contributed by
Susan J. Herdman, Ph.D., P.T.
Assistant Professor
Department of Otolaryngology-Head and Neck Surgery
Johns Hopkins University
Baltimore, Maryland

Case Studies Contributed by

Lois Deming Hedman, M.S., P.T.
Instructor in Clinical Physical Therapy
Programs in Physical Therapy
Northwestern University Medical School
Chicago, Illinois

Mary M. Castiglione, P.T.
Coordinator of Physical Therapy at
Meadowbrook of Atlanta Community
Reentry Rehabilitation Program,
Atlanta, Georgia

Editorial Consultant
Marilyn J. Lister P.T.
Berryville, Virginia

Stokesville Publishing Co.

Table of Contents

Why Read This Book?

The major reason a physical or occupational therapist or a student of those disciplines picks up a book of this nature is to gain insight into the causes of neurologic disorders and the treatment of clients who are afflicted with them. Clients with neurologic deficits provide a particularly challenging problem to therapists. The clients' abnormal movement patterns and muscular weaknesses cause their movements to differ from the smooth, coordinated movement and skills seen in most individuals. Attempts to improve these abnormal movements and skills is usually fraught with frustration and sometimes met with limited success.

As clinical therapists, our ways of knowing are often less than optimum. According to Kerlinger (Doudlah 1981), there are four ways of knowing: (1) tenacity--we know it because we always believed it; (2) authority--we know because some expert said it; (3) a priori--we know because it seems reasonable from a known or assumed cause based on theory rather than experience or experiment; and (4) scientific method--we know because there is documentary evidence to support conclusions. Doudlah (1981) rightfully suggests that therapists rely too heavily on authority, tenacity and reasonableness rather than on science.

Physical therapy and occupational therapy professions both suffer from the lack of a body of scientific research that yields data to support and explain the interventions applied to clients. While exciting projects are in the offing, it will be some time before even half of what is used in the clinic can be verified. Until that happens, though, it will be necessary to base any therapeutic approach on as sound a foundation as is possible.

> We must reevaluate our approaches to clients with neurologic disorders, and base our practice on current advances in the movement sciences.

Some approaches, such as that developed by the Bobaths, were based on intuitive insight from clinical observation of inputs and responses. Other practitioners, such as Margaret Rood, immersed themselves in the current neurophysiologic literature and attempted to develop techniques logically from a scientific knowledge base. All of these therapists had the ability to tune in to their clients, which led to exceptional clinical success. Difficulties arose when others, on viewing the apparent successes of these pioneers, wanted to adopt these new techniques for their own clients. These pioneering therapists and others attempted to describe and provide explanations for the techniques, some based on theory and knowledge current at the time and some not. The most likely major element of success, rapport with the client, was the one element often not credited and the one most difficult to teach to another.

As might be expected, techniques were often based on or explained by interpretations of physiology that would be inaccurate today. As physiologic information and knowledge have increased among professionals, the old explanations and techniques have had to be modified. Unfortunately, much of the old information and many of the techniques continue to be perpetuated in the classroom and in clinical practice. As authors of texts relating to neurologic foundations of therapeutic intervention, we are well aware of the problems associated with providing accurate, up-to-date, scientific information. As insight and knowledge change, a new edition or a new book is needed. This book is intended to fill that need.

Students frequently ask, Why should we study this stuff? It sometimes seems that they want to learn only "how" to do something. We believe that to learn "why" something is done is as important, if not more so, than how it is done. Therapists with only the precise, technical, hands-on information and skills will find themselves at a loss when those facts and skills do not lead to solutions to client problems. Therapists with a solid background of appropriate knowledge for their skills will be able to devise effective programs for each client no matter what problems are encountered.

The information presented in this book is intended to help the learner develop an understanding of the basis of clinical practice with neurologic clients. In the process, old techniques may be challenged or at least, their rationale may be altered. This is as it should be. Professional growth requires that the acquisition of new or more complete knowledge results in appropriate changes.

> Tthe scientific principles on which treatment should be based are emphasized in this book.

Some insights into client treatment and evaluation will be presented in this book, but the major emphasis will concern the neurophysiologic knowledge and principles on which treatment will be based. The first part of the book is devoted to theories of motor control and to theories of motor development and their possible relationship to each other. Most neurologic intervention is based on some knowledge of motor control systems and motor development schemes. Some of the previous misconceptions about these areas will be explored because they are still prevalent in therapy today. There are many theories or versions of theories of motor control. We have not described them all. We have chosen to emphasize the systems theories because we believe they provide the most functional view of motor control and suggest many avenues for intervention. It will be the job of the learner, whether he be a student or a practicing therapist who is updating himself, to add to the dissemination of newer information and hasten the demise of the outdated or ill-conceived data.

The second section of the book is devoted to an understanding of reflexes and their role in movement. The prevalent model of motor control used by therapists in the clinic is probably the reflex-hierarchical view. Insight into the current models and theories of motor control and motor development should help to put reflexes in their proper perspective.

The problem with semantics relative to reflexes and reactions is also addressed. Some would have us dispense with the word reflexes because it seems to imply a hierarchical scheme. Others suggest that by definition a reflex requires a stimulus and results in a response. This presents difficulties because we know that some movements we identify as being reflexive are not of a stimulus-response nature. It may be possible to rename reflexes to avoid the stimulus-response connotation, but such maneuvering does nothing to clarify the matter. In this book, we will redefine reflexes and make an attempt to determine the nature of these reflexes and to relate this information to current views of movement and movement dysfunction. Included will be a review of fetal movements recorded through new technology and of the relationship of these movements to reflexes and motor development.

The third section is devoted to the vestibular system. This information is included in this volume because of a relatively new understanding of the role and function of the vestibular system. The vestibular system is undoubtedly involved in many reflexes or movements generated by the human body; therefore, information concerning the vestibular system and righting and equilibrium reactions will constitute a large portion of this book.

The vestibular system is included in this text because it is an integral component of motor control and disorders of this system are amenable to therapeutic intervention.

Many theoretical viewpoints revolve around the vestibular system because it has a powerful influence on the motor neurons and therefore muscle activity. Equilibrium and righting reactions remain an important component of client evaluation and treatment. We have made assumptions about the role of the vestibular system in balance and equilibrium and have often concluded that poor balance and equilibrium result from a problem with the vestibular system; however, we have had inadequate tools with which to investigate these assumptions.

New, sophisticated technology has led to an increased understanding of the function of the vestibular system. It is now possible to differentiate and identify clinical problems associated with vestibular deficits. A whole new area of insight and intervention in problems associated with vestibular diseases and disorders, such as head trauma, that often involve the vestibular system is available to therapists. It would appear, therefore, that in-depth insight into the vestibular anatomy and physiology as well as the pathologic conditions would be most valuable and timely. The last portion of the section will include treatment of clients with vestibular disorders.

The fourth section contains information and guidelines for the evaluation and treatment of clients with disorders of motor control. Principles of motor learning, derived from scientific laboratory experiments and practical applications in psychomotor learning, are presented in this section. These principles have powerful potential for assisting therapists in structuring treatment sessions and in evaluating and providing proper feedback for clients' motor learning. The latest motor control theories do not suggest new tools for treatment. Thus the therapist will need to use the currently available clinical tools, such as proprioceptive neuromuscular facilitation patterns, handling techniques, and sensory stimulation methods, for different reasons and with new perspectives from past approaches. It will be up to the clinical therapist to apply the principles derived from knowledge of motor control and motor learning theories.

Should the recipients of our ministrations be patients or clients?

In this text, we have elected to use the term client instead of patient. The noun patient is defined as an individual awaiting or under medical care, or one that is acted upon. Within the medical community, patients are often forced into passive, dependent roles. Treatments and procedures are done *to* them; they are very literally *acted upon* as the definition suggests. The change of terms from patient to client symbolizes a shift in attitude from passive to active. It serves to further enforce our belief that those individuals with whom we have the privilege to assist in their health are indeed our partners. It is through this active participation and shared responsibility that we therapists can truly assist our clients in reaching and maintaining their maximal functional ability and goals.

We have attempted to develop this text into a tool for facilitating learning by using less technical language, by developing a layout designed to promote interaction with the material, and by providing study questions throughout the text. A conscientious attempt to answer these questions will undoubtedly result in a better retention and understanding of the concepts presented. We hope that you will enjoy working your way through this text and that you will become a better therapist for having done so. Have fun!

Carolyn Crutchfield
Marylou Barnes

Note: Reference for this preface can be found in the bibliography for Section I.

Section I

Theoretical Constructs in Motor Control and Motor Development

Chapter 1 - Theories of Motor Control

NOTE: Portions of this chapter are originally from Crutchfield (1989), reprinted with permission.

An understanding of the theories that attempt to explain motor acts is of paramount importance in developing treatment strategies aimed at correcting or overcoming abnormalities in motor control. If such knowledge is not in the physical therapist's background, any treatment applied to a client will be the result of mimicry of someone's technique for ameliorating neurologic deficits. Motor control deficits and resulting movement dysfunction plagues all clients who have suffered nervous system insults, and insights into the mechanisms underlying this dysfunction are critical to appropriate therapeutic intervention.

> Each of us has a model of motor control on which treatment is based, irrespective of whether the model is conscious to us.

When a physical therapist treats a neurologically involved client, either consciously or unconsciously a model of motor control comes to mind and treatment is based upon it. Certain assumptions are associated with the model the therapist has chosen to accept. For example, you might espouse what is considered to be a mostly outmoded view that cerebral spasticity results from a hyperactive muscle spindle system. In this case, it is likely you will assume that the client with brain damage who demonstrates resistance to passive stretch has a short and sensitive muscle spindle. Treatment will thus be aimed incorrectly at desensitizing the muscle spindle and gaining control over the system by gradually increasing the length the muscle can attain before resistance appears. If our model is incorrect, our assumptions will lead us astray, and the treatment procedures devised are most likely to be incorrect. Even if the treatment technique is a useful one, it may be applied either for the wrong reason or with inappropriate expectations of the result.

For at least 80 years, researchers have been attempting to answer the question of how movement is generated to produce complex motor patterns of behavior. The available technology for studying neurologic phenomena has increased or improved by quantum leaps in recent years; however, the level of understanding nervous system function is still far from that required to generate consistently effective treatment interventions. It is clear, however, that ignorance of at least basic information about movement control and development renders the clinician inflexible and unable to develop creative alternatives.

No past or present theory of motor control is universally acceptable. Research results can be found that will at least suggest support for any one or a number of theories, depending on the interpretation of the findings. Many results can be and are interpreted to support totally opposite points of view. Theorists provide extremely divergent views of what structures are actually in control of movement. For some, the cortex of the brain and its neural networks are in charge of activating specific muscles to produce the movements. Some theorists, while acknowledging the complexity and power of the nervous system, believe that the system does not function in a vacuum and is not always in direct control of all neuromuscular responses. For the latter theorists, it is not necessary to identify specific neural circuits or areas of the brain in order to understand movement and perhaps to develop interventions when abnormal movements occur.

Because insight into these differing views is important to developing one's own view of movement mechanisms, several of these theories will be discussed. We will attempt to identify some of the assumptions that are likely to accompany these theories and to suggest how the theories may relate to the understanding of clients with movement dysfunction and treatment approaches that may be allied with them. It is important to understand that many theories of motor control exist. We have chosen a few that have been in favor in therapy circles or that currently appear to hold promise for clinical understanding. Theories are rarely ever proven or disproven--they are used as a framework for developing research and clinical questions designed to support or change them.

| Many theories of motor control exist, but not one of them is universally accepted. |

Reflex Theories

Sherrington's (1906) experiments, early in this century, have often been interpreted in a manner that suggests that complex human behavior can be reduced to certain reflex reactions or combinations of reflex behaviors. To interpret reflex theories that address movement, it is extremely important to discuss what constitutes a reflex. In many cases, the semantic issues concerned with the term reflex have added to the problem. Theorists and practitioners have used the term differently and have perpetuated misunderstanding of various views of movement origin. In its strictest definition, a *reflex* requires a stimulus and results in a response. The simplest example of such a phenomenon is the monosynaptic spinal reflex, or the deep tendon reflex, which is mediated by the muscle spindle. A tap on the tendon excites the stretch receptors in the muscle. These impulses stimulate the motor neurons to the muscle that contracts; in turn, a movement at the joint occurs.

| Reflex theories assume that a stimulus is necessary for a response to occur. |

Other early researchers, such as Magnus and de Kleijn (1912), using cats whose nervous systems had been transected surgically at increasingly higher and higher levels, observed more complex behaviors. Perhaps the real problem with the term reflexes occurred when these animal behaviors were referred to as reflexes; undoubtedly, they were so labeled because the stimuli appeared to be necessary to elicit the resultant patterns of activity.

Further, patterns of complex activity have been described from observing not only newborn humans but also clients with central nervous system (CNS) insults. Proponents of reflex-based behavior have attempted to

2

explain such complex motor behavior as resulting from the chaining of simple reflexes into combined patterns of activity (Delong 1971). To preserve the sensory input requirement for a reflex in this chaining effect, theorists suggest that one reflex becomes the stimulus for another. The basic unit of movement in this theory would be the reflex (Easton 1972).

Movements result from the activation of muscle groups in characteristic spatial-temporal relationships. The muscle groups are involved in the pattern through a specific relationship, or sequence, to each other (spatial) and with particular timing of onset, peak contraction, and cessation of activity (temporal). When this activation is relatively invariant (ie, does not change very much), a readily identifiable movement is observed that is often called a reflex. The movements are, or can be, associated with specific sensory stimuli; thus these stimuli are often believed to be necessary to elicit the motor response. This coupling of the sensory stimulus with the response fulfills the definition of a reflex. Newer research and different interpretations of the literature challenge the view that such complex behaviors as the flexor withdrawal, automatic walking, asymmetric tonic neck, tonic labyrinthine, and Moro reflexes that can be elicited in normal neonates and young infants can be reduced simply to a stimulus-response categorization.

As noted by Barnes et al (1978), many researchers have had problems with the concept of reflexes as classically defined. Sherrington (1906) himself wrote that "a simple reflex is probably a purely abstract conception, because all parts of the nervous system are connected together and no part of it is probably ever capable of reaction without affecting and being affected by various other parts, and it is a system certainly never absolutely at rest."

It is apparent that the term reflex must be more broadly defined if we are to continue to use it to describe certain movement patterns. This topic is discussed further in Chapter 4, which addresses the nature of reflexes in more detail.

Because muscles are activated in characteristic relationships, the movement is somewhat stable and thus recognizable.

It is not possible to define complex behaviors as being reflexes in the classical sense.

Hierarchy Theories

Reflex Hierarchy

The term *hierarchy* relates to the idea of a series of levels of control with each succeeding level having control over all the previous levels. Such systems of control are common in the military, business, and government. Figure 1-1 shows a hierarchical system with the general in control of the troops. Captains are directly in control of the sergeants assigned to them, although captains are able to command the other sergeants if necessary. The sergeants have the same relationship with the privates.

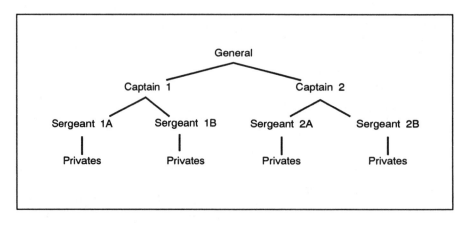

Figure 1-1 A hierarchical system.

Theorists have also attempted to categorize certain reflex patterns into a specific hierarchy of neural organization. The first of such hierarchies was vertical in nature; that is, it was assumed that some area of the nervous system is responsible for generating or controlling the reflex. Through ablation experiments it was concluded that the lowest level in a vertical system would be reflexes generated in the spinal cord. Next up the vertical climb are the brain stem and midbrain reflexes, and finally in that hierarchy are the cortically governed reflexes. The fact that a reflex, or movement pattern, does not manifest itself after section or destruction of a particular level of the CNS, however, can have several interpretations, only one of which is that the region is responsible for generating or controlling the reflex.

Hierarchy. A series of levels of control with each succeeding level controlling the previous level.

Although the primitive, or early, reflexes as well as the higher, or more mature, reflexes have been presented in this hierarchical manner (Bobath 1971; Fiorentino 1973), there are some distinct problems associated with such attempts. One major problem with describing integration centers for the various reflexes is that no absolute assurance exists that these movements are indeed associated with the areas suggested. But even if it is assumed that all knowledge about such centers is true, many additional problems remain. For example, the Moro reflex, one of the earliest and most primitive reflexes, is supposedly generated or controlled in a higher center, the medulla. Stepping movements have been assumed to be an intrinsic reflex property of the spinal cord. However, because stepping is relatively uncommon in the human with a spinal cord injury, it has been hypothesized that the reflex is controlled from the brain stem and possibly the diencephalon (Brooks 1986). It quickly becomes apparent that the assumed hierarchy relating to primitive and mature reflexes does not always hold true.

Theories that combine reflexes into movements and suggest that those reflexes are ordered in a hierarchical organization rests heavily on animal studies of the early 1900s. This perspective has dominated our view of motor control in physical therapy for so long that it still probably provides the most prevalent underpinnings of therapeutic intervention.

> Using a hierarchical model, therapists assume that one reflex inhibits the expression of another.

Assumptions that physical therapists have made in accepting a reflex-hierarchical model of motor control are either that the higher level reflexes will inhibit the lower ones or that the primitive reflexes prevent the development of the righting and equilibrium reactions. It is also assumed that the primitive reflexes interfere with the development of normal movement or the elaboration of normal movement. It has already been pointed out in the earlier section concerning reflexes that in normal children the primitive patterns are an expression of early normal movements. The patterns are adaptive, that is, they become modified according to the changes in the environment (context). Abnormal infants exhibit these patterns in an abnormal manner from the beginning. In children with abnormalities the patterns are dominant and nonadaptive. The more complex postural patterns involving equilibrium and weight shift also are impaired in the abnormal child and are more difficult to acquire. These stereotyped movement patterns can also be elicited in adults who experience neurological insult, leading to the assumption that the higher systems of organization have been damaged. According to a hierarchical view, this damage releases the higher level of control over the lower, or more primitive, system.

> Assuming that a stimulus is necessary to perform a movement makes the client a passive recipient of therapy.

Treatment approaches based on a reflex and a reflex-hierarchical view of motor control bring with them the assumptions that a specific stimulus is required to elicit the response and that sensation is necessary for movement. Therapists espousing such a theoretical construct are likely to assume that the higher centers are in charge of coordinated movement and that the lower centers never dominate unless some pathologic condition arises. It is then assumed that if the lower levels dominate the movements, they will be primitive and stereotyped in nature. Therefore, treatment may be directed first at attempting to decrease the dominant effects of the primitive patterns and then to eliciting the more desirable equilibrium and righting reactions. The assumption is that the primitive reflexes prevent the elaboration of the higher reactions and that the latter assist in the integration of the former. Treatment programs in this case are highly organized around specific reflexes. The client often becomes the passive recipient of therapy.

Hierarchical Aspects of Other Theories

It should be noted that there are still proponents of reflex-oriented motor development and motor control (Zelazo 1983). It should also be noted that what constitutes a reflex, an automatic movement, a coordinative structure, or a pattern confuse the issue. Because such patterns of movement (reflexes) are central to many other views of motor control, they cannot simply be tossed aside. The actual presence of such motor patterns as the asymmetric tonic neck reflex cannot be denied. What is important for physical therapists to consider is that some treatment

5

approaches have been designed to treat the client for a presence or absence of reflexes based on a hierarchical arrangement in which the presence of one reflex is believed to interfere with or enhance the development of another. Later in this book, further discussion of evaluation and treatment involving reflex patterns will be presented.

It is not possible to dispense with the concept of hierarchy in modern theories of motor control. Several proponents of different theories including patterns (Brooks 1986) and systems (Woollacott et al 1986; Nashner and McCollum 1985) describe some hierarchical aspects of movement control. These hierarchies could be considered vertical or horizontal depending on the interpretation placed on the information presented.

Again, it is most important for physical therapists to become familiar with the nuances of the terms involved in order to help determine the intent of a research or a theoretical article. It is also important to remember that in the past, reflexes were considered within the framework of a vertical organization of control, and we often believed that one type of reflex directly inhibited the development of another one. It is this unsubstantiated, assumed causal relationship in a hierarchical arrangement that brings some treatment approaches into question.

| Reflex-based theories continue to be proposed. |

| Many theories contain hierarchical aspects. |

Servomechanistic (Loop) Theories

The advent of computers and the information processing used to develop them have had an effect on theories of motor control. You may have often heard the brain referred to as a computer. We do not intend to present much specific information concerning theories that have sprung from the background of information processing, because they are generally believed to be inadequate for explaining brain behavior. Elements of these views do appear in other theories, however, so the basic elements or principles should be understood.

Open Loop

With the open-loop theory, the central command center issues a command that contains all the information necessary to produce a movement (Fig 1-2). The movement is completed without any alteration in variables such as direction, velocity, and amplitude. No feedback loops occur, and the neurons are activated only in one direction. While it has been out of date for some time as a complete explanation for motor control, at least some aspects of this theory are resurrected in other theories, particularly those that suggest movements may be programmed in advance.

This view of the nervous system has been quite common in physical therapy. In many approaches to client treatment the therapist attempts to trigger the desired movement by manipulating input to the client. The client is often a passive recipient of the technique and not an active participant in his treatment.

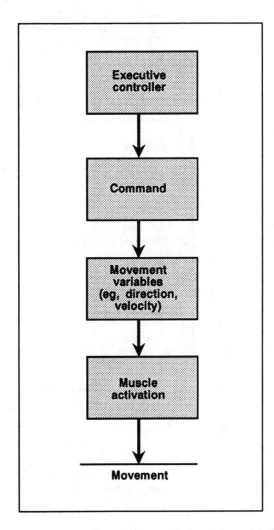

Figure 1-2 Open-loop model of motor control. From Crutchfield (1989), reprinted with permission from J B Lippincott Co.

Closed Loop

The major difference between the open- and closed-loop approaches to motor control is that in the closed-loop model the executive controller needs to be given the result of the response. As seen in Figure 1-3, the neurons are arranged in circular fashion, providing feedback for error detection and correction (Adams 1976). In a closed-loop model, the individual must be an active participant in the controlling, manipulating, and generating of behavior. Thus, when elements of a closed-loop system are assumed, the therapist will expect the client to become an active agent experiencing and exploring the environment. This view is extremely important in patient care. Undoubtedly, some aspects of this theory are useful and will resurface when certain other theories of motor control are explored. As a complete explanation of motor control, however, the view is inadequate.

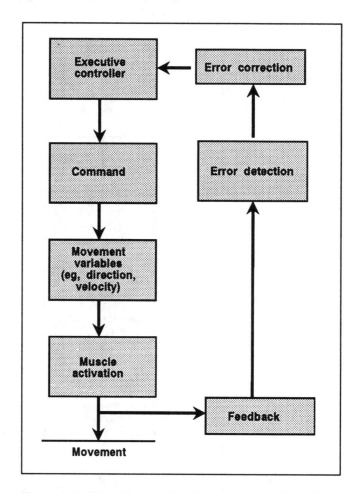

Figure 1-3 Closed-loop model of motor control. From Crutchfield (1989), reprinted with permission from J B Lippincott Co .

Cognitive Theories

Cognitive theories relate in particular to highly skilled and rapid movements. Some theorists have suggested that two major components enter into a skill: a decision component and an action component. Experience that allows the performer to anticipate the action results in a faster decision time or reaction time. The more a skill is practiced, the more it improves. Keele (1982) suggests that highly skilled behavior may be as much cognitive as it is perceptual or motor.

The lessons that can be applied to treatment from such theories relate to concentration and practice. Undoubtedly, practice and repetition are key elements in learning new or improving old motor behavior. It is not likely, however, that basic posture and movements underlying average everyday activities are to be equated with highly skilled athletic or artistic acts. Most neurologically involved clients lack these fundamental movements that are likely to be much less cognitive in nature. Nonetheless, cognition, concentration, and participation are important in all movements; valuable lessons can be obtained from a brief look at cognitive theories.

Study Questions:

1. **Explain the difficulties that may arise if a therapist has based treatment on invalid theoretical constructs.**

2. **What is an assumption and why does it matter to therapists?**

3. **List the main elements of a reflex theory.**

4. **Describe a hierarchy as it might relate to the nervous system.**

5. **Explain how both reflex and hierarchical aspects may exist in some current theories of motor control.**

6. **Explain why an open-loop theory does or does not require feedback for the continuation of movement?**

7. **What differences in treatment approaches may occur when therapists, knowingly or unknowingly, espouse the following models or theories of motor control: a) a reflex model; (b) a hierarchical model; c) an open-loop model; d) a closed-loop model; or e) a cognitive model?**

8. **Are all of these theories in conflict with one another? Must you decide which one (if any) to accept?**

9. **If a therapist accepts a reflex-hierarchical model of motor control, what assumptions are likely to be made?**

Pattern Generator Theory

Some selected major theories that likely hold the most promise for understanding motor control and providing a firm basis for developing evaluation and intervention techniques are systems theories, particularly the self-organizing systems theory. Another somewhat older view of motor control is explained in the pattern-generation theory. Although probably not a stand-alone theory for motor control, pattern generation underlies much of systems theory as well as pattern theory. Thus the former may be easier to understand if a detailed look at pattern generation is encountered first.

The existence of predeveloped patterns of activity would be a mechanism for simplifying motor activity. With patterns of movement, muscles are activated in certain spatially and temporally organized relationships. For instance, in certain circumstances the plantar flexor, hamstring, and paraspinal muscles may functionally be linked together, with every muscle contracting at a specific time and in a particular sequence to produce a characteristic movement. It has been suggested that perhaps the most classic movements that might result from a pattern generator occur during gait and locomotion. According to Brooks (1986), we know that locomotor patterns are programmed because neural control signals associated with locomotion are recorded even in animals who have been paralyzed with curare or some other such agent.

Nashner and Woollacott (1979), through elegant human experiments, identified specific patterns of muscular activity that result from particular sets of circumstances. When a subject is standing on a platform that provides forward or backward perturbations, predictable movement patterns occur in response to the disturbances in balance produced by the moving platform. These patterns have been called the hip and ankle synergies, or strategies. If the perturbation is small, the control of the center of gravity is achieved by postural sway, a pendulum motion controlled from the ankles. The pattern of muscular activity is very specifically timed and organized (Fig 1-4).

> A pattern of muscles linked together functionally would decrease the complexity required for muscle activation.

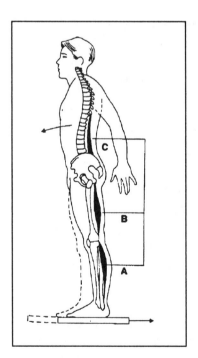

Figure 1-4   Posterior platform perturbation induces a forward sway of the body, which is counteracted by a specific sequence of muscle contractions: (A) Gastrocnemius, (B) hamstring, and (C) paraspinal muscles. From Crutchfield (1989), reprinted with permission from J B Lippincott Co.

> Nashner's platform perturbations: Ankle *synergy* (backward perturbation--the body reacts as if someone pulled a rug out from under you from behind, and you sway forward.

If the center of gravity is perturbed too far for the ankle synergy to bring it back into equilibrium or if the ankle synergy cannot be effective in a given environmental context such as standing cross-wise on a beam, a more proximal strategy is elicited. This strategy is called the hip synergy, and either the hamstrings and paraspinal muscles or the quadriceps femoris and abdominal muscles are activated with little or no activity from the ankle musculature. This synergy, like the ankle synergy, is used in an attempt to return the center of gravity to a stable position, and its activation results in a much wider excursion of the body (Fig 1-5).

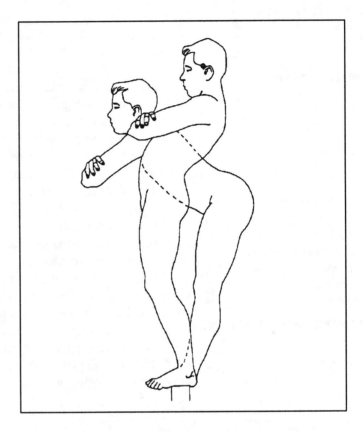

Figure 1-5 The hip synergy. From Crutchfield (1989), reprinted with permission from J B Lippincott Co.

If the perturbation is such that the platform under the feet is jerked backward, it causes a forward displacement of the body. To correct this displacement, the gastrocnemius, hamstring, and lumbar paraspinal muscles contract in that specific order to return the center of gravity to a more stable position (Fig 1-5). A forward perturbation resulting in a backward displacement of the body produces an activation of the opposite muscles: the anterior tibialis, quadriceps femoris, and abdominals.

According to Nashner (1990), synergy patterns of muscular activation occur too quickly to be voluntary and are too slow to be considered reflexive. At least these patterns are too slow to be the result of a simple

The ankle and hip muscle synergies act to bring the body back over the base of support.

11

monosynaptic reflex elicited from stretch of the involved muscles during perturbation. Nashner believes, however, that these movements are preprogrammed linkages of specific muscles constrained to act together in particular patterns. In this particular case, these specific patterns are activated under certain conditions in which there is a destabilization of the center of gravity.

How many patterns are there? Where do they come from? Do all our movements consist of predictable patterns of muscular activity? These are questions that will be considered throughout this discussion.

> **Complete movement patterns are seen in the fetus.**

Some evidence suggests that at least some of these patterns may be determined genetically because they are present before birth. Milani-Comparetti (1981) and others have observed the spontaneous activity of fetuses by using ultrasonography. Very competent and complex movements have been documented. Reaching, grasping, thumb sucking, and changing positions are a few. Because no stimuli could be identified to elicit many of these behaviors, Milani-Comparetti concluded that motor actions result from pattern generators. Thus pattern generators would be considered the underlying neural basis for such spontaneous movement. Chapter 4 on the nature of reflexes contains further information concerning fetal movements.

> **At birth, the fetus must cope with gravity, a circumstance that has tremendous influences on the movements expressed.**

It is likely that the failure of the neonate to demonstrate many of these same movements competently at birth relates to the environmental states that occur before and after birth. Before birth, the fetus is floating in a fluid medium in which the antigravity effects could provide a most suitable environment for expressing such movements. Once the child is born, the effects of gravity completely alter the environment in which movements are to occur. In some cases, the infant is undoubtedly too weak to produce the pattern against gravity. Learning and maturation are needed to perform in this new set of circumstances. Other mechanical or developmental factors also may influence the expression of these motor behaviors.

Neuroanatomical Substrata

Because neurons are highly differentiated cells, they are not capable of cell division and multiplication once the differentiation has taken place. Therefore, at the time of birth all the neurons the child will ever have are present, but many of the connections between neurons have not been completed. One clear difference between the nervous tissue of neonates and more adult animals is the connections, or synapses, that are completed and activated. The processes of learning and maturation apparently have strong influences on the development of synaptic connections and the activation of synapses present. Therefore, the basic structure for some program generators that are not expressed at birth or in utero may be present at birth, but their connections are not yet complete.

Myelination also is an important process of maturation. Myelination is not completed in the newborn and continues for some years after birth. In patterns the critical timing factors that are influenced by the amount of myelin present may have an influence on the accessibility of any given pattern or system of activation.

It has been postulated that the generator may be accessed from peripheral stimulation of sensory receptors. However, early animal studies on locomotion showed that even if the sensory input was eliminated by cutting the sensory roots, a locomotor pattern could still be generated. The question that arises then is how is the pattern accessed. Some theorists have proposed that the pattern is expressed from within the CNS itself. Combination theories suggest that the spinal and supraspinal centers function together with the interaction of continuous sensory input and cortical refinement to modify motor pattern activity.

If the first elaboration of motor patterns is spontaneous and occurs without sensory input, the role or value of such input may be questioned. Classical reflex models of motor control clearly indicate that sensory mechanisms are active by definition and cannot be separated from the motor response. In Milani-Comparetti's (1981) view, even though movement is initially spontaneous, later in prenatal development the link between sensory input and motor output is observed. Even if specific stimuli are not necessary to elicit a movement, they may be of value for feedback to the CNS for motor learning. This feedback would bring into the central mechanisms a knowledge of the movement and its results. The results of the act can be used to make the next movement more refined or better suited to the purpose.

Fatigue studies in humans have supported the theory that some learned human movements may be stored as motor patterns. If an act is repeated until the subject is fatigued, the following question arises: What is fatigued--the arm, the pattern, or the program? Measurements showed that once fatigue results from repetition of one arm pattern, greater fatigue occurs in the same pattern in the opposite arm than when a different pattern is performed. That is, if a pattern of activity is performed by the left arm until it is fatigued and then the pattern is repeated by the right arm, the right arm will more easily be fatigued performing that particular activity than if a completely different activity is attempted (Rosenbaum 1977).

Experiments with handwriting have shown that the trajectory, or shape, of the writing is similar whether written with the right hand, the right hand with enlarged letters, the left hand, the foot, or the pen in the mouth. Thus the writer's style was recognizable no matter how the writing was produced. This observation suggests that the same program is drawn on by diverse muscle systems.

How the Nervous System Controls Programs

According to Brooks (1986), motor acts consist of "hold" programs, which are postures, and "move" programs, which are transitions from one posture to another. Complex actions are produced by overall plans composed of several programs. The programs themselves are further composed of smaller subroutines, or subprograms. Subprograms contain the code for actual muscle activity and also initiate other subroutines that execute patterns of muscle contractions and so forth. This hierarchical system of plans, programs, and subprograms ultimately converge on neurons executing nonlearned automatic, or reflex, adjustments we might call patterns. Movements are learned when successful combinations of certain patterns occur and the entire sequence of action is planned thereafter as a single unit or another larger pattern. This process suggests that continued practice is essential to learning new motor tasks. In addition, synaptic strength is reduced when the pattern is unused. So the old adage "use it or lose it" makes sense.

According to Brooks (1986), the sensorimotor areas of the brain are concerned with sensations and motor programs. The brain directs the elaboration of movement in a command hierarchy that may be thought of as occurring on three levels. The highest level is the association cortex. At this level, the overall plans are developed. The middle level, consisting of the sensorimotor cortex, the cerebellum, the basal ganglia, and the brainstem, converts the plans into subprograms and programs. The lowest level, consisting of the spinal cord, executes the programs through motorneuron activation. Brooks states that this hierarchy is not to be thought of as a rigid vertical line of command. Levels interact through internal feedback loops to correlate ascending and descending messages.

Two kinds of errors may occur with programs when attempting to achieve a goal (Schmidt 1988). These are errors in either selection or execution. In selection errors, the subject will choose the wrong program. For example, a batter who expects a fast ball sets the spatiotemporal program that will allow him to hit it effectively. He is thrown a slow curve instead. The bat swing that he executes is inappropriate, and he is not successful.

> According to Schmidt, there are two types of program errors: those in selection and those in execution of the program.

Errors in execution occur when the program is correct, but it is not run or executed correctly. The muscles do not do what they were intended to do. If muscles are fatigued, for example, the variation in timing that results from fatigue will alter the execution of the pattern. In this case, reduction in fatigue will correct the error in execution. Errors in selection are thought to involve the central mechanisms while those in execution may involve spinal or cerebellar mechanisms. Attention, or cognitive awareness, is probably necessary to correct selection errors.

Those who espouse the view that there are pattern generators within the nervous system would be expected to incorporate them into treatment programs. If a movement package, or pattern, exists, then it would possible to use it if the pattern could be accessed. The first step would be to identify patterns in normal individuals, with an attempt to observe how they are altered or whether they even exist in clients afflicted with nervous system disorders.

Anyone who has treated clients with neurological deficits knows that the motor organization is not normal. The client may demonstrate consistent movement patterns, or synergies, but these synergies are dominant and nonadaptable, and the client has a limited repertoire of movements.

For instance, analysis of the muscular activation patterns found in the perturbation studies noted earlier showed differences between those with nervous system disease and normal individuals. In some cases, the order of muscular activation was altered. As might be expected, such alteration in sequence would result in the elaboration of a different movement than that produced with the normal sequence.

From a clinical perspective, it would seem logical that when treating clients an approach might be to attempt to change the abnormal patterns that they demonstrate. Undoubtedly, our understanding of the mechanisms of movement is ahead of clinical methods of intervention. There is no proof that it is possible to access a new synergy or to correct an abnormal one. Nonetheless, it appears more prudent to attempt such a feat with logical reasoning based on available knowledge than to persist in treatments based on clearly outmoded concepts. So be creative!

Perhaps the wrong sequence, or synergy, is used in the activity. Possibly the synergy itself is abnormal, with alterations in the activation sequences of the muscles. The direction of treatment, then, would be to foster the elaboration of the correct pattern, or synergy, for the appropriate task and the diminution of the improper one. These objectives might be accomplished in any number of ways. Biofeedback, electrical stimulation, or cutaneous stimuli might be used to trigger the appropriate order of muscle activation. Situations may be contrived, such as using a balance beam or a soft support surface, that will force the elaboration of a specific pattern. Allowing the individual to move while providing useful guidance and support through handling might be a good approach, at least early in the treatment. See Chapter 14 about how such guidance and support might most effectively be given.

> Clients with a disease of the CNS demonstrate abnormalities in the synergies elaborated in response to platform perturbations.

> An appropriate treatment goal would be to alter the abnormal synergy if possible.

Motor Schema

Schmidt (1988) has described problems with the concept of patterns and programs. Such questions arise as, How many programs are there? Does changing the speed of a baseball pitch require a new pattern generator? Is there a pattern generator for every possible combination of new pitches? If a pattern was required for every one of the infinite variations of throwing, hundreds or thousands of pattern generators and programs would be necessary. This need would present a major problem for storage of such programs. Another problem with programs is the novelty problem. How does one make a movement never made before? We are quite capable of executing movements for which no evolutionary purpose can be construed.

> In schema theory, the nervous system stores general plans rather than individual patterns.

It has been observed that repeated movements may be similar, but they are never identical. Schmidt (1988) suggests that movements, rather than resulting from specific pattern generators, result from programs that are more generalized. If the controlling centers are supplied with informational data, such as they are in computer programs, the program could be run off in a variety of ways depending on the goal. This would eliminate the massive storage required for individual patterns. He indicates that about four kinds of information might be stored: (1) variable data such as duration, force, spatial relationships, and movement size; (2) movement outcome, such as what happened; (3) sensory consequences, such as what it felt like; and (4) initial conditions, such as the weight and size of objects to be manipulated and the initial state of the body. In the course of running a given program, the subject briefly stores these four pieces of information after each response. The brain then abstracts the relationships among the stored bits of information and generates or updates any rules that describe the relationship between them. Thus a motor schema, or general plan, is stored rather than vast numbers of individual patterns.

Study Questions:

1. Describe the hip and ankle synergies reported by Nashner. Under what conditions is each strategy elicited?

2. Why might a neonate not demonstrate the complex movement patterns seen in the fetus before birth?

3. List some of the maturational factors present in the development of the nervous system.

4. What is a pattern? Discuss the evidence in support of preprogrammed patterns in humans.

5. How does Brooks fit in a hierarchical scheme?

6. How could pattern theory be incorporated into clinical practice?

7. Explain the differences between patterns and schema.

Systems Models of Motor Control

> With a systems model of motor control, the whole is greater than the sum of the parts as the control is broadly distributed among the parts.

The idea of a systems, or distributed control, approach to motor control probably has many roots. Underlying a systems view of control is the concept that the whole is greater than the sum of the parts and that the control does not reside within one area but is broadly distributed. There are properties and behaviors that are exhibited that cannot be understood by investigating or by limiting the investigation to the component parts. For example, the elements sodium and chloride can be studied through many avenues such as with electrochemistry or in solution. But when the elements are combined into sodium chloride, or table salt, they exhibit properties that could not be ascertained from studying only the elements themselves. Flour and sugar do not make a cake.

In the systems view of motor control the common thread is that all of the parts are interrelated to all the other parts and the recording of the behavior of an isolated circuit or unit fails to explain the functioning organism as a whole. In a heterarchy there is no strict order of command. The unit in charge will vary with the requirements of the task. Although there are many areas of basic agreement, various researchers have viewed the systems approach somewhat differently.

> In a heterarchy, there is no strict order of command. The unit in charge will vary with the requirements of the task.

A systems view of control could be considered a *heterarchy*. A heterarchical system (Fig 1-6) can be structured very similarly to a hierarchy, with one important difference. In a heterarchical system, a particular response may not require the highest level of control. At a busy military airport, the air controller may be only a sergeant, but when it comes to deciding who lands and takes off and in what order, it has to be the decision of the sergeant and not that of the captains, who may be flying the planes. A *heterarchical system* is one that acknowledges the basic flexibility of the human motor system.

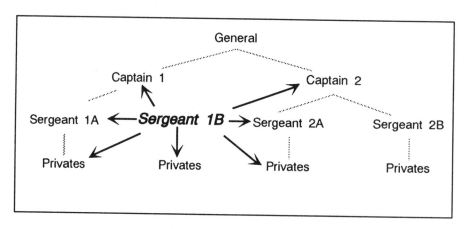

Figure 1-6 A heterarchial system.

Biomechanical Aspects of Systems Theories

Some investigators have proposed models of specific motor behaviors that include the importance of biomechanical factors as well as nervous factors. These models are part of systems theory, but they are not totally inconsistent with such concepts as central pattern generators or motor programs and are incorporated into some other models.

In movement, there is what has been termed the degrees of freedom problem. That is, how free is each component of movement to perform independently. Bernstein (1967), a Russian physiologist, was probably the first to address this problem. Each joint in the body may have up to three degrees of freedom; that is, it may move in flexion, abduction, and rotation. The degrees from each joint then may be combined with those of other joints because most movements involve a multisegmental or multijoint action. Such combinations produce a very large, if not infinite, number of possible joint positions. How to control all of those possible combined degrees of freedom becomes a problem for the nervous system.

> The need to control multiple joints (many degrees of freedom) would be lessened by linking muscles and joints together in a functional synergy.

Additional components are involved in defining the degrees of freedom. Each individual muscle has to be controlled. Further, each motor unit within the muscle is controlled. Given that there are different types of motor units, something must provide for the proper selection of each type. The number of components a controlling system has to manage exponentially expands to mind-boggling proportions. Some solutions to controlling multiple motor units are presented in the companion volume to this book; the size principle of motor unit activation is described. Selection of motor neurons to be activated according to their size would present a simple order of activation and thus decrease some of the

18

tremendous demands for activating specific motor units. In addition, the existence of a pattern generator that automatically selects certain muscles and links them together to produce a synergy acting as a single unit would greatly reduce the degrees of freedom that would burden an executive controller in comparison to having the controller select each muscle individually. That is, if the brain is the executive controller and if it must determine which of each of the millions of motor neurons must be activated at a given movement, the demands placed on it would be excessive.

Anatomical factors provide context variability.

Bernstein (1967) also defined three major sources of variability that are conditioned by the context, or the environment, in which they occur. The first of these is the variability that results from anatomical factors. For example, the pectoralis major will either flex or extend the shoulder depending on the position of the arm in relation to the trunk in horizontal adduction. The muscle, therefore, changes its role based on the biomechanical function of its angle of pull. The biceps brachii muscle will provide slow elbow extension, lowering the arm as a result of gravity, but the triceps brachii will perform the same motion if it is fast or if resistance to extension is encountered. Thus the context, or condition, in which the act occurs varies.

Mechanical or nonmuscular forces such as inertia are sources of variability.

The second source of context variability is mechanical. There are many nonmuscular forces at work such as gravity and inertia. Depending on conditions, a given amount of muscular contraction of a specific muscle will have different movement consequences. The result depends on the context, or external environmental conditions, in which the muscle is activated and the relationship between one joint and another as they are functionally linked together. When one link is controlled or changed, the other joints or links must necessarily change. A skilled performer learns to use the nonmuscular forces to her advantage. Muscular and nonmuscular forces complement each other.

A third source of context variability is physiological.

The third source of context variability, or variability that depends on the state of other elements, is physiological variability. For instance, rather than having a strict order of control, the supraspinal or higher neural mechanisms do not dominate the spinal ones. The interneurons in the spinal cord change the descending information and do not simply relay it. The large number of inputs to any interneuron provide horizontal and vertical connections that give the spinal cord an organization of its own that does not solely depend on messages from the cortex.

One way to control the degrees of freedom (actions across several joints) is to make the body stiff.

Bernstein (1967) implied that the highly skilled athlete has discovered ways of controlling the degrees of freedom involved in the movement under consideration. When one is just beginning to learn a skill, the first approach is to eliminate as many of the degrees of freedom as possible by making the body relatively rigid. These movements are stiff and unskilled. As improvement occurs, some of the degrees of freedom are released. As skill increases, the adult learner or the developing child learns to release more of the degrees of freedom and to work with the

19

reactive forces. When a batter swings at a ball and his hips rotate, a certain rotation in the upper part of the body will occur (Fig 1-7). The batter can exploit the reactive forces and thus does not actually have to control his entire trunk through every part of the movement. Acquiring skill primarily involves two processes. One is finding ways of controlling the degrees of freedom. The other is to make use of the forces provided by the context in which they occur. Any coordinated activity requires an environment of forces for its proper expression (Turvey et al 1982).

Figure 1-7 When hitting a baseball, the player's shoulders follow the movements imparted by the hips and pelvis. From Crutchfield (1989), reprinted with permission from J B Lippincott Co.

Role of Coordinative Structures, or Synergies

Bernstein stated that a muscle never enters into a complete movement as a separate entity.

The fundamental problem in motor control is how to regulate systematically the many degrees of freedom of the body within a wide variety of contexts, or environmental conditions, while involving an intelligent executive system as little as possible. Bernstein (1967) suggested that this could at least in part be solved by what is termed a muscle linkage, or coordinative structure (functional synergy). A coordinative structure consists of a group of muscles constrained to act as a single functional unit. These muscles often span several joints. Bernstein stated that a muscle never enters into a complete movement as a separate entity. Muscles and joints are linked together so that movement in one changes the response in the other. For instance, when performing a task such as aiming a gun, the joints are linked through the muscles and act together. When the shoulder moves in one direction, the wrist moves in another, keeping the aim on target. Skill is developed by learning to activate such constraints.

A mechanical example of constrained activity is an automobile. There are four wheels on the car. To simplify successful guiding of the vehicle, the designers built in some very specific relationships. Mechanisms were designed to link the two front wheels together. If the steering

20

wheel is turned to the right, both of the wheels turn to the right. Independent control over each wheel is not possible. The rear wheels are set in concert with the front wheels with a much simpler and less flexible linkage than that between the steering wheel and the two front wheels. In this case, the rear wheels simply follow the front wheels and are not controlled directly from the steering wheel. Thus the multiple problems of controlling all four wheels independently has been simplified to one control, the steering wheel, which permits only the rotation of the steering device to provide full control over all four wheels simultaneously, determining the direction of the vehicle.

The steering wheel and the four wheels of a car permit it to move as a coordinative structure.

An example of constraint in the body occurs when the abdominal muscles contract to rotate the pelvis into posterior tilt; the gluteal muscles can usually be felt to contract as well. These contractions would imply that functional linkages occur between various muscles in the performance of tasks. These functional linkages could also be called reflexes, or patterns, so you can see that terms and definitions are very important in understanding the intent of the author, theorist, or researcher.

There are multiple ways of linking joints and producing movements, but only certain ones of them appear, depending on the biomechanical context. For instance, if you reach for a large and close target with your hand, you will accomplish the task faster than if you reach for a little target that is further away. This observation is a result of Fitts' law, a mathematical computation about target size and distance to the target that we will not burden you with at this time. However, Kelso (1982) attempted to apply Fitts' law to two-handed movements rather than one-handed movements. This experiment involved reaching for a large close target with one hand and simultaneously reaching for a small more distant target with the other hand. If both targets were reached for at the same time, you would expect the hand aiming at the large close target to get there first. In fact, both hands got to their respective targets at the same time. This result challenges that law under the conditions of a two-handed activity. Some other lawful relationship has been in effect in which both of the upper extremities have been linked together, putting constraints on the activity and simplifying the control.

Movements always involve multiple muscles linked together over several joints. Muscles do not work in isolation.

Self-regulatory Components of Systems Theories

Nesting Constraints

When independent muscles are constrained to act together, a self-regulatory system is created. When a horse walks, for instance, the complete step cycle can be defined in 4 phases as shown in Figure 1-8. Phase 1 is the support phase. Phases 2, 3, and 4 are extension and flexion phases. When locomotion in the horse is analyzed, it becomes apparent that the different types of gait, such as a walk, trot, rack, and gallop, are very similar to the walking phase. The relationships of the

21

positions of the joints of the limbs change very little. As the speed increases and the horse changes to a gallop, the time required to go from flexion to extension and the time from extension to landing on the hoof do not change. The only change that occurs is a decrease in the duration from landing on the hoof to the next flexion of the extremity; therefore, only the support time changes (Tuller et al 1982).

Figure 1-8 A complete step cycle of the horse proceeds from 1 to 4, in which 1 represents the support phase. As velocity increases, only the duration of the support phase is decreased. Flexion and extension phases are changed very little or not at all. From Crutchfield (1989), reprinted with permission from J B Lippincott Co.

The differences in the gait patterns of a horse result from what might be called nesting constraints; that is, there are larger constraints governing smaller linkages. For instance, there are linkages for the forelimbs and the hind limbs. There must also be linkages over the pelvic and scapular girdles. Thus the synchronization differences noted in the trot, rack, and gallop depend on what girdles and what limbs are in phase with each other. When two limbs are moving, the position of the one in relation to the other is described by the term phase. This relationship can be expressed in degrees. For instance, when the two limbs are doing exactly the same thing they, are in phase or at 0 degrees. When they are in totally opposite positions, the limbs are 180 degrees out of phase with each other.

In the trot gait pattern of the horse, the right forelimb and left hind limb are in phase (Fig 1-9). The right forelimb and right hindlimb are in phase in the rack gait (Fig 1-10).

Figure 1-9 Opposite limbs of the shoulder and pelvic girdles are synchronized in the trot gait. From Crutchfield (1989), reprinted with permission from J B Lippincott Co.

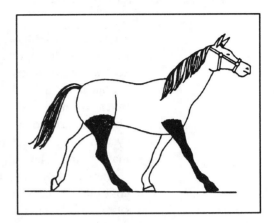

Figure 1-10 Limbs of the same side of the shoulder and pelvic girdles are synchronized in the rack gait. From Crutchfield (1989), reprinted with permission from J B Lippincott Co.

In the gallop, both the right and left forelimbs are in phase with each other as are both hindlimbs (Fig 1-11).

In the walking or alternate-step gait, any limb is one-half cycle out of phase with the other limb of the same girdle (Tuller et al 1982) (Fig 1-12). By simply increasing the energy delivered to the system, which results in increasing muscular contraction and gait speed, different patterns appear.

Figure 1-11 Both limbs of the same girdle are in phase with each other in the gallop. From Crutchfield (1989), reprinted with permission from J B Lippincott Co.

Figure 1-12 Alternate-step gait. From Crutchfield (1989), reprinted with permission from J B Lippincott Co.

Mass-Spring Models

Another hypothesis about how muscle action relates to constraints is proposed in the mass-spring model. According to Bernstein (1967) and others, the mass-spring is a simple mechanical device in which a spring is attached to a fixed support at one end and a mass is suspended at the other. No matter what the elongation or compression of the spring, it always returns to the same length (Fig 1-13). In such oscillatory systems, no error correction is necessary because the position of the mass-spring is lawfully specified by the relationship between the spring's stiffness and resting length and the magnitude of the mass. No executive controller is necessary to direct it. It is possible to model the muscular system as a mass-spring system. Experiments by Kelso (1982), described earlier, which showed that movement is accurate even when sensory input from joints and muscles is removed, support the mass-spring model for movement in living systems. Thelen's work, described in Chapter 2, also provides evidence for mass-spring characteristics.

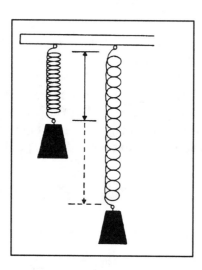

Figure 1-13 A mass-spring system. After being stretched, the spring always returns to the same position. From Crutchfield (1989), reprinted with permission from J B Lippincott Co.

Fel'dman (1986) further developed the mass-spring model into what he calls the equilibrium-point model of motor control. He maintains that joint stiffness and position are regulated by the length-tension characteristics of the agonist and the antagonist muscles. Some of these characteristics are the viscoelastic, mechanical, and neural conditions influencing the state of muscle contraction and stiffness. The equilibrium point is where the plots of length-tension curves of the agonist and the antagonist intersect. In the equilibrium-point hypothesis, the limb position can be changed by selecting a new characteristic, such as increased contraction, for the contributing muscles (Fig 1-14). Muscle stiffness is regulated through the stretch reflex, which represents regulation from many avenues including descending tracts in the nervous system.

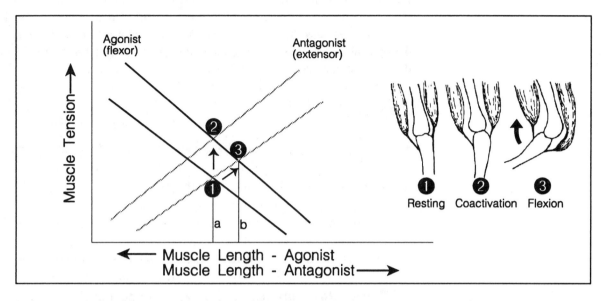

Figure 1-14 The relationship of muscle characteristics in the agonist (dark line) and the antagonist (light line) to their length-tension changes. At rest the equilibrium point resulting from the tension produced between the two muscles at *point 1* produces no joint movement at *length a*. If the tension is raised equally in both so that the equilibrium point is now at *2*, coactivation results, the joint is stiffer, but the muscle lengths do not change and remain at *a*. If tension is increased in the agonist, a new joint position of flexion is seen, and the equilibrium point at *3* results in a change in respective muscle lengths. At *length b* the agonist is shorter and the antagonist is longer. Note that the increase in lengths for the two muscles (along the abscissa) are in opposite directions.

Sensory Components in Biomechanical Aspects of Systems Theory

In motor control, the multitude of sensory-perceptual processes are no less demanding on the controller than are the modes of motor output or muscular expression. In terms of sensory perception, the job of dealing with all possible combinations of perceptual states is as overwhelming as coordinating all possible muscle responses.

Fel'dman's (1986) hypothesis also presents a dynamic alternative to the requirement for monitoring proprioceptive information continually and comparing it with some internal memory of the movement. The mass-spring concept allows the limb to assume a specified position even without feedback. He argues that the nervous system sets the desired position by adjusting the length-tension relationships of the muscles involved. The spring will always reach a final or equilibrium point depending on the system's dynamic factors such as mass and stiffness. Muscles have only to be adjusted by those factors and the desired behavior, including the trajectory of the limb, is closely approximated by

25

mechanical principles. That is, the amount of stiffness is determined by the level of coactivation present, and the mass relates to the load on the muscle, including such conditions as bearing weight, the number of levers involved, and the speed of the contraction. No constant feedback is necessary unless the resulting equilibrium point does not match the desired end-point because some unwanted and prolonged mechanical disturbance occurs.

Study Questions:

1. In your own words, describe a systems model of motor control.

2. How is control determined in a heterarchy?

3. Define degrees of freedom.

4. What is meant by the phrase "the degrees of freedom problem"?

5. How can the many degrees of freedom be managed?

6. Define constraint as it relates to motor control.

7. What element causes the horse to switch gait patterns?

8. Describe how a muscle can behave as a mass spring.

Neurological Approaches to Systems Theory

Sensory

Sensory information:

1) somatosensory

  a) exteroceptive

  b) proprioceptive

  c) interoceptive

2) vestibular

3) auditory

4) visual

Sensory information may be considered to be of three main types. The first relays information about the environment and may be termed exteroceptive. The second relays information about the relationship of body parts, most usually referred to as proprioceptive. The last relays information about the internal environment and is termed interoceptive. Although important, the latter will not be considered further. Sensory information can be classified further according to specific function: somatosensory, vestibular, auditory, or visual. Somatosensory receptors include both exteroceptors (cutaneous receptors) and proprioceptors (muscle, joint, and tendon receptors).

The sensory information is certainly used for feedback to control and to adjust subsequent movements. Another important concept, however, is that of feedforward. In feedforward, the control system uses sensory

26

information, especially vision, to change reactions or movements in advance of some condition. An example would be to use vision to avoid obstacles before bumping into or stumbling over them.

Actually, the exteroceptive and proprioceptive receptors can work together in producing what might be called exproprioception: information about the environment in relation to the observer. For instance, researchers have determined that vision resulting from actively moving in the environment provides a far richer source of information than simply passively observing the environment. The retina receives light rays reflected from objects in the visual field. The rays strike the retina in a unique location for each position of the eye in relation to the object. Thus movements of the head change the location on the retina that the light rays strike. The changes in the pattern of retinal stimulation that occur when the eye moves from one position to another is called the optical flow. This term implies that the visual environment flows past us as we move and tells us about the environment itself in ways that could not be achieved when the body is still (Schmidt 1988).

An important question is what role all these sensory inputs play in motor control and how important is that information. Vision seems to be a dominant source of information for movement and thus has a proprioceptive role as well as an exteroceptive one. One aspect of the role of vision has been studied as it relates to the control of standing, a very basic activity. Lee and Aronson (1974) studied infants who had a limited experience in standing and walking. They fabricated a moving room, a device with a fixed floor in which three walls and the ceiling were suspended so that they could be moved back and forth over that floor (Fig 1-15). When the room moves toward the infant, it will produce an optical-flow pattern that is interpreted by the infant the same way as if he were moving forward. Thus, if the child were using vision to maintain posture, we would expect that the compensatory movement made would be made by the posterior muscles in response to falling forward. All of the children swayed, stumbled, or fell backward. The reverse is true if the room is moved away from the child, and the child falls forward. This is direct evidence of the postural role that vision can fulfill.

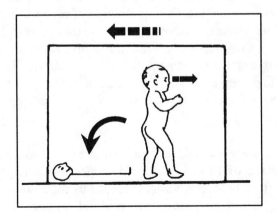

Figure 1-15 The moving room experiment. Moving the room toward the child is interpreted by the child's sensory system as if he were moving forward. Thus the child induces compensatory muscle action in the backward direction and falls backward.

The child also has proprioceptive information being relayed from the skin, muscles, and joints that should signal to him that he himself is not actually moving and thus would not need a compensatory movement. The infant, however, has not yet had sufficient experience with proprioceptive information to use it effectively. Vision is thus dominant and in this case is providing misleading information that still has a dramatic effect on posture. Adults seem to be more attuned to proprioceptive information and sway much less when in the same condition.

A form of exproprioceptive information that can be computed mathematically is the "time-to-contact" between an object and an individual observing it. It would seem important for a performer to be sensitive, whether walking through a crowded room, hitting a ball, or driving a vehicle such as a car or boat. One compensates for the perceived difference in time-to-contact with the object. Hitting a tennis ball or participating in other such athletic events is regulated by this lawful relationship between optic flow and time-to-contact. Visual exproprioceptive information may bias reflexes underlying motor activities, as seen in the moving room experiments. Sound and tactile information will produce the same results. That is, many different sources of information may alter the muscular responses, but the responses are also constrained to some internal reference system. The existence of this reference seems to be clear because conflicting information, such as visual evidence of moving counteracted by proprioceptive evidence of standing still, is usually sufficiently resolved in the adult to prevent an over-reliance on false information that will produce instability and falls. Numerous sources of information exist that will affect the activity of the muscle (Fitch et al 1982).

The human body has a posture-preserving system and a movement system. The first system, the posture-preserving system, produces movements designed to keep the body upright. Superimposed on these postural movements are those generated by the movement system that produces movements of the body or parts of the body. All activities are performed in terms of these two classes of movements. Every movement of the body or its parts acts to disturb the upright posture, so it is necessary to be sensitive to what can be done and still remain upright. One must in some way be aware that there is a region of reversibility; that is, the effects of the movement can be reversed so the individual does not fall. Within this region, any movement that disturbs balance may be counteracted by another movement that restores balance. Given a system engineered to preserve upright posture, an individual must choose movements that will not go beyond this region in which the balance can be restored.

The posture-preserving system is tailored to all movements. Before a movement occurs, the rest of the body makes adjustments in anticipation of the movement. Different movements are preceded by different postural adjustments. Thus the movement and postural systems

In the systems approach, many systems share information and work together.

28

constrain each other. This is accomplished cooperatively, not by one dominating the other. Much of skill acquisition focuses on discovering the relationship between these two systems.

Motor

A systems, or distributed, model of motor control revolves around a network of neural connections that are not vertically oriented as some of the previous hierarchical models would suggest. Rather, the entire nervous system can be considered to consist of complex systems and subsystems that interact in a flexible manner rather than in a strict hierarchical fashion. The various systems and subsystems would share information and work together to control movement.

In this approach the area, unit, subsystem, or system responsible for being the controller in motor control varies from circumstance to circumstance. The subsystem with the most accurate information relative to the demands of the environment and the state of the individual has the greatest effect on the resulting actions.

With a systems approach the control is shared, and whichever system has the most accurate information determines the response.

If the somatosensory system is registering accurate information about the condition of the supporting surface, it should have major influence on the motor outcome. This is especially true if some other system such as the visual system is registering inaccurate information. Some other system or subsystem will determine which information is accurate and influence the selection of the appropriate response.

With a distributed view of motor control, some of the closed-loop aspects of neural organization become apparent. In such a system, feedback is part of the loop. When feedback is present, a system of comparison arises that is postulated by some theorists to be active in motor learning. A feedback mechanism provides knowledge of results to the motor control system. When such knowledge of results is present, the result can be compared with the intention, and the next movement can be modified accordingly. This aspect of systems theory is little different in principle from Schmidt's (1988) schema theory presented earlier.

In motor learning, do we have to learn all of the subsystems down to the smallest muscle twitches? At least to some extent the final coordination of different muscles is already built into the organism. What the learner does is learn particular goals at an abstract level. At lower levels, some part of those goals are automatically translated into action. The human body has many more ways to move than it actually uses because body movements are partly constrained by patterns already built into the organism. We have already suggested this is true of locomotion patterns in animals. This constraint is also true of the specific patterns of activity producing ankle and hip synergies that result when anterior-posterior balance is disturbed.

Further, consider the asymmetric tonic neck reflex, one set of many movement patterns of the human body. This reflex is present in young infants and is also exhibited by children with CNS dysfunction. Normal adults do not exhibit this reflex in such stereotyped fashion. However, studies have shown that under conditions of fatigue or need for greater strength, the normal adult will turn the head toward the arm producing extension movements and away from the hand producing flexion movements (Fig 1-16). When movements combine with the reflex activity, additional strength is conferred. This illustration is highly suggestive of the notion that much final selection of movement is based on already existing motor patterns.

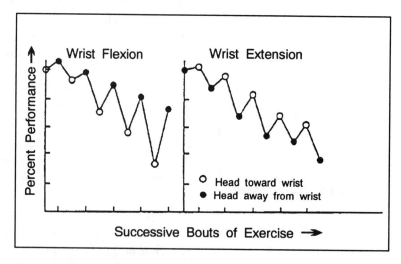

Figure 1-16 The strength of the performance of successive weight lifting bouts with the hand decreases in comparison to the first bout. The percentage is greater for flexion when the head is away from the wrist and less when the head is toward the wrist. The reverse is true for wrist extension.

This reflex pattern, as well as others, appears in movement patterns in sports and dancing (Fig 1-17). Given certain circumstances, the effects of a different reflex, such as the labyrinthine reflex, may influence the output and thus alter the tonic neck reflex pattern. Some consider that a motor program itself is a hierarchical representation of action. The action begins with determining general goals and proceeds to the selection of specific muscles. Much of the learning may take place at higher levels that plan the general sequence of action. Final details may be woven into the movement by innate reflex patterns. It must be kept in mind that these reflexes are complex movement patterns, not a strict stimulus-response tendon tap followed by a knee jerk (see Chapter 4). Reflex and voluntary performance gradually blend into one another.

They are connected by activities that may be automatic in nature but may also be modified by cognitive influences.

Figure 1-17 Asymmetric tonic neck reflex patterns in various movements.

Study Questions:

1. Compare feedback and feedforward concepts.

2. Describe visual flow and its relationship to movement.

3. How do reflexes fit into the concepts of systems theory and pattern theory?

Self-organizing Aspects of Systems Models

Theorists attempting to understand the neurologic determinations of motor control have discovered that the requirements for identifying even one pattern generator is a task almost beyond comprehension at the present time. The pattern generator, no matter how it is viewed, is a theoretic concept that may or may not be valid. This situation is true of all theories of motor control. Adding to the confusion is the fact that the same research results can often be interpreted in such a manner as to either support or refute a given theory.

A large problem that occurs when defining neurological substrata in motor control is establishing the link between the neural levels and the behavioral levels. Therefore, the dynamic, or self-organizing, theorists suggest that it might be more profitable to study motor control from a completely different perspective. Perhaps it is more useful to identify principles of organization that might underlie motor behavior.

Physicists have known for centuries that there are basic laws that govern the universe. Identifying and applying these laws has provided a much simpler base for understanding the universe and has ultimately enabled us to make headway in conquering it. It is through the application of these laws that space travel and much of our scientific technology has developed.

In this systems approach, it is necessary to define the total system and interactions of the parts of the system. Of basic interest is the change of motion in a system and the flow of energy within it. For example, consider a pot of water. Just sitting on the stove it would contain a quiet, smooth volume of consistent, even fluid. If heat is added, the water boils and is no longer quiet. The relationship of the parts or molecules to one another has changed. If heat is continually applied, the water turns to steam. Now the parts are again in a different relationship. There is no mechanism in the pot of water that made an executive decision to start boiling. It simply followed basic laws of physics. There may be, therefore, basic laws that govern living systems and result in the spontaneous self-organization of parts into different relationships.

Self-organization in biological systems means that pattern and order can emerge from the interaction of the components in a complex system. There is no need for commands or explicit instructions. A complex system likely has a huge number of degrees of freedom. When there is a thermodynamic condition in which there is a directed flow of energy, the elements can self-organize in a pattern of behavior that has many or few degrees of freedom. This can schematically be represented as in Figure 1-18. In A, the elements are randomly arranged and represent many degrees of freedom. Under certain conditions the elements can be arranged into patterns that dramatically reduce the degrees of freedom in the system, as can be seen in B. Figure C shows that the resulting system can exhibit behavioral complexity through multiple stable configurations.

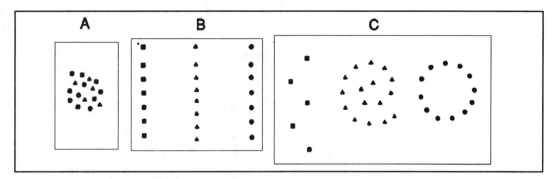

Figure 1-18 (A) Schematic depiction of self-organization in a complex system consisting of many degrees of freedom. (B) Under thermodynamic conditions, such systems can self-organize to produce a dynamic arrangement with less degrees of freedom. (C) The system, in turn, can exhibit multiple patterns, multiple stable states, and adaptable configurations. From Thelen (1989*c*), reprinted with permission.

This phenomenon can be demonstrated in nonbiological systems, such as in certain chemical reactions. Simple ions of bromate placed in a medium that is highly acidic will suddenly show a spontaneous burst of activity that produces beautiful spirals and other complex forms (Fig 1-19). In this chemical reaction, the patterns will decay as energy is used up. In biological forms, a continual supply of energy is provided through metabolic processes, and thus, the patterns would not have to decay. Furthermore, these patterns can be mathematically modeled by a computer further suggesting a lawful phenomenon has occurred.

The question arises as to whether laws or principles exist that transcend the biological properties of the system just as they do for nonbiological systems and that will help us to understand the complex patterns of movement. Some theorists suggest that principles of self-organization can be discovered that do not limit us to the anatomy or physiology of the organism. If so, it might be expected that those principles would be applicable to such diverse biological organisms as the centipede, cockroach, cat, horse, and human.

In the early 1900s some extraordinary experiments were conceived and implemented by Erich von Holst (1973). Working with a centipede, he systematically removed pairs of legs until six legs or three pairs remained. The animal immediately assumed the gait of a six-legged animal. If another pair was removed, the animal demonstrated a quadruped gait. Thus the original gait in which each leg was one seventh out of phase with each other completely changed to a new organization.

> Nonliving ions can self-assemble into complex patterns if energy is supplied.

> A centipede, deprived of all but four legs, assumes a four-legged gait, producing a completely new organization of behavior.

33

Figure 1-19 Evolving forms in a special reaction. The spontaneous development of structure can be seen in a sequence of photographs (left panels of each pair) that shows waves of chemical activity. These complex forms can remarkably be well modeled by a simple computer simulation (right panels). From Madore and Freedman (1987), reprinted with permission.

The role of the environment is critical in the systems view of motor control because all movements are done within the context (ie, the conditions and constraints of the environment). An example of contextual influences on motor control has been demonstrated through research on animals and human infants using a split-belt treadmill. On such a treadmill each belt can be run independently. When the belts are run at different speeds, complex interlimb patterns emerge. Infants shortened the stance on the slow belt and increased the stance on the fast belt to maintain regularly alternating steps (Thelen et al 1987c). This was an instantaneous change in the pattern of activity to meet demands resulting from changes in the environment, or the context of the movement.

Both the centipede experiments and the split-treadmill experiments cast doubt on the presence of central pattern generators dedicated for locomotion. It does not seem reasonable that the centipede has hard-wired programs available just in case it loses certain pairs of legs. The same conclusion is reached relative to walking on split treadmills. Such activity would not be expected for any species. These experiments suggest that there must be more all-encompassing principles or laws that govern, or at least play a crucial role in governing, the activity of living organisms.

Other examples of instantaneous changes in patterns of activity were encountered earlier in this section relative to the different gaits found in horses. Similar studies on humans suggest that when certain factors are changed, the pattern of activity changes. For instance, if subjects alternately flex and extend their wrists, they may do so either in phase or out of phase. That is, both wrists may be flexed and both extended or one may flex while the other extends (Fig 1-20). When a factor change is imposed during an out-of-phase pattern, such as increasing the energy delivered to the system to speed up the movement, the subjects shift to an in-phase pattern and an out-of-phase pattern cannot be sustained (Kelso and Scholz 1985). Try moving your wrists as shown in Figure 1-20B. As you try the alternating pattern, speed it up. Note that you will reach a speed at which you cannot keep the alternating pattern going and either you switch patterns or the pattern disintegrates.

These types of experiments show that the nervous system is not in charge of every little detail of the movement. For instance, when walking, a lot of movements happen just by momentum. Elastic energy is stored in the muscles and the tendons through stretch, and potential energy is changed to kinetic energy as movement takes place. Perhaps some elaborate program is not necessary to produce a gait sequence. Remember that horse studies show there is a specific gait that is most energy efficient for a particular speed or range of speeds. The horse will walk until a certain speed is reached and then the gait pattern changes.

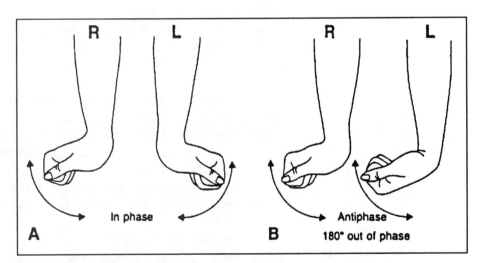

Figure 1-20 (A) When both the left and right wrists are extending or flexing, the pattern is considered to be in phase. (B) When one wrist is flexing and the other is extending, they are in an out-of-phase pattern. From Crutchfield (1989), reprinted with permission from J B Lippincott Co.

The new pattern will persist at a higher speed until it is more energy efficient to change the organization of movement by switching to a trot.

The speed of an activity may determine the pattern used. The principle may be one of energy efficiency, or conservation of energy.

Perhaps, rather than having an elaborate neural switching of programs, the system reorganizes itself when the energy requirements reach a certain level. Just as with the pot of water, a reorganization of the system occurs that is going to be more efficient. Try walking fast as opposed to jogging. You will discover how much more difficult and energy consuming it is to maintain the speed of a fast walk than to change to a jog. Beyond a certain speed, walking cannot be maintained.

> Gait comes about through the exploitation of elastic properties of tissues and inertia and through the activation of specific muscles.

Studies covering the past 50 years on a wide variety of animals, such as cockroaches, cats, dogs, and stick insects, have shown some results that are striking. Past and recent studies indicate that the initiation of swing phase in gait depends in part on reflexes that appear to be identical in all the species studied. Swing phase is initiated when the support leg is unloaded. Some pathway signals the decrease in load at the end of stance and that signal triggers the initiation of swing on the opposite limb (Pearson and Duysens 1976).

A second mechanism in triggering swing in these animals is the position of the hip joint at the transition point between stance and swing. Movements in 7-month-old infants who performed little or no stepping patterns were studied by supporting them over a treadmill. The infants immediately produced alternating stepping movements that closely resembled mature walking. It is possible that providing the full extension stretch to the stance leg, together with unloading the ankle and producing a weight-shift, supplies the passive energy required to overcome gravity and swing the leg forward (Thelen 1986a). Theories proposing that maturation of the executive control system is required to allow stepping in a developing child are being challenged.

If full extension and limb unloading are important events in triggering swing phase, consider how many clients with stroke or cerebral palsy never achieve full hip extension and appropriate unloading of the limb during gait. It may be that studies such as these will allow us to begin identifying some of the critical factors causing the system to reorganize itself. If the client can be helped to establish that critical factor, perhaps that human organism can spontaneously reorganize itself.

Many of the biomechanical principles or observations made about motor control, such as muscle constraints and mass-spring models, contribute to the self-organizing theories of motor control. These factors describe lawful relationships and behaviors concerning some aspects of living systems. In this approach, the environment becomes a crucial element in the elaboration of movement and may play a role as important as that of the nervous system itself.

The task to be addressed by the dynamic systems, or self-organizing, theorists is to identify the principles at work that may govern biological movement. At this juncture, it is apparent that altering the speed, velocity, or frequency of an activity would be important in clinical evaluation and treatment.

The question arises as to just what happens in the case of a stroke. If the system self-organizes, what is the organizational change occurring that results in the readily identifiable gait and posturing of the client with such a neurologic deficit? The first understanding that must be had is to recognize that the dynamic systems theorists are not denying that the nervous system has a role in movement. It is viewed, rather, that areas of the nervous system participate in or produce the self-organizing behavior and that strict neural circuits destined to become pattern generators and so forth may not exist. Some studies with monkeys, for instance, have shown that an area of the sensory cortex that is activated upon stimulation of the hand is no longer responsive when the hand is deafferented. The area reorganizes itself to participate in other sensory activities. If the afferentation is restored, the cortex reorganizes itself, and once again that area responds to hand stimulation. The brain itself may be a self-organizing system that is even more dynamic than we suspected.

Are All Theories in Conflict?

As we have noted, there are many theories of motor control. At this important point in our history, movement scientists who are therapists are contributing significant insights into these processes. Many of the research studies cited in this text were performed by such individuals. Researchers necessarily work on problems that are narrowly defined so that they are amenable to investigation. Even if the scientists are therapists, both they and we are then required to make larger interpretations of the material.

For example, Leonard (1992) has attempted to correlate motor patterns generated in normal development and disability with structural changes in the CNS. Such an attempt requires the inclusion of nonhuman animal studies and their extrapolation to the human condition. He and his colleagues have described the developmental differences between the infant and adult brain in the cat and have developed human studies to compare these observations in humans by investigating motor activities in individuals with cerebral palsy or who have suffered strokes.

Leonard et al (1991) studied the development of walking in children with cerebral palsy. They determined that locomotor patterns in children with cerebral palsy are similar to those of normal infants during supported locomotion. As the children with cerebral palsy mature, however, they retain some of the characteristics of the infant patterns.

Some projects suggest that the age of the developing brain at the time of injury has significant influence over the clinical manifestations of the

37

lesion (Leonard 1992). It appears that cortical influences become more apparent later in development and that autonomous segmental reflexes come increasingly under cortical control with age. Leonard it al (1991) propose that the major cause of the locomotor abnormalities in individuals with cerebral palsy is the lack of development of descending corticofugal projections and the repercussions of this failed development. These researchers indicate that their studies reaffirm the existence of a locomotor central pattern generator (CPG) and its presence in humans, at least early in ontology.

Most, if not all, systems theorists would agree that the nervous system exists and that one of its primary roles is pattern generation. We do not believe these theorists would fail to acknowledge that developmental processes occur and that maturation of structures has an effect. Some investigators assert that the CPG is modified when necessary for function as when encountering an obstacle or a potentially destabilizing force during gait and is thus responsive to context (Leonard 1993). Although neither the systems or pattern theorists would probably agree, we believe that most of the research outcomes of both are reasonably compatible. One of the major differences in interpretation is the extent to which patterns are hard wired, or genetically predetermined, or dynamically assembled to accomplish the task.

We believe that the more responsive to context and variable these movements are found to be, the more we are able to push our interpretation toward a less demanding role for the cortex, and a softer assemblage of pattern generation. A role for the cortex, however, is undisputed and, undoubtedly, many of the problems displayed by patients with movement dysfunction relate to damage in this area. The attraction of a systems approach is that other elements are also important and these elements may be more amenable to intervention by the practioner. All these researchers are providing valuable and exciting information. It is up to us as clinical therapists to interpret these findings for ourselves and find ways to apply them in our own clinical practice.

Summary

From this relatively short exploration it is apparent that much is yet to be discovered before a full understanding of motor control is possible. Only the major or most familiar theories have been presented here. Numerous other aspects or approaches to motor control have not been mentioned. Some theorists have approached motor control by attempting to identify the areas or specific structures of the brain that appear to be responsible for variations in movement. Brooks (1986) probably best represents the neurophysiologist who can integrate the anatomy and physiology of the brain into a story of movement. Much of the work on movement patterns and integrated systems has been postulated by Nashner and Woollocott (1979) and colleagues.

Other theorists have approached the problem of motor control from the perspective of identifying general laws and principles that may govern movement. They suspect that there are natural laws that govern the biologic systems just as there are lawful relationships that govern the universe. Bernstein (1967) and Fel'dman (1986) have contributed biomechanical models to a dynamic self-organizing systems approach to movement that has been expanded upon by Kelso (1982) and his colleagues. The most all encompassing theory that incorporates self-organizing systems theory is the dynamic action theory proposed by Thelen and her colleagues.

Even if we do come to know exactly what part of the brain contains a program, if programs exist, this knowledge in and of itself may not likely be very helpful in selecting treatment protocols in physical therapy. The same is not true for those in medicine who may discover drug or surgical treatments for such disorders. Information presented from these theorists leads us to expect that more of these laws, principles, and relationships will be discovered. The knowledge of such laws and principles will provide guidance for understanding movement deficits and developing rehabilitation procedures for intervention.

These principles may ultimately prove to be the most valuable to the practicing clinician because they may provide the clearest suggestions about which factors may be altered for rehabilitation. It is quite possible to vary clinically such factors as velocity, speed, and frequency. Muscular timing and sequencing may be amenable to change, and the ability to produce an adequate peak tension in the muscles when the task demands it may change. Identification of prerequisite acts, such as full hip extension for the triggering of swing phase in gait, will provide reliable guidance as to the choice of activities within a rehabilitation program. Of course, careful clinical observation of the resultant patterns of movement may give us clues as to the normal and abnormal nature of such a pattern and guide us to find methods of altering undesirable patterns.

| Mechanical components of movement must be considered equally with other components. |

The mechanical issues of movement have been ignored for too long. Although those theories do not really explain what the CNS is doing, an explanation may not be critical to understanding movement or correcting movement disorders. Perhaps no one area must necessarily be in control. Possibly all of the parts of the system are equally important in causing a reorganization. In terms of abnormal motor control, perhaps when any part is atypical the entire system is going to reorganize itself around that.

Another modality that has received minimal attention in therapy is vision. From many of these studies it is clear that vision is an extremely important sense for balance and coordination and for development of motor skills. Both the incorporation of the visual system in therapeutic intervention and an awareness and concern for visual deficits in clients merit more intensive consideration.

From a nervous system perspective, a therapist can fairly be certain that she can influence the anterior horn cells. This can be done simply by adding some sensory input such as vibration. But the more synapses, reflexes, loops, and structures that can be identified that also might influence the outcome, the less confident one becomes about what is actually being manipulated or changed. But in some sense the concept of self-organizing systems and biomechanical principles provide better access to treatment. It is very possible, for instance, to observe and change the amount of hip extension in a child.

It is an exciting and frustrating time to be involved in clinical physical therapy because the complete understanding of motor control awaits some future date. Even further in the future is the understanding of abnormal motor control. The exact approach to take with a client eludes us, but many new thoughts, experiments, and theories are providing new insights into treatment and evaluation. Clinical application necessarily lags behind the discovery of facts, laws, and principles; however, by keeping up to date and approaching the problems with flexibility, more appropriate clinical applications will be made.

We have chosen to emphasize systems theories in this text because we believe they hold the most promise for a functional understanding of motor control. We have further chosen the dynamic action theory as developed by Esther Thelen and her colleagues to represent self-organizing systems theory because it is the easiest to comprehend (for us at least) and because we are able to derive many practical insights for therapeutic intervention from it. This theory is presented in the next chapter.

Study Questions:

1. Describe self-organization in biological systems.

2. What happens when legs are removed from a centipede?

3. Define context.

4. What was the point of the treadmill experiment with infants?

5. Explain how walking is more than a sequence of muscle activity.

6. Compare and contrast the various theories of motor control.

7. Are all theories in conflict and must the therapist choose one or another as the sole guide for treatment application? Defend why or why not with specific examples.

Chapter 2 Dynamic Action Theory

Bridge Between Motor Control and Motor Development

As you learned earlier, researchers in this country who have developed the systems and self-organizing systems theories from the work of N.A. Bernstein are J.A.S. Kelso, M.T. Turvey, and B. Tuller. Esther Thelen and her colleagues have expanded and applied much of this information and have developed a theory of motor development from observing movements in newborn and young infants. Through this work she has unveiled her own view of motor control that incorporates and confirms many principles of systems theory. Hers is a total systems approach in which many subsystems, or elements, of which the nervous system is only one, interact dynamically to determine the final outcome of any movement. She indicates that "infants are born as moving systems with body segments that obey the principles of movement just as surely as those of the most highly trained athlete" (Thelen et al 1987*a*, p 41).

> Prescriptive theory relies on the *instructions* for movement rather than an explanation of the inner mechanisms.

Thelen (1989*a*) views the reflex-hierarchical, loop, pattern, and schema theories as *prescriptive* in nature. Prescriptive theories of motor control are those in which movement is determined through a series of commands, or instructions. The instructions for movement are believed to be a hard wired part of the nervous system and to come from a specific neural network that exists before any movement is exhibited. In a hierarchy, the highest level of the nervous system, the cortex, is the command center that distributes instructions for movement to the lowest level, the spinal cord.

In a reflex-hierarchical view, the higher level reflexes inhibit elaboration of the lower level, or primitive reflexes, as development proceeds. In this view, the reflexes result from hard wired patterns in the nervous system. The more cognitive theories previously discussed, such as schema and some pattern theories, may incorporate some interaction with the environment. The emphasis in these cognitive theories, however, is on the formation of progressively higher plans, instructions, and commands for producing behavior. Skills then are the linking of plans, instructions, and commands and thus become hierarchically assembled. Clearly, these theories are prescriptive in nature.

Motor Development

Thelen brings motor control theory and motor development theory together to explain how movement begins, how it is controlled, and how changes proceed throughout the developmental span. Many current and past developmental theorists have concluded that motor development, along with cognitive development, is a natural result of the maturation of the nervous system. The neural-maturationists such as Arnold Gesell and Myrtle McGraw suggest that infants come to control and coordinate their movements as the part of the nervous system responsible for them matures. These predetermined movements are not changed, or modified, by the environment. Both the maturational motor development and the hierarchical motor control theories are limited to one dimension, or one system, because the development of movement is solely attributed to the central nervous system (CNS).

Prescriptive theories lack the ability to explain the inner mechanisms of how movements occur (Thelen et al 1987*a*). For example, a stop sign prescribes that a driver must stop the car but does not contain any information about *how* to stop it. The fact that a neural network, or a pattern of movement, may exist does not explain how it actually participates in the form and quality of the movements, especially novel or new forms of movement. Further, such postulated networks do not account for the changes that occur in movement over time as development proceeds. For instance, these theories do not satisfactorily explain how children shift from one level of performance to a higher level, such as from creeping to upright locomotion.

> According to dynamic action theory, movement is not prescribed but emerges in relation to the external environment and the internal biologic environment.

Thelen has formulated a profoundly different theory of motor development. A good way to begin gaining insight into this theory is to consider the terms chosen for its name, dynamic action theory. In general terms, we usually think of *dynamic* as meaning simply energetic, vigorous or forceful, or causing energy or motion--the opposite of static. Thelen's theory uses principles from the relatively new science of dynamical systems, including the fields of synergetics, thermodynamics, and nonlinear systems. In movement theory, she uses this term in a broader sense than pure biomechanics. She includes the concept that movement is not prescribed *before* its elaboration, but that the movement emerges *during* its execution in relation to the physical environment of the external world and the biologic environment of the internal world. A working insight into the rather broad use of this term is difficult to achieve, although the major idea is that a dynamic system is any system in which behavior changes over time. As you progress through this material and gain further insights into the dynamic action theory, you should begin to get the concept.

> Action is movement.

The other word used in naming this theory is *action*. Thelen's theory is grounded in action. It is a movement-based account of behavior. That is, she has investigated specific movements that infants spontaneously generate during the experimental observation periods. This could be termed real-time action, or activity. That is, the action is occurring at a specific and real moment in time (during the experiment). From these events she has proposed a general theory that explains changes during developmental time, that is, changes through the span of an infant's development. Real-time events are happening here and now while developmental time spans the history of an individual. Other developmental theorists may begin with the evidence observed over developmental time, such as the gradual attainment of competence in motor skills, and attempt to discover the real-time processes that possibly explain it.

Thelen indicates that "most developmental theorists are most interested in the development of complex symbolic and affective processes--the 'life of the mind' and have paid less attention to the translation of ideas into movement--a 'life of the limbs.' Infants are born with much movement and few ideas so they lack symbolic and verbal mediating mechanisms between their mental state and the expressions of their bodies" (Thelen and Fogel 1989*b*, p 23).

An important element of Thelen's work, which differentiates it from most other researchers, is that her initial observations were of spontaneous activity of newborn and young infants. Other researchers manipulated the subjects by handling them or requiring them to perform tasks. Thelen made observations of movements the children performed themselves and carefully analyzed the video recordings of those movements. Children were not required to perform in any way. In her later studies, some environmental changes were made to observe how the children would respond to them, but they were not required to perform particular tasks.

The dynamic action theory incorporates self-organizing principles of movement. Self-organization in biological systems means that pattern and order can emerge from the interaction of the components in a complex system. There is no need for either commands or explicit instructions.

Central to systems theories is the hypothesis that individual muscles and joints never work in isolation. You will remember from material earlier in the previous chapter that one of Bernstein's (1967) major points was that a muscle never acts as a single independent element in a total movement. Each muscle participates in a movement that involves other muscles and many body parts and segments. One of the ways that the nervous system controls the large number of parts is by linking specific muscles together and constructing a pattern of activity, which has been called a functional synergy, or coordinative structure (Bernstein 1967).

Thelen believes that muscles work together in patterns, or functional synergies, to accomplish common goals. Thus the function to be performed is what determines how and which muscles will be linked together to produce the movement. This view is directly contrary to models of motor control that are based on hierarchically recruited, hard wired, or reflex-like subunits of behavior. Such reflex models suggest that there is a strict mapping of the relationships between these muscles that exists before the movement takes place.

The dynamic action theory addresses the fundamental question of the sources of order in movement over space and time. Functional synergies, or coordinative structures, represent just one system or subsystem in the total systems view. Because muscles are linked together consistently under each circumstance, they produce an order and regularity of movement. It is this order that makes movements assume recognizable forms such as kicking, smiling, or serving a tennis ball. This order cannot be predicted by studying the muscles and joints as individual units in a movement. These synergies emerge, or arise, as a new development from the function they will produce; thus they are sources of information. In contrast, the muscles and joints in prescriptive theories serve only as vessels of information as they become the recipients of commands (Thelen et al 1987*a*).

Other biomechanical elements, or subsystems, are important in the dynamic action theory. Movement outcome cannot be predicted by muscle forces alone. Movement is the result of both muscular and nonmuscular forces, including the inertial and reactive forces from the moving body and the forces resulting from contact with the supporting surface.

Movement is the result of both muscular and nonmuscular forces.

A good example of systems' properties involving many subsystems occurs in the coordination and control of a single extremity during gait. During locomotion, the joints are not controlled as individual units. The joints and muscles are linked together as a whole synergy that involves the entire extremity. This linkage is maintained despite changes in the speed or the force of the movement.

These consistent patterns are not completely explained by the nervous system activation of the muscles involved. The final movement is also the result of passive forces generated by the length and the resting condition of the muscles. In addition, there are effects resulting not only from the mechanical linkages between the muscles and the ligaments in the joints but also from the pull of one segment in relation to another. The effects of gravity also are very important in locomotion. There is little muscular activity in the leg during the swing phase of normal speed walking because the effects of the nonbiological elements, such as gravity and inertia, contribute to the movement. The pattern that we see thus emerges from the relationships of both the physical and the neural components contributing to the movement (Thelen and Cooke 1987).

In dynamic systems, the pattern emerges from the relationship of both physical and neural components.

Perhaps the best way to gain a more complete understanding of Thelen's model of motor control and motor development would be to review some of her experiments. They will be presented in the order in which she performed them, so that we can build her theoretic approach in steps.

Rhythmical Movements in Infants

Thelen's (1979) first research project involved investigating the presence of rhythmical stereotypies in normal human infants. She described 47 movement patterns of rhythmical and highly stereotyped behaviors involving the legs and feet; the head and face; the arms, hands, and fingers; and the whole torso in various postures. Some of these movements included kicking, banging on objects, waving arms, rocking, and bouncing (Fig 2-1).

These movements seem to be performed for their own sake, and it is difficult to ascribe a purpose, or goal, to them. The movements emerged at specific times and persisted for a certain period in the child's developmental time span. For instance, kicking and other movements of the legs appeared at birth and reached a peak of activity between 14 and 32 weeks of age. Rocking and other patterns exhibited on hands and knees appeared at about 24 weeks and declined at 32 weeks. Thus, within the first year of life, each movement had a specific time it appeared, reached a peak, and then declined.

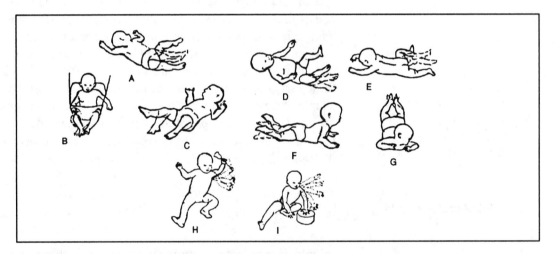

Figure 2-1 Rhythmical stereotypies of the legs and arms. (A) Alternate leg kicking; (B) foot rubbing; (C) and (D) single leg kicking; (E) and (F) single leg kicking in prone; (G) both leg kicking; (F) both leg kicking with back strongly arched; (H) arm waving with object; (I) arm banging against surface and arm sway. From Thelen 1979, reprinted with permission of Academic Press Ltd (London).

In addition to the observation that the stereotypies appeared and diminished with a recognizable regularity, their appearance was correlated with the results of other tests of neuromuscular maturation such as the Bayley Scales of Infant Development. Thelen thus showed that these rhythmical movements had a significant relationship with motor milestones and that the age of onset of such stereotypies are predictive of the speed with which motor development will proceed.

Apparently, these behaviors result from spontaneous motor patterns that have a high degree of intrinsic organization. *Organization* may be defined as any unified consolidated group of elements; a systematized whole. Thelen concluded that the rhythmic behaviors represent a unified group of elements (eg, muscles, joints, neurons, and biomechanical effects) working as a systematized whole for a specific purpose. Further, these behaviors are not dependent on external circumstances, or stimuli, for their elaboration but are self-generated and spontaneous.

Stereotyped behavior in a muscle group appears either before more complex activities are demonstrated or just as the infant is gaining postural control over a new position. Thelen's (1979) conclusions were that there is some central control of the patterns and that they reflect some degree of functional maturity of a particular neuromuscular pathway before there is perfect voluntary control.

Kicking

The next step in Thelen's investigations was to study more carefully one specific stereotypic behavior of normal infants. She chose to investigate one of the earliest stereotypies observed--rhythmic kicking--in order to gain insight into the inherent motor organization of the very young infant (Thelen et al 1981). These first studies examined the dynamic components of early movements of the legs. The next question is how these early movements, present at or before birth, could possibly be adapted later into movements that relate to the external environment of the child. Thelen was particularly interested in the development and maturation of locomotion as an example of how motor control and motor development evolve.

Experimental Procedure

Infants were videotaped during spontaneous kicking, and the tapes were analyzed frame by frame. By knowing the number of each frame and the speed by which each frame was generated, a very exact picture of the component movements of kicking was obtained. Some of these movement components were the temporal factors (eg, the time movements began, the time between phases, and the point the movement changed directions).

The kick was divided into the flexion phase; the intrakick pause (the interval between the cessation of flexion and the initiation of the extension phase); the extension phase; and the interkick pause (the interval between the end of extension and the initiation of the next flexion). See Figure 2-2.

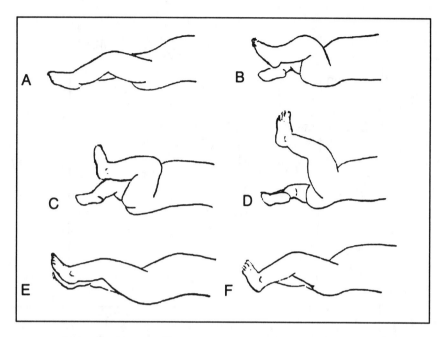

Figure 2-2 Characteristic positions of the leg in the infant single-leg kick cycle, shown in a 6-week-old girl. (A) Interkick interval, leg extended; (B) initiation of flexion phase, ankle begins dorsiflexion; (C) hip, knee, and ankle fully flexed; (D) initiation of extension phase; (E) extension phase; and (F) end of extension phase, with heel on the supporting surface and the ankle still dorsiflexed. In rapid kicking, the heel did not often rest on the supporting surface between kicks. Drawn from Thelen et al (1981).

> Intrakick and interkick intervals are more variable than the movement phases.

These experiments showed a close synchrony of the joints in space and time. Interjoint coordination was highly structured so that the hip, knee, and ankle joints moved predictably together (Fig 2-3). For all the infants, flexion and extension phases were relatively stable, and the flexion phase was shorter in duration than the extension phase. Intrakick and interkick intervals were more variable than the movement phases, and the interkick, or the time between kicks, was the most variable of all.

An important observation was that the repetitive cycle of leg flexion and extension in kicking looked quite similar to the movements of a single leg in mature gait. Mature gait can be divided into two general phases: stance and swing. Remember from Chapter 1 that it is the duration of the stance phase that decreases when the velocity of the gait increases. The duration of the swing phase remains relatively constant.

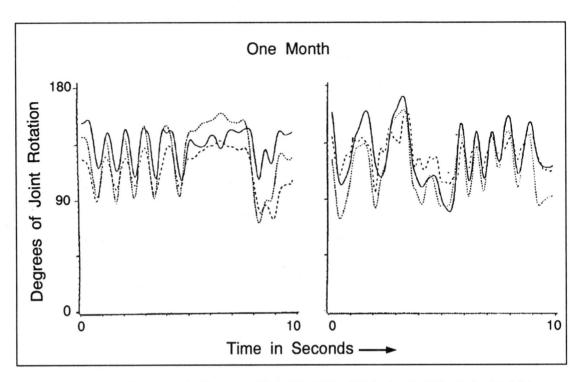

Figure 2-3 Joint rotations recorded from two different 1-month-old infants. Solid line is the hip joint, short dashed line is the knee joint, and long dashed line is the ankle joint. Decreasing joint angles indicate flexion movements; increasing angles indicate extension. Note how the three joints move together into flexion or extension. Thelen and Fisher 1983a, reprinted with permission.

The kicking of infants produced a parallel phenomenon to the division and action of mature gait. The sum of the flexion, the intrakick pause, and the extension phases in the infants may be considered equal to the swing phase of adults. The interkick interval corresponds to the stance phase of mature gait. The diagram in Figure 2-4 shows the mathematical manipulation comparing stance and swing phases in kicking infants and in adults and certain animals. It is easy to see that the lines are almost identical, particularly between the human infants and adults.

> The interkick interval corresponds to the stance phase of gait.

This study suggests several important points about the development and control of locomotion. Human infants produce very predictive and patterned movements. These cannot be classified as reflexes because no stimulus is required to elicit them. These coordinated motor activities occur early in development before either true voluntary or goal directed and purposeful movements emerge. Finally, the pattern generators involved in these prelocomotor activities are present and active long before functional locomotion appears.

> Infants move in predicted and patterned ways that are not reflexive in nature.

The patterns observed in kicking suggest that humans have some type of central pattern generator capable of generating consistent movements. These pattern generators are likely to be subcortical in nature because the infant cortex is poorly developed at this stage, especially in the areas associated with the legs (Thelen et al 1981; Conel 1941).

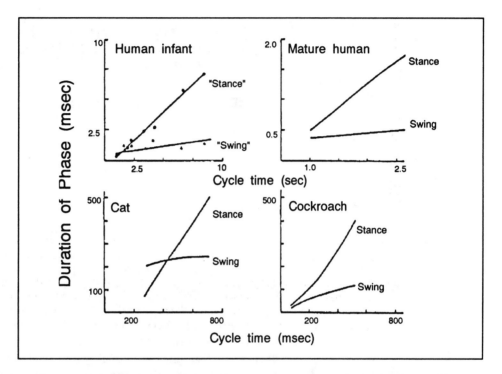

Figure 2-4 Comparisons of the duration of the "stance" and "swing" phase of the single-leg infant kicking to the duration of phases of the step cycle in the mature human, the cat, and the cockroach. In the infant, "swing" phase was defined as the sum of the flexion, intrakick pause, and extension phases: "stance" is the interkick interval. From Thelen et al (1981, p 51), reprinted with permission.

Study Questions:

1. How does Thelen's dynamic action theory differ from neuromaturationist theory?

2. What constitutes a prescriptive theory?

3. Explain the following statement: Movement is an emergent property of the relationship between both the physical and the neural components contributing to the movement.

4. What are rhythmical stereotypies?

5. Are the spontaneous movements of the infant's extremities random and unstructured? Defend your answer.

6. Describe and explain the linkages between the hip, knee, and ankle during the newborn kicking movements.

7. Explain how an infant kick can be compared to adult gait.

8. Describe the evidence that suggests that the development of coordinated motor patterns follows the development of voluntary or goal directed movement.

9. Define real time and developmental time.

State

Another critically important aspect of Thelen's investigations is her interest in the relationship of the infant's state to the movements observed. *State* refers to the general arousal level of the infant which reflects the state of the nervous system. Six states have been identified: the infant is (1) in deep sleep, (2) in light sleep, (3) drowsy, (4) alert, (5) active, or (6) crying (Brazelton 1984). Thelen noted that the amount of kicking or other rhythmical activity changes as the state, or arousal level, changes. Kicking is more reliably observed in infants who are active or crying (states 5 and 6) than in those who are quiet and alert (state 4). Therefore, increasing arousal, or levels of generalized behavioral activation, appears to facilitate the activity of these generator circuits.

> *State* reflects the level of arousal in the nervous system and relates to the amount and type of movement generated.

The relationship of the state of the nervous system and the amount of muscle activity is very important in determining the shape the movement pattern assumes. The type of kicking the infant demonstrates is also directly related to his state. Thelen and Fogel (1989*a*) indicate that the infant's movement is indexed by state; that is, he will shift from one pattern to another by increasing arousal and thus increasing the amount of muscle activity within the same generator pattern.

Muscle Activity in Kicking

The addition of electromyographic (EMG) studies to her behavioral descriptions of movements provided Thelen with information about how the muscle groups actually work together to produce a kick. Thelen and Fisher (1983*a*) added EMG analysis of hip, knee, and ankle musculature during kicking.

If we were to perform a movement analysis of an infant kick based on kinesiologic principles, we would expect the flexor part of the kick to be initiated by hip flexor muscles and the extensor phase by hip extensors. An EMG analysis showed that the kicks were initiated principally by short strong activation of the hip flexor muscles. The ankle dorsiflexors were also active. Contrary to what you might expect, there was often coactivation of the antagonist, or extensor groups, but the flexors were the most dominant; thus the movement performed was flexion (Fig 2-5).

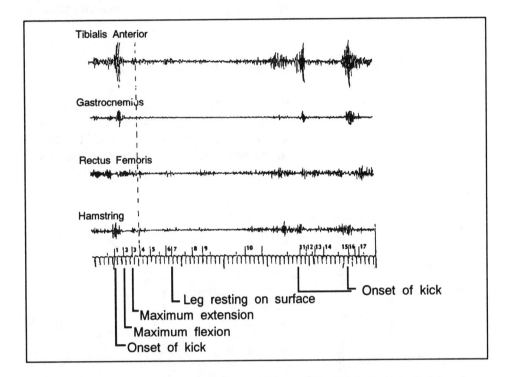

Figure 2-5 Electromyographic recordings from a 2-week-old infant. Note that the kicking frequency is low because the kicks are relatively slow. Two kicks are recorded in this time segment. The kicking segments are similar to those described in Figure 2-2. Note the weak extensor activity and the relative amount of coactivation present at the onset and through the duration of the flexion phase of the kick. From Thelen and Fisher (1983a), reprinted with permission.

Even more contrary to what you might expect was the observation that no EMG activity was present in either the extensor or the flexor muscles during the extension part of the kick. Thelen and Fisher (1983b) concluded that these newborns relied heavily on passive mechanical forces as an integral part of the movement. There was no braking of the flexor movement but simply a cessation of the active flexor thrust before the end of flexion. It would appear that combining the relaxation of flexor activity, viscoelastic properties of the muscle and other tissues of the leg, and the effects of gravity on the flexed limb, an extension of the leg was produced through a recoil phenomenon. Occasionally during the flexion phase, an infant would hold his legs in a flexed posture for a little longer than ordinary. When this prolonged flexion occurred, the posture was maintained by continuous low-level activity of the flexor muscles.

Infants may rely on passive forces such as that produced by the recoil phenomenon to produce some movements.

51

Therapists have often described the kicking in infants as a reciprocal movement because the kicking leg oscillates between flexion and extension and the movement alternates between right and left leg. In fact, Margaret Rood, a pioneer in neurotherapeutic approaches in physical and occupational therapy, described the earliest patterns in developmental sequence as reciprocal innervation patterns, which were mass flexion or extension movements. Thelen and Fisher (1983a) showed that there was little evidence of reciprocal activation of the antagonistic muscles in the newborn kicking pattern.

Maturational Changes

In one experiment, 2-week-old infants were compared with 4-week-old infants to observe possible maturational changes (Thelen and Fisher 1983a). The experiment confirmed the close synchrony of the joints in the kicking movement. In addition, this synchrony appeared to get even stronger between 2 and 4 weeks of age (Fig 2-6).

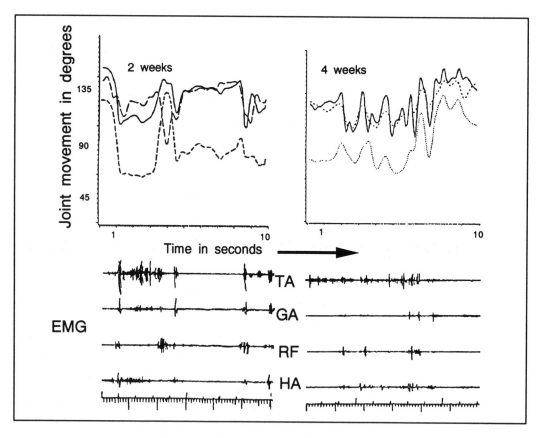

Figure 2-6 Concurrent EMG records and joint rotation records from a 2-week-old infant and a 4-week-old infant. Note that the three joints are more highly synchronized in the 4-week-old infant. Note also that most EMG activity is recorded from the flexor muscles in either flexion or extension phases. TA (tibialis anterior); GA (gastrocnemius); RF (rectus femoris); HA (medial hamstring). From Thelen and Fisher (1983a), reprinted with permission.

Note the differences in the EMG recordings of rapid kicking in a 6-month-old infant (Fig 2-7) compared with those of a 1-month-old shown in Figure 2-6. By 6 months of age strong extension is seen, with less coactivation of flexors and extensors.

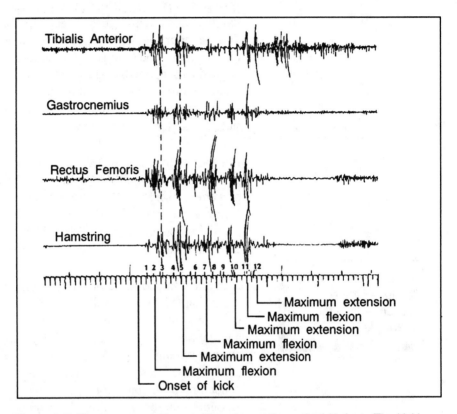

Figure 2-7 Electromyographic recordings from a 6-month-old infant. The kicking is relatively rapid, with 5 kicks recorded in the center portion of the graph. At this age, note the strong extensor activity. From Thelen and Fisher (1983a), reprinted with permission.

Developmental and Motor Control Principles

Traditionally, the spontaneous movements of infants have variously been described as being disorganized, random, thrashing, or mass movements (Peiper 1963; Doudlah 1981). Thelen's work just described has shown this to be otherwise. The pattern of the joint movements in space and time is shaped by the interplay of the active muscular forces supplied by the infant and the reactive forces either supplied by the environment or resulting from the physical properties of the tissues involved. Because of the constancy of the relationships observed in the joint measurements, there appears to be an active interaction among body parts. This means that the limb as a whole acts as a unit, rather than individual muscles or joints acting independently. This follows Bernstein's (1967) thesis that a muscle never enters into a movement as an isolated entity but that groups of muscles are constrained to act together as functional units.

The limb behaves as a unit.

53

Another of Bernstein's observations is borne out with Thelen's research. Remember that muscles have been modeled as an attached spring loaded with a specific mass. No matter what the elongation or compression of the spring, it always returns to the same length. The position of the spring is specified by the relation between the spring's stiffness, resting length, and amount of mass attached. Thelen et al (1987*b*) have shown that the leg movements of the newborn obey the same laws as the mass-spring. The stiffness of the infant's spring is set by the relative activation of agonists and antagonists. The more powerful movements require more muscle force and thus a stiffer spring. Once compressed, the spring recoils back to the resting position of extension without further activity in the muscles.

It is the relative timing of the muscles in the functional synergy that produces the recognizable form of the movement. Thus we recognize the movement as a kick. The speed and force of the muscular activity is controlled by central mechanisms that result in a relative activation of the agonist and antagonist muscles. Thus the role of the nervous system is to determine the stiffness of the spring.

Higher levels of state produce different movements in the infants' legs.

It should come as no surprise, then, that in these infants the stiffness of the spring is intimately related to the state of the child: the higher the state, or arousal level, the stiffer the spring. In state 5 kicking may show alternating activity of the legs while in state 6, with the infant intensely crying, kicking is observed as both legs kicking simultaneously and stiffly. This is a shift to a whole new movement. The basic pattern generation has remained the same, but the increase in one factor, the amount of muscle activation, has produced a new movement--a bilateral straight leg position. Therefore, early in development, the level of activity in the muscles is a function of the state of the infant, and the amount of muscular activity governs the shape the kicking pattern takes (Thelen et al 1987*b*).

Voluntary, or Goal Directed, Movement

Thelen and Fisher (1983*b*) performed an ingenious addition to her basic approach in order to investigate voluntary movement and early motor learning. The investigators attached a control line from the infant's leg to a mobile so that the mobile would move with movements of the leg. They found that in 3-month-old infants there was an increased kicking frequency associated with the presence of the mobile. This reflects the infant's ability to voluntarily move the mobile, presumably for his pleasure and interest. The patterns of the kick remained identical to the spontaneous patterns that were observed earlier. Thus, it would appear that the very young infant is capable of purposeful voluntary movement and that the patterns of movement he will use are those currently available--the flexions and extensions of the kick.

It is further interesting to note that developmental doctrine has indicated that neuromuscular maturation progresses in a cephalocaudal direction. Yet, according to Thelen and Fisher (1983a), newborn infants show their most highly patterned gross movements in the legs. Rhythmical and synchronized arm movements also have been observed in newborns, but the most reliable patterns are found in the legs. Clearly, developmental theory based on developmental-time observations, rather than on real-time observations, has produced some apparently erroneous rules.

Thelen's work challenges the concept of cephalocaudal development.

Study Questions:

1. Define *state* and describe how it affects movement.

2. Explain how the muscles are activated in the newborn kicking pattern.

Development of Locomotion as a Model for the Development of Motor Control

Comparison of Stepping and Kicking

Until Thelen's work, most early infant behavior had been described as being the result of reflex arcs. Spontaneous movements had not been studied. *Spontaneous movements* are those that occur naturally in the everyday life (or real time) of the infant and that are not elicited by someone else manipulating the child (Thelen et al 1981). Certain reflexes were thought to be the precursors of particular movements. For instance, spontaneous stepping, which is elicited by tactile stimulation on the bottom of the feet while the infant is held vertical, has been thought to be a developmental precursor to walking. This reflex disappears in the first 2 months of life.

Zelazo (1983) discovered that automatic stepping can be maintained through exercise. The infants in which this reflex has been maintained also seem to ambulate earlier than those in whom it was not. Zelazo extends this work to a more general theory of the development of locomotion. He suggests that by maintaining the movement through use, the reflex converts to goal-directed behavior based on higher plans

55

through developing cognitive skills and through maturing motor pathways. Thus the reflex forms the basis for the stepping pattern of independent walking. This reflex disappears without practice, to resurface later when the cognitive development is sufficient to trigger it. Zelazo is clearly in the maturationist camp.

> **Kicking and stepping are identical movements.**

Thelen used her established laboratory techniques for studying kicking in order to compare kicking with spontaneous stepping in 2-week-old infants. An analysis showed that kicking and stepping are essentially identical patterns of movement (Thelen and Fisher 1984). Any differences, such as the extent of joint flexions, could be explained by the effects of gravity on the infant's limbs in the upright position as opposed to the supine position. In the upright position, we have interpreted the movements as stepping and in the supine position we name them kicking.

Although the traditional belief is that tactile sensations from the bottom of the feet and the upright posture are the stimuli eliciting the stepping reflex, Thelen and Fisher's (1984) comparisons showed that infants were no more stimulated to step in the upright position than to kick while in the supine position. Once again, as in kicking, the elaboration of the alternating step-like patterns of the legs was more clearly associated with general arousal, or the infants state, than with the upright posture.

Many observers have clearly indicated that the stepping reflex disappears at about 2 months of age (Barnes et al 1978; Zelazo et al 1972). Thelen (1983) points out that the upright position makes the infant work against gravity to lift the legs. Alternatively, gravity is less effective and may even provide some assistance in the final degrees of flexion in the supine position. As infants mature, the mass of the legs increases dramatically, especially in fatty tissue, in relation to their length. This change in mass alters the dynamics of the moving limb. There is a relative decrease in muscle mass and, therefore, a lack of sufficient strength in the muscles to lift the legs against gravity or support full weight when the body is upright. As a result, the stepping movement, or reflex, disappears. Infants who practice stepping have likely increased their muscular strength through physical training.

To prove this point, Thelen et al (1984) added weights to the legs of younger infants who were stepping to simulate the expected weight gain. These infants then produced less stepping. Infants with and without weights were then submerged in water up to the waist to lessen the effects of gravity. Not surprisingly, there was an increase in stepping activity. Thus, it should be safe to conclude that stepping disappears because of nonneural factors rather than through elaborate inhibitions of the developing cognitive brain (Fig 2-8).

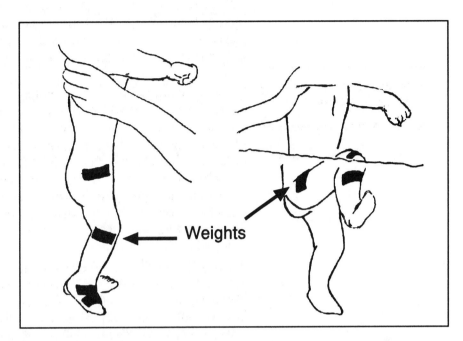

Figure 2-8   The effect of reduced mass on the stepping of a 1-month-old boy. Left, held erect out of water, boy performed 6 steps; joint angles average hip = 125 degrees, knee = 112 degrees, and ankle = 97 degrees. Right, held erect with legs under water, boy performed 23 steps; joint angles averaged 94, 77, and 86 degrees, respectively (drawn from Thelen et al 1984).

Evolution of Walking Patterns

Thelen and Cooke (1987) wanted to determine whether walking was a gradual process occurring across developmental time or the result of maturation of some particular neurological substratum that occurs at a particular point in developmental time. The investigation included analyzing stepping and walking patterns in infants from 1 month of age and comparing them to older infants who were beginning to walk.

> Locomotor patterns evolve over developmental time.

Although infants attain independent walking at about 1 year of age, the refinement of patterns of joint angle rotations does not reach the mature form for some years. It appears that pattern modification develops gradually during the first year, and evidence suggests that the steps of the new walker are indeed derived from the more simple patterns available at birth.

The EMG recordings also show an evolution of muscle activity from early patterns to later ones. You will remember that in newborns extensors are coactivated with the flexors at the onset of the flexion portion of the kick and are silent during the extension portion. As infants develop, the extensive coactivation is gradually replaced with

57

more phasic muscle activation. Older infants begin to show coactivation of flexors and extensors during the extension phase of the kick. With further maturity, there comes a more true reciprocal pattern of flexor and then extensor activity. These EMG patterns continue to change, and some coactivation of muscles continues even after the children have attained independent locomotion (Okamoto and Goto 1985). These findings indicate that a gradual refinement, or developmental, process is in place (Thelen and Cooke 1987; Thelen et al 1983).

Systems Contributing to Locomotion

Remember that earlier in this chapter it was noted that experiments with a variety of animals showed that the initiation of swing phase in gait depends on the effective stretch to muscles of the stance leg and is followed by the unloading of that leg. In human adults, the major force for the initiation of swing comes from the plantar flexors at push-off. These muscles are assisted by the hip flexors, which contract at the beginning of the swing phase. All of these muscles have been stretched beyond their resting length as body weight is shifted forward during stance on the single weight-bearing limb before swing begins (Figs 2-9, 2-10).

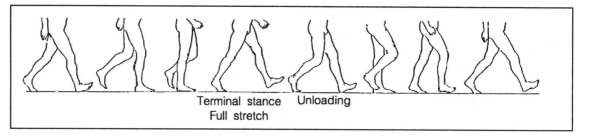

Terminal stance   Unloading
Full stretch

Figure 2-9 The normal gait cycle. Note the phases of the cycle that produce maximum stretch on the plantar flexors and unloading of the pre-swing leg.

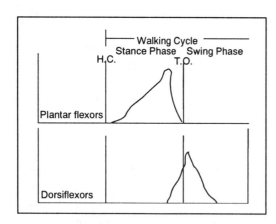

Figure 2-10 Muscle activity profiles of the plantar flexors and dorsiflexors. Note the relatively little overlap, suggesting that coactivation is not part of the mature form of gait.

To investigate how these circumstances might be observed in developing infants, Thelen (1986a) created an elegant experiment in which 7-month-old nonwalkers were held over a moving treadmill. Although these infants failed to attempt many steps on the quiet treadmill, they showed mature stepping patterns as soon as it was turned on. Thelen suggests the possibility that the treadmill provides an energy boost for the passive and mechanical backward stretching of one leg. This stretching action allows the underlying coordinative linkages to materialize. The infants will provide this stretch by themselves once they have gained sufficient strength and balance control. The treadmill provides a biomechanically appropriate environment, or context, that shapes a specific complex pattern from a general existing pattern-generating system. This shaping illustrates just how the environment can affect the task (Fig 2-11).

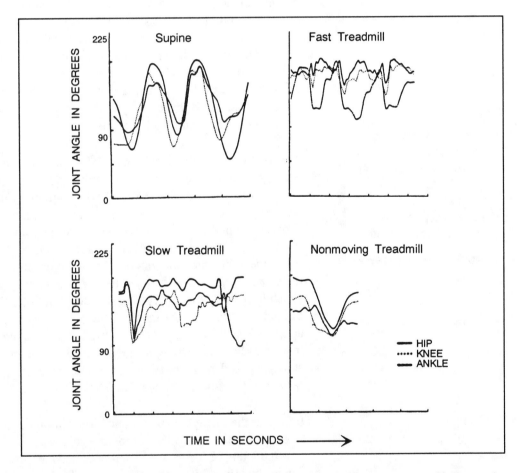

Figure 2-11 Joint angle excursions of a 7-month-old infant during spontaneous kicking and stepping on a nonmoving treadmill and a treadmill moving at two speeds. The infant performed no steps in the baseline condition on the nonmoving treadmill. Note the smooth, synchronous excursions of the supine and baseline conditions and the more elaborated and complex fashions with the treadmill. From Thelen and Fogel (1989b), reprinted with permission.

The appropriate neural substrata for increasing sophistication in movement, such as balance control, is necessary for infants to acquire the patterns of mature stepping, but it is not sufficient in itself. Thelen (1986a) believes that the gradual changes she has observed in the months before and after walking result from maturation and experience in all the contributing subsystems, including balance, posture control, and strength. In addition, the environmental context that incorporates the dynamic functional demands of upright locomotion contributes to the patterns that emerge. The specific elements of the pattern involved in walking are not set down in detail by the nervous system before walking occurs. These details are emergent with the task of walking itself. The details arise from the system self-organizing around the task of walking .

The environment is a critical system that influences the movement that emerges.

Infants just beginning to walk are unstable and show variable patterns of activity. A factor that greatly contributes to this instability is that infants lack the strength to remain balanced on one leg. If the child cannot remain balanced for long on a single leg, he cannot effectively stretch the muscles and tissues of the stance leg. Therefore, he cannot effectively use the viscoelastic and inertial properties of the stretched muscles to initiate swing. It will then be necessary to use excessive active muscle contraction to produce flexion movements in stance by bringing in muscles not used during mature gait. The use of extra muscles will alter the gait pattern, but this activity will diminish as strength and balance improve (Thelen and Fogel 1989a).

Most of the characteristics of gait in infants can be explained by lack of balance because of insufficient strength.

This lack of strength leads to many of the characteristic observations of early gait such as flexed knees and ankles, short stride, and increased cadence (Sutherland et al 1980). At the beginning, infants are toe walkers. Because they cannot stand on one leg for very long, they have a short swing phase, with reduced flexion at the joints producing a small swing movement. This small swing does not give them sufficient time to rotate the ankle into enough dorsiflexion to produce a heel strike; therefore, they land on the toes first. Besides being somewhat out of synch for a heel strike, they lack sufficient strength to cushion the impact of landing with the more mature knee-flexion wave that is present in adults. Thus the acquisition of strength in the stance leg is very important in allowing the most dynamically efficient coordination strategies, as demonstrated by more mature walkers, to emerge in the gait pattern of the developing walker (Thelen and Fogel 1989a).

It is clear that many nonneural and biodynamic factors are just as important in the acquisition of mature gait as are neurologic maturation or remodeling. Most of the differences between infant gait and adult gait can be explained by these mechanisms (Thelen and Fogel 1989a). There is a gradual evolution from the simple pattern generation of the newborn period. Essential to the development of mature gait is the ability of the joints to produce more individual movements rather than the obligatory synergy of the newborn period. More than likely this tight synergy results, at least in part, from the coactivation pattern of the muscles newborns use to produce their kicks. If the hip and ankle muscles are always activated together, the joints will also be locked together. As less coactivation occurs, muscles become more free to be active in other spatiotemporal patterns such as plantar flexion of the ankle with flexion of the hip. This freedom from coactivation permits more flexibility between the joints.

These observations confirm another of Bernstein's (1967) formulations concerning the degrees of freedom in a system. He said that to control the many degrees of freedom in a new movement, we will restrict the movement initially through coactivation and tight synchrony of the muscles in the synergy. This produces an increased stiffness in the joint activity and produces a tightness and relative inefficiency in the movement. As more control is gained through practice, some of the degrees of freedom are relaxed and less coactivation is used.

| Movements will be stiff when the degrees of freedom are first restricted and controlled by coactivation, or cocontraction. |

Thelen et al (1987c) suggest that when more independent control of the joints has been accomplished, the muscles and joints work together in a way that results more from certain constraints than from that of specific neuronal networks generating patterns of action. These constraints are produced by the weight of body segments, viscoelastic and other nonneural properties of the extremity, and the biodynamic demands of the task. The treadmill experiments show that such a dynamic environment, or context, can elicit a more complex movement pattern. A dramatic remodeling of the neurological substrata or inhibition of the networks is not necessary for refinements to take place.

| Changing the environment may cause a more complex movement to be produced. |

Interlimb Coordination

Evidence is fairly clear that functional synergies involve at least the entire extremity. A further question would be whether the synergy involves the contralateral extremity or other parts of the body. Because locomotion involves at least both lower extremities in a predictable synchronized fashion, the question becomes a practical one.

Through an even more sophisticated locomotion experiment with infants using a split-belt treadmill, Thelen et al (1987c) found that human infants would adjust the components of the stepping pattern within a dynamically different context to maintain alternating leg movements. This alternating pattern is what maintains a stable center of gravity in normal locomotion.

| Functional synergies involve both extremities. |

Most of the time the alternating pattern with different belt speeds was maintained through changes in the duration of the stance leg on each belt. For instance, when the left leg was on the faster belt the right leg initiated swing earlier to maintain the alternating pattern. Thus the activity of one limb modified the activity of the opposite limb (Fig 2-12).

This study showed that the synergy responsive to the dynamic context of the treadmill involved both limbs. The treadmill drove each leg at a different speed, but both limbs responded in a cooperative manner to preserve an alternating gait. Thelen et al (1987c) concluded that cycle and step phase timing was not solely the result of either a pattern generator or the treadmill belt speed alone. It is logical that if the belt speed determined the stance duration, each leg would have its own cycle rather than having the cooperative cycles that were produced.

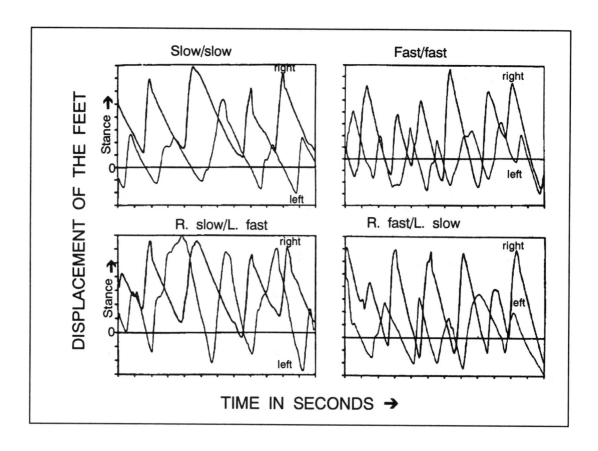

Figure 2-12 Displacements of the right and left feet in the horizontal direction of a single infant as a function of treadmill direction. Movement in the positive direction is the stance phase of the step. The figure illustrates the influence of the belt speed on step rate in the tied-belt condition (slow/slow; fast/fast) and the maintenance of regularly alternating steps in both the tied and split-belt conditions. From Thelen et al (1987c), reprinted with permission.

Interlimb coupling is improved by supporting beginning walkers with the hands.

The pattern of interlimb coordination demonstrated by a 1-year-old child who is beginning to walk independently is similar to the coordination elicited on the treadmill. Supporting beginning walkers by holding their hands improves the interlimb coupling. Holding the hands provides enough support to compensate somewhat for the lack of strength and postural control that are problems for the young child (Thelen and Fogel 1989a). Walking is a difficult task for a human because bipedal gait is inherently unstable. There are extreme requirements for maintaining balance over a small base of support that is constantly moving as weight shifts are performed for forward movement. Infants must then generate the functional synergies necessary to move the body forward simultaneously with synergies required to maintain dynamic balance (Thelen 1989*b*). Constant interaction with the environment maintains a flow of information into the nervous system along with the flow of activity out to the muscles. Movement in each new posture produces multiple new sensory experiences as infants learn the limits of their stability in the upright posture.

Thelen believes that the neuromuscular system must maintain functional coherence of the two legs by transmitting information about the dynamic status of one leg to the other leg. The CNS monitors the task rather than monitoring the specific pattern of muscle activation. The result is that the particular pattern involving coupling of the two legs emerges to fit the task. Because the infant's cortex is not fully developed, it is more likely that these adjustments originate in segmental or other subcortical structures (Thelen and Fogel 1989*a*).

> The dynamic status of one leg is transmitted to the other leg by the CNS, which monitors the task rather than the specific muscle patterns.

Another experiment was performed by Thelen and Jensen (1989) that illustrates a similar dynamic linkage between the two legs. Small weights were attached to one leg of 6-week-old infants to observe any changes in supine kicking. Surprisingly, the frequency, amplitude, and velocity of the kicks were maintained in the weighted leg. The extra weight appeared to have no effect. However, the number of kicks and the frequency and amplitude were increased in the unweighted leg. The experimenters assumed that the infants sensed the weight change and increased the energy delivered to both legs in the kicking pattern. The effect would be most noticeable in the unweighted leg because the extra energy used by the weighted leg would just maintain the number and size of kicks of the weighted leg. The synergy apparently involves both legs because the weight change was applied to only one leg, but both legs responded.

All of these experiments performed by Thelen and her colleagues have led her to construct a developmental plan for locomotion. This plan relies on the development of various systems involved when upright locomotion is produced. She has shown how certain reflexes, such as automatic stepping, are composed of movements identical to those spontaneously generated by the newborn. The pattern produced is a general one, and the specifics are determined by the context and the task. She has provided evidence that these patterns change gradually to a more recognizable mature form in upright gait through the involvement of many systems or subsystems, not just the nervous system.

Complex interaction between the two limbs appears to be monitored and controlled by the nervous system. Clearly, the state of development of one component, such as strength of muscles, has a profound effect on the ability of other systems to manifest their effects.

Another question to be answered was whether infants could detect the changing array of forces as they move and compensate for them with active muscle participation. In natural movements, adults control the passive forces from the other segments and from gravity by adjusting their active muscle contractions. Through the use of refined techniques of analysis, Thelen and Jensen (1989) have shown that infants do know about the status of their movements. By comparing slow and fast kicks, it was possible to determine that even at 2 months of age the infants could detect and manage the different passive forces present in the two conditions by their precise use of active muscle contraction.

Possible Control Variables in Locomotor Development

A dynamical system shows nonlinear changes over time. The rates of physical growth occur in spurts and plateaus, not as a straight line. These spurts and plateaus also are reflected in changes in the nervous system serving perceptual and motor functions. The result is that development itself is nonlinear. Thus no single mechanism of change will apply across a developmental-time scale but rather each analysis must account for the capabilities of the infant in relation to the task in a particular environment. Thelen has detailed how such mechanisms might influence the development of upright locomotion.

Thelen (1986*b*) suggests that a systems view of the development of locomotion involves many levels and types of components. She has proposed a hypothetical developmental profile for each proposed subsystem, or component, and illustrated it through the use of a simple stylized graph. The span for each profile is approximately the first year of life. Each profile represents a possible *control variable*, that is, a crucial variable whose changes can cause system-wide reorganization. She cautions that these components are only possible control variables and that the list is not likely to be all inclusive. The graphs are not always based on large amounts of data, are drawn in approximation, and have arbitrary units (Thelen 1986*b*). They are, however, extremely valuable in visualizing how some possible crucial factors, or control variables, could affect the development of locomotion.

> Thelen suggests that there may be eight hypothetical variables that could contribute to locomotor development.

The development of locomotion serves well as a model for motor development in general, and it also provides insight into motor control. Thelen (1986*b*) describes eight hypothetical components that contribute to locomotor skill: pattern generation, joint synchrony, postural control, body constraints, extensor strength, control of antagonists, visual sensitivity to movement, and motivation. Some of these have already been discussed in detail in Chapter 1 and will be summarized along with other components to help you visualize how these control variables affect the development of locomotion.

Pattern Generation

Thelen believes that some type of pattern generation is present. Again, you will remember that pattern generation is the assembly of muscles into relationships that produce recognizable movements such as kicking, stepping, and walking. The generation of these patterns is the responsibility of the nervous system. The patterns are likely of a general nature. The graph represents the pattern generation as a straight line, suggesting that at least this particular generator does not undergo significant change itself throughout this developmental time scale of one year (Fig 2-13).

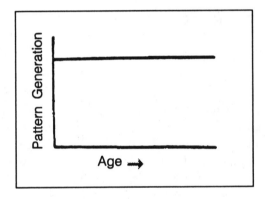

Figure 2-13 Stylized graph of a hypothetical pattern generation. Note that the pattern is hypothesized to be relatively unchanging across the first year of life. Figures 2-13 to 2-21 are modified from Thelen (1986*b*), reprinted with permission.

Joint Synchrony

We noted earlier that the ankle, knee, and hip joints in the newborn are very tightly synchronized in the kicking movement. As the infant matures, this tight synchrony diminishes and the joints are able to work in more flexible and variable linkages. This view is consistent with the proposals by Bernstein (1967) that movements begin with very tight controls over the degrees of freedom until we learn to release them efficiently. This tight synchrony is probably the result of the extensive cocontraction of the muscles and the heavy reliance on passive forces in early kicking. Mature locomotion requires more flexibility between the joints than those present in the newborn. Figure 2-14 shows, then, that the synchrony is tightest at about 1 month of age, when the graph dips downward. Although there is a overall steady decrease in the tight relationship between the hip, knee, and ankle throughout the first year, these changes are not linear. Undoubtedly, the ups and downs reflect the tighter synchrony that comes from the coactivation that is usually present in learning new tasks and the subsequent relaxing of it as mastery occurs.

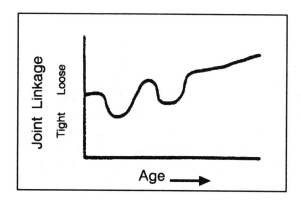

Figure 2-14 Stylized graph tracing the possible history of the relative tightness and looseness of the joint linkages. When the joints are highly synchronous, there is likely to be considerable coactivation of agonists and antagonists.

Postural Control (Balance and Equilibrium)

The infant develops appropriate behavioral adjustments to vestibular, proprioceptive, and visual stimuli that are necessary for balance and equilibrium to manifest themselves. Balance and equilibrium contribute to the ability to support body weight on one leg, which is required for locomotion. Synergies used by older children and adults in response to platform perturbations that potentially destabilize the balance have been described by Nashner and Woollacott (1979), and you read about them earlier in the first chapter during the discussion of pattern generator theories. Even the very young infant produces directionally appropriate responses to perturbations (Woollacott 1986). Postural responses are age-related, that is, they evolve over the life span. The adult synergies are not fully present until about 6 years of age. Studies in the elderly show that age-related changes occur in all segments of the life span. The stair-step nature of the graph of this component in Figure 2-15 reflects postural control over an increasingly greater number of body segments and arrangements within the first year of life. For instance, the infant begins to develop appropriate adjustments in the supine position before they are available in sitting and then in standing.

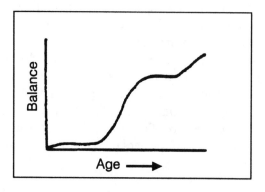

Figure 2-15 Stylized graph representing the acquisition of postural control over the first year. The step-like quality of the graph represents the ability to control multiple segments at different postures such as in sitting, all-fours, standing, and walking.

Body Constraints

Thelen (1986*b*) points out that newborns are not designed at all well for bipedal locomotion. As you can see in Figure 2-16, their heads are very large and the center of gravity is too high so they are very top-heavy. Their trunks are too long, shoulders are too narrow, and legs are too short.

In addition, body fat rapidly begins to increase after birth. The net effect of this accumulation of fat is an increase in body weight and a relative decrease in the muscle mass necessary to move this increased weight. Figure 2-17 reflects this sudden increase in fat at about 1 month of age that greatly increases constraints on the body. Then there are gradual changes in body proportions and composition of tissue that are likely to limit upright locomotion. This is shown on the graph as a steady drop in the line representing how the weight places constraints on the body, impairing the ability to produce certain movements.

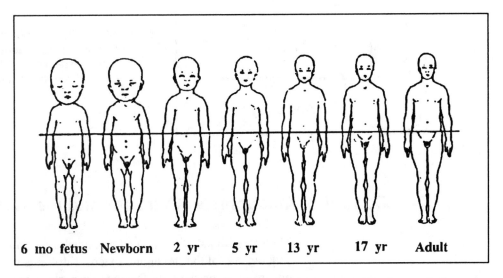

6 mo fetus   Newborn   2 yr   5 yr   13 yr   17 yr   Adult

Figure 2-16   The change in position of the center of gravity with increasing age. From Palmer (1944), reprinted with permission of the Society for Research in Child Development.

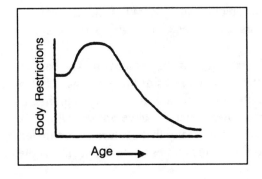

Figure 2-17 Stylized graph showing the possible body constraints such as weight, fat content, and density of tissues. After the first month or so, the baby rapidly gains weight, most of which is fat. This increase in weight becomes a constraint on the ability to produce certain movements.

Extensor Strength

As noted before, Thelen (1986*b*) has proposed that many of the early movement changes observed in infants are the result of relative lack or gain of muscular strength, particularly in the extensor muscles. As infants mature they actually gain in strength through activating their muscles and practicing movements against gravity. The first increase in extensor strength is likely to be in the legs during kicking while supine. The dip in the graph probably represents the relative lack of extensor strength in trunk muscles when changing from supine to sitting postures. The gradual incline suggests there is increasing strength in extensor muscles involved in sitting then standing and walking (Fig 2-18).

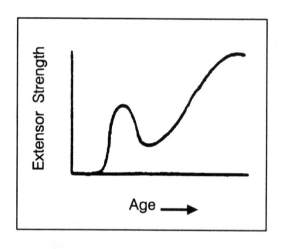

Figure 2-18 Stylized graph representing the relative effectiveness of extensor strength. This graph is shaped to suggest that different demands are present in different positions.

Control of Antagonists (Extensor and Flexor Control)

Thelen's EMG studies showed that newborn infants initiate kicks with coactivation of the flexor and extensor muscles with greater activity occurring in the flexors. The extension phase is a passive one resulting from recoil phenomena. This pattern begins to be modified and by 5 months of age there are active muscle contractions in both the extension and flexion phases of the kick. It is not until 7 months, however, that even the most rudimentary reciprocal activity is seen. Even at 1 year of age coactivation of flexors and extensors may still occur to some extent.

The bilateral control of flexors and extensors also shows phases of development such that the right and left sides may not have balanced flexor and extensor activity at a particular time. The graph illustrates an alternate swinging up and down pattern of development (Fig 2-19). This reflects the observations made by many that posture is dominated by either flexors or extensors at various times along the scale. Thelen has observed that this dominance determines what movements will occur at a particular time no matter what the underlying pattern generation may be.

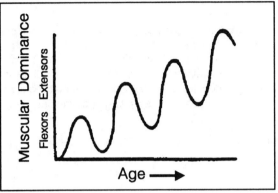

Figure 2-19 The child encounters alternating flexor and extensor muscle dominance. As the child ages, the muscular activity becomes more balanced and the swings into flexion and extension become less marked.

Visual Sensitivity to Movement

Vision is important in regulating movements, particularly in locomotion (Kelso 1982). Vital questions are: when do infants become visually aware of movement and when is this awareness used to help regulate their movements? Earlier in the chapter on motor control, you noted that infants would fall in response to a moving room. This suggests that both sitting and standing infants control their posture through what is called optic flow. One type of optic flow produces the sense that the body is moving when movement is actually being produced in the environment. Adults rely more on proprioception for postural stabilization, while young children appear to use vision more for postural control. Recent studies indicate that vision is used to control equilibrium during walking as well. We likely learn to use vision in a feedforward manner to tune the motor system adaptively to meet the environmental demands of the task (Kelso 1982).

Infants even a few weeks old have been shown to respond to looming objects. Woollacott (1986) has shown that young infants produce more errors in their behavioral responses to perturbation when vision is present. This suggests that learning to use vision appropriately in movement is a developmental process. This component of locomotion is graphed in step-like increases (Fig 2-20). Once again, these steps most likely reflect the use of visual sensitivity in the various postures, such as supine, sitting, standing, and walking, which are mastered in a steplike fashion on a developmental-time scale.

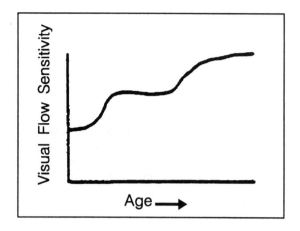

Figure 2-20 A general representation of the acquisition of sensitivity to visual flow. The newborn makes directionally appropriate responses to visual looming of objects. This ability continues to develop in different positions that require body stability such as sitting and standing.

Motivation

Thelen (1986*b*, p 114) states "by motivation I mean the infant's ability to recognize the task at hand and to desire to act upon it." This would involve some measure of cognitive development. The high level reached by the middle of the year, as shown in Figure 2-21, is supported by the observation that infants at this age will find some way to get to desired objects, depending on the skills available to them. Thus they may scoot, roll, rock, crawl, creep, or walk toward their goals.

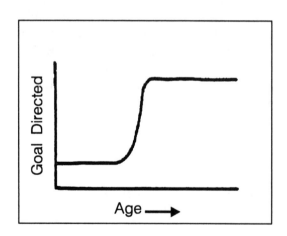

Figure 2-21 To walk, the infant must desire to accomplish some goal. If a toy is the motivator, for instance, it is apparent long before walking, and the child will get to the object in whatever manner is available at the time.

Context

All of these graphs are then layered to illustrate the multileveled nature of the systems involved (Fig 2-22). Developmentally, they are not only existing in parallel but also interacting with each other. The circle that interacts with all of them is the context. A characteristic of a dynamic

70

systems approach that must also be considered is the context in which the movement takes place. By *context*, we mean the internal (biological) environment of the individual, the external environment in which the movement occurs, and the functional goal that the person is trying to reach. Figure 2-22 shows that the outcome at any time depends on the context. The greater system organizes itself through the subsystems around the task, and the resultant movement emerges from these relationships. The environment may either support the movement or constrain the movement. The treadmill experiment is an example of how the environment can support the elaboration of a movement.

This environmental context may be both social and physical. For instance, parents are likely to provide support for toddlers by holding their hands, which improves the interlimb coupling. Thus a systems model, or perspective of movement and movement development, dictates that the final outcome of movement cannot be determined by any one system but is determined by the interaction of the elements of the system within a specified context. To be sensitive to the context, the nervous system must continually monitor the periphery and adjust to it. It is through the interaction with the environment that new patterns of movement are selected by the individual. Over time, some patterns become preferred by the individual and are thus repeated, practiced, and strengthened, but they do not become so strong or ingrained that they are singularly dominant and obligatory (Thelen 1989*a*).

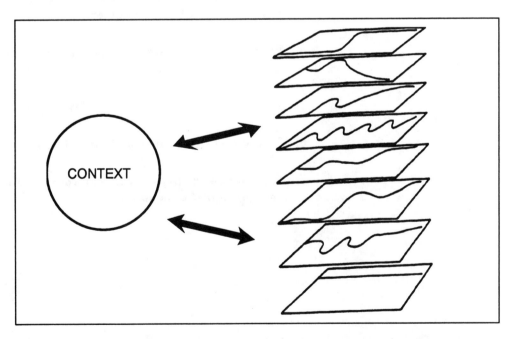

Figure 2-22 A conceptual representation of the systems or subsystems involved in motor control in the acquisition of locomotion. Each system has its own developmental profile and interacts with the other systems. Any system can be rate limiting. All these body systems interact with the context, which is as important a determinant in the movement as any of the systems. Modified from Thelen (1986*b*).

We have assumed that the movements of newborn infants are random and disorganized. Thelen's careful observations, however, have shown that there are many recognizable patterns of coordination that are stable enough to be recognized. These may be elicited through particular stimuli to serve certain adaptations. For example, rooting, sucking, and hand-to-mouth patterns may serve early feeding adaptations. She indicates that we should think of these movements as continuums of relative stability and flexibility rather than as being rigidly determined reflexes or patterns. For example, the Babinski reflex may be less flexible than an adaptive reach for a toy, but even this movement is responsive to context (Thelen et al 1989).

Study Questions:

1. Explain why some early reflexes, such as spontaneous stepping, may disappear.

2. How do the treadmill experiments explain emergent properties of a self-organizing system?

3. Explain the characteristic patterns of gait in infants as they compare to adult patterns in terms of the dynamic action theory.

4. What do the responses prove to both the split-belt treadmill and the weighting of the infant's extremity?

5. What is meant by the statement development is nonlinear?

6. Describe Thelen's concept of context and explain its importance.

7. Explain how the hypothetical control variables affect the development of locomotion.

Developmental Implications

From her classic experiments, Thelen reached several conclusions concerning motor development and motor control. The overall conclusion is that there are multiple systems involved in the attainment of developmental milestones. From the perspective of this theory, the onset of walking and other developmental milestones cannot be explained by cortical maturation alone.

Any system, or component, of development can be a rate-limiting factor relative to developing a given ability.

It is clear that the various systems or subsystems do not mature at the same rate. One of the most important concepts is that the developmental state of any of the subsystems may be a rate-limiting factor relative to the motor abilities the child displays. For instance, the sudden increase in body fat resulting in overall decrease in the proportion of muscle mass produces a resistance to stepping that cannot be overcome. Thus the stepping reflex disappears. The ability to make stepping movements upright against gravity is limited by the strength of the muscles in relation to the body constraints present at the time.

Synergies

Synergies, or coordinative structures, subserve spontaneous movement, elicited or reflex movement, and voluntary movement. For example, the movement pattern demonstrated by kicking in an aroused infant may be the same pattern elicited from a pinprick that we have called the flexor withdrawal reflex. The same kicking pattern may be used in a voluntary act by the infant such as moving a mobile attached to the leg. In all these instances, the movement pattern is similar, but the movement has come about as a result of the different environmental conditions.

Synergies are linkages that serve spontaneous, reflex, or goal-directed movement.

Other researchers have proposed that locomotion in nonhumans is the result of *spinal rhythm generators*, a group of interneurons capable of generating coordinated limb activity, and that human locomotion may also be under strong central control. This view is strongly espoused by Brooks (1986), as you discovered earlier in the first chapter during the discussion of pattern generation.

It is believed that patterns are softly assembled to accomplish the task rather than being hard wired, or anatomically preset.

Evidence is rapidly accumulating to show that patterns of coordination are not "hard wired" anywhere in the nervous system. These patterns are more likely to be "softly assembled," specifically in response to the total task context (Thelen and Jensen 1989). "For movement to be shaped and assembled dynamically, there must be a continual sharing of information between the CNS and the changing conditions of the limbs and body segments. Self-generated movements provide constant information to infants on the status of their own bodies, and at the same time, on their interactions with the physical environment, thus exploring a universe of motor and sensory possibilities. Because the contexts in which infants

73

move change dramatically during the first year (fluid to gravity, bearing weight on the feet, dynamic balance while walking), development itself sets new challenges for the nervous system" (Thelen and Jensen 1989).

Because the elements are free to assemble or reassemble in response to the task, any variety of coordinative solutions to a task are possible within a given maturational level. Some solutions, or patterns, are either easy or preferred by the individual. Thus infants prefer to move in a certain way but do not necessarily have to do so because the patterns of movement are not preassembled in a fixed manner. Other motor patterns may be possible but difficult, while still others are not sufficiently stable to appear at all. As development proceeds, the preferred solutions to the task will come to dominate the repertoire. They will more frequently be used and will become accurate and efficient. Thus they become a skilled activity.

> A pattern may become a favorite or preferred one, but it is never obligatory or required.

"Nonetheless, the number of response configurations to a particular task, although variable both between and within performers, is not infinite" (Thelen 1989a, p 25). This happens because the human has a basic structure (just as a dog has a basic structure that makes him a dog) and must interact within the human motor system and its biomechanical constraints. The task itself and the objects commonly associated with such tasks produce enormous influence on the execution of the movement. The properties of the objects themselves constrain the choice of movements (Thelen 1989a).

> The movement form is constrained or influenced by any objects involved in that movement.

Synergies are also used to preserve balance when the center of gravity is lost (Nashner and Woollacott 1979). These synergies, which appear as a result to platform perturbations, are so predictable that it is often suggested that they are hard wired into the system. Another view, however, shows that because the testing circumstances are so predictable and uniform; because all the subjects are human with similar arrangements of muscle, bone, body proportion and other biological components; and because the subjects are obeying the same physical laws, it should not be surprising that the softly assembled patterns are quite similar from individual to individual (Thelen 1989a). It should be noted that even Nashner (1990) states that the synergies he has reported in the literature represent the purest and most common responses, but that everyone does not produce identical patterns.

The coordinative structure, or synergy, has components that preserve stability of the form of the movement and components that allow for flexibility of the movement to meet functional demands. The relationship of the muscles and joints to each other provides the stability of the movement. For example, although different people walk differently, we know that the motor skill these people are doing is walking; we can identify the movement of throwing a ball or kicking a ball. The small differences that you see in walking by which you can identify your friend are provided by the flexibility of the coordinative structure. This flexibility results from the control we have over such

74

variables as how much energy to deliver to the muscles to scale up the speed of the movement or how stiff to make that muscular spring.

The flexibility of the synergy not only provides an explanation for individual variability but also provides the infant, child, or adult the opportunity to adapt the synergy, or fine tune the movement, to meet the functional demands of the task (Thelen 1986*b*; Thelen and Fogel 1989*b*; Thelen et al 1987*a*). The movement itself does not retain flexibility; a movement is the result of the interactions of subsystems. Each subsystem retains the right to interact differently during succeeding movements. Therefore, it is the subsystem that retains flexibility.

No privileged one-to-one relationship exists between the pattern of nervous system output and the resulting movement because many forces other than those generated by the muscles influence the movement. Thus a particular arm or leg movement will use different functional synergies in different positions such as lying supine or standing erect. Conversely, the same functional synergy, or muscular innervation pattern, will produce different movement outcomes in these two different postural conditions (Thelen 1989*b*).

> **Flexibility occurs because each subsystem retains the right to interact differently in the next movement.**

Phase Shifts

Another vital element of self-organizing systems theory is the presence of phase shifts. Although a phase shift is not limited to movement, it explains the development, or change, of one movement into a new form of movement. There are no stable intermediate forms of movement; that is, the change from movement to movement appears to be stagelike, or discontinuous. For instance, there is no intermediate stable movement between walking and running. In the example of the horses, it is clear that increasing the speed of the gait produces completely new forms of locomotion: walk, trot, canter, and gallop. These are completely different forms of locomotion requiring different relationships among extremities and between limb girdles. In the example of the bilateral wrist movements cited earlier in Chapter 1, remember that one either can move both wrists in flexion and extension or can alternate with flexion in one and extension in the other if the movements are slow. When the control variable of speed is increased to a critical level, only the simultaneous flexion and extension movements remain.

> **If walking is one phase and running is another, then a phase shift is one in which walking changes, or shifts, to running.**

In development, the different milestones infants display may represent such stagelike developmental phase shifts. An example would be the shift from creeping to walking. It might appear that some intermediate stage exists because new walkers stumble, fall, lack smoothness and rhythm in their steps, and thus are quite variable. There are, however, no true stable intermediates between creeping and walking.

To produce this stagelike, or nonlinear result, either a particular control variable or several variables are scaled linearly (are built up from slight to strong). For example, in kicking patterns of the newborn, the control variable is the infant's state that governs the amount of muscular activity in the legs. The active child kicks in a relatively alternating pattern, but as the excitability increases, a linear increase occurs in the energy delivered to the pattern. The result is a completely different movement: stiff simultaneous kicks with both legs. The underlying pattern generation remains the same (Fig 2-23).

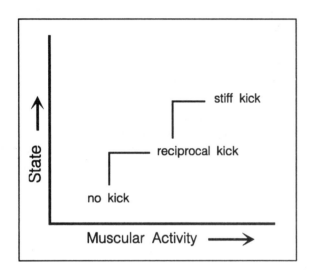

Figure 2-23 A conceptual model to illustrate the relationship between the state of the nervous system and the amount of muscle activity. As the energy delivered to the system increases, muscle contractions increase. As this relatively linear scaling occurs, phase shifts appear. That is, movement is shifted from one stable form to another stable form, as represented by the types of kicking performed by an infant under such conditions.

In development, these phase shifts explain some of the apparent discontinuities such as the loss of stepping or the relatively sudden beginning of upright stance. These scalar changes in control factors can be linear, incremental, or continuous, and they can trigger transitions in one of two ways. First, they may reach a critical value that initiates a phase shift. A further example of this is the scalar, or incremental, change in body weight that shifts the system from a stepping mode to a nonstepping mode at 3 months of age. Second, environmental factors may also affect the production of new forms of movement. Social interaction with the parents may provide physical support and encouragement. Parents may also model the activity and provide access to objects. These factors may facilitate or substitute for capabilities that the child would develop later independently. These contextual factors allow the child to shift to a more mature form of the movement while the support is being given. This practice may also result in the child permanently shifting to the new forms far earlier than would have been the case without the supported practice (Thelen 1989a).

Thelen demonstrated the use of such contextual factors when she either added weights to the infants' legs or placed the infants in water or on treadmills. The environmental contexts were changed and that in turn

Demands from the environment can produce a phase shift from one movement to another.

76

altered the biomechanical demands on the legs. Under certain conditions, such as having adequate muscle strength, stepping represents a preferred and stable output of the system. Changing the internal or external conditions, such as by gaining weight or being placed on a treadmill, causes the system to reassemble into another preferred and stable action, such as nonstepping or walking.

Let us consider once again the development of upright stance. A good question to ask is, What control variables shift the infant from such forms of locomotion as creeping or crawling to independent upright locomotion? Recall that Thelen has hypothesized at least eight control factors for gait. At the stage of creeping and crawling, perhaps the two most important variables are the postural control of balance and the extensor muscle strength.

When a child performs "combat crawling," his belly is on the floor so his trunk is supported. The infant moves from one place to another by pushing and pulling with his arms and legs. There is no requirement for balance mechanisms to be active, because the center of gravity never falls outside the base of support. Nor does the center of gravity fall outside the wide base of support afforded by achieving the all-fours posture on hands and knees. To creep, however, at least one limb must be lifted from the support surface to establish a new base for forward progression. Nonetheless, with a four-point stance, it is possible to move from one static balance position to another by moving only one limb at time. This process produces a tripod posture that also maintains the center of gravity within it. There are no demands for dynamic balance (Thelen et al 1989).

It has been noted that once the infant achieved hands and knees posture, the pattern first used for progression tended to be as follows: left knee, then left hand, then the right hand, and then the right knee. This pattern demands less strength and balance than any other pattern, particularly patterns requiring simultaneous movement of two limbs. As a child practices creeping and gains experience in the movement, she may begin to unload two support limbs simultaneously, either diagonally or ipsilaterally. This change allows for greater speed but provides less stability (Thelen et al 1989).

According to Thelen, then, when infants creep they use all the critical elements needed for walking except the final requirements for achieving erect stance and bearing weight on a single limb while shifting forward on the other. They have appropriately patterned interlimb and intralimb coordinations. They have adequate body proportions, visual sensitivity to movement, and the desire to move from one position to another. The missing elements needed to switch into the new phase of upright locomotion are strength and dynamic balance.

After 7 to 8 months of age, the rate-limiting factors that are not fully developed and that limit the ability to walk are strength and dynamic balance.

Even the half-upright posture of sitting, which is much simpler than upright stance, requires adequate strength and balance. Consider all the articulated segments that must be managed and the body mass that must be supported. The trunk has 32 articulated segments, and connected to it are upper extremity segments and a relatively large head. All this rests on a pelvic base that is further enlarged by partially extended legs. In the beginning, the infant sits with a rounded trunk in which the center of gravity is placed forward by flexion at the hips. This position is not maintained by active muscle contraction but by restraint of the ligaments, shape of the joints, passive muscle stretch, and stiffening of the trunk from increased intrathoracic and intraabdominal pressures. Stable independent sitting requires sufficient strength, especially in the trunk extensors, to control the body mass. It also requires sufficient mechanisms of equilibrium to integrate a large number of segments (Thelen and Jensen 1989).

Multiple Forces in Movement

> Multiple forces interact to produce a movement.

When an adult or older child kicks a football or a soccer ball, the movement at the hip joint is a consequence of multiple passive and active forces. First, there are muscle forces acting on the hip. There are motion-dependent forces that result from the associated movements of the thigh, leg, and foot. Reactions from the viscoelastic properties of various connective tissues occur, and forces come from gravity acting through the centers of mass of the limb segments. But only the muscle forces are actively controlled by the CNS. It is clear, however, that the CNS must be able to use and accommodate to these multiple, interacting forces because we humans are able to produce smooth coordinated movements despite being able to control only one type of force.

> Movement matures when we learn to control and exploit passive forces.

You will remember, from Chapter 1, that Bernstein considered the acquisition of skill to be not only the controlling of passive forces but also the exploiting of them to maximize the effectiveness of muscle contractions. The relationship between the pattern of muscle activation and the resulting movement of the limbs is not a one-to-one, stereotyped relationship because the forces do not come only from muscles.

To gain further insight into movement development, Thelen and her colleagues (Schneider et al 1990) have begun to analyze movements in such a way as to partition the torques generated by infants as they kick into active and passive components. The torques arise from 3 sources: from the effects of gravity, from the accelerations and velocities of interconnected segments (motion-dependent torques), and from muscle. The muscle torque is that which results from both active muscle contraction and from passive deformation of muscle and related tissues.

This compartmentalization can be illustrated by the analysis of a cat shaking its paw rapidly at high velocity to shake off an irritant placed on the pad of its paw. The torques acting on the paw were generated almost entirely by the muscle component. At the knee, however, the muscle torques were generated not to create movement but to counteract the large torques transmitted to the knee by the action of the paw. These knee torques are thus called motion-dependent torques (Schneider et al 1990). One way to help visualize these motion-dependent forces is to imagine a jointed puppet. Strings are attached from each jointed extremity to the control mechanism of the puppeteer. A single pull of one string may result in the movement of all of the connected joint segments.

By examining kicks of varying intensity and in different positions, the Thelen group was able to explore how the young infant controls a range of active and passive forces to produce a stereotypic, nonintentional movement. Three positions were used to produce different contexts in terms of how the leg relates to gravity (supine, angled, and vertical). If muscle action alone were the prime component, we would expect the forces to be turned off and on in a stereotyped fashion, and one would not expect the muscle to change activity with different gravitational contexts.

Figure 2-24 shows a summary of torque contributions to hip reversal in the context of body posture and kick intensity. You can see that the muscle forces are not simply turned off and on to reverse the kick. The muscle forces, for instance, are strong in flexion in all positions, but there was an extensor action during vigorous kicks in the supine position that was required to overcome gravity. This gravitational influence was present because of the greater hip flexion accompanying a vigorous kick although and the limb was oriented to diminish the effects of gravity. Thus the reversal was context-dependent (depended on the position). Also in the vigorous kick a large, flexor, motion-dependent torque was produced that required a large muscle extensor torque to counteract it. Both in the inclined and vertical kicks and in the nonvigorous kick in the supine position, gravitational forces produced the reversal of the action. This is a very different picture than would result if the muscles were reciprocally turned on and off in a stereotyped fashion by a rigid "motor program" (Thelen 1990).

Animal studies show the same phenomena (Bradley 1990). In cats walking at high speeds, the forces that accelerate the knee into extension are very large and must be countered by flexor muscle activity. At slower speeds the passive elastic forces of the knee flexors and connective tissues are sufficient to counteract acceleration of the knee into extension, and thus opposing flexor forces are not required.

These experiments appear to provide further evidence that muscle patterns of activation are soft assembled to accomplish the goal within the context of the movement. Thelen (in press) suggests that although these early movements are probably precursors to later locomotion, these patterns are not similar to walking in any measure of muscle action, joint phasing, or interplay of passive and active torques. Rather, these early movements represent only the rough outline of future patterns. Walking is accomplished by learning to control muscle torques in an interaction

A jointed puppet is useful for visualizing motion-dependent forces.

Even infants are able to control active and passive forces.

with peripheral events and sensory experiences and the specific details are carved in by function (Thelen in press).

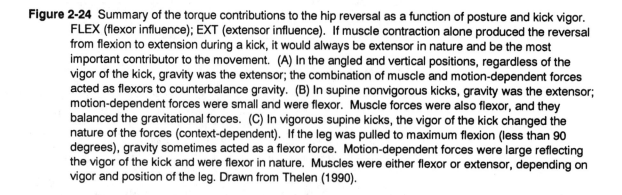

ANGLED AND VERTICAL KICKS

A   Vigorous and Nonvigorous

Gravitational forces	Ext
Motion-dependent forces	Flex
Muscle forces	Flex

Reversal was a function of GRAVITY
MUSCLE remained FLEXOR force even when leg extended

SUPINE KICKS

B   Nonvigorous

Gravitational forces	Ext
Motion-dependent forces	Flex (small)
Muscle forces	Flex

Reversal was a function of GRAVITY
MUSCLE remained FLEXOR force even when leg extended

C   Vigorous

Gravitational forces	Ext/Flex
Motion-dependent forces	Flex (large)
Muscle forces	Flex/Ext

Reversal was context-dependent--vigor and position
MUSCLE modulated to EXTENSOR to counterbalance MOTION-DEPENDENT forces

Figure 2-24 Summary of the torque contributions to the hip reversal as a function of posture and kick vigor. FLEX (flexor influence); EXT (extensor influence). If muscle contraction alone produced the reversal from flexion to extension during a kick, it would always be extensor in nature and be the most important contributor to the movement. (A) In the angled and vertical positions, regardless of the vigor of the kick, gravity was the extensor; the combination of muscle and motion-dependent forces acted as flexors to counterbalance gravity. (B) In supine nonvigorous kicks, gravity was the extensor; motion-dependent forces were small and were flexor. Muscle forces were also flexor, and they balanced the gravitational forces. (C) In vigorous supine kicks, the vigor of the kick changed the nature of the forces (context-dependent). If the leg was pulled to maximum flexion (less than 90 degrees), gravity sometimes acted as a flexor force. Motion-dependent forces were large reflecting the vigor of the kick and were flexor in nature. Muscles were either flexor or extensor, depending on vigor and position of the leg. Drawn from Thelen (1990).

Perceptual Motor Loops

Muscle contractions are not isolated from sensory systems (Thelen 1990). Through their own movements, individuals detect patterns of their perceptual fields (eg, visual, haptic, proprioceptive, vestibular, acoustical). As the movements occur, they are mapped together with their sensory consequences. According to Newell et al (1989), improvements in skill either during development or through practice by older individuals are achieved through such a discovery process.

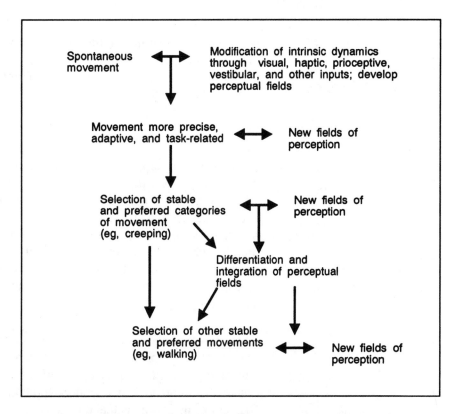

Figure 2-25 Perception-action loops. As movement (action) is generated, sensory consequences are experienced (perception). The sensory memories become associated with the movement (mapped) and are further developed and modified as the cycle continues in a spiraling manner.

Movements produced by infants are accompanied by concomitant visual, haptic, proprioceptive, and vestibular consequences. As the task is further explored through repeated movements, the interaction between the information from these modalities regulates the movement so that stable and preferred patterns of movement emerge in an adaptive, functional and self-organizing manner (Fig 2-25). Motor development then can be thought of as a recurrent perception-action loop. Thelen

81

(1990) suggests that the process of skill acquisition requires not only knowledge of the outside world but also knowledge of the capabilities and limitations of one's own body as it acts in a world of forces.

> All the senses need to be included in practice activities for the most effective motor learning.

If this is the process of skill development, then anyone, infant or adult, who is learning or fine tuning movements needs to experience success through activities that incorporate all the perceptual senses that will help to develop preferred forms of movement that are efficient and stable (Thelen et al in press).

Transition From Spontaneous to Voluntary Arm Movements

It may be easy to assume at this point that these investigations relate only to more automatic events in the lower extremities and cannot be generalized to the acquisition of more voluntary or skilled motor acts. To delve further into the acquisition of early skills, Thelen et al (1991a) began a series of experiments to evaluate the development of reaching in infants.

Infants appear to thrash their arms in random and uncontrolled movements. You will recall that kicking appears to lack organization when it is simply observed. According to von Hoftsen (1984), newborns show some directed arm extensions, which have been called prereaching actions, but voluntary directed reaches are not consistent until 3 or 4 months of age. To gain knowledge about the development of voluntary reaching, Thelen et al (1991a; 1991b) performed extensive longitudinal studies on four infants beginning at 3 weeks of age and continuing until 1 year of age.

These experiments were designed to provide information about how babies solve the problems of voluntary control using their ongoing spontaneous nongoal-directed movements. The infants began with apparently undirected waving, or "flapping," movements and then began to alternate these with actual directed attempts to contact a toy.

The first two important observations derived from the study were that the infants produced goal-directed reaches at very different ages. The first baby to reach was 12 weeks of age and the last was 22 weeks of age. It is thus difficult to suggest a built-in time clock for such developmental activities. Second, the infants began their reaches in two distinctly different styles. The ultimate outcomes, however, were functionally equivalent as each infant contacted the toy. By 4 months of age, all had accomplished the motor milestone of reaching for an object.

Two of the infants began with what was described as a "flap and swipe" style. That is, the babies used large, vigorous, high-velocity movements that appeared to be uncoordinated and busy. The spontaneous flap thus had high motion-dependent torques that were counterbalanced by high muscle torques. Although the directed reach looked very similar to the spontaneous flap, both the muscle torques and motion-dependent torques were damped considerably by cocontraction of the muscles. Within 2 weeks of first making contact, however, these two babies had lowered the level of muscular activity and were using the muscle forces at the shoulder primarily to raise the arm against gravity. They thus appear to have discovered a more optimal level of muscular activity suited for the task. That is not to say that cocontraction does not remain at some level during these early times.

The other two infants began with much slower velocities, thus producing smaller inertial forces that had to be controlled. However, they also routinely produced muscular cocontraction that stiffened or stabilized the shoulder joint against the motion-dependent torques generated by the distal segments of the upper limb. But these movements were much slower and thus the torques were less than those of the more vigorously moving babies. The babies with lower levels of activity used muscles primarily to counteract gravity, but within 2 weeks these infants began to "scale up" their muscular contractions and began to appear more like the first two babies did at their beginning contact.

It is clear that there is more than one way for an individual to develop the early skill of reaching for a toy and that the reaches were organized by the task (contact with the toy). It would seem, therefore, that some hard wired, predetermined, CNS generated pattern could not account for this development. The infant has softly assembled the movement patterns that are successful from the spontaneous, rhythmical, intrinsic movements occurring and available at birth. The early unskilled movements form the neuromuscular bases from which skills such as reaching, sitting, and walking are built.

Apparently, for infants to acquire voluntary control of their movements they must interrupt the natural stereotypies, or oscillations. They do so by stiffening the muscles through cocontraction, which slows the velocity of oscillatory movements and decreases the motion-dependent forces generated by such uncontrolled or flapping movements. Once the infants have gotten general control by stiffening their muscles, further practice will increase their accuracy, and the movements will become more stable and reliable. Eventually, the infants can change their speed and stiffness to become more efficient and actually begin to use the passive forces created by gravity and motion rather than simply resisting them. The infants self-discover the dynamics necessary to accomplish the specific task and learn to convert their flapping movements into goal-directed reaching when they have been presented with a toy.

Adults are very adept at using passive forces from inertia and the elastic properties of the system. As a result, they contract muscles only to complement those forces. Schnieder and Zernicke (1989) performed torque analyses on adults after they practiced novel, rapid arm movements. The analyses showed that subjects' movements became faster and the hand trajectories smoother as they made more efficient use of passive forces.

Voluntary control begins to develop as the infants first learn to modulate the stiffness of their muscles through cocontraction. Stiffening the limbs to dampen reactive forces allows the infant to get the extremity into the general area and position for the task. Remember the degrees of freedom problem stated first by Bernstein (see Chapter 1)? These experiments confirm that the initial method of controlling the vast numbers of degrees of freedom through cocontraction occurs from the beginning of motor development.

Other Developmental Principles

With respect to developmental time, there are additional principles of systems theory that we should review. First, each subsystem in the system has its own developmental timetable, and the contributing components may not mature in a synchronous fashion, that is, the ratio of change may vary drastically. For example, at any point in time, the child may have an immature motor system and highly developed sensory capabilities, have one sensory system advanced and the others retarded, or even have one highly selective neural tract accelerated in function. Nevertheless, the movement outcome at that point in time is a product of the multilevel, relational, dynamic interaction of the subsystems within their individual maturational level.

One or more subsystems may compete with, inhibit, or facilitate each other. An explanation, then, for a disappearing movement, or reflex, such as stepping may be that the increased weight of the legs without concomitant increase in strength of the leg muscles may inhibit the expression of stepping. Therefore, any subsystem may act as a rate-limiting factor. Whatever the developmental readiness of other components, new developmental movement may occur only when the slowest component matures (Thelen 1986*b*).

Finally, at every stage in the life cycle, it is function rather than the formation of some motor command instruction issued by the cortex that drives behavior. The developing child has the ability to reach the same functional goal from many different initial conditions and pathways. As a result, a variety of coordinative structures, or synergies, may be used for the same functional task, and conversely, the same coordinative structure may be used for a variety of tasks.

The impetus to move is task oriented whether the infant is hungry or wants a toy. The source of behavior is function, and it is context-specific. This principle provides an explanation for why variability is seen in children's movement performance and why some children arrive at a developmental task using different pathways. Haley

84

(1986), Fishkind and Haley (1986), and Doudlah (1981) demonstrated that considerable variability occurs in the developmental sequence of postural reactions for individual infants. Even though there is a general sequence for the acquisition of postural reactions, not all infants pass through the sequence in a similar order. Thus variability can be considered a *normal* sign of development, whereas stereotyped behavior in this context can be considered a sign of dysfunction.

In development, there are also components that allow for stability of movement and for flexibility in the face of functional demands. Dynamic action systems predict that transitions from one stable form of movement to another may not be linear, or continuous, but may be discontinuous. Movement forms are stable, but if you increase a scalar quantity such as arousal level a different form of movement may emerge.

Key Principles

In summary, the following are key principles of a dynamic systems approach to movement in real and developmental time:

1. Movement is the product of multilevel subsystems dynamically interacting within the supports and constraints of the environment.

2. Across both real- and developmental-time scales, there are components that preserve the stability of form and components that allow for flexibility.

    a. Behavior exhibits stable forms because of coordinative structures, or synergies, generated; coordinative structures arise in development in relatively invariant, or structured, sequences because of inherited maturational timetables and convergent task demands.

    b. Behavior exhibits flexibility because coordinative structures have adjustable tuning variables and during development, function dictates the pattern, or coordinative structures, used.

3. Transitions from one stable form of movement to another may not be linear or continuous.

4. Each subsystem may not mature at the same rate.

5. One subsystem may be rate limiting.

6. Function drives behavior.

Study Questions:

1. What are the purposes of synergies, or patterns? How are they developed?

2. Explain phase shifts and give examples. Try to develop one example not given in the text.

3. What is meant by the following statement: A given system or subsystem may be a rate-limiting factor in development.

4. Explain the following statement: Function drives behavior. Contrast that statement with this statement derived from McGraw's work in Chapter 3: Structure determines function.

5. What do the experiments concerning the differentiation of forces generated in movement tell us about motor control?

6. Explain what the observations made as the infants developed reaching patterns contribute to the understanding of motor control?

7. Define cocontraction (coactivation) and describe its role in motor pattern development.

8. How could or should we approach the evaluation and treatment of clients with motor control problems based on the existence of the possible control variables for locomotion?

9. How are perception and movement related? How do they develop?

10. What does variability have to do with motor control?

Chapter 3 - Motor Development

Developmental Theories

Healthy children are active creatures. Children expend enormous amounts of energy in exploring, learning about, and mastering their world. The hallmark of the first 2 years of life is the relentless pursuit of competence. Between the ages of 11 and 15 months, children become fully capable of walking, climbing, manipulating small and large objects, and feeding themselves. Also at this time, children are poised on the brink of language development, are acquiring significant social skills, and demonstrate some level of intellectual capacity. How are all these skills acquired?

Systematic observers of children have noted three characteristics of development: (1) general behaviors and capabilities develop with a remarkable similarity among children, (2) the appearance of the behaviors and capabilities usually occur along a similar timetable and in a similar sequence, and (3) any deviation from the normal course of development tends to be short-lived and of temporary influence in terms of overall developmental progression. All this occurs despite wide variations in the environments in which children grow and develop (Horowitz 1987).

> **Motor behaviors are seldom addressed by developmental theorists.**

Many theories of child development treat development in general terms while other theories address motor development more specifically. Most of the theorists, however, were and are mainly concerned with cognitive processes and behavioral acquisition and are interested in motor acts only as an expression of these processes. There are psychoanalytic theories, such as that expressed by Sigmund Freud, that relate primarily to the development of personality through the psychosexual stages of development. In this scheme, all development in the first 18 months is lumped into the oral stage, and the child gets very little credit for significant changes in the early months of life.

Behavioral theorists stand in sharp contrast to psychoanalytic theorists, who are interested in the mental and emotional processes that shape the personality. Behavioral theorists are interested in how people learn to behave in particular ways. These interests have produced various learning theories. B.F. Skinner's (1971) operant behavioral theory is usually considered to be of such genre. Skinner has little interest in what goes on inside the organism. Instead, such behaviorists stress the part that learning processes play in the acquisition of certain behaviors. Motor behaviors, especially early ones, are not particularly addressed. In the nature-nurture controversy, this group represents the extreme environmentalist view, believing that the environment has the greatest influence on developmental change.

Humanistic theorists stress the uniqueness of the human condition. Abraham Maslow and Carl Rogers represent this group, and they are concerned with maximizing the human potential for self-direction and freedom of choice. They have developed a hierarchy of needs in which the top of the pyramid is the need to fulfill this unique potential called self-actualization. Clearly, the individual is not in charge of these phenomena until after infancy.

Ethological, or organismic, theorists study the behavioral pattern of organisms from a biological point of view because organisms are proposed to have some genetically determined responses. Jean Piaget, whose theories are based on inherent biological characteristics, is often referred to as a cognitive theorist because he was interested in the internal factors of the process of knowing (cognition). Another preeminent organismic theorist was Arnold Gesell. The basic approach embodied in the theories of Piaget and Gesell have been dominant in American developmental psychology for almost 30 years (Horowitz 1987). These theorists mostly represent the nature side of the nature-nurture controversy, believing that genetic make-up determines the greatest portion of developmental change.

Structure: Unit of organization that provides shape and form.

Stage: Developmental periods that govern behavior.

The center of the Piaget-Gesell orientation involves a notion of *structure.* Structure has been defined in various ways by different theorists. For Gesell, it was a physical entity that permitted behavioral function; for Piaget, it was a system of rules and transformations that governed thought processes at a particular point in time. In its most generic sense, structure is used to refer to a unit of organization that by its existence exerts functional control over behavior. A structuralist approach also posits developmental periods, or *stages,* that embody a set of organizing characteristics that govern behavior during each developmental epoch. Although the concepts of stage and structure have been dominant ideas in developmental psychology and developmental biology, in more recent times developmental psychologists have taken up the concept of *system,* with considerable attention being given to general systems theory. Systems theory relating to motor control was encountered in Chapter 1, and Esther Thelen, as you discovered in Chapter 2, certainly represents the latter group.

System: Units organized to exert functional control over motor behavior.

Piaget, who has had more influence on mainstream developmental psychology than anyone, has also been called a transactional theorist. That is, he believed the child develops as an outcome of adaptive processes that involve interaction with the environment. Even though Gesell was more biologically oriented than Piaget, he did not deny the necessity for the environment in the process of development. You have already seen the role of the environment in the dynamic action theory of Thelen presented earlier. In current times, the nature-nurture split seems to be less of an issue because theorists suggest that both environment and genetics play significant roles in development throughout the life span. Perhaps one may be more important at one time than the other.

Although many therapists are familiar with Piaget and incorporate some of his concepts in the evaluation of children, no further insight into Piagetian theory will be offered here because his theory does not address motor skills and their development. Because motor, or movement, abnormalities are our special interest in therapy and are usually the focus of the professional intervention, knowledge of this area of development is of greater concern in the medical arena than it is in many others where the major concern is how children function and how they learn.

Not so very long ago the newborn human was thought to be an incompetent entity that does little more than eat, sleep, breathe, and perform other automatic physiologic functions such as eliminating waste. Many theorists, including Piaget, have considered the first few months of life as nothing more than the expression of reflexes or "a general wiring for a set of actions" (Horowitz 1987). However, through the years, often with the benefit of more advanced technology, research has shown that the newborn is truly an amazing creature with functioning sensory systems, some communication abilities, and many patterns of movement that have often gone unrecognized because they seem to pale when compared with the inability to walk, talk, and manipulate objects.

Motor development research has primarily been done by investigators who were or are still more interested in the intellectual, or cognitive, aspects of development and consider that the motor behavior of the preverbal infant is the only evidence available, as Thelen puts it, to investigate the "life of the mind" (Thelen and Fogel 1989*b*). Despite Piaget's emphasis on action as an essential organizer of the first stage in development, which he called the sensorimotor period, his theory devotes little attention to movement. Until Thelen and a few of her contemporaries of the 1980s sparked new interest in movement, the field of motor development had been dormant for a relatively long time.

Neuromaturationist Theories

Two investigators who could be considered to be the towering giants of the field of developmental research involving movement were Gesell, mentioned previously, and Myrtle McGraw. These two researchers produced an incredible collection of observations of infant behavior. Both of them photographed infants extensively, with the best technology available during the 1920s and 1930s. Gesell has written at least 22 books on the subject, including two large atlases of photographs representative of those taken while observing children during the first 2 years of life.

What is best remembered from their monumental works are the milestones, or stages, of development. These stages, or milestones, are

> Nature and nurture both have significant roles in mental and motor development.

> The infant is not an immature, incompetent adult.

fundamental to most, if not all, of the various tests and screening devices devised for establishing developmental normality. It is on these norms and descriptions that therapists have come to rely for both the rules and the standards of motor development.

As Doudlah (1981) points out, therapists are quite aware of the observations of McGraw and Gesell but are not at all familiar with the purposes and goals of their research and the scientific context in which they worked. Thelen (1989a) believes that neither of them meant the exquisite descriptions of movement to be an end in themselves. Their orientation was thoroughly biological, and they were profoundly influenced by the embryologists working in the 1920s to 1950s. They both sought to answer the fundamental question of whether the sources of developmental change were maturational or experiential and to discuss the relationship between structure and function in generating developmental change. Although their theoretic conclusions were somewhat different, both used the emergence of posture and movement to study this relationship.

Myrtle McGraw

McGraw sought to correlate observable changes in the nervous system, usually based on histological studies in other animals, with overt changes in behavior. Her goal was to prove that behavior emerged in a lawful manner from the structural growth and maturation of the nervous system. Thus McGraw was a neuromaturationist. To discover the relationship between structure and function, she believed it was necessary to observe the onset and form of behavior and to correlate the behavior with its anatomic and physiological substrata (McGraw 1935; 1945). The studies in embryology current at that time most often involved the descriptions of the movements made by various species. McGraw therefore chose human movement, specifically emergent posture and locomotion, to study because of their relationship or similarity to behaviors in other species rather than language or other cognitive skills (Thelen 1989a).

Neuromaturationist: Everything occurs as a result of CNS activity, and thus CNS maturation is important.

McGraw observed the patterning of prone progression, sitting, swimming, grasping, adjustment to inversion, and erect progression, and she sought to correlate the changes in these patterns over time with neurogenesis. She attributed the driving force in developmental change to the increasing maturation and role of the cerebral cortex in improving function. In short, function emerged from structure. It should be noted that there are contemporary researchers and theorists who continue to place maturation of the cerebral cortex, or encephalization, as an explanation for such events as the disappearance of the stepping reflex (Leonard et al 1988).

Neonatal Swimming

One of the most fascinating observations McGraw (1945) performed was of aquatic, or swimming, behavior of newborn and older infants (Fig 3-1). At 11 days of age, the new infant submerged in the prone position shows a very orderly swimming pattern that McGraw labeled reflex. After the first few months, the pattern becomes disorganized, and then the baby tends to rotate from a prone to a dorsal position and to struggle with the extremities. McGraw describes the third phase of swimming movements, which occurs about the time of independent walking, as deliberate, or voluntary, movements. The baby remains submerged in the prone position while the flexor and extensor motions of the extremities propel the body through the water.

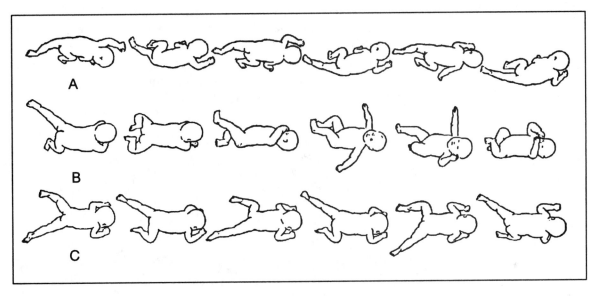

Figure 3-1 Three phases in the development of aquatic behavior of the human infant. (A) Reflex swimming movements; (B) disorganized behavior; and (C) voluntary or deliberate movements. From McGraw 1945, reprinted with permission.

McGraw (1945) interprets these observations as beginning with automatic reflex activity, which is present in other species embryologically. The second stage is representative of the development of some neural mechanism that serves to disrupt the organization of reflex activity. She describes this as a period of transition in which neither the cortex nor the subcortical nuclei function for the optimum benefit of the baby. The final phase reflects more deliberate and apparently voluntary movements that differ from the rhythmical movements of the newborn. McGraw indicates that the quality of the movements and the child's awareness of his environment proves that the cerebral cortex is participating in the activity.

Thelen (1989*b*) suggests that the spontaneous kicking movements exhibited by newborns when placed supine is a general pattern that

> Stepping, supine kicking, and swimming movements are the same pattern.

results in swimming when the baby is placed prone in water. This is identical to the earlier observation in which Thelen indicated that stepping movements when the child is placed upright are the same as kicking when placed supine. Additionally, about the time the swimming pattern is lost, infants gain a rapid burst of extensor muscle strength so that a prone infant tends to arch his back and extend his arms. This type of posture would certainly facilitate rolling over, especially in water, and also would naturally disrupt the flexed position needed to float while in the prone position. Thus this apparent regression can be explained by a change in one control factor, muscle strength, just as it was with the disappearance of automatic stepping. See Chapter 2.

Inversion

In another unusual situation, McGraw (1945) held the infants by the ankles and suspended them upside down. She then observed the infants' attempts to adjust themselves to the position. Figure 3-2 shows the phases observed. This procedure particularly shows the alternating development of flexor and extensor dominance.

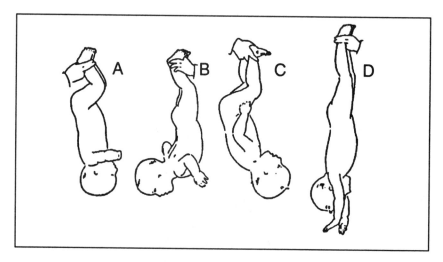

Figure 3-2 Four phases of postural adjustment to suspended inversion. (A) Flexor dominance; (B) active extension; (C) antigravity active flexion; and (D) mature stage, neither flexion nor extension dominates. From McGraw (1945), reprinted with permission.

Phase A noted in the figure shows the predominance of flexor activity in the newborn up to about 1 month of age as he makes an effort of maintain the position of flexion against gravity.

After about 6 weeks of age, there is a rapid increase in extensor muscle strength. Phase B is representative of this change, which also includes more active power in the extremities, particularly the upper extremities. McGraw suggests that the emergence of extension is the result of selective cortical inhibition of the flexion present in the newborn. Phase C shows another switch to flexor activity that appears to be more deliberate in nature. McGraw's interprets this pattern as evidence of cortical activation of muscular movement.

Phase D has been labeled the mature stage. Neither flexion nor extension dominates. Figure 3-3 is a graphic presentation of the alternation in muscular dominance at different ages. You have learned that it is not necessary to invoke elaborate cortical inhibitory and facilitatory systems to account for these patterns of muscular activity. The alternating muscular dominance between flexor and extensor muscles undoubtedly depends on a number of factors and is another movement control variable proposed by Thelen. Whether the flexors or the extensors are the strongest or most dominant at any point in time does have significant affect on what kinds of patterns can be elaborated.

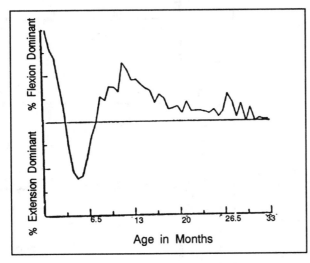

Figure 3-3 The percentage of distribution of flexion and extension in the adjustment to inversion between birth and 33 months of age. From McGraw (1945), reprinted with permission.

Rolling

In addition to these unusual activities of newborn swimming and inversion, McGraw (1945) studied the development of rolling from supine to prone, sitting, creeping and crawling (prone progression), and assuming the upright posture. Figure 3-4 shows the stages in rolling from the supine to the prone position. The newborn has a flexed posture and insufficient strength to roll over. The infant may either roll from supine to side as a tight unit or turn the head to the side without affecting the body (Fig 3-4 A1, A2). Next, axial extension begins to develop and the baby either may roll all the way over or may fail to time the flexion adequately in order to roll over and will roll back to supine (B1, B2). At about 6 months the baby arches in extension and completes the roll, which occurs as the infant develops better flexor and extensor control. McGraw labeled this phase activity as automatic rolling (C1, C2), because the child does not roll to perform some continued function such as sitting up or getting to all fours. Phase D is considered deliberate, and the child rolls for the express purpose of attaining either all-fours or

93

sitting postures. Figure 3-5 shows the percentage occurrence of each phase of rolling over.

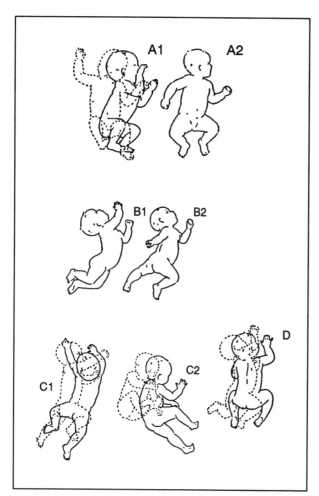

Figure 3-4 Four positions involved in rolling from a supine to prone position. From McGraw (1945), reprinted with permission.

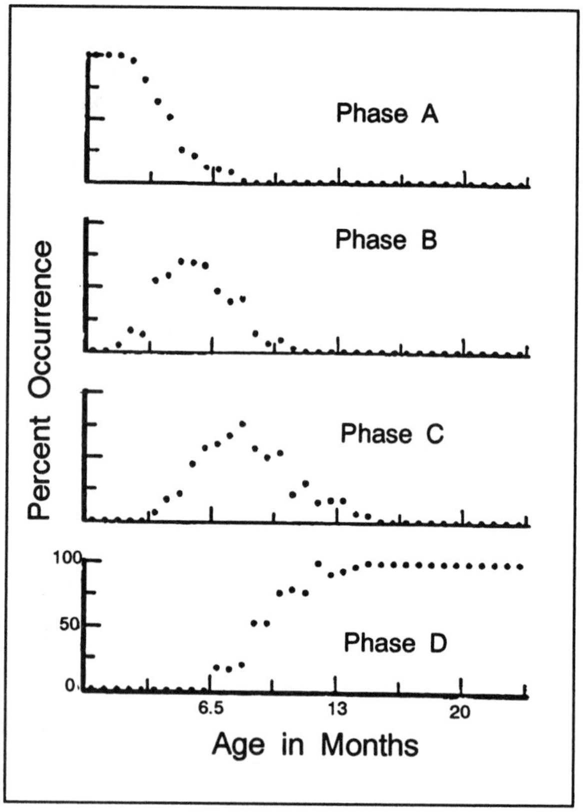

Figure 3-5 The percentage of occurrence of each phase of rolling over from birth to 20 months of age. Each dot represents 21 days. From McGraw (1945), reprinted with permission.

Prone Progression

Prone progression is a nine phase progression to creeping and crawling from the prone position. McGraw (1945) indicates that no other neuromuscular function that she observed had more individual variation than this progression. Figures 3-6, 3-7, and 3-8 show the phases she described and the ages when they are displayed most frequently. The newborn shows considerable flexion and extension activity of the lower extremities (Fig 3-6 A). Again, this is the supine kicking pattern, or the swimming pattern seen in the water. As will be seen later, some people have called this activity primary crawling. Phase B in Figure 3-6 shows

94

beginning spinal extension, and it is easy to see the development of head control and the elaboration of head righting reactions.

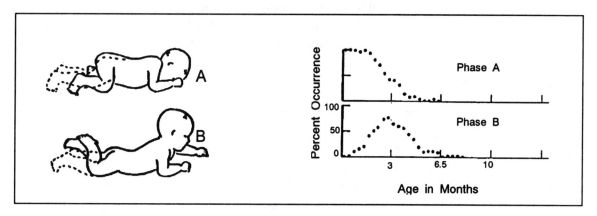

Figure 3-6 First two stages in the prone progression as described by McGraw. Graph shows the percentage of occurrence at each phase by age. From McGraw (1945), reprinted with permission.

In Figure 3-7, phase C is called advanced spinal extension because the extension has moved down the spine from the cervical area to the thoracic spine and the extensor muscles have become stronger. The head and chest are lifted from the surface and can be maintained in that posture for some time. Propping on arms begins, and it is this addition that really permits the elevation of the chest from the surface. If you do not believe that, lie down prone and attempt to raise your head. Notice that it is extremely difficult and in some cases impossible to bring the head to a full upright position without using the arms to help elevate the chest. Phases D and E show incipient, or beginning, propulsion of the upper and lower extremities, respectively. Phase F is the assumption of the creeping position. The ages at which these phases appear and the percentage of occurrence are graphed on the right of Figure 3-7.

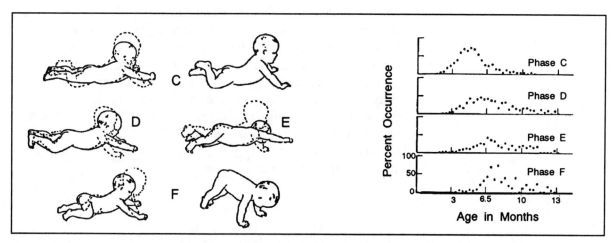

Figure 3-7 Four middle stages in the prone progression. Graph shows the percentage of occurrence at each phase by age. From McGraw (1945), reprinted with permission.

95

Phase G is an unorganized attempt at progression (Fig 3-8). Phase H shows organized propulsion in the creeping position. Phase I is an integrated propulsion in which the movements involved work together as if they were one. The age when these phases appear and the percentage of occurrence are shown on the right of Figure 3-8.

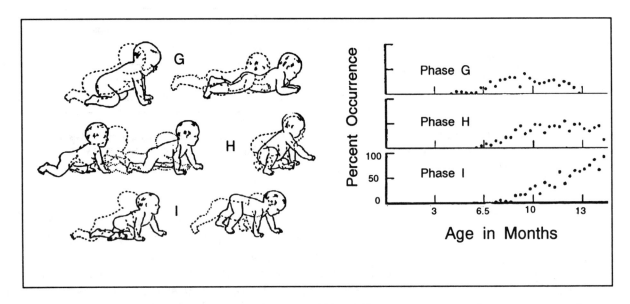

Figure 3-8 Last three stages in the prone progression. Graph shows the percentage of occurrence at each phase by age. From McGraw (1945), reprinted with permission.

Throughout this series of descriptions, McGraw continues her attempt to correlate the observed patterns of function with cortical maturation either resulting in effective inhibition of earlier components or manifesting cortical control over posture and movement. Look again at these series of movements as she describes them. If you review the ages for prone progression with the ages recorded for swimming and inversion, it is easy to see that major factors influencing these progressions could be muscular strength, especially extensor strength, and the relative imbalances in flexor and extensor activity. Muscular strength has been described as a control factor, that is, a crucial variable that can affect developmental changes. It does not become necessary to invoke maturation of cortical structures as the driving force for this development. Of course, maturation is indeed taking place and the pattern generation is being modified and fine tuned as part of this occurrence, but it is not likely to be the sole dimension or the only system participating in these events.

Sitting

McGraw was interested in the development of a sitting posture. She suggests that the appraisal of behavior changes resulting in the assumption of independent sitting presented problems different from the other patterns that she had analyzed. She stated that "most behavior patterns developing during the first year of life are activities of phylogenetic origin. In ontogenetic development, a primitive reflex pattern, controlled at a segmental level, usually characterizes the newborn phase" (McGraw 1945, p 62). Her embryological roots and orientation are obvious. The swimming and progression activities are common to many species. McGraw was concerned that there was an absence of a reflex phase in the development of sitting posture and believed this phenomenon indicated that sitting was an achievement of recent phylogenetic origin.

Phylogeny: Evolution of a genetically related *group*.

Ontogeny: Development of the *individual*.

She further indicated that "the newborn infant offers little resistance to gravitational force, but at some time, usually during the third quarter of the first year of life, he gains the ability not only to resist the force of gravity sufficiently to maintain an erect sitting position but also to overcome the force in order to assume independently a sitting position. In order to study the nature of development that culminates in the infant's independent and coordinate assumption of a sitting position, it was found convenient *to pull the child by the hands* from a recumbent sitting position and then gently *push him forward* so as to test his growing resistance and sense of balance. By this method it was possible to detect neuromuscular development before the child was able to gain an independent sitting position" (McGraw 1945, p 62) (italics are our emphasis).

Was McGraw observing manipulated responses or spontaneous movements?

As when the child was held upside down in the inversion procedure, here we can see the effect of interfering with the child's natural spontaneous movements. We have already noted McGraw's reasons for engaging in these experiments. The problem is that over the years therapists and others, who were either developing screening tools or trying to understand and summarize developmental sequences, have often placed different objectives and interpretations on McGraw's observations. It has already been stated that one great contribution of more recent research is that investigators have observed and measured spontaneous movements. This issue will arise again later when other approaches to developmental sequence are discussed. For now, it is important to recognize simply how and for what purpose these experiments were done. Later, we will try to interpret the data in light of more recent experimental findings. The existence of these infant patterns cannot be denied; however, the interpretation of their roles in development can be challenged.

McGraw (1945) described the aspect of rising to sitting in phases. The first three phases of the rising aspect have been termed pull-to-sit (Fig 3-9). The progression of infant participation in this maneuver clearly suggests a role for increasing muscular control, especially flexion against gravity. Phases D and E are spontaneous aspects of rising to the sitting position using a ventral push or a dorsal push, respectively. Again, in the early months, the child uses rotational aspects to accomplish this task, most probably because he lacks the strength in the flexors, particularly the abdominal muscles, to arise without rotation. The parent's, caretaker's, or therapist's role in the pull-to-sit is to provide the support for abdominal muscles throughout the first 6 to 7 months and to substitute for inadequate neck flexors early in the infant's development.

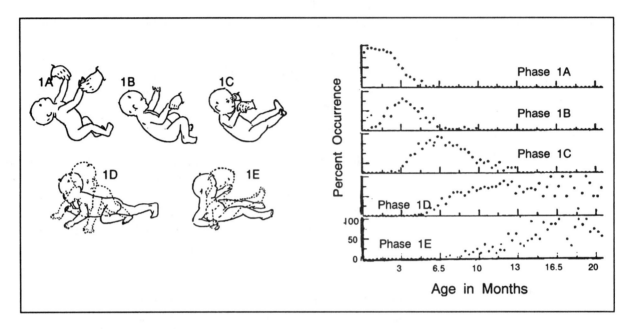

Figure 3-9 First three stages of the rise-to-sit sequence. These have been termed the pull-to-sit components (1A-C). 1D and E show the spontaneous aspects of rising to the sitting position. Graph shows the percentage of occurrence at each phase by age. From McGraw (1945), reprinted with permission.

There are six phases in what McGraw termed the resistive aspect of neuromuscular development in achieving a sitting position (Fig 3-10). Again, muscular strength becomes the prime issue; in this case, it is the trunk extensors. When placed in a sitting position, the newborn has no appreciable resistance to gravity at all (Fig 3-10 2A). Around 3 months of age, some incipient resistance to forward flexion can be observed, as is seen in Phase 2B (Fig 3-10 2B).

Between 5 and 7 months of age, the infant shows exaggerated resistance (Fig 3-10 2C). As extensor strength is developing, the child has difficulty controlling it as precisely as is necessary to remain sitting. A sudden thrust backward may result if too much energy is supplied to the muscles. The child thus often topples backward or sideward and also has no protective arm movements to catch himself and prevent the fall. Eventually, the infant is able to bear weight on the arms and hands while leaning forward, and he can sustain sitting for longer periods as he continues to refine extensor strength and postural control of the many segments of the spine to accomplish erect sitting around 8 months of age.

Actually achieving the sitting position independently occurs a little later than sitting with stability when placed in that position. If you look at prone progression and the age at which weight bearing on elbows and hands occurs, these abilities just precede the ability to sit while leaning forward and bearing weight on hands.

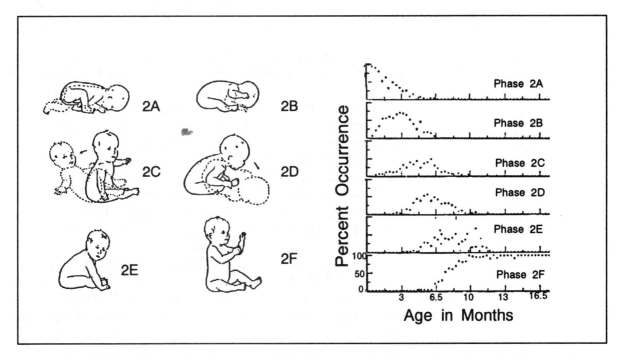

Figure 3-10 Six phases of the resistive aspect of neuromuscular development when placed in a sitting position. Graph shows the percentage of occurrence at each phase by age. From McGraw (1945), reprinted with permission.

Assumption of Erect Posture and Upright Locomotion

McGraw (1945) investigated two other sequences of patterns: the assumption of the erect posture and the accomplishment of upright locomotion. She divided these into two separate series of movements, or phases, but the overlap and interdependence of these phases is evident. Again, because the infant does not achieve the erect position independently until 12 to 15 months of age, McGraw decided to *place* the subjects in the upright position, *support* them, and *observe* the developmental changes that were apparent before independent assumption of the posture or locomotion. McGraw assumed that they represented an orderly progression of function resulting from an orderly developmental maturation of the nervous system. Unfortunately, we have sometimes concluded from these descriptions that responses obtained through manipulation at an earlier point in time are direct prerequisites of a particular function.

It should be understood that there is nothing inherently wrong in manipulating children to discover answers to questions. Thelen also

99

manipulated infants when she held them on the treadmill. The purpose was to discover whether a mature locomotion pattern could be made manifest before that pattern was demonstrated naturally. McGraw also had specific reasons for performing these manipulations, as noted earlier. The problem arises when therapists place different interpretations on the information obtained and assume the information for their own purposes without being thoroughly familiar with both the methods and the goals of the research.

Figure 3-11 shows the phases of erect locomotion as McGraw described them. Automatic stepping is demonstrated in phase A, and the loss of it in phase B. Phase C shows the various bouncing and stamping activities a suspended child will demonstrate between 4 and 12 months of age. Also noted is the better control of head position and activity developing in the upper extremities. In phase D the child takes steps when supported by an adult. The differences between phases E, F, and G are mainly the refinement of upright postural control and balance. This control allows the gradual lowering of the arms from the high hand-guard position of phase E and the beginning of their rhythmical participation in forward stepping in phase G. Recall that Thelen (Chapter 2) provided a description of the components, or subsystems, that participate in this progression, including the development of adequate strength in the lower extremity muscles and sufficient balance and postural control to integrate all the joints involved especially those of the spinal column. The ages for these phases are on the right of Figure 3-11.

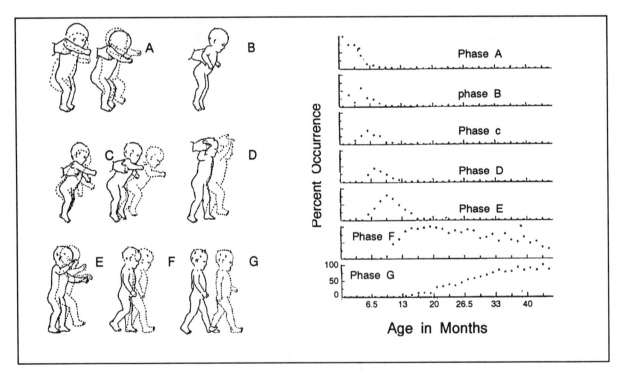

Figure 3-11 Seven phases of erect locomotion as defined in the text. Graph shows the age and percentage of occurrence at each phase of locomotion described. From McGraw (1945), reprinted with permission.

In Figure 3-12, seven selected phases of assumption of the upright posture are shown. Again, these begin with five phases in which the child is supported or manipulated. In the newborn, pull-to-stand from pull-to-sit is essentially passive. Considerable muscle strength is necessary for active participation to take place. At around 5 to 6 months, the child shows an incipient, or beginning, urge to push himself upward by raising his buttocks slightly, but he cannot sustain the position. With the development of extensor muscle strength the infant can extend his lower extremities, but his shoulder girdle is usually in a plane posterior to his feet. In phases D and E, the child first leans forward to align his scapula over his feet and, later, pushes more ventrally to assume this posture.

Phases F and G represent two methods that are used independently to assume the upright posture. In phase F, the child rolls to prone, gets up on all fours, and then stands upright. In phase G, there is slight rotation from supine, with arm support to get to standing. Phase F usually occurs before G, but both patterns may be used alternately for some time.

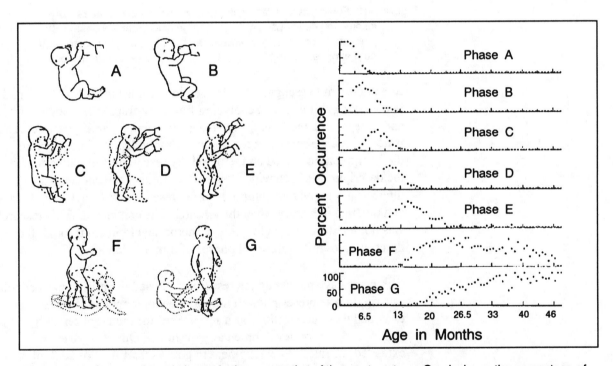

Figure 3-12 Seven selected phases in the assumption of the erect posture. Graph shows the percentage of occurrence at each phase by age. From McGraw (1945), reprinted with permission.

Figure 3-13 shows the footprint patterns of three stages in developing gait. The changes in surface contact show the progression from walking on the toes to a wide based foot-flat type of contact. The heel-to-toe progression with a more mature base width occurs last.

101

If these phases just discussed were put together without those requiring adult support, another sequence of patterns would be demonstrated. Additionally, what is missing in McGraw's sequence is not only the pull-to-stand the infant actively performs when pulling on furniture or other objects to achieve upright posture independent of another person but also the side walking patterns of cruising while holding on to furniture for support.

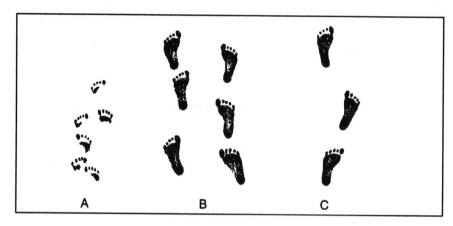

Figure 3-13 Footprints illustrating changes in surface contacts as upright locomotion develops. (A) Digital progression, narrow base; (B) plantigrade progression, wide base; and (C) heel-toe progression, normal base. From McGraw (1935), reprinted with permission.

It is important to recognize the tremendous contribution McGraw made in observing, filming, and analyzing frame-by-frame thousands of photos and in recording the findings in as objective a manner as possible. There is no argument about what the photos actually depict. The problem is in the interpretation placed on them both by researchers and others who use the descriptions of behavior. It is easy to understand McGraw's interpretation, given the purpose for the research effort in the first place and the time in history when the research was conducted. This research was not intended as a rigid guide to motor development through the description of milestones and phases of motor behavior.

Clinicians have picked up the research and used the milestones described as a rigid order prescription of normal development and, further, extended these descriptions as a set of rules for intervention with children who were developmentally disabled. Others have even extended the rules of development to govern treatment of adult clients with neurological deficits. The sequential features of erect locomotion were not McGraw's sole concern. She believed they would help determine the dynamic element of change that leads one form of behavior to give way to the next (McGraw and Breeze 1941). The phases shown were selected to prove her points, not to provide a screening device or guidelines for therapeutic intervention. McGraw clearly believed that maturation of the nervous system was the single force driving the development of motor behavior in infants and she set about to prove it.

Arnold Gesell

Gesell, a contemporary of McGraw's, also used patterning of posture and movement as his primary data. He also was firmly rooted in embryology. His developmental theory, however, was much more far reaching than McGraw's generalizations. More than any other developmentalist, Gesell saw human ontogeny, including the development of the mind, as a specific application of the very general laws of embryology. Fundamental to his theory and research process was the conviction that development was a morphological process. He envisioned behavior as having shape, or structure, and he believed that mental processes were manifested in motor behavior and could thus be understood through study of the shape, or form, of development. Gesell saw his mass of descriptive data on stages of motor, adaptive, language, and social behavior of children as much more than a catalog of expected age norms (Thelen 1989a).

| Gesell believed that mental processes could be understood through studying motor behavior. |

Developmental Principles

Gesell (1954) proposed five principles of developmental morphology, developed from his studies. Some of them have been and continue to be widely quoted and used. One of these was the *Principle of Developmental Direction*. He suggested that development proceeds from head to toe and proximal to distal. This principle was derived from the phenomena of gradients and polarities in embryology in which embryologists showed that the fate of an organ was determined by its position in the egg. It is necessary to realize that this principle was applied to human development through visual inspection of sequential photos of infant movement. No strict analysis of the movements themselves were performed and no investigation into actual processes were possible, such as using electromyography to gain insight into infants' muscular patterns. While observations, especially highly structured ones, provide excellent insights into phenomena, they can also greatly mislead theorists and practitioners when inappropriate interpretations are placed on the behaviors observed. This is a tremendous problem in our profession because vast numbers of techniques and evaluation procedures are based on observations. We are struggling to find better and more valid ways of quantifying observational data to help with documenting therapeutic value of particular techniques and determining appropriate intervention.

| Observations can mislead practitioners when inappropriate interpretations are placed on them. |

Gesell's *Principle of Functional Asymmetry* resulted from the recognition that some asymmetric elements occur in development. The asymmetric tonic neck reflex is one example.. He suggested that these asymmetries promote handedness and eye dominance and permit a higher access to information about the environment than if only one form of orientation were involved.

The *Principle of Individuating Maturation* suggests that maturational mechanisms are in basic control of development and that specific training and environment cannot be prime influences on movement. His data for this position came from his famous studies on twin training (Gesell 1954). One identical twin was given early training in stair climbing before the structures necessary to perform the task were thought to be developed. The other twin was given a few short direct instructions when he reached the age that it was thought the stair-climbing structures would have been developed. There seemed to be little affect or advantage for early training.

There are numerous studies, by other investigators, in the literature that suggest that much of development is somewhat predetermined. Carmichael (1926) prevented the activity of tadpoles by keeping them in an immobilizing solution while control tadpoles were allowed to develop swimming in water. When the controls were swimming, the drugged tadpoles were put into water and were soon swimming like the others. This suggests that maturation rather than exercise or environmental experience was responsible for swimming. Studies have been done that significantly restrict the activity of human infants, although it is neither ethical nor wise to restrict activity entirely. Restrictions are sometimes present culturally, as when infants are kept bound to cradle-boards by their Hopi Indian parents. Motor activities that develop in the first year are not greatly, if at all, retarded by such limited restrictions of activity.

Some cultures also emphasize different types of parenting in which sitting and standing may be encouraged early by such methods as scooping out a hole in the earth and placing the child in a sitting position while the adults are engaged in other activities. In these cases, certain milestones appear to be advanced in terms of the time of their occurrence. Clearly, maturation and underlying pattern generation have considerable influence on development. When children have been abandoned in the wild or abused through social and physical restrictions, however, both mental and physical problems have been observed that are not always amenable to correction. Thus, while partial restrictions or differences in cultural parenting may have somewhat transient or relatively minor effects on development, severe and long lasting restrictions may have permanent effects. If the latter is true, then it is clear that environmental conditions also are extremely important to development.

Gesell's other principles, such as the *Principle of Reciprocal Interweaving* and the *Principle of Self-Regulatory Function,* which also arose directly from embryology, resulted in a complex model of dynamic morphology of behavior. His time-space conception of development was perhaps an early forerunner of the systems view that "holds that the living organisms are characterized by the time-space dimensions of their interrelated parts" (Thelen 1989a, p10). Gesell differs from McGraw's linear view of development and explicitly invokes waxing and waning (advances, regressions, consolidations) of components, or traits, that

For Gesell, nature was the prime influence on the development of movement.

Some studies seem to suggest that maturation is responsible for motor development.

Other studies show that environment is extremely important to motor development.

Where McGraw had a linear view of development, Gesell developed a spiraling view of development.

104

intermesh in myriad ways in a spiral course in which sequential forms of behavior are reincorporated with newer forms at an increasingly higher level.

Gesell's Developmental Research

Unfortunately, Gesell is best remembered for his incredible catalog of developing infant behaviors and age-based developmental norms. Of major interest to therapists are the descriptive and photographic records of infant movement. Because therapists have proposed hypotheses and devised treatment programs for developmentally disabled children based on these norms and descriptions, it seems important to delve into the processes and procedures Gesell used to gather his data.

His longitudinal studies were relatively limited. At least five children were studied for 1 year. Most of the other studies were cross-sectional in nature. The cinematographic methods used to record infant behaviors were outstanding for the time. These studies produced hundreds of yards of film and thousands of photographs. A two-volume atlas of infant behavior was published (Gesell 1934) that included 3,200 action photographs. The introduction to the volume and the description and photographs of the methods and materials used raise some startling points.

Gesell used highly structured, manipulative procedures in cataloging infant behaviors.

The sessions that were recorded were highly structured. Figure 3-14 shows some of the materials used. Just viewing the equipment gives some insight into what was done with the children. Note that special chairs and supports were used in the crib if the child could not sit up independently. Figure 3-13 also shows a grid for the precise presentation of objects to the child.

Gesell's procedures were highly structured and manipulative. Some of the activities were the same as those noted in McGraw's work, such as pull-to-sit and pull-to-stand and holding the children upright before they could stand or pull themselves to standing. Children were given very specific toys, or very specific objects were presented to them. There is no indication in his works as to why these items were chosen or how the scales and topics for analysis were actually developed. No reasoning or pilot data is given for such selection.

It is important, once again, to remember Gesell's purpose in these studies. He was interested in mental growth, with an ultimate view as to how it could be correlated with embryological principles and laws. The title of his first book is *The Mental Growth of the Pre-School Child;* the sub-title is *A Psychological Outline of Normal Development from Birth to the Sixth Year, Including a System of Developmental Diagnosis.* This book was rewritten in 1940 as the popular *The First Five Years of Life.* His system of developmental diagnosis, which includes motor development, language development, adaptive behavior, and

105

personal-social behavior, forms the basis of several developmental screening tools such as the Denver Developmental Screening Test.

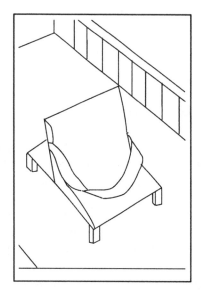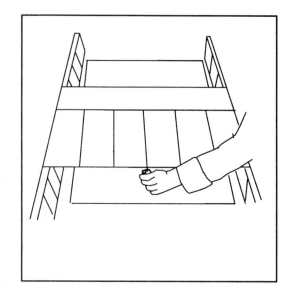

Figure 3-14 Items used in Gesell's evaluation procedures and special chair with straps for securing infants who could not yet sit independently. Drawn from Gesell (1934).

We will not present a step-by-step analysis as was done with McGraw's sequences because much of the motor behaviors are similar. Numerous other researchers have studied infants and made the same general observations. A general developmental sequence can be found in an untold number of texts concerning the growth and development of children. Figure 3-15 is such a general sequence showing the ages at which 25% to 90% of children achieve the behavior listed.

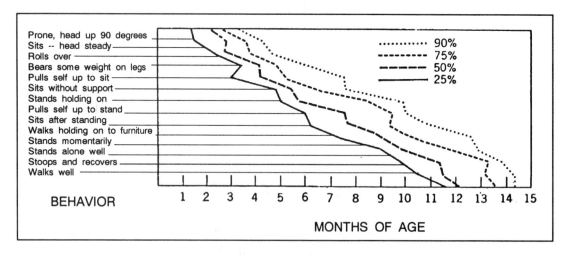

Figure 3-15 The percentage of infants displaying a given behavior at a particular age. Note the wide range of normal between the time when 25% of the infants demonstrate the behavior and when 90% of them display the behavior. Based on the Denver Developmental Screening Test.

Developmental Sequence

The meaning of *developmental sequence* is often in the eye of the beholder and dependent on the interests of the investigator or clinician who attempts to describe it. Developmental sequence is a term we could define as the order in which characteristics or traits of interest, such as movement patterns, are expressed as the individual ages. Thus almost anything of interest could be traced through its progression. Even with motor behavior of children, investigators have had specific agenda for their observations. For instance, we have already noticed that McGraw selected what she believed were specific continuous sequences such as prone progression, independent sitting, and upright locomotion. So the items or patterns that are followed, photographed, or described are the choice of the investigator or the observer, and as we have seen, the objectives underlying these recordings or observations are quite likely to be different among investigators. These objectives should be known and understood before the reports of an investigator are used for other purposes.

Some of the first sequences of infant behavior to be described were derived by the biographical method. That is, accounts of the behavior were described by observers, usually a parent. With this method, the possibility of bias in the judgment of the beholder is less discernible than when using photographic records that may be examined by anyone.

Dennis (1952) studied 40 biographical investigations published by several investigators and found 50 items relating to motor development (Fig 3-16). The median age for the elaboration of these behaviors was determined along with the age range of their appearance. The latter provides a very graphic insight into the individual differences in rates of development.

Shirley (1931) observed 25 infants until they were 2 years old. Parents reported on progress during intervals between the investigators observations. Figure 3-17 graphically represents the median age and age ranges for 25 items chosen for examination. Compare these findings with those of Dennis.

The data are similar; however, the age of initial appearance and the median age of appearance are somewhat earlier in the biographical studies. Quite likely this represents parents that were sufficiently interested in keeping the diaries and who were with the children continuously and thus available when the activities may have actually begun. Of course, biases of proud parents may also influence the biographical data. Studies by Gesell (1928, 1934), Bayley (1969), McCarthy (1972), and others result in profiles of similar items or activities, but the norms usually differ from one test to another (Munn 1974). In some cases it is completely clear how and why the study was

107

performed, but in other cases it is not. The result here, however, is that the items from test to test are relatively similar. Gesell and others who initially thought that the rate of motor development is indicative of later mental growth have not been proven to be correct. We now know that motor development, although positively correlated with later mental development as measured by intelligence tests, is correlated only to a very low degree (Goodenough 1949; Bayley 1968).

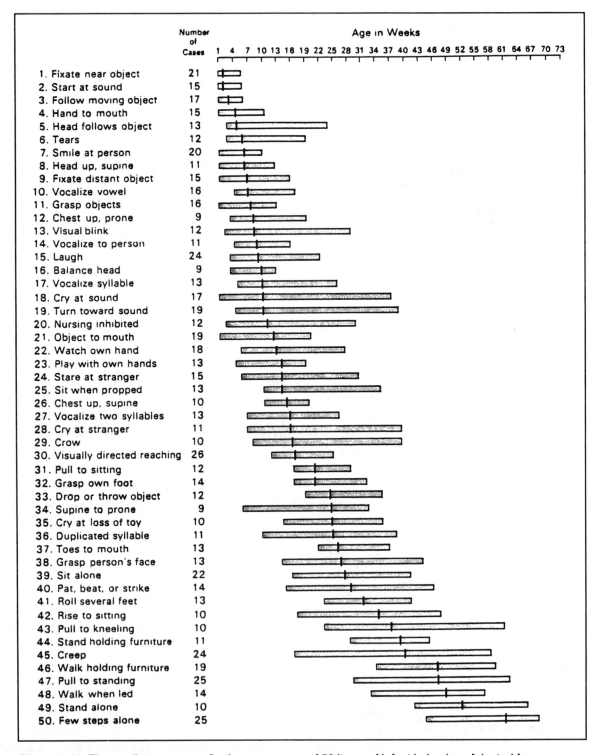

Figure 3-16 The median age range for the appearance of 50 items of infant behavior. Adapted from Dennis (1952).

108

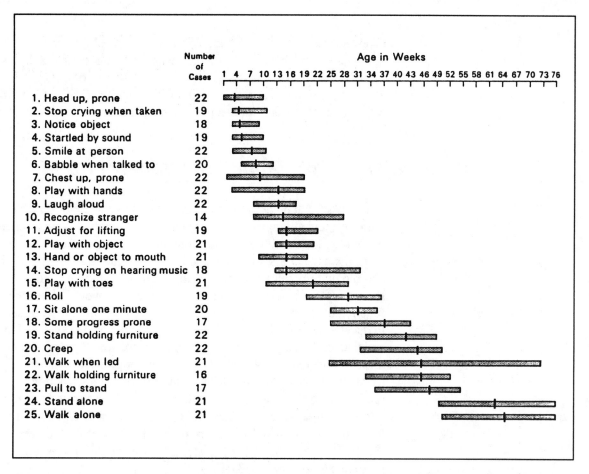

Figure 3-17 The age range for the appearance of 26 items of infant behavior. Adapted from Shirley (1931).

One of the most striking and most important elements to extract from these norms and others like them is the tremendous variation in individual accomplishment of any item. Some children walk by 7 months of age, while others will not walk independently until 18 months. Doudlah (1981) made an interesting observation about determining developmental age. She showed participants at a conference videotapes of 12 samples of motor performance by normal children. She asked the audience to estimate the ages of the children demonstrating the behavior. The conference attendees were therapists and other professionals from all over the country who work with children and often observe such behaviors. These professionals estimated the ages to range from 7 months to 18 months. In actuality, the children were all the same age, but their skill levels varied considerably. Such an observation brings into question whether age is a significant issue or whether other aspects of developmental sequence are more meaningful.

Normative studies show the age at which various motor accomplishments are to be expected, but they really do not provide insight about the development of a particular activity from its initial to its final stages. McGraw attempted to describe stages of a particular activity, but we have already indicated the weakness in her approach. Therapists have long considered the order of developmental events to be

There is considerable variation in skill development.

109

a key element in the understanding of normal development. Treatment approaches have been based on the assumption that certain activities are prerequisite to, or are components of, later or more complex skills. These assumptions have been derived from interpretation of the old body of literature that has just been presented in this text.

Developmental Interpretations of Margaret Rood

Therapists, both physical and occupational, have made observations of their own and attempted to answer the question of how development is related to motor activity and motor control. Margaret Rood was one of those therapists. She immersed herself in the literature and devised neurologic principles from the information she gathered. From this data she attempted to devise treatment techniques that would affect the function of the nervous system. She believed that the order, or sequence, in development held lessons for understanding nervous system function and that such a sequence provided rules for treatment progression. It must be understood that she, along with other pioneers in neurologic treatment, were quite up-to-date for their time and provided the profession with a new maturity and considerable progress from the traditional treatments in vogue at the time. We owe them a great debt for their courage and insight. Unfortunately, Rood contributed very little to the literature, and most of her insights have been interpreted and presented by others (Fig 3-18).

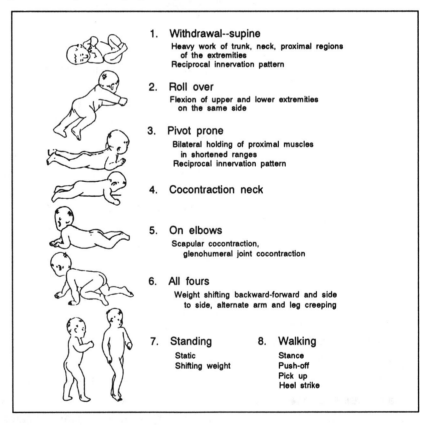

1. Withdrawal--supine
   Heavy work of trunk, neck, proximal regions of the extremities
   Reciprocal innervation pattern

2. Roll over
   Flexion of upper and lower extremities on the same side

3. Pivot prone
   Bilateral holding of proximal muscles in shortened ranges
   Reciprocal innervation pattern

4. Cocontraction neck

5. On elbows
   Scapular cocontraction, glenohumeral joint cocontraction

6. All fours
   Weight shifting backward-forward and side to side, alternate arm and leg creeping

7. Standing
   Static
   Shifting weight

8. Walking
   Stance
   Push-off
   Pick up
   Heel strike

Figure 3-18 The skeletal function sequence as described by Rood. Redrawn from Stockmeyer (1966).

110

Rood chose certain motor milestones evident in children and attempted to place those milestones on a grid that reflected nervous system maturation (Stockmeyer 1966). Her maturational scheme had relatively little to do with the cortex of the brain but was based on her current understanding of the development of peripheral connections

Clearly, Rood chose certain motor milestones to emphasize, and she changed this emphasis throughout her career as she and other therapists added to or modified this sequence (Fig 3-19). It is interesting that at particular times in the evolution of her approach, the sequence did not include rolling or sitting but did include some patterns of questionable origin, some of which have never been listed on developmental scales. It is also important to recognize that these choices were not made from scientific research but some opinion formed by the therapist through unspecified types of clinical observation and interpretation of the neurophysiological literature available at the time.

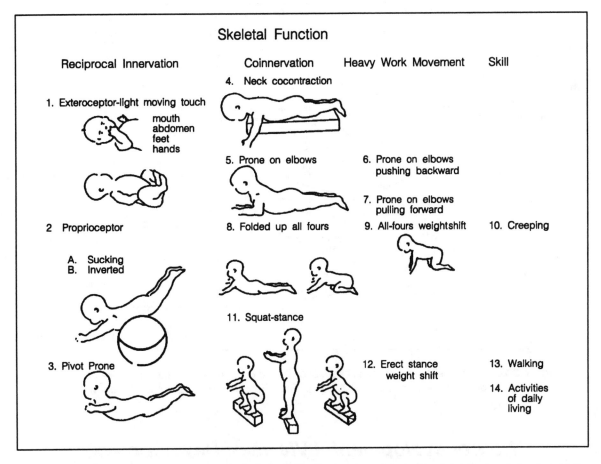

Figure 3-19 The 14 developmental steps of skeletal function arranged under the four stages of development according to Rood. From Heiniger and Randolph (1981), reprinted with permission.

Therapists at that time and later on incorporated the same basic model with certain alterations. Figure 3-20 shows a similar developmental

111

sequence scheme that is in current use. Therapists have attempted to update the information and answer questions that have arisen through the years. The names of the categories show such attempts to reconcile differences. Mobility has been equated with reciprocal innervation, coinnervation has been interpreted as stability, and controlled mobility has described heavy work movement. Skill remains on all sequences. The basic definitions of the terms have changed in some cases and remained the same in others. The term *mobility* in proprioceptive neuromuscular facilitation has been defined as the range of motion available for a motion to take place and sufficient motor unit activity to initiate a muscle contraction. That is a good operational definition for mobility and better than using the term reciprocal innervation, which we have noted is incorrect. The basic concept of stability still remains linked to the neurological phenomenon of coactivation, or cocontraction, of agonists and antagonists. We will deal with the relevance of this assumption later.

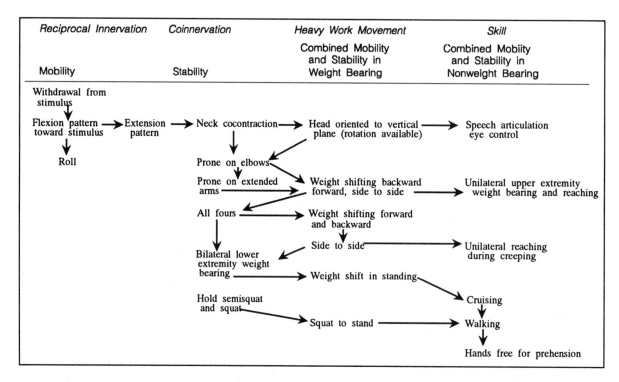

Figure 3-20 A composite developmental sequence based on Rood's and other approaches such as proprioceptive neuromuscular facilitation. From Farber (1982), reprinted with permission.

Neurodevelopmental Views of Development

Karl and Berta Bobath also were pioneers involved in developmental evaluation and treatment of neurologically involved clients. Their approach has been developed into the neurodevelopmental treatment approach. They, too, deserve respect for their contributions to the field. Therapists associated with this approach (Bly 1981a; 1981b; Laren 1982) have attempted to break the motor behaviors into more elemernts

112

than those previously described. These descriptions involve detailed changes in joint positions as the child accomplishes the motor milestones. Particular emphasis is placed on rotational movements, weight-shifts, antigravity extension, and antigravity flexion. Again, these scales are descriptive in nature and are heavily based on prior literature concerning reflexes, particularly righting and equilibrium.

The descriptions are not known to be wrought from controlled observational research but merely from observation. The conclusions and explanations of the relationship of components is based on logical supposition emanating from observation and the literature.

Developmental Research

Fishkind and Haley (1986) studied the relationship between certain movements that therapists have assumed to be components of independent sitting. The phases of sitting described by McGraw and the motor components proposed by others were observed in 10 infants between the ages of 3 and 5 months. The presence or absence of the following were noted in relation to the level of sitting ability: integrated Moro and asymmetrical and symmetrical tonic neck reflexes; protective reactions; equilibrium reactions prone, supine, and sitting; prone progression; Landau reaction; pull-to-sit; rolling; and hip flexion while in the supine position.

We should know why as well as how an investigator collects data before we formulate possible interpretations of the results.

Fishkind and Haley found little support for the popular concept that there is a consistent pattern of underlying motor components required for the development of sitting. Contrary to their expectations, there was a wide range in ages for the attainment of each sitting performance level and wide differences in the rate of progression through the levels. For instance, they found that it is not necessary for the child to have protective extension reactions to sit for a specified duration. There was no consistent sequential pattern of components that were stable prerequisites for the first two levels of sitting. It is difficult to make a final determination about all possible prerequisite motor patterns because all of the components were present by the time the third level of sitting was achieved. Statistics do not provide cause-effect information but rather the correlation of the presence of one pattern with another. The data could not be interpreted in a manner that indicates that the activities and reflex patterns were specifically prerequisite for that level of sitting.

Research shows no pattern of components is required for the development of sitting.

It is quite possible to interpret the Fishkind and Haley (1986) study as supporting the concept that sitting is a synergy that is independent of other patterns of movement such as rolling or prone progression. The basic requirements that allow the synergy to be expressed are probably muscular strength and some balance and postural control over multiple spinal segments and the extremities. Sitting, therefore, may rely on other mechanisms in association with the pattern generation for goal accomplishment, as does locomotion. This study and others suggest also

113

that there may be many paths to the same end point in development and that each child does not have to complete one specific track to achieve motor skills and independence.

It also seems clear that if the child does not have protective extension reactions backward and sideward, he may be able to maintain sitting for some time if unperturbed but is unable to control his balance if the center of gravity is thrown too far outside the base of support. Even with adequate muscular strength, a point is reached in which balance cannot be regained solely through muscular resistance. In this case, the arms must extend in the direction of the fall and bear weight if a fall is to be prevented. Protective extension is another independent synergy that is neither required for nor a part of upright sitting, but it is called on if the center of gravity is disturbed under certain conditions. Therefore, certain cooperative combinations exist to permit the elaboration of a particular synergy in relation to the demands of the environment.

Horowitz and Sharby (1988) studied the development of prone extension postures in normal infants. They wanted to find out whether there was a sequence for the head, upper extremities, and lower extremities in the prone extension (pivot prone) posture and whether the acquisition of this posture was required for prone-on-hands and prone-on-elbows postures. For many years, therapists believed that muscles must work in a shortened position in a nonweight bearing pattern to prepare them for weight bearing functions. This concept was developed by Rood from her integration of the literature available at that time and her observation of infant development and abnormal patterns of movement found in children with such problems as cerebral palsy.

Horowitz and Sharby showed that the full development of the pivot-prone position was not necessary for the child to perform prone-on-elbows but followed the development of head and lower extremity extension. Development did not follow a head-to-toe pattern because head development was followed by lower extremity extension and then by upper extremity extension. Some children achieved the prone-on-hands and prone-on-elbows positions without ever achieving the pivot-prone pattern. These data also suggest that there are variable paths to development and that it cannot be determined that one specific movement is a component or prerequisite pattern to another. It clearly shows that Rood's old concept about the necessity for shortened range nonweight bearing patterns before weight bearing ones does not bear up under careful scrutiny.

Developmental Research Project--Anna Doudlah

Anna Doudlah (1981), a therapist who has performed developmental observations within a strict research orientation, studied a significant number of children (25) over a longitudinal course of several years and has provided another view of a developmental sequence. Her studies are published in video format. As a researcher, she strongly believes that the only appropriate medium for studying and reviewing this sequence is through videotape recordings, which is a medium not directly amenable to publication. The information presented here is extracted from the proceedings of a conference presentation. The methods used are clearly described, and the goals of the research are explicitly stated. It seems most reasonable to present this information in narrative and picture format in order to spark new inquiry and to suggest possible alternative approaches to intervention of movement dysfunction.

To enhance the motor development in developmentally disabled children, she first sought to understand the process of how function in normal children is regulated and changed. Identifying the sequence of motor events from birth to walking became the objective of her research program, which began in 1967. The research was also undertaken to help clarify the confusion resulting from the differences in emphasis and description of developmental sequence used in the assessment tools and treatment approaches by therapists who were involved with developmentally disabled children. She believed also that therapists use a wide variety of approaches that are considered to be developmental and are often ineffective in the remediation of the multiply handicapped.

> Doudlah filmed *spontaneous* movement in children.

Doudlah (1981) noted that the motor development sequence in normal children, based on observation of spontaneous movement over time, had not been described. To fill this void, she filmed 20 children, on a monthly basis, who were moving about freely in their own homes. At no time were the children directed to move in any particular way.

The questions to which Doudlah sought answers were as follows: (1) Is there a motor development sequence representative of normal children as they progress from birth to walking? (2) Is the motor performance the same for all normal children as they progress through the sequence? and (3) What is the sequence?

> **Phase 1** - Movement in place.
>
> **Transition 1** - Rolling.
>
> **Phase 2** - Movement through space in a quadrupedal position.
>
> **Transition 2** - Being upright in space.
>
> **Phase 3** - Movement through space in the upright position.

Films were viewed at regular, fast, and slow speeds and frame-by-frame. Motor behaviors seen were listed by month for each child. The motor development sequence that was identified had resulted from selecting performances common to all children and was presented in a checklist (Fig 3-21). Motor events were numbered from 1 to 35 for convenience and discussion. In reality, however, these motor events occur as clusters of actions rather than in a rigidly ordered list. Doudlah observed that motor items naturally grouped themselves, enabling description of the child's position or performance in space. She described these as three phases and two transitions (Figs 3-22 to 3-26).

Name DATE																								
PHASE 1 -- MOVEMENT IN PLACE																									
1. Random movement: on back																									
2. Turns head																									
3. Lifts head in midline																									
4. Extension of body axis																									
5. Weight bearing: elbows																									
6. Push/pull with legs/arms																									
7. Weight bearing: forearms /hands																									
8. Extension of body axis / push up																									
TRANSITION 1 -- ROLLING																									
9. Back to side																									
10. Belly to side																									
11. Back to belly																									
12. Belly to back																									
PHASE 2 -- MOVEMENT THROUGH SPACE QUADRUPEDAL POSITION																									
13. Pivots																									
14. Pushes back																									
15. Weight bearing: hand/knee																									
16. Crawls																									
17. Oscillates: hands/knees																									
18. Creeps																									
19. Sits: unilaterally																									
TRANSITION 2 -- BEING UPRIGHT IN SPACE																									
20. Kneels: both knees																									
21. Push / pull to stand																									
22. Stands on toes																									
23. Sits: upright independent																									
24. Kneels: knee / foot																									
25. Oscillates: kneeling both knees																									
26. Raise / lower body: kneeling																									
27. Oscillates: standing																									
PHASE 3 -- MOVEMENT THROUGH SPACE IN THE UPRIGHT POSITION																									
28. Walks around objects																									
29. Stoops with assistance																									
30. Squats with assistance																									
31. Walks with assistance																									
32. Climbs																									
33. Walks independently																									
34. Stands up in space																									
35. Squats in space																									

Figure 3-21 The developmental checklist. From Doudlah (1981), reprinted with permission from The Central Wisconsin Center for the Developmentally Disabled, Madison, Wis.

Figures 3-22 to 3-26 provide a pictorial and narrative description of the events occurring in these phases and transitions. Drawn from Doudlah (1981) and other sources. Originals were in photograph form. Text is reprinted with permission of Anna Doudlah, PhD.

Figure 3-22 -- PHASE 1. MOVEMENT IN PLACE (1-6 months)

The earliest spontaneous movements seen in a child are influenced by the position in which the child is placed on a supporting surface; that is, in the supine or prone position. If placed on the back, the infant will move arms and legs in what appears to be random patterns. Thelen showed that the leg patterns in particular are not random but are quite well organized although predictable action patterns involving head, arms, and legs are not apparent to the <u>casual</u> observer of the normal child at this time. When prone, the infant below struggles to turn her head (A) and then raises and holds her head up in line with the trunk (B). Later, her head, upper trunk, and arms are lifted off the supporting surface in the action of extension of her body axis (head, neck, and trunk) (C). The infant next supports herself on elbows (D) and later on forearms or hands (E). The actions of extension of, body axis and pushing up on arms are frequently done together as a repetitive exercise (F). During this phase infants may be seen pushing with legs and pulling with arms as if to move their bodies forward (G). However, actual movement of the body is limited if it occurs. Action patterns during this phase are best described as bilateral, that is, both arms or legs move together in the same way.

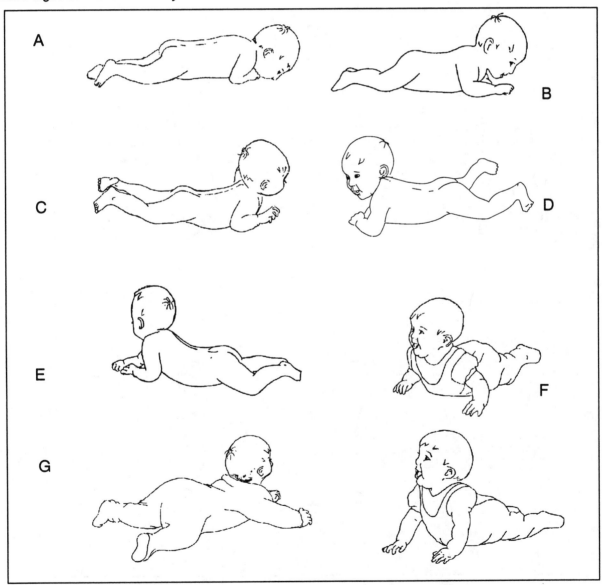

Figure 3-23 -- TRANSITION 1. ROLLING (3-7 months)

The infant uses rolling to change her position in space, which is limited to either the prone or supine position. Initially, the infant may roll from supine (A) or prone to the side and return to the original position. Action is initiated by turning her head in the direction of the roll; her legs lead the action of turning the rest of her body. Later, the infant rolls all the way from supine to prone (B) and prone to supine (C). Actions during this time are unilateral as one arm or leg bends, or flexes, and the other extends. The 20 children in this project preferred the prone position at this time. All motor events in phase 2 involve the prone position.

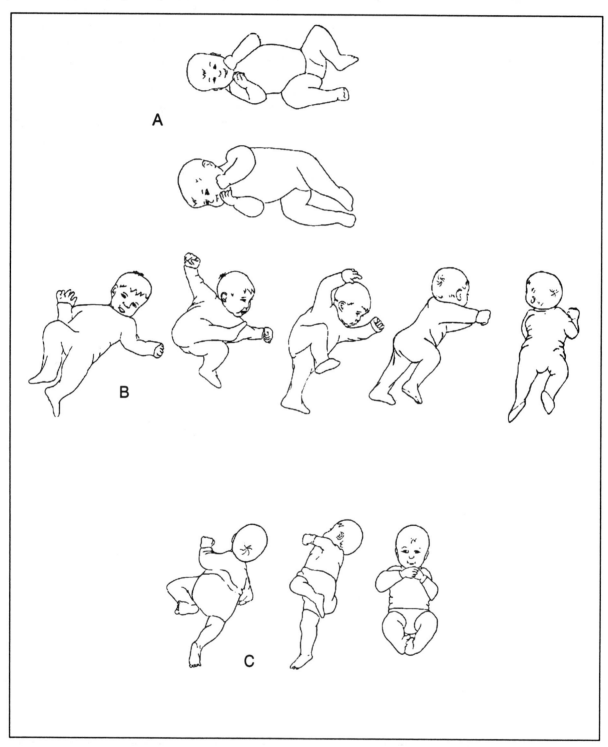

Figure 3-24 -- PHASE 2. MOVEMENT THROUGH SPACE--QUADRUPEDAL POSITION (4-12 months)

During phase 2, skills in weight bearing on hands and unilateral functions of arms and legs are used to raise the chest off the supporting surface (A); pivot, or turn, in space and push the body backward (B). Pushing back takes the form of moving backward or, later, getting to the weight bearing position on hands and knees (C). The child may briefly maintain this position but will likely appear unstable in it. Later, the child oscillates in the all-fours position, an action that might be a series of either short quick jerks or a vigorous rocking. Oscillation in each newly achieved position appears to be important before moving into action from that position. The child crawls, moving forward with the belly in contact with the surface, or creeps, moving forward on hands and knees (D). Not all children crawl (12 of those in this project did), but if they do, they crawl before creeping. At this time, children sit unilaterally, that is, they shift their weight from the hands-knees position to sitting on one hip while bearing some weight on the arm that is extended to the same side (E).

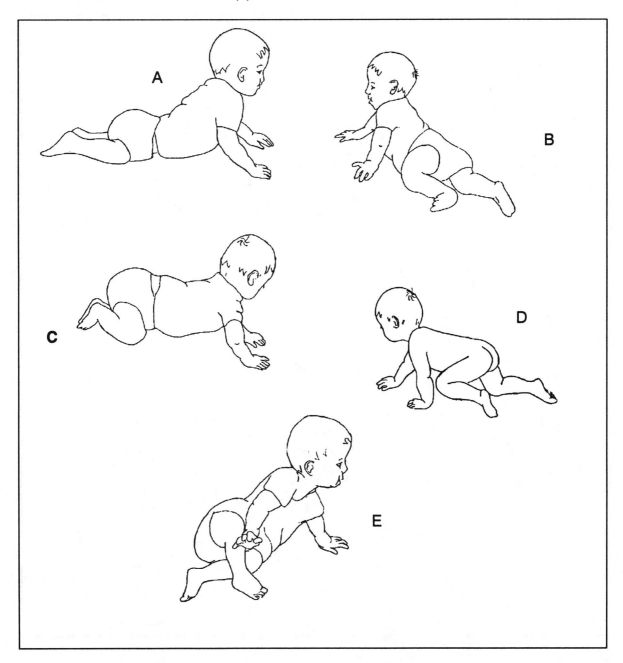

Figure 3-25 -- TRANSITION 2. BEING UPRIGHT IN SPACE

In this transition, the child's actions are directed toward kneeling, sitting upright independently, and standing. Getting to kneeling, either on both knees (A) or on one knee and one foot (B), is usually done by reaching for an object at arms length and raising the body so the trunk makes a 60-75 degree angle with the supporting surface. The child can be observed to oscillate when kneeling on both knees. Initially, standing is accomplished in a manner similar to early kneeling, that is, the child pulls or pushes to the upright position at arms length and at an angle to the supporting surface (C). After achieving the upright position, the child stands on her toes and oscillates in standing. The position of the foot in standing is noteworthy; it is placed with toes pointing to the side, with full body weight taken on the inner border. Later, the child raises or lowers her body to or from kneeling by extending or flexing her weight bearing leg (D). Sitting upright independently is accomplished by shifting the weight backward from the creeping position without using her arms (E).

Figure 3-26 -- Phase 3. MOVEMENT THROUGH SPACE IN THE UPRIGHT POSITION

Once the child has achieved the upright position, she begins to cruise, or move around objects, usually furniture, with steps taken to the side (A). The child raises and lowers her body by stooping or bending over from the waist; by squatting through the raising or lowering of her body by flexing or extending the legs (B); or by kneeling (C) while holding on to an object. Later the child walks with assistance using an object such as a chair or toy or a person (D). Once the upright position has been achieved, climbing up and off of objects becomes an important part of the child's movement routine. The child then walks independently (E), stands up in space (F), and squats in space free of any object or person (G).

121

Doudlah's (1981) research method allowed her to make several interesting observations about motor development. She emphasized the importance in the first phase of extension of the body axis (neck and trunk) in the prone position as preparation for weight bearing on elbows and later on forearms and hands. She also observed that the children underwent oscillations in positions before moving in the position. This observation is similar to those made by Thelen (1979) who described the oscillations as rhythmical stereotypies.

Doudlah observed that each time a child achieved a new position in space he oscillated in it, that is, moved repetitively and somewhat rhythmically in the position before moving to a new position or to a new place in space. Oscillations were always in the direction of the evolving movement, or action. Rocking on hands and knees is a very common example of an oscillation. Doudlah observed that this type of motor event appears in many developmental schedules simply as an event without any particular developmental significance, although Thelen considered the rhythmical stereotypy to be of considerable importance and predictive of developmental rate. The oscillations Doudlah identified were as follows: (1) extension of the body axis followed by pushing up on forearms or hands and oscillating up and down similar to a push-up; (2) rocking on hands and knees; (3) bouncing up and down on the knees; and (4) bouncing up and down on the toes in the standing position. She also noted that children stand on their toes in preparation for weight bearing on the entire foot. This was seen in children who did not wear hightop shoes early in their development.

> **Oscillations or stereotypies are evident in a position before movement occurs.**

Doudlah, as have many others, observed tremendous differences in performance and in rates of development as children progress through the motor development sequence. Children will demonstrate their motor skills spontaneously and quickly if they are comfortable in the immediate environment and will not attempt motor behaviors outside their skill and comfort range. Doudlah believes that the child's spontaneous motor performance is the most representative of the true developmental status and provides more reliable information than responses to physical manipulation by an adult.

Interpreting Developmental Rules

Therapists are and have been interested in the order and rules, or principles, of development because it has been assumed that movement dysfunction could be determined from possible deviations from this order. A plan for treatment intervention could then be established from the knowledge of the order of development. It is assumed that all children march to an internal drummer and that those who demonstrate developmental abnormalities will be treated effectively if they are carried through or forced or guided into those patterns that have been described.

A serious problem with this approach is that if the laws and principles and the specifics behind the sequences are in error, modeling a treatment progression based on it is likely also to be fraught with error. Therefore, it would seem worthwhile to investigate a few of those principles.

Cephalocaudal Directional Development

Remember that the principle of cephalocaudal development was articulated by Gesell from the concepts of eddies and currents in the cellular flow during embryologic development. If one is limited only to observation, this rule seems to be quite true. The child appears to develop head control followed in order by control of the upper trunk, lower trunk, arms, and then legs. Perhaps such observation can be deceptive. Thelen showed clearly that the most organized and regular movements of the newborn are in the legs--not in the arms or the head and trunk. (See Chapter 2). For many years, it was assumed that the kicking movements of the lower extremities were random and disorganized, because the human eye lacks the mechanism to record and compare movements and relationships as finely as a camera can record them and a computer can analyze them.

> **Thelen casts doubt on the long held head-to-toe rule of development.**

> **All areas of the body appear to develop concurrently.**

The major reason that movements appear to develop in a head-tail order is that sufficient strength in key muscles and adequate balance control develop later, and they are requirements for attaining such lower extremity functions as sitting or standing balance and gait. In actuality, it appears that all areas of the body develop concurrently, but some rate-limiting factors such as lack of muscular strength prevent certain types of movement from being expressed earlier in development.

Development Proceeds From Proximal to Distal

The proximal to distal principle was also proposed by Gesell. However, some studies have shown that both proximal and distal components are developing concurrently rather than sequentially (von Hofsten 1984). For example, individual finger movements and other forms and patterns of wrist and finger movements occur at the same time shoulder movements are seen. It is quite likely that some of the hand movements and manipulations that do not appear until later in development are more dependent on either proximal control or coordination of the total synergy rather than on distal control. In other words, the basic movements for hand function are present very early but are not fully functional until the entire synergy is expressed. In addition, other components such as strength, muscle balance, visual control, and motivation are involved in the attainment of function.

> **Function depends on a combination of**
>
> **synergy,**
>
> **strength,**
>
> **balance,**
>
> **vision,**
>
> **and motivation.**

Movements Proceed From Gross to Fine

The assertion that movement proceeds from gross to fine rests on the observation that such fine motor skills as handwriting appear much later in development than more gross motor skills such as walking. The categorizations of *gross* and *fine* must have been determined from the supposition that large muscles and more proximal joints are primarily involved in the former and small distal muscles and joints are called on in the latter.

> Walking is a highly skilled activity.

It is possible, however, that these suppositions and categorizations are somewhat in error. Walking, for instance, is not really a gross skill. The exquisite timing and coordination among muscles used for walking belies the traditional gross-skill title given to it. Review the development of locomotion described by Thelen and see if you can then continue to justify the traditional concept. Various forms of manipulation of large and small objects with the hands are significantly developed before the child can walk. Handwriting, painting, knitting, and other such fine skills are more than finger manipulations. They are certainly dependent on some intellectual maturity and practice--but, of course, so is perfectly coordinated running, jumping, dancing, and other skills that depend significantly on movements of the lower extremities.

> Coordinative structures, or movement synergies, involve multiple muscles and joints.

Actually, there are probably few gross movements. All movements involve synergies, or coordinative structures, that incorporate multiple muscles across several joints rather than being isolated muscle or joint actions. The manipulation of fine objects with the hand depends on other muscles and joints as well as those of the hand. These synergies are influenced by such conditions as the position of the arm, that is, if it is resting on the table or being held in front of the body. Additionally, if the position of the object is high, or low, or to the front or to the side of the individual. All of these conditions require different synergies of muscles and joints to accomplish one particular task such as handling an object.

Variability in Developmental Sequence

There are variations in the way children progress through developmental sequences. Children accomplish patterns at different times and often with some noticeable variation in the patterns or in the order in which the patterns are expressed. For instance, not all children crawl before creeping or creep before walking. Thus it would seem risky to propose that there is some set pattern of movement to which all children with developmental abnormalities should adhere.

Use of the Developmental Sequence With Adults

Another assumption often made is that the recovery from injury or disease to the central nervous system follows the same set of rules that govern motor development in infants. Much of this assumption rests on the observations that there is some predictability and orderly progression in recovery of function. The adults demonstrate abnormal synergies, reemergence of primitive reflexes, and an inability to perform such tasks as rolling over, standing up, and walking. Thus it may be assumed that they have regressed and must be taken back through the developmental sequence.

> Adults with neurologic disorders do not necessarily have the same problems as do children with neurologic disturbances.

Much recent research has shown that individuals with cerebral vascular accidents or other neurologic disorders often have problems with the onset of muscular activity, the ability to reach an adequate peak tension (weakness), and the ability to shut the muscle off at the proper time. Certain synergies cannot be accessed (Crutchfield 1989; Crutchfield et al 1989). It would seem to be a great leap of logic to equate the problems of an adult neurologic client who fails to perform certain patterns of movement with the lack of developmental sequence of movements in a child who has yet to exhibit mature patterns of activity.

> Some patterns within the developmental sequence are suitable for adults because of the safety factor.

The patterns of movement usually described in developmental sequence may be used with adults for other purposes. For instance, the ability to roll is important for bed mobility. Many developmental patterns are safer than standing because there is a wide base of support and the center of gravity is close to the supporting surface. Certainly, it is reasonable to expect an adult to be able to perform rolling, creeping, and other such patterns. The point is that these activities are useful for purposes other than being direct prerequisites to some higher activities. Thus waiting to work on gait until the client can roll or creep because some relationship supposedly exists between these movements does not appear to be a sound approach to treatment

Study Questions:

1. Compare the views of McGraw, Thelen, and Doudlah concerning development.

2. What is the significance of observing spontaneous movement?

3. **Why are the rules cephalocaudal, gross-to-fine, and proximal-to-distal called into question?**

4. **What is the danger in treating adults by using a developmental sequence?**

Other Rules of Developmental Sequence

Divide Work Into Two Limits

Rood originally divided developmental sequence into particular categories and implied that specific neurophysiological phenomena governed movements in these divisions. For instance, she divided work into two limits: light work and heavy work (Stockmeyer 1966; Heiniger and Randolph 1981). *Light work* was defined as the movement of the light lever, as when the arm flexes and the hand traces an arc. *Heavy work* results when the distal part of the extremity is fixed on a supporting surface and the body (heavy lever) moves over the distal pivot point. Students will remember from their anatomy that this phenomena is often referred to as reversing the origin and insertion of the muscle.

There is much about this concept that makes sense and is useful; however, the suppositions made by Rood when using these types of muscular actions are unproven and questionable. Rood stated that the light work activities involve more cortical participation, are more skilled activities, use superficial two-joint muscles, and are biochemically costly and inefficient for use, particularly when using these muscles during activities better performed by heavy work muscles. The latter are deep, one-joint muscles most often acting as stabilizers.

> Two important types of functional movement experiences are weight bearing and nonweight bearing activities.

It is possible to sift out of this over-interpretation of the literature the idea that in general, function can be divided into two major types of movement experiences: weight bearing and nonweight bearing. Creeping on all fours and push-ups are weight bearing functions. Typing a letter and feeding oneself might be considered to be nonweight bearing activities, at least of the hands. It would be possible to rest the elbows on the table and thus partially bear weight through the shoulder joint. Many activities, therefore, are obviously combinations of such movements. In walking, for instance, approximately one half of the cycle is weight bearing and the other half is nonweight bearing.

126

A strictly cadaver-oriented kinesiological analysis of muscular action suggests that certain muscles act as the prime movers in a particular activity, so a diagnosis and remediation of a muscular problem is often performed on this basis alone. When that happens, isolated muscle exercise is certain to be prescribed. In truth, feeding oneself is most likely a synergistic pattern involving far more muscles than shoulder abductors, elbow flexors, and hand muscles. Bernstein's thesis, so well articulated by Thelen, that all movements are the result of multiple muscles and joints assembled to solve the motor problem or complete the motor task, cannot be ignored. Thus feeding oneself involves trunk and other muscles that are needed to support the more obvious muscular activity. Activities of feeding oneself while sitting, standing, or lying in bed are not likely to be composed of the same synergy patterns.

An important lesson from this light-work--heavy-work classification is that as therapists, we often fail to work in functional patterns that are weight bearing, because the client cannot attain the position required to do so or does so in a manner we do not consider acceptable. This mistake is further compounded by our being committed to the idea that many nonweight bearing activities are prerequisites to or components of weight bearing ones.

Studies show that different muscles are often used in weight bearing and nonweight bearing activities. The synergy for standing and raising an arm is different than for lying supine and raising an arm. It is possible that the motor units involved in the same muscles are different between such tasks (Moffroid 1989). When recording EMG, for instance, a maximum, isometric, nonweight bearing contraction of the quadriceps femoris muscles will produce a heavy pattern of activity, with densely packed potentials being recorded. If the subject then performs a squat or semisquat, the pattern is much different, with smaller amplitudes and much more sparse activity when recording from the same electrodes. This latter pattern will prevail even though tremendous strain is put on the subject by using only one leg and adding resistance to the body weight. It might appear that the subject is now performing maximal contractions, but the electromyographic pattern is not identical with that recorded during maximal contraction of knee extensors when engaging in a nonweight bearing activity.

There are likely to be several reasons that such results are observed. The most obvious one is that it does not seem reasonable to compare an isolated muscle contraction with a movement that is obviously composed of a complete synergy involving multiple muscles and joints. In a squat-to-stand activity, the hamstring muscles will assist knee extension, and the ankle, hip, trunk, and upper extremities are also involved in the movement. Does it seem reasonable, then, that knowing how much weight the client can lift on a quadriceps exercise table will indicate how well the client can perform a squat?

> To solve a motor problem or complete a motor task, we use multiple muscles and joints acting in concert.

> Achievement in nonweight bearing functions does not necessarily lead to effective weight bearing.

127

Evaluation and treatment should emphasize the desired movement in its functional form because there is not likely to be a significant carry over or transfer of training from one activity to another. This observation will be discussed more thoroughly in Chapter 14 in the presentation of motor learning principles. Even different weight bearing activities, such as balance in standing and balance in walking, fail to transfer to each other. If this is the case, there will certainly be little relationship of nonweight bearing patterns to weight bearing ones. It is, therefore, useful to remember that function is the important and ultimate goal, and it may require weight-bearing synergies or nonweight bearing synergies or both, either simultaneously or sequentially. One should not infer from this information that balance in standing or nonweight bearing activities have no relevance to the problem at hand. Obviously, if the client cannot sit, there are other components of the movement that can be enhanced in other positions, such as assuming the prone position for muscle strengthening. It is rather that the therapist should not expect this latter work to transfer directly to sitting. Ultimately, for sitting to be accomplished, the work must be performed in the sitting position.

| Function is the key word in both evaluation and treatment. |

Dividing Function Into Four Stages

The four stages of developmental sequence that Rood described (reciprocal innervation, coinnervation, heavy work movement, and skill) present additional problems in light of current knowledge. Rood suggested that the first stage, reciprocal innervation, represents the state of the nervous system at birth. This concept is refuted by Thelen's (1983) studies on newborns. Remember that Thelen showed through electromyographic recordings that the first movements of kicking, while they appear reciprocal in nature, are in fact the result of coactivation of agonists and antagonists. Thelen suggests that cocontraction is a more immature pattern of muscular activation and that true reciprocal activity of agonists and antagonists occurs later in development. This observation is supported by other researchers as well (Woollacott 1986).

| It is unlikely that one activity must precede another, especially in treatment. |

Rood concluded that these sequences as she described them were invariant and that one was prerequisite to another. Thus the first three stages were thought to be building blocks of skill, the final stage. Skill in her sequence consisted of functional movements such as creeping, walking, and activities of daily living. Rood believed that if the first three stages could be completed, these skills would automatically develop. Again, current research suggests otherwise, as noted in the study by Fishkind and Haley (1986) described earlier. Each function consists of its own pattern and produces minimal transfer to another.

Abnormal Development

Although the emphasis of this text is on normal development and motor control, some discussion of abnormal development may be useful and appropriate. Some therapists have believed there is an abnormal sequence of motor development that leads to abnormal movement and motor control. Those therapists who have a neurodevelopmental treatment orientation suggest that there are significant milestones in abnormal motor development (Bly 1981*b*). These conclusions appear to be based on a general observation of children with motor problems and how their course of development compares with normal development. These milestones are presented as blocks to normal development. In the presence of these blocks, the infant must make compensations in order to move, and those compensations lead to abnormal motor development.

Are there milestones of abnormal development?

These therapists recognize also that in early normal development there is a dominance of axial extension. Several months later the child begins to become competent in antigravity flexion activities. In children with motor disabilities, antigravity flexion does not develop or extension remains dominant. If the baby cannot stabilize himself properly for distal movement, he will fix the joints by excessive effort and improper coactivation of muscles. When this fixation occurs, other movements become altered or impossible to accomplish, and as they are practiced and repeated, they lead to abnormal development. Four particular blocks are usually described: at the neck, shoulder girdle, pelvis, and hips.

Neck Block

In the development of normal head control, the infant tucks the chin in midline, producing some flexion of the head on the neck that results in an easy upright posture of the head and neck. Children without sufficient head control hold their heads steady by elevating their shoulders to stabilize their heads. The final position is one of hyperextension of the head on the neck and a stacking of the head on the neck and shoulders. This posture becomes locked in and prevents or modifies other movements such as sitting. Try sitting and strongly elevate your shoulders and hyperextend your head on your neck. Notice that your arms are less mobile for balance or manipulation, your back becomes rounded, and your sitting balance is more difficult.

Shoulder Girdle Block

It is postulated that dynamic scapular muscle activity provides holding of the shoulder girdle for arm and forearm motions, especially in weight bearing patterns such as prone on elbows and prone on hands. Without the proper scapular function, the infant will fix his shoulders in position by holding his arms to the sides. Logically, this posture would appear to

129

interfere with the ability to freely move the humerus. Reach and grasp and manipulation skills could be affected as well as creeping and other patterns involving the upper extremities.

Pelvic-Hip Block in Anterior Tilt

Early in development, normal infants appear to have a relatively passive anterior pelvic tilt, whether in the prone or supine position. The hips are usually placed in abduction and external rotation. As more control of movements and position is gained, the infant begins to have active pelvic control and can rock between anterior and posterior tilt.

If muscular control does not develop, the child remains in the anterior tilt condition, with his hips in flexion, abduction, and external rotation. In this posture, other movements such as rolling over or creeping, tailor or side-sitting, and standing are very difficult.

Pelvic-Hip Block in Posterior Tilt

With the development of abdominal muscle strength, the normal child performs active posterior tilt of his pelvis, with an interplay between anterior and posterior tilt. With an extensive posterior tilt, the child will develop tight hip extensors. As a result, he will sit on his sacrum, which further requires an abnormal flexion, or rounding, of the spine in order to sit. It will also be necessary to further hyperextend his head and neck to see what is going on around him. He will usually be stable in W-sitting because these joint positions can be maintained with a very stable base of support.

It seems quite likely that most of these movements and postures result from muscular weakness, muscular imbalance, and possible problems with proper synergy development. As time proceeds, contractures develop, and abnormal postures become set from these and other biomechanical effects and through continued practice of inadequate patterns.

Other Views of Abnormal development

Developmentally disabled children use movement patterns that are similar to those of normal children, according to Doudlah.

Doudlah (1981) also was interested in the motor performance of developmentally disabled children. She attempted to answer the question of whether their motor performance as they progress through the developmental sequence is different from normal children. Films were taken of children with such problems as hemiparesis, Down syndrome, hydrocephaly, arthrogryposis, or blindness. Her films, taken as the children progressed through the developmental sequence, demonstrated that the developmentally disabled used similar action patterns to those of normal children.

130

Doudlah (1981) suggests that the effects of the children's disorders on their motor performance are readily observed if the therapist is committed to objective systematic observation and documentation of ongoing developmental progress. If economically feasible, a permanent visual record of the child's progress recorded on videotape becomes an invaluable tool for learning about motor development and provides a permanent sequence of events that can be analyzed for research and documentation purposes.

Through her research on the progress of developmentally disabled children and the effects of some forms of developmental treatment, Doudlah came to the following conclusions:

1. Following programs founded on existing developmental guidelines in which positions and manipulation of the child in the performance of motor events is stressed does not result in improvement of developmental status in the motor domain.

2. Developmentally disabled children can be made to perform certain motor events or to perform in specific environments such as a clinic. This on-command performance cannot be judged as a program success unless the child spontaneously demonstrates a similar performance during play.

3. The therapist cannot expect to modify motor performance and skill involving more advanced motor events by failing to account for early spontaneous movement.

4. Remediation strategies founded on older developmental theory may not provide therapists with sufficient information for modifying the developmental status of developmentally disabled children.

Doudlah (1981) concluded, through film analysis, that developmentally disabled children follow the same motor development sequence as the normal child *if one observes their spontaneous performance.* Movement patterns are modified by the physiological manifestation of the child's condition, be it one of weakness, inappropriate muscle activity, or structural abnormality. Doudlah believes that motor development can be slowed, or delayed, in both normal and developmentally disabled children by insisting on specific motor performances that are out-of-phase with the child's developmental level. Therefore, the use of devices that limit or inhibit a child's spontaneous movement are not recommended.

Doudlah indicates that in providing services to the developmentally disabled, the most critical decisions are made during the observation and evaluation of motor performance. We have yet to understand, clearly, motor development in normal and developmentally disabled children;

> We should be interested in spontaneous movement, because that is what a child will do when we are not present.

131

there are many discoveries yet to be made in this domain of human performance.

Summary

The purpose of this chapter was to orient you to the various views of child development. A very important current theory of motor development has been proposed by Thelen and her colleagues. Remember that her theory was presented in Chapter 2, and it should be read before or concurrently with this chapter.

Much detail has been given to the sequences described by McGraw and expanded on by many therapists. This has been done mostly to provide a detailed description of developmental milestones as observed by many, including Gesell. It is imperative that the purposes and contexts of these early researchers be known and understood before applying either their sequences or principles to handicapped populations.

Doudlah's descriptions are included because they represent a different view of developmental sequence and are based on scientific analysis of longitudinal data. The sequences that were filmed and analyzed contained no manipulations of the children, and all movements described were spontaneous. Comparing her sequence with those of others should provide useful insight into development itself and possible uses of a developmental approach to treatment and evaluation.

In the real world, children are certainly manipulated. That is, mothers will place the child in a sitting position or do pull-to-sit activities long before the child can participate independently in such activities. The mother, however, places no particular inference on these activities. She is unlikely to assume that pull-to-sit has any particular relevance to the sitting position itself, only that it is an activity that is pleasurable for her and the child. It is we therapists who have placed some value judgment on the maneuver. The parents' handling of the child will provide experiences the child cannot yet engage in alone, which will perhaps enhance muscular strength and coordination through such augmented practice.

The detail in some approaches has been presented to permit a critique of these views in light of more recent investigations. Because therapy is strongly based on these views, in many cases for reasons that are not even in accord with the original researchers themselves, it would seem reasonable and valuable to study them thoroughly and determine, as far as possible, their current relevance.

Bibliography Section I

Adams JA. Issues for a closed-loop theory of motor learning. In: Stelmach GE, ed. *Motor Control: Issues and Trends*. San Diego, Calif: Academic Press Inc; 1976.

Bayley N. Behavioral correlates of mental growth: birth to 36 years. *Am Psychologist. 1968;23:1-17.*

Bayley N. *Bayley Scales of Infant Development*. New York, NY: Psychological Corp; 1969.

Barnes MR, Crutchfield CA, Heriza CB. *The Neurophysiological Basis of Patient Treatment, II: Reflexes In Motor Development*. Atlanta, Ga: Stokesville Publishing Company; 1978.

Bernstein NA. *The Coordination and Regulation of Movements*. New York, NY: Pergamon Press Inc; 1967.

Bly L. The components of normal movement during the first year of life. In: Slaton DS, ed. *Development of Movement in Infancy*. Chapel Hill, NC: The University of North Carolina Press; 1981*a*.

Bly L. Abnormal motor development. In: Slaton DS, ed. *Development of Movement in Infancy*. Chapel Hill, NC: The University of North Carolina Press; 1981*b*.

Bobath B. *Abnormal Postural Reflex Activity Caused by Brain Lesions*. London, England: William Heinemann Medical Books Ltd; 1971.

Bradley NS. Animal models offer the opportunity to acquire a new perspective on motor development. *Phys Ther.* 1990;70:776-787.

Brazelton T. Neonatal Behavioral Assessment Scale. In: *Clinics in Developmental Medicine, No. 50. Spastics International Medical Publications* 2nd ed. Philadelphia, Pa: J B Lippincott Co; 1984

Brooks VB. *The Neural Basis of Motor Control*. New York, NY: Oxford University Press Inc; 1986.

Carmichael L. The development of behavior in vertebrates experimentally removed from the influence of external stimulation. *Psychol Rev.* 1926;33:51-58.

Conel JL. *The Postural Development of the Human Cerebral Cortex, II: The Control of the One-Month-Old Infant*. Cambridge, Mass: Harvard University Press; 1941.

Crutchfield CA. Neuromuscular causes of movement dysfunction. In: Scully R, Barnes MR, eds. *Physical Therapy*. Philadelphia, Pa: J B Lippincott Co; 1989.

Crutchfield CA, Shumway-Cook A, Horak FB. Balance and coordination training. In: Scully R, Barnes M, eds. *Physical Therapy*. Philadelphia, Pa: J B Lippincott Co; 1989.

Delong M. Central patterning of movement. *Neuroscience Research Program Bulletin.* 1971;9:10.

Dennis W. *Age and Behavior I: A Survey of the Literature*. Pittsburgh, Pa: American Institute for Research; 1952.

Doudlah AM. Potential or pathology: in the eye of the beholder. In: Slaton DS, ed. *Development of Movement in Infancy*. Chapel Hill, NC: The University of North Carolina Press; 1981.

Easton TA. On the normal use of reflexes. *American Scientist.* 1972;60:591-598.

Farber SD. *Neurorehabilitation: A Multisensory Approach*. Philadelphia, Pa: W B Saunders Co; 1982.

Fel'dman AG. Once more on the equilibrium-point hypothesis for motor control. *Journal of Motor Behavior.* 1986;18:17-54.

Fiorentino MR. *Reflex Testing Methods for Evaluating CNS Development*. Springfield, Mass: Charles C Thomas Publisher; 1973.

Fishkind M, Haley SM. Independent sitting development and the emergence of associated motor components. *Phys Ther.* 1986;66:1509-1514.

Fitch HL, Tuller B, Turvey MT. The Bernstein perspective, III: tuning of coordination structures with special reference to perception. In: Kelso JAS, ed. *Human Motor Behavior: An Introduction*. Hillsdale, NJ: Lawrence Erlbaum Associates Inc; 1982:253-270.

Gesell A. *Infancy and Human Growth*. New York, NY: Macmillan Publishing Co; 1928.

Gesell A. *An Atlas of Infant Behavior*. New Haven, Conn: Yale University Press; 1934.

Gesell A. The ontogenesis of infant behavior. In: Carmichael L, ed. *Manual of Child Psychology*. 2nd ed. New York, NY; John Wiley & Son Inc; 1954:335-373.

Goodenough FL. *Mental Testing*. New York, NY: Rinehart Publishers; 1949.

Haley SM. Sequential analyses of postural reactions in nonhandicapped infants. *Research*. 1986;66:531-536.

Heiniger MC, Randolph AR. *Neurophysiological Concepts in Human Behavior: The Tree of Learning*. St. Louis, Mo: C V Mosby Co; 1981.

Horowitz FD. *Exploring Developmental Theories: Toward a Structural/Behavioral Model of Development*. Hillsdale, NJ: Lawrence Erlbaum Associates Inc; 1987.

Horowitz L, Sharby N. Development of prone extension postures in healthy infants. *Phys Ther*. 1988;68:32-39.

Keele SW Component analysis and conceptions of skill. In: Kelso JAS, ed. *Human Motor Behavior: An Introduction*. Hillsdale, NJ: Lawrence Erlbaum Associates Inc; 1982.

Kelso JAS, ed. *Human Motor Behavior: An Introduction*. Hillsdale, NJ: Lawrence Erlbaum Associates Inc; 1982.

Kelso JAS, Scholz JP. Cooperative phenomena in biological motion. In: Haken H, ed. *Complex Systems: Operational Approaches in Neurobiology, Physical Systems, and Computers*. New York, NY, Springer-Verlag New York Inc; 1985.

Laren H. Introduction to neurodevelopmental technique. *Course Handout*. Chicago, Ill: Chicago Institute of Rehabilitation, 1982.

Lee DN, Aronson E. Visual and proprioceptive control of standing in human infants. *Perception and Psychophysics*. 1974;15:529-532.

Leonard CT, Hirschfield H, Forssberg H. Gait acquisition and reflex abnormalities in normal children and children with cerebral palsy. In: Amblard B, Berthoz A, Clarac E, eds. *Posture and Gait: Development, Adaptation, and Modulation*. New York, NY: Elsevier Science Publishing Co Inc; 1988.

Leonard CT, Hirschfeld H, Forssberg H. The development of independent walking in children with cerebral palsy. *Dev Med Child Neurol*. 1991;33:567-577.

Leonard CT. Neural and neurobehavioral changes associated with perinatal brain damage. In Forssberg H, Hirschfeld H, eds. *Movement Disorders in Children*. Switzerland; Karger; 1992.

Leonard CT. Integrating science and practice in the rehabilitation of the neurologically involved patient. *Course Syllabus*. Morro Bay, Calif: Tricounties District California APTA, 1993.

Madore BF, Freedman WL. Self-organizing structures. *American Scientist*. 1987;75:252-259.

Magnus R, de Kleijn A. The influence of the head on the tone of the muscles of the extremities. *Pflugers Arch*. 1912;145:455-458.

McCarthy D. *McCarthy Scales of Children's Abilities--Ages 2 1/2 to 8 1/2*. New York, NY: Psychological Corp; 1972.

McGraw MB. *Growth: A Study of Jimmy and Johnny*. New York, NY: Appleton-Century-Crofts; 1935.

McGraw MB. *The Neuromuscular Maturation of the Human Infant*. New York, NY: Hafner Press; 1945.

McGraw MB, Breeze KW. Quantitative studies in the development of erect locomotion. *Child Dev*. 1941;12:267-303.

Milani-Comparetti A. The neurophysiologic and clinical implications of studies on fetal motor behavior. *Semin Perinatol*. 1981;5:183-189.

Moffroid M. Musculoskeletal causes of movement dysfunction. In: Scully R, Barnes M, eds. *Physical Therapy*. Philadelphia, Pa: J B Lippincott Co; 1989.

134

Munn NL. *The Growth of Human Behavior.* 3rd ed. Boston, Mass: Houghton Mifflin Co; 1974.

Nashner LM, Woollacott MH. The organization of rapid postural adjustments of standing humans: an experimental-conceptual model. In: Talbott RE, Humphrey DR, eds. *Posture and Movement.* New York, NY: Raven Press; 1979:243-257

Nashner LM, McCollum G. The organization of human postural movements: a formal basis and experimental synthesis. *The Behavioral and Brain Sciences.* 1985;8:135-172.

Nashner LM. Sensory, neuromuscular, and biomechanical contributions to human balance. In: Duncan PW, ed. *Balance.* Alexandria, Va: American Physical Therapy Association; 1990:5-12.

Newell KM, Kulger PN, van Emmerik RE, et al. Search strategies and the acquisition of coordination. In: Wallace SA, ed. *Perspectives on the coordination of movement.* New York, NY: Elsevier Science Publishing Co Inc; 1989:85-122.

Okamoto T, Goto Y. Human infant pre-independent and independent walking. In: Kondo S, ed. *Primate Morpho-physiology, Locomotor Analyses and Human Bipedalism.* Tokyo, Japan: University of Toyko Press. 1985:25-45.

Palmer CE. Studies of the center of gravity in the human body. *Child Dev.* 1944;15:99-180.

Pearson KG, Duysens J. Function of segmental reflexes in the control of stepping in cockroaches and cats. In: Herman RM, Grillner S, Stein PSG, Stewart DG, eds. *Neural Control of Locomotion.* New York, NY: Plenum Press; 1976.

Peiper A. *Cerebral Function in Infancy and Childhood.* New York, NY: Consultants Bureau; 1963.

Rosenbaum D. Selective adaptation of "command neurons" in the human motor system. *Neuropsychologica.* 1977;15:81-91.

Schmidt RA. *Motor Control and Learning: A Behavioral Emphasis.* 2nd ed. Champaign, Ill: Human Kinetics Publishers Inc; 1988.

Schneider K, Zernicke R. Jerk-cost modulations during the practice of rapid arm movements. *Biol Cybern..* 1989;60:221-230.

Schneider K, Zernicke R, Ulrich BD, et al. Understanding movement control in infants through the analysis of limb intersegmental dynamics. *Journal of Motor Behavior.* 1990;22:493-520.

Sherrington CS. *The Integrative Action of the Nervous System.* New Haven, Conn: Yale University Press; 1906.

Shirley MM. *The First Two Years: Postural and Locomotor Development.* Minneapolis, Minn: University of Minnesota Press: 1931

Skinner BF. *Beyond Freedom and Dignity.* New York, NY: Alfred A Knopf Inc; 1971

Stockmeyer SA. An interpretation of the approach of Rood to the treatment of neuromuscular dysfunction. *Am J Phys Med.* 1966;46:900-956.

Sutherland DH, Olson R, Cooper L, Woo SL. The development of mature gait. *J Bone Joint Surg [Am].* 1980;62:336-353.

Thelen E. Rhythmical stereotypies in normal human infants. *Animal Behavior.* 1979;27:699-715.

Thelen E. Learning to walk is still an "old" problem: a reply to Zelaso. In: Zelaso PR. *Journal of Motor Behavior.* 1983:15:139-161.

Thelen E. Treadmill-elicited stepping in seven-month-old infants. Child *Dev.* 1986*a*;57:1498-1506.

Thelen E. Development of coordinated movement: implications for early human development. In: Wade MG, Whiting HTA, eds. *Motor Development in Children: Aspects of Coordination and Control.* Boston, Mass: Martinus Nijhoff Publisher; 1986*b*:107-120.

Thelen E. The role of motor development in developmental psychology: a view of the past and an agenda for the future. In: Eisenberg N, ed. *Contemporary Topics in Developmental Psychology.* New York, NY: John Wiley & Sons Inc; 1989*a*.

Thelen E. Evolving and dissolving synergies in the development of leg coordination. In: Wassace SA, ed. *Perspectives on the Coordination of Movement.* New York, NY: Elsevier Science Publishing Co Inc; 1989*b*:259-281.

Thelen E. Self-organization in developmental processes: can systems approaches work? In: Gunnar M, Thelen E, eds. *Systems and Development: The Minnesota Symposia on Child Psychology, Vol 22.* Hillsdale, NJ: Lawrence Erlbaum Associates Inc; 1989*c*:77-117.

Thelen E. Coupling perception and action in the development of skill: a dynamic approach. In: Bloch H, Bertenthal BI, eds. *Sensory-Motor Organizations and Development in Infancy and Early Childhood*. Norwell, Mass: Kluwer Academic Publishers; 1990:39-56.

Thelen E. The development of locomotion from a dynamic systems approach. In: Hirschfeld H, Forssberg H, eds. *Theory and Practice in the Treatment of Children With Movement Disorders*. New York, NY: S Karger. In press.

Thelen E, Bradshaw G, Ward JA. Spontaneous kicking in month-old infants: manifestation of a human central locomotor program. *Behav Neural Biol*. 1981;32:45-53.

Thelen E, Cooke DW. Relationship between newborn stepping and later walking: a new interpretation. *Dev Med Child Neurol*. 1987;29:380-393.

Thelen E, Fisher DM. The organization of spontaneous leg movements in newborn infants. *Journal of Motor Behavior*. 1983a;15:353-377.

Thelen E, Fisher DM. The organization of spontaneous to instrumental behavior: kinematic analysis of movement changes during very early learning. *Child Dev*. 1983b;54:120-140.

Thelen E, Fisher DM, Ridley-Johnson R. The relationship between physical growth and a newborn reflex. *Infant Behavior and Development*. 1984;7:479-494.

Thelen E, Fogel A. Self-organizing systems and infant motor development. *Developmental Review*. 1989a;7:39-65.

Thelen E, Fogel A. Toward an action based theory of infant development. In: Lockman J, Hasen N, eds. *Action in Social Context*. New York, NY: Plenum Publishing Corp; 1989b:23-63.

Thelen E, Corbetta D, Konczak J, et al. First reaches in human infants: a kinematic, kinetic and EMG analysis. Presented at the 21st Annual meeting of the Society for Neuroscience; November 1991a; New Orleans, La.

Thelen E, Kelso JAS, Fogel A. Self-organizing systems and infant motor development. *Developmental Review*. 1987a;7:39-65.

Thelen E, Ridley-Johnson R, Fisher DM. Shifting patterns of bilateral coordination and lateral dominance in the leg movements of young infants. *Dev Psychobiol*. 1983;16:29-46.

Thelen E. Skala K, Kelso JAS. Spontaneous kicking in young infants: evidence for a dynamic bilateral system. *Dev Psychol*. 1987b;23:179-186.

Thelen E, Ulrich BD, Niles D. Bilateral coordination in human infants: stepping on a split-belt treadmill. *J Exp Psychol* 1987c;13:407-410

Thelen E, Ulrich BD, Jensen JL. The developmental origins of locomotion. In: Woollacott M, Shumway-Cook A, eds. *The Development of Gait Across the Lifespan*. Columbia, SC: University of South Carolina Press; 1989:25-47.

Thelen E, Jensen JL. An "outside-in" approach to the development of leg movement patterns. In: von Euler C, Forssberg H, Lagercrentz H, eds. *Neurobiology of Early Infant Behavior*. New York, NY: Macmillan Publishing Co; 1989:107-118.

Thelen E, Ulrich BD. Hidden skills: a dynamic systems analysis of treadmill-elicited stepping during the first year. *Monogr Soc Res Child Dev*. 1991;56:1-90.

Thelen E, Jensen J, Kamm K, et al. A kinematic, kinetic, and EMG analysis of the transition from spontaneous movements to voluntary reaching. Presented at the Biennial meeting, Society for Research in Child Development; April 1991b; Seattle, Wash.

Thelen E, Jensen JL, Kamm K, et al. Infant motor development: implications for motor neuroscience. In: Stelmach G, Reyuin J, eds. *Tutorials in Motor Neuroscience*; Norwell, Mass: Kluwer Academic Publishers. In press.

Tuller B, Turvey MT, Fitch HL. The Bernstein perspective, II: the concept of muscle linkage or coordinative structure. In: Kelso JAS, ed. *Human Motor Behavior: An Introduction*. Hillsdale, NJ: Lawrence Erlbaum Associates Inc; 1982.

Turvey MT, Fitch HL, Tuller B. The Bernstein perspective I. In: Kelso JAS, ed. *Human Motor Behavior: An Introduction*. Hillsdale, NJ: Lawrence Erlbaum Associates Inc; 1982.

von Hofsten C. Developmental change in the organization of pre-reaching movements. *Developmental Psychology*. 1984;20:378-388.

von Hofsten C. Mastering reaching and grasping: the development of manual skills in infancy. In: Wallace SA, ed. *Perspectives on the coordination of movement*, New York, NY: Elsevier Science Publishing Co Inc; 1984:223-258.

von Holst E. Relative coordination as a phenomenon and as a method of analysis of central nervous function. In: Martin R, ed. *The Collected Papers of Erich von Holst: The Behavioral Physiology of Animals and Man*. Coral Gables, Fla: University of Miami Press; 1973;1:33-135.

Woollacott MH. Postural control and development. In: Whiting HTA, Wade MG, eds. *Themes in Motor Development*. Boston, Mass: Martinus Nijhoff Publishers; 1986.

Woollacott MH, Shumway-Cook A, Nashner LM. Aging and posture control changes in sensory organization and muscular coordination. *Int J Aging Hum Dev*. 1986:23:97-114.

Zelazo PR. The development of walking: new findings and old assumptions. *Journal of Motor Behavior*. 1983;15:99-137.

Zelazo PR, Zelazo NA, Kolb S. Newborn walking. *Science*. 1972;177:1058-1059.

Section II

Coordinated Motor Patterns --
Reflexes and Reactions

Chapter 4 - Nature of Reflexes

When therapists talk about movement, what is it that we really mean? What are movements? What is the relationship between reflexes and movement or the beginnings of movement? What are reflexes? In this text, we will consider *reflexes* and *reactions* to be coordinated patterns of movement that may be demonstrated spontaneously by the infant, child, or adult and that may also be elicited by external stimuli. In this chapter, we will attempt to discover the answers to the above questions and to enlarge upon the concepts of reflexes and other coordinated patterns of movement.

Where Does Movement Begin?

Naturally, we would suspect that the origins of movement must begin before birth, because infants can be felt to move inside the womb, and infants are certainly born moving. The first observations of fetal movements occurred in animals. Finding acceptable ways of observing human fetuses was another matter. The early studies of human fetal behavior were done earlier in this century by Hooker (1952) and Humphrey (1944), but these studies were of fetuses that had been removed from the womb. The investigators stimulated the fetuses in various ways and recorded the results. As you have already learned, manipulating the organism to elicit movement presents problems in the interpretation of that movement.

The development of real-time ultrasound equipment has permitted investigators to witness the movements generated by the fetuses themselves in a safe, noninvasive way. This was first accomplished in 1971 (Prechtl 1986). Video taping technology added to ultrasound has further enhanced our knowledge of these early movements because the taped movements can be viewed over and over again, making a correct analysis of what is transpiring much less subject to error or controversy.

Most of us probably know young parents-to-be who proudly flaunt ultrasound photographs of the off-spring-to-be. Unfortunately, when the fetus grows too large, in the second half of pregnancy, we can no longer see the entire body of the fetus and the still pictures become much less interesting to us. In the near future, no doubt, equipment that will photograph the last 4 months of fetal growth in its entirety will be developed. Only then can we be more certain of the exact nature of fetal movement patterns during the entire prenatal period.

As a result of the rash of studies on fetal motility that have taken place in the decades of the 70s and 80s, we need to alter some of our thinking relative to the concept of developmental movement patterns. We also need to adopt some new terms and revise some of the well-used semantic expressions we therapists use to communicate with our colleagues.

Beginnings of Fetal Movement

In the beginning, there are random movements and coordinated patterns.

And there are gross movements and fine movements.

Normal gestation is 40 weeks, or about 9 months. According to Prechtl (1985), the first fetal movements are seen at around 7 to 8 weeks of postmenstrual age. At about 9 weeks, some jerky, startle type movements are seen along with more tonic movements. So the presumption we had before the advent of real-time ultrasound that the random, amorphous, jerky movements preceded the slower, smoother movements is not valid. Also no longer necessarily valid is the old idea that random movements precede distinct, coordinated motor patterns, because the evidence seems to indicate that coordinated patterns are available from the beginning. Generalized movements of the trunk and limbs appear only several days before isolated arm and leg movements. This finding suggests that the principle of movement developing from gross to fine is invalid even in fetal life. Further, arm and leg movements have a simultaneous onset and thus do not follow a craniocaudal or head-to-toe developmental sequence (Prechtl 1986). Figure 4-1 shows the onset of certain fetal movements as they relate to each other.

One of the most surprising observations Prechtl made was that by the fifth and sixth months of fetal development the repertoire of fetal movements consists entirely of motor patterns or reflexes that are seen after birth. The reverse circumstance is not true because there are behavior patterns in the newborn that are not available to the fetus (Prechtl 1984).

Nature of Fetal Movements

The fetal brain can generate motor patterns and react to the environment.

According to Touwen (1978), there are two main abilities of the infant brain. First, the developing brain can generate both phasic and rhythmical motor patterns such as sucking, breathing, and stepping. The side-to-side movements present in the rooting reflex seen in hungry young infants is another example of a rhythmical, centrally generated motor pattern (Prechtl 1958). Second, the infant brain can react to stimulation it receives from the environment. The interaction between these two abilities leads to the complex, variable, and very individualized quality of motor behavior. If the brain is severely damaged, this interaction is impaired, and only the ability to react to stimulation may be retained.

142

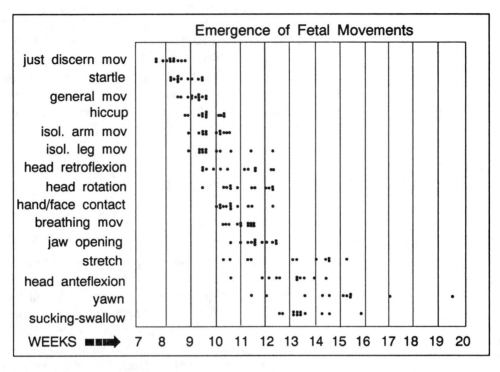

Figure 4-1 Postmenstrual ages of fetuses at which certain motor patterns were observed for the first time. From De Vries et al 1984, reprinted with permission.

It appears that these fetal movements are endogenously generated, that is, they are spontaneously created by the fetus and are not elicited by external stimuli. Although the intrauterine and extrauterine environments are so different, the fetal movements are very similar before and after birth. This observation lead Prechtl to believe that peripheral sensory control does not play a significant role in the development of these movements. We do know from the studies of both Hooker (1952) and Humphrey (1944) that the fetus is capable of responding to direct stimuli, even if it is not receiving it in utero.

However, as Wolf (1986) states, there is impressive experimental and clinical evidence to indicate that exercise and proprioceptive feedback mechanisms profoundly influence the development and coordination of motor patterns in animals, infants, children, and adults. It seems unlikely that those same variables would have no effect on fetal motor development, and thus Wolf does not believe that it is possible to conclude that these movements are controlled solely by maturational time tables independent of experience or exteroceptive stimulation.

Wolf (1986) believes that Prechtl's own observations suggest that fetal movements are modified by their activity. That is, two different patterns will become partially synchronized and will give rise to new stable patterns. For example, "toward the end of pregnancy, eye movements,

143

general movements, heart rate patterns and other coordinated movements are sufficiently synchronized so that distinct ensembles of behavior patterns, which are analogous to the behavioral states described for full term neonates, can be identified" (Wolf 1986, p 66). The original patterns either may be the expression of the developing nervous system or may be assembled for specific intrauterine demands or both. Thus the dynamic interaction among established patterns will cause novel patterns to emerge from those elements. This idea is in line with the emergent properties of the motor system as proposed in the dynamic action theory of motor control described in Chapter 2.

Purpose of Fetal Movements

Researchers who have observed the patterns of fetal motility have speculated on the functional significance of the movements and why the fetus moves so frequently and in so many different ways. It is quite likely that some fetal movement patterns exist in order to help the fetus adapt to conditions in the uterus (Prechtl 1986). The fetus may change position frequently to prevent stasis and adhesions to the uterine wall or between different parts of the fetus. Two different motor patterns produce these postural changes. One is a rotation along the body axis. This fetal rolling pattern is initiated by a lateral rotation of either the head or the hips. The other motor pattern is one of alternating leg movements that produce a somersault if the legs are properly positioned against the uterine wall. Positional changes may occur up to 20 times an hour during the first half of pregnancy. The rate decreases as the pregnancy proceeds, probably as a result of a lack of space within the uterus as the fetus grows.

> Fetal movements may have the purpose of preventing stasis and adhesions and preparing the fetus for birth.

It is also possible that the fetus has intrinsic mechanisms that play a significant role in its own birth process. For example, the attainment of the normal vertex position may be the result of active behavioral mechanisms. Fetuses that were initially in the breech position have been found to have shifted to the vertex position before birth. It has been suggested that reflex stepping and crawling movements may also serve to position the fetus in a vertex position (Prechtl 1984) .

Sucking and swallowing movements have been recorded, and because the stomach becomes distended immediately after these movements, it is almost certain that the fetus is swallowing amniotic fluid. Swallowing may reduce the amount of amniotic fluid in preparation for birth, or it may supply additional nutrients to the fetus (Oppenheim 1981). Obviously, it is not completely clear as to just why this phenomenon takes place.

Early fetal motility may be necessary for the normal development of the structure of bones and joints. Lack of such early movement may lead to

144

joint and bone defects, such as ankylosis and clubfoot. Even the fine structure of the central nervous system itself may be somewhat dependent on the neural activity and the motor effects it produces (Oppenheim 1981). How much such mechanisms play a role in human fetal development is far from being understood.

It seems wise to exhibit some caution in these interpretations so that the meaning of fetal movements is not over-interpreted and intentional behavior is not attributed to either the fetus or the newborn infant. Such interpretations go far beyond the available evidence and are purely speculative (Prechtl 1986).

Antecedent Traits

Antecedent generally means something existing or occurring before in time or order. In developmental biology, it also means that whatever occurs before bears some functional cause-and-effect relationship with an event that follows. There are few known examples of antecedent events for human neural and behavioral development because it is very hard to perform experiments that establish such links. Nevertheless, almost everyone believes that early events in development bear an antecedent relationship to later events. It is just as possible, however, that all traits or events are not solely direct antecedents of specific adult characteristics. That is, we should not ignore the phenomenon of transient adaptations that may occur in immature organisms (Oppenheim 1984).

> In development, early events may have an antecedent relationship to later events.

Newborn humans demonstrate reflexes, or patterns of behavior, that are rarely exhibited after the first year of life. These include sucking, rooting, stepping, grasping, reaching, crawling, swimming, and the Moro response. It is quite likely that at least some of the early patterns, or reflexes, do represent antecedents of their voluntary counterparts. As noted in Chapter 2, Thelen's work on the kicking-stepping pattern and its relationship to later walking patterns provides strong support for this conclusion.

Developmental theorists such as Piaget believed that each stage of cognitive development is a necessary antecedent of later stages. This approach to motor behavior, however, fails to recognize the possibility that the ontogenetic adaptations have a purpose of their own at each stage. For instance, the idea that embryonic activity promotes the development of joint and muscle structure suggests that such activity has a greater role than simply that of being the necessary antecedent of some later behavior.

Adaptive Behavior

According to Oppenheim (1981; 1984), ontogenetic adaptation refers to structural, physiologic, or behavioral characteristics that primarily are associated with a period of an organism's life history.

Some fetal motor patterns are regularly performed spontaneously long before they fulfill a meaningful task as part of a complex adaptive function. Breathing is a classical example of this behavior. The early rhythmical breathing movements and such patterns as sighs, yawns, stretches, eye movements, and side-to-side movements of the head all have similar or identical characteristics to neonatal patterns and to adult patterns (Prechtl 1984). The observation that many movement patterns exhibited by the human fetus persist into postnatal stages does not rule out the possibility that these movements subserve a unique function in utero. Whatever their effects during prenatal development, many of these patterns reach their full adaptive function only after birth. After birth, they are not only spontaneously generated but also come under afferent control. According to Prechtl (1984), to be fully adaptive the patterns should be responsive to the context at the appropriate moment in the situation for which they are required. The patterns then become associated with a sensory trigger.

> Development of muscle strength may be the vital adaptive link that enables the infant to begin to function appropriately in its environment.

According to Prechtl (1984), except for vital functions such as respiration, circulation, and nutrition, the human newborn infant is very poorly suited to the requirements of the extrauterine environment. He suggests that the newborn has obvious signs of incompetence, such as poor muscle power, weak or absent postural control of the head and limbs, and limited vision. Social behavior is rudimentary at best, and goal directed movements lack necessary precision. This incompetence continues until about the end of the second month when a major transformation of the behavioral repertoire and sensory capacities occurs. Many of these observations can be explained, as was pointed out in Chapter 2, by a lack of muscular strength against gravity. Much of the activity that the infant is able to accomplish by 2 to 3 months of age relates to the development of competence against gravity.

Oppenheim (1984) indicates that a characteristic is adaptive if it is genetically controlled to increase an organism's fitness and chance of perpetuating its genes. Throughout the life span, organisms exhibit characteristics by which they adjust to the changing requirements of their life history. These characteristics may be transient and require the creation of structures and functions that are necessary for one stage of development but may be unnecessary for or incompatible with survival at later stages.

It has been suggested that the grasp response of hands and feet and the Moro reaction are examples of mechanisms in the infant that are related

146

to clinging to the mother. We might consider these vestigial movements because they have lost their adaptive function in man, but they are present in other mammals. Compared with other mammals, the excess in neonatal body weight, composed primarily of fat, may be another specific adaptation in the human. White subcutaneous fat may be an adaptive compensation for loss of fur that acts as thermal insulation.

It would seem necessary, then, for the adaptations that are developed throughout the life history of an individual (ontogeny) to become reorganized, suppressed, or eliminated as development proceeds. Some of the structures and processes created for survival at one point in development may be incompatible with later adaptive requirements. An example of such a condition relates to the changes in structure of the developing heart. The shunts and holes that are required for embryonic circulation are not compatible with circulatory requirements that exist after birth when blood must circulate through the lungs. When these holes persist as congenital heart defects, they are often incompatible with life itself.

The suckling activity is an example of an ontogenetic adaptation that undergoes pattern changes to other forms of sucking and is ultimately replaced by completely different forms of ingestive behavior. In adult humans, reflex-like rooting and sucking behaviors are present only in certain neuropathological conditions. It would appear that ontogenetic adaptations may be more prevalent and may continue to be expressed through a greater share of the life cycle than previously thought (Oppenheim 1984).

Continuity-Discontinuity and Regressive Phenomena

From fetal observations it is possible to suggest that there are continuities and discontinuities in development. Some developmental conditions and adaptations might continue in a linear fashion while others come and go or reach abrupt stages. There are likely to be losses as well as gains. Oppenheim suggests that ontogeny is both destructive (or retrogressive) and constructive (or progressive) in nature. He states that "life histories are often complex and frequently involve dramatic transitions, regressions and losses which give the appearance of discontinuity" (Oppenheim 1984, p 17).

At birth, the infant may have a huge capacity to adapt to the new environment because of preadaptive fetal behaviors.

After birth, the mechanics of movement change because there is a considerable difference between the experience of floating in fluid and being exposed to the full force of gravity. There is a difference in the space to which movements are restricted, and the quality of tactile stimuli is also considerably different before and after birth. There are changes in environmental conditions such as temperature, noise level, and exposure to light. Drastic physiological changes occur because the

147

lungs now require active ventilation, and nutrition must purposefully be sought as it is no longer continuously supplied.

These changes in conditions and responses require an enormous adaptive capacity. The full-term infant has this capacity to respond, but this ability does not simply develop and emerge at term. Although most of the stimuli encountered do not exist in the uterine environment and the fetus has not used the capacity to respond to such stimuli before birth, the general processes are developed gradually from a much earlier age. So even though it might appear that the newborn would have to make large changes to adjust to the new demands of the environment, only a few vital adjustments are necessary. It seems that this adaptive ability results from the existence of preadaptive functions that appeared early in gestation and remain essentially intact until the infant reaches 2 months of age (Oppenheim 1981).

What conditions in the nervous system account for the variety of both regressive and progressive changes that occur throughout prenatal and early postnatal development and perhaps even up to and beyond sexual maturity? The major structural changes that accompany regressive adaptations are neuronal death, axon and dendrite retraction or degeneration, and loss of synapses. New adaptations are associated with cell production, new axon growth, and new synapse development. It is also possible that changes in biochemical, physiological, and hormonal systems underlie both destructive and constructive adaptations that may not produce obvious structural changes (Oppenheim 1981). In addition, changes in other systems, such as an increase in fat content, may result in apparent regressions because such a change may prevent some other function from occurring. The disappearance of the stepping reflex as a result of increased body weight is an example of such apparent regressions.

"In reality all these issues become inextricably blurred since what one is really interested in is what an organism is doing at a stage (behavior description), how it got that way (development, antecedents), why it is doing this behavior and not another one (survival value, adaptiveness) and finally whether the behavior will persist, disappear or be reorganized (transient or permanent adaptation)" (Oppenheim 1984, p 22).

A new hypothesis has been suggested concerning the maturation of the human nervous system and the duration of pregnancy. Because so many of the neural functions of the human neonate and young infant are relatively immature, it has been suggested that the human baby is born too early and that development is incomplete at the time of birth (Prechtl 1986). Thus the early neonatal period might be considered to be a later stage of fetal development as is the case with certain others of the animal kingdom.

Use in Diagnosis

De Vries et al (1984) believe that because the movements of young fetuses are not uncoordinated and random but are specifically and recognizably patterned, this makes them potentially useful for diagnostic purposes. In abnormal first-trimester pregnancies, slow, sluggish movements have been observed, and the excursion of the movements was also lower than those seen in normal pregnancies. The quality of fetal motility provides an indicator of the chronic neurological condition of the fetus.

Prechtl (1984) indicates that the postnatal continuation of many fetal neural mechanisms has repercussions on the validity of neurological and behavioral assessment. Because many of the tested functions are transient fetal mechanisms, any abnormal signs or deviant behavioral characteristics of the newborn may disappear during the major transformation at the end of the second month. It is true that many of the conditions that suggest an infant will be at risk for serious problems do not always prove to be predictive.

The study of fetal movements provides much insight into the origin of movement and the nature of patterns that have been labelled as reflexes. Further inquiry into the nature of reflexes should enlarge our understanding of these movements

Fetal movements may have diagnostic or predictive value.

What Are Reflexes?

A tendon tap produces a knee jerk. Touching a hot stove results in a rapid reflexive withdrawal of the extremity. The athlete is said to have quick reflexes. What exactly are these reflex activities? In Webster's Unabridged Dictionary, a *reflex* is defined as "a movement performed automatically and without conscious volition...." Reflex activity may also be defined as the whole neurological process comprising reception, transmission, and response that involuntarily assists in motor coordination (Easton 1972).

In the classical sense, at least, a reflex response is usually considered to be a motor output that follows some specific sensory input such as the tendon tap. It can be inferred that the final result is inevitable, but this is not necessarily true. The type of response will vary as the result of different influences. One such influence might be level of excitability, or state of the nervous system, when the stimulus enters it (Thexton 1973). This means that any ongoing activity in the central nervous system that will alter the level of arousal and awareness of the organism will have an effect on the response produced by further input. The response will also depend on previous learning that has occurred in the system. In other words, the nervous system is in a constant state of flux, and the output need not be stereotyped, or automatically predictable.

> **Reflex patterns reflect both stimulus-response and endogenous conditions.**

Furthermore, the definition of a reflex usually emphasizes the stimulus-response condition; that is, a stimulus must always precede the movement or response. This view might be true for such reflexes as the monosynaptic spinal stretch reflex. More complex movements, however, have been observed to be spontaneous in nature and produced in the absence of demonstrable sensory stimuli, particularly peripheral ones (Prechtl 1984; de Vries et al 1984). Sherrington (1906) himself commented, "A simple reflex is probably a purely abstract conception, because all parts of the nervous system are connected together and no part of it is probably ever capable of reaction without affecting and being affected by various other parts, and it is a system certainly never absolutely at rest."

A spinal stretch reflex produces a muscular response in about 50 to 70 milliseconds. Voluntary movements have the longest latencies for muscular response, usually 150 milliseconds or greater (Keshner 1990). Nashner (1990) has termed the responses to platform perturbations as automatic movements because they generally occur within 100 milliseconds and are thus somewhere between reflex and voluntary. Thus, in his classification, a reflex does depend on external stimuli and is limited to the very fast patterns resulting from such stimulus-response mechanisms as the monosynaptic myotatic reflex from the muscle spindle system. Note the characteristics in Figure 4-2 of the three types of movements as described by Nashner (1990).

According to Keshner (1990), however, complex movements that are well learned can confound these response definitions. That is, voluntary responses can occur as early as those of reflexes. The major point here is that many well known and complex movements that are produced in relatively stable forms with minimal variability, have been named reflexes (such as the Moro reflex or the sucking reflex), but these movements are not in the same class of movements as represented by the stretch reflex.

> **Reflexes, by definition in this book, may be complex motor patterns that are not necessarily activated by external stimuli.**

The fact that therapists deal with reflexes clinically has been criticized. There is a view that stimulating these movements makes the client a passive entity in treatment. There is also the concern that the approach is a hierarchical one and that stimulating movements is not natural. What is important to understand is that these movements have been generated spontaneously before they have ever been brought under stimulus control. The infant moves in whatever patterns are available, whether the movements are self-generated or elicited. As you will find in this section of the book, both methods have some value, depending on the therapist's objective. It is important to recognize that these movements cannot be classified as reflex and simply dispensed with, because it is possible to elicit them in a stimulus-response mode. They are complex movements that are often self-generated and thus should not be considered significantly different from automatic movements.

Key Characteristics of the Three Types of Movements			
	Reflex	**Automatic**	**Volitional**
Type of stimuli	External	External	External or self-motivated
Comparative latency of response	Fastest	Intermediate	Slowest
Variability of response	Little	Some	Great
Factors modifying the response	Musculoskeletal or neurological abnormalities	Musculoskeletal or neurological abnormalities	Musculoskeletal or neurological abnormalities
		Configuration of support	Conscious effort
		Prior experience	Prior experience
			Task complexity

Figure 4-2 Key Characteristics of three types of movements. From Nashner (1990, p 9), reprinted with permission of the American Physical Therapy Association.

It does not seem reasonable, or necessary, to rename these movements so that the terms reflex or reaction are altered or eliminated. If these movements were renamed when the names are so familiar and universally recognized, it would most likely cause more confusion than already exists. Should we rename the asymmetric tonic neck reflex, for example, and call it the asymmetric tonic neck coordinative structure? And the Moro reflex might be called the Moro synergy. We will not presume to solve this problem in this text. Simply realize that the reflexes presented in this book are complex motor patterns, are not limited to activation by external stimuli, and may appear to be relatively invariable but are still responsive to context. As you have already noted from earlier sections of this book, these reflexes can be considered to be coordinative structures or patterns of muscular activity that are the result of the linking of specific muscles together as described by Bernstein (1967) and Thelen (1985).

Early (Primitive) Reflexes, or Synergies

Prechtl (1984) suggests that spontaneous movements cannot solely be attributed to autonomous pattern generators or instinctual energies. Motor responses to discrete external sensory stimuli cannot be reduced to direct reflex relationships. Remember, from studies noted in Chapter 2, that the state produces changes in the movement outcome that do not appear to be continuous, or linear, in nature. Increasing the infant's state from quiet and alert to hard crying changes the kicking pattern abruptly from an alternating pattern to a rigid bilateral extension of the legs. Fluctuations in state presumably induce spontaneous motor activity. The finding that the same motor pattern can either be provoked by exteroceptive stimulation or be induced as an emergent property of transient-state fluctuations thus eliminates the need for making categorical distinctions between stimulus-elicited and spontaneous motor patterns.

Prechtl et al (1979) and others suggest that although the motor patterns are spontaneously generated in the fetus, they will come under afferent control after birth. Movements such as rooting and sucking become a complex function in which peripheral sensory stimulation of the oral region plays an increasingly important role. Because these movements do not persist throughout life, they are called primitive reflexes. But Prechtl believes that the clear history of their existence throughout prenatal and into postnatal life is the strongest argument against considering them to be of reflex origin. To extend this reasoning, it would seem then that reactions that can be elicited in the developing healthy infant cannot be called reflexes in the proper sense.

Are newborn patterns primitive? The term primitive suggests that the infant's brain is underdeveloped, incompetent, and deficient relative to the standard of the adult brain in which reflexes are replaced with cortically controlled voluntary movement (Touwen 1984).

Touwen, Prechtl, and other more recent theorists suggest that such a limiting and reductionist view is inaccurate and misleading. Infants have biologically different brains from animals and adult humans, from both species and age perspectives. In addition, animals that have been reduced surgically and adults who have suffered brain damage do not make reasonable models for comparison when describing movements of the developing healthy infant. The former might rightly be called primitive because they have lost much of their differentiation and variability.

Touwen (1984, p 123) states, "In a conception of the developing brain that emphasizes the involvement of the whole system in all changes during development, and that considers the healthy infant's brain as an age-specific and age-adequate organ system, it is no longer valid to use the term 'primitive reflexes.' The word 'primitive' is simply inadequate. Purely stereotyped reflexes do not occur, although reflex mechanisms may be hidden by the variable display of the infant's complex brain. Reflexes and reactions, and their developmental course, are useful in the neurological examination of infants but their existence in itself is not an adequate explanation of how the brain works."

Another view of reflex behavior and developmental progression is that it appears or follows a very predictable, stereotyped, and invariable course. Thus we would expect to elicit a reflex, or synergy pattern, from a neonate with exactly the same result if the same stimulus is used each time. The patterns may be similar and recognizable, a movement may be repeated, but it is never identical from trial to trial. Others have suggested that development proceeds along an invariable course. According to Touwen (1978), the most normal circumstances are those in which there is variability. Each individual proceeds through development following general guidelines but varying from individual to individual and within individuals.

> Motor development follows general guidelines but varies between and within individuals.

Walking is an excellent example of what is meant by such variability. Each of us knows that we can recognize different people by their gaits even when they are so distant that their features cannot be recognized. So there is subtle variation in gait, but the overall general pattern of gait is sufficiently the same as to be recognized as such. Winter (1987) has observed that definite intraindividual gait patterns exist as well. That is, subtle changes in the gait characteristics occur within the same individual from trial to trial and especially from day to day.

According to Touwen (1978), the more abnormal circumstances occur when the reflex responses or motor acts are much more stereotyped and predictable from trial to trial and day to day. Unfortunately, most authors of developmental literature have equivocated on these descriptions and have led to confusion by indicating that development is quite variable in normal infants and yet talk about the normal stereotyped sequence. The ultimate result is that most of us have interpreted these discourses to mean that stereotyped is normal and variability is abnormal. It would appear that such a view must be changed.

> Fetal movements are not primitive or immature movements. They are simply early movements.

In view of the systems approach to motor control theory that motor patterns--or reflexes, synergies, or coordinative structures--must be adaptable to allow pursuit of the behavioral goal of the moment, it is reasonable to believe that variability is necessary for adaptability to occur. Additionally, fetal movements should not be considered primitive in the sense that the system is not fully developed when they are observed. The nervous system is fully developed in utero and at birth to meet the needs of those periods.

It would be foolhardy to disregard the notion of reflexes even if the term encourages confusion. The movement patterns do exist postnatally and can be observed both as spontaneous movements or as elicited ones. In both cases, they are useful to therapists in evaluation and treatment. It may be more important to observe those behaviors spontaneously than to elicit them in a stumulus-response mode, because the former depicts the behavioral state of the infant at that point in time. In the event the therapist finds it necessary, an elicited reflex movement might yield appropriate information.

Various authors have called primitive reflexes by other names: primary reflexes--a term that suggests a sequence (primary, secondary, tertiary); basic reflexes--a term that suggests a hierarchy; and initial and infantile reflexes--terms that imply age specificity (Touwen 1978).

Therapists have often thought of reflexes as occurring in one of three categories: 1) simple spinal reflexes such as those mediated by the muscle spindle and Golgi tendon organ, 2) primitive reflexes that are not evident after the first year of life, and 3) equilibrium and righting reactions that persist throughout life (Barnes et al 1978). We believe that reflexes, particularly the complex movement patterns seen in fetuses, infants, children, and adults, are recognizable synergies that span many body segments. These movement patterns may be called reflexes, reactions, synergies, coordinative structures, or other such terms for patterns of movement. In this case, all these terms are relatively interchangeable, even though reflexes have often been categorized as primitive movements occurring in the fetus and infant, and reactions categorized as movement patterns that persist throughout life.

In this text, we have chosen to refer to the reflexes, synergies, or coordinative structures that are apparent in fetal life and in early infancy as *early reflexes*. Further, they have been divided and organized into major categories: vital or survival reflexes, vestigial reflexes, and functional reflexes. Some early patterns that appear to have more mature forms later in development are presented together as continuous entities. The various forms of righting and equilibrium responses are presented last.

Study Questions:

1. Write a definition of the term reflex as it is used in this book. How does your definition differ with the traditional understanding of the meaning of the word?

2. Write your own definition of antecedent traits, adaptive behavior, continuity-discontinuity, and regressive phenomena.

3. Clarify why the above mentioned phenomena are important in understanding infant development.

4. What do the experts believe to be the purpose of fetal movement?

5. Why do you think the authors of this text prefer to use the term early reflexes as opposed to the traditional term--primitive reflexes?

Chapter 5 - Survival and Vestigial Reflexes

Survival Reflexes

Rooting and sucking-swallowing reflexes have been associated with the emergence of early eating behaviors (Parmelee 1963; Prechtl 1958). They have also been associated with the organization of developmental oral motor behaviors and thus have often been called survival reflexes (Bosma 1975; Sheppard and Mysak 1984). Feeding is the single necessary point of engagement between the infant and the environment, for the child's biological survival. The prenatal coordination of the feeding pattern, beginning with stimulation of the cheek and leading to turning of the head, latching onto the nipple, sucking and swallowing, permits the newborn to be maximally adaptive to a variety of environmental variations in the source of nutrition. The infant must be capable of responding to a variety of human and artificial nipples if she is to survive (Sameroff 1973).

Rooting Reflex

The coordinated movement pattern of rooting is seen spontaneously before and during feeding and can be elicited by tactile stimuli. The infant responds either to hunger or to slight tactile stimulation of the perioral region by moving the tongue, mouth, and head toward the point of stimulation and, therefore, actively achieving rotation, extension, and flexion of the head (Fig 5-1). This response allows the infant to search for nourishment and to grasp with his mouth so that he can take his mother's breast or a bottle without using his hands (Peiper 1963).

Test Procedure

The presence or absence of the rooting reflex can be evaluated either during feeding in which it is observed as a spontaneous activity or during a session in which it is stimulated by the therapist under the stimulus-response mode of triggering the reflex. Place the infant supine with his head in the midline. Using a nipple or pacifier, gently stroke first the perioral skin at the corner of the mouth, moving laterally toward the cheek, then the upper lip, and finally the lower lip. After stimulation of the corner of the mouth, there should be head turning directed toward the stimulated side. With stimulation of the upper lip, there is opening

157

of the mouth and extension of the head (Fig 5-2). After stimulation of the lower lip, the mouth opens, and the jaw drops. The infant tries to suck the stimulating nipple or pacifier.

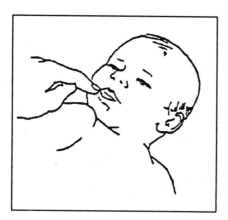

Figure 5-1   The rooting response.

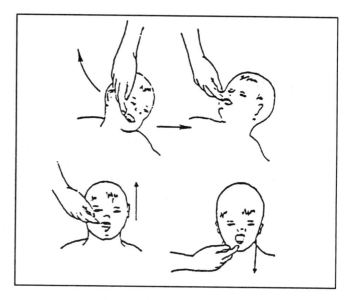

Figure 5-2   Eliciting movements of the lips, jaw, and head with the rooting reflex.

By definition, a full-term infant is 40 weeks of gestational age.

Full-term gestation is usually 40 weeks of gestational age (GA). The movement pattern of rooting is present in the infant of 28 weeks GA upon tactile stimulation of the corner of the mouth, but there is no response upon stimulation of the lower lip and only a faint response when the upper lip is stimulated (Saint-Anne Dargaisses 1972). It is not until 37 weeks GA that the response is perfect in all four directions. The pattern of rooting is active through 3 months (Mueller 1972), 4 months (Provost 1980), 6 months (Prechtl 1958), and 8 months (Sheppard and Mysak 1984). With age, the frequency and complexity of the response tends to decline.

Hooker (1952) and Humphrey (1969) observed similar stimulus response patterns when tactile stimulation was applied to human fetuses as early as 11.5 weeks GA. Recent real-time ultrasound studies have described isolated rotation of the head at 9 to 10 weeks GA and spontaneous head rotation from side to side, described as rooting movement patterns, at 14 weeks GA (deVries et al 1984).

Although some reflexive movement patterns may appear earlier in fetal development, we are concerned with movement activity at 28 weeks GA because that is the age of viability. That means that infants born less than 28 weeks GA do not usually survive. It is possible that you may be

158

The age of viability: The age at which a premature infant is expected to survive is 28 weeks GA.

working with such premature infants who would be expected to survive. As a general rule, these early reflexive patterns, which appear to disappear, are suppressed, or are organized or integrated into the expression of voluntary movement at about 4 to 6 months postterm age. Postterm age is defined as months after the time when the baby should be born, that is, after 40 weeks GA.

The infant will turn away from the stimulus if he is satiated or if the stimulus is too noxious. There usually will be no response to perioral stroking if the infant is preoccupied. So if he is voiding or crying he may not respond. This reflex is absent in depressed infants, especially those depressed by barbituates. Before evaluating the rooting movement pattern, the examiner needs to know the behavioral state of the infant, that is, whether the infant has just been fed, is voiding, or is under the influence of drugs.

The rooting pattern is believed to serve functions in normal development other than the feeding function. Repeated spontaneous head turning precipitated by hunger results in rotation of the neck that elicits the neck righting reaction. As you encounter the neck righting later on in this section, you will find that it enables an infant to learn to roll over. It is possible that the rooting response also enhances the development of certain expressions such as head shaking, nodding, and perhaps smiling (Peiper 1963).

Failure to obtain a rooting response may indicate general depression of the central nervous system (CNS). The persistence of the rooting reflex may indicate sensorimotor dysfunction. Asymmetrical results may be indicative of an insult to one side of the brain or an injury to a facial nerve or muscle. If the infant should be hungry and is not preoccupied and you fail to elicit a rooting response, you should look for further signs of sensorimotor facial nerve dysfunction, CNS depression, or muscle injury.

The rooting reflex is more pronounced in brain damaged infants than in normal infants. If the response persists well beyond the age when it normally would disappear, be suppressed, or be integrated into the expression of voluntary movement, it appears to interfere with sucking and other oral behaviors (Farber 1974; Sheppard 1964). It is also possible that the circumstances allowing the pattern to persist may prevent the expression or development of other oral activities.

Sucking-Swallowing Reflex

The sucking-swallowing reflex, elicited by placement of a nipple or pacifier into an infant's mouth, allows the neonate first to close his lips automatically around the source, then to suck repeatedly using a rhythmical pattern, and then to swallow. This rhythmical sucking pattern can be observed spontaneously during feeding or can be elicited

159

by placing a pacifier into the infant's mouth. The purpose of the reflex is to obtain nourishment. A cycle of lip closure and sucking finally culminate in swallowing.

Test Procedure

This movement pattern can be evaluated either during nutritive sucking when the infant is actually feeding or during nonnutritive sucking. Place the child supine with his head in the midline and then place a nipple or pacifier into his mouth. This should elicit the sucking-swallowing response. The examiner should feel strong rhythmical sucking movements. In some cases, you might wish to use a finger covered with a sterile finger cot. This permits you to actually feel the movements inside the mouth (Fig 5-3).

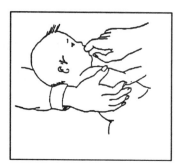

Figure 5-3   Eliciting a sucking reflex.

There are some differences in the response, depending on whether you use the nipple and bottle (nutritive sucking) or the pacifier (nonnutritive sucking). When a pacifier is used, sucking-swallowing is characterized by bursts of sucking alternating with rest periods. The studies by Wolf (1968) characterized nonnutritive sucking as consisting of 8 sucks per burst at a rate of 2 sucks per second with a 6 second rest between bursts. According to Sameroff (1973), a burst may contain 5 to 20 sucks lasting about 7 seconds, followed by a rest period of equal length. In nutritive sucking, there is a continuous stream of sucks at a rate of 1 suck per second (Sameroff 1973; Wolf 1968). Toward the end of feeding, rest periods are present.

> The sucking movement pattern is flexible and varies according to the task or goal to be accomplished.

The slower rate of sucking seen in nutritive sucking may be necessary to coordinate this pattern with respiration and swallowing in the feeding process. In addition, there is a higher rate of swallowing in nutritive sucking in comparison with nonnutritive sucking. The differences in the rate of sucking and swallowing in the two types of sucking demonstrate that infants can adapt their sucking patterns with respect to a given context (environmental conditions, demands). Thus the sucking movement pattern is not fixed, but it is flexible, varying systematically with the context and assembled to accomplish the particular task or goal. The infant can change the sucking behavior as a function of the consequences of the activity. Remember that these conditions are likely to be the result of a dynamic systems aspect of movement development that you studied in Chapters 1 and 2.

The rhythmical suck-swallow movement patterns are present at 28 weeks GA (Saint-Ann Dargassies 1966). By 33 to 36 weeks GA, preterm infants demonstrate the same pattern of sucking as full-term infants, but the rate of sucking is slower (Wolf 1968). The sucking-swallowing reflex comes under volitional control between 2 and 5 months of age (Mueller 1972). As the movement pattern becomes volitionally controlled, the sucking pattern is no longer rhythmical.

Hooker (1952) and Humphrey (1969) observed similar stimulus response patterns to tactile stimulation in human fetuses at 24 weeks GA. Recent real-time ultrasound studies have shown rhythmical sucking and swallowing movements as early as 12 weeks GA (deVries et al 1984).

As with the rooting pattern, the sucking-swallowing movement depends on the behavioral state of an infant, especially if he is satiated. If the infant has recently been fed, you will not be able to elicit sucking movements by inserting a nipple or pacifier into his mouth. Thus, always ask the caretaker when the infant was last fed.

> A poor or absent sucking or swallowing pattern is life threatening.

Weakness or absence of the sucking-swallowing movement pattern is of great concern because it decreases the infant's ability to derive nourishment normally and consequently deprives him of normal oral sensory stimulation. This situation can be life threatening, and complete absence may require either permanent or temporary methods of providing nutrition, such as surgically inserting a tube into the stomach for external feeding. A persistence of the sucking-swallowing reflex interferes with the development of voluntary sucking movements. This process interferes with normal tongue movements that later are incorporated into patterns of sound production and are used for a variety of feeding movements, depending on the type and texture of the food eaten. Ineffective suck-swallow movements may contribute to drooling as well.

Study Questions

1. Why do you think it is important for the therapist to understand survival reflexes?

2. Why is nutritive sucking slower than nonnutritive sucking?

3. If you fail to elicit a rooting reflex in an infant who should be hungry, you should look for signs of dysfunction. What might they be?

161

Vestigial Reflexes

Vestigial reflexes are seen in the fetus and in infants up to 4 months of age. Their purpose is not clear at this time.

One explanation for the presence of what we are going to call vestigial reflexes is that they represent a phylogenetic memory of the time when young animals were clinging to the fur of its mother's abdomen, as young monkeys do today. These movements are still displayed by human infants, although they are no longer of adaptive value to the human species. You should remember this discussion from the first chapter in this section concerning fetal movements. It is also possible that these movements are present for other purposes that currently cannot be determined. In any event, these early reflexes are present in the fetus before birth and appear to disappear by becoming integrated or masked through the development of more mature and voluntary movements by the third or fourth month of postnatal life.

Moro Reflex

The Moro reflex is one of the most commonly tested early coordinative patterns, or reflexes, in the evaluation of the neurological status of a newborn infant. This movement pattern can be elicited either by movements the infant makes himself that might result in a sudden drop of the head or by an external stimulus. Generally, it is triggered by a sudden change in position of the head in relation to the trunk and results in two distinct movement patterns: (1) extension and abduction of the upper extremities, opening of the hands, and crying followed by (2) flexion and adduction of the upper extremities across the chest, resembling an embrace (Fig 5-4).

There is some disagreement as to the exact movements produced by the lower extremities during this response, although most authorities agree that the lower extremities extend. It has been observed, however, that if the lower extremities are in extension before the response is elicited, they will move in a pronounced flexion posture. Also, during the response, a slight tremor or shaking of all extremities may be observed.

The functional significance of the Moro reflex is subject to controversy among many investigators. Milani-Comparetti (1981) considers the Moro to be a survival competence that is needed for the first inspiration at birth. Andre-Thomas and Autgaerdeen (1963) suggest that the Moro breaks up the predominant flexion posture of the newborn. Moro himself suggested that it is a vestigial movement pattern used in lower animals to catch a hold of their mother's fur if they begin to fall. Other investigators believe that it serves no functional purpose.

Test Procedure

The Moro reflex may be elicited by the head drop, the body drop, or the hit method. Dropping the infant's head backward about 30 degrees from the trunk is the most widely used method. You can elicit this by placing the infant supine with his head in the midline and the upper extremities on his chest. Then place one hand under his head and the other hand under the upper part of his trunk. Begin to bring the infant to a sitting position and then suddenly drop your hand at his head a few centimeters, allowing his head to fall backward about 30 degrees (Fig 5-4). Remember to keep your hand under his head so that you can catch his head when it drops.

Another method used does not include dropping the head of the infant. Called vertical acceleration, or body-drop, the infant is positioned as described above, but instead of the head being dropped, the entire body of the infant is accelerated downward as a result of the examiner bending her knees. The response consists of slight dorsiflexion of the head and, abduction and extension of the arms with fanning of the fingers. The embrace response is not observed (Eviator and Eviator 1978).

The hit method of eliciting the response is to sharply strike the bed upon which the infant is lying in a supine position. The most effective hit is near his head. This produces a loud noise and vibrations of the bed. Again, the embrace part of the response may not be seen.

It is important that you make sure the infant is not grasping an object in his hand, because this will inhibit the response on one or both sides (Andre-Thomas et al 1960). Observe the response and note the movement pattern (Fig 5-5). Do the upper extremities extend or abduct? Do the hands open? Do the lower extremities extend? Does the infant cry? Is the embrace response present? Whatever method you use, the first time you elicit the response it will probably be as upsetting to you as it is the child. Remember that the head really does not drop very far to get into your hand. The secret is to drop the hand back rapidly, not to drop it far. A little follow-through with your arms and body by gently flexing everything also helps. Because this procedure is threatening to the child, it should not be elicited until the end of your assessment. This procedure will probably alter the state of the infant.

The pattern of the Moro reflex is somewhat different in babies that have been born too early. The movement response evolves over time as the baby ages and reaches the age when full-term infants are born at 40 weeks GA. As the infant gets older, more components of the response are added. The onset of this movement pattern can be observed in a premature infant of 28 weeks GA in which the response consists of only extension of the fingers. It is not until 32 weeks of gestation that the response consists of three movements (extending and abducting the upper extremities, opening of the fingers, and crying) and not until 41

163

weeks GA that the embrace portion of the movement pattern is present, with adduction and flexion of the upper extremities (Saint-Anne Dargassies 1966).

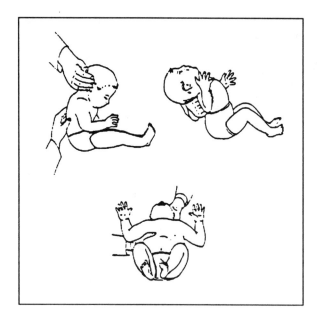

Figure 5-4 Eliciting a Moro response.

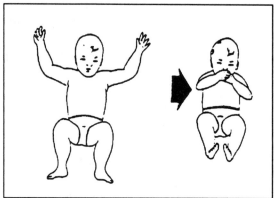

Figure 5-5 The abduction and embrace components of the Moro reflex.

The advent of real-time ultrasound has permitted us to study the beginnings of this movement in fetuses that are not old enough to survive outside the uterus. Researchers, using ultrasound, have described a movement pattern consisting of extension of the back, retroflexion of the head, and external rotation and elevation of the arms in a fetus of 10 weeks GA. This is pictured in Figure 5-6 (deVries et al 1982). Ianniruberto and Tajiani (1981) also reported movement patterns of extension of the legs, head, and trunk, accompanied with flexion and elevation of the arms in fetuses of 16 weeks GA. Some fetuses showed an extended-downward position of the arms. These movements are similar to those seen with the Moro reflex.

With ultrasonography, these researchers also described startle patterns in fetuses between 8 and 13 weeks GA. These startle movement patterns were initiated in the legs and consisted of either flexion or extension movements that may have spread to the neck and trunk (Fig 5-7).

An important point to remember is that the Moro reflex is not the same as the startle reaction. The startle and the Moro have often been confused. The startle reaction is a flexor response while the Moro is primarily one of extension. A sudden loud noise is the best stimulus for eliciting the startle reaction, whereas a specific change in the position of the head in relation to the trunk is the best stimulus for eliciting the Moro reflex. In some instances, both the startle and Moro result from sudden loud noises. In these cases, the startle is rapid and precedes the slower Moro reflex (Goldstein et al 1938). Unlike the Moro reflex, the startle reaction remains throughout life.

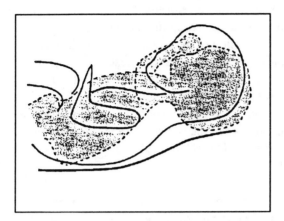

Figure 5-6   Moro type pattern of movement observed with ultrasound in a fetus of 10 weeks GA. Initial position is white and the end position is gray. From deVries et al (1982), reprinted with permission.

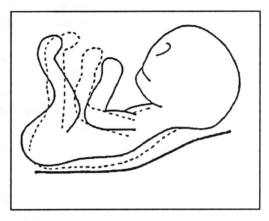

Figure 5-7   Startle movements as observed with ultrasound. The end position is shown with dashed lines. From deVries et al (1982), reprinted with permission.

The Moro pattern is strong from birth until about 2 to 3 months of age, and then it progressively becomes weaker until the response no longer can be elicited by 5 to 6 months of age (Peiper 1963). According to Touwen (1976), the disappearance, suppression, or integration of this movement response is attributed to the older infant's neck muscles being strong enough to contract and prevent a backward drop of the head. Cowie (1970) observed that the Moro reflex persists longer in infants with Down syndrome. This finding can perhaps be ascribed to the decreased tension of neck muscles in children with Down syndrome that prevents effective use of neck muscles. Thus the inability to elicit a Moro response may be related to the development of muscle strength rather than to an inhibition of this early movement pattern that might occur through maturation of the CNS. The Moro response has also been observed to persist in premature babies, infants with very low birth weight, and narcotic-addicted neonates (Chasnoff and Burns 1984; Marguis et al 1984; Parmelee 1964).

> An inability to elicit a Moro response may be related to the amount of muscle strength the infant has developed.

As with most early reflexes, problems can be anticipated when the response cannot be obtained at all, when it is not performed equally on both sides of the body, or if it persists into life beyond the time when it should be seen. Failure to obtain this movement at birth indicates general depression of the CNS. Late persistence of the Moro reflex may suggest a sensorimotor dysfunction. Asymmetry of the response may indicate an insult to one side of the brain. Peripheral injuries at birth also are encountered. There may be damage to the peripheral nerves of the extremity, as seen in Erb's paresis. The clavicle or humerus may be fractured, or the muscles of the involved extremity might be injured.

165

It has been stated that late persistence of the movement pattern affects the development of motor milestones and the appearance of postural reactions, such as righting and equilibrium reactions. It is true that other changes are progressing during development as the Moro response is changing in character and diminishing in response. During this time, there is progressive acquisition of head control and ability to sit by propping on the hands in front of the body. Researchers have noted that when this reflex is present there is less ability to sit without support, to roll, to reach for toys, and to ambulate independently. Postural reactions such as the Landau reflex, protective reactions, and tilting reactions do not occur or are impaired when the Moro reflex is present (Bleck 1975; Capute et al 1982b; Fishkind and Haley 1986; Marquis et al 1984; Molnar and Gordon 1976).

The problem with relationships is that the research statistics only suggest that there is something in common with the presence of one thing and the presence or lack of another. The mathematics do not prove that there is a cause-effect relationship. Thus we do not yet understand the underlying process of development that might produce such relationships. That is, we do not know whether the presence of the Moro prevents the development of other movement patterns or whether that finding simply represents the present condition of the nervous system that prevents the generation of more advanced and complex patterns of movement. Therefore, the persistence of the Moro reflex may be a useful predictor of some future ability and does not necessarily actually affect that ability itself.

> **It is more accurate to think of primitive reflexes as early reflexes.**

Another concept that is important for you to understand is that one early coordinated pattern, by itself, cannot promote or retard development. Single findings are rarely predictive of anything. As you proceed through this chapter, you will discover that persistent early reflexes usually occur together or in clusters. Therefore, in this section there will be continuous statements about the persistence of a certain early, or primitive, reflex and how it might affect development. Keep in mind that it is necessary to present these patterns one at a time in order to facilitate learning about them but that the conditions encountered usually involve more than the reflex under discussion at the moment.

Remember that development is a dynamic process occurring in both real and developmental time and that many components interact simultaneously to produce movement within a given context with respect to a specific goal. For example, if the goal of the child is to sit independently and reach for a toy, the infant will practice this activity over and over again, perfecting the movement pattern and gaining strength in order to do this activity. Once the strength is present, this may prevent the elicitation of the Moro reflex because the head does not fall backward. The movement pattern of the arms in a forward flexed position that is required to reach for a toy is opposite the pattern of the Moro reaction and thus may mask or prevent this response. It would seem, then, that it is quite possible that the acquisition of adequate strength against gravity and the development and learning of motor skills suppress the expression of the Moro movement pattern. If so, the concept is incorrect that the Moro itself prevents the acquisition of the ability of the infant to sit and reach and therefore must disappear before reaching can be done. If an infant does not have the opportunity to practice these skills or is prevented from doing so by a damaged nervous system, the Moro may indeed still be demonstrable.

Reaching and Grasping

Traction Response

Infants display their first voluntary reach and grasp activities between 3 to 4 months of age. Before this, newborn infants have a characteristic flexor dominance in their limbs, which only gradually wanes during the first 6 months. Therapists and neurologists test the decline of this flexor preference by grasping the arms of an infant and pulling the infant to a sitting position. In the newborn, the resultant flexion of the arms probably results mostly from stretch of the flexor muscles; it has been called the traction response. You have undoubtedly seen a traction response in an infant. Notice that when you attempt to pull a baby to sitting she helps with her arms. You can feel that contraction and see the body come toward the arms as flexion at the shoulders occurs. Remember from Chapter 2 that the neonatal patterns involve multiple joints and muscles and that much cocontraction occurs. Thus the shoulder muscles not only produce flexion but the fingers tighten in flexion, producing a strong grasp pattern of the hand. In addition to the flexion of the arm muscles, you will also see that the trunk and leg muscles are activated.

As noted in Chapter 3, McGraw (1945) performed the pull-to-sit test on infants as they matured from the newborn stage. The flexion movement seen in the older infant is a result of active extensor muscles. The baby's hands are fixed on your hands so that his extensor muscles pull his body toward your hands by extending his shoulders. The child truly helps actively with the movement as opposed to depending mostly on stretch. The trunk flexors and lower extremity muscles also strongly participate in the active pull-to-sit of the older infant. Perhaps the best indicators of the presence of a true traction response in older infants are the continuation of head lag, the lack of participation by the abdominal and lower extremity musculature, and obvious activity in the shoulder flexors and other arm flexor muscles.

Testing Procedure

When testing for the traction response, place the infant supine, grasp his forearms, and pull him to sitting. The total flexor response is usually of sufficient strength for the infant to support his weight. The early flexor dominance of the traction response and linking of all upper extremity joints, as seen in Figure 5-8, permits the infant to momentarily grasp a rattle or other object if placed in his hand (Twitchell 1970). As flexor dominance wanes, cocontraction diminishes, and other patterns are developed.

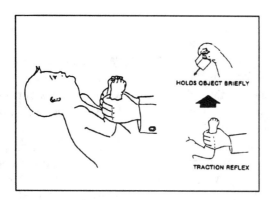

Figure 5-8 Traction response. A pull on the forearms provides stretch to the flexor muscles of the upper extremity. This produces a total flexion pattern, including the flexors of the fingers.

At 4 to 5 months of age, when infants first demonstrate an active reach, the traction response is no longer elicited through a stimulus-response mode. The relationship between the traction response and first reaching has not been studied. Whether the traction response is organized into voluntary reaching or whether voluntary reaching suppresses the traction response is open to debate. It is possible that as new patterns of voluntary movement are developed for active reach and grasp, the traction response is masked because active reach requires control of the extensor muscles of the arm in conjunction with the flexor muscles of the hand that are necessary for the infant to grasp the toy with a full palmar grasp. Whatever the underlying mechanism might be, other factors are necessary to promote voluntary reaching, one being visual regard of the object (von Hofsten 1983).

In cases of defective development where flexor dominance persists, the traction response can be adapted for purposeful prehension (reach and grasp), but development of this prehensile ability is long delayed as compared with the normal condition in which it begins to develop by the third or fourth month. The synergistic wrist flexion of the traction response causes weakness of grasp by placing the finger flexors at a mechanical disadvantage (Twitchell 1965). Try this on yourself. Flex your wrist and notice how finger flexion weakness results.

Palmar Grasp Reflex

The palmar grasp reflex is probably the same movement pattern seen when eliciting the traction response. In this case, the stimulus used to elicit the response is different because an object or the investigator's finger is placed into the hand itself (Fig 5-9).

Test Procedure

To test for the palmar grasp, place the child supine with his head in midline. Insert your index finger into the palm of his hand, from the ulnar side, and press gently against the palmar surface. Two responses are seen: first, there is a *catching phase,* consisting of quick flexion and adduction of the fingers; second, there is a *holding phase,* consisting of sustained flexion of the fingers when traction is maintained on the flexor tendons (Twitchell 1965). Halverson (1937) found that the closing, or catching, response results from contact or light pressure while the holding phase requires more proprioceptive input, such as the stretch that occurs when traction is maintained on the tendons.

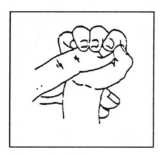

Figure 5-9 Palmar grasp reflex.

In addition, the response spreads to involve the wrist, forearm, and arm. The infant can be lifted from the bed by raising your hand or the object that is grasped. On occasion, full body weight can be supported with this grasp. The palmar grasp is present at birth in full-term infants. The neonate's hands show grasping responses that have been interpreted as having a clinging function. The infant's hand attempts to grip on almost anything that comes in contact with the palms.

Again, the movement is different in premature babies, and the pattern evolves as the infants reach 40 weeks GA. At 28 weeks GA, pressure to the palm of the hand causes the fingers to bend, but the reaction remains localized and does not spread to the rest of the arm. The arm remains inactive. At 32 weeks GA, the tonic reaction of flexor muscles spreads to the wrist, forearm, and arm; by 34 weeks GA, the tonic reaction spreads to the shoulder muscles, causing the infant to be raised from the support, but his head is not raised. By 37 weeks GA, pulling upward raises the whole body, but participation of the head is poor because the neck muscles do not participate effectively. By 41 weeks GA, the neck muscles play an active part.

Studies of fetuses removed from the womb also showed that this response is present before viability. Hooker (1952) noted closing of the fingers at 10.5 weeks GA, with total fist closure by 16 weeks GA. By 20 weeks GA, a thin glass rod placed in the palm of the hand resulted in finger closing, and by 22 weeks GA, the grip was so strong that the tester could move the whole arm with the glass rod.

169

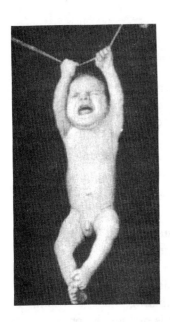

Figure 5-10 A newborn infant suspending total body weight through the palmar grasp response. From Peiper (1963), reprinted with permission.

Between 2 months and 5 months of age, infants explore objects that vary in substance and texture.

Again, while studying spontaneous movement before birth, with ultrasound, investigators have noted that in fetuses of 18 to 19 weeks GA, the hands clasp each other, grasp the umbilical cord, and explore other parts of the body (Ianniuberto and Tajani 1981). The advent of ultrasound has ushered in a wonderful opportunity to observe the developing infant.

Peiper (1963) calls the above response the tonic palmar grasp. If a rope is placed in the hand of a newborn, his hands grasp it, and he can cling to the rope in this manner so that for a short time, his hands carry the weight of his freely suspending body (Fig 5-10). According to Peiper, the traction and palmar grasp response represents a phylogenetic memory of the time when young animals clung to the fur of their mothers with the aid of this movement pattern.

The intensity of the traction and grasp response tends to increase during the first 30 days of life (McGraw 1945). Between 1 to 2 months of age, the flexion response can be facilitated by contact stimulation to the palm of the hand (Twitchell 1970). The ability to elicit the flexion response declines with the emergence of the contact grasp response, although fragments may persist up to 5 months of age (Twitchell 1965; 1970). The ability to elicit the palmar grasp declines with the emergence of voluntary grasping, around 4 to 5 months of age.

In a grasp, the fingers may be either tightly clenched or lightly flexed; the distinction is not exact. Functionally, tightly clenched fingers lack mobility. If the amount of flexion present prevents independent finger movements, then the grip is said to be clenched (Connolly and Dalgleish 1989). Grasp patterns in infants can be classified along two dimensions: rigidity-flexibility and appropriateness-inappropriateness. A grasp that does not permit the manipulation of the object by movements within the hand is a rigid, or clenched, grasp, whereas one that does permit intrinsic movement is flexible. The dimension of appropriateness-inappropriateness relates to the constraints imposed by the grasp in relation to the particular task. Young infants demonstrate rigid, clenched grasps that have the advantage of greater stability while older infants tend to use more flexible grasp patterns (Connolly and Dalgleish 1989). The clenched grasps of young infants may also be influenced by the flexor dominance at this early age.

Although neonates have rigid, clenched grasps, these grasp patterns are not controlled solely by automatic mechanisms. Rochat (1987) noted that the grasp pattern is guided by what the grasped objects afford for functional actions. Infants show different types of gasping to different objects that vary in substance and texture. The observation suggests that the infant has an early ability to detect the object's affordances, such as its graspability. That is, does the object invite touch? Is it too big to be grasped? Is it soft or hard? The infants response to toys is controlled by the object's characteristics on the basis of what it affords for functional actions. Spontaneous exploration of a novel object put in the infant's hand for grasping develops rapidly between 2 and 5 months of age. During this period, infants' manual activities evolve from passive holding (clinging) of the object to an active manipulation of the object.

Rochat (1987) also showed that from birth infants show differential responding to a hard or soft object when placed in the hand. A hard object is squeezed more frequently than a soft object. Two types of squeezes could be differentiated based on the relative duration of the pressure on the object. The first was a squeeze-release pattern of response, described as pressure lasting less than 1 second. The other squeeze was a clutch pattern in which the response lasted longer than 1 second (Fig 5-11). At birth, infants tend to show more clutch patterns when a soft object is placed in the hand and more squeeze-release patterns when hard objects are offered. The hard object provides more support for a squeeze grasp and too much rigidity for clutching. Thus, in neonates, grasping is adaptable to the type of object placed in the hand and is not under the control of purely hard-wired mechanisms.

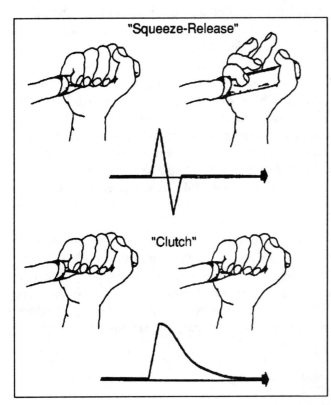

Figure 5-11 The two patterns of grasp: the squeeze-release and the clutch. The bottom traces show the corresponding polygraph record over the recording period. From Rochat (1987), reprinted with permission.

These observations support systems theory of motor control and motor development that suggests movements are assembled to accomplish a goal. Even if the movement can be stimulated by a particular stimulus and appears at certain times to have an obligatory nature, it is adaptable. Grasping is not a stereotyped response triggered indiscriminately by any kind of stimulation, but rather, it is actively modulated according to the object's characteristics. Grasping, then, may be only the first step in exploring an object, and the pattern initially encountered may not be reducible to a compulsive CNS-generated reflex pattern. Rather, the pattern may be the result of many subsystems acting together along with the specific neurologic pattern generated, such as the manner in which muscles are constrained to act together, the presence of flexor domination, and the cocontraction of the muscles involved (Palmer 1989).

The child or adult in whom the palmar grasp predominates as a mass pattern will have difficulty reaching for and grasping objects. Once grasped, he will have difficulty releasing objects.

> The variability of palmar grasp movement patterns seem to support the notion that movements are responsive to context and assembled to accomplish a goal.

Plantar Grasp Reflex

Just as the name implies, the plantar grasp is a grasping reaction of the toes. Spontaneous grasping of the foot is often seen in infants. The grasping pattern can also be facilitated by pressing your thumb into the ball of the infant's foot. If you place an infant in supported standing, his toes will curl as if to grip an object on the floor.

The plantar grasp is present at birth and has been observed in premature infants at 28 weeks GA. This response has not been described by ultrasound studies in young fetuses. This is the last early movement that can be elicited under a stimulus-response mode because it is integrated by about 9 months of age. Most of the early reflex patterns cannot be elicited after 4 to 5 months of age. The response is variable over the first 4 months of life and has been seen in children at 1 year of age (Touwen 1976).

Peiper (1963) also considered this grasp response to represent a phylogenetic memory of the time when the young animal clung to the fur of its mother's abdomen. As you can see in Figure 5-12, the neonate can be stimulated to grasp a rope with both hands and feet and suspend the body weight. This is a rare observation, and the infant can maintain himself in arm and leg suspension for only a short time.

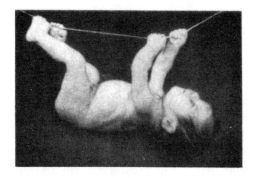

Figure 5-12 Suspension the body weight through the plantar and palmar grasp reflexes. From Peiper (1963), reprinted with permission.

Test Procedure

To test for this flexor movement in a stimulus-response mode, place the infant supine with his head in the midline. Press your thumb into the ball of the infant's foot and observe for flexion of all five toes (Fig 5-13). The plantar grasp can also be tested in the standing position. Pressure on the ball of the foot from contact with a supporting surface results in flexion of the toes.

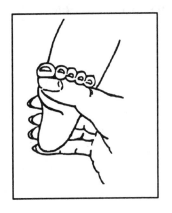

Figure 5-13 The plantar grasp reflex.

According to Milani-Comparetti and Gidoni (1967a; 1967b), you should not be able to elicit the plantar grasp after a child learns to pull-to-stand, stand at a support, and walk independently. However, when using a supine testing method, Touwen (1976) found no relationship between the disappearance of the plantar grasp and the onset of walking unsupported in normal infants. On the other hand, Effgen (1982), eliciting the plantar grasp in developmentally disabled children when they were in a standing position, did find a relationship between the disappearance of the plantar grasp and the emergence of independent walking. Infants in whom the plantar grasp was ultimately integrated later developed independent ambulation. However, she found no relationship between the suppression of the plantar grasp and the ability to pull to stand and stand at a support. Infants who could pull to stand and stand at a support also displayed a plantar grasp.

As with the other reflexes discussed, suppression of the plantar grasp may occur through the infant's experience with standing at a support, cruising, and walking with and without assistance because these activities promote more functional postures for the toes. This hypothesis is shared by other researchers who state that the plantar grasp disappears when the infant begins to stand up and walk (Poeck, cited in Touwen 1976).

The presence of a tonic plantar grasp usually gives parents considerable trouble when they try to put on a child's shoes. The contact of the ball of the foot with the sole of the shoe immediately results in flexion of all toes, and it is virtually impossible to push the foot into the shoe unless the foot is relaxed.

As with other early elicited responses, failure to obtain the plantar grasp indicates depression of the CNS, and absence of the response may indicate a defect in the spinal cord (Beintema 1968). The late persistence of the response may suggest sensorimotor dysfunction or deficit. Asymmetry of the response could indicate insult to one side of the brain, to the peripheral components of the nervous system, or to the muscles.

173

Study Questions:

1. There are two survival reflexes and four vestigial reflexes. Write a brief description of each.

2. Describe the testing procedures you would use to elicit each of the above reflexes.

3. During what period of time would you expect to be able to elicit these reflexes?

Chapter 6 - Kicking Patterns

Although kicking and stepping have traditionally been considered two different discrete motor patterns, Thelen and Fisher (1982) have demonstrated that these two movements are identical. The differences between them are related to the position in which the movement is produced. When the baby is lying supine, it will kick. If you pick up that baby and place her in the upright position, the same movement pattern occurs, although in this position it is called stepping. Other early reflex patterns of the lower extremities such as flexor withdrawal, crossed extension, and neonatal positive supporting also would appear to be derived from the kicking pattern. Again, the position of the infant or the specific manipulations of the therapist make the patterns appear to be different movement patterns.

> Externally elicited kicking patterns are often stereotyped, whereas spontaneous kicking patterns are varied.

From the traditional viewpoint of motor development--the reflex perspective--therapists have tested for the crossed extension reflex and the flexor withdrawal reflex in the supine position and for the spontaneous, or automatic, stepping in supported standing. The movement patterns produced from these input-output, or stimulus-response, modes are similar to that seen in infant kicking. Although the movement patterns are similar, whether elicited by an outside stimulus or produced spontaneously, a difference between the types of movement patterns is that kicking is adaptable to changes in the environment, be it internal or external, whereas movement patterns elicited from external stimuli are often more stereotyped and less adaptable.

Flexor Withdrawal Reflex

The flexor withdrawal reflex has been referred to variously as the flight reflex, the defense reflex, or the negative supporting reaction. Thus, it would appear that the neonate, child, and adult automatically uses the reflex movement as a defense or protective mechanism against noxious stimuli.

Test Procedure

Place the infant supine and gently prick the sole of his foot with a pin (Fig 6-1). As the name implies, the infant will extend his toes, dorsiflex his foot, and flex his extremity at the knee and hip joints in order to withdraw his foot from the stimulus. The opposite lower extremity also may be included in withdrawal and, if the stimulus is noxious enough, the leg will respond with vigorous flexion alternating with extension

175

(Fig 6-2). The entire body may also react by withdrawing from the stimulus (Andre-Thomas and Autgaerdeen 1963; Brazelton 1984).

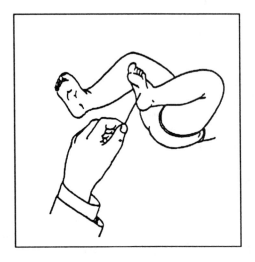

Figure 6-1 Flexor withdrawal reflex.

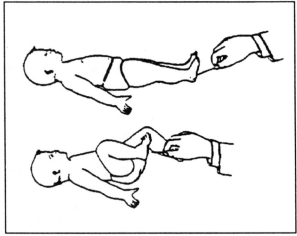

Figure 6-2 The entire lower extremity participates in the flexor withdrawal pattern, and the opposite extremity also may respond.

The withdrawal reflex is present at birth and has been elicited in preterm infants as young as 28 weeks gestational age (GA). Preterm infants less than 30 weeks GA have low thresholds to noxious stimuli, that is, it takes less stimulus to the foot to cause it to withdraw. By the time the premature infants reach term age, they have similar thresholds as full-term infants.

Repeated stimulation of the foot in preterm infants results in sensitization of the flexion reflex, that is, repeated stimulation results in a build-up of the reflex response. Under these conditions, the child either demonstrates continuous rhythmic flexor and extensor movements (kicking) or holds the extremity completely in flexion. The other leg and the trunk also may become involved in a mass body movement. This sensitization occurs until the infant reaches 32 weeks GA. After 32 weeks GA, repeated stimulation results in habituation, or a lessening, of the response when the stimulation is repeated. This habituation to the stimulus is observed in term infants and adults (Fitzgerald et al 1988).

Although traditionally it was believed that the total flexor withdrawal reflex is not elicited after 1 or 2 months, evidence indicates that the reflex shows no changes from birth to independent walking (Touwen 1976). If that is the case, flexor withdrawal is certainly the last of the early reflexes to be integrated, or modified.

Adults and children also produce withdrawal patterns. The stimulus threshold needed to elicit a flexor withdrawal is different for infants and adults than for premature babies. At 40 weeks GA, or term age, the threshold for stimulation is considerably less than it is for an adult or

176

even for someone with spinal cord injury. Using vonFrey hairs to stimulate the foot, Fitzgerald et al (1988) found that it took less than 2 g of force to elicit a flexor withdrawal in infants. Thirty to 75 g of force from the hairs was required to elicit a withdrawal response from the adults and 30 g were required to elicit a response from the paraplegic client. We do not know if the threshold for responding increases gradually during childhood or if there is a more sudden increase to adult levels in the postnatal period.

Thus the vigor and extent of the response is dependent on the intensity of the stimulus and the age of the client. A young preterm infant will need less stimulus to elicit a response than a full-term infant. The infant will require less stimulus than the older child or adult. If a weak stimulus is applied to an adult or older child, the response may simply be either dorsiflexion of the ankle or inversion or eversion of the foot to avoid a noxious stimulus. This is another example of the probable effect of the strong cocontraction of muscles seen in infant movements. With a decrease in the coactivation, more flexibility between movements of the hip, knee, and ankle are possible. Thus the adult has more flexibility in the manner in which he may respond.

Absence of the response may reflect inadequacy of the CNS. Late persistence of the full flexion response to a mildly noxious stimulus may indicate a delay in postural maturation. Asymmetry of a response may indicate either an insult to one side of the brain or a peripheral nerve or muscle injury to one side. Infants born in breech presentation (feet first) may show a weak or absent reflex, or a noxious stimulus may result in greater extension of the legs rather than flexion (Beintema 1968).

If the flexor withdrawal reflex is strong, it may be the result of a bias toward flexor dominance that may prevent extensor development for weight bearing in the upright position and for subsequent walking. When the infant is held upright and does not bear weight while in the upright position, the flexor withdrawal reflex pattern is often called a negative supporting reaction. You must also keep in mind, however, that there is a period of time during development, called astasia, in which the normal infant may not bear weight in the erect position (Andre-Thomas et al 1960). As indicated earlier, this period of nonweight bearing can be explained as being the result of an increase in weight, primarily fat, without a concomitant increase in muscle strength. Thus the baby cannot lift his heavy legs.

Crossed-Extension Reflex

The crossed extension reflex gets its name because either a noxious stimulus or pressure applied to the ball of the foot of one extremity produces an extension response on the opposite side. Thus this movement pattern is concerned with action in both legs.

177

Test Procedure

As in testing for the previous reflexes, first place the infant supine with his head in the midline. Then extend one lower extremity and keep it straight by holding it at the knee. With your other hand, put firm pressure on the ball of the foot (Fig 6-3). A noxious stimulus also may be used, but it is more threatening to the infant (Beintema 1968). After the stimulus is applied, observe the response of the contralateral leg, keeping in mind the appearance and integration sequence of the reflex.

The contralateral lower extremity will first flex, then adduct and extend (Fig 6-4). Or, if the stimulated extremity is not fixed, the stimulated leg will withdraw (a flexor withdrawal), and the opposite extremity will extend. Thus this movement pattern also resembles kicking, in the infant.

The crossed extension reflex begins to appear at 28 weeks GA. At that time, only flexion and extension of the lower extremity appear as a response to the stimulus. Later on, adduction appears in the middle of the sequence so that by 40 weeks GA, all three components of the reflex pattern are present--flexion, adduction, and extension. As the response becomes integrated and begins to diminish, adduction is the first movement component to disappear; flexion is the last phase to be integrated (Humphrey 1964). Generally, the reflex in its early form can no longer be accessed by 4 months of age. After that age, infants are capable of directing the extension phase of the movement toward the stimulus, and the flexion component becomes more variable. This change indicates that the movement pattern is developing into an active movement that remains through life. This active movement has been called an active defense pattern (Touwen 1976).

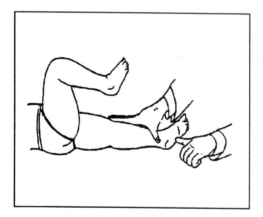

Figure 6-3 Eliciting the crossed extension reflex. The extremity must be immobilized during stimulation.

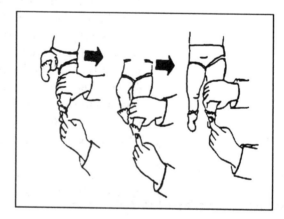

Figure 6-4 The three phases of the crossed extension reflex: flexion, adduction, and extension.

178

Figure 6-5 Possible use of the crossed extension reflex pattern.

The movement pattern of the crossed extension reflex is observed when an adult walks barefoot across an open field and steps on a piece of glass. The extremity is immediately withdrawn (flexor withdrawal), and the contralateral leg will have to bear the weight of the body to prevent falling (Fig 6-5). This increased extensor posturing is reinforced by a combination of a movement pattern that is part of, or similar to, the crossed extension reflex and the positive supporting reaction (which you will encounter later). When someone steps on a noxious stimulus, the contralateral leg begins to go through the first phase of the reflex--flexion and adduction. Only a partial range of motion occurs before the last component, extension, comes in for weight bearing. Obviously, balance reactions also must be present for this task to be achieved.

If the crossed extension reflex persists in its early form beyond the time of its integration into voluntary behavior and becomes obligatory, it will dominate the individual's posture and movement. A client may learn to use this automatic movement pattern to walk, but he will be unstable because the base of support is too narrow. There is also an inability to vary the movement pattern within the environmental context and conditions. Early in life, an infant that retains the dominant pattern will not demonstrate good reciprocal movements in the legs. If the infant does not kick in a reciprocal pattern, the ability to walk and perform other movements may be endangered.

Kicking

The arousal level of the infant will dictate the kicking movement pattern you will see.

An alternative to eliciting the crossed extension and flexor withdrawal reflexes during an evaluation of movement is to observe the infant during kicking. Although reciprocal, or alternating, kicking is present throughout the first year and is a preferred movement pattern, the infant also demonstrates other types of kicks, such as unilateral kicking and simultaneous kicking of both legs. A longitudinal study of the evolution of kicking patterns showed that the infant initially kicks alternately, then unilaterally, and then returns to bilateral kicking, either alternating the legs or reciprocally kicking both legs simultaneously (Thelen et al 1983). The frequency of kicking declines at the time of independent locomotion (Thelen 1979).

The frequency of kicking is influenced by the arousal level, or behavioral state, of the infant. When infants are in sleep states, they show minimal or no kicking; in awake states, they show reciprocal kicking; but if crying hard, they will show rigid extension of the legs in an extensor pattern (Thelen et al 1982; 1983). Thus, although infants can produce the reciprocal type of kicking you are expecting to see, their arousal level will either facilitate, inhibit, or change the pattern.

Early kicking is a spontaneous movement and is related to the patterns eventually used in walking. By 3 months of age, infants have been observed using early kicking patterns to control an overhead mobile. Thus the infant can recruit this early spontaneous movement pattern to voluntarily control a device that she wishes to move (Thelen and Fisher 1983).

During the first year, kicking becomes differentiated into finer movements and integrated with other system components, producing more flexible and adaptive movements. The newborn kicks with a very tight and predicable linkage of the hip, knee, and ankle joints. By 4 to 6 months of age, the tight relationship is relaxed somewhat, and the infant is able to move the hip, knee, and ankle more independently of one another. However, after 6 months of age, the joints once again are locked together in the kicking movements. By 10 months of age, the joints again show greater individual action (Thelen 1985).

As noted in Chapter 2, the organization of movements between the legs also changes during the first year. In the newborn period, infants predominantly demonstrate reciprocal leg movements, but by 1 to 4 months of age, the infant prefers to kick only one leg. The amount of kicking in one leg and the leg preference varies among and within infants. By 4 to 6 months of age, there is a return to bilateral coordination, including both alternating and synchronous kicking. The individual joint action and bilateral coordination available by the age of 7 to 12 months allows a recombining of elements into more complex functional patterns needed for crawling and walking (Thelen et al 1983).

> Volitional motor control, weight changes, and dominance of flexor and extensor influences determine kicking patterns.

Although these changes in kicking during the first year were once ascribed to maturation of the CNS, Thelen suggests that the uneven course of kicking during the first year is attributable to not only the development of voluntary motor centers but also to early weight gains and the relative dominance of flexor and extensor influences (Thelen 1985). Other subsystems that may contribute to these pattern changes are arousal level, perception, and motivation. From this viewpoint, changes in kicking cannot be attributed to one single cause but to the dynamic interaction of many subsystems.

Ultrasound studies have shown alternating kicking movements in utero as early as 10 weeks GA (deVries et al 1982). In addition to reciprocal limb movements, fetuses also demonstrate symmetrical leg movements at 13 to 14 weeks GA (Ianniruberto and Tajani 1981). You will remember from the chapter describing fetal movements that these early coordinated movement patterns may allow the fetus to move around in the uterine cavity, possibly to prevent adhesion and stasis and to find the correct presentation for birth (Milani-Comparetti 1981; Prechtl 1986).

These early movement patterns may be the direct precursors of later forms of movement in postnatal life. Thelen et al (1987) believe that early leg movements gradually change and merge into those required for mature locomotion. The authors suggests that locomotion occurs as a result of the need to move around in the upright position.

Preterm infants as young as 28 weeks GA also demonstrate coordinated kicking movements that are identical in organization to newborn movements (Heriza 1986). However, there are subtle differences between the movement pattern seen in full-term infants and those preterm infants when they reach 40 weeks GA. Preterm infants are more extended at all joints, especially the ankle, in comparison with full-term infants. The premature infants also paused more during kicking and kicked less than full-term infants. These differences were attributed to the arousal level and to the longer time the preterm infant spent in a gravitational environment, which inhibits flexion. The long confinement in the intrauterine space for full-term infants contributes to the flexor dominance of these full-term infants; this confinement has been missed by the preterm infant (Heriza 1988).

Placing

There are a variety of placing reactions--visual, tactile, and proprioceptive--that can be demonstrated, or elicited, in both the upper and lower extremities. As the name implies, in response to certain stimuli, the infant will flex his proximal joints and place his hands or feet onto a supporting surface. In this section, the placing reactions in the lower extremities will be presented as they relate to stepping. Upper extremity placing reactions also will be described.

Visual and tactile placing are exhibited in the older infant. Developmentally, proprioceptive placing in the feet is correlated with spontaneous stepping (Halsey 1968), whereas visual placing is closely associated with independent walking.

Proprioceptive Placing

Test Procedure

To test for proprioceptive placing in the legs, support the child under his shoulders and keep him in a vertical position. Lift one leg and support it in the flexed position. Then lift the child so that the dorsum of his free foot is pressed up against the edge of a table. This procedure will place a stretch on the ankle dorsiflexors (Fig 6-6). The response in the lower extremity consists of flexion at the hip and knee and dorsiflexion at the ankle, as if to clear the table. This is followed by extension of the extremity so that the foot is placed squarely on the table top. This placing may or may not be accompanied by weight bearing (Touwen 1976).

Figure 6-6 Eliciting proprioceptive placing in the lower extremities.

Proprioceptive placing, or neonatal placing as it is sometimes called, of the lower extremities is considered a residual form of fetal locomotor patterns modified by gravity (Milani-Comparetti 1981). As stated earlier, fetal locomotion is present at 10 weeks GA (deVries et al 1982). In the preterm infant, proprioceptive placing in the legs can be elicited at 35 weeks GA (Carter and Campbell 1975; Saint-Anne Dargassies 1966).

> Early placing (up to 2 months of age) is without weight bearing; placing at 9 to 10 months is accompanied by weight bearing.

Although traditionally the proprioceptive placing reaction was considered to be integrated by 6 weeks of age and definitely by 2 months (Halsey 1968), a longitudinal study of infants from birth to the time of independent walking reported variability of performance of the placing reaction (Touwen 1976). During the first 2 months of age, more than 80% of the infants showed a brisk placing response with no weight bearing. This percentage decreased during subsequent assessments, so that during the 4th and 5th months only about half of the infants showed a brisk response. This decrease in the elicitation of placing by 4 to 5 months of age is supported by Provost (1980). Subsequently, the percentage of brisk responses increased, and from the 9th to 10th month, more than 80% of the infants again showed a brisk placing response accompanied by weight bearing.

Again, in contrast to earlier findings, the placing reaction was elicited primarily by tactile stimulation after the first month or so, and proprioceptive reinforcement of the tactile input did not enlarge the response. From about 6 to 12 months of age, proprioceptive influences played an increasing role. This period coincides with the initial phase of standing-up behavior, and Touwen (1976) suggested that the mechanisms for the initial placing reaction were incorporated into the organization of voluntary standing behavior.

Proprioceptive placing, however, can be obtained at any age if traction is exerted against the ankle or wrist to the point of discomfort. You may have used this reaction when walking or running across uneven ground or going up stairs and stumbling across an object you did not see in your path. The early reflex pattern is not a preferred response later in life because most of the time visual placing responses occur first and prevent the opportunity to exert traction on the ankle.

Proprioceptive placing resulting from traction occurs throughout life.

The presence or absence of the proprioceptive reflex as it relates to the development of independent walking was studied by Bleck (1975). He found that a persistent proprioceptive placing reaction was not predictive for locomotor progress in children with cerebral palsy, suspected cerebral palsy, or developmental delay. Bennett et al (1981) also found no ability to predict cerebral palsy from the presence or absence of the proprioceptive placing reaction, just as did Harris (1987).

Asymmetry of responses may indicate insult to one side of the brain, muscle weakness, or peripheral nerve injury. Stereotyped simultaneous placing of both feet after initial contact of only one foot is probably abnormal (Paine et al 1964).

Visual and Tactile Placing Reactions

Visual and tactile placing reactions are protective mechanisms that help prevent destabilization and falling when objects are seen or encountered or, in some cases, when support surfaces are unexpectedly changed or are of considerable variation.

Test Procedure

To evaluate visual placing, hold the child vertically, as previously described for proprioceptive placing, and advance the child toward a supporting surface. The response is the same as seen in proprioceptive placing; that is, the lower extremity flexes and then extends to bear weight on the supporting surface. The visual placing reactions are associated with independent walking. Remember that vision is a dominant force in the acquisition of balance in the developing child; a child relies on visual input in gait probably for both postural control and guidance for locomotor progression.

In an upper extremity response, the shoulders and elbow joints flex and extend to position the extremities on the surface and to bear weight with the wrist extended and the fingers extended and abducted. In the hands, visual placing is quite likely used for accurate placing of the hands during creeping and visual reaching and grasping.

The placing reaction is elicited as the infant sees the table approaching (Fig 6-7). After the visual placing develops, it is usually impossible even to attempt to test for proprioceptive placing because the child will place her foot or hand before the surface is touched.

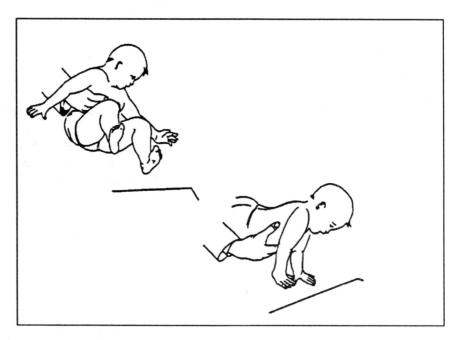

Figure 6-7 Visual placing of the lower and upper extremities.

Tactile placing reactions occur in response to tactile stimuli. The reaction is identical to visual placing and to test for it the infant must be blindfolded. Because this procedure is not well tolerated in children, and because the two reactions appear at about the same age, it is not necessary to test for tactile placing reactions.

The visual and tactile placing reactions in the upper extremities appear between 3 and 4 months of age, although in the lower extremities they appear between 3 and 5 months. As one might expect, the visual and tactile placing reactions persist throughout life.

Failure to obtain visual placing reactions after 5 months of age may indicate general depression of the CNS or sensorimotor dysfunction. In testing for these reactions, note whether there is a difference in stimuli needed to elicit the response. For example, visual placing may be elicited in the hands, and only proprioceptive placing may be elicited in the feet. This difference between hands and feet may suggest more involvement of the upper extremities than of the lower extremities.

184

Positive Support

An infant placed in the vertical upright position will bear weight. Likewise, a child or an adult who is standing will bear weight on his legs. There is a difference, however, in the type of posture that is demonstrated under the two conditions. In the infant, weight is only partially borne, and the hips and knees are partially flexed (Fig 6-8). Remember that the newborn period is a stage of flexor dominance and that the extensor muscles are not sufficiently strong to support full body weight. The older child or adult bears total body weight in an extended posture. These two types of postures have traditionally been called the neonatal positive support and the weight bearing, or mature positive support.

Test Procedure

When testing, support the infant in the vertical position with your hands under her arms and around her thorax. Allow her feet to make firm contact with a table top or other flat surface. Note the response. Does the child bear weight? How much? What is the position of the hips and knees? Are they partially flexed or are they extended?

There are two points to consider when testing for the positive support: the amount of weight that is borne and the amount of hip and knee flexion or extension that is present. Depending on the age and skills of the child, instead of supporting the weight of the child under her axilla you may want to support her by holding on to her hands or by using only one hand (Fig 6-9). By 11 months of age, the child may be able to stand without support. Thus where you support the infant or child will determine how much voluntary effort the child will need to stand erect. Both support and effort need to be attended to carefully during your testing.

> Posture and movements that look very similar to positive support have been seen in fetuses.

The early form of standing is present at birth and is seen developing in premature infants at 35 weeks GA. In studies using ultrasound equipment, researchers have observed a posture and movement similar to the supporting reaction. Fetuses at 10 and 16 weeks GA have been observed to position their legs in extension against the uterine wall. By pushing the legs against the wall, they have propelled themselves off the wall, producing a somersault resulting in rotation along the transverse axis (de Vries et al 1982; Ianniruberto and Tajani 1981). It is suggested that this fetal posture and movement continue as the supporting reaction of the newborn in postnatal life (Milani-Comparetti 1981).

Andre-Thomas et al (1960) indicated that the neonatal positive support disappears around 2 months of age, when there is a period in the infant's development (2-6 months) during which the infant does not bear any

185

weight when placed in the standing position. Again, this is referred to as physiological astasia (Fig 6-10). At the end of this period, the child actively bears weight in the standing position. This biphasic developmental course was not seen in a study by Touwen (1976).

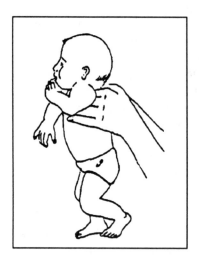

Figure 6-8 Positive supporting responses in a neonate.

Figure 6-9 Standing with assistance.

Figure 6-10 Physiological astasia--refusal to bear weight in the standing position.

Touwen (1976) found that it was difficult to distinguish between neonatal positive support and active standing because one gradually merged into the other. Thus not all infants may show a period of time when they will not bear weight in the standing position, but other infants may demonstrate this developmental stage. When evaluating an infant, however, you should be aware of the possibility that this stage may exist. Do not consider nonweight bearing as an abnormal response. As discussed previously, Thelen and Fisher (1982) suggest that any disappearance of weight bearing, or period of nonweight bearing, may be the result of an increased weight gain that occurs early in infancy, so that some infants do not have the muscle strength to support the heavier body.

When placed in the standing position, preterm infants stand on their toes as a result of the predominance of extensor posture and ankle plantar flexion. This extensor posture is the result of the preterm infant living in an unhampered extrauterine environment and coming under the influences of gravity. Paine et al (1964), however, state that a tendency to stand on tiptoes is not confined to preterm infants but also may be observed in full-term infants.

The neonatal positive support is a prerequisite for spontaneous stepping (Peiper 1963). It is not intended for prolonged maintenance of posture but more as a posture preparatory for motion (Paine et al 1964).

Spontaneous Stepping

When a newborn is held vertically and tilted forward, the infant appears to take steps and to be walking. This pattern of spontaneous stepping is identical to kicking but different from early true walking.

Test Procedures

To test for spontaneous stepping, support the infant in a vertical position, with your hands under her arms and around her chest, and allow her feet to touch the supporting surface. The infant should bear some weight on her legs (neonatal positive support). Next, incline the infant anteriorly and slowly move her forward to accompany any stepping. The infant will make alternating stepping movements with both legs (Fig 6-11). The coordination of this spontaneous walking is good, and its rhythm is regular. The heel is placed down first, with strong dorsiflexion of the foot. There are no balancing or associated movements of the upper extremities. The heel-first step is a result of strong dorsiflexion of the foot. The dorsiflexion is part of the kicking pattern, and the strong flexion components of the kicking pattern may, in part, result from the mechanical influences of intrauterine positioning and from the predominate flexor posture present in the newborn.

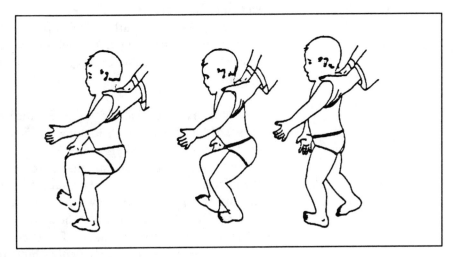

Figure 6-11 Automatic or spontaneous stepping movements elicited in the neonate.

Preterm and full-term infants will stand on their toes because of extensor dominance.

Spontaneous stepping, or automatic walking, begins to develop at 35 weeks GA in the premature infant (Saint-Anne Dargassies 1966). The

187

preterm infant will often walk on the toes and be more extended than the full-term infant. The preterm infant has not spent significant time in the confined space of the uterus and has been exposed to the influences of gravity. Thus the muscles and joints are not biased for flexor dominance but for extensor dominance. As noted under the discussion of kicking, reciprocal movements of the legs appear as early as 10 weeks GA.

Spontaneous stepping often disappears at 2 months of age in parallel with the neonatal positive support reflex. As with the neonatal positive support of the lower extremities, there is a period of time, between the fourth and sixth months, during which the child may not take steps. The nonweight bearing stage is called astasia; the nonstepping phase is called abasia (Saint-Anne Dargassies 1972).

As with neonatal positive support, the disappearance of spontaneous stepping has traditionally been thought to be the result of maturation of the CNS. Some researchers (Forssberg 1985; Leonard et al 1988) continue to consider that early infant stepping and the adult locomotor pattern are controlled solely by motor programs in the CNS and that development from the early pattern to the adult pattern is reflected by changes within the nervous system and by learning. These researchers lean toward the hierarchical control of movement. They do not consider early infant stepping to be a reflex, because an external stimulus is not needed to produce the movement; however, these authors do believe that this early stepping is an innate motor pattern--a hard-wired central pattern generator.

These researchers suggest that the inactive period results from excitability changes in the central neural network as descending locomotor systems develop and establish contact. When supported stepping reappears, the child can stop or start the movement. Over the next few months, this early stepping pattern undergoes dramatic changes in order to become adapted for adult locomotion. Major systems that must be present for adult locomotion are the visual and equilibrium systems.

Infants with cerebral palsy demonstrate the same gait pattern during early supported walking as do normal infants of the same age. In contrast to normal children, these children do not change the early gait pattern to a pattern resembling that of adults but retain several features of the infantile gait pattern. Several authors believe that movement deficits in children with cerebral palsy can be attributed solely to supraspinal mediated deficits which prevent the ability to refine movement and to adapt to a changing environment (Forssberg 1985; 1986; Leonard et al 1988). These processes--refinement of movement patterns and the ability to adapt to the environment--require integration from higher brain centers. It must be remembered that those who espouse a systems approach to movemement do not suggest that motor patterns do not exist nor that maturation of the cerebral systems is not important. The systems theorists have approached the problem from a nonneurological perspective and suggest that other systems and the context are equally as important. From this perspective it is reasonable to believe that such factors as limb weight and muscular strength also influence the ability to perform a given movement. Most of both approaches are actually compatible, the main difference being how much of a given pattern is actually hard wired into the system.

Can spontaneous stepping be preserved and thus facilitate true walking at an earlier age? Andre-Thomas and Saint-Anne Dargassies exercised infants several times a day but could not prevent the disappearance of the initial stepping movements (Peiper 1963). Zelazo et al (1972) had mothers exercise their infants daily and were able to maintain spontaneous stepping and facilitate earlier walking (Fig 6-12).

According to Zelazo et al (1972), with practice through assistance by the infant's family, stepping appeared to develop from a reflexive pattern to an instrumental (goal-directed) behavior during the first year of life. From a behavioristic viewpoint, it is supposed that stepping was found to be a pleasurable response and thus was a rewarding experience for the infant. With exercise, it is assumed that the infant gains the capacity to both activate and inhibit the reflexive pattern. By gaining on-off control, the reflexive stepping pattern is transformed gradually from an automatically elicited behavior to one that the infant can start and stop.

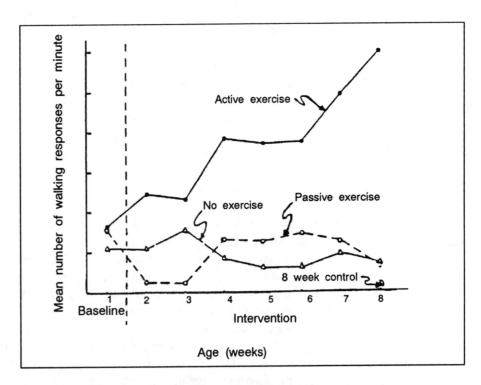

Figure 6-12 Mean number of walking responses for the experimental group (practice stepping) and the control groups (no exercise; passive exercise) during the first 8 weeks of life. From Zelazo et al (1972), reprinted with permission.

189

Although the disappearance of early stepping was delayed, children still did not walk before 9 months of age. This observation suggests that there is a maturational limit to the onset of unaided walking. Zelazo (1976) proposes that this constraint may be cognitive in origin. It was concluded that earlier walking by the exercised infants was attributable to underlying changes in information processing ability, which probably is the ability to access stored memories in rapid succession that may characterize both the cognitive changes that occur around the end of the first year and the onset of erect locomotion. Thus the development of unaided walking can be accounted for by two principles: (1) the development of instrumental control of reflexive patterns during early infancy and (2) a centrally mediated change in information-processing ability occurring from about 8 to 12 months of age. This cognitive change is considered a necessary condition for the expression of human motor abilities (Zelazo 1976; 1983; Zelazo et al 1989).

In contrast, you are familiar with a series of studies, by Esther Thelen and her collaborators, that have shown that the disappearance of stepping seems to be the result of the dramatic increase in the mass of the legs, which can no longer be raised against the pull of gravity (Thelen and Fisher 1982). When these researchers submerged 4-week-old-infants to chest level in warm water, functionally reducing the leg mass, they found that stepping increased dramatically in rate and amplitude. The frequency of stepping was influenced not only by the weight of the legs but also by the arousal level. Infants who were more highly aroused stepped more. This suggests that when more energy is delivered to the muscles, the biodynamic limitations of mass can be overcome.

In summary, the precursors to mature walking are newborn stepping and kicking. Remember that spontaneous kicking is similar in coordination and temporal organization to erect stepping movements. Unlike the stepping response, which can no longer be elicited after about 2 months, infants continue supine kicking throughout the first year. Thus this evidence suggests that the disappearance of stepping need not be solely ascribed to the maturation of the CNS but, rather, may be the result of, or influenced by, physical conditions.

Remember that in addition to submerging infants in water during the period of nonstepping, Thelen and Ulrich (1991) also placed these infants on a treadmill so that they took steps. These steps were more mature than the step patterns seen in either stepping without the treadmill or kicking supine, however, so the infants demonstrated not the immature pattern of early stepping but the mature pattern of adult locomotion. Thelen proposed that the movement pattern for later adult gait, therefore, is present but masked by the lack of extensor strength and balance. Thus Thelen considers that the early pattern of stepping is modified with age into mature locomotion, as do Forssberg and Zelazo. Unlike Forssberg and Zelazo, however, she believes that rather than rely solely on the maturation of cognitive processes, other variables necessary for change are such factors as body weight, extensor muscle strength, and balance. These subsystems dynamically interact with other subsystems such as the nervous system, motivation, cognition, and other psychosocial factors within a specified context. Two crucial variables in this picture appear to be muscle strength and balance.

Study Questions

1. Explain the relationship of kicking to stepping, according to Thelen and Fisher.

2. What other lower extremity patterns are related to kicking?

3. What is the rationale for grouping these movement patterns together?

Chapter 7- Attitudinal Postural Reflexes

There are a group of reflexes, or postural patterns, that involve the entire body. They influence total postures of the infant, child, or adult, and they are usually called attitudinal, or tonic, reflexes. Individually they are identified as the asymmetric tonic neck reflex (ATNR), the symmetric tonic neck reflex (STNR), and the tonic labyrinthine reflex (TLR).

Asymmetric Tonic Neck Reflex

The ATNR is elicited by rotation of the cervical vertebrae. Because it is easier to visualize the rotation of the neck by observing the head, we will describe the stimulus for the ATNR and other neck reflexes relative to movement of the head.

If the ATNR is present, when the individual's head is turned to one side a typical postural pattern occurs in the extremities (Fig 7-1). This pattern is most easily remembered by visualizing it as an archer's bow and arrow position or a fencing posture. If you were to draw a bow with your right hand, your head rotates to the left, your left elbow extends to hold the bow, and your right elbow is flexed to draw the bowstring. The lower extremity on each side assumes the same position as the upper extremity. Thus, if the head turns to the right, the left upper and lower extremities flex and the right upper and lower extremities extend. The terms *skull arm* or *chin arm* have been used to designate the arm that is being described. The arm to which the back of the skull points when the head is turned would be the skull arm. The chin arm would be the arm to which the chin points.

Research studies indicate that the asymmetric tonic postural pattern contributes to the supportive framework of nonstressful movement (Hellebrandt 1962; Hirt 1967; Ikai 1950; Tokizane 1951; Waterland and Hellebrandt 1964). This is interpreted to mean that there is some facilitation of extension in the extremities toward which the head is rotated. Overt movement may not be seen, but there is an advantage to extension in this position.

In an important study by Hellebrandt et al (1956), such advantages were found. They asked people to repeatedly move a lever by either flexing or extending their wrists until a point near exhaustion was reached. In addition, subjects either looked toward the moving wrist or away from it. If the asymmetric tonic neck pattern influences the movement, a gainin extensor strength would be expected by looking at the wrist and a gain in flexor strength would be expected when turning the head away. In Figure 7-2, there is a striking confirmation of these predictions. Most striking was the observation that subjects would spontaneously turn their heads when they were fatigued, even though they were not instructed to do so. Through this mechanism they gathered additional power when fatigued.

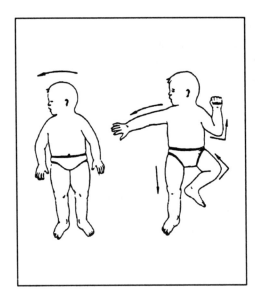

Figure 7-1 Typical postural response of the asymmetric tonic neck reflex. Note the extension of the extremities on the chin side and the flexion on the skull side.

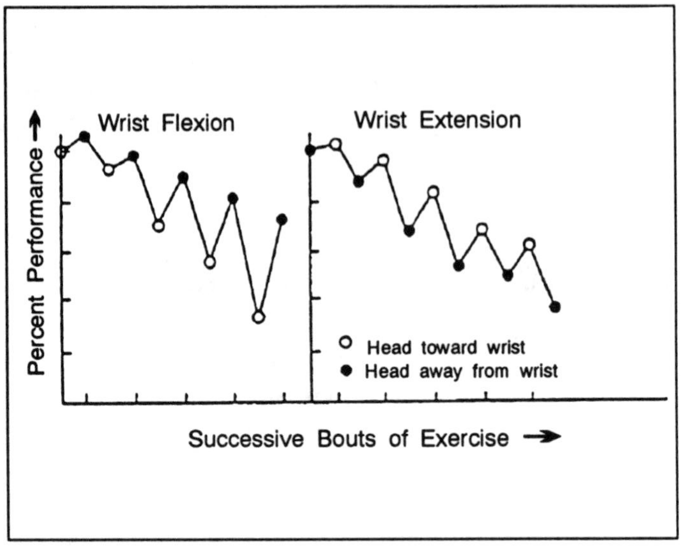

Figure 7-2 This graph shows the strength of performance of weight lifting with weights in the hand while performing wrist flexion or extension movements. The strength of the response declines with fatigue, as noted by plotting subsequent bouts against the performance of the first bout (100%). When wrist flexion is performed, the strength is greater when the head is turned away from the wrist. When extension is performed, the strength is greater when the head is turned toward the wrist. Based on Hellebrandt et al (1956).

Given that the ATNR pattern facilitates certain postures, one might expect it would commonly be used in stressful activities such as sports. In the classic study by Fukuda (1961), many skilled performers were, in fact, captured on film showing the classic ATNR position in a variety of activities (Fig 1-17, Chapter 1). Although these studies suggest that the ATNR supports movement, it is possible that the athlete is merely looking or reaching in that direction and the reflex is not producing the pattern. Additional research is necessary to determine whether the ATNR observed in young children is important in determining those movement patterns observed in adults (Schmidt 1988).

Looking in the direction of the extended arm seems to give it added strength.

Gesell (1954) believed that the infant first observes his hand (hand regard) while lying supine in the ATNR position. This hypothesis was confirmed by Coryell and Henderson (1979), who found that the ATNR posture tends to place the infant's hands within the field of vision, thus helping to ensure that the hands are seen and examined. Therefore, the

194

ATNR could be said to begin the developmental process of coordinating eyes and hand for later functional skill in reach and grasp. However, a restricted small sample study reported by Larson et al (1990) showed there was no relationship between reaching behaviors and the presence or absence of the ATNR in a sample of 2- to 4-month-old infants.

The ATNR posture is also seen in the prone position and is believed to influence pivoting and low creep, which is defined as movement with the abdomen on the ground (Goldfield 1989). During pivoting while prone and performing the low creep, infants extend an arm in the direction of the orientation of the head. Thus, when an infant actively orients his head to look to one side, his arm on that side is more likely to be extended than flexed, which prepares the infant to reach out in the direction of gaze.

Test Procedure

When testing for this postural pattern in normal infants, place the neonate supine. Next, using a visual stimulus, encourage the infant to focus and follow the stimulus visually through an arc of 180 degrees, observing the posture of his upper and lower extremities (Fig 7-3).

When observing and testing for the ATNR posture, you must make a distinction between the extent this posture is assumed by the individual upon active rotation of the head and the extent to which this posture is imposed by passive rotation of the head by the examiner. The pattern cannot be imposed on a normal infant, child, or adult to a completely obligatory extent, that is, to the extent that as long as the head is held to the side, the individual cannot escape the pattern (Paine et al 1964). It is often difficult to elicit this pattern in normal children, and it is most often observed as a posture the infant will spontaneously assume (Fig 7-4).

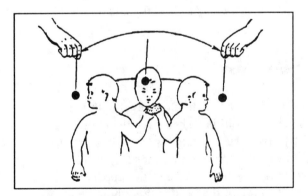

Figure 7-3 Evaluate ATNR response by presenting a visual stimulus and encouraging the infant to follow it through 180 degrees. Note the position of the extremities.

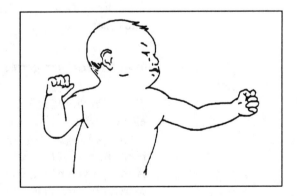

Figure 7-4 Spontaneous assumption of the ATNR position.

195

If you do not see the typical fencing, or bow and arrow, posture when the infant actively turns his head, you may turn his head first to one side and then the other and observe the position of his upper and lower extremities (Fig 7-5). Of course, an imposed ATNR should not be so obligatory that the infant cannot move the extremities out of the fencing posture. The postural pattern may be stronger in the upper extremities or the lower extremities, depending on the age of the infant, (Carter and Campbell 1975; Coryell and Cardinali 1979). Additionally, the postural set may be stronger on the right side than on the left side (Bobath 1954).

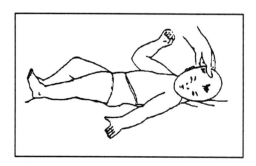

Figure 7-5 Attempt to elicit the ATNR by passively turning the head to one side. Wait for the response to develop.

The same testing situation for the neonate and the infant also can be used for the older child or the adult. In addition, you can passively move the extremities through extension and flexion and note the muscular resistance that occurs in relation to the position of the head. If the ATNR is present and the client's head is turned to the left, you would expect there to be an increase in the resistance to passive flexion of the left elbow that reflects a change in extensor activity.

You may evaluate the presence of the ATNR in older children by observing motor behaviors such as sitting and reaching, grasping toys, eating, creeping, walking, running, and skipping. Note the position of the upper and lower extremities relative to the position of the head. In addition to your observations, which are extremely important, there are some testing activities that can be performed by a child 6 years of age and older.

(1) Railroad track, or arm extension, test

The child should stand with the arms flexed to shoulder level with his elbows extended and wrists in neutral position. Then have the child close his eyes and remain quietly erect. Next rotate his head passively to both sides and observe the posture of his upper extremities (Fig 7-6). Although you may not observe an ATNR positioning of the upper extremities, resistance to passive turning of the head is thought to be an attempt by the child to avoid the disorganizing influence of the ATNR (Ayres 1972; Silver 1952).

Figure 7-6 Railroad track test for the presence of the ATNR. Passively turn the head and note the posture of the upper extremities.

(2) Quadruped position

The child assumes the all-fours position, and the therapist either passively rotates the child's head to both sides or he is encouraged to turn his head by looking at a visual target. Observe the amount of flexion in his skull arm and note the amount of head resistance (Fig 7-7). Ayres (1972) considers a slight degree of elbow flexion to be indicative of the influences of the ATNR, whereas Parmenter (1975) states that visible muscle activity changes and that elbow flexion to 30 degrees in the skull side arm would be considered normal. Parr et al (1974) indicate that as much as 49 degrees of flexion is normal. Again, resistance to passive movement of the head is believed to be a function of a child's attempt to avoid the disorganizing influences of eliciting the ATNR.

Another test using the all-fours position is the quadruped reflex inhibiting posture in which the skull hand is on the hip and the knee on the side of the face is off the floor (Fig. 7-8). Observations are made of the ability to maintain this posture during active head rotation (Connolly and Michael 1984; Sieg and Schuster 1979).

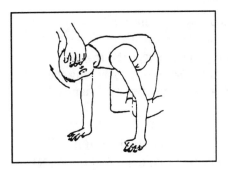

Figure 7-7 Quadruped position for evaluating ATNR.

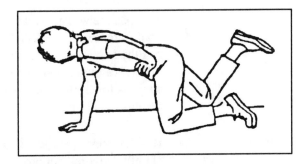

Figure 7-8 Quadruped reflex inhibiting posture. Note the ability to maintain this posture during active head rotation.

197

(3) Supine position

The child lies supine with his shoulders flexed and elbows extended in front of his body. Place your hands on the child's hands and apply some resistance by pushing down steadily. Then ask the child to turn his head to the right and left. As you resist the extension of both arms, note the amount of elbow flexion of his skull arm (Fig 7-9). If the ATNR is influencing the muscle activity, the child may not be able to keep his skull arm in complete extension.

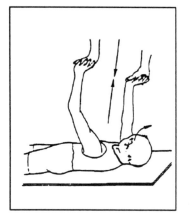

Figure 7-9 Supine test position for the influence of the ATNR.

Another test that can be done using the supine position requires the child to rest his arms beside his body, with his palms down and about 6 inches from his hips. Turn the child's head to both sides. When this position is used, measurement of flexion of the skull arm is made with an electrogoniometer.

Studies have been performed to determine if one position is better than another in detecting the presence of the ATNR in preschool children. The quadruped test posture produced significantly larger responses, a mean of 29 degrees, than did the supine test posture, which had a mean of 6 degrees (Zemke and Draper 1984). These results support those by Sieg and Schuster (1979), who looked at the differences between the quadruped position, the quadruped reflex inhibiting posture, and the standing position. Although all three postures revealed the presence or absence of the ATNR, the quadruped reflex inhibiting posture more readily revealed the presence of the ATNR position when compared with the other positions in children with learning disabilities.

Another maneuver was examined in which tension was added to the supine posture by moving the child's body down the table until his legs hung over the table edge, with his hips and upper body still supported. The child was then asked to raise his legs up even with the table and hold them there. The added tension produced significant increases in elbow flexion. In boys, the mean elbow flexion increase was from 6 to 10 degrees with added tension. The girls' mean responses changed only slightly, from 3 to 4 degrees. Blindfolding did not produce significant changes in the amount of elbow flexion of the skull arm in either group.

Test posture was also addressed in a study by Warren (1984), who found no differences in the ATNR between a supine or a seated position in healthy adults or in adults who had hemiplegia. Stress did make a difference in the quality of the response. Stress, added by having the subjects forcefully squeeze a hard rubber pad in their normal hands, resulted in a larger ATNR response.

Besides using specific test postures, using good observation of the client's activities can provide additional insight into the effect the ATNR may be having on posture and movement. When either performing posture examinations or observing how a client performs movements

198

and executes tasks, keep an eye open for subtle changes in the character of extremity postures or strength in relation to position of his head. Include active head movement in your evaluation procedures in order to examine these influences routinely.

(4) Walking on heels

Have the child or adult walk on her heels and observe the position of her head and of her upper extremities. Having the child or adult do this backward or blindfolded increases stress, which may elicit an ATNR.

(5) Standing on one foot

As the child or adult stands on one foot, observe the position of her upper extremities in relation to her head. Closing her eyes may make the activity more stressful.

(6) Tandem walking

While the child or adult walks with one foot in front of the other (tandem walking), first forward and then backward, observe the posture of her upper extremities in relation to the position of her head. Performing the task backward is more difficult and may add stress, and closing her eyes may make the activity more difficult.

(7) Walking a balance beam

While the child or adult walks forward and backward on a balance beam, observe her head and arms as mentioned above. Walking backward is more difficult than walking forward, and closing her eyes makes the activity even more difficult.

You should be concerned about the presence of the ATNR only if it is observed in more than half of the test or task situations. If you observe the ATNR posture only once, it should be noted for future reference and comparison, but it is not possible to conclude that the ATNR is definitely present or having significant effect on posture or movement.

The ATNR posture is evident at birth. There is a difference in the posture of the arms and the legs that follows a sequence of appearance. The reason it is important to know some of these seemingly little details is that you will be evaluating infants of different ages and at different stages in their development. These relatively subtle changes, or progressions, may become meaningful when you attempt to make a judgment as to the child's condition or state of development. If a particular posture or movement is more apparent at 6 months than at 3 months, you will know what to expect and will be able to use the information in subsequent examinations.

The legs show a maximum response 1 week after birth; the response declines in overt expression by 12 weeks. The posture of the arms becomes increasingly apparent until 6 weeks, after which it declines (Coryell and Cardinali 1979). This history of appearance can be described as an inverted-U model in which the pattern begins, reaches a peak, and then declines (Fig 7-10). This was confirmed by Paine et al (1964) and Provost (1981), who reported that the peak incidence occurs between 4 and 8 weeks of age, with a gradual decline of the posture by 4 to 6 months. You can see that researchers continue to report a range of ages in which some activity occurs. Again, these ages are relative guides. The life history of a particular child will begin to become more clear as you perform repeated evaluations. It is not possible to make an absolute decision at a single point in time, but you will begin to get an idea about what may be expected to happen.

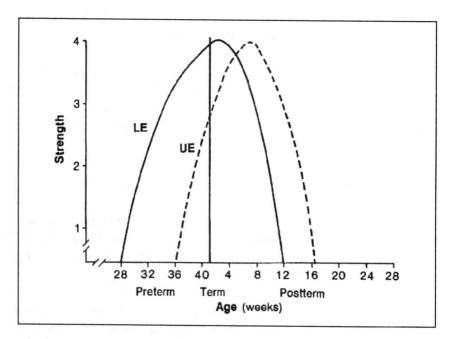

Figure 7-10 This graph represents the history of the appearance of the ATNR. Note that this history follows an inverted-U model. The lower extremities demonstrate ATNR postures earlier than the upper extremities, and the postures disappear, or become integrated, earlier in the lower extremities than in the upper extremities. From Stengel et al (1985), reprinted with permission.

The ATNR posture has been noted in fetuses between 8 and 20 weeks gestational age, with frequency increasing with increasing age (Hirt 1967). Saint-Anne Dargassies (1977) described the ATNR posture in a premature infant of 32 weeks gestational age, yet a picture published in the same article shows a 28-week-old infant demonstrating the posture in his lower extremities. The evolution of the ATNR posture was observed in one preterm infant. The presence of the posture was noted in his legs at 32 weeks, his arms at 26 to 37 weeks, and his trunk at 41 weeks

(Carter and Campbell 1975). This study illustrates the additive character of the reflex before birth. Do not forget that this study is of only one infant. It is difficult to make broad generalizations from a sample of one. Nonetheless, the observations are valuable in providing insight into the nature and timing of the components of the response.

Although the asymmetric tonic posture declines in intensity by 4 to 6 months of age, it can be elicited in the older child or adult under stressful and nonstressful situations. At no time, however, should it interfere with motor activity, but rather the reflex pattern should enhance the supportive framework of a voluntary motion. An obligatory response is never normal.

The presence of an ATNR is important if it is obligatory.

If the ATNR neck posture either is strong or is obligatory at any age, symmetry of posture may not be attained, and many movement patterns may not develop. An obligatory ATNR will prevent the infant from touching and exploring his own body. The infant will not be able to bring his hands to the midline and play with them or to bring his hands to his mouth and suck on his fingers. All of these activities are performed by normal infants in the course of their development. It would appear that these activities are necessary for developing body image and for acquiring everyday skills, such as self-feeding and dressing. In children that retain the ATNR pattern, these skills do not develop, are delayed in developing, or are deficient in quality.

The argument may be made that the ATNR itself is not directly responsible for these deficits. It is true that cause-effect proof does not exist. It seems clear, however, that if the child is limited in the variety of motor patterns available, completely normal adaptive movements will not occur. If the few patterns available are directly antagonistic to the movement desired, then the new movement either will not be expressed or will of necessity be a less than effective and efficient movement. For instance, try rolling over using an ATNR pattern. Hold the position rigidly while attempting to do so. What difficulties were encountered and how did you compensate for them? If only your arms are considered, you can see that extension will block rolling beyond side lying. To roll over, the child will have to use unusual and inefficient patterns if rolling is to occur at all. It does not seem important clinically whether the posture itself is the problem or whether the conditions that limit the movements are the problem. Treatment is not so much a matter of inhibiting or preventing the expression of the posture as it is helping the child develop new varieties of movement. When other choices are available, the ATNR will be less used and thus less dominant. The more a pattern is used, the more preferred it becomes.

Persistence of this posture may therefore prevent the child from becoming functionally independent. The infant dominated by the ATNR posture will not be able to raise his head symmetrically when prone or supine. Reach and grasp will be impaired. Visualize how this posture would interfere with his ability to sit unsupported or maintain balance

201

well enough to walk. In the presence of a persistent influence of the ATNR on movement, almost every important motor skill will fail to develop.

In addition, a persistent obligatory posture may result in structural deformities, such as a scoliosis or a subluxation or dislocation of the hip of the skull leg. Soft tissues are quite plastic and adaptable so that if a particular posture is maintained for an extended period, muscle tissue develops contractures, connective tissue shortens, and the joint mechanics become altered. In fact, the addition of the ATNR testing in the quadruped-reflex-inhibiting position has proven beneficial in the early identification of scoliosis in healthy school children. Children who demonstrated a positive ATNR showed a relationship between the convexity of the curvature and the side of the ATNR. For instance, children who showed a left lumbar or thoracic curve had a left ATNR (Connolly and Michael 1984).

A child with a dominate ATNR pattern of movement will have difficulty visually tracking an object across an arc of 180 degrees. The infant may be able to focus on an object and begin to follow it visually on the chin side of the ATNR, but he appears to have difficulty following the object to the midline or past the midline. The lack of visual attention and tracking may affect not only reaching and grasping, but in the older child, it could affect reading and writing across a paper. Gesell noted the inability of normal infants to follow objects visually beyond the midline if an ATNR was present.

It has been suggested that the older child and adult with a persistent but not obligatory ATNR will have impaired motor planning skills and bilateral motor coordination (Ayres 1972). Reading comprehension may also be compromised (Parmenter 1975).

After cerebral catastrophes, such as stroke or brain trauma, or with degenerative diseases, the ATNR pattern may appear or reappear, depending on your point of view. Whether this ATNR posture is equivalent to that seen in infants is open for debate. The presence of the ATNR in adults with brain injury and in developing children has traditionally been considered to result from of a lack of inhibitory influences that higher centers of control exert over lower centers. Obviously, this is a reflex-hierarchical view of the problem. If more contemporary theory is considered, the explanation may be that this early postural pattern is easier for the individual to assume and maintain than are complex postures.

When the brain is damaged, it is possible that certain integrative functions are compromised, eliminating the control or expression of a variety of movements. The ability to control the amount of tension generated in the muscle or the timing of when to turn the contraction on or off produces stiff and ineffective movements that no longer resemble the smooth coordinated ones. Gravity presents a new challenge to balance and muscle power. Some of the once preferred patterns that were expressed as far back as fetal life may be simpler and more readily available than complex patterns. The ability to generate novel movements is impaired because at least one system--the nervous system--is not functioning normally. The requirements of the activity or skill may be too difficult for the client, so postures and movements that require less strength and balance are used.

Generally, a stereotyped and obligatory response that cannot be counteracted by spontaneous movement is observed in only pathological conditions. The ATNR posture seen in normal infants is characterized by variability of their patterns and is readily changed through the generation of another movement.

Symmetric Tonic Neck Reflex

The STNR posture, like the ATNR, is influenced by changes of the relative position of the head and the trunk. When the head is extended, extensor activity predominates in the upper extremities and flexor activity predominates in the lower extremities. Upon flexion of the head, flexor activity predominates in the upper extremities and extensor activity predominates in the lower extremities (Fig 7-11).

Controversy exists concerning the possible influence of the STNR on posture in the adult in stressful activities. Hellebrandt et al (1956) demonstrated classical STNR responses in normal adults. With the subjects in the modified quadrupedal position, ventroflexion of their heads was associated with elbow joint flexion while dorsiflexion of their heads evoked elbow extension. However, Tokizane (1951) indicated that in normal adults, flexion of their heads resulted in flexion of all extremities while extension promoted extension of all extremities.

The STNR posture appears later in development than the ATNR and thus appears to replace the asymmetric patterns with more symmetric ones. This event would make bilateral manual activities such as bringing the hands to the mouth easier to develop or perform. This pattern could also help to diminish extensor activity in the prone position by assisting the four-point kneeling, or high-creep, position.

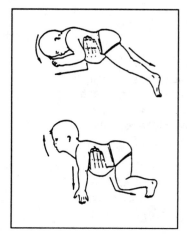

Figure 7-11 The symmetrical tonic neck reflex. Note the positioning of the extremities in relation to flexion or extension of the head.

203

In the four-point position, both arms are extended and both legs are flexed, symmetrically. The knees are forward under the trunk, in adduction, lifting the abdomen and chest from the supporting surface. The head is well up from the floor, making it possible for the eyes to gaze directly ahead. Attaining the high-creep position requires sufficient muscular strength in the upper extremities to allow the infants to push against the surface, raising the head, abdomen, and chest off the surface, and to shift the center of mass backward. Infants will rock forward and backward in this position. Generally, infants do not perform forward progression in this posture because their hands are needed to support their trunks above the ground. However, some infants will move forward from the high-creep position by rocking back on their heels to support their body weight and then extending both arms forward. As their arms bear the weight, both knees are brought forward in a hopping movement.

When weight bearing is gradually released from the hands during rocking in the high-creep position, the infant becomes able to support the body above the ground with a tripod stance of one arm and both legs. Rocking with reciprocal movements of the extremities and with the abdomen off the ground generally precedes the advent of creeping forward (Gesell 1954; Goldfield 1989; Thelen 1979). Remember in the previous discussion that the ATNR supports the asymmetric pattern of the arms and legs during pivoting while in the prone position. This support now becomes useful for locomotion because there are adequate balance reactions and sufficient muscular strength to eliminate the need to support the body with both hands.

Before eliciting the STNR, observe the infant, child, or adult during posture and movement. Note the position of his extremities in relation to the position of his head. The hopping done in an attempt to creep that was described earlier is often called the bunny hop, and it is a characteristic movement in the presence of a dominant STNR. The STNR may also be observed when the child is supine and attempts to sit up. As shown in Figure 7-12, the child may first flex his head and then flex his upper extremities while his lower extremities extend, adduct, and may even cross (Bobath and Bobath 1972).

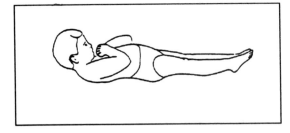

Figure 7-12 A child with STNR influences demonstrates a stereotypical pattern when attempting to sit up. With flexion of his head, his upper extremities flex and his lower extremities extend, adduct, and may even cross.

Test Procedure

The STNR may be elicited in any of five positions, depending on the age of the individual: (1) ventral suspension over the examiner's hand, (2) prone over your lap, (3) supported sitting, (4) all-fours, and (5) standing plantigrade. First flex the head and note the response of the extremities, and then observe the extremities when the head is extended.

One way to remember the response is to visualize a dog crawling under a fence. As the head is flexed to go under the fence, his front legs flex and the hind legs extend. As the dog comes up under the other side of the fence, his head extends, the front legs extend, and the hind legs flex in order to bring the body under the fence.

If you do not see a response when manipulating the head in these positions, passive manipulation of the extremities when the head is flexed or extended may demonstrate some change in muscle tension that is consistent with the position of the head.

Bender (1976) also describes testing for the STNR in the all-fours position by resisting forward creeping at the shoulders and backward creeping at the buttocks. The entire creep pattern is observed to note the position of the head, upper extremities, trunk, and lower extremities. The static hand and knee position has also been used by Berk and DeGangi (1983) to assess the influences of the symmetrical tonic neck posture. In this test, the head is passively extended or flexed. The amount of elbow flexion present when the neck is flexed is noted and the body position with the neck extended is described.

Considerable controversy exists over whether there is a presence of the STNR in normal development and what its significance is when observed or elicited. The STNR is observed transiently, with the greatest frequency occurring between 4 and 6 months of age (Capute et al 1984). The postural set is suppressed or incorporated into other postures and movements by 8 to 12 months of age (Milani-Comparetti and Gidoni 1967). The possible role of the STNR in development appears to be limited. It emerges at a time when the Landau (a righting reaction you will encounter later) is already developed, so it probably also influences the positional response of lower extremities, causing them to flex in response to head extension. It is possible that the STNR is not a distinct entity but, rather, reflects the intersection of a decreasing tonic labyrinthine influence in the supine position with an evolution of muscle tension changes in infancy (Capute et al 1982*b*).

The STNR supports the all-fours posture by promoting flexion at a time when extensor activity has been dominant. The all-fours position is symmetrical in nature and thus the STNR counters the asymmetry promoted by the ATNR. The STNR must be modified and incorporated into functional postures and movements in order for a child to creep with

205

reciprocal movements of his extremities. As noted earlier, if the STNR is dominant in the all-fours position, when the head is extended it is accompanied by extension of the arms and flexion of the legs, so that the buttocks rest on the heels. When the child attempts to creep, he hops forward like a rabbit because he is unable to lift his buttocks from his heels without falling on his face.

In addition, the presence of an obligatory STNR may cause difficulties with walking and with getting onto the floor from standing. A persistent obligatory STNR may cause spinal flexion deformities, and sitting posture is affected when the child persistently sits back on his heels.

Tonic Labyrinthine Reflex

The TLR is named after the labyrinths, which are sensory organs that are stimulated by the position of the head in relation to gravity. It is thus assumed that the vestibular, or labyrinthine system, is responsible for the postural patterns noted. This reflex is described as producing different responses, depending on the position of the head. When the body is supine, the posture is one of greater extension, and when the body is prone, flexion dominates.

Posture, muscle strength, and the environment must be considered when looking at the TLR.

Although this postural dominance has been assigned to the labyrinths, muscle strength and environmental constraints also must be taken into account when considering this reflex. The posture of full-term infants is generally biased toward flexion as a consequence of being confined in the uterus before birth. In contrast, preterm infants' posture is more extended as a result of being in an unconfined environment at an earlier age.

When placed prone, the newborn full-term infant remains in a posture dominated by flexion. When the infant is placed supine, there is less flexion. Although this postural change has been ascribed to the TLR, it may actually be the result of the pull of gravity on the extremities. Remember that the newborn infant has little capability against gravity.

Let us review the development of movements in prone and supine in order to study any possible relationship the movements may have with the TLR. As the child develops and gains strength, the flexed postures in the prone position are replaced with extension. Initially, the infant lifts his head against gravity by developing extensor strength, or control, in the cervical spine. Initially, there is no support when on his elbows or hands. As extensor strength is increased, with control further down the spine, the infant lifts his head and thorax off the floor and supports the weight of his head and upper trunk on his elbows. Later, the child practices an axial extension posture that has been described variously as a plane-like posture, a swimming posture, or a pivot prone position. At this time, the infant lifts his head and thorax and supports his upper trunk on open hands and extended arms. The child learns to roll first from prone to supine and then from supine to prone. Lastly, the child will rock back by flexing his hip and knee joints and assume the all-fours position, bearing weight on extended arms and flexed knees.

In the supine position, the newborn engages in active kicking and what appear to be random movements of his arms. As strength develops, the child actively moves against the gravitational field by bringing his hands to the midline and toys to his mouth. Next, his legs are lifted high in extension, and the baby grasps his feet by bringing his hands to his feet and begins to lift his head in flexion against gravity. Later, the infant brings his feet to his mouth. After this time, the infant develops good flexion control against gravity but no longer tolerates the supine position and rolls to prone.

In the adult, Tokizane (1951), using electromyographic recordings, demonstrated that the vertical position produces more activity in the flexor muscles in all the limbs while in the prone inverted position; with the head down, extensor muscles show more spontaneous activity in all the limbs (Fig 7-13). Because adults should show little TLR and show strong righting reactions, it may be argued that the head down, or inverted, position facilitates extension through the action of the righting reactions rather than the TLR. In treatment, the inverted position may be used to facilitate extension, even though we may not correctly identify the underlying reflexes involved.

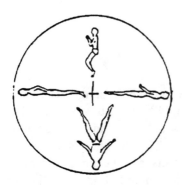

Figure 7-13 Increased electromyographic activity in flexor muscles when vertical compared with increased activity in extensor muscles when positioned head down.

Test Procedure

To test for the TLR in the neonate or young child, place the infant prone and then supine with his head in the midline and let his extremities rest by his side. Observe the infant's posture and movement. Are there a variety of resting postures? Does the child move into and maintain age-appropriate antigravity postures that we just summarized above? Are there a variety of individual extremity movements?

In addition, the following manipulations can be done with the infant in the prone or supine position. Passively move the extremities and note whether there is less or more flexor muscle activity, or resistance to extensor movements, when the child is prone than when he is supine. In the supine position, place your hand behind the child's head or shoulders and begin to bring him to a sitting position. Note whether there is more resistance than normal to head and shoulder flexion, because this indicates an increase in extensor muscle activity. Resistance of his shoulders to forward flexion can be tested by bringing his upper extremities forward and across his chest. If the TLR is present, excessive resistance will be felt or his arms will pull backward. You can also lift the child's hips and bring his knees toward his chest. If the reflex is present, you will feel increased resistance to trunk flexion.

The following tests can be done with the child prone. First, raise his head into extension and note the amount of resistance. Second, bring his shoulders into extension and note the resistance (Fig 7-14). Other tests have also been developed that quantitatively examine the amount of flexor and extensor dominance in the prone and supine positions. The prone extension postural test is used as part of certain test batteries to look at sensory integrative dysfunction in children (Ayres 1972; Bowman and Katz 1984; Harris 1981; Gregory-Flock and Yerxa 1984).

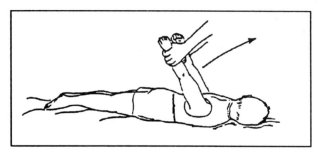

Figure 7-14 To test for flexor influences of the TLR with the child prone, bring his shoulders into extension and note the amount of resistance to the movement.

A game called airplane is used on the DeGangi-Berk Test of Sensory Integration (Berk and DeGangi 1983). In this test, the child assumes an antigravity extensor posture with his shoulders abducted to 90 degrees and his elbows fully extended. The amount of support provided by the examiner, the posture of the arms, and the amount of extension of his trunk and hips are scored. The amount of time that the child can maintain the posture is also obtained.

A game called monkey is also used on the DeGangi-Berk test to evaluate supine flexion. The child holds onto a pole and crosses his legs at the knees over the pole. How the child assumes the antigravity posture of flexion is scored. The amount of time that the child can maintain the position is obtained.

Another test that can be used to evaluate supine flexion is to ask the child of 6 or more years of age to curl up from the supine position without the advantage of clasping his arms around his knees. A normal child should have sufficient antigravity flexion to perform this task. The antigravity supine flexion posture is also a clinical observation on the Sensory Integration and Praxis Tests (Ayres 1989). In severe cases of increased flexor muscle activity while prone, the child's hips will be flexed extremely and cannot be extended, and the child cannot be placed on his abdomen (Bobath and Bobath 1972).

The prone extension posture is shown in Figure 7-15. With age, children demonstrate the ability to assume and maintain this posture. Children who have been identified as learning disabled are unable to assume and maintain this posture at age-appropriate ages. However, these children do not compare differently from a group of 4 year olds. Thus, the prone extension test should not be used as an evaluation tool for 4-year-old children to differentiate between normal or learning disabled. By age 5 years, this test can discriminate between normal and learning disabled children. Clinically, it was believed that a child 6 years and older could assume and maintain the prone extension posture for 20 to 30 seconds. Recent evidence indicates that the expected duration for children 6 years and older is 60 seconds (Gregory-Flock and Yerxa 1984).

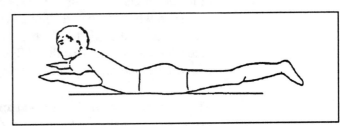

Figure 7-15 Prone extension, or pivot-prone, posture.

The inability to assume and maintain the prone extension posture has been considered to be the result of either an inadequate integration of the TLR or an immature labyrinthine neck righting reaction. More recently, Ayres (1989) indicates that the inability to assume this position should be interpreted as insufficient vestibular processing rather than as a poorly integrated TLR or immature labyrinthine neck righting reaction. The inability of children to assume and maintain the prone extension posture often has been considered a primary indicator of a vestibular syndrome (Ayres 1972).

However, as will be noted in Section IV, recent studies by have shown that the postural abnormalities found in children with learning disabilities are not the result of peripheral vestibular dysfunction (Shumway-Cook et al 1987; Horak et al 1988). The problems appear to be in the central functions of integrating visual, vestibular, and somatosensory information because these children have great difficulty when faced with intersensory conflicts (see Chapter 11). The authors suggest that this condition is likely to be the case with many types of central dysfunction, including cerebral palsy. It appears that the standing balance and prone extension postures cannot be used as vestibular tests but rather as general balance tests. Difficulty in performing these tests cannot be ascribed to the vestibular system. (See Chapter 15).

The reason these research results are important is that if we assume the problems that have just been described are the result of vestibular dysfunction, then the conclusion that will be reached after the evaluation is that this system is faulty. Treatment will then be aimed at "normalizing" vestibular sensitivity. Traditionally, this has been accomplished by having the child engage either in spinning or rotating activities or in bouncing, rolling, rocking, and other such activities assumed to be vestibular in nature. Obviously, these treatments will be based incorrectly and thus will be less effective than programs designed to improve intersensory integration or to correct biomechanical problems or other mechanisms that may be involved.

Clearly, it has been observed that children with developmental disabilities will have dominance of either flexion or extension, depending on the position either they assume or in which they are placed. They will demonstrate difficulty with prone and supine activities as they have been described. This information is useful for prediction purposes in evaluating whether the difficulty is ascribed to the labyrinths or to something else. For this purpose, the name is not important. However, when faced with clinical evaluation on which treatment will be based, it is another matter. These old assumptions should be reconsidered, and perhaps this reflex, if this constellation of responses can be considered to be a single entity, should be named something else.

The TLR, or postural changes that appear when in the prone and supine positions, is considered to be present at birth, but the exact ages of onset or integration are unknown. Heriza (1984), in a study of 30 preterm infants, indicated that the strength of the TLR followed an inverted U-shaped developmental profile, with the strength of the reflex reaching a peak by 38 weeks GA and decreasing in strength by 8 months postnatal age. In a study of 149 full-term infants, the TLR in the prone position (TLR-prone) was present in 80% of infants at 2 weeks of age, persisted throughout the first 18 months of life, and diminished to less than 30% of the children by 2 years of age (Capute et al 1982b). In a subsequent study of 381 infants, the TLR-prone did not peak until 4 to 6 months of age and overlapped with the presence of the Landau response (a righting reaction). The TLR-supine peaked at 2 months of age and steadily declined through the first year (Capute et al 1984).

The persistence of obligatory flexor and extensor patterns, in relation to these particular postures, may prevent the acquisition of motor skills. When prone, the child cannot lift his head or support his weight on forearms or later on extended arms because either the flexor activity is too strong or the extensor activity is ineffective. If the child's body is held stiffly in flexion, he cannot roll from prone to supine.

When in the supine position, flexor weakness or extensor dominance prevents the child from coming to a sitting position. His hands cannot be brought to the midline and, consequently, cannot be placed in his mouth. The child cannot roll to prone. All these motor skills can be prevented by the overpowering extensor muscle activity, and all further developmental milestones will be difficult or impossible to attain.

If you would like to get some idea of how dominant extensor activity would affect the ability to perform simple movements, do the following exercise. Attempt to assume a sitting position while holding your neck, trunk, and extremities in a rigidly extended posture. Let your head fall back as you try to sit up. In this same posture, try to roll over.

Summation and Combined Effects of the ATNR, STNR, and TLR

Remember that a problem reflex rarely, if ever, occurs in isolation. Findings usually occur in clusters, which compound the difficulty for the child who is dominated by them. Naturally, we might expect that the ATNR, STNR, and TLR will exert their influences together. The resulting body posture might be described as resulting from the algebraic sum of the patterns of flexor and extensor dominance that occurs with each one. For example, if a child who exhibits both the TLR and STNR is placed in the prone position and has his head subsequently flexed, his upper extremities may be flexed strongly because of the combined influence of the TLR and the STNR, while his lower extremities may demonstrate normal postural activity because of the opposite effects of the TLR and the STNR.

Because of the combined effects of these postural patterns, it often is difficult to determine which one is the most dominant or if all are exerting the same amount of influence. A clear and detailed description of the movements and postures may provide the best record for further reference. Note that two or three of the postural patterns appear to be present.

It is quite possible that the STNR and the TLR, in particular, are not actual postural patterns as the ATNR appears to be. These two reflexes may simply involve the response of the body to ineffective capacities. Clearly, clients with central nervous system deficits suffer from the inability to generate adequate muscle tension in a properly timed and sequenced activation of muscles (see Crutchfield and Barnes, 1984, for a thorough discussion of these conditions). In addition, newborn infants go through sequences of flexor and extensor dominance, and they are initially very weak and ineffective against gravity, so that muscle strength is a major factor in the appearance of motor patterns. Many of the effects described can be explained on these bases. The patterns clearly seem to exist but may not be the result of neck reflexes or vestibular dysfunction.

Lack of knowledge of the exact mechanism does not render invalid either the evaluation or the treatment of the affected child or adult. The importance of evaluation is to use the predictive data, which has been generated, to help determine the child's status. This information is provided in Chapter 10. Evaluation of how the client moves spontaneously and under manipulations provides insight into the strengths and deficiencies the client must capitalize on or overcome to improve in motor control. Treatment should be aimed at assisting the client in developing a variety of movement abilities rather than specifically inhibiting or facilitating a particular reflex. These motor patterns may simply represent a limited repertoire of movements, and because they are available and provide the easiest methods for the client to move, they are practiced and practiced until they become more dominant, or preferred, by the child. Whatever the child is asked to do or wishes to do, it will be accomplished with the motor patterns that are available, just as the infant steps with the kicking pattern of muscular activity. Additionally, problems with solving intersensory conflicts may contribute to the patterns that evolve.

Study Questions:

1. Why is it said that the ATNR coordinates the eyes and hand for later functional skill?

2. Why must you distinguish between a spontaneous ATNR and one elicited by passive turning of the head?

3. In reading about reflexes and reactions you may encounter the word obligatory. Exactly what does it mean and why should you be concerned with it?

4. Some people think that the STNR and the TLR do not really exist. Defend their stance.

Chapter 8 - Righting Reactions

Before delving into righting and balance reactions, it is necessary to realize that all standing and moving reactions to the forces of gravity are governed by somatosensory, visual, and vestibular influences acting in concert when the three inputs are available and functioning appropriately (See Chapters 11 and 15). Certainly, for testing purposes, either one or two of the systems may be negated, forcing the body to react under the influence of the third system only. Under normal circumstances, however, all three systems will be called into play as the body attempts to maintain balance and an upright posture.

Righting reactions, thus, are those reactions that either bring the head into relation with the trunk or orient the head in a normal functional position relative to the ground. They are automatic reactions that enable the body to assume the normal standing posture and to preserve its balance in the process of changing from lying to sitting to standing, through head control. In the absence of head control, a baby will not learn to sit or stand up.

There are two kinds of righting reactions: those that orient the head and body when rotation occurs and those that serve to orient the head in space and in relation to the ground. You will also encounter the righting reactions that align the trunk with the head when either is turned or rotated. These reactions are the neck-on-body (NOB) and body-on-body (BOB) reactions, and they will be described later in this chapter under rolling.

There are three reactions that work together to adjust tne position of the head in space so that the head is vertical and the mouth horizontal is with the ground. These are the optical, labyrinthine, and body on head righting reactions. Another reaction will be discussed in this section: the Landau reflex. The Landau reflex is a particular combination of some righting reactions.

As you study righting reactions, you will notice that the reactions follow a definite sequential development and that the stages in the sequence coincide with certain stages in motor development. Much of this sequential expression is probably related to the gain in muscular strength the infant achieves over time. Thus, to roll over, get up on hands and knees, sit-up, and stand, righting reactions must be available, and the underlying muscle strength and control necessary to use the reactions in these functional ways also must be present.

Even though righting reactions appear to work in concert, it is important to be able to recognize and elicit each one separately, because the

> Righting reactions:
>
> Labyrinthine
>
> Optical
>
> Body on head
>
> Landau

> Muscle strength and control must be available in order for righting reactions to work.

knowledge gained from ascertaining the status of each not only gives a clue as to the infants stage of motor development but may also enable us to perform more definitive evaluations to help diagnose the client's difficulties.

Initially, the therapist should observe the movements of the child or adult who is prone, supine, sitting, and standing. The first clue to look for is how the head position is controlled and how well it is controlled under different demands. For example, on the pull-to-sitting maneuver, does the individual have either complete head lag or partial head lag? Will his head right if the baby is supported by the therapist around his shoulders or upper trunk? Will the child momentarily right his head and then let it drop? What are the biomechanical restrictions?

Many times the position of the trunk and extremities dictates the position of the head. Try sitting on a high stool with your pelvis tilted posteriorly so that you are sitting on your sacrum. Now take away any support from your legs and maintain this position for a minute or so. Undoubtedly, you will find your abdominals quivering, your lower extremities held stiffly out in front of you in extension, and your upper extremities held away from your body and moving about to maintain balance. What about your head? In this precarious, rounded trunk position, the head is very difficult to right fully. Thus the child who sits in this manner may not be lacking righting reactions as much as proper posture of his trunk and adequate muscular strength and endurance to assume and maintain an appropriate position. And do not forget range of motion, because soft tissue, bony, or other restrictions will also affect these abilities.

> Each individual righting reaction may give clues as to the stage of development and the infant's diagnosis.

Labyrinthine Head Righting Reaction

The labyrinthine head righting reaction keeps the head in the normal upright position in space or brings it into the normal upright position. By normal position we mean head vertical, mouth horizontal. Stimuli from the otoliths of the labyrinths and the resulting contraction of the muscles of the neck will right the head.

The beginnings of this reaction are only faintly demonstrable in the neonate (Peiper 1963). Shaltenbrand (1928) states that when a newborn is held under the axilla in the vertical position, the head of the neonate usually sinks downward in response to the pull of gravity. If the head falls forward, then weak, repeated countermovements that temporarily lift the head into the normal vertical position may occur.

If the infant is tilted sideways, then the head falls sideways, and countermovements are very indistinct, as in Figure 8-1. The influence of this righting reaction on the head becomes more and more distinct with increasing age. Again, it would seem quite likely that the basic patterns required to elaborate the head righting reactions are present at or before birth. The neonate does not have sufficient strength in his neck

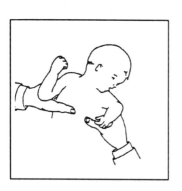

Figure 8-1 Lack of head righting reactions.

214

musculature to demonstrate the response. As he gains strength, the relative size of his head also decreases, thus permitting the full righting reaction to manifest itself.

There has been considerable argument as to whether the labyrinthine head righting reaction is present at birth. At birth, the baby is probably unable to right his head because the tiny muscles are simply not developed well enough to hold up the relatively huge head that he has. By 2 months of age, however, the infant is strong enough to begin to right his head.

Test Procedure

After observing head control in functional positions and activities, the therapist can alter the environment in an attempt to isolate the reactions. To test for this reaction you should hold the baby in space and use a blindfold on him. If you do not blindfold the baby, you may be witnessing a combination of the labyrinthine head righting and the optical righting reactions. In the normal testing position when the examiner holds the infant under his axilla, his head and body should assume a vertical position with his mouth in the horizontal plane (Fig 8-2).

When the baby is held prone or supine and blindfolded, does he attempt to lift his head (Fig 8-3)? Because we have not eliminated the pull of gravity on the head, he may right his head with the labyrinthine head righting reaction. If he does not attempt righting when blindfolded, will he attempt to do so with the blindfold removed? An affirmative answer may suggest that vestibular responses are not up to par. Toddlers and older children will often inhibit this reaction, especially if the examiner is trusted. Extreme care should be exercised that this intentional inhibition is not considered pathological.

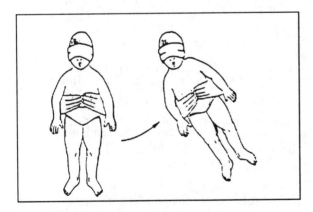

Figure 8-2 Testing for the labyrinthine righting reaction. Note that the child is blindfolded to eliminate the optical influences. Proper righting position is with the head vertical, mouth horizontal.

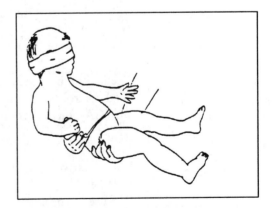

Figure 8-3 Labyrinthine righting reaction when suspended in supine.

215

Perhaps you can recall a time as a student when you stayed up too late at night. The next day in class, as the lecturer droned on and on about some obscure topic, your eyes closed slowly as your chin descended toward your chest. Suddenly the head snapped upright, the eyes opened wide, and you were again alert. Your stature with the professor was saved by the influence of the labyrinthine head righting reaction.

Divers must volitionally inhibit this reaction in executing a forward dive, because the labyrinthine head righting reaction causes the head to extend against the gravitational forces acting on it. Anyone who has attempted diving knows what happens when the chin is not tucked into the chest and the body does not enter the water headfirst--a painful and embarrassing belly flop. This is an example of the control we may exert on the labyrinthine righting reactions, which are with us throughout life.

Optical Head Righting Reactions

Normal head control is dependent on visual cues in addition to labyrinthine input. Therefore, in addition to gravity acting on the labyrinths for head control, vision also plays an important role. In fact, vision may play a more dominant role in the development of head righting than does the vestibular system. Lee and Aronson (1974) performed moving room experiments (see Chapter 1) in which children fell over when the room moved toward or away from them. Adults, on the other hand, increased body sway during the same activity, but they did not fall. The conclusion from this and other studies is that postural control in infants is more dependent on visual cues, but in adults it is more dependent on somatosensory inputs. However, when visual reactions are abolished in an otherwise normal individual, such as when blinded, little disturbance of the other righting reactions is apparent (Martin 1967). We also know that if vision is present in individuals who have had their labyrinths ablated, little disturbance is seen. Because there are redundant inputs from the vestibular, visual, and somatosensory systems that are used for postural control, it is quite possible to compensate for the loss of one system under most conditions.

The labyrinthine head and optical righting reactions combine to facilitate head control on the pull-to-sitting maneuver. At 37 weeks gestational age (GA), there is complete head lag on pull to sitting (Fig 8-4). By 41 weeks GA, the maneuver results in some straightening of the head, with increased activity of the neck flexors muscles. The ability to right the head improves greatly with maturation. At 2 months of age, there is little head lag as the infant is pulled into a sitting position. This is because the neck flexor muscles are sufficiently strong and both the labyrinthine head righting reaction and the optical righting are operational.

By 3 to 4 months of age, there is virtually no head lag because the head tends to follow the trunk (Fig 8-5). At 6 to 7 months of age, the child anticipates being pulled to a sitting position and can actually assist and lift his head from the supine position spontaneously, as seen in Figure 8-6 (Illingworth 1966).

Righting reactions will be inhibited severely if there is abnormal muscle activity present. Normal head control, then, is dependent on the appropriate muscle strength and the presence of righting reactions. The combined actions of the labyrinthine head and optical righting reactions result in the head being righted, as for upright locomotion, in relation to the ground and in space.

 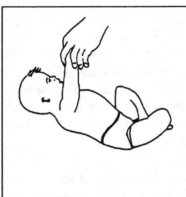 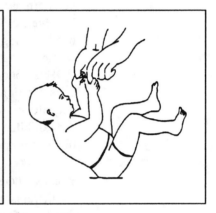

Figure 8-4 Complete head lag occurs in pull-to-sit maneuver in preterm infants.

Figure 8-5 At 3 or 4 months, there is no head lag.

Figure 8-6 By 6 or 7 months, active head flexion precedes the pull-to-sit maneuver.

Test Procedure

Evaluating the optical righting reaction requires the same procedures as for the labyrinthine righting except that the blindfold will not be used. The optical righting reflex may be present at birth and persists throughout life. Just as with the labyrinthine head righting reaction, however, it is not distinctly seen until 2 months of age, and as before, this lag may relate to the required gainin muscular strength.

Body Righting Reaction Acting on the Head

A third head righting reaction, the body righting reaction acting on the head (BOH), produces the same responses as do the labyrinthine head and optical righting reactions in that all three reactions cooperate in righting the head. The BOH also serves to right the head in response to

217

some portion of the body having touched a supporting surface. Therefore, stimulation of some pressure sense organs in those parts of the body that are resting on a surface causes a movement response of the head

An infant makes use of these righting reactions to lift his head when lying prone (Fig 8-7). In the absence of righting reactions, it would be dangerous to place an infant prone because he could not free his air passages and might smother; therefore, in addition to their function relative to balance, early righting responses are also important for the safety or protection of the infant.

According to Twitchell (1965), the BOH is the reflex used by the newborn to right his head from the prone position, because the labyrinthine righting reaction is not present in the newborn. Because the newborn has no means of exhibiting labyrinthine and optical righting, however, we have little justification in support of the notion that the head righting reactions are not present. The continued debate over whether the labyrinthine head righting reaction is present at birth and the BOH is not or vice versa does not have to be resolved for practical consideration. Because of the weakness in head righting muscles of the neonate, we may assume that if either or both are present at birth, they are exhibited very weakly and therefore do not become distinctly obvious until 2 months of age.

Because there are three reactions that are responsible for head control, the therapist must keep in mind possible interactions when testing for these reactions. If we test for the BOH reaction when the baby is prone and blindfolded, we have not eliminated the pull of gravity on his head; therefore, it is also possible that the labyrinthine head righting reaction is present and reacting (Fig 8-8).

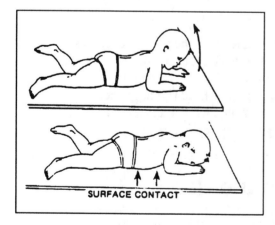

Figure 8-7 Surface contact stimulates the body on head righting reaction. The infant attempts to right the head while prone.

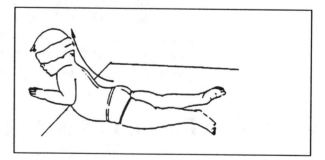

Figure 8-8 The optical influences in prone righting can be eliminated by blindfolding the child. It is not possible to eliminate any vestibular influences on the body on head righting reaction.

Landau Reaction

The Landau reaction is believed to represent the combined effects of the labyrinthine head righting reaction, the BOH reaction, the optical righting reaction, and perhaps the NOB and BOB. As such it is useful clinically for assessment of motor maturity. This reaction is also referred to as the sagittal plane righting reflex (Milani-Comparetti and Giodioni 1967a) and the symmetrical chain reflex in the abdominal position (Peiper 1963). The Landau reaction begins to appear at 3 months of age and reaches its peak at about 5 to 6 months, coinciding with the emergence or establishment of the labyrinthine head and optical righting reactions.

Test Procedure

To test for this reaction, the child is held in horizontal suspension by supporting the child prone and horizontally in space with your hand between his nipple line and his umbilicus. In testing for this reaction, note the degree of active extension of his head from the righting reaction influences (Fig 8-9).

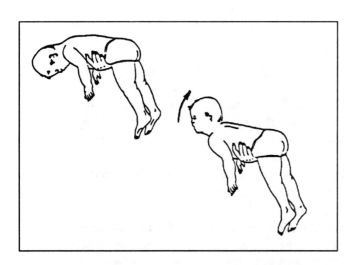

Figure 8-9 The Landau reaction. Note the position of the extremities and the extension of the trunk and head.

There is subsequent extension of the spine, with the concavity upward, that may be partly supported by tension on the back extensors. There is partial extension of the hips that may occur in response to the gravitational pull on the hip extensor muscles. Rhythmical kicking is also present at 4 months of age in 80% of the infants (Cupps 1976).

In this reaction, the arms never hang down but are retracted at the scapula, with the shoulders extended and the elbows either flexed or extended and the forearms pronated, as shown in Figure 8-10 (Cupps 1976). When this posture is spontaneously assumed by the child when prone on the floor, it is sometimes called the pivot prone position (Fig

219

8-11). How it got that name is not clear; however, at this same stage of development the child is practicing axial extension and, according to Doudlah (1981), moving in place by such actions as pivoting. Thus this activity has been called pivot prone (Martin 1989). The name really does not matter, what is important is that all of these patterns appear to be similar or identical and differ only in how they are elicited or observed. Naturally, they occur at the same time developmentally.

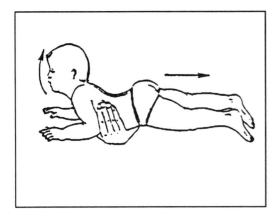

Figure 8-10 The Landau reaction. When fully developed, the trunk and lower extremities extend. Note that the arms also are extended at the shoulder.

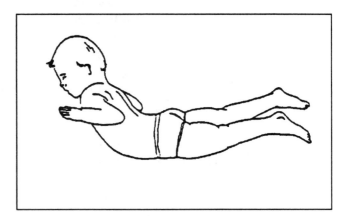

Figure 8-11 The ability to assume the prone extension, or pivot-prone posture, coincides with the appearance of the Landau reaction.

Although passive flexion of the head in this position is not part of the Landau (Mitchell 1962), this maneuver is useful in identifying motor problems. Therefore, once the infant has attained an extended position, passively flex his head and observe the reaction of the rest of his body. His trunk and lower extremities also should flex. Then remove your hand from the child's head and observe the return of the extension pattern. A normal child will again resume the same extended position with his head 90 degrees above the horizontal.

Children with inappropriate muscle activity may be unable to reassume this extended position with their heads above the horizontal. In addition, these children either may have a paucity of leg movement and not demonstrate any kicking movement or may hold their legs in an abnormal, rigid, extended pattern (Cupps 1976).

Remember that at the time the Landau appears, the child is going through a stage of extensor dominance. The reaction is so strong that it seems as if the baby is almost forced to produce the position simply by being suspended over your hand. After this time in development, the pattern is no longer shown in such an obligatory manner. The extremities become heavier as the child grows, and the position is not automatically assumed. You can ask an older child or an adult to assume this position on the floor if you want to evaluate the extension

220

posture and muscular power. Individuals with normal muscle strength should be able to maintain this position for 20 to 30 seconds (Ayres 1972).

McGrew et al (1985) showed that the Landau could be evaluated in subparts, including neck extension, trunk extension, hip extension, knee extension, and kicking activity during the testing period. Their study showed that full-term and preterm infants demonstrated age-related differences in the subscores. More preterm infants were noted to have full hip extension and atypical kicking patterns. The full-term infants showed a greater variability in response, a phenomenon noted earlier that is the hallmark of normalcy. Thus the Landau test that evaluates the different components may be useful in predicting infants at risk for future motor problems.

Absence of the Landau may be associated with motor weakness, motor neuron disease, or mental retardation (Mitchell 1962). An infant who droops limply in an inverted-U pattern, even as early as at birth, can be suspected of having decreased extensor activity or muscle weakness. This posture is often seen in the floppy infant syndrome. Even a neonate without the benefit of full righting reactions will indicate that he has some extensor capacity against gravity (Fig 8-12). An exaggerated Landau, or too much extensor muscle activity, may be present in children who have other abnormalities of muscular activity such as spasticity (Cupps 1976).

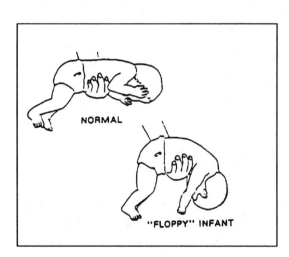

Figure 8-12 When suspended in the prone position, the normal infant shows some extension posture in the neck and trunk compared with the floppy infant who has no antigravity capability when suspended prone.

Rolling

The ability to rotate the body around the vertebral axis is important for rolling from supine to prone and from prone to supine. Children and often adults use rotation or partial rotation to attain sitting and standing positions; therefore, an excellent way to evaluate the ability of the infant, child, or adult to perform axial rotation is to observe the movement patterns that each uses to perform these activities. Rotation has been described as a righting reaction, because as the head rotates the rest of the body twists, or rotates, to become realigned with it or as one part of the body rotates, the other parts realign with it.

The earliest spontaneous axial rotation is seen in the fetus of 10 weeks GA (deVries et al 1982). Rotation around the longitudinal axis results either from rotation of the head followed by trunk rotation or from leg movement with hip rotation. A total change in fetal position can be achieved in as little as 2 seconds. Researchers believe that these movements permit the fetus to change position and orientation from time to time in the uterus, probably to prevent adhesions and stasis (Prechtl 1986). The important feature of interest to therapists is that this rotation in the uterus is segmental in character. That is, one part of the body initiates the rotation and other parts follow in segmental fashion. This information will be useful later when the different forms of rotation that are present in the neonate and young children are discussed. The NOB and BOB righting reactions are rolling patterns. The are described later as elicited rotational righting patterns for testing purposes..

Observing Spontaneous Patterns

Rolling from prone to supine or from supine to prone can be encouraged in a young infant by placing the infant on a flat surface in either position and presenting an interesting toy to one side and then the other. In our culture, on the average, babies first roll from the side-lying position to the supine position at 1 to 2 months of age and then from the supine to the side-lying position at 4 to 5 months. Infants first roll from prone to supine at 4 months of age and then from supine to prone at 6 to 8 months.

Infants start with a partial roll (side lying to supine) at 1 to 2 months of age and complete a full supine-to-prone roll at 6 to 8 months.

The quality of the movement pattern of rolling changes with age. When the infant rolls from back to side lying or the reverse, there is a total body response rather than a segmental pattern. This pattern has often been described as log rolling, because the whole body rolls as a unit (Fig 8-13). Some infants are able to roll from supine to prone by using segmental rotation, or rotation of successive vertebrae around the trunk axis, at 4 months of age. This movement is initiated by head rotation, not by hip rotation. There are extension movements of the spine and the extremities (Fig 8-14). By about 7 to 8 months of age, most infants roll into the prone position easily and smoothly; however, only half of these infants exhibit trunk rotation. By 9 months of age, the majority of infants use segmental rotation of the body on the pelvis during rolling behavior, as seen in Figure 8-15 (Folio and Fewell 1983; McGraw 1945; Touwen 1976).

Figure 8-13 The early form of the neck on body reflex.

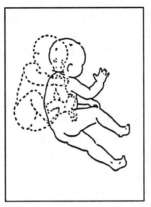

Figure 8-14 Later rolling with extension of the spine and the extremities.

Figure 8-15 Segmental rotation between the trunk and the pelvis during more mature rolling behavior.

Trunk rotation during rolling from prone into supine starts to occur between 6 and 7 months of age, about 4 weeks earlier than it does when rolling over from supine to prone. This rotation pattern occurs at about the same time that infants start to support themselves on extended arms in the prone position. Thus, because this pattern is seen first, it must be easier for infants to push up on extended arms and then rotate the upper half of the body on the pelvis in order to turn over to supine than it is to lift the head and shoulders in supine position and rotate them on the pelvis in order to turn over into prone. Between 9 and 10 months of age, infants rotate into a sitting position from the prone position and do not return to supine because they seem to dislike this position or they find it too limiting.

A question that might be asked is, Why is rotation around the trunk axis seen in fetuses at 10 weeks GA but not seen in infants in the first few weeks of life? There are a couple of possibilities. One is that newborn infants are without sufficient strength to move against gravity in either direction, so that initial rolling from side lying to supine at 1 to 2 months and supine to side lying at 4 to 5 months may be assisted gravitationally. Perhaps increased tension in some muscle groups initiates the rolling that is then followed by gravitational assist to complete the half roll. Rotation in the trunk axis probably does not begin until the infant has developed sufficient muscle strength to not only initiate movement but also to complete the roll to prone or supine.

A second, or additional, possibility relates to the type of muscular contractions that the neonate exhibits. From the work of Thelen (1985) and others as noted in Chapter 2, we know that the newborn and young infant primarily uses coactivation of agonists and antagonists to produce certain movements. Thus the joints are bound, or linked, tightly together because this cocontraction does not permit the individual joint action required for the various segments of the spine to rotate somewhat sequentially instead of simultaneously. The ability to produce axial rotation coincides with the relaxing of joint linkages observed in early kicking patterns and the diminishing of cocontraction patterns seen in leg musculature.

> **Normal adults roll in a variety of movement patterns.**

Adult rolling movements have been described by Richter et al (1989). Rolling was described according to three body regions: upper extremities, lower extremities, and head and trunk. Although these researchers found a variety of movement patterns used by adults to roll, four patterns tended to be observed most often. The most frequent arm pattern used was a lift and reach above the shoulder level; the leg pattern varied between a unilateral lift, a unilateral push, or a bilateral lift; and the head and trunk pattern began with either the shoulder girdle leading in the rolling task or by changing the relationship between the pelvis and shoulder girdle during the roll (Fig 8-16). The most important finding from this study is that normal adults use a variety of movement patterns to roll. This variation is in contrast to those of brain injured adults who tend to use only a few patterns or one stereotyped pattern to roll. In addition, although lack of rotation between the shoulder girdle and pelvis has been considered to be an abnormal movement pattern, 3% to 4% of the normal adults in this study used this trunk pattern. Figures 8-17, 8-18, and 8-19 show the other common forms of rolling present in the Richter study.

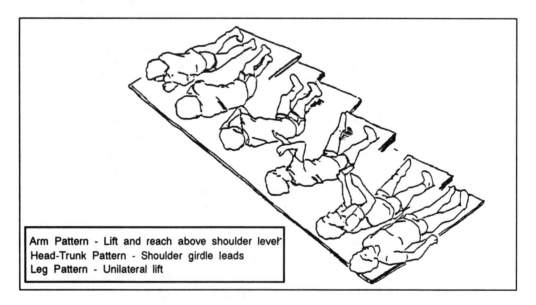

Arm Pattern - Lift and reach above shoulder level
Head-Trunk Pattern - Shoulder girdle leads
Leg Pattern - Unilateral lift

Figure 8-16 A common form of rolling. Pattern begins in the lower right-hand corner and is completed in the upper left-hand corner. From Richter et al (1989, p 81), reprinted with permission of the American Physical Therapy Association.

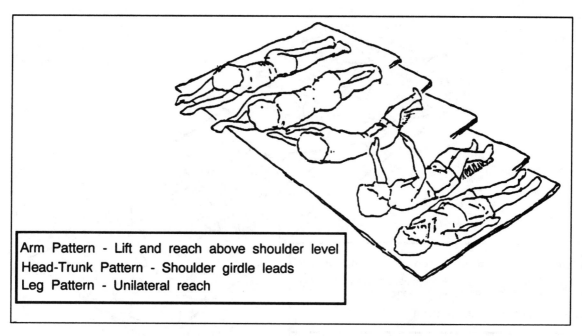

Arm Pattern - Lift and reach above shoulder level
Head-Trunk Pattern - Shoulder girdle leads
Leg Pattern - Unilateral reach

Figure 8-17 A second common form of rolling. Pattern begins in the lower right-hand corner and is completed in the upper left-hand corner. From Richter et al (1989, p 82), reprinted with permission of the American Physical Therapy Association.

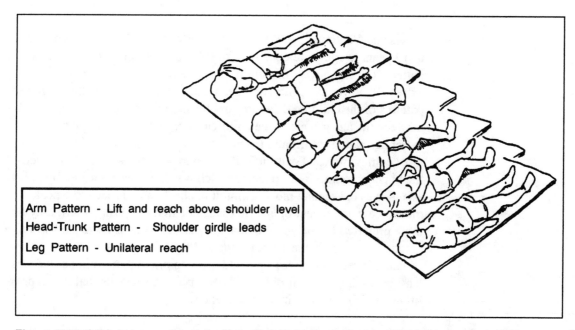

Arm Pattern - Lift and reach above shoulder level
Head-Trunk Pattern - Shoulder girdle leads
Leg Pattern - Unilateral reach

Figure 8-18 A third common form of rolling. Pattern begins in the lower right-hand corner and is completed in the upper left-hand corner. From Richter et al (1989, p 82), reprinted with permission of the American Physical Therapy Association.

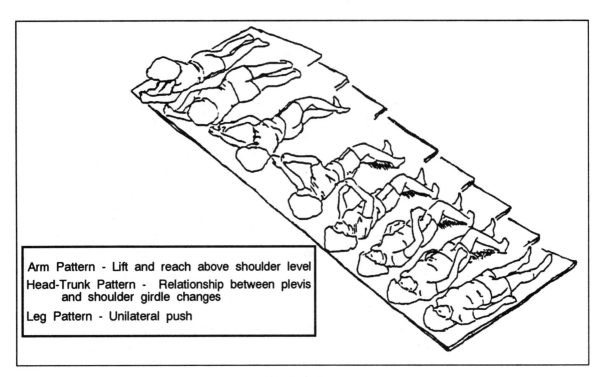

Arm Pattern - Lift and reach above shoulder level
Head-Trunk Pattern - Relationship between plevis and shoulder girdle changes
Leg Pattern - Unilateral push

Figure 8-19 A fourth common form of rolling. Pattern begins in the lower right-hand corner and is completed in the upper left-hand corner. From Richter et al (1989, p 82), reprinted with permission of the American Physical Therapy Association.

Lewis and VanSant (1990) reported a study in which 64 children from 6 to 10 years of age were observed for rolling behavior. The same basic patterns of rolling were present in the three body areas of upper extremity, lower extremity, and head and trunk. However, the preferred patterns of the children differed from those of the adults and differed between the age groups of the children. For instance, the upper extremity pattern of lift and reach at or above shoulder level was the most commonly used pattern, just as it was with the adults. However, the upper extremity push pattern, which was the least preferred by adults, was the second most common in children and reached a peak incidence in the 8 year olds. This suggests that the push pattern may be more preferred by the younger age groups. The push and reach showed a greater incidence in the 10 year olds and the lift and reach above shoulder level, which was a second most common pattern in adults, was least prevalent in 6 year olds. This observation suggests that this type of lift and reach develops in later sequences.

Rolling patterns are age-related and change across the life span.

In this same study the lower extremity patterns of the children were also the same as those found in adults, but they were preferred in a different order and varied among the three age groups of children. The unilateral push, which was third in preference for adults, was most preferred by the children and was most common in the 6 year olds, suggesting an early

226

preference pattern. The same observation occurred for the children's second choice pattern of unilateral lift without push, which was also a second choice for adults. Bilateral push increases with age and is more common after childhood. The adults preferred pattern of bilateral lift was last among children and most prevalent in the 10 year olds, again suggesting that it is a later pattern.

The head and trunk, or axial, patterns showed the most agreement in order with adults but incidences varied with the ages of the children. The most preferred pattern in both groups was the aligned pelvis and shoulder girdle, but it was the least prevalent in the early age groups. The pelvis-leads and shoulder-leads patterns changed little across age groups, so that it was not possible to propose a sequence for them. The pattern in which the relationship changes between the pelvis and shoulder girdle was common before 6 and after 10 years of age.

These studies provide insight into common movement patterns that have not systematically been observed in the past. They tell us that there is a great variety in these patterns, and even though they change with age groups, an individual may be found performing patterns outside the age group. This knowledge allows therapists to offer a wide variety of movements for their clients, and it certainly indicates that no one way of rolling should be imposed on all clients. The age divisions also suggest that more age appropriate forms may be selected or expected for the particular age of the client.

Elicited Rotational Righting Reactions

If the infant, child, or adult does not voluntarily roll, you can elicit a rolling pattern either by turning the head on the trunk or by rotating one leg across the other. The NOB does exactly what the name implies. Rotate the neck and observe the resultant movement of the body. If the head is rotated to the side, the body follows in a rolling pattern. With a normal neonate, this rolling does not have segmental sequences (first the shoulders, then down the vertebrae to the pelvis, and then the legs), as is usually the case with the more mature infant. As noted earlier, the neonate rolls as if the body were a bound unit. Thus a descriptive way to remember this early pattern is to call it log rolling. The movement pattern observed in the neonate resulting from the elicitation of the NOB reflex is similar to that seen when the young infant rolls from side lying to supine or from supine to side lying.

Test Procedure

NOB

The NOB is elicited in the newborn infant by placing the infant supine with his head in the midline and then rotating his head to one side. The body follows as a whole toward the side to which the head is turned.

Robinson (1966) described this reflex in preterm normal-weight infants and in small-for-date infants, showing that the reflex usually appears between 34 and 37 weeks GA. The reflex is modified by 4 to 5 months of age when the mature form of the reflex (segmental rolling) appears.

BOB

The BOB is basically the reverse movement from the NOB. Place the neonate supine with his head in the midline, flex one leg up toward his chest, and rotate the leg across his body to force the baby to roll over. With the BOB, the thorax, chest, and head will follow the pelvis. Thus the type of rolling pattern is the same as seen with the NOB, although in this case, the lower extremities begin the movement and the trunk and neck twist to realign the head with the trunk. As with the NOB, the rolling pattern of the BOB is similar to the rolling pattern that the infant uses to roll from side lying to supine or from supine to side lying. Unlike the more mature infant, the neonate demonstrates a log rolling response and does not roll all the way from supine to prone. Figure 8-20 shows the mature response.

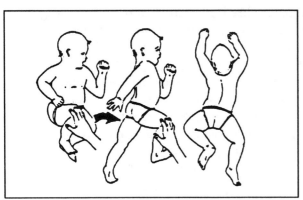

Figure 8-20 The mature form of the body-on-body righting response. Note the segmental nature of the pattern, with the trunk and head following the hips and pelvis.

The persistence of the neonatal, or immature, form of rolling (with no rotation between the shoulders and pelvis) or the persistence of the neonatal, or immature, form of the NOB and the BOB is of clinical significance. In children in whom rolling is limited to these early forms of movement patterns, whether spontaneously produced or elicited by the examiner, there will be a lack of variety of rolling movements. It can be said, then, that whatever the causes the persistence of these immature, or limited, forms likely will interfere with the development of segmental rolling found in the more mature infant of 4 to 5 months of age and in the child and adult. If segmental rolling does not develop, the older infant, child, or adult may have difficulty with other movement patterns that require rotational components or may fail to develop a variety of movement patterns and thus be limited to more stereotypical responses.

Persistence of the early form of rolling or the NOB or the BOB at 4 months of age was predictive of central nervous system dysfunction at 12 months of age and specifically of cerebral palsy between 3 and 8 years (Bennett et al 1981; Harris 1987). The presence of the log rolling form at 6 months of age was significantly predictive of cerebral palsy and developmental delay (Campbell and Wilhelm 1982); persistence after 10 months of age was a significant signal of developmental delay (Molnar 1974; 1978; 1979). With respect to ambulation, there are inconsistencies as to the effect of a persistent neonatal NOB. Bleck (1975) found that a persistent neonatal NOB was predictive of the inability to ambulate, whereas Capute (1979) did not find a relationship between the early form of the NOB and later ambulation.

> There is no wrong or right way to roll, but there seems to be age appropriate sequences in rolling.

Because segmental rolling has been seen in the fetus with ultrasound, the notion that it is a more mature form of rolling is not exactly accurate. Nonetheless, the neonate reverts to or engages in a form of rolling that evolves with age; thus it is not inaccurate to describe these differences of form in terms of extrauterine maturity. As other voluntary motor patterns become more preferred by the infant, NOB form of rolling is gradually replaced by them. Therefore, by 4 or 5 years of age and on through adulthood, we see a tremendous variety of rolling patterns, which should lead us to the conclusions that there may be no right or wrong way to roll, but that there may be more age-appropriate sequences. By knowing these sequences, the therapists will have a wide range of methods to teach clients to roll and a general guide as to the possible method of first choice.

The pattern that emerges in rolling either may be simply a matter of preference or may be the result of muscle strength, speed in rolling, timing and sequence in muscular activity, or purpose of the roll. For example, the adult might roll without segmental movement because it is more effective, especially for very rapid rolling. Rolling to approach an object may be different than rolling on command or for a nonpurposeful reason (McGraw 1945).

It should be noted that the response should not be stronger to one side than it is to the other, particularly in infants (Paine 1961). If you see a stronger response to one side, you should consider the possibility of a pathological state, or central nervous system dysfunction, or if seen in the older child or adult, it could be attributed to right or left handedness, muscle strength, habit, and the like. Certainly, any illness, disease process, joint malfunction, or medication must be taken into consideration when evaluating an individual. It is the therapist's job to determine whether there is a serious problem meriting attention.

Righting reactions can serve two main purposes for therapists: (1) They can be used to evaluate an individual's ability to produce effective movements and to gain insight into his developmental status and the presence of abnormalities in nervous system function and (2) they can be used therapeutically to facilitate movement or control where it does not exist.

Achieving the Erect Position From Supine

Generally, an infant first gets into an erect position by first rolling supine to prone, then backing up on her knees to an all-fours position, and then using a pull-to-stand method to get up. When the pull-to-stand method is no longer needed, the child usually gets on all fours, straightens her knees in plantigrade, and pushes up from the floor. In the experience of Paine et al (1964), the NOB reaction could no longer be demonstrated once the infant could attain the standing position from a sitting position without rotation. We might extend Thelen and Fisher's (1982) observations on the disappearance of the stepping reflex that show quite likely that stepping ceases because of a relative lack of sufficient muscular power against the imposed load (see Chapter 2). Therefore, the pattern a child or adult uses to go from the supine position to an erect stance is probably in some measure dependent on the muscle strength available. When the abdominal and hip flexor muscles have attained sufficient strength for the task, a sit-up type of maneuver would seem to be most efficient.

> Strengthening exercises exclusive of other movement mechanisms *may not* constitute effective treatment.

It should be noted that the concept of strength is a complex one. Certainly, strength has not been satisfactorily defined or acceptably measured. Nonetheless, whatever the phenomenon, an adequate amount of force, or tension, must be exerted in the correct performance of a given task. The ability to perform an activity may certainly involve more than the additive contraction of motor units. Underlying mechanisms of neuromuscular efficiency, such as appropriate recruitment of motor units and the timing of muscular sequences in a synergy, are components required for the effective use of the musculoskeletal system. Thus outright strengthening exercises, particularly in clients with neurological deficits, may not provide an adequate result. Strength may also be obtained through practicing the appropriate activity, using coordinated natural patterns such as those described in proprioceptive neuromuscular facilitation techniques, and using other approaches such as electrical stimulation and many possible forms of biofeedback.

Schaltenbrand (1928) observed the activity of the BOB in a changing sequence of movements in children attaining the erect position from supine lying. From the time the child can assume a standing position from supine (10-12 months) until 2 years of age, she will roll prone from supine with a complete rotational pattern, attain the all-fours position, and then stand up. From about 15 months to 2 years of age, therefore, the child uses a relatively pure NOB or BOB pattern to get into a standing position from supine lying.

Between the ages of 2 and 3 years, there is a transition from the complete rolling over pattern to rolling to the side to attain sitting. Schaltenbrand (1928) and others have indicated that the so-called mature form of attaining the erect position occurs between the ages of 4 and 5, as the child rises from supine to sitting to standing with symmetrical movement patterns similar to a sit-up. It has been assumed that this symmetrical movement is the final form and that changes are not expected later in life.

VanSant (1988a; 1988b) clearly showed that attaining the upright position from a supine position is a developmental task that continues into adulthood and most likely changes throughout the life span. Therefore, the assumption that righting movements reach a particular form (symmetrical pattern) in early childhood and remain unchanged through later childhood and adulthood seems to be unfounded. She studied children between the ages of 4 and 7 years and young adults between the ages of 20 and 35 years. The conclusions reached in these studies included the observation that the general pattern of movement seen in adults may also be seen in children; however, some of those patterns seen in the very young children may not be seen in young adults.

VanSant (1988a; 1988b) divided the body into three components for her studies: upper extremities, lower extremities, and trunk (axial). By so doing, it was possible to determine when multiple combinations of movements in those three areas occurred. Subjects varied greatly in the movement patterns they used to rise from supine to erect stance. A single form of rising is not present in children from ages 4 to 7 years, nor is it present in adults. Only one fourth of the adults studied used the same method of rising. The method most commonly used involved symmetrical patterns of the trunk and extremities (Fig 8-21). Figures 8-22 and 8-23 show the second and third most common forms of rising that VanSant observed. VanSant (1990) also suggests that body topography and mass are likely to affect rising patterns. In a preliminary study when young adults were burdened with 10% of their body weight they changed from symmetrical patterns to asymmetrical ones. This information further supports the importance of body weight and strength to function. Longitudinal studies need to be performed to determine whether there is a changing sequence within individuals. Studies of the older population need to be performed also to ascertain similarities and differences with younger adults and children.

From studies on 123 children, VanSant (1988b) showed that the task varied with age, and a trend toward increasing symmetry with increasing

231

age was noted. However, even the oldest subjects (7 years) did not use the symmetrical pattern in the majority of cases. Two patterns that were used by children that were not found in adults were a jump-to-squat pattern in the lower extremity component and a full-rotation abdomen-down pattern described in the axial component. Figure 8-24 shows the most common form of rise to stand in young children. The upper extremity movement pattern is an asymmetrical push, the axial pattern is forward with rotation, and the lower extremities produce an asymmetrical wide-based squat.

Figure 8-21 The most common form of rising to a standing position. Upper extremity component: symmetrical push; axial component: symmetrical; and lower extremity component: symmetrical squat. From VanSant (1988*b*), reprinted with permission of the American Physical Therapy Association.

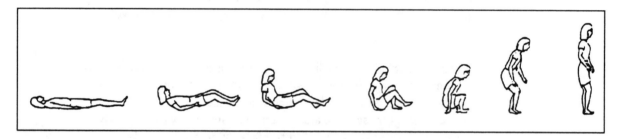

Figure 8-22 The second most common form of rising to a standing position. Upper extremity component: symmetrical push; axial component: symmetrical; and lower extremity component: symmetrical squat. From VanSant (1988*b*), reprinted with permission of the American Physical Therapy

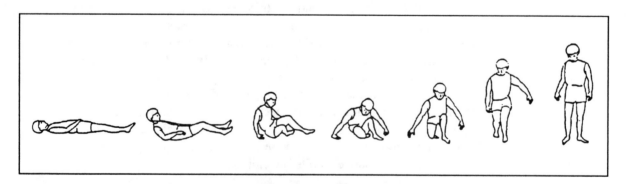

Figure 8-23 The third most common form of rising to a standing position. Upper extremity component: asymmetrical push and reach; axial component: partial rotation; and lower extremity component: half kneel. From VanSant (1988*b*), reprinted with permission of the American Physical Therapy

Again, significant variation was noted in the patterns used to rise from supine. Figure 8-25 shows five other forms of rise patterns that were observed by VanSant. It is clear the changes in form are age-related, but a richness of variation exists that has not been so graphically described before. These studies support the idea that variability is the normal condition in human movement and development and that restricted and stereotypical patterns reflect abnormality.

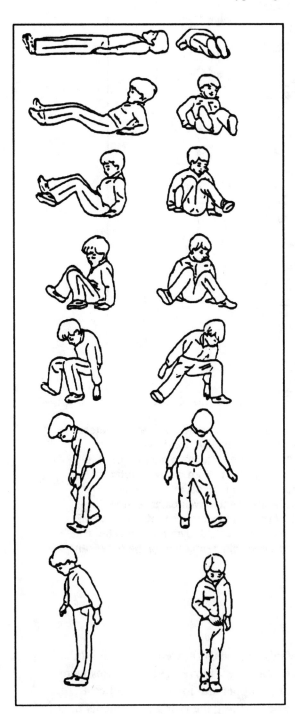

Figure 8-24 The most common form of rising to standing in young children. Taken from frames of film of the side (on the left) and foot (on the right) views. This 5-year-old boy demonstrates the characteristic form of rising in young children. Starting from the top in the supine position and moving successively downward to the standing position, the upper extremity movement pattern is characterized as an asymmetrical push. The axial region movement pattern is termed forward with rotation, and the lower extremity movement pattern is an asymmetrical wide-based squat. From VanSant (1988*a*), reprinted with permission of the American Physical Therapy Association.

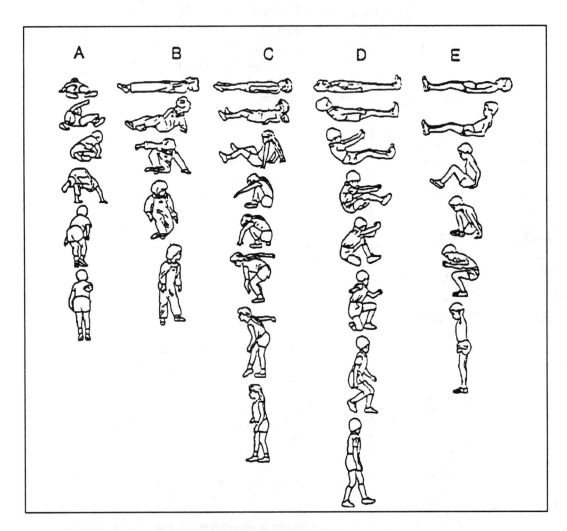

Figure 8-25 Various forms of rising to standing in young children. (A) This 4-year-old boy demonstrates upper extremity (UE) movement pattern of push-and-reach to bilateral push, axial (AX) region pattern of full rotation, abdomen up; and lower extremity (LE) pattern of jump to squat. (B) This 5-year-old girl demonstrates an UE pattern of asymmetrical push; AX pattern of partial rotation; and LE pattern of half kneel. (C) This 5-year-old girl demonstrates an UE asymmetrical push; AX movement forward with rotation; and LE symmetrical narrow-based squat with balance step. (D) This 7-year-boy demonstrates UE symmetrical reach; AX movement forward with rotation; and LE half kneel. (E) This 7-year-old boy demonstrates UE symmetrical push; AX symmetrical pattern; and a LE narrow-based squat. From VanSant (1988a), reprinted with permission of the American Physical Therapy Association.

In another study, Luehring and VanSant (1990) showed that older adults used the same general patterns, but three new movement categories were used to describe the movements in the upper and lower extremities. They concluded that the categories describing the rising movements in young adults and children were generally accurate but not comprehensive descriptors of patterns used by older adults. In this study, the 64- to 85-year-old subjects were divided into two groups: those who were involved in organized exercise activities and those who were not. The patterns used differed between the two groups. The active group preferred to rise by pushing with one upper extremity and reaching with the other while rotating the trunk to side-facing and moving through half-kneel to standing. The inactive group reached across the body with one upper extremity so that both hands were on the floor. They then assumed the all-fours posture, and then moved to kneeling, then to half kneeling, and then to standing. Thus, even though the ages were the same, the activity level of the subjects had an influence on the patterns used. This suggests that preexisting conditions in clients with other problems will undoubtedly affect either their ability to perform certain tasks or the manner in which they will perform. This information is extremely valuable to therapists because they must consider these conditions when evaluating clients and prescribing treatment. Linde et al (1995) investigated the supine-to-standing position with individuals afflicted with multiple sclerosis. They showed that the disease process, rather than aging factors, is largely responsible for changes in patterns. In this case trunk movements may be more influential than extremity movements in restricting mobility.

McCoy and VanSant (1993) used these video techniques to investigate the movement patterns adolescents, ranging in age from 11 to 17 years, use in rising from a bed. Again, it was found that the patterns varied with age, and the greatest variability was noted in the youngest age group of 11-year-old subjects. In general, the adolescent groups were quite variable as 89 different forms of rising were observed.

This investigation further brings into question some of our assumptions about how people should move. For instance, Carr and Shepherd (1987) indicate that clients should be taught to come to a sitting position from a side-lying position and should be discouraged from using their tendency to pull on the edge of the bed. The form of rising that McCoy and VanSant (1993) found to be relatively common across all age groups did not eminate from a side-lying position but rather involved a push pattern in the far extremity and a grasp of the side of the bed and a push pattern of the near upper extremity as the subjects achieved a sitting position from supine (Fig 8-26 A-D). Clearly, not allowing the client to pull on the edge of the bed is contrary to a natural approach to this task. It is most likely that the therapist is not in a position to know what is the best way for the client to accomplish the task. The client needs to be an active problem solver and should be allowed to explore a variety of methods and to help decide on the most effective ones to use.

> Body constraints and other non-neural elements may be control parameters that determine the patterns demonstrated.

Green and Williams (1992) used the same research protocol to study 30-39-year-old adults coming from a supine to erect position. In this study the activity level of their subjects was recorded. The results of their study showed that the adults who were more active demonstrated more advanced patterns than did their less active counterparts. Thus movement patterns appear to be influenced by life style choices. This study further supports the VanSant studies of this nature. In addition, the study suggests that strength and flexibility and other nonneural elements of movement have measurable influences on motor control. Dhawan and VanSant (1995) added weight packs to young adults and found they changed their patterns. This provides further evidence of non-neural control parameters in movement (see Chap. 2).

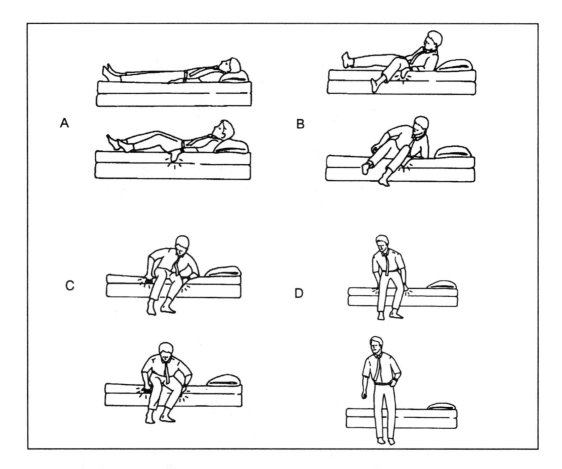

Figure 8-26 A fairly common rising-from-bed pattern used by all adolescent age levels. From McCoy and VanSant (1993), reproduced with permission of the American Physical Therapy Association.

Study Questions:

1. **Why may it be incorrect to assume that the inability to move appropriately will be corrected by mere strengthening of muscles through weightlifting?**

2. **Describe the difference between immature and mature forms of rolling.**

3. **What do you think will be the most significant finding of the VanSant studies relative to your treatment planning for your clients?**

Chapter 9 - Balance Reactions

Balance reactions are automatic reactions used for maintaining or controlling the center of gravity. Anytime the center of gravity is moved in any direction--up or down, forward or backward, or side to side--some response occurs. We have divided balance reactions into two categories: (1) those that humans use to protect the body from pain and injury from falling once the center of gravity is displaced too far for recovery, herein labelled protective reactions, and (2) those that enable us to keep the center of gravity within the base of support to prevent falling either by anticipatory weight shifts or by movement patterns, herein labelled tilting or postural fixation reactions. Obviously, all of the balance reactions persist throughout life.

> **Balance reactions:**
>
> Protective extension UE, protective extension LE, tilting, and postural fixation.

Before delving into balance reactions, it is necessary to recognize that all standing and moving reactions to the forces of gravity are governed by visual, vestibular, and somatosensory influences, acting in concert when the three inputs are available and functioning appropriately (see Chapters 11 and 15). Certainly, for testing purposes, either one or two of the systems may be negated, forcing the body to react under the influence of the third system only. Under normal circumstances, however, all three systems will be called into play as the body attempts to maintain balance and an upright posture.

Protective Reactions

Protective Extension Reactions

Protective extension reactions protect the body when it is displaced by horizontal or diagonal forces (Martin 1967). These reactions automatically enable the body to protect itself against the effects of falling. Because the body needs to protect itself from infancy through adulthood, these reactions remain throughout life. In the literature, protective reactions are also referred to as parachute reactions (Milani-Comparetti and Giodioni 1967a; Paine et al 1964); propping reactions, and precipitation reflexes (Andre-Thomas et al 1960).

> **Protective reactions serve to protect the body against the effects of falling.**

Protective extension reaction is a good term to be used to describe what happens as the body starts to fall toward the ground. As a child topples over toward the ground, you will notice that she extends her elbows, wrists, and fingers ahead of her body to break the fall and to protect the rest of her body from injury. Similarly, if you were to watch a child jump into water, you would see extension at her knee joints. And observe the same child diving head first into water and you should see protective extension at her elbow joints. These reactions can also be observed by having the child or adult reach for objects placed relatively far from the center of gravity.

Protective Extension of the Upper Extremities (Forward)

For clarity, we will first discuss protective reactions of the upper extremities and then consider the lower extremities. You will note the terms protective reaction forward, protective reaction sideward, and protective reaction backward. Obviously, displacing the center of gravity forward will elicit the protective reaction forward. The expression of the protective reaction forward coincides with the infant's ability to bring her extended upper extremities forward for reaching out and bearing weight at around 6 to 7 months of age.

Test Procedure

To test for the protective extension reaction forward, support the prone infant around his thorax, in a horizontal position. Plunge his head and upper trunk downward toward a table top and observe the presence or absence of flexion at his shoulders and extension of his elbows. In addition to elbow extension and shoulder flexion, you should see his fingers extend and abduct as if to break a fall (Fig 9-1). Once his forearms are extended at the elbows and his hands touch a surface, positive supporting reactions of his upper extremities are observed because the child will support himself on extended arms.

The protective extension reaction forward can also be tested from a sitting or upright kneeling position. The protective extension forward reaction also permits the examiner to observe any differences in reaction of the two extremities so that any subtle asymmetry may be noted.

Protective Extension of the Upper Extremities (Sideward)

The onset of the protective reaction sideward is generally at 7 months of age. This reaction permits the child or adult to do exactly what the name implies, that is, protect himself when falling toward either side (Fig 9-2).

The protective extension reaction sideward is easy to elicit in an adult. Briskly shove a seated individual on one shoulder with enough force to cause him to completely lose his balance. Notice how his opposite arm abducts at the shoulder joint and extends at the elbow. Extension of his wrist and abduction and extension of his fingers also can be seen. (Again, the protective reaction sideward is followed by the positive supporting reaction as soon as contact is made with a supporting surface.)

Protective Extension of the Upper Extremity (Backward)

The protective reaction backward is the third protective reaction of the upper extremities. It can be elicited at about 9 to 10 months of age. Haley (1986*a*) noted that the protective reactions did not always appear in a specific order, so times of onset should be considered approximate and most likely overlap considerably. As the name implies, the reaction is an attempt by the individual to protect his body against a fall when the center of gravity has been displaced backward.

To test for this backward reaction, place the child in a symmetrical sitting posture with his legs out in front or in tailor fashion. Then push the child backward with enough force to displace his center of gravity and offset balance. A full reaction is backward of extension of all joints of both arms (Fig 9-3).

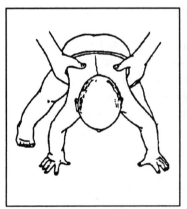

Figure 9-1 Protective extension forward.

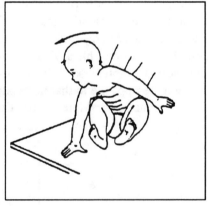

Figure 9-2 Protective extension sideward.

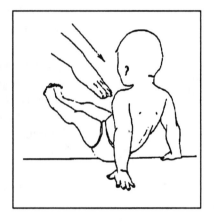

Figure 9-3 Protective extension backward.

All three of the protective reactions enable a baby or an adult to protect his body against pain or injury as a result of a loss of balance that results in falling. Failure to obtain or a delay in the acquisition of protective reactions may indicate general depression or developmental deficits of the central nervous system. Asymmetry of response in a movement that should produce a symmetrical response may be indicative of an insult to one side of the brain or perhaps a peripheral nerve or muscle injury.

Protective reactions can cause problems.

NOTE: An important concept to consider relative to protective reactions of the upper extremity is that they can cause injury in adults if we do not remember to or do not have time to inhibit them during a fall. Colles' fractures, subluxation of the elbow joint, and fractures of the clavicle are common results of failure to suppress the forward and sideward protective extension reactions. Failure to suppress the protective

239

reaction backward may also result in an anterior rotator cuff tear. This fact indicates the necessity for teaching paraplegics, actors, dancers, and anyone else who may be subject to falling just how to fall properly.

Protective Reactions of the Lower Extremities (Downward)

There are two types of lower extremity protective reactions. One is elicited in nonweight bearing (the protective reaction downward) and the other type is elicited during weight bearing (protective staggering reactions). The protective reaction downward is usually the first to appear in the lower extremity at about 4 months of age. During protective extension reactions of the lower extremities, also called parachute reactions, the most obvious motion seen is extension of the knee joints for the purpose of protecting the body against the effects of a fall.

Test Procedure

Hold a child vertically and rapidly plunge his feet downward toward a table top and you will see this rapid extension of the knee joints. In the normal child, you will also see hip abduction and external rotation accompanied by dorsiflexion of his ankles (Fig 9-4). In a child with motor problems, you may notice extension of his knees, but all other motions are likely to be opposite to that normally seen. In this event, you can expect hip adduction and internal rotation and ankle plantar flexion.

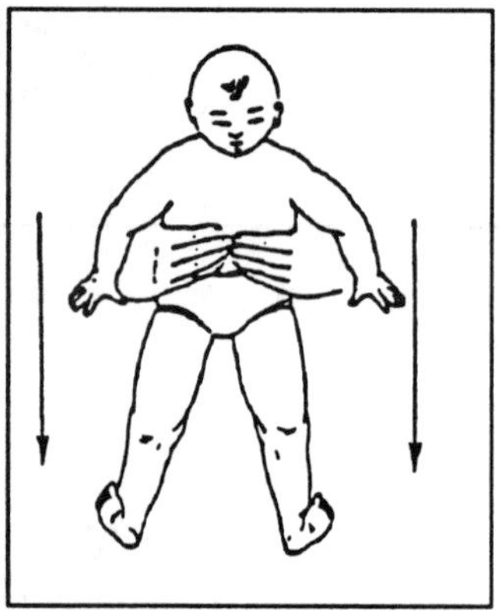

Figure 9-4 Protective reaction downward.

Protective Reaction of the Lower Extremities (Staggering)

The staggering reactions in the lower extremities become apparent during 15 to 18 months of life and persist throughout life to maintain upright erect posture of humans when their bodies are displaced by a horizontal force. When children first learn to walk, they do not have staggering reactions, which is one reason why they fall so frequently. The child can protect himself somewhat with the protective reactions of his upper extremities, but he cannot keep his body from falling.

240

Ask a friend to stand in front of you. Give her a sharp shove in a forward direction and notice how she recovers balance by taking one or more steps forward. If pushed backward she will take one or more steps backward. Push the individual sideward and you may notice something a little different. She may take a step sideward or she may cross one foot over the other to regain her balance. This response to sideward perturbations is termed staggering.

These stepping type of responses to disturbances of the center of gravity are synergies that have been described by Nashner (1990) (See Chapter 1). The synergies of choice when standing will be either the ankle strategy or the hip strategy if the center of gravity is not disturbed so drastically as to require stepping to prevent falling. Shumway-Cook and Woollacott (1985) studied children from 15 months to 10 years of age, using the platform perturbation system that Nashner developed. They found that children under the age of 6 years were able to produce some responses that were in the appropriate direction for the perturbation. They found, however, that the adult form of the responses with appropriately timed proximal and distal muscle sequences did not occur until after 6 years of age. Children in the age group of 4 to 6 years demonstrated responses that were in transition from those seen in infancy and those elicited from adults.

Children or adults who have neither perfected nor developed staggering reactions will not be safe, independent walkers. Any change in the center of gravity will cause the such individuals to lose their balance and fall. The problem may be further compounded when such individuals do not have the protective reactions of their upper extremities.

Balance Reactions: Preserving the Center of Gravity

Tilting Reactions

Balance reactions occur to maintain the body's center of gravity over the base of support. One category of balance reactions is referred to as tilting reactions. These reactions occur when the center of gravity is shifted and the base of support is unstable, such as when using a tiltboard. The other type is the postural fixation reaction that occurs when the center of gravity is shifted but the base of support is stable, such as when standing on the floor or sitting in a chair.

Tilting reactions occur in whatever position the individual has assumed. Thus you would expect to observe them when the base of support is tilted during such activities as lying prone or supine, kneeling, sitting, and standing.

Test Procedure

When using a tilt board, as the board is tilted downward to the left you should expect to see a concavity of the individual's spine toward the right, or upward side (Fig 9-5). These responses are controlled by the interaction of the vestibular, visual, and somatosensory inputs. If the amount of tilt or the speed of tilt are sufficient, the entire synergy produced in response to the tilting is the curvature of the vertebral column, a turning of the head toward the upward side, and an extension and abduction of the extremities on that side (Fig 9-6). In addition, if you push an individual beyond the point where tilting reactions would be adequate to sustain balance, you would see protective reactions come into play to catch his body or break the fall (Fig 9-7).

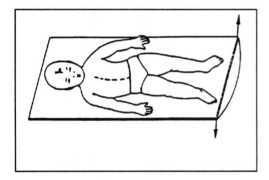

Figure 9-5 Tilting supine. Note the curvature of the spine with the concavity on the upward side.

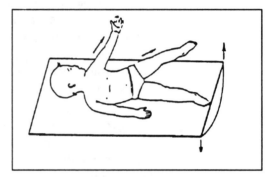

Figure 9-6 Tilting supine. Further tilting produces extension and abduction of the extremities on the upward side as well as the curvature of the spine.

Older literature suggests that the curvature is a labyrinthine response and that the head and extremity movements are proprioceptive responses. Actually, the various sensory systems are redundant, that is, they all participate in generating the postural or balance responses that in the past were believed to be the domain of only one sensory system.

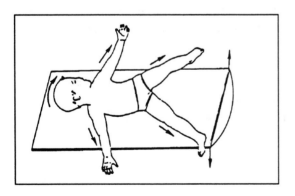

Figure 9-7 When the tilting stimulus is too large to maintain the center of gravity effectively, protective extension reactions appear in the downward extremities to help break the fall.

Because vision, proprioception, and the vestibular system play roles in tilting reactions, it is sometimes desirable to attempt to elicit the responses under conditions that eliminate one or more of the senses. This will perhaps provide insight as to which system the client is relying on most for his postural stability. To eliminate vision, you may blindfold the client. Eliminating the other systems is much more difficult. Some of the more elaborate methods of diminishing the proprioceptive inputs and of fooling the vestibular system are covered in Section III and IV of this book. You should study this chapter again after you have read those sections and establish an understanding of the role of these systems in motor control and balance, and of how those roles relate to the evaluation procedures used to examine these responses. Do not forget that most research has shown that adults tend to rely most heavily on proprioceptive inputs for postural orientation and, conversely, that children rely more heavily on vision. These facts should be kept in mind when evaluating clients of different ages.

A child or adult devoid of vestibular function or one having a central nervous system disorder affecting the functioning of the labyrinths shows little postural disability provided normal vision and a stable base are present. When two of the three systems are not functioning effectively, however, an individual may experience great difficulty in keeping his center of gravity in its proper position relative to his base of support.

Try this on a friend. Place a board on a floor mat and have your friend sit on one end of the board. Slowly raise your end of the board about 6 to 8 inches off the mat. Notice the spine curvature that is caused by moving your friend's center of gravity. Continue to lift your end of the board until something happens with the friend's arms and legs. Finally, jerk the end of the board upward very rapidly to a height of 12 to 15 inches so that your friend is literally thrown off balance. Do you see the responses just described? Remember that all of these are appropriate responses. It should seldom be your objective to throw an individual totally off balance. Most likely you will be looking for more subtle responses. For instance, you might wish to record how many degrees of tilt a client can adjust to properly at different speeds of imposed tilt. This will provide a baseline of information for future reference.

The chapters concerning the evaluation of balance and posture in Sections II I and IV provide more insight into techniques of evaluation. These reactions are present in many different positions. As children achieve control in such positions as supine, prone, sitting, kneeling, and standing, the presence of the appropriate tilting reactions can be evaluated (Fig 9-8).

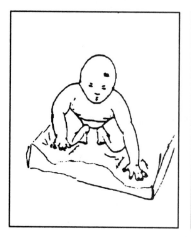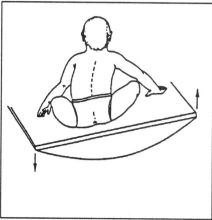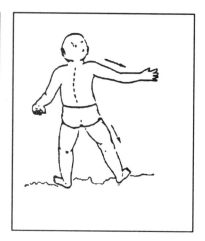

Figure 9-8 Tilting reactions in all fours, sitting, and standing.

There are general time guides for the appearance of tilting reactions. The reaction while in the prone position appears at 5 months, supine at 7 to 8 months, sitting at 7 to 8 months, all fours at 9 to 12 months, and standing at 12 to 21 months. All persist throughout life. Milani-Comparetti and Giodioni (1967a) state that incipient, or beginning, prone tilting reactions are needed for weight bearing on extended arms when prone. Therefore, you should be able to see an infant weight bearing on extended arms while prone at about 5 months of age. It has been suggested that full tilting reactions in the prone and supine positions and beginning reactions in the sitting position are needed for an infant to sit without hand support (Milani-Comparetti and Gidoni 1967a; Molnar 1974). Because an infant can usually sit without support at 7 to 8 months of age, you should expect to elicit full prone and supine tilting reactions and incipient sitting tilting reactions at this age.

The same investigators have stated that full tilting reactions in sitting and incipient reactions in all fours are needed for creeping. Full tilting reactions in all fours and incipient reactions in standing are needed for standing and walking. Thus incipient or beginning tilting reactions in a specific developmental position are needed for the acquisition of the developmental milestone, although perfection of the tilting reaction does not take place until the child has advanced developmentally one stage beyond it.

Remember the discussion in Chapter 3 on motor development concerning the current lack of proof that one pattern is a definite prerequisite to another? The statements above concerning the need for certain tilting patterns to be present before certain other movements can be accomplished is based on observation and correlation studies. These

244

patterns usually do appear in the sequences described in association with the movements they are purported to influence. That makes them of predictive value at the very least. Balance reactions are necessary for maintaining stability within whatever base of support and condition of the support surface is present. Using the information in this chapter in conjunction with the presentation of balance functions in Sections III and IV will provide you with a rich array of possibilities for both definitive evaluation and treatment approaches.

Postural Fixation Reactions

Another balance reaction is called the postural fixation reaction. This reaction automatically sustains and balances the baby as a whole and his individual parts--head, trunk, and extremities--in a position appropriate to the activity of the moment and to any external forces that may be acting on him (Martin 1967). As with tilting reactions, postural fixation reactions appear with the development of competence against gravity in the basic milestone positions (prone, supine, sitting, all fours, standing) and persist throughout life.

Postural fixation reactions are similar to tilting reactions except that (1) the former reactions occur during voluntary activity or because of external forces having been applied to the body when the base of support itself is stable and (2) the latter reactions occur in response to changes in the base of support.

In evaluating postural fixation reactions, either you may encourage a child or adult to engage in voluntary activities while you observe what takes place or you may exert the external force. As with tilting reactions, you should notice a curving of the vertebral column toward the external force, with abduction and extension of the extremities on the side to which force was applied (Fig 9-9). Again, if the force is so intense that it becomes impossible for the individual to use postural fixation to recover balance, you should expect to see protective reactions (Fig 9-10).

Test Procedure

In testing for postural fixation reactions, either a force can be applied when the infant is prone but supported on extended arms or a voluntary goal-directed activity can be used that requires a shift in the center of gravity. Pushing the infant at one shoulder will cause a bracing of his opposite arm and possibly extension and abduction of the arm on the side the examiner touched. The same reaction may be observed when the child is reaching for an object while bearing weight on one arm. Observe the quality of the trunk reactions. There should be an elongation on the weight bearing side as the weight shift occurs. Many clients with inadequate responses and control will sink into the support surface and collapse on the weight bearing side, thus gaining stability

245

from the support surface itself rather than through control of trunk patterns.

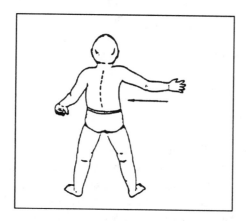

Figure 9-9 Postural fixation reactions. With a stable base of support, the individual receives an external destabilizing force such as a push. Note the curvature of the spine and position of the extremities on the side of the force.

Figure 9-10 If the destabilizing force is sufficient to overcome the postural fixation reactions, protective extension reactions are seen in the opposite extremities.

Obviously, testing and observing during volitional activity can be done while the child or adult is also in the sitting position. You have already determined that if you apply force to the right side of a body, the body will curve toward the right. What do you think would happen were you to push a sitting child backward? Try it. Notice how the body curved forward. If you had a child or adult in a sitting position and you wanted to facilitate the back extensors, how would you do it? If you answered that you would displace the center of gravity forward, you are correct.

You now have a concept that balance reactions may be used to evaluate the neuromuscular and developmental status of the individual and to provide you with a means of treatment. As a child attains such motor milestones as sitting, creeping, standing, and walking, it should be apparent to you that balance reactions can be tested in any position the child is developmentally able to attain. Again, this testing can be done by applying force or simply by observing how the child reacts to the environment spontaneously. You may also change the environment and observe his responses.

As with the other positions, a child or adult can be encouraged to attempt many volitional activities while standing. By observation you can note postural adjustments being made by the individual to maintain the upright position. Additionally, you can apply external force anteriorly, posteriorly, or laterally, noting compensatory movements.

Many adjustments to changes in the center of gravity while standing are accomplished by initiating contraction of muscles in the ankles and feet. As you know from Nashner's studies described in Chapter 1, many parts of the body are involved in the adjustment to such perturbations. Thus muscles of the knees, hips, and trunk are usually involved as well as the ankles and feet. The sequence and timing of the muscles in these synergies are not fully developed until 6 years of age, but they are present to some degree from the time the child is able to stand (Shumway-Cook and Woollacott 1985). In response to an anterior force on the body, the subject will be pushed backward, and you should see dorsiflexion of his ankles. There will be some contraction of his knee extensors and his trunk and hip flexors.

Exactly what muscles respond to the perturbation and how strongly they respond also depends on the point where you apply the force. A push at the shoulders may not result in exactly the same pattern that would occur if the push occurs at the pelvis. A force applied from back to front may cause the individual to rise up on his toes by plantar flexing his ankles. A lateral force applied to the subject's left side should produce eversion of his left ankle and inversion of his right ankle. Of course, other joints and muscles will be involved in these synergies as well.

It should be noted once again that the observation of spontaneous balance reactions under the condition of functional movements is most important. These responses should be observed by the therapist, and possibly, attempts should be made to quantify the results for evaluation records.

Study Questions:

1. What are the purposes of righting reactions?

2. How do they differ?

3. Describe how you would test for each. How do protective reactions actually serve to protect human beings?

4. What is so important about the ability to stagger?

5. Elaborate on the rich array of possibilities for evaluation and treatment of balance problems, including tilting and incipient standing reactions.

Chapter 10 - Evaluation of Early Coordinated Patterns

The evaluation of spontaneous or elicited coordinated patterns of movement, which we have called reflexes and reactions, is one of many methods used for the analysis of posture and movement in infants, children, adolescents, adults, and elderly people. Traditionally, therapists have assessed reflexes and reactions based on the assumption that these early forms of movement were the building blocks of later motor control and skill (Easton 1972). Changes in movement from simple reflexes to voluntary motor control were considered to be reflective of inhibition of early subcortical motor responses through the growing influence of the cortical motor control systems. As you have discovered by now, those assumptions are probably not valid.

Contemporary therapists, who are versed in more current theory, will assess these early coordinated patterns based on the assumption that these movements are the expression of the dynamic interaction of many interrelated subsystems from which movement emerges to accomplish functional tasks. These early movements may serve to facilitate or constrain the emergence of later motor control or skill. By assessing reflexes and reactions, the clinician acquires a better understanding of the development of movement in individuals of all ages.

With young children, this evaluation should be accomplished in a sequential fashion in order to monitor the developmental course of reflexes and reactions when determining whether the rate of development is normal, advanced, or delayed (Campbell and Wilhelm 1985; Smith et al 1982). Sequential evaluations also are more accurate than single examinations in predicting developmental outcome (Capute et al 1978a). The persistence of early reflexes, or movement patterns, beyond the time of their normal disappearance has been shown to be predictive of later central nervous system (CNS) dysfunction, whereas delayed development in children with Down syndrome or mental retardation has been associated with delayed acquisition of postural reactions such as righting and equilibrium responses.

Role of State in the Evaluation

Because responses obtained during evaluation of reflexes and reactions depend on the state of the nervous system, testing should be administered at optimal times for the infant and child and should be recorded (Stengel et al 1985). As noted in Chapter 2, Brazelton (1984) identified six states reflecting the status of the nervous system.

There are two sleep states:

State 1. Deep sleep--characterized by eyes closed, regular breathing, and no spontaneous activity except startles or jerky movements.

State 2 Light sleep--denoted by rapid eye movements at regular intervals under closed lids; irregular respirations; and low activity level with random movements, startles, or startle equivalents.

There are four awake states:

State 3. Drowsy--eyes may be open or closed, and activity level is variable with interspersed, mild startles from time to time.

State 4. Alert--eyes are open, and motor activity is at a minimum.

State 5. Active--eyes are open, and there is considerable motor activity with thrusting movements of the extremities.

State 6. Intense crying.

State and *context* are two important concepts that every therapist should master.

The most optimal state for assessing reflexes and reactions is state 4 in which the infant is quiet and alert. State influences how much muscle tension is present at any point in time and thus how much movement and the type of movement that will be expressed (Prechtl 1977). Thelen et al (1987) have suggested that arousal level in the infant may be a scalar element, or one scaled in a linear fashion, that produces phase shifts. Remember from Chapter 2 that a phase shift is the change into a new movement pattern and that such shifts may be instantaneous. For example, you will remember that in states 1, 2, and 3, reciprocal kicking is not observed; in states 4 and 5, smooth reciprocal movement of the legs in the supine position is present; in state 6, reciprocal kicking again is not present but the legs are held stiffly in extension. Results of a study by Smith et al (1982) suggest that state influences the motor pattern of the tonic labyrinthine reflex, asymmetric tonic neck reflex, symmetric tonic neck reflex, crossed extension, and Moro reflex patterns in children who have cerebral palsy with spastic quadriplegia. The higher the state, or the more agitated the child, the less consistent were the responses to the stimuli.

State must be taken into consideration when evaluating reflexes and reactions in order to make meaningful clinical decisions. Behavioral state should be monitored throughout the examination to provide a dynamic state profile (ie, a description of the movement patterns you observe or elicit along with the state in which they appear) as an additional index from which to make clinical decisions. To be valid, it is essential that the examination instructions indicate, for each item, the

250

optimal state of the infant in which the examiner should carry out the testing and for which states the item cannot be appropriately completed (Prechtl 1982). There are some tests available that indicate in what particular state the infant should be for specific items to be administered. These tests, which are described in Appendix A, include the Assessment of Preterm Infant Behavior, the Neonatal Behavioral Assessment Scale, and the Neurological Assessment of the Preterm and Full-term Newborn Infant. The latter test provides space for the examiner to identify the state of the infant at the time of the elicitation of the behavior. Obviously, responses that do not tend to influence the state significantly should be carried out early in the examination, while those upsetting the infant, such as the Moro and the ATNR, should be performed last.

Observation of Spontaneous and Elicited Postures and Movements

Because reflexes and reactions are related to posture and movement, evaluation should be done under two conditions: (1) observing spontaneous and voluntary postures and movements and analyzing them with respect to the components of movement associated with the specific posture and (2) providing specific hands-on examination in a stimulus-response mode, if indicated. Studies comparing spontaneous and stimulus-elicited responses will be described next.

Observation of Spontaneous Movements

It has been asserted that observing the child move provides more reliable diagnostic information than handling the infant and stimulating responses. This assumption was supported in a study on the reliability of the Movement Assessment of Infants in which reliability of observed items was greater than that of elicited items (Haley et al 1986). In addition, 7 of 17 items that were highly significant for prediction of cerebral palsy in low-birthweight infants were observational items not involving handling (Harris 1987). An effective supplement to observation is videotaping the child, because it allows you to review the tape, repeatedly if necessary, for a more valid and reliable examination of the components of movement.

Evaluation of Elicited Responses

With respect to the elicitation of reflexes and reactions, you may want to choose one of the following tests. Each has one or more sections that require the examination of reflexes and reactions. Each of the following screening and evaluation tools is described in Appendix A.

Assessment of Preterm Infant Behavior (APIB).
Chandler Movement Assessment of Infants-Screening Test
     (CMAI-ST).
Milani-Comparetti Motor Development Screening Test.
Movement Assessment of Infants (MAI).
Neonatal Behavioral Assessment Scale (NBAS).
Neonatal Neurobehavioral Examination (NNE).
Neurological Assessment of the Preterm and Full-term Newborn Infant
     (NAPI).
Neurological Examination of the Full-Term Newborn Infant .
Primitive Reflex Profile (PRP).
Reflex Profile.

The evaluation of reflexes and reactions has long been an essential ingredient of the analysis of movement in infants and children. Specifically, such examination provides the clinician with a yardstick for the analysis of motor development by yielding some or all of the following information (Stengel et al 1985):

1. Index of development.
2. Assessment of muscle strength.
3. Identification of movement dysfunction.
4. Identification of motor delay.
5. Prediction of future developmental outcome.
6. Establishment of baseline for treatment.
7. Determination of success of treatment.
8. Aid in research in movement development.

In most examinations, the following are considered to be significant observations:

1. Failure to observe a posture or movement or to obtain a response may indicate general developmental delay or a sensorimotor dysfunction.

2. Persistence of early coordinated movement patterns, or responses, beyond the time when they should disappear or become integrated may indicate either general developmental delay or sensorimotor dysfunction.

3. Specific clusters of deviant postures and movements, or responses, are more predictive of future outcome than a single abnormal response. Item clusters also may be more clinically reliable and useful than individual items (Haley et al 1986; Schneider et al 1988).

4. Presence of asymmetries may indicate the following:

     a) injury to peripheral nerves of the extremity as seen in infants with Erbs palsy,

b) injury to muscles of an extremity,

c) muscle weakness, or

d) insult to one side of the brain.

Although the presence of asymmetries has traditionally been thought to indicate insult to one side of the brain or unequal injury and has been found important in the early detection of cerebral palsy, recent evidence has shown that asymmetries are normal in development (Thelen et al 1983). At 4 months of age, asymmetries are frequently observed and may be a normal component of movement (Gratton et al 1986; Schneider et al 1988). In addition, the presence of asymmetries has not been shown to be predictive of central nervous system dysfunction (Ellenberg and Nelson 1981; Harris 1987). Reliability in identifying and scoring asymmetries also has been shown to be poor (Haley et al 1986).

The evaluation of reflexes and reactions as coordinated patterns of movement is only one component of an evaluation. A complete evaluation should be done by therapists, including biomechanical components of the musculoskeletal system such as muscle strength, range of motion, flexibility, and postural alignment; movement components such as elicited reflexes and reactions; and spontaneous and voluntary movements. Other necessary components are motor development, sensory components, perception, and anthropometrics (body measurements such as height and weight). Assessment of motor milestones, which have been described as appointments with function, may better delineate poorly functioning infants than will reflex assessment alone (Campbell and Wilhelm 1985; Milani-Comparetti 1981). The information in this section can be applied most readily to infants and children. However, recall from the discussion on rolling that these coordinated synergies and patterns of movement generally have a life span aspect. The therapist will certainly apply the principles gained in evaluation and treatment to clients across their life span. In Section IV on treatment considerations, this point will be emphasized.

Prediction

A fair number of studies have been performed that were designed to determine whether certain activities or patterns or tests are predictive of later function. A summary of many of these studies is presented in Appendix B. This information is vitally important for helping the clinician decide what to use in the evaluation of clients. As with much research, the answers are not completely clear. Some studies support a relationship between a particular observed item and later function but others may not. Because the research conditions will vary, as will the approach of the investigators, you, the consumer of such information, must make the final judgments as to the relevance of any such study to your own practice.

Early coordinated patterns (primitive reflexes) can be used as early developmental markers, that is, an index of the state, or stage, of development. The earliest indication of the presence of a significant motor disability may be either the delay in the disappearance of an early reflex pattern or the presence of such a coordinated pattern to an abnormal degree. Obligatory early reflexes, those that control the posture and movement of an infant or child, may signify the presence of a severe motor disability. Such dominant patterns are always considered pathologic, and one might suspect that the child who has such reflexes also has cerebral palsy (Capute 1979; Capute et al 1984). The obligatory responses of the asymmetric tonic neck reflex, symmetric tonic neck reflex, tonic labyrinthine reflex-prone, and tonic labyrinthine reflex-supine should always be a cause for concern. Persistence of obligatory reflexes as the child grows is a definite sign of absent motor control (Badell-Ribera 1985). If the normal timetable for the appearance or disappearance of early reflexes is significantly delayed, cerebral palsy is predicted (Paine et al 1964; Stern 1971). Thus changes in the evolution of such reflex patterns may be one of the earliest indicators of motor dysfunction.

It is important to keep in mind that rarely do findings appear as single isolated entities and, if they do, that no significant conclusions can usually be drawn from them. Try to keep in mind that these studies ultimately are designed to determine whether the presence of findings at a particular early age will predict the diagnosis or status of the child at a later point in time. In some cases, the research was done retrospectively, that is, after the diagnosis was made the subjects files were studied to determine what evidence existed earlier that might have led to the diagnosis being made earlier. Keep these overall goals in mind, and do not let the various methods of investigating them confuse you.

From these and other studies, the following primitive, or early, reflexes appear to be late in integration and, if obligatory, may differentiate those infants who have cerebral palsy from those with developmental delay:

> tonic labyrinthine reflex--prone and supine,
> asymmetric tonic neck reflex
> exaggerated neonatal positive support,
> plantar grasp,
> spontaneous stepping, and
> Galant's. (NOTE: the Galant reflex is elicited by suspending the infant prone and stroking along the infant's spine with the back of your fingernail. The result is a curving of the trunk toward the side that was stroked .

One must keep in mind, however, the following:

1. A cluster of aberrant reflexes has better predictive value than does a single persistent reflex.

2. There is a phenomenon of transient dystonia in which infants may appear to have cerebral palsy but will develop normally.

3. Young and sick preterm infants may have greater numbers of aberrant reflexes early in life.

Transient Findings

Although early reflex retention, which is associated with delayed acquisition of motor milestones and delayed postural reactions, is often suggestive of a diagnosis of cerebral palsy, several investigators have shown that there is a transient nature to these clinical signs. Drillen (1972) was the first to describe the behavioral and motor components of transient dystonia in the first year of life in low birthweight infants (in this case less than 2000 g). These infants exhibited either decreased muscle tension or increased muscle tension in addition to increased extension in their trunks and lower extremities and a flexor pattern in their upper extremities. Also present were delayed motor development, exaggerated or prolonged early reflexes, brisk phasic reflexes, and delayed postural reactions. Sixty percent of those infants classified as having moderate to severe dystonia recovered spontaneously. Twenty percent were neurologically normal at 1 year of age, but abnormal signs reappeared shortly after ambulation. Twenty percent were diagnosed as having cerebral palsy. Those children who showed transient dystonia in the first year of life exhibited more school difficulties than did a control group at 6 years 8 months (Drillen et al 1980). The authors concluded that the residual effect of minor disability cannot be estimated until after school entry.

Transient dystonia has also been detected in full-term normal weight infants after perinatal stress (Amiel-Tison 1986; Drillen 1972). In earlier studies, investigators had also commented on infants with noted motor dysfunction and persistent early reflexes early in life who later developed normally (Paine 1961; Solomons et al 1963; Illingworth 1966). Subsequent studies confirm that although some infants diagnosed with cerebral palsy outgrow cerebral palsy, these children often exhibit subtle neurological signs or behavior problems, deficits in prehensile skills, and intellectual or other deficits by 4 to 7 years of age (Kitchen et al 1987; Stewart et al 1988).

Those studies suggest that a diagnosis of cerebral palsy early in life does not always remain stable and that many of these children do not demonstrate motor abnormality in later years. However, many of these children do demonstrate problems in learning at school age. Thus, infants and young children who demonstrate persistent early reflexes, delayed postural reactions, and delayed motor milestones should be evaluated sequentially through age 8 years in order to determine accurately the infant and young child's individual progress. It is also useful to clarify early impressions of cerebral palsy, developmental delay, and minor neurological problems affecting learning and behavior.

Lastly, it can be determined if the infant is normal and has outgrown cerebral palsy.

In all of these studies, the authors indicate that the process underlying these changes is not understood and may not be the same in each case. If one took a dynamic systems perspective in regards to these changes, a number of factors could be postulated to influence such changes. Each subsystem, such as muscle strength, flexor or extensor dominance, and balance control, participating in development has its own schedule of changing structures and processes as growth proceeds. These subsystems act as a cooperative whole and are sensitive to minute deviations in each of the participating subsystems. This means that at any point in the developmental life history (ontogeny), small pushes or nudges from within the infant, such as the number and severity of medical problems, or without the infant, such as the home environment or other socioeconomic factors, can direct the subsequent outcome (Thelen 1988). If you need further information on dynamic systems, please read Chapter 2 and the last part of Chapter 1.

Ontogeny of Early Reflexes and Postural Reactions

Several studies have addressed the developmental profile, or history, of early reflexes and postural reactions: Burns and Bullock (1980); Capute et al (1982a; 1984); Carter and Campbell (1975); Haley (1986a; 1986b); Heriza (1984); Paine (1960); Paine et al (1964); Provost (1980; 1981); Saint-Anne Dargassies (1977); Touwen (1976); and Shepphard and Mysak (1984). All studies except those by Haley (1986a; 1986b) were longitudinal. Six studies followed normal full-term infants from birth; two studies to 4 months (Provost 1980; 1981); one to 8 months (Shepphard and Mysak 1984); one study to 12 months (Paine 1960); one study to independent walking (Touwen 1976); and two studies to 2 years (Capute et al 1982b; 1984).

Four studies addressed the ontogeny of early coordinated movements in preterm infants: Saint-Anne Dargassies (1977) from 28 weeks gestational age (GA) to 40 weeks; Carter and Campbell (1975) from 34 weeks to 42 weeks; Burns and Bullock (1980) from 35 weeks to 12 months corrected age, although information is only available from 1 month of age; and Heriza (1984) from 32 weeks GA to 8 months corrected age. Haley (1986a; 1986b) looked at nonhandicapped and Down syndrome infants, between 2 and 10 months of age for the nonhandicapped infants and between 2 and 24 months for the infants with Down syndrome.

From these studies, five general models of the change in the complexity and quality of movement can be derived (Stengel et al 1985).

1. Inverted-U model (Fig 10-1): Linear increase in the response followed by a decrease. The profile of the asymmetric tonic neck reflex is a good example.

2. N-shaped model: Linear increase in the response, followed by a decrease, and again, followed by an increase (Fig 10-2). An example of a reflex that follows this ontogenic profile is the stepping reflex.

3. Period of no change in the response followed by a decrease (Fig 10-3). The Galant's follows this type of development.

4. No change in a response over time (Fig 10-4). Clearly, the deep tendon reflex would fit in this category.

5. Linear increase in response (Fig 10-5). Postural reactions such as righting and equilibrium follow this pattern of appearance.

By assessing reflexes and reactions in a sequential fashion, the clinician acquires a better understanding of the life history, or ontogeny, of the child and can better predict developmental outcome. In other words, the pattern of development may implicate a possible central nervous system dysfunction. For example, the rooting reflex has a developmental course following the inverted U-shaped model, that is, a gradual increase in the complexity of the response from 28 weeks GA to 40 weeks, followed by a decline in the response from 6 postnatal weeks to 4 to 8 months.

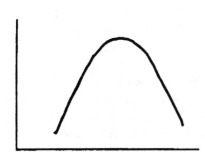

Figure 10-1 The inverted-U model.

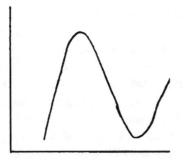

Figure 10-2 The N-shaped model.

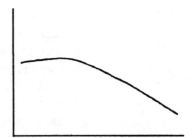

Figure 10-3 No-change-followed-by-a-decrease model.

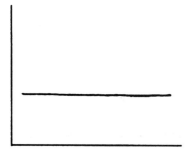

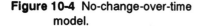

Figure 10-4 No-change-over-time model.

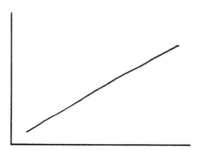

Figure 10-5 Linear increase model.

Hypothetically, a preterm (premature) infant could demonstrate a normal developmental course of this reflex from birth to the equivalent of 40 weeks GA, that is, an increase over time, but later fail to exhibit the integration of the reflex at the appropriate age, resulting in a persistence of the response that may endanger appropriate development at a later age. In other words, initial normal expression of a reflex does not guarantee uneventful development at later points in time. Sequential testing can uncover these patterns and provide substantial predictability, and this testing should be more widely used by clinicians.

An interesting phenomenon is becoming apparent as research is increasing with premature infants (less than 37 weeks GA). Many of the reflexes elicited at birth that later disappear or become integrated (an ontogenic pattern of no change and then linear decrease as described in #3) are being noted to be present before to 38 weeks GA. In the preterm infant, these reflexes often show a developmental pattern of emergence such that with increasing gestational age the response of the reflex becomes heightened. From these observations, it might be postulated that it is unlikely that any early coordinated pattern follows a model of absolute linear decrease. Rather, most reflexes probably follow an inverted U-shaped model of development in which there is a linear increase in the response before 40 weeks GA and a linear decrease after. Examples of reflexes following this model of evolution include the rooting reflex, sucking-swallowing reflex, Moro reflex, crossed extension reflex, asymmetric tonic neck reflex, and placing reactions in the upper and lower extremities (Burns and Bullock 1980; Capute et al 1984; Carter and Campbell 1975; Heriza 1984; Paine 1960; Provost 1980, 1981; Saint Anne-Dargassies 1977; Touwen 1976).

The asymmetric tonic neck reflex is an explicit example of the inverted-U model (Fig 10-2). For this reflex there are two profiles to be shown, however, one for the upper extremities, and one for the lower. If the profile only included postterm infants, it would not exactly follow the inverted U. It would be more like a no-change model or have a slight rise and then a decrease. When preterm findings are included, the profile clearly follows an inverted U.

Spontaneous stepping and positive supporting reactions follow a three stage, or N-shaped model, as do the neck righting reaction acting on the body and the body righting reflex acting on the body. During gestation, there is an increase of strength of the response followed by a decline with concomitant appearance of the mature response and gradual merging into voluntary activity (Fig 10-3). Some children do not bear weight between 2 and 6 months of age, the so-called physiological astasia, which is reflected in the return to the zero line in the N-shaped model.

All balance and equilibrium reactions, including visual placing, protective reactions, tilting reactions, and postural fixation reactions, follow a linear increase model beginning after birth (Andre-Thomas et al 1960; Connolly 1981; Haley 1986a, 1986b; Paine 1960; Touwen 1976).

The interpatterning of the righting, protective, and equilibrium reactions are discussed in more detail by Haley (1986b), who demonstrated that the developmental profile of these postural reactions over the first year of life have both cumulative and unidimensional properties; that is, early level responses are retained as higher level responses are acquired. For example, the infant will demonstrate partial equilibrium reactions in the all-fours position while showing full reactions in the sitting position. *Unidimensionality* refers to the fact that the postural reactions emerge over time in one direction, showing few regressions or interruptions in the sequence. Although 68% of the infants studied followed the same developmental sequence of the emergence of postural reactions, other infants deviated from this sequence.

There is a sequence to the ontogeny of early reflexes and of postural reactions, and these reflexes can be used in the examination of infants. However, you must be aware that variability is normal and that not all infants will demonstrate the expected sequence. Variability in performance is common in infant movement during the first months and years just as it is in normal adult movement (Richter et al 1989; VanSant 1988a, 1988b). Therefore, frequent documentation of development is necessary to gainan accurate picture of an infant's progress, to reveal various types of patterns of recovery or delayed deficits that are in need of close follow-up, and to determine which infants will resolve problems (Campbell and Wilhelm 1985; Heriza 1991).

Study Questions:

1. Discuss the word state as it relates to infants, children, and adults.

2. Why is observing spontaneous movement emphasized?

3. Manipulating a child is not all bad. Explain.

Bibliography - Section II

Als H, Lester BM,Tronick EC, Brazelton TB. Towards a research instrument for the assessment of preterm infant's behavior (TPIB). In: Fitzgerald HE. Lester BE, Yogman MW, eds. *Theory and Research in Behavioral Pediatrics, I.* New York, NY: Plenum Publishing Corp; 1982.

Amiel-Tison C. A method for neurologic evaluation within the first year of life. *Curr Probl Pediatr.* 1986;7:1050.

Andre-Thomas D, Chesni Y, Saint-Anne Dargassies S. The neurological examination of the infant. In: *Clinics in Developmental Medicine, No. 1. Spastics International Medical Publications.* London, England: William Heinemann Medical Books Ltd; 1960.

Andre-Thomas C, Autgaerdeen S. Location from pre-to-post natal life. In: *Clinics in Developmental Medicine, No. 24. Spastics International Medical Publications.* London, England: William Heinemann Medical Books Ltd; 1963.

Ayres AJ. *Sensory Integration and Learning Disorders.* Los Angles, Calif: Western Psychological Services; 1972.

Ayres AJ. *Sensory Integration and Praxis Tests.* Los Angeles, Calif: Western Psychological Services; 1989.

Badell-Ribera A. Cerebral palsy: postural locomotor prognosis in spastic diplegia. *Arch Phys Med Rehabil.* 1985;66:614-619.

Barnes M, Crutchfield C, Heriza C. *The Neurophysiological Basis of Patient Treatment, II: Reflexes In Motor Development.* Atlanta, Ga: Stokesville Publishing Company; 1978.

Beintema DJ. A neurological study of newborn infants. In: *Clinics in Developmental Medicine, No 24. Spastics International Medical Publications.* London, England: William Heinemann Medical Books Ltd; 1968.

Bender ML. *The Bender-Purdue Reflex Test and Training Manual.* San Rafael, Calif: Academic Therapy Publications; 1976.

Bennett FC, Chandler LS, Robinson NM, Sells CJ. Spastic diplegia in premature children. *Am J Dis Child.* 1981;135:732-737.

Berk RA, DeGangi GA. *DeGangi-Berk Test of Sensory Integration.* Los Angeles, Calif: Western Psychological Services; 1983.

Bernstein NA. *The Co-ordination and Regulation of Movements.* New York, NY: Pergamon Press Inc; 1967.

Bleck EE. Locomotion prognosis in cerebral palsy. *Dev Med Child Neurol.* 1975;17:18-25.

Bobath B. A study of abnormal postural reflex activities in patients with lesions of the central nervous system. *Physiotherapy.* 1954;40:259-280.

Bobath K, Bobath B. Cerebral palsy. In: Pearson P, Williams C, eds. *Physical Therapy Services in the Developmental Disabilities.* Springfield, Ill: Charles C Thomas, Publisher; 1972:31-185.

Bosma JF. Anatomic and physiologic development of the speech apparatus. In: Tower DB, ed. *The Nervous System, III. Human Communication and its Disorders.* New York, NY: Raven Press; 1975.

Bowman OJ, Katz B. Hand strength and prone extension in right-dominant 6 to 9 year olds. *Am J Occup Ther.* 1984;8:367-376.

Brander R, Kramer J, Dancsak M, et al. Inter-rater and test-retest reliabilities of the movement assessment of infants. Pediatric Physical Therapy. 1993;5:9-15.

Brazelton T. Neonatal Behavioral Assessment Scale. In: *Clinics in Developmental Medicine, No.50. Spastics International Medical Publications.* 2 ed. Philadelphia, Pa: J B Lippincott Co; 1984

Burns YR, Bullock MI. Sensory and motor development of pre-term infants. *Australian Journal of Physiotherapy.* 1980;26:229-243.

Campbell SK, Wilhelm IJ. Developmental sequences in infants at high risk for central nervous system dysfunction: the recovery process in the first year of life. In: Stack JM. *The Special Infant: An Interdisciplinary Approach to the Optimal Development of Infants.* New York, NY: Human Sciences Press; 1982.

Campbell SK, Wilhelm IJ. Development from birth to 3 years of age of 15 children at high risk for central nervous system dysfunction: interim report. *Phys Ther.* 1985;65:463-469.

Capute AJ, Accardo PJ, Vining EPG, et al. Primitive reflex profile: a pilot study. *Phys Ther.* 1978a;58:1061-1065.

Capute AJ, Accardo PJ, Vining EPG, et al. *Primitive Reflex Profile.* Baltimore, Md, University Park Press; 1978b.

Capute AJ, Palmer FB, Shapiro BK, et al. Primitive reflex profile: a quantitation of primitive reflexes in infancy. *Dev Med Child Neurol.* 1984;26:375-383.

Capute AJ, Shapiro BK, Accardo PJ. Motor functions: associated primitive reflex profiles. *Dev Med Child Neurol.* 1982a;24:662-669.

Capute AJ, Wachtel RC, Palmer FB, et al. A prospective study of three postural reactions. *Dev Med Child Neurol.* 1982b;24:314-320.

Capute AJ. Identifying cerebral palsy in infancy through study of primitive-reflex profiles. *Pediatric Ann.* 1979;8:589-595.

Carr JH, Shepherd RB. *A Motor Relearning Program for Stroke*, ed 2. Rockville, Md, Aspen Publishers Inc; 1987.

Carter RE, Campbell SK. Early Neuromuscular development of the premature infant. *Phys Ther.* 1975;55:1332-1341.

Chandler LS. Screening for movement dysfunction in infancy. In: Sweeney JK. *The High-Risk Neonate: Developmental Therapy Perspectives.* New York, NY: The Haworth Press Inc; 1986.

Chandler LS, Andrews MS, Swanson MW. *Movement Assessment of Infants: A Manual.* Rolling Bay, Wa: Infant Movement Research; 1980.

Chasnoff IR, Burns WJ. The Moro reaction: a scoring system for neonatal narcotic withdrawal. *Dev Med Child Neurol.* 1984;26:484-489.

Connolly K, Dalgleish M. The emergence of tool-using skill in infancy. *Developmental Psychology.* 1989;255:894-912.

Connolly BH, Michael BT. Early detection of scoliosis: a neurological approach using the asymmetrical tonic neck reflex. *Phys Ther.* 1984;64:304-307.

Connolly KJ. Maturation and the ontogeny of motor skills. In: Connolly KJ, Prechtl HFR, eds. *Maturation and Development, Biological and Psychological Perspectives: Clinics in Developmental Medicine, No. 77/78.* Philadelphia, Pa: J B Lippincott Co; 1981;216-230.

Coryell J, Cardinali N. The asymmetric neck reflex in normal full-term infants. *Phys Ther.* 1979;59:747-753.

Coryell J, Henderson A. Role of the asymmetrical tonic neck reflex in hand visualization in normal infants. *Am J Occup Ther.* 1979;33:255-260.

Cowie VA. *A Study of the Early Development of Mongols.* Oxford, England: Pergamon Press Ltd; 1970.

Crutchfield CA, Barnes ML. *The Neurophysiological Basis of Patient Treatment, III: Peripheral Components of Motor Control.* Atlanta, Ga, Stokesville Publishing Co; 1984.

Cupps C, Plescia MG, Houser C. The Landau reaction: a clinical and electromyographic analysis. *Dev Med Child Neurol.* 1976;18:41-53.

deVries JIP, Visser GHA, Prechtl HFR. The emergence of fetal behavior, I: qualitative aspects. *Early Hum Dev.* 1982;7:301-322.

deVries JIP, Visser GHA, Prechtl HFR. Fetal motility in the first half of pregnancy. In: Prechtl HFR, ed. *Continuity of Neural Functions From Prenatal to Postnatal Life: Clinics in Developmental Medicine, No. 94.* Philadelphia, Pa: J B Lippincott Co; 1984.

deVries JIP, Visser GHA, Prechtl HFR. The emergence of fetal behavior, II: quantitative aspects. *Early Human Dev.* 1985;12:99-120.

Dhawan LD, VanSant AF. The effect of two levels of added weight on the movement patterns used to rise from supine to standing. Presented at the 12th International Congress of the World Confederation for Physical Therapy, June, 1995, Washington DC.

Dietz JC, Crowe TK, Harris SR. Relationship between infant neuromotor assessment and preschool motor measures. *Phys Ther.* 1987;67:14-17.

Doudlah AM. Potential or pathology: in the eye of the beholder. In: Slaton DS, ed. *Development of Movement in Infancy*. Chapel Hill, NC: The University of North Carolina Press; 1981.

Drillen CM. Abnormal neurologic signs in the first year of life in low birth weight infants: possible prognostic significance. *Dev Med Child Neurol*. 1972;14:575-584.

Drillen CM, Thomson AJM, Burgoyne K. Low-birthweight children at early school age: a longitudinal study. *Dev Med Child Neurol*. 1980;22:26-47.

Dubowitz L, Dubowitz V. The neurological assessment of the preterm and fullterm infant. *Clinics in Developmental Medicine, No. 79*. Philadelphia, Pa: J B Lippincott Co; 1981.

Easton TA. On the normal use of reflexes. *American Scientist*. 1972;60:591-598.

Effgen SK. Integration of the plantar grasp reflex as an indicator of ambulation potential in developmentally disabled infants. *Phys Ther*. 1982;62:433-435.

Ellenberg JH, Nelson KB. Early recognition of infants at high risk for cerebral palsy: examination at age four months. *Dev Med Child Neurol*. 1981;23:705-716.

Eviator L, Eviator A. Neurovestibular examination of infants and children. *Adv Otorhinolaryngol*. 1978;23:169-191.

Farber S. Sensorimotor evaluation and treatment procedures for allied health personnel. In: *Occupational Therapy Curriculum*. Indianapolis, Ind: Indiana University Medical Center; 1974.

Fishkind M, Haley SM. Independent sitting development and the emergence of associated motor components. *Phys Ther*. 1986;66:1509-1514.

Fitzgerald M, Shaw A, MacIntosh N. Postnatal development of the cutaneous flexor reflex: a comparative study of preterm infants and newborn rat pups. *Dev Med Child Neurol*. 1988;30:520-526.

Folio MR, Fewell RR. *Peabody Developmental Motor Scales and Activity Cards*. Allen, Tex: DLM Teaching Resources; 1983.

Forssberg H. Ontogeny of human locomotor control, I: infant stepping, supported locomotion, and transition to independent locomotion. *Exp Brain Res*. 1985;57:480-493.

Forssberg H. Development and integration of human locomotor functions. In: Goldberger ME, Murray M, eds. *Development of Plasticity of the Mammalian Spinal Cord, III: Fidia Research Series*. Padova, Italy: Liviana Press; 1986.

Fukuda T. Studies on human dynamic postures from the viewpoint of postural reflexes. *Acta Otolaryngol(Stockh)*.. 1961;161:1-52.

Gesell A. The ontongenesis of infant behavior. In: Carmichael L, ed. *Manual of Child Psychology*. 2nd ed. New York, NY: John Wiley & Son Inc; 1954.

Goldfield EC. Transition from rocking to crawling: postural constraints on infant movement. *Developmental Psychology*. 1989;25:913-919.

Goldstein K, Landis C, Hunt W. Moro reflex and startle pattern. *Archives of Neurology and Psychiatry*. 1938;40:322-327.

Gratton MP, McClintock MK, Levy J. Laterality as an early indicator of infants at risk for developmental disability. *Phys Ther*. 1986;66:741. Abstract.

Green LN, Williams K. Differences in developmental movement patterns used by active versus sedentary middle-aged adults coming from a supine position to erect stance. Phys Ther. 1992;72:560-568.

Gregory-Flock JL, Yerxa EJ. Standardization of the prone extension postural test on children ages 4 through 8. *Am J Occup Ther*. 1984;38:187-194.

Haley SM. Postural reactions in infants with Down Syndrome: relationship to motor milestone developmental age. *Phys Ther*. 1986a;66:17-22.

Haley SM. Sequential analyses of postural reactions in nonhandicapped infants. *Phys Ther*. 1986b;66:531-536.

Haley SM, Harris SR, Tada WL, Swanson MW. Item reliability of the Movement Assessment of Infants. *Physical and Occupational Therapy in Pediatrics*. 1986;6:21-39.

Halsey JH. Chronic decerebrate state in infancy: neurologic observations in long surviving cases of hydrocephaly. *Arch Neurol.* 1968;19:339-346.

Halverson HM. Studies of the grasp response in early infancy. *J Genet Psychol.* 1927;51:371-449.

Harris NP. Duration and quality of the prone extension position in four, six, and eight-year-old normal children. *Am J Occup Ther.* 1981;35:26-30.

Harris SR. Early neuromotor predictors of cerebral palsy in low-birthweight infants. *Dev Med Child Neurol.* 1987;29:508-519.

Harris SR, Haley SM, Tada WL, Swanson MW. Reliability of observation measures of the Movement Assessment of Infants. *Phys Ther.* 1984a;64:471-475.

Harris SR, Swanson MW, Andrews MS. Predictive validity of the Movement Assessment of Infants. *Developmental and Behavioral Pediatrics.* 1984b;5:336-342.

Hellebrandt FA. Methods of evoking the tonic neck reflexes in normal human subjects. *Am J Phys Med.* 1962;41:56-66.

Hellebrandt FA, Houtz, Partridge MJ, Walters CE. Tonic neck reflexes in exercises of stress in man. *Am J Phys Med.* 1956;35:144-159.

Heriza CB. *Early Intervention for Premature Infants.* St. Louis, Mo: St Louis University; 1984. Unpublished manuscript.

Heriza CB. *Kinematic Analysis of Leg Movements in Premature and Fullterm Infants.* Edwardsville, Ill: Southern Illinois University; 1986. Unpublished dissertation.

Heriza CB. Comparison of leg movements in preterm infants at term with healthy fullterm infants. *Phys Ther.* 1988;68:1687-1693.

Heriza CB. Implications of dynamical system's approach to understanding infant kicking behavior. *Phys Ther.* 1991;71:222-235.

Hirt S. The tonic neck reflex mechanism in the normal human adult. *Am J Phys Med.* 1967;46:362-369.

Hooker D. *The Prenatal Origin of Behavior.* Lawrence, Kan: University Press of Kansas; 1952.

Horak FB, Shumway-Cook A, Crowe TK, Black FO. Vestibular function and motor proficiency of children with impaired hearing, or with learning disability and motor impairments. *Dev Med Child Neurol.* 1988;30:64-79.

Humphrey T. Primitive neurons in the embryonic central nervous system. *J Comp Neurol.* 1944;81:1-45.

Humphrey T. Some correlations between the appearance of human fetal reflexes and the development of the nervous system. *Prog Brain Res.* 1964;4:93-135.

Humphrey T. Postnatal repetition of human prenatal activity sequences with some suggestion on their neuroanatomical basis. In: Robinson RJ, ed. *Brain and Early Behavior: Development in the Fetus and Newborn.* San Diego, Calif: Academic Press Inc; 1969.

Ianniruberto A, Tajiani E. Ultrasonographic study of fetal movements. *Semin Perinatol.* 1981;5:175-181.

Ikai M. Tonic neck reflex in normal persons. *Jpn J Physiol.* 1950;1:118-124.

Illingworth RS. The diagnosis of cerebral palsy in the first year of life. *Dev Med Child Neurol.* 1966;8:178-194.

Keshner EA. Reflex, voluntary, and mechanical processes in postural stabilization. In: Duncan PW, ed. *Balance.* Alexandria, Va: American Physical Therapy Association; 1990.

Kitchen WH, Ford GW, Richards AL, et al. Children of birth weight (less than) 1000g: changing outcome between ages 2 and 5 years. *J Pediatr.* 1987;110:283-288.

Larson MA, Lee SL, Vasque DE. Comparison of ATNR presence and developmental activities in 2-4 month old infants. Presented at the 65th Annual Conference of the American Physical Therapy Association; June, 1990; Anaheim, Calif.

Lee M, Aronson E. Visual and proprioceptive control of standing in human infants. *Perception and Psychophysics.* 1974;15:529-532.

Leonard CT, Hirschfield H, Forssberg H. Gait acquisition and reflex abnormalities in normal children and children with cerebral palsy. In: Amblard B, Berthoz, Clarac F, eds. *Posture and Gait: Development, Adaptation, and Modulation.* New York, NY: Elsevier Science Publishing Co Inc; 1988.

264

Lewis AM, VanSant AF. Age differences in children's movement patterns in the task of rolling from supine to prone. Presented at the 65th Annual Conference of the American Physical Therapy Association; June, 1990; Anaheim, Calif.

Linde S, Conklin M, Hanon J, et al. Rising from a supine position to a standing position: a study of individuals with multiple sclerosis. Presented at the 12th International Congress of the World Confederation for Physical Therapy, June, 1995, Washington DC.

Luehring SK, VanSant AF. Movement patterns of active and inactive older adults in the task of rising to standing from the floor. Presented at the 65th Annual Conference of the American Physical Therapy Association; June, 1990; Anaheim, Calif.

Marguis PJ, Ruiz NA, Lundy MS, Dillard RG. Retention of primitive reflexes and delayed motor development in very low birth weight infants. *Developmental and Behavioral Pediatrics*. 1984;5:124-126.

Martin JP. *The Basal Ganglia and Posture*. Philadelphia, Pa: J B Lippincott Co; 1967.

Martin T. Normal development of movement and function: neonate, infant, and toddler. In: Scully R, Barnes MR, eds. *Physical Therapy*. Philadelphia, Pa: J B Lippincott Co; 1989.

McCoy JO, VanSant AF. Movement patterns of adolescents rising from a bed. *Phys Ther*. 1993;73:182-193.

McGraw MG. *The Neuromuscular Maturation of the Human Infant*. New York, NY: Hafner Publishing Co; 1945.

McGrew L, Catlin PA, Bridgford J. The Landau reaction in fullterm and preterm infants at four months of age. *Dev Med Child Neurol*. 1985;27:161-169.

Milani-Comparetti A, Giodioni EA. Pattern analysis of motor development and its disorders. *Develop Med Child Neurol*. 1967a;9:625-630.

Milani-Comparetti A, Giodioni EA. Routine developmental examination in normal and retarded children. *Develop Med Child Neurol*. 1967b;9:5.

Milani-Comparetti A. The neurophysiologic and clinical implications of studies on fetal motor behavior. *Semin Perinatol*. 1981;5:183-189.

Mitchell RG. The Landau reaction (reflex). *Dev Med Child Neurol*. 1962;4:65-70.

Molnar GE. Motor deficit of retarded infants and young children. *Arch Phys Med Rehabil*. 1974;55:393-398.

Molnar GE. Analysis of motor disorder in retarded infants and young children. *Am J Ment Def*. 1978;83:213-222.

Molnar GE. Cerebral palsy: prognosis and how to judge it. *Pediatric Ann*. 1979;8;596-605.

Molnar GE, Gordon SU. Cerebral palsy: predictive value of selected clinical signs for early prognostication of motor function. *Arch Phys Med Rehabil*. 1976;57:153-158.

Morgan AM, Koch V, Lee V, Aldag J. Neonatal neurobehavioral examination: a new instrument for quantitative analysis of neonatal neurological status. *Phys Ther*. 1988;68:1352-1358.

Mueller HA. Facilitating feeding and prespeech. In: Pearson P, Williams C, eds. *Physical Therapy Services in the Developmental Disabilities*. Springfield, Ill: Charles C Thomas, Publisher; 1972:283-310.

Nashner LM. Sensory, neuromuscular, and biomechanical contributions to human balance. In: Duncan PW, ed. *Balance*. Alexandria, Va: American Physical Therapy Association; 1990:5-12.

Oppenheim RW. Ontogenic adaptations and retrogressive processes in the development of the nervous system and behavior: a neuroembryological perspective. In: Connolly KJ, Prechtl HFR, eds. *Maturation and Development: Biological and Psychological Perspectives: Clinics in Developmental Medicine, No. 77/78*. Philadelphia, Pa: J B Lippincott Co; 1981.

Oppenheim RW. Ontogenic adaptations in neural and behavioral development: toward a more ecological developmental psychobiology. In: Prechtl HFR, ed. *Continuity of Neural Functions from Prenatal to Postnatal Life: Clinics in Developmental Medicine, No. 94*. Philadelphia, Pa: J B Lippincott Co; 1984.

Paine RS. Neurological examination of infants and children. *Pediatric Clinics of North America*. 1960;7:471-510.

Paine RS. The early diagnosis of cerebral palsy. *Rhode Island Medical Journal* 1961;44:522-527.

Paine RS, Brazelton TB, Donovan DE, et al. Evolution of postural reflexes in normal infants and in the presence of chronic brain syndromes. *Neurology*. 1964;14:1036-1048.

Palmer CF. The discriminating nature of infants' exploratory actions. *Devlopmental Psychology.* 1989;25:885-893.

Parmelee AH. The hand-mouth reflex of Babkin in premature infants. *Pediatrics.* 1963;31:734-740

Parmelee AH. A critical evaluation of the Moro reflex. *Pediatrics.* 1964;33:773-788.

Parmenter C. The asymmetric tonic neck reflex in normal first and third grade children. *Am J Occup Ther.* 1975;29:463-468.

Parr C, Routh DK, Byrd MT, McMillan J. A developmental study of the asymmetrical tonic neck reflex. *Dev Med Child Neurol.* 1974;16:329-335.

Peiper A. *Cerebral Function in Infancy and Childhood.* New York, NY: Consultants Bureau; 1963.

Piper MC, Darrah J, Byrne P. Impact of gestational age on preterm motor development at 4 months chronological and adjusted ages. *Child Care, Health and Development.* 1989;15:105-115.

Prechtl HFR. The directed head turning response and allied movements of the human body. *Behavior.* 1958;13:212-242.

Prechtl HFR. The mother-child interaction in babies with minimal brain damage. In: Foss BM, ed. *Determinants of Infant Behavior, II.* New York, NY: John Wiley & Sons Inc; 1963.

Prechtl HFR. The neurological examination of the fullterm newborn infant. *Clinics in Developmental Medicine, No 63.* Philadelphia, Pa: J B Lippincott Co; 1977.

Prechtl HFR. Assessment methods for the newborn infant: a critical evaluation. In: Stratton P, Chichester J, eds. *Psychobiology of the Human Newborn.* New York, NY: John Wiley & Sons Inc; 1982.

Prechtl HFR. Continuity and change in early neural development. In: Prechtl HFR, ed. *Continuity of Neural Function from Prenatal to Postnatal Life: Clinics in Developmental Medicine, No. 94,* Philadelphia, Pa, J B Lippincott Co; 1984.

Prechtl HFR. Ultrasound studies of human fetal behavior. *Early Hum Dev.* 1985;12:91-98.

Prechtl HFR. Prenatal motor development. In: Wade MG, Whiting HTA, eds. *Motor Development in Children: Aspects of Coordination and Control.* Boston, Mass: Martinus Nijhoff Publisher; 1986.

Prechtl HFR, Fargel JW, Weinmann HM, Bakker HH. Posture, mobility, and respiration in low-risk preterm infants. *Dev Med Child Neurol.* 1979;21:3-27.

Provost B. Normal development from birth to 4 months: extended use of the NBAS-K, I. *Physical and Occupational Therapy in Pediatrics.* 1980;1:39-51.

Provost B. Normal development from birth to 4 months: extended use of the NBAS-K, II. *Physical and Occupational Therapy in Pediatrics.* 1981;1:19-34.

Rast MM, Harris SR. Motor control in infants with Down Syndrome. *Dev Med Child Neurol.* 1985:27:675-685.

Richter RR, VanSant AF, Newton RA. Description of adult rolling movements and hypothesis of developmental sequences. *Phys Ther.* 1989;69:63-71.

Robinson RJ. Assessment of gestational age by neurological examination. *Arch Dis Child.* 1966;41:437-447.

Rochart P. Mouthing and grasping in neonates: evidence for the early detection of what hard or soft substances afford for action. *Infant Behavior and Development.* 1987;10:435-449.

Saint-Anne Dargassies S. Neurological maturation of the premature infant of 28-41 weeks gestational age. In: Falkner F, ed. *Human Development.* Philadelphia, Pa: W B Saunders Co; 1966.

Saint-Anne Dargassies S. Neurological symptoms during the first year of life. *Dev Med Child Neurol.* 1972;14:235-263.

Saint-Anne Dargassies S. *Neurobiological Development in the Full Term and Premature Infant.* New York, NY: Excerpta Medica; 1977.

Sameroff AJ. Reflexive and operant aspects of sucking behavior in early infancy. In: Bosma JF, ed. *Fourth Symposium on Oral Sensation and Perception: Development in the Fetus and Infant.* Bethesda, Md: US Department of Health, Education, and Welfare; 1973.

Schmidt RA. *Motor Control and Learning: A Behavioral Emphasis.* Champaign, Ill: Human Kinetics Publishers Inc; 1988.

Schneider JW, Lee W, Chasnoff IJ. Field testing of the Movement Assessment of Infants. *Phys Ther*. 1988;68:321-327.

Shaltenbrand G. The development of human motility and motor disturbances. *Archives of Neurology and Psychiatry*. 1928;20:720-730.

Sheppard JJ. Cranio-oropharyngeal motor patterns in dysarthria associated with cerebral palsy. *J Speech Hear Res*. 1964;7:373-380.

Sheppard JJ, Mysak ED. Ontogeny of infantile oral reflexes and emerging chewing. *Child Dev*. 1984;55:343-348.

Sherrington CS. *The Integrative Action of the Nervous System*. New Haven, Conn: Yale University Press; 1906.

Shumway-Cook A, Horak FB, Black FO. A critical examination of vestibular function in motor-impaired learning-disabled children. *International Journal of Pediatric Otorhinolaryngology*. 1987;14:21-30.

Shumway-Cook A, Woollacott MH. Dyamics of postural control in the child with Down syndrome. *Phys Ther*. 1985;65:1315-1322.

Sieg DW, Shuster JJ. Comparison of three positions for evaluating the asymmetrical tonic neck reflex. *Am J Occup Ther*. 1979;33:311-316.

Silver A. Psychologic aspects of pediatrics: postural and righting responses in children. *J Pediatr*. 1952;41:493-498.

Smith SL, Gossman MR, Canan BC. Selected primitive reflexes in children with cerebral palsy: consistency of response. *Phys Ther*. 1982;62:1115-1120.

Solomons B, Holden RH, Denhoff E. The changing picture of cerebral dysfunction in early childhood. *J Pediatr*. 1963;63:113-120.

Stengel TJ, Attermeier SM, Bly L, Heriza CB. Evaluation of sensorimotor dysfunction. In: Campbell SK. ed. *Pediatric Neurologic Physical Therapy*. New York, NY: Churchill Livingstone Inc; 1985.

Stern FM. The reflex development of the infant. *Am J Occup Ther*. 1971;25:155-158.

Stewart KB, Deitz JC, Crowe TK, et al. Transient neurological signs in infancy and motor outcomes at 4 1/2 years in children born biologically at risk. *Topics in Early Childhood Education*. 1988;7:81-83.

Stuberg WA, Dehne PR, Miedaner JA, White P. *Milani-Comparetti Motor Development Screening Test: Test Manual*. Omaha, Neb: Media Resource Center, C. Louis Meyer Children's Rehabilitation Institute, University of Nebraska Medical Center; 1987.

Swanson M. *Written communication*. Seattle, Wa: Child Development and Rehabilitation Center, WJ-10, University of Washington; April 1990.

Thelen E. Rhythmical stereotypies in normal human infants. *Animal Behavior*. 1979;27:699-715.

Thelen E. Developmental origins of motor coordination: leg movements in infants. *Dev Psychobiol*. 1985;18:1-22.

Thelen E. On the nature of developing motor systems and the transition to extrauterine life. In: Smotherman W, Robinson SA, eds, *Behavior of the fetus*. Bloomfield, NJ: Telford Press; 1988.

Thelen E, Fisher D. Newborn stepping: an explanation for a "disappearing" reflex. *Developmental Psychology*. 1982;18:760-775.

Thelen E, Fisher D. From spontaneous to instrumental behavior: kinematic analysis of movement changes during very early learning. *Child Dev*. 1983;54:129-150.

Thelen E, Fisher D, Ridley-Johnson R, Griffin NJ. Effects of body build and arousal on newborn infant stepping. *Dev Psychobiol*. 1982;15:447-453.

Thelen E, Ridley-Johnson R, Fisher D. Shifting patterns of bilateral coordination and lateral dominance in the leg movements of young infants. *Dev Psychobiol*. 1983;16:29-46.

Thelen E, Kelso JS, Fogel A. Self-organizing systems and infant motor development. *Developmental Review*. 1987;7:39-65.

Thelen E, Ulrich BD. Hidden skills: a dynamic systems analysis of treadmill stepping during the first year. *Monogr Soc Res Child Dev*.; 1991;56:1-99.

Thexton AJ. Some aspects of neurophysiology of dental interest. *J Dent*. 1973;2(2):49-54.

Tokizane T. Electromyographic studies on tonic neck, lumbar and labyrinthine reflexes in normal persons. *Jpn J Physiol.* 1951;2:130-145.

Touwen B. Neurological development in infancy. *Clinics in Developmental Medicine, No. 58.* Philadelphia, Pa: J B Lippincott Co; 1976.

Touwen B. Variability and Stereotypy in Normal and Deviant Development. In: Apley J, ed. *Care of the Handicapped Child: Clinics in Developmental Medicine, No. 67.* Philadelphia, Pa, J B Lippincott Co; 1978.

Touwen B. Primitive Reflexes--Conceptual or Semantic Problem? In: Prechtl HFR. ed. *Continuity of Neural Function from Prenatal to Postnatal Life: Clinics in Developmental Medicine, No. 94*; Philadelphia, Pa, J B Lippincott Co; 1984.

Tremblath JT, Kliewer D, Bruce W. *The Milani-Comparetti Motor Development Screening Test.* Omaha, Neb: Media Resource Center, C Louis Meyer Children's Rehabilitation Institute, University of Nebraska Medical Center; 1977.

Twitchell TE. Normal motor development. *Phys Ther.* 1965;45:419-423.

Twitchell TE. Reflex mechanism and the development of prehension. In: Connolly KJ, ed. *Mechanisms of Motor Skill Development.* San Diego, Calif: Academic Press; 1970.

Vanderlinden D. Ability of the Milani-Comparetti developmental examination to predict motor outcome. *Physical and Occupational Therapy in Pediatrics*, 1985;5:27-28.

VanSant AF. Age differences in movement patterns used by children to rise from a supine position to erect stance. *Phys Ther.* 1988a;68:1130-1138.

VanSant AF. Rising from a supine position to erect stance: description of adult movement and a developmental hypothesis. *Phys Ther.* 1988b;68:185-192.

VanSant AF. Life span development in functional tasks. *Phys Ther.* 1990;70:788-798.

Von Hofsten C. Catching skills in infancy. *J Exp Psychol[Learn Mem Cogn].* 1983;9:75-85.

Warren ML. A comparative study on the presence of the asymmetrical tonic neck reflex in adult hemiplegia. *Am J Occup Ther.* 1984;38:386-392.

Waterland JC, Hellebrandt FA. Involuntary patterning associated with willed movement performed against progressively increasing resistance. *Am J Phys Med.* 1964;43:13-30.

Winter DA. *The Biomechanics and Motor Control of Human Gait,* Waterloo, Ontario, Canada: University of Waterloo Press; 1987.

Wolf PH. The serial organization of sucking in the young infant. *Pediatrics.* 1968;42:943-955.

Wolf PH. The maturation and development of fetal motor patterns. In: Wade MG, Whiting HFA, eds. *Motor Development in Children: Aspects of Coordination and Control.* Boston, Mass: Martinus Nijhoff; 1986.

Zelazo PR. From reflexive to instrumental behavior. In: Lipsitt LP, ed. *Developmental Psychobiology: The Significance of Infancy.* Hillsdale, NJ: Lawrence Erlbaum Associates Inc; 1976.

Zelazo PR. The development of walking: new findings and old assumptions. *Journal of Motor Behavior.* 1983;15:99-137.

Zelazo PR, Weiss MJ, Leonard E. The development of unaided walking: the acquisition of higher order control. In: Zelazo PR, Barr R, eds. *Challenges to Developmental Paradigms: Implications for Theory, Assessment, and Treatment.* Hillsdale, NJ: Lawrence Erlbaum Associates Inc; 1989;139-165.

Zelazo PR, Zelazo N, Kolb S. Walking in the newborn. *Science.* 1972;176:314-315.

ke R, Draper DC. Notes on measurement of the magnitude of the asymmetrical tonic neck reflex response in normal ol children. *Journal of Motor Behavior.* 1984;16:336-343.

Section III

Vestibular System

Chapter 11 - Role of the Vestibular System in Motor Control

In therapy, our concept of balance often has restrictions and narrowness of definition because it is envisioned that someone without balance simply falls easily, is dizzy, or demonstrates shaky--or ataxic--movements. Clinical tests for balance have been limited to having the clients stand on one leg with eyes open and eyes shut and telling them not to allow the clinician to push them over as their equilibrium is disturbed by supplying thrusts on the trunk or by rocking a tiltboard.

Balance is an essential part of movement and skill. Balance is the ability to maintain equilibrium, that is, the ability to maintain the center of body mass over the base of support.

> **Equilibrium:** The normal oriented state of the body, involving adjustment to changing gravitational and spatial relationships.

For example, normal walking is considered to be a perfectly timed sequence of muscle activity that produces internal forces for interaction with external environmentally produced forces. It is easy to consider walking as a task requiring muscular coordination as well as balance. If the ankle is sprained, however, altered joint kinematics and the presence of pain change the pattern of muscle activity, producing a movement dysfunction that is recognized as a characteristic limp. A dysfunction in balance has occurred because the body's center of mass is displaced over the uninvolved leg such that the center of body mass lies closer to its limits of stability. In this case, the problem is easily localized in the clinical assessment, and effective treatment is undertaken to help heal the tissue disruptions and diminish the pain. The result after healing is a restored balance and a coordinated gait pattern.

Multiple Roles of Sensory Information

In a systems view of motor control, balance and coordination are dynamic integrative functions that make use of multiple sensory inputs. Motor output must be flexible, adaptable, and responsive to changes in the environment. Sensory systems interact with motor systems at all levels, ensuring environmental adaptation. The response to a particular stimulus depends on the environmental context in which it is presented. The same stimulus may result in different responses in different contexts.

> **Different sensory systems may relay information about the same conditions, producing redundant sensory cues.**

Sensory information assumes multiple roles in the control of movement. Sensory cues may trigger a postural response. Sensory cues containing essential information about the environment may be used when learning new movements or when fine tuning movements. The use of multiple senses in postural control preserves freedom of movement while retaining effective automatic stabilization for the maintenance of balance. The nervous system uses multiple sensory inputs for postural orientation. These senses include vision, vestibular input, and somatosensory inputs.

The organization of redundant sensory cues is a complex process. The nervous system must determine which senses are giving useful information and which ones are giving conflicting information about the environment and the relationship of the body to it. This information is necessary for the nervous system to determine the position of the center of mass in relation to gravity and to determine the nature of the supporting surface on which the body stands or sits or lies. Once the correct information is determined, the motor system will select, or assemble, the appropriate package, or synergy, that will move the center of mass to equilibrium.

Redundant information is helpful in determining the exact conditions present.

Postural control depends on the redundant inputs from the visual, somatosensory, and vestibular systems. The visual system registers the movements of objects in the environment and our movements within the environment. It is possible, however, for our eyes to deceive us. Have you ever been sitting in a bus, train, or car and when the adjacent object such as another train moved, you suddenly felt that you were moving? In this case, the information the visual system was relaying about your movement in relation to gravity was not correctly interpreted.

The nature of the supporting surface on which you are standing, walking, sitting, or lying is registered by somatosensory inputs from muscle spindles and joint and cutaneous receptors. These receptors tell us whether the supporting surface is slick, rocky, soft, hard, and so forth. These receptors also provide information that assist the nervous system in judging such self-to-self information as the position of the various joints of each limb in relation to each other.

The vestibular system acts to resolve intersensory conflict.

The vestibular system registers the position and movements of our bodies relative to gravity. It has been suggested that the role of the vestibular system in balance is to act as the body's internal reference system for determining the appropriateness of other sensory information. The vestibular system likely provides for the resolution of intersensory conflicts arising when information from other sensory systems are misinterpreted and the correct information is not conveyed. Thus, in the moving bus and train example, when misinterpretation of the visual input tricked you into believing that you were moving, the somatosensory system was relaying information to the contrary.

Theoretically, the vestibular system helps resolve the conflicts that may occur when interpreting information arising from these two senses. Once the conflict has been resolved, you quickly know that you were not moving but rather that the adjacent train or bus was moving. Such intersensory conflicts are frequently encountered in our everyday functioning within the environment. If we cannot resolve these conflicts intersensory conflicts are frequently encountered in our everyday functioning within the environment. If we cannot resolve these conflicts rapidly, inappropriate motor responses will occur, and movement dysfunction results.

To gain insight into how the vestibular system works, we will present the results of studies by one investigator who developed a moving platform with which sensory inputs were eliminated or, alternatively, inaccurate orientation information was provided (Nashner 1982). Body sway was measured under six conditions (Fig 11-1).

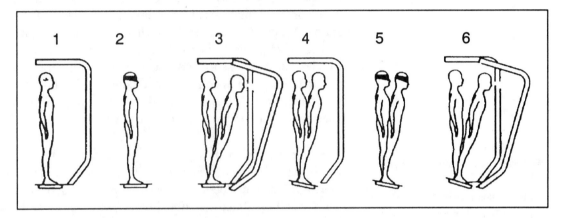

Figure 11-1   The six sensory conditions (see text). From Nashner (1990), reprinted with permission of the American Physical Therapy Association.

In condition one, the subject was standing quietly. In condition two, he was standing and blindfolded so that vision could be eliminated. A box with a visual pattern surrounded the subject in condition three. The box moved as the subject swayed resulting in a lack of visual flow; therefore, the visual system failed to register the movement. Because the body was actually moving, the visual system was not presenting information concerning sway that could be interpreted accurately to the central mechanisms. In condition three, therefore, an intersensory conflict existed between the visual system and the receptors registering motion in the ankles. When this conflict was resolved, the normal subjects swayed very little. As might be expected, a slightly greater sway was evident in condition three.

In a fourth condition, the platform was rotated in conjunction with the body sway. Usually, as the body swayed forward the ankles would move in relative dorsiflexion and the joint receptors and muscle spindles would register this movement. In the experimental condition, however, the platform rotated into plantar flexion in concert with the forward inclination of the body such that the relative dorsiflexion did not occur; therefore, the joint and muscle receptors could not register movement at the ankle, although body movement was clearly taking place. With condition four, normal subjects had a greater sway than with the first three conditions.

The greatest sway occurred in the fifth and sixth conditions. In condition five, the subject was blindfolded to eliminate vision, and the platform was rotated to provide inaccurate support surface information. The sixth condition combined the rotating platform and the visual box so that the subject received inaccurate information from both the somatosensory systems and the visual systems.

Several conclusions were suggested from these experiments. First, as noted earlier in the moving room experiments, as adults we rely most heavily on our somatosensory systems for orientation for postural control. You will remember from Chapters 1 and 2 that infants rely more on vision than proprioception. Second, the greatest sway is produced when both somatosensory and visual information either is removed or is inaccurate for postural control, most likely leaving only vestibular inputs to mediate balance. These inputs alone do not appear to be as effective as somatosensory and visual inputs may be under certain conditions.

> Subjects without vestibular function did not fall when standing with eyes closed because somatosensory information was sufficient for orientation.

Once the normal responses to the experimental conditions were established, subjects who had vestibular system disorders were put through the same protocol. It was surprising to discover that subjects with reduced vestibular function did not sway significantly more than normal subjects in the first two conditions that duplicate the Romberg test. Yet the Romberg test has been accepted for many years as the basic evaluation procedure to detect abnormal vestibular function. Because the subjects still had accurate information about the support surface from the somatosensory system, they fared quite well.

> If one or more sensory cues are misinterpreted, other cues help to interpret information correctly.

Thus balance is usually maintained by both vision and proprioception unless they conflict with one another. The vestibular system is not as critical to maintaining certain conditions of balance as was once believed, that is, balance is not provided by the vestibular inputs alone. Clients with complete loss of the vestibular system do very well unless there is a conflict between vision and somatosensory inputs. Of course, these conflicts are often present in everyday life. Thus, although the vestibular system is not the only contributor to balance, it is very necessary for the everyday activities of most individuals who are required to function within a wide variety of environmental conditions.

Other Components of Balance

Balance is a complex function that depends on a complex interaction of component processes of which the intersensory organization is but one. The eye and head stabilization process described earlier are also important components of balance. In addition, the appropriate performance and structural soundness of the musculoskeletal system provides a biomechanical basis for balance. The joints must function properly, and muscle strength and flexibility must be adequate. Weakness of ankle musculature or restrictions of the ankle joint will prevent the proper elaboration of any pattern involving ankle neuromuscular activity such as the ankle strategy described by Nashner in Chapter 1.

The client must also perceive his limits of stability, that is, how far can he sway in all directions without falling or changing the position. In addition, that perception must be consistent with the actual biomechanical limits. For example, clients with hemiplegia commonly list to the involved side despite the adequate strength of the musculature involved. The client is quite likely to insist that he is sitting up straight; thus the client has an erroneous concept of the upright position and the limits of his stability.

> **What are the limits of stability?**

Proper balance requires activity patterns that are anticipatory. Horak et al (1984) demonstrated that voluntary movements are coupled with anticipatory postural activity. Electromyographic recordings on subjects who did rapid flexion movements of their arms showed activity in their legs and trunks that preceded deltoid muscle activation for arm movements. Thus preparatory postural adjustments are important in reducing disequilibrium associated with a rapid coordinated movement. These movements are most likely entire synergies programmed, or assembled, to accomplish the goal; thus the postural adjustment is packaged along with the desired movement as a functional unit. It is important that the client have preparatory synergies and be able to learn to adjust motor responses to repeated conditions.

> **There is a postural set required as preparation for every movement.**

Performers must process sensory information appropriately in order to use it in conjunction with other senses. Visual system problems may result from the inability to ignore inappropriate information as might occur in clients with head injuries.

Balance is a complex process relying on the interaction of many systems, including the vestibular system. Physical therapists who base their treatments on this systems view of movement control will provide a variety of experiences for their clients to help them become responsive to environmental demands, keep them flexible, and increase their functional capacity.

Study Questions:

1. How does the vestibular system function in the maintenance of balance?

2. List several components, or systems, that are necessary for the maintenance of balance.

3. Explain how an injury or pain can disturb balance.

Chapter 12 - Anatomy and Physiology of the Vestibular System

Introduction

It is important for therapists to understand the structure and function of the vestibular system because it has widespread influence on muscular activity and movement. Specifically, the system has two primary functions: one, it acts to stabilize the eyes in space during head movements; and two, it contributes to postural stability in stance and in ambulation. With postural stability, it may act as the body's internal reference system for determining the appropriateness of other sensory information. Recent research has given us new insights as to how the system works, particularly as it relates to other systems in the body. An effective evaluation and treatment of clients with specific vestibular disorders, such as labyrinthitis, is now a reality on which further insights and improvements can be anticipated. The vestibular system has a pivotal role in the maintenance of balance and equilibrium, but that role has proved to be somewhat different than the one on which some of our clinical assumptions may have been based. It appears, therefore, that it would be very useful to delineate the proper role of the system in movement and its relationship to the rehabilitation of clients with movement disorders.

> The vestibular system stabilizes the eyes and contributes to postural stability.

This system, complicated by the multiple interactions of the vestibular pathways with many other parts of the brain, can be divided rather easily into two major anatomic and functional components. It has a *peripheral component* known as the labyrinths, or vestibular apparatus, and a *central component* made up of vestibular nuclei and ascending and descending tracks. The peripheral apparatus is the sensory component of the system--the part that generates the nerve signals that are transmitted to the central component and which ultimately may influence motor activity somewhere in the body. We will begin by describing and depicting the peripheral component. Considering together the anatomy and physiology of the peripheral part of the system should enhance the understanding of this sensory apparatus. The central component of the vestibular system will be presented in the same manner. Once the structure and function of the system is understood, the clinical evaluation and treatment of clients with movement dysfunction related to this system will be encountered.

Peripheral Component

Labyrinths

The labyrinths are located on either side of the head in the temporal bones of the skull. This whole component is about 2.5 cm long in an adult. It lies in the bone, on an angle, roughly between one ear and the opposite eyeball. In other words, if you were to stick a pencil in your right ear (not a good idea) with the intent that it emerge from the left eye socket, the pencil would pass through the labyrinth in the approximate plane in which it lies within the head. See Figure 12-1. This angle, or position, will become most important later for understanding the way the sensory receptors in the labyrinths are turned on, or activated.

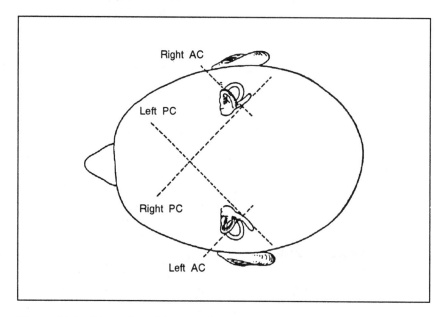

Figure 12-1 Orientation of the semicircular canals within the head. AC, anterior canals; PC, posterior canals. From Baloh (1984), reprinted with permission.

The peripheral vestibular apparatus is made up of a hollow bony system of tubes or ducts. Inside this bony structure are three membranous tubes, or canals, that are connected to two membranous sacs forming a continuous tubular system. This whole membranous system is connected with the adjacent auditory, or cochlear, system that also is encapsulated in bone. The three ducts, or semicircular canals, are arranged at right angles to each other in such fashion that one is relatively horizontal and lateral to the others, one is superior and anterior, and one is more posterior and inferior than the other two. Thus these canals may be referred to in the literature either as the horizontal, superior, and inferior semicircular canals or as the lateral, anterior, and posterior canals.

278

Sometimes, they are referred to simply as the horizontal canal and the vertical canals.

One of the membranous sacs is named the utricle; the other is the saccule. The utricle is in a superior position relative to the saccule when the head is in an upright position. Together these sacs are known as the vestibule, from which the entire system may have gotten its name (Fig. 12-2). Carefully study the figure at this time and identify the parts.

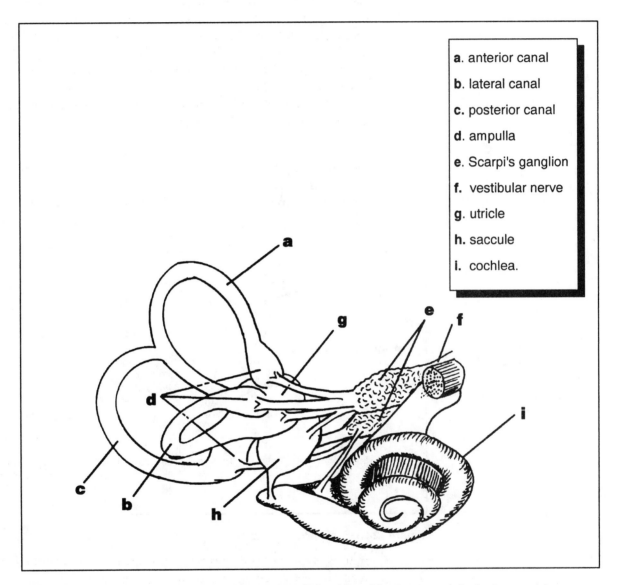

a. anterior canal

b. lateral canal

c. posterior canal

d. ampulla

e. Scarpi's ganglion

f. vestibular nerve

g. utricle

h. saccule

i. cochlea.

Figure 12-2 Human vestibular system showing the relationships of the three canals to the two macular organs and the vestibular apparatus to the auditory apparatus.

There is a bulbous enlargement on the each of the canals at the point where they join the utricle. These bulges are known as the ampullae. Figure 12-2 also shows that one trunk of the vestibular nerve sends branches to the ampulla of the superior and horizontal canals and one

279

branch to each the utricle and the saccule. From another trunk, the nerve branches to the saccule and to the ampulla of the posterior canal. The vestibular ganglion, also known as Scarpi's ganglion, contains the cell bodies of the vestibular nerve and is represented by the two fusiform enlargements on the nerve branches.

You may wish to stop here, cover the box with the labels above Figure 12-2, and see if you can identify all the parts correctly.

Inside the bony labyrinth is a fluid called perilymph that completely surrounds the membranous labyrinth. Inside of the membranous labyrinth is another fluid, known as endolymph, that has a density and viscosity that is slightly greater than water. The latter fluid, because of its viscosity, tends to remain inert. It is this characteristic of the endolymph, this inertia, that is responsible for the initiation of the sensory messages that will be sent from the canals to the central nervous system (CNS).

Inside each ampulla are two structures: the crista and the cupula. The crista is attached to the bottom surface of the ampulla and resembles a dumbbell in shape. Covering the dumbbell is a carpet-like layer of hair cells (Fig 12-3).

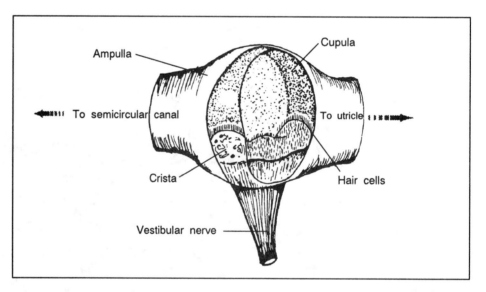

Figure 12-3 Schematic drawing of the ampulla depicting the crista with its hair cells projecting upward into the gelatinous cupula.

The fibers of each hair cell project upward and are embedded in the base of the gelatinous cupula. As seen in Figure 12-3, the cupula extends upward and is in contact with the topmost surface of the ampulla. In this resting, upright position, it effectively blocks the canal so that it divides the ampulla into two chambers.

Each hair cell has 40 to 70 or more fibers called stereocilia and one fiber known as the kinocilium. It is easy to pick out the kinocilium in pictures or electronmicrographs because it is always the thickest and tallest of the hairs, or cilia, in each hair cell. The stereocilia are of varying lengths and are arranged in steps from the shortest to the tallest, with the tallest being those closest to the kinocilium (Fig 12-4).

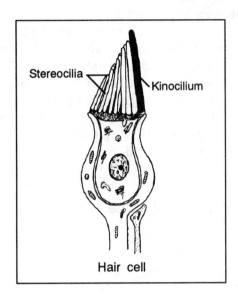

Figure 12-4 A hair cell depicting the varying lengths and the stair step arrangement of the stereocilia and kinocilium.

In Figure 12-5 you can see the orientation of all five sensory receptors within the peripheral vestibular apparatus. Notice how the crista in the horizontal, or lateral, canal is oriented almost vertically while those of the other two canals are more or less horizontal within the ampullae. The macula of the utricle is mostly horizontal. The anterior one third of this macula is inclined upward against the anterior wall of the utricle. The macula of the saccula is almost vertical against the medial wall of that vestibule.

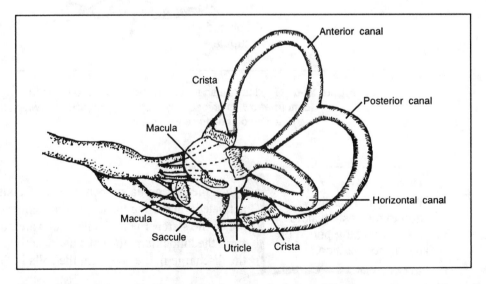

Figure 12-5 Schematic drawing showing the orientation of the five sensory receptors of the vestibular apparatus.

281

Activation - Deactivation of Hair Cells

Horizontal rotation of the head is a form of angular acceleration.

Endolymph can move only longitudinally along the tubes because the canals are narrow and almost completely filled with endolymph and because the endolymph tends to be inert. Movements that will alter the flow in the canals are angular rotations of the head. An angular movement could be either rotating the head to the left or right or moving the head forward and downward toward the floor. During a rapid, horizontal rotation of the head, the fluid initially tends to maintain its relative position in space and the cupula of the ampulla is pressed against it. When the cupula containing these hair cells and the endolymph are pressed together, the cupula bulges, or bends, in the opposite direction, causing the enclosed hair cells to bend with it (Fig 12-6). When the hair cells are thus bent, an electrical discharge occurs.

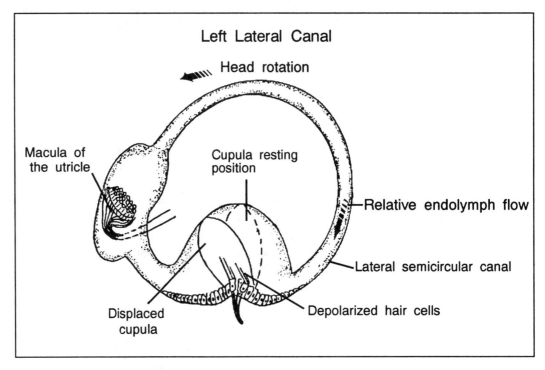

Figure 12-6 The lateral canal. When the head is rotated to the left (top arrow), the endolymph (bottom arrow) is pressed against the resting cupula, which moves it into a new position in the direction of the utricle.

Notice in Fig 12-7 that there is more activity during the resting state than during the period of hyper-polarization.

When the stereocilia are bent toward the kinocilium the hair cell is activated, increasing the discharge frequency of the afferent nerve. When the stereocilia in the hair cells are pushed in the direction away from the kinocilium, the cells are deactivated, resulting in a decrease in the discharge frequency from the cells in the displaced cupula (Fig 12-7).

282

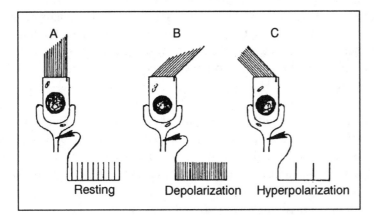

Figure 12-7 Scheme of the electrical situation at rest. (A) no deviation, showing the resting discharge; (B) during deviation of the cilia toward the kinocilium, resulting in depolarization; and (C) during deviation away from the kinocilium, causing hyperpolarization.

In the canals, the kinocilia are always oriented toward one side of an ampulla. They will be oriented either toward the side of the vestibule or toward the canals. For example, in the ampulla of the horizontal canal, the kinocilium of each hair cell is located on the anterior, or utricle, side while the stereocilia are on the posterior, or canal, side of each hair cell. Thus, when turning the head quickly to right side, the fluid in the right horizontal canal would bump into the cupula of that canal, bending it anteriorly toward the utricle. Because the kinocilia in the horizontal canal are oriented toward the utricle, the stereocilia would be bent toward the kinocilia, causing the hair cell to be activated (Fig 12-8).

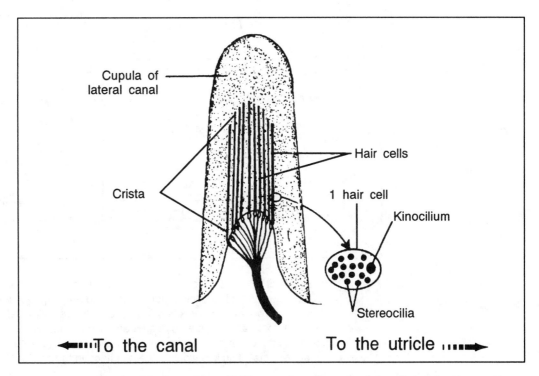

Figure 12-8 Cupula of the lateral canal, with an enlargement of a hair cell showing the position of the kinocilium and the stereocilia in a hair cell of that canal.

Think about this process until you are able to visualize just how the hair cells in the right horizontal canal will be bent toward the utricle during a rightward rotation of the head. At the same moment, the hair cells of the left horizontal canal will be bent in a direction away from the left utricle. In this manner, the activity in the right horizontal canal receptors will be increased while the activity from the receptors in the left horizontal canal will be decreased.

Activation is depolarization.

Deactivation is hyperpolarization.

As is the usual case with any receptor, there needs to be an adequate stimulus to activate it. In the case of the labyrinthine receptors, it takes a shearing force to bend the hair cells. As shown in Figure 12-9, the force is most effective when it is applied parallel to an imaginary line that bisects the hair cells straight through the middle of the stereocilia and on through the kinocilium (Hudsputh 1983).

It is important to understand this arrangement in order to visualize how certain movements would stimulate the hair cells minimally while others occurring in the exact plane in which most of the hair cells lie would be in line to produce a maximal stimulation. Thus some movements may produce a greater output from the hair cells than others, even though the movements may appear to be quite similar.

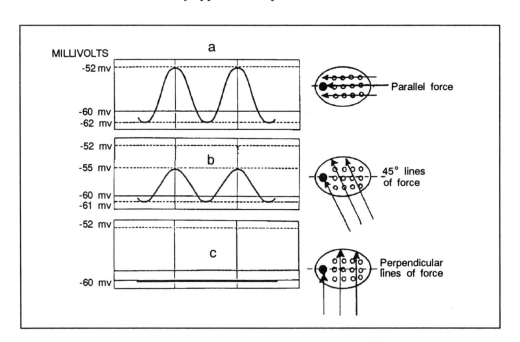

Figure 12-9 Effects of different directional forces on a hair cell. (a) A force that displaces the stereocilia toward the kinocilium, that is parallel to an imaginary line through the stereocilia and on through the kinocilium, and that bisects the cell is the most effective force. (b) A force applied at a 45 degree angle to the imaginary line is effective in depolarizing the cell but is less so than a parallel force. (c) A force perpendicular to the imaginary bisecting line would have no effect on the hair cell.

Because each semicircular canal is approximately parallel with a canal on the other side of the head (review Fig 12-1), the canals on both sides of the head form functional pairs. The two horizontal canals form one

284

The CNS will recognize either depolarization or hyperpolarization to detect the direction and velocity of head movements.

pair while each anterior canal is paired with the contralateral posterior canal. Remember though, that movement that excites one canal causes hyperpolarization in the opposite canal. This is referred to as the *push-pull* arrangement of the vestibular system. The CNS is apparently able to use either signal to detect the direction and velocity of head rotation within certain limits. Obviously, different semicircular receptors are excited by head movement in different planes, but the canals are oriented to each other in a manner that is optimal for detection of head movements in all directions.

Activation-Deactivation of the Lateral Canals

Before delving further into the functions of the canals, it is necessary to look at the anatomic structure of the hair cells relative to several principles of physics. Again, in the lateral canals, the kinocilia are always situated on the hair cells such that they are on the utricular side of the crista while stereocilia are on the canal side. And again, pressure applied to the hair cells of the lateral canals that tends to push the stereocilia in the direction of the kinocilia and toward the utricle activating this sensory system. This directional flow of the endolymph toward the kinocilia is referred to as an *ampullopetal flow* (Fig 12-10).

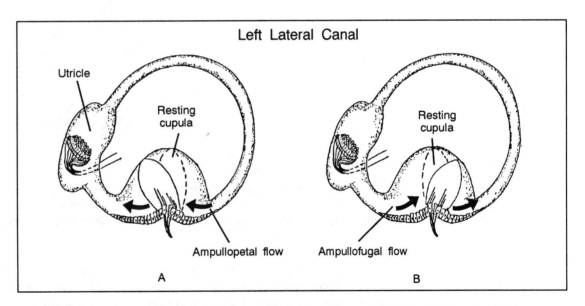

Figure 12-10 Diagrammatic representation of the position of the cupula in the left lateral canal during (A) ampullopetal pressure of endolymph and (B) ampullofugal pressure.

A directional flow of the endolymph that pushes the ampulla away from the utricle of the lateral canal is called an *ampullofugal flow*. This ampullofugal flow would occur when the endolymph in the canal is pulled away from the cupula and the endolymph in the utricle is pushed

285

against it, effectively bending the hair cells toward the canal and away from the kinocilia—an action that tends to deactivate the canal receptor (Fig 12-10).

If you were to turn your head quickly to the right, the right lateral canal would have a tendency for ampullopetal (toward the kinocilia) flow of endolymph. At the same time, in the left lateral canal, there would be an ampullofugal (away from the kinocilia) flow. A turning of the head to the right, therefore, would result in an activation of the right lateral sensory organ and a deactivation of the nerve cells in the left lateral canal (Fig 12-11).

> The lateral canal is activated by ampullopetal pressure, or flow, of endolymph.

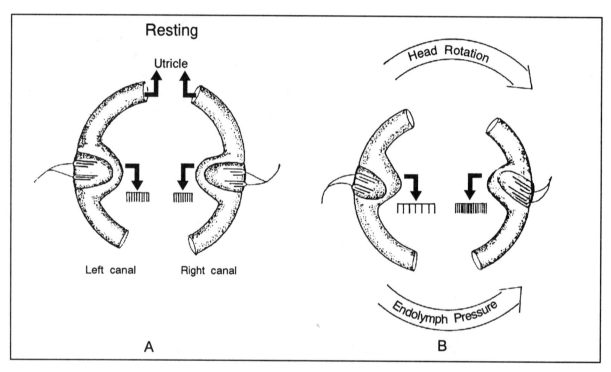

Figure 12-11 The firing frequency, or push-pull relationship, of the lateral canals: (left) with the head in a resting position and (right) with the head being rotated to the right. Note in the right diagram the increase in the firing frequency of the right canal and the concurrent decrease in the firing frequency of the left canal.

Another point that needs to be understood about these lateral, or horizontal, canals is that they are not exactly horizontal when the head is held in its normal upright position. If the face is tilted downward about 30 degrees from horizontal, the lateral canal is then positioned more nearly horizontal in space. The receptor will function more efficiently with the canal in this more level position because it is then in the best plane for ampullopetal and ampullofugal flow to take place. If the head is then quickly rotated to the right or left, one of the crista of the horizontal canals will be activated maximally while the crista in the canal on the opposite side of the head will be deactivated maximally (Fig 12-12).

286

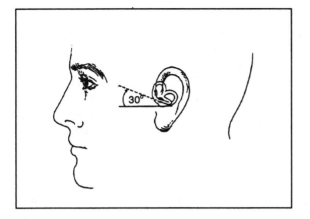

Figure 12-12 The plane of the lateral canal in (dotted line) the normal resting position of the head and (solid line) the nose downward position that places the canal in the most horizontal position. Redrawn with permission of Baloh (1984).

Activation-Deactivation of the Vertical Canals

Vertical canals respond more to ampullofugal flow of endolymph.

There is a big difference in the manner in which the anterior and posterior canals function compared with the lateral canal. That difference is related to the anatomic structure of the hair cells. Unlike the lateral canal hair cells, those in the anterior and posterior canals are situated such that the kinocilia are located on the canal side of the crista while the stereocilia are located on the side closest to the utricles. Therefore, unlike the lateral canals, an ampullofugal (away from the utricle) flow of endolymph produces a greater response than does an ampullopetal (toward the utricle) flow. If the neck is quickly flexed, the endolymph in the anterior canal will tend to lag behind, and the cupula would bump into the endolymph on the utricular side of the canal, effectively pushing the stereocilia toward the kinocilium. Thus, it is the ampullofugal flow of endolymph that pushes the stereocilia and the kinocilium in a direction away from the utricle in the anterior canal and that activates its receptor most effectively.

Canals are paired functionally (ie, when the right anterior canal is depolarized the left posterior canal is hyperpolarized).

The orientation of the hair cells in the posterior canal are the same as those of the anterior canal, that is, the stereocilia are on the utricular side of the crista while the kinocilia are on the canal side of the crista. The posterior receptor also responds to ampullofugal flow of endolymph in the same way as does the anterior canal. Remember, though, that the posterior canal is oriented differently than is the anterior canal. Thus rotation of the head downward and to the right would activate the right anterior canal because this movement causes an ampullofugal flow of endolymph. The left posterior canal would be deactivated because of the ampullopetal flow of endolymph in that canal. Again, we see the push-pull relationship of these two functionally paired canals. The normal resting discharge rate of the other two vertical canals may not be sufficiently changed because with the head in this position they are not in the most perfect plane for activation or deactivation to take place effectively. Therefore, the usual background level of electrical activity in the inactive vertical canals would remain largely unaffected. The

287

same is true of the lateral canals in that they also are not in position to be affected by this motion.

Summary of Canal Activity

There are three concepts that should be understood relative to canal activity: one is that the canals operate as matched pairs; another is that the canals have a push-pull relationship, which means that when one of a pair is depolarized, the other of that pair is hyperpolarized; and the third one is that the movement most likely to increase or decrease the firing rate of a canal is in the plane in which that canal lies.

The lateral canals function best when the head is tilted downward 30 degrees, putting the canals in their most perfectly horizontal position. The lateral, or horizontal, canal is the most responsive to ampullopetal endolymph flow. The vertical canals also function best when the motion of the head is most nearly in the plane in which these canals lie. These motions would be neck flexion or extension or diagonal patterns such as bending the head forward and to the right or backward and to the left. These vertical canals respond most favorably to an ampullofugal flow of endolymph.

Study Questions:

1. **Why do some movements minimally excite a receptor while others produce maximal excitation?**

2. **Describe the conditioned under which the right lateral canal would be deactivated maximally.**

3. **What causes hair cells to be depolarized?**

Macular Receptors

Macular organs of the vestibule are sometimes referred to as otolith organs.

The sensory receptors in the utricle and saccule are usually referred to as macules but are sometimes called otoliths. These organs differ in both structure and function from the sensory organs of the semicircular canals. Again, there are hair cells with hairs that project upward or outward into a gelatinous mass, but the mass is not attached to or in contact with any structure at its outer surface. Located on that outer surface, or membrane, are little calcium carbonate crystals known as otoconia, or otoliths, that adhere to the membrane because of its tacky, or sticky, surface. It is possible that the fine fibrous network that comprises the

288

outer membrane of the macula may also serve to hold the otoliths in place. We do know that when one of the macular organs is removed from the body, the sticky surface loses its tackiness and the stones fall off. It is the weight of these stones producing a gravitational shearing force on the hair cells when the head moves that increases or decreases the activity of the hair cell (Fig 12-13). The macular receptors are particularly situated to respond to linear or straight plane movements--side to side, up and down, or anterior to posterior.

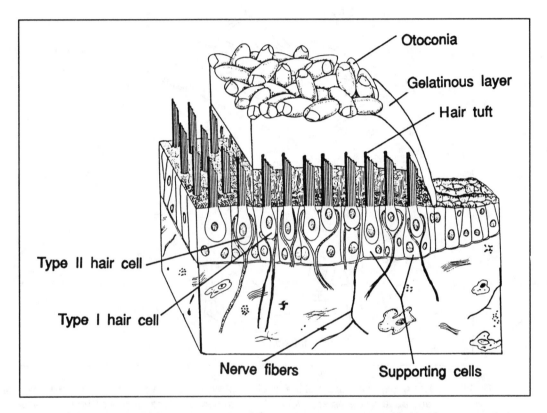

Figure 12-13 Diagrammatic representation of the components of a macular receptor, showing the otoconia, gelatinous mass, hair tufts projecting into the gelatinous mass, Type I and Type II nerve fibers, and supporting cells.

Macular Activation-Deactivation

There is another anatomical feature of both the utricle and the saccule that should be known in order to have an understanding of the complexity of the manner in which these sensors monitor movement. Look at Figure 12-14A and notice that there is a C-shaped line drawn through the diagrammatic representation of the macula of the utricle. This line is called the striola, and on each side of the line there are arrows drawn toward it. On one side of the line, the kinocilium is on the side of the hair cell facing the striola while the stereocilia are located laterally, or to the outside. On the opposite side of the line, the same thing is true,

289

that is, the kinocilium is always nearest the striola while the stereocilia are to the medial side. Figure 12-14B represents a cross section of the macula, showing the positions of the kinocilium and stereocilia of the hair cells relative to the striola.

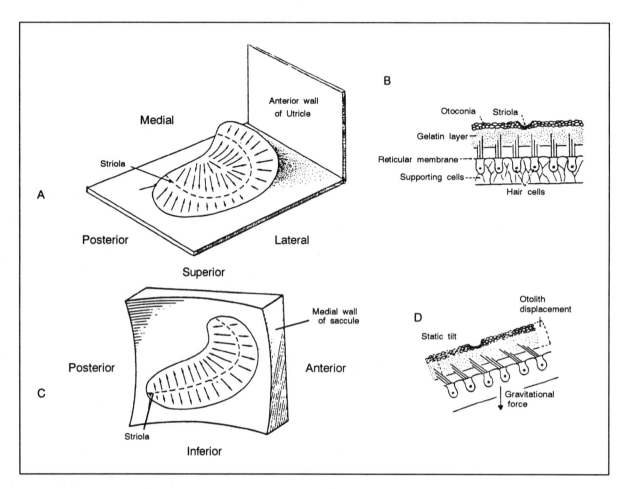

Figure 12-14 (A) The macule of the utricle depicting its striola and its mostly horizontal position against the floor and abutting the anterior wall. (B) Cross section of the macula of the utricle showing the positions of the hair cells relative to the striola. (C) The saccule showing its striola, its vertical orientation in the medial wall, and the position of the kinocilia on the side of the hair cell away from the striola. (D) A cross section of the striola showing activation and deactivation of the hair cells of the utricle during head tilt. Also shown (A and C) are arrows indicating the direction in which the kinocilia are arranged relative to the stereocilia in the two macular organs. From Baloh (1984), reprinted with permission.

As you study that diagram closely, it should be easy to visualize that some of the hair cells will be in the best position to be activated by a linear movement in a straight forward direction while some of the opposite cells will be deactivated by that same movement. Other cells may be little affected because they are not in a good position to read the movement. Recall that the shearing force applied to hair cells causes maximal activation or deactivation only when that force is directed through the middle of the bundles of stereocilia to the kinocilia. Visualize how keeping your head in the same straight forward orientation but moving your body forward and 10 degrees to the right

290

would bring different hair cells into play more strongly than those activated during the first movement. Perhaps you can also draw a mental picture of the many hair cells in the utricle that would be sensitive to a backward or forward tilt of the head because of the position of those cells relative to the striola and the curvature of the receptor. Notice just how it is possible for the labyrinths to monitor every exquisite movement of the head.

Otolith organs are sensitive to linear motion or tilt in any direction.

In the representation of the macula of the saccule (Fig 12-14C), the arrows are pointing away from the striola indicating that the kinocilia are on the side of the hair bundles facing away from the striola. Thus, during any vertical linear acceleration some of the hair cells would be highly activated while the bundles on the opposite side of the striola would be deactivated. It would appear that some of the bundles, especially those near the top of the striola, would be situated such that they also would be sensitive to anterior-posterior acceleration. It is clear that together these two otolithic organs are sensitive to linear movement or tilt in any direction and will pick up any movement, however slight. It is also clear that these two organs work together to inform us of our position in space and that their functions are complimentary. Figure 12-14D shows the hair cells on one side of the striola being activated while those on the opposite side are deactivated by a tilt of the head.

Nerves and Hair Cells

There are nerve fibers leading to and from the hair cells of both the crista and the macula. There are two different types of hair cells (types I and II), and the nerve endings are different on each type (Fig 12-15). The afferent nerve ending on the type I hair cell resembles a wine glass. Its fiber is one of the largest in the nervous system. The efferent nerve ending on this cell is of the familiar bouton type, but notice how it has a synapse on the afferent nerve ending. This efferent fiber brings impulses from the central areas to the sensory ending.

Most sensory receptors receive efferent input, which probably comes from the sympathetic nervous system. This arrangement serves to increase the discharge rate of the afferent fiber and is believed to modulate its response to the mechanical stimuli produced by the deformation either of the cupula or of the macular gelatinous mass.

The type II hair cell also has direct bouton type endings from both afferent and efferent nerve fibers. The afferent neurons are bipolar, and their cell bodies are in Scarpi's ganglion. From there, the fibers carry nerve impulses to the CNS. The efferent fibers originate in the brain stem and terminate in the periphery on the receptor hair cell. The efferent synapses on the type II cell also increase the discharge rate of the afferent fibers. These type II cells are thought to be less sensitive than the type I hair cells.

291

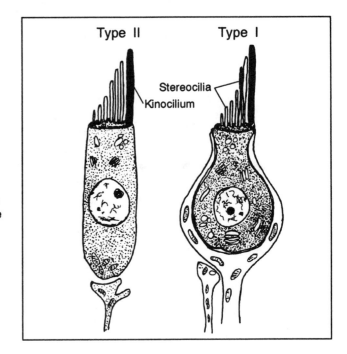

Figure 12-15 Representation of the components of type I and type II hair cells showing the chalice ending on type I and the bouton endings on the type II cell.

The hair cells in the five sensory organs of each labyrinth are in positional orientations such that it is possible for them to read every movement of the head, however slight, in any angular or linear direction. For example, the macula of the utricle is positioned more or less horizontally, with its hair cells projecting vertically (Fig 12-16). It is easy to imagine that any linear and horizontal movement (backward, forward, or side to side) would result in a bending of the hair cells.

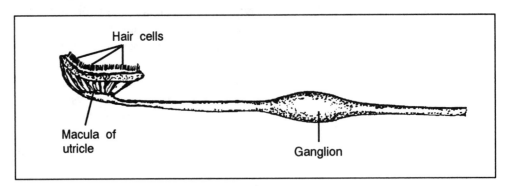

Figure 12-16 The sensory receptor of the utricle showing its horizontal position, with the vertical projection of the hair cells.

The macula of the saccule, on the other hand, is oriented vertically with its hair cells projecting outward, or laterally (Fig 12-17). Because the hair cells project outward into their gelatinous mass, with the otoliths sticking to the surface, it is also easy to imagine that when jumping up off the floor in a vertical linear motion, the shearing forces of the otoconia would displace the hair cells downward. This receptor is believed to function even during the subtle vertical up and down movements that occur with ambulation.

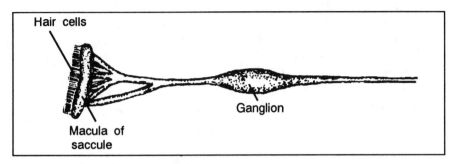

Figure 12-17 The sensory receptor of the saccule depicting its vertical orientation with a horizontal projection of the hair fibers.

Firing Characteristics of the Vestibular Receptors

The 10 sensory receptors in the external vestibular apparatus are never totally electrically silent for any length of time. Even though one canal is in the best position to monitor some movement, it does not mean that the other 5 receptors are totally deactivated. It simply means that one is more activated than are the others. Even though any angular or rotational acceleration of the head definitely would be monitored best by one of the canals, it is also possible that the receptors in the utricle and the saccule would also be activated by that same movement.

> Activation and deactivation of vestibular receptors do not occur in an all-or-none fashion.

The receptors respond to brief movements of the head rather than to prolonged unidirectional movements. With prolonged head movement, the endolymph tends to settle back into its original position in the canals or the macular organs, permitting the hair cells to start to return to their original resting positions.

It is fortunate that the vestibular system is arranged so that it does not remain in a highly activated state when the stimulus is continuous. Think about what happens when flying from New York to California. Initially, you would be very much aware of just when the airplane took off down the runway. Very soon, the sensation that the body is being thrust backward by the forward motion of the plane has died out. This sensation is diminished because the receptors respond only to acceleration, and when its ceases, they return to their resting state. That is, the vestibular receptors begin to slow down their firing rate and return to the resting level of activity they had before the plane took off. If this decrease in the firing rate did not take place, the trip would be exhausting and irritating because of your constant awareness of the forward motion of the plane.

293

Again, the fact that a sensory receptor may be depolarized or hyperpolarized by any movement or tilt of the head does not mean that it will stay that way for any length of time. (Most authorities agree that activation of the canal hair cells lasts from 20 to 30 seconds after rotary acceleration starts.) If the rotation continues but acceleration ceases, it takes the cupula about 6 seconds to return to its resting position, and the cells are deactivated. If the rotation is stopped, the endolymph will flow in the opposite direction and will deflect the cupula in the opposite direction. This reversal of direction effectively renders the cupula silent for a period of 20 to 30 seconds, after which it again returns to its resting position and resting potential because the endolymph has stopped circulating.

In similar fashion, a tilt of the head is read by the macular organs only for a short period of time--literally seconds. We sometimes are aware of the position of the head when it is first tilted in order to read a book held in the lap, but again, it is fortunate that the end organs are depolarized for a matter of seconds and then return to their resting state or else we might not be able to concentrate on reading.

The concept to be remembered here is that to activate the vestibular sensory organs beyond their resting state, a linear or angular acceleration must take place, with the key word being acceleration. The system does not respond to continuous movement or tilt, only to an acceleration of that movement or tilt.

It should be clear, however, that while canals respond mostly to angular acceleration and the otolith organs respond mostly to linear acceleration, any one of the sensory organs may respond to either type movement under the right circumstances. In fact, it has stated that "the vestibular receptors are the most precise and sensitive of all sense organs in the animal world." (Jongkees 1975, p 233). No doubt the multidirectional positions of the hair cells around the striola within the macular receptors contribute to that precision and sensitivity. The fact that these organs are never completely electrically silent because of the constant pull of gravity accounts for their extremely low threshold. Because of this low threshold, the smallest of movements in one direction will increase the resting frequency by depolarization and decrease the resting frequency through hyperpolarization of cells in the opposite side. This low threshold, therefore, becomes another big factor in the precision and sensitivity of the system in reading body position and head movement.

"The resting discharge plays an integral part in all aspects of vestibular function. The labyrinth must be considered one of the most important sources of general muscle activity. The resting discharge furnishes a continuous influx of 'excitation' via the vestibular nuclei into the motor centers associated with postural and locomotor muscle systems. It is known that loss of vestibular input results in prolonged general muscular debility that may even extend to the visceral musculature " (Lowenstein 1975, p 101).

Activation lasts 20 to 30 seconds--returns to resting level--rebounds in opposite direction, causing cupular silence that lasts another 20 to 30 seconds before resting potential is resumed.

To activate the system, linear or angular *acceleration* must take place.

Vestibular sense organs are never deactivated completely.

Why is the resting discharge so important to body function?

294

Vision, the Vestibular System, and Other Proprioceptors

A number of years ago an interesting experiment was conducted that showed what happens to humans when we receive conflicting information from the vestibular, visual, and somatic receptors. Subjects were seated on a rotating platform and then were blindfolded. Subjects were rotated to a certain level of angular velocity that was held constant for a period and then was decreased, and then the rotation stopped. Figure 12-18 shows what was actually done to the subjects. During the period marked (a), the subject was stationary in the chair. Line (b) indicates the period when acceleration was begun by rotating the chair in a clockwise movement. During period (c), the chair was rotated at a constant velocity for 2 minutes. During period (d), deceleration was initiated, and line (e) indicates that period during which all movement stopped (Parker 1980).

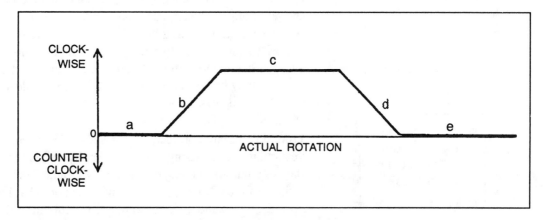

Figure 12-18 Actual rotation of subjects. From Parker (1980), reprinted with permission.

Figure 12-19 diagrammatically shows the perceptions the subjects had as to just what was taking place. Line (a') indicates that the subjects were aware that they were sitting still. Line (b') indicates that the subjects knew that they were being rotated in a clockwise direction. After a few seconds during the period of constant velocity (line c'), the subjects perceived that they were being slowed down and stopped. During the actual slowing down period (line d'), the subjects thought that they were being rotated in a counterclockwise direction. During the second stationary period (line e'), the subjects thought that they were being slowed down in the counter-clockwise direction. This misleading reaction to rotation is potentially dangerous to individuals who do not have a means such as vision to help solve this conflict (Parker 1980).

295

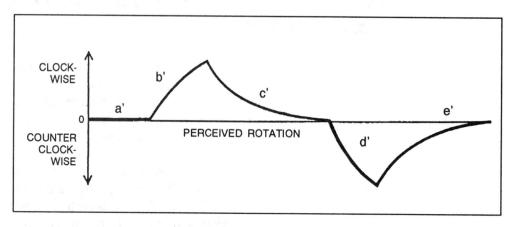

Figure 12-19 Perceived rotation of subjects. From Parker (1980), reprinted with permission.

The false interpretation by the subjects occurred because the vestibular system reads acceleration only and is not responsive to continuous motion. The sensation by the subjects that they were being turned in the opposite direction (line d') occurred because the endolymph, which initially deflects the cupula upon acceleration, will then settle back into its original state, causing the effect of deflecting the cupula of the opposite canal. When this opposite canal deflection occurred, the subjects had the sensation of being turned in that opposite direction, and because they had no vision, there was no available sensory system to tell them that this was not so.

From this research project, we can see that humans may be fooled by a vestibular system acting alone. Normally, when the peripheral portion of the system is stimulated, the central vestibular system and other higher centers of the CNS will exert an influence on what happens. Other body proprioceptors and vision also play a modulating role. Vision can also fool us when the vestibular system and other proprioceptors are not functioning together appropriately. For example, when sitting inside an automobile in a car wash, if you watch the whirling brushes pass back over your car, there is a strong sensation that the car is moving forward. Intellectually, we know that the car is not moving but it certainly seems to be doing so. This false reading can be corrected by simply moving our heads or bodies, thus calling into play the vestibular system or other proprioceptors.

It is possible to become accustomed to a stimulus if exposed to it repeatedly. The term habituation refers to this reduction in response with repeated stimulation. This phenomenon occurs over time. We humans may suffer severe problems with balance and equilibrium when we cannot adapt to stimuli of long duration or habituate to repeated stimuli, or when we cannot overcome erroneous information from vision and proprioception. In some individuals, particularly children, the vestibular system does not always habituate to repeated stimuli. In those cases

> What happens to endolymph when acceleration but not motion ceases?

> Habituation means a reduction in response with repeated stimulation.

296

when the system is not inhibited, sea sickness from boating or motion sickness from riding in a car occurs. When we do not purposely override the vestibular system during a swan dive by positioning the head straight down at the point of entry into the water (when that system would normally tell us to keep the head in an upright position throughout the dive), a belly flop occurs. Throughout life, in these and many other instances, we learn to suppress the system.

Study Questions:

1. What is it about the vestibular receptors that makes them so sensitive to movement?

2. Because the vestibular system is so sensitive, how is it that humans are not overly stimulated by the system every time we move or are transported from one place to another?

3. The labyrinth must be considered one of the most important sources of what type of activity?

4. What is likely to happen to an individual who cannot habituate to the system?

5. Explain the term resting discharge, or discharge frequency, and elaborate on just why it is of such importance to us.

Central Component

Sensory information from peripheral components of the vestibular system is transmitted via cranial nerve VIII mostly to four vestibular nuclei. These nuclei are located in the floor of the fourth ventricle of the brain stem, at the junction of the medulla and the pons. Vestibular afferent fibers also have pathways directly to the cerebellum that bypass the four nuclei. From these two major locations, second order neurons may do two things: one, they may project down the spinal cord and ultimately converge on the anterior horn cells where they may help to activate the final common pathway (the motor nerve) producing muscle activity; or two, they may ascend with synapses on motor nuclei in the brain stem where they may summate sufficiently to produce eye movement. There are also second order neurons to the cerebellum, the reticular formation, the thalamus, and the cortex. The vestibular nuclei also receive inputs from the spinal cord, the cerebellum, the reticular formation, and higher centers.

Vestibular Nuclei

Depicted in Figure 12-20 are the four vestibular nuclei: the superior, the lateral (sometimes referred to as Deiters' nucleus), the medial, and the inferior (sometimes called the spinal, or descending, nucleus). Vestibular reflexes are all transmitted over pathways that begin in these nuclei. The lateral vestibular nucleus receives input primarily from the utricle and the cerebellum. Input to the medial nucleus comes primarily from the utricle, the cerebellum, and the semicircular canals. Most afferent fibers to the superior vestibular nucleus originate in the cerebellum or in the semicircular canals. In fact, this nucleus is considered to be the major relay center for ocular reflexes mediated by the semicircular canals. The inferior vestibular nucleus receives its major input from the utricle, the saccule, and the cerebellum.

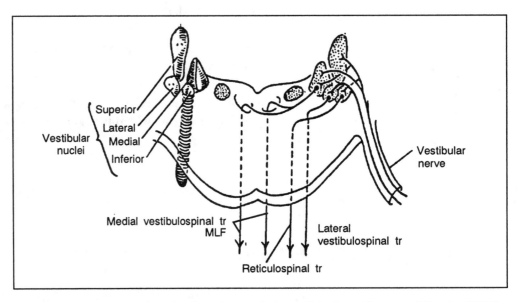

Figure 12-20 Input to and outflow from the vestibular nuclei. From House and Pansky (1967), reprinted with permission.

Descending Tracts From the Nuclei

From the lateral nucleus, tracts descend as far down the cord as the lumbosacral segments where the axons terminate on the anterior horn cells or on interneurons. These lateral axons make up what is known as the lateral vestibulospinal tract (LVST). All LVST axons are believed to

298

be excitatory in nature. However, because the major function of the LVST axons is to activate extensor, or antigravity, muscles and to deactivate flexor muscles, some of the synapses of the secondary neurons must excite inhibitory interneurons to flexors while the excitatory fibers have synapses directly on anterior horn cells to extensor muscles of the neck, trunk, and legs (Fig 12-21).

From the medial, lateral, and inferior nuclei, axons descend both sides of the cord in the medial longitudinal fasciculi and form the medial vestibulospinal track (MVST). Most of the fibers making up the medial tracks descend to the cervical area of the cord where they probably have synapses on both excitatory and inhibitory interneurons controlling input to the motor neurons innervating flexor and extensor muscles of the neck. A few MVST fibers also reach the thoracic area of the spinal cord. The neurons of the medial track have an important functional role in the reflex interactions between the neck muscles, the vestibular system, and the muscles of the eyes.

> The LVST activates antigravity muscles and inhibits trunk flexor muscles.

> The MVST carries messages to cervical and some thoracic muscles.

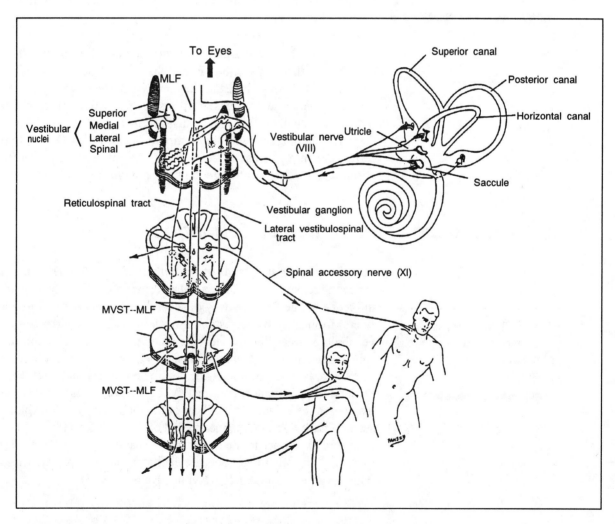

Figure 12-21 Descending tracts carrying input from the sensory organs to the periphery. From House and Pansky (1967), reprinted with permission.

299

Vestibulospinal Reflexes

The major function of the vestibulospinal reflexes (VSRs) is to interact with the somatosensory and visual systems in controlling postural stability in standing and during ambulation. The VSR makes its contribution by stabilizing the body in space while head movements occur during maintenance of posture and during movement. The vestibular apparatus detects the movement and position of the head and then sends this information to specific structures within the CNS where it is used to generate compensatory postural responses. Although there is some overlap in the activity of these systems, each makes a unique contribution to postural stability.

> Postural stability is controlled by the VSR interacting with visual and somatosensory inputs.

When the vestibular system is disrupted, the symptoms that occur reflect both the vestibular abnormality and the altered interaction among the vestibular, visual, and somatosensory systems (Brandt and Daroff 1980). Thus, in designing a treatment regimen, the therapist will need not only to work on the abnormality but also to consider the changing roles of the other two systems.

Note also just how VSRs may influence ocular reflexes, which will be discussed in the next section. Recall that nerve fibers in the MVST descend to the cervical area of the cord where they have synapses with neurons innervating muscles of the neck. You will later learn that there is a cervico-ocular reflex (COR) that originates in the deep muscles of the neck and interacts with the vestibulo-ocular reflex (VOR) to produce certain eye movements. In this manner, eye reflexes may interact with postural reflexes to contribute to postural control.

Influence of the Reticular Formation

> The MRT and PRT make important contributions to static and dynamic posture.

Few if any of the thousands of fibers that make up the vestibular nerve have a direct synapse in the reticular formation (RF). Most vestibular influence on the RF is by way of secondary fibers (vestibuloreticular fibers) from each of the vestibular nuclei. "There is evidence that the vestibuloreticular fibers contribute much to the vestibular control of spinal mechanisms" (Nyberg-Hansen 1975, p 82). From the reticular formation, two sets of tracts--the pontine reticulospinal tract (PRT) and the medullary reticulospinal tract (MRT)--have fibers that descend all the way down the spinal cord. Fibers of the medullary reticulospinal tract seem to have a function opposite that of the LVST and PRT. The MRT fibers are excitatory to the flexor muscles and inhibitory to extensor muscles. The other two tracts are excitatory to extensor muscles and inhibitory to flexor muscles (Nyburg-Hansen 1975).

Ascending Tracts

Neurons project directly from the superior nucleus through the ipsilateral medial longitudinal fasciculus (MLF) to the motor nuclei of the extrinsic eye muscles (see Fig 12-21). Other fibers originate in the medial vestibular nucleus, which receives its major input from the canals, the utricle, and the cerebellum, and ascend to the oculomotor nerves via the contralateral MLF.

Most of the fibers leaving the inferior vestibular nucleus project to the reticular formation and to the cerebellum. Many of the outgoing fibers also cross the brain stem to the contralateral medial, lateral, and inferior nuclei. Because some fibers from the inferior nucleus pass to the cerebellum, the reticular formation, and three nuclei on the opposite side, the major function of this nucleus is thought to be the coordination of signals from both sides of the brain stem with the cerebellum and the reticular formation.

Sensory signals from the vestibular nerve are modified by inputs from many sources.

Although it may be interesting to categorize form and function in order to better understand how parts of the system work, it is important to understand that the vestibular system does not really operate that way. It may be true that sensory signals from the vestibular nerve initiate the process, but once the signals have started on their way from the periphery, they are modified, reorganized, and integrated by inputs from other parts of the body. In changing afferent impulses to efferent responses, a vast array of signals is sent forth to other organizing and mediating systems before those signals arrive at their final destination--the motor nerve.

It must clearly be understood that signals pour into the vestibular nuclei from the labyrinths, the cerebellum, the muscle proprioceptors, the reticular formation, the cerebral cortex, and other places and that signals also go forth to all these same places. All the intricate parts of the vestibular apparatus are arranged such that it would be impossible to activate a single receptor and witness a simple result, even if that were desirable. A physician or scientist may test an isolated part of the system, but when rehabilitation is attempted, the responses obtained by therapists generally represent the sum of all the activity taking place in both the peripheral and central parts of the system.

Sources of input to vestibular nuclei are labyrinths, cerebellum, reticular formation, proprioceptors and the cortex.

Once this concept is understood, it becomes clear that while we may manipulate the vestibular system and speak in terms of certain inputs yielding certain outputs through a given sensory receptor or motor nerve, we are in effect using the system much more globally. Even relatively simple reflexes produced by the system actually have influences of a far wider nature. Most movements of the head are accompanied by movements of the eyes. Some of these head movements evoke the vestibulo-ocular reflexes which you will read about next. Sources of

301

input to vestibular nuclei are labyrinths, cerebellum, reticular formation, proprioceptors, and cortex. They are presented in the following section in their simplest form. Please keep in mind that these head movements occur within a more global and complex background setting.

Study Questions:

1. Name the descending tracks and describe the function of each.

2. Why is it so difficult to isolate the functioning of any one of the 10 sensory receptors in the peripheral apparatus?

3. How is it that the eyes contribute to postural control?

Vestibulo-Ocular Reflexes

Horizontal VOR

The VOR is responsible for gaze stability.

As stated before, one of the primary functions of the vestibular system is to stabilize the eyes in space. This is done by the VOR. The VOR is important because it allows us to see stationary objects while the head is moving. It does this by producing an eye movement of equal velocity to the velocity with which the head is moving, but the eye movement is in the opposite direction (Fig 12-22). This gives us gaze stability, and were it not for this stability, everything in our surroundings would become blurred each time the head moved.

Test your VOR!

There is an interesting experiment that can be done to test your own VOR. Place your hand about 10 inches from your face and stare at the creases in the palm. Now move your hand rapidly to the left and right and notice that you can no longer see the creases because the palm is blurry. Again, hold the palm in the same position and fix your gaze on the creases. This time move your head back and forth, as is done when you shake your head to mean "no." Notice how the creases remain distinct. If you can clearly see the creases with the head moving in this left to right pattern, your VOR is working properly.

302

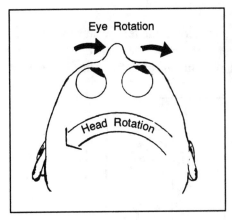

Figure 12-22 The vestibulo-ocular reflex producing gaze stability during rotation of the head.

The VOR consists of a simple three neuron pathway. The receptor is located in the semicircular canals. As depicted in Figure 12-23, when the head is turned to the right, the endolymph in the right horizontal canal presses against the cupula in that ampulla (ampullopetal flow), which results in an increased firing rate in the right vestibular nerve. This in turn excites neurons in the right medial vestibular nucleus. The outgoing fibers project to the ipsilateral oculomotor nucleus. Motor neurons from this nucleus cause the right medial rectus muscle to contract, pulling the eye to the left.

> For your eyes to move in concert, there must be simultaneous facilitatory and inhibitory inputs to both eyes.

Since our eyes normally operate in concert, when the right eye moves there is a mechanism to coordinate a comparable movement in the left eye. During the same time that impulses are being sent to the muscles of the right eye, an impulse travels from the right medial vestibular nucleus to the contralateral abducens nucleus on the left side of the brain stem and on to the left lateral rectus muscle, causing it to contract (Fig 12-23). This results in the movement of the left eye to the left.

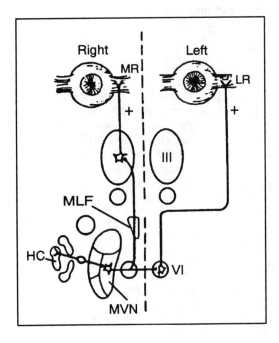

Figure 12-23 The three neuron pathways showing facilitation to the left lateral rectus and right medial rectus muscles resulting from acceleration of the head to the right. MLF - medial longitudinal fasciculus; HC - horizontal canal; MVN - medial vestibular nucleus; MR - medial rectus; LR - lateral rectus; III - oculomotor nucleus; VI - abducens nucleus. From Baloh and Honrubia (1979), reprinted with permission.

Both eyes move simultaneously to the left because additional inhibitory messages have been sent to the motor neurons of both the right lateral rectus and the left medial rectus muscles from that same right horizontal canal (Fig 12-24).

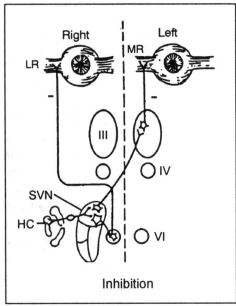

Figure 12-24 Inhibition to the right lateral rectus and left medial rectus muscles resulting from rotatory acceleration of the head to the right. SVN - superior vestibular nucleus; HC - horizontal canal; LR - lateral rectus; MR - medial rectus; III - oculomotor nucleus; IV - trochlear nucleus; VI - abducens nucleus. From Baloh and Honrubia (1979), reprinted with permission.

Figure 12-25 clearly shows the facilitation and inhibition originating in the same canal and ending on the four ocular muscles. If the right lateral rectus muscle is to be able to pull the right eye to the right, the right medial rectus muscle must be inhibited. And, if the left medial rectus muscle is to be able to pull the left eye rightward, the left lateral rectus muscle must be inhibited so that the left eye will also turn to the right, producing conjugate eye movement.

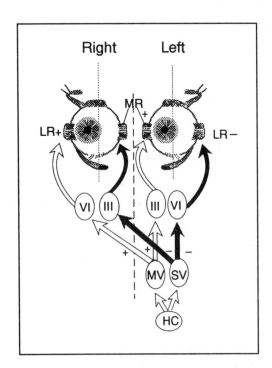

Figure 12-25 Facilitation and inhibition from the left horizontal canal. Note that the white arrows represent facilitation while the black arrows depict inhibition. HC - horizontal canal; MV - medial vestibular nucleus; SV - superior vestibular nucleus; MR - medial rectus; LR - lateral rectus; III - oculomotor nucleus; VI - abducens nucleus.

Notice also in Figure 12-25 that the inhibitory mechanism so necessary for the horizontal turning of the eyes has a little different route than do the facilitatory impulses. Inhibitory impulses travel from the superior vestibular nucleus while the facilitatory impulses are carried from the medial nucleus. From the superior nucleus, inhibitory secondary neurons have synapses in the left abducens nucleus, with a nerve supplying the lateral rectus muscle of the left eye. At the same time, impulses travel from the superior nucleus across the brain stem to the oculomotor nucleus (III) where there is an inhibitory synapse with the nerve supplying the right medial rectus muscle.

Vertical VOR

There is also a vertical VOR. When the head is flexed on the neck, excitation of the anterior canals occurs because endolymph presses against the cupula from the utricular side of the ampulla, pushing the stereocilia into the kinocilium. There is a small satellite nucleus near the other vestibular nuclei. It provides a relay for certain extraocular muscle activity. Impulses from the anterior canal go to this satellite vestibular nucleus and to the oculomotor nucleus and nerve, causing a contraction of the inferior oblique and superior rectus muscles. These two muscles, working in concert, pull the eyes upward (Fig 12-26). Notice the accompanying inhibition to the superior oblique and inferior rectus muscles that originated in these same anterior canals but are relayed through the superior nucleus.

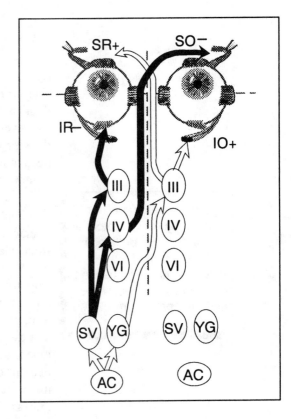

Figure 12-26 The vertical vestibulo-ocular reflex showing the eyes raised as a result of stimulation of the two anterior canals. Depicted are the facilitatory (white) and inhibitory (black) pathways from the right anterior canal only. The left canal initiates the same sensory message for the opposite muscles. YG - satellite vestibular nucleus ("y" group); AC - anterior canal; SV - superior vestibular nucleus; SO - superior oblique muscle; SR - superior rectus; IR - inferior rectus; IO - inferior oblique; III - oculomotor nucleus; IV - trochlear nucleus; VI - abducens nucleus.

When the head is extended on the neck, posterior canal receptors are facilitated, and signals from them ultimately arrive at the superior oblique and inferior rectus muscles, which then pull the eyes down in the orbit. Again, there must be simultaneous inhibition to the inferior oblique and the superior rectus muscles of both eyes (Fig 12-27).

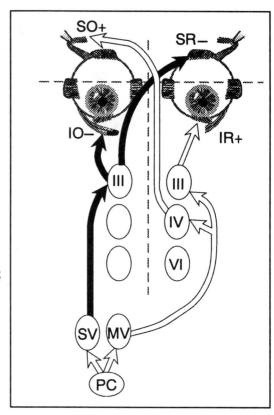

Figure 12-27 The vertical vestibulo-ocular reflex showing the eyes lowered as a result of stimulation of the two posterior canals. Depicted are the facilitatory (white) and inhibitory (black) pathways from the right posterior canal only. The left canal initiates the same sensory message for the opposite muscles. PC - posterior canal; SV - superior vestibular nucleus; MV - medial vestibular nucleus; SO - superior oblique muscle; SR - superior rectus; IO - inferior oblique; IR - inferior rectus; III - oculomotor nucleus; IV - trochlear nucleus; VI - abducens nucleus.

The strongest facilitation to eye muscles and the strongest inhibition to their antagonists is that which arrives from the same canal (Ito 1975). However, there are several other neural mechanisms that contribute to the efficiency of the VOR. These mechanisms include the effects of head movement on the contralateral canal, the effects of commissural inhibitory pathways, and the influence of the cerebellum.

Eye movements are initiated by the receptors in the canals. Smoothness and efficiency of the movements are influenced by commissural pathways and the cerebellum.

The inhibitory commissural system also contributes to the push-pull interaction of the vestibular inputs (Fig 12-28). These pathways are somewhat confusing, and you will need to work through them carefully. When turning the head to the left, start with the primary afferent neuron from the left semicircular canal. The primary afferent neuron excites the type I neuron in the medial vestibular nucleus. The type I neuron, in turn, projects to the oculomotor nucleus, but it also has a collateral fiber that excites a type II neuron in the contralateral vestibular nucleus. The type II neuron is inhibitory and decreases the firing rate of the type I neurons on that side. Therefore, when the head turns to the left, the ipsilateral type I neuron to the left medial rectus muscle will have an increased firing rate because it is facilitated by the increased firing of the primary afferent neuron. This type I neuron will also be affected by the removal of inhibition (disinhibition) as a result of the decreased firing of the inhibitory type II neuron that normally would be driven by the contralateral type I neuron. Remember, the contralateral type I neuron will have a decreased firing rate because of the decreased firing of the primary afferent neurons from the semicircular canals on that side and because it will be inhibited by a type II neuron.

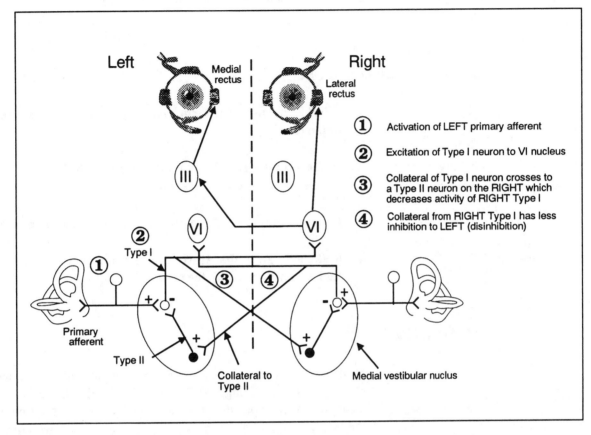

Figure 12-28 The inhibitory commissural pathways showing how the additional inhibition may contribute to a smooth VOR by furnishing extra inhibition to the push-pull relationship.

One contributing factor to the normal VOR is that a head movement in one direction will result in a decrease in firing in the vestibular nerve from the contralateral semicircular canal. When the head is turned to the left, there will be a diminution of the normal tonic firing in the right vestibular nerve. That right nerve does not become entirely silent, but the normal flow into the central part of the system when the canal receptor is at rest will be diminished. The right side of the peripheral system can then be said to be eliminated effectively during acceleration to the left.

Another contributing factor influencing the vestibular system in eye movements is the interaction of the cerebellum with the vestibular nuclei. The cerebellum influences the vestibular nuclei in two principal ways. Purkinje cells in the cerebellar cortex, through monosynapses, inhibit

Disinhibition, disfacilitation, and cancellation are related but different phenomena.

307

cells in the vestibular nuclei; and the fastigial nucleus of the cerebellum facilitates vestibular nuclei. The fastigial nucleus, however, receives inhibitory input from purkinje cells so that the latter cells can influence the vestibular nuclei either by direct inhibition or through disfacilitation through the indirect route. It is thought that the role of the cerebellum in this case is to inhibit the VOR in order that humans might have visual fixation when the head and the visual world are moving in the same direction. This inhibition is called VOR cancellation.

Study Questions:

1. What is meant by the term gaze stability and why is it so important?

2. Write out a short definition for the words disfacilitation, disinhibition, and cancellation.

3. How is it that normal eye movements are smooth and efficient?

4. Make a diagram that traces inputs from the vestibular system that are influenced by the cerebellum.

Nystagmus

Nystagmus is an involuntary, alternating sequence of quick phase and slow phase (eye tracking) movements of the eyes. Usually there is a slow movement in one direction followed by a much faster movement in the opposite direction. In vestibular nystagmus, the slow movement is initiated by the semicircular canals while the quicker component of the movement is a resetting of eye position through CNS pathways.

If you were to seat normal individuals in a chair that can be rotated slowly for a minute or two and ask them to keep their eyes closed while they are being rotated, when the movement is stopped you would very likely see postrotatory nystagmus, so called because it follows the rotation. Just to be sure, you may want to have this activity demonstrated for you.

The pathway for horizontal nystagmus is depicted, in part, in Figure 12-25. When the head is rotated to the right, the eyes move to the left because of the activation of the right horizontal canal. If the rotation continues, the eyes will move slowly away from the direction of the rotation and then will be jerked rapidly back in the direction of the rotation. This pattern of slow movement away from the direction of the rotation and fast movement in the direction of rotation is repeated as the rotation continues, until a constant speed is reached (acceleration ceases).

308

When the rotation stops, the eyes will begin to move back and forth in the opposite pattern because the endolymph will try to settle back into its resting position, causing it to push against the cupula of the right horizontal canal. This will cause the slow beat of the eyes to be in the same direction that the individual was rotated, that is, to the right. The fast beat will be to the left, in the direction opposite of the original rotation. The reversal of the eye movement pattern resulting from this rotational activity is termed postrotatory nystagmus.

In addition to the horizontal to and fro movement, there are also up and down, or vertical movements, and circular movements of the eyes that may be seen and tested. In other words, the movement may be in any direction, but it is always involuntary and, except for the circular, pendular, and other nonlinear movements, has slow and fast components that are in opposite directions to each other.

> Nystagmus is a normal reaction to rotatory or angular acceleration.

Motion of the head or motion of objects would result in an inability to keep an object in focus were it not for compensatory reflex movement of the eyes during which we attempt to fix our eyes on, or gaze on, an object. Thus nystagmus can be a normal reaction to either rotatory or some other angular movements of the head, and when it does occur, it is generally termed physiologic nystagmus (Fig 5-29a). When it persists or when it occurs without head movement, however, some pathologic problem probably exists either in the periphery or in the central part of the nervous system (Fig 5-29b). Of course, the absence of postrotatory nystagmus may be indicative of nonfunctional labyrinths.

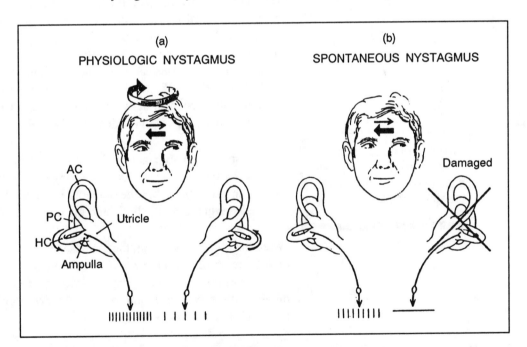

Figure 5-29 Primary afferent nerve activity associated with (a) rotationally induced physiologic nystagmus and (b) spontaneous nystagmus resulting from a lesion of one labyrinth. The thin straight arrow is the direction of the slow component; thick straight arrow is the direction of the fast component. Curved arrow is the direction of endolymph flow, or pressure, in the HC (horizontal canal). From Baloh (1984), reprinted with permission.

As clarified by Brandt et al (1977), nystagmus may be elicited by other stimuli such as torsion of the cervical vertebrae, vibration applied to the neck, a moving sound source, imagining that a visual image is moving, or hypnotic suggestion that a motion is being seen.

Optokinetic Nystagmus

Optokinetic nystagmus (OKN) is an eye movement generated in response to movement of a large visual stimulus. Like rotary nystagmus, this is a jerk nystagmus in that there is a slow-phase eye movement (to follow the moving target) and a quick-phase eye movement in the opposite direction to reset the eye position and make it ready for another slow phase. The OKN in primates has an initial pursuit component (cortical) that brings the eye velocity up to the same velocity as the object that is being tracked and a subcortical component (the nystagmus) that continues the tracking of the moving object. An old name for OKN was train nystagmus. A common laboratory experiment for evoking OKN is to have the subject watch a rotating drum on which lines or some similar pattern has been printed.

Visual-Ocular System

The visual-ocular system enables individuals to follow, without turning the head to do so, an object in the environment that is moving rapidly across their visual fields. This is called *pursuit*, and it is done by the visually mediated ocular responses and not by VORs. In other words, the visual-ocular system is cortically, or volitionally, driven. These visual-ocular responses can work independently of the VORs, work together with the VORs, or work at cross purposes with the VORs. When there is a conflict between the two ocular responses, the visual-ocular responses override the VORs (Baloh and Honrubia 1979).

> Visual-ocular responses are not vestibular reflexes but they sometimes work together with them.

These responses enable us to follow an object that is moving through space when the body is motionless. They are also used when the body is moving through space but the object to be viewed is motionless, and they are needed when both the body and the object are moving.

When the object is moving, the visual-ocular response enables us to pursue the object with the eyes in a relatively smooth movement and to fix the eyes on that object. These cortically driven, smooth pursuit, eye movements are voluntary and relatively slow (maximum velocity of 60°/sec).

When the body is moving and the object to be viewed is motionless, the visual-ocular attempt to fix the eyes on the object may cause what are called *saccadic* movements. These movements are rapid back and forth movements initiated by the visual reflex in the effort to fix the fovea of the eye in the correct position for clear vision of the moving object.

There are different types of saccadic eye movements: voluntary, reflexive, and spontaneous. Voluntary saccades are used to change fixation between two stationary targets. The velocity of saccadic eye movements is high (300°-900°/sec), and the acceleration also is high (3000°/sec/sec or more).

Cervico-Ocular Reflexes

Another system that interacts with the VOR in maintaining stability of the eyes is the cervico-ocular system. Not much is known and understood as to just how the COR operates in humans because not much research has been done on humans. It seems clear that such a reflex does exist and that it is probably induced by change in sensory feedback from the deep rotator muscles and facet joints of the neck. It is believed that if the neck is turned, the neck reflex complements the reflex produced by the horizontal canal, giving better eye stability than if either of the reflexes acted alone. According to Baloh (1979), the VOR and COR interactions occur because of a convergence of neck and semicircular canal afferents on secondary vestibular neurons. It is probable that the neck reflex serves to enhance the function of the VOR. The neck reflex is mentioned here, however, for two reasons: one, it exists; and two, there are several study results in clients with bilateral vestibular loss that suggest that the COR may substitute in part for the missing VOR in producing eye-head coordination and gaze stabilization.

Feedback from muscles and joints in the neck may affect eye stability.

An understanding of the functions of the COR, the VOR, and the visual-ocular reflexes becomes important to you as a therapist as you attempt to evaluate and design treatment programs for clients with vestibular, somatosensory, or visual deficits. If you are to help your clients function in space, as effectively as each is capable of doing, you must understand the relationships of the three systems in normal movement and just how you might use one or two of the systems to train the third.

Summary of Ocular Reflexes and Responses

In summary, there are VORs, CORs, and a visual-ocular system, all of which serve to allow you to see clearly. The VOR is a compensatory eye movement that occurs in response to head movement but is in the opposite direction of the head movement. The purpose of the VOR is to keep the eyes stable in space during a head movement so that the image of a stationary object being viewed remains on the fovea of the retina, giving the best visual acuity. During VOR cancellation, the eyes move with the head, that is, in the same direction as the head, to follow a

311

moving target. When this same direction movement of the eyes and head occurs, the VOR is said to have been canceled because the eyes did not move in the opposite direction as they usually do in the VOR. The VOR cancellation is cortical and involves some of the same cortical areas (parietal lobes) as do pursuit eye movements.

The CORs probably enhance the VOR and may partially substitute for it in the event of bilateral vestibular loss. These CORs may interact with postural reflexes to contribute to postural control by coordinating head and neck movements.

Pursuit movements allow tracking of moving objects when the head is still.

Saccadic movements allow tracking of stationary objects when the head is moving.

The visual-ocular system, sometimes called the pursuit system, allows humans to pursue an object across the visual field without moving their heads or to fixate on an object either when the object is motionless but the body is moving or when both the body and the object are moving.

Study Questions:

1. Describe postrotatory nystagmus.

2. Sketch the pathways for nystagmus.

3. What is the difference between physiologic nystagmus, pathologic nystagmus and optokinetic nystagmus?

4. Name some of the ways that nystagmus may be elicited.

5. What are the differences in function of the VOR and the visual-ocular system?

Chapter 13 - Assessment and Treatment of Clients with Vestibular Disorders

Note: Portions of this chapter are from Herdman (1990a), reprinted with permission of the American Physical Therapy Association.

Introduction

Disorders of the vestibular system affect both oculomotor and postural control. The signs and symptoms that occur reflect both the vestibular abnormality and the altered interaction among vestibular, visual, and proprioceptive cues. Clients may complain of vertigo (the perception that the world is turning) or of disequilibrium (a sense of imbalance, falling), and they may have nystagmus and ataxia; however, as you will see, the specific problems are dependent on the type of vestibular dysfunction.

Several different mechanisms may account for the remarkable ability of the vestibular system to recover after injury or disease. One of the most important of these mechanisms is *adaptation*, the vestibular system's ability to make long-term changes in how it responds to an input. When there is no remaining vestibular function, visual and proprioceptive systems substitute in part for the lost vestibular function.

Several exercise approaches have been developed to treat different types of vestibular problems; the type of approach used depends on the type of vestibular disorder. The purpose of this chapter is to 1) discuss the impact of different vestibular lesions on function, 2) review some of the common tests used to assess the function of the vestibular system, and 3) present some of the exercise approaches used in the management of clients with vestibular disorders. Three main categories of vestibular dysfunction will be discussed: vestibular hypofunction (unilateral loss), complete bilateral vestibular loss, and positional vertigo.

Assessment

Clients with complaints of either vertigo or disequilibrium are usually referred to otolaryngology or neurology departments for assessment. Among the many tests the client may have are some that are specific for vestibular system function, including caloric and vertical axis rotational tests. In addition, the client will usually also have a hearing test. These

313

tests, along with a clinical examination, blood tests, and either computerized tomography or magnetic resonance imaging, are used to determine whether the client has a vestibular disorder and, if he does, whether it is unilateral or bilateral, whether there is any remaining vestibular function, and whether there are central nervous system structures involved.

The question of central nervous system involvement is particularly important. First of all, vertigo and disequilibrium can be the result of central as well as peripheral lesions of the nervous system; therefore, the treatments used would be different. Second, many different central nervous system structures are involved in recovery after peripheral vestibular lesions. These structures include not only the vestibular nuclei, the vestibular commissural system, and the cerebellum, all of which are probably involved in adaptation, but also the visual system and the spinal cord, which are involved in the development of strategies that substitute for the lost vestibular function. The information gained from the clinical assessment and from the various tests, therefore, is used in making a diagnosis and also in determining the treatment of the client and the expectations for recovery. A brief introduction to the clinical exam and to some of the tests used to assess the client with dizziness is appropriate.

> Vertigo is a nonspecific symptom. It can result from many causes.

Caloric Tests

> Heat or cold may produce a movement of endolymph.

The caloric test is used to assess function of the peripheral vestibular system. In this test, the external canal is irrigated with cool or warm water or air. The temperature of the irrigant is different than the temperature of the inner ears so that the resultant temperature gradient causes movement of the endolymph in the adjacent horizontal canal. (The vertical canals are not close enough to be affected by the temperature gradient.) The direction of the fast phase of the nystagmus that occurs after stimulation of a single horizontal canal depends on the temperature of the water and on how the client is positioned. The client is usually positioned supine. When cold water is used, the movement of the endolymph in the horizontal canal is ampullofugal, and the fast phase of the nystagmus will be directed away from the irrigated ear. When warm water is used, the movement of the endolymph will be ampullopetal, and the fast phase of the nystagmus will be toward the irrigated ear. The pneumonic "COWS" is often used to recall the expected results (cold opposite, warm same). You should work through what to expect if the person is placed in a prone position. Figure 13-1 shows the electrooculogram of a normal subject to cool and warm water irrigation of the right and left ears. By convention, the direction of the nystagmus is always given as the direction of the quick-phase eye movement, although the stimulus is actually producing the slow-phase eye movement. The quick-phase eye movement is believed to occur to reset the eye position. Notice the direction of the fast-phase eye

> **COWS**--cold opposite side, warm same side.

314

movements to cool and warm water for each ear and see if it follows the pneumonic COWS.

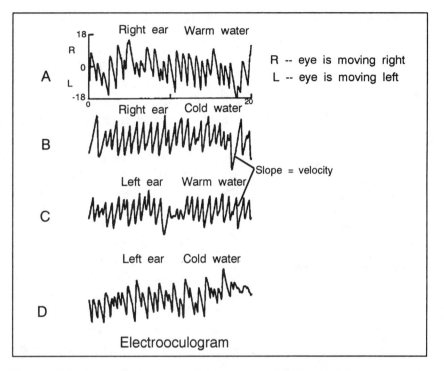

Figure 13-1 Normal caloric response to warm and cold water irrigation. Eye movements are recorded by electrooculography; eye movements to the right are up and to the left are down. The scales are the same for all figures as in A. Note that warm water irrigation of the right ear produces a slow-phase eye movement to the left with a quick phase resetting eye movement to the right. The slope of the line indicates the velocity of the eye movement. Cold water irrigation of the right ear (B) causes slow-phase eye movements to the right and fast to the left. Check the responses in (C) and (D) to make certain that they also follow the pneumonic COWS.

Caloric stimulation, of course, is not a naturally occurring stimulus, but the advantage in using it is that it is possible to test the function of each horizontal canal separately, enabling its use to identify the side of the lesion. A disadvantage of the test is that the results depend on the success of the irrigation, which can vary considerably with variations in the anatomy of the external canal.

Vertical Axis Rotational Tests

The rotational test also measures horizontal canal function, although with modification of the test vertical canal function also can be measured. During the test, eye movements are recorded during controlled, *en bloc*

315

rotation of the body in the dark. En bloc refers to turning the entire body as a single unit. Rotation of the head (with the body) results in excitation of one horizontal canal and inhibition of the other horizontal canal. In this way, the rotational test mimics natural stimulation of the vestibular system. The limitation of this test is that it cannot differentiate which side is affected in a unilateral lesion, although it can identify that there is a unilateral lesion. An advantage of this test over the caloric test is that it can be used to identify bilateral decreases in vestibular function. Because the results of the caloric test are interpreted by comparing the response to irrigation of one ear with the response to irrigation of the other, bilaterally decreased function is not always obvious. Both tests, therefore, are often required for a complete exam.

The vertical axis rotational test can be used to determine the gain of the vestibulo-ocular reflex (VOR). The VOR gain is computed by dividing the slow phase eye velocity by the head velocity. At slow head velocities, the VOR gain should equal 1 (Fig 13-2).

The second measurement of vestibular function obtained from the rotational test is the time constant (Tc). The Tc is defined as the time it takes for the slow-phase eye velocity to decrease to 37% of its peak velocity once rotation has stopped. Figure 13-2 also shows the Tc. A normal Tc indicates that there is a normal input from the peripheral vestibular apparatus to brain stem structures, called the velocity storage system, and that the brain stem structures are normal.

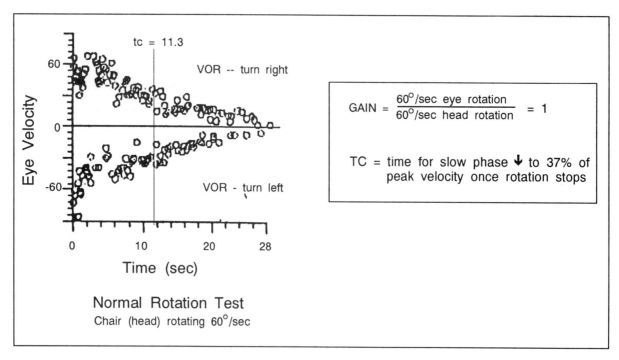

Figure 13-2 Normal response to vertical axis rotational test using a 60 °/sec step. Eye velocity is on the abscissa and time is on the ordinate. The gain of the response (eye velocity/head velocity) is approximately 1. The Tc is 11.3 seconds.

Auditory and Other Tests

Many disorders affecting the vestibular system are associated with changes in hearing. Tests of the auditory system are used to determine whether the hearing problem is unilateral, bilateral, conductive (ossicular chain), or sensorineural (cochlea or nerve). The frequencies at which hearing is diminished and the pattern of hearing loss sometime aid in determining the diagnosis of a vertiginous client. In Meniere's disease, for example, there is often a low-frequency fluctuating hearing loss. A progressive high-frequency loss often occurs in ototoxicity.

Several other tests performed by the audiologist are useful in diagnosis. These include Brain Stem Auditory Evoked Responses and electrocochleography. The former tests the integrity of the auditory pathway (cochlear nerve, cochlear nucleus, superior olive, lateral lemniscus, inferior colliculus). The electrocochleography is a new test that has potential use in identifying clients who have certain vestibular disorders such as Meniere's disease or fistula, both of which will be discussed later.

Clinical Assessment

The clinical exam of the dizzy client by the physician is very important for diagnosis and also aids in the development of the treatment program. The client's general medical and surgical history identifies problems that may affect the client's response to treatment. The client who has diabetes may also have poor vision or poor proprioception or both; the client with arthritis of the cervical spine or with a cervical injury from an automobile accident may not be able to perform the head movements used in some of the exercise programs. It is also important to know what precipitates the vertigo or dizziness, if anything, and the duration and frequency of the attacks. An important consideration is whether the client experiences more vertigo and disequilibrium when stationary in a moving environment or when moving through the environment, because this information will aid in developing the treatment program.

Knowing the conditions that precipitate vertigo can be useful in developing treatment.

The complete clinical exam would include assessment of strength, range of motion, sensation, reflexes and cerebellar function in addition to vestibulo-ocular and vestibulospinal function. It is difficult to isolate vestibulospinal responses from other mechanisms of postural control. Clinical tests of the vestibulo-ocular system are used more frequently to assess vestibular function than are tests of the vestibulospinal system because the observed behavior is less contaminated by other systems. Still, it is important to recognize that the results of the clinical examination reflect the interaction of many inputs to the nervous system and the interactions among different nervous system structures.

317

The complete oculomotor exam (Tab 13-1) might include assessment of ocular alignment, pursuit and saccadic eye movements, and vestibular function. The vestibulo-ocular exam includes assessment of VOR during slow head movements, both horizontally and vertically. Another test assesses the function of the vestibular system during high-velocity head movements. The client must maintain visual fixation on a stationary target during single, unidirectional passive head movements. People with normal VOR can maintain fixation without difficulty. If there is a decrease in vestibular function, the eyes will move off the target during the head movement, and the client will have to make a corrective saccade to regain target fixation. Changes in visual acuity during gentle oscillations of the head, as would occur in clients with bilateral vestibular lesions, should also be assessed.

Table 13-1

Oculomotor Examination

Ocular alignment--one eye elevated or scewed in relation to the other; strabismus
Pursuit and saccadic eye movements
VOR and VOR cancellation
Halmagy maneuver--while subject looks at a target, examiner rapidly turns the head
    passively in one direction at high velocity; look for corrective saccades
Visual acuity with head movement
Tragal-pressure induced--push on tragus of the external ear inducing pressure in the
    external auditory canal; look for nystagmus and eye deviation
Hennenbert's test--pressure is increased in external auditory canal with air pressure
    device; look for nystagmus and eye deviation
Nystagmus*
    spontaneous
    gaze evoked
    hyperventilation induced
    head-shaking induced
    positional--Hallpike position (see Fig 13-7)

---

*NOTE: All tests in which nystagmus is evoked require the use of Frenzel lenses (special glasses) to prevent the subject from visually fixating.

Other tests of vestibular function involve attempting to induce nystagmus, using a number of different procedures. These include pressure to the tragus (cartilaginous projection) of the external ear, positional changes, hyperventilation, and head shaking. Nystagmus induced by tragal pressure, or applying pressure to the middle ear through the external canal, may indicate that there is a fistula between the middle and inner ear (Hennenbert's sign). Positional changes that induce nystagmus may indicate either a central or a peripheral vestibular lesion. Hyperventilation induced nystagmus may occur in multiple sclerosis but also may occur in some metabolic disorders. Head-shaking induced nystagmus is most common in unilateral peripheral lesions and would not be seen in normal individuals nor in clients with symmetrical bilateral deficit.

Many different clinical tests can be used for assessing postural stability (Tab 13-2). In should be emphasized, however, that these tests are not specific for the vestibulospinal system but are simply ways of assessing postural stability.   These tests include the Romberg, the sharpened Romberg, and the measurement of one-legged standing balance, all with eyes open and eyes closed. Normal values by age are available for many of these tests. In addition, dynamic postural stability can be assessed using tests such as the walk-on-floor-eyes-closed (tandem walking) test, and Fukuda's marching test. The clinical exam should be designed to test both static (quiet stance) and dynamic (moving) stability under conditions that isolate various sensory cues and under conditions that stress balance, such as decreasing the base of support or requiring head movement. For instance, clients can be required to maintain balance with eyes open and eyes closed while standing on foam rubber to distort proprioceptive feedback. The client might also be asked to walk while turning the head from side to side, because such movements frequently result in ataxia.

Table 13-2

Postural Examination

Romberg--stand, arms folded across chest
Sharpened Romberg (tandem)--stand with feet aligned heel-to-toe, arms folded across
        chest
Stand on one leg eyes open, eyes closed
Walk on floor eyes closed (tandem walk)--arms across chest

Note: on all standing tests, the amount of sway time is recorded in seconds per trial. Numbers of steps taken are recorded in walking tests. There are norms that have been published for comparison. When using these norms the exact procedures described must be followed (Fregly et al 1972; Fregley et al 1973; Bohannon et al 1984).

Fukuda's stepping test--march in place, 50 steps; eyes open and closed; measure how much the individual turns to the left or right. Normal values are available. Some trends have been found, such as with changes in propioception, which way the turn occurs may reflect the problem; weakness also will make the subject turn (Watanabe et al 1985).

Gait analysis

Note: Because the norms for all tests vary with different age groups, it is important to compare the client against the correct age group if meaningful interpretations
are to be made.

Balance can also be quantified using a force platform. These tests may simply measure anterior-posterior or lateral sway with the subject standing on a stationary surface (static posturography) or they may measure automatic responses to sudden translational or rotational perturbations of the support surface (moving platform posturography). Translational perturbations could include horizontal movements of the support surface in either an anterior-posterior or a side-to-side direction. Rotational perturbations would move the support surface so that the toes go up or down (pitch). A system, described in Chapter 11, also is available that quantifies the client's ability to use different sensory cues (visual, vestibular, somatosensory) to maintain balance (Neurocom International, Inc). Although these tests may provide information about different aspects of the client's postural instability, they do not necessarily identify that the problem is in the vestibular system and do not localize the problem within the vestibular system itself.

> Postural stability can be assessed a number of ways, but the clinical tests do not necessarily localize the problem to the vestibular system.

The clinical examinations by physical therapists may include many of the same tests used by physicians. The goal of the physical therapy assessment, however, is not to diagnose but rather to establish the baseline data needed for developing a treatment plan and for determining whether the client's condition is changing as a result of treatment. Some test results are descriptive only, such as head-shaking nystagmus. Other subjective results may be quantified using a visual analogue scale similar to that used in the assessment of pain perception. Data may also be kept on the duration and frequency of the vertigo and disequilibrium. Clinical assessment of balance can usually be quantified by timing the ability of the client to maintain balance during the different tests. Careful documentation is extremely important.

Study Question:

1. Describe the various ways that vestibular function and postural stability can be evaluated.

Vestibular Hypofunction, or Unilateral Loss

Symptoms and Signs

The exact presentation of symptoms in a client with vestibular lesions and the client's subjective complaints reflect changes in both the VOR and the vestibulospinal reflex (VSR). Listening carefully to the client's description of what he feels is often helpful in determining the type of vestibular lesion.

Clients have a multitude of complaints ranging from vertigo and disequilibrium to light-headedness; blacking-out; sensations of swimming, being pushed or pulled, rocking, tilting, or walking on foam rubber; or sensations that the room is sideways or even up-side-down. Of course, these sensations are sometimes from nonvestibular problems. Lesions of the semicircular canals usually produce the symptoms of vertigo and disequilibrium. Otolith dysfunction also produces disequilibrium, but clients additionally complain of a tilting sensation, or the sensation that they are moving vertically or in an anterior-posterior direction. Examination of oculomotor control helps identify the nature of the dysfunction.

Unilateral lesions of the semicircular canals usually result in nystagmus; unilateral lesions of the otoliths result in a skew deviation (one eye positioned lower in the orbit than the other). Often, both the semicircular canals and the otoliths appear to be involved. With these diverse complaints and with the multitude of problems that can cause these complaints, a careful clinical examination is a necessity.

Vestibulo-ocular Function

Some review of normal vestibular function will be helpful before describing the effect of unilateral vestibular hypofunction or loss. Several concepts to keep in mind are as follows:

1. Vestibular neurons have a tonic firing rate at rest.

2. The canals work in a push-pull relationship (ie, with head movement, the firing rate of one canal will increase while the firing rate on the other side will decrease).

3. The best stimulus for each canal is movement of the head in the plane of the canal, and the eye movement produced will be in the same plane.

4. The otolith contribution to oculomotor control is to keep the eyes aligned along the horizontal line and to generate the small (5°) torsional, or circular, eye movement that keeps the eyes horizontal when the head is tilted laterally.

> The VOR stabilizes gaze during head movement.

As has already been discussed, one of the most important functions of the vestibular system is the generation of the VOR. When the VOR is functioning normally, it stabilizes gaze (eye position in space) during head movements by producing an eye movement that is of equal velocity

321

as the head movement but 180 degrees out of phase. Under most conditions, the gain (eye velocity/head velocity) of the VOR is 1, although this varies with how attentive (alert) the subject is and with other factors such as the velocity and acceleration of head movement and the client's anticipation of the head movement. Figure 13-3a is a recording of the velocity tracing of the horizontal VOR in a normal person. Note that the eye velocity (bottom trace) matches the head velocity (top trace) during both acceleration and deceleration phases. This can be seen even more clearly in Figure 13-3b in which head and eye velocity are plotted against each other. When eye and head velocities match, overlapping straight lines are formed for both acceleration and deceleration.

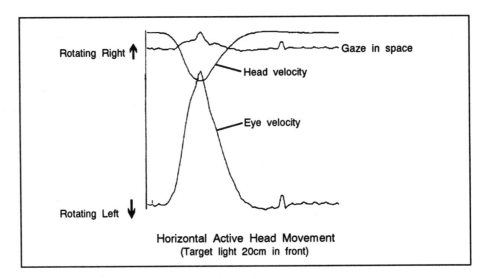

Figure 13-3a Normal horizontal VOR during active head movement. Head velocity and eye velocity match each other during the acceleration and deceleration phases. This can be seen more clearly in Figure 13-3b in which the velocities are plotted against each other.

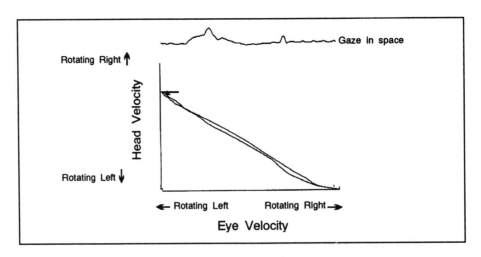

Figure 13- 3b Eye and head velocity plotted against each other.

322

Oculomotor disturbances from vestibular lesions

A decrease in activity on one side has the effect of increasing activity on the other side.

Unilateral lesions of the peripheral vestibular system result in both static and dynamic disturbances of the VOR. Normally when the head is stationary, the firing rate of the right and left vestibular nuclei are in balance with each other. With an acute unilateral lesion of the labyrinth or of the vestibular nerve, the resting firing rate of the vestibular nucleus on the side of the lesion decreases. The apparent effect is as if the intact side is being stimulated although there is no change in head position nor is there any head movement. This is called a static disturbance.

The slow phase of nystagmus is toward the side of the static VOR lesion.

Static disturbance of VOR causes a spontaneous nystagmus, with the slow-phase eye movement being toward the side of the lesion. Initially, this can be seen in room light. This spontaneous nystagmus disappears in the light within a few days as the resting tone of the vestibular nucleus recovers. Also, clients use visual fixation to stabilize the eyes. In the dark, spontaneous nystagmus may be present for many years.

The loss of input from the otolith unilaterally results in a static disturbance of ocular alignment and an eye lower on the side of the lesion than on the contralateral side. The skew deviation causes a vertical diplopia; that is, the client complains of seeing double with the images overlapping vertically. The skew deviation recovers quickly, usually within 4 to 5 days, as the balance between the two otoliths is reestablished.

Gain is abnormal in dynamic disturbances in the VOR after unilateral lesions.

The dynamic disturbance in the VOR after a unilateral lesion is characterized by a decrease in the gain of the vestibular system. Remember that gain is the relationship of the output of the system (eye velocity) over the input to the system (head velocity). In the acute stage of a unilateral lesion, when the head moves toward the side of the lesion the compensatory eye movement is very poor. The gain is dependent on the velocity of the head movement and on whether the client is viewing a stationary target or is being tested in the dark. Gain can vary from 0.25 to 0.5 in clients with unilateral lesions. As you should recall, normal gain equals 1. Initially, VOR gain also will be low when the head moves toward the intact side. Although the oculomotor deficit after unilateral vestibular loss varies from client to client and varies with different test conditions, the VOR is clearly abnormal after unilateral loss. During passive head movement in the light, clients may make corrective saccades (high-velocity eye movements) to refixate on the target. With time after the unilateral lesion, the dynamic disturbance in the VOR recovers. This is most obvious in the increased gain (eye velocity/head velocity) with rapid head movements toward the side of the lesion.

Remember the push-pull relationship of the two labyrinths in the normal ear? Again, with head movement in one direction there is an increase in the firing rate in the ipsilateral labyrinth and a decrease in the firing rate in the contralateral labyrinth. With a unilateral lesion, the brain receives only the decreased firing rate from the contralateral labyrinth as the head moves toward the side of the lesion. The brain uses that signal to determine direction and velocity of head movement. The faster the head velocity, the lower the firing rate of the primary afferents and the faster the compensatory eye movements in the direction opposite the head movement. The firing rate of a neuron, however, can only decrease to zero. Therefore, with high-velocity head movements toward the side of the lesion the firing rate of the contralateral neurons may decrease to zero; with even higher velocity head movements it remains at zero. Eye velocity, therefore, can not increase further even if head velocity increases. That is, there is a saturation of the responses such that eye velocity peaks below head velocity. The gain of the slow-phase eye velocity will be lower than normal, and the client will use other strategies, such as catch-up saccades, to keep the eyes on the target.

> With unilateral lesions, eye velocity in the opposite direction cannot increase to equal the head movement; therefore, the client may use catch-up saccades as one way of keeping the eyes on the target.

Postural Stability

As noted in Chapter 11, postural stability is maintained through complex interactions among sensory inputs, biomechanical constraints, and voluntary motor control. Three sensory systems--visual, vestibular, and somatosensory--provide the main inputs to the automatic postural reflexes and contribute to voluntary postural control. Several concepts are particularly important to understanding the changes in postural control that occur after vestibular lesions. They are as follows:

(1) Role of visual cues

> The effectiveness of visual stabilization is influenced by the distance from objects in the visual field.

a. *Movement of the body relative to a stationary visual world.* Visual inputs provide several different cues that affect postural stability. As a person sways, even with quiet standing, retinal slip (movement of an image across the retina), eye velocity, and head velocity information are used to determine body movement relative to environmental movement. Changes in image size and retinal disparity, which would occur with anterior-posterior sway, are additional cues. Visual stabilization of balance under these conditions appears to be primarily dependent on central vision and is related to the distance from the eyes to the visual target. When the distance exceeds 1 m, visual cues become less effective. Brandt et al (1985) suggest that the differences in the distance between the subject and the stationary world may account for the variability often noted in the Romberg test results. Essentially, if you test clients while they are looking at a stationary object within arms length away, they will sway less than if they are looking down a long corridor. It is important, therefore, to be consistent in your testing procedures.

b. *Movement of the visual environment around a stationary person.* Movement of the visual world results in the perception of self-movement and, in fact, can cause an increase in postural sway. This effect is more dependent on stimuli in the peripheral portions of the visual field than on stimuli in the central portions of the field. Most people have experienced this effect at one time or another. Remember the example of your sitting in a stationary car or train and when an adjacent car began to move, your feeling as if you were moving for a brief moment. The direction of the induced postural response is related to the direction of stimulus movement. When you are facing a visual stimulus that suddenly moves toward you, you will feel as if you are swaying forward and therefore will correct for this perception by swaying backward. Clients with peripheral vestibular lesions frequently complain of greater postural instability when moving through complicated visual environments or when in a visual environment that is moving. A complicated visual environment may not provide sufficient cues to help them maintain their balance. A moving visual environment may cause a greater induced postural response than the response in a normal person because the client with a vestibular deficit cannot rely on vestibular cues to decide whether the world is moving or not. This phenomenon is common, and it is called the shopping aisle syndrome.

(2) Role of proprioceptive cues

Inputs from skin, muscle, and joint receptors may affect postural responses in several ways. Neck proprioceptors initiate the cervicocollic reflex that acts to align the head with the body, thus complementing the vestibulocollic reflex. Somatosensory information from the lower extremities also is used to maintain postural stability. A study by Diener et al (1984) suggests that proprioceptive inputs may play a more significant role in postural stability during slow perturbations than during rapid perturbations of balance.

(3) Role of vestibular cues

The role of vestibular signals in postural control is not completely understood. Several studies have reported an early electromyographic (EMG) response in lower extremity muscles that is present in normal subjects but absent in clients with bilateral vestibular loss after sudden rotational or translational perturbations of the support surface. However, the significance of this rapid vestibular response is not clear.

Horstmann and Dietz (1988) demonstrated fast-acting vestibulospinal responses when they displaced the heads of normal subjects in an anterior-posterior direction by 2 cm. This response was absent in clients with bilateral vestibular loss. They determined that the EMG response induced by this perturbation of the head was only 10% of the EMG response that occurs when the head moves after perturbations of the support surface. They therefore concluded that the fast vestibulospinal contribution to postural stability is small. Additionally, Dichgans and

325

Diener (1989) showed that changing the head position, which presumably would alter vestibular inputs, has no effect on the latency or amplitude of the responses to rapid rotational perturbations of the support surface. The response to slow platform movements, however, were altered by changes in head position. Despite this confusion, it is obvious that lesions of the peripheral vestibular system have profound effects on postural stability: during the acute stage of a unilateral peripheral vestibular lesion, clients tend to fall or deviate toward the side of the lesion.

Postural Disturbances

Postural Disturbances From Removing Sensory Cues

> Usually the loss of one sense causes little problem because redundant information from other sources will compensate.

In general, optimal postural stability requires two sensory inputs. In normal subjects, removing one sensory cue (eg, vision) does not cause a marked increase in postural sway; even when walking with eyes closed a normal subject's performance is fair. Clients with complete bilateral vestibular loss have normal postural stability when standing quietly. Removing two sensory cues, however, is much more devastating. Normal subjects can stand with eyes closed (no vision) and with proprioceptive input minimized, but there will be a large decrement in their postural stability (Fig 13-4).

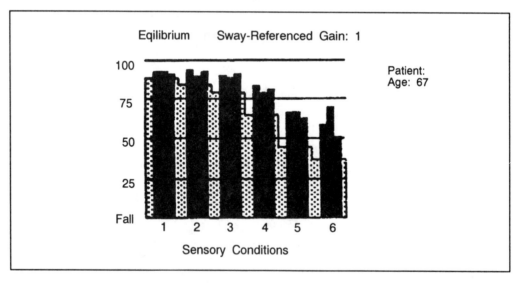

Figure 13-4   Normal anterior-posterior sway in a 67-year-old subject. The sway is indicated as a score from 100 (perfect stability) to zero (loss of balance) for each of six test conditions. Test 1: normal visual, proprioceptive, and vestibular cues; Test 2: normal proporioceptive and vestibular cues, eyes closed; Test 3: normal proprioceptive and vestibular cues, distorted visual cues; Test 4: normal visual and vestibular cues; distorted proprioceptive cues; Test 5: normal vestibular cues, distorted proprioceptive cues, eyes closed; Test 6: normal vestibular cues, distorted proprioceptive and visual cues. Each test was repeated three times.

Thus, when normal subjects are forced to rely solely on vestibular cues, anterior-posterior sway may increase from < 1 degree (normal quiet stance with eyes open or closed) to > 6 degrees. The effect of removing sensory cues is important when considering the treatment of clients with vestibular deficits. Many of these clients are at risk for losing visual or proprioceptive cues or both because of conditions such as diabetes.

Postural Disturbances From Vestibular Lesions

The VSRs have a static disturbance (abnormality during quiet stance) after a unilateral lesion. The static disturbance is seen in the asymmetry in lower extremity EMG activity when the client is standing quietly. Like spontaneous nystagmus, this asymmetry in EMG activity is probably the result of the imbalance in the tonic firing rate of the vestibular nuclei. The asymmetric stance can be corrected when using visual cues and, therefore, is best detected if the client is standing with eyes closed. Clinically, the static disturbance in the VSR appears to recover in about 1 month.

The dynamic disturbance (abnormality during movement) in the VSR is evident as a disruption of the locomotive equilibrium of these clients. Clients with peripheral vestibular deficits have no limb or truncal ataxia and, when seated, appear to be very stable as long as there is no head movement. When ambulating, however, they have a markedly ataxic gait. Even when compensated (ie, other systems make up for the vestibular loss), some ataxia can be produced by having the clients turn around quickly or turn their heads from right to left repeatedly while walking. To summarize, both the VOR and VSR demonstrate static and dynamic changes in function following unilateral vestibular lesions. This is in contrast to clients with symmetrical bilateral vestibular loss.

Treatment

The use of exercises to treat clients with vestibular dysfunction was introduced in the 1940s by Sir Terence Cawthorne, an otolaryngologist, and F.S. Cooksey, a physical therapist. They did not differentiate among the different vestibular problems; they simply noted that clients with vestibular disorders tended to avoid moving their heads and reasoned that to have normal function head movement should be encouraged. Although some of the exercises advocated here are based on Cawthorne's work, the current approaches differ in two important ways. First, they reflect our increased knowledge of vestibular system function and second, they apply only to specific vestibular disorders. The main goals of these exercises are to improve 1) gaze stability during head movement, 2) visual-vestibular interactions during head movement, and 3) static and dynamic postural stability.

Study Questions:

1. What symptoms are usually seen with a unilateral semicircular canal lesion and with lesions of the otoliths?

2. Explain the push-pull relationship between each pair of canals.

3. When the head is moving but the gaze is stabilized, by producing an eye velocity equal to the head velocity, what is the value of the gain? Gain =   ?

4. Differentiate between static and dynamic oculomotor disturbances found in vestibular lesions.

5. How are the eyes kept on a target when the head is moving if the client has a unilateral vestibular lesion?

6. If the vestibular lesion is on the right side, describe the vestibular responses on both sides when the head turns to the right.

7. Compare the visual events when the body moves in a stationary world with the events occurring when the body is stationary and the visual environment moves.

8. Under what circumstances do proprioceptors play the most significant role in postural stability?

9. What happens when sensory inputs are removed?

10. Explain static and dynamic disturbances in unilateral lesions.

Mechanisms of Recovery

Adaptability of the VOR contributes to the recovery of gaze stability.

There are a number of ways gaze stability might recover following unilateral vestibular lesions. Recovery in part may result from recovery of the VOR itself. One of the most significant characteristics of the vestibular system is its ability to adapt--to make long term changes in how the neurons respond to a stimulus. The VOR can function normally (have a normal gain) after unilateral loss under certain conditions, such as low-velocity head movements or high-velocity head movements, if the client knows which direction his head is to move before the movement occurs.

The substitution of proprioceptive inputs also may contribute to recovery of gaze stability. Maoli and Precht (1985) suggest that neck

328

proprioceptive inputs have an increased influence on gaze stability after unilateral lesions compared with normal conditions. During head movement, neck proprioceptive inputs drive a compensatory eye movement, the COR, which is similar to the VOR, but it functions at much lower frequencies of head movement. Kobayashi et al (1988) found that nystagmus occurring when a vibratory stimulus is applied to the muscles of the neck (neck vibratory nystagmus) increased after unilateral vestibular lesions in human beings, implying an increased COR.

> The COR proprioceptors in the neck can produce compensatory eye movement.

Clients may also develop alternative strategies to maintain gaze stability. Segal and Katsarkas (1988) found that clients used combinations of the VOR and saccades to maintain gaze stability after unilateral vestibular lesions. The use of saccades would not appear to be a particularly useful alternative strategy for a poor VOR because clients would not be able to see during head movements. Clients may also opt to restrict head movements in order to see more clearly, because with a poor VOR vision would be poor while the head is moving. Restricting head movements would not be a particularly successful substitution for the VOR because ultimately it would limit everyday activities and still would not provide a mechanism for seeing clearly during head movements. Human beings probably use a variety of strategies, which may be different from client to client, in an effort to maintain visual fixation on a target during head rotations. However, the most effective mechanism for improving gaze stability during head movements would seem to be to increase the VOR gain. Methods by which the VOR gain can be increased will be discussed later.

> When the VOR is lost, clients will adopt other strategies to maintain visual fixation.

There also are several mechanisms by which postural stability might improve following unilateral vestibular loss. Recovery may result from recovery of the VSR. Black et al (1989) found that in the acute stage after acoustic neuroma resection, which involves removing the vestibular nerve, clients were unable to maintain their balance on tests in which they had to rely on vestibular cues alone. With time, however, they recovered their ability to maintain balance on these tests, suggesting an improved ability to use vestibular cues.

> Other senses may substitute for lost vestibular function.

Recovery might also result from the substitution of visual or proprioceptive cues. Several studies have shown that clients with unilateral vestibular lesions may become less stable when visual cues are removed. In the acute stage after resection of acoustic neuroma, subjects had decreased postural stability when proprioceptive cues from the feet and ankles were distorted and when forced to rely on vestibular cues. This suggests that initially these subjects were relying on proprioceptive cues for postural stability in stance. Neck proprioceptive cues also may contribute to improved postural stability. In cats, neck proprioceptive inputs caused increased responses in dcLVN (one of the vestibular nuclei in the cat) neurons after unilateral vestibular neurectomy (58% in normal, 69.5% in acute stage, and 74.2% in chronic stage).

There is considerable redundancy in the contributions of the different sensory inputs to postural stability, and each sensory input appears to have optimal frequencies at which it acts to stabilize balance. For both gaze and postural stability, visual and proprioceptive cues would substitute only in part for the decreased vestibular response. Thus the best treatment approach would seem to be to improve the function of the remaining vestibular system rather than to foster the substitution of visual or proprioceptive cues.

Improvement Through Activity

Studies on the effect of unilateral and bilateral vestibular loss in animals support the concept that visuomotor experience shortens the recovery time of the dynamic vestibular reflexes. Mathog and Peppard (1982) demonstrated that after unilateral labyrinthectomy, cats given exercises recovered postural stability faster than a nonexercised control group. Igarashi et al (1981) found that specific exercises resulted in a more rapid recovery of dynamic postural stability in squirrel monkeys when comparing a control group (nonexercise) with an exercise group after unilateral vestibular lesions.

> Exercise or practice in movement of the eyes, head, and body enhance recovery of function.

Several studies have noted the importance of early visuomotor experience after unilateral vestibular lesions. There is a delay in the recovery of the dynamic vestibulo-ocular response in cats and in monkeys deprived of vision immediately after unilateral labyrinthectomy. Lacour et al (1976), in a study of the effects of unilateral vestibular neurectomy in baboons, found that when motor activity was restricted, the initiation of recovery of otolith-spinal reflexes was delayed and the course of the recovery was prolonged when compared with nonrestrained animals. Furthermore, if visuovestibular interaction is allowed in the immediate postoperative period after unilateral labyrinthectomy in monkeys, recovery begins quite promptly. Fetter et al (1988) found that changes in VOR gain occurred within 1 hour after unilateral labyrinthectomized animals were exposed to light.

Exercises for Adaptation

As mentioned before, one of the more remarkable characteristics of the vestibular system is adaptation. The response of vestibular neurons to a particular stimulus changes or adapts as a natural part of development and aging. The response of the system also changes or adapts in response to disease or injury. Research shows the gain (eye velocity/head velocity) of the vestibular system can be increased by manipulating visual inputs.

> Adaptation of the vestibular system to loss can be facilitated by manipulation with visual inputs.

Exercises to induce adaptation of the vestibular system should incorporate several important concepts (Tab 13-3).

1. The best stimulus to produce adaptation of the vestibular system is movement of an image across the retina (retinal slip), combined with head movement. If a person is trying to see an object clearly and the object begins to move on the retina, vision degrades (poor acuity) and eye movement is generated to again see the object clearly. Retinal slip, a normal phenomenon, is therefore the error signal that results in an increase in the VOR gain. The brain alters the firing rate of the neurons to try to minimize the error signal. Movement is also necessary to regain normal (or near-normal) postural stability after vestibular lesions, presumably so that the brain can correct for a different error signal.

2. Adaptation of the vestibular system is specific to the stimulus used. For instance, if a single frequency of head rotation is used in the exercises, vestibular adaptation will be greatest at that frequency, with less change at other frequencies. To increase the VOR gain across many frequencies, which would mimic normal movement, the exercises would have to require that the client perform head movements at many different frequencies.

3. Another important point is that the gain of the vestibular system is affected by voluntary motor control. Several studies have shown that if subjects are asked to fixate on an imaginary visual target in the dark while making head movements, vestibular gain will increase over what it was without fixation. In practical terms, this suggests that clients cannot be lazy when practicing the different exercises; they must try to maintain fixation of the visual target and concentrate on the task. The exercises require effort on the part of the client.

4. Adaptation takes time. Although some adaptive changes occur quickly, even instantaneously, the stimulus probably needs to be maintained for several minutes to assure adaptation.

5. Another concept is that in the normal individual there is an interaction of vestibular, visual, and proprioceptive cues. To ensure optimal recovery, therefore, exercises should incorporate vestibular, visual, and proprioceptive experience. Having the client practice horizontal head movements while maintaining fixation on a stationary target to improve gaze stability, for instance, might be done both with a small target that will use the voluntary smooth pursuit system (primarily cortical pathways) and with a large, full-field target that will engage the optokinetic system (primarily subcortical pathways). Exercises to improve postural stability during head movements should be practiced without as well as with visual cues.

6. The last point is that these exercises should produce the symptoms of vertigo and disequilibrium in the clients. The therapist needs to explain to the client that the dizziness is a sign that the brain is trying to learn how to deal with that input and that the only way the brain will recover is if it experiences that sensory conflict. For instance,

331

clients with peripheral vestibular disorders frequently complain of a greater sense of disequilibrium and of greater postural instability when they are moving through a richly textured environment or when the visual environment moves with respect to themselves. The exercise in which the client tries to maintain fixation on a moving full-field target while simultaneously moving his head would be an appropriate choice because it may evoke disequilibrium and postural instability. In addition, the client should not avoid situations that make him dizzy, whether it is moving his head or walking in shopping malls, simply because it exacerbates the symptoms. Basically, if something makes the client dizzy, it is probably good for him.

Table 13-3

Exercises to Enhance Vestibular Adaptation[a]

---

1. Vestibular stimulation (X1 viewing)[b]

    Tape a business card on the wall in front of you so that you can read it.
    Move your head back and forth sideways keeping the words in focus.
    Move your head faster but keep the words in focus.
       Continue to do this for 1-2 minutes without stopping.
    Repeat the exercise moving your head up and down.
    Repeat the exercises using a large pattern such as a checkerboard (full-field stimulus}.

2. Visuovestibular interactions (X2 viewing)[b]

    Hold a business card in front of you so that you can read it.
    Move the card and your head back and forth horizontally in opposite directions keeping the words in focus.
    Move your head faster but keep the words in focus. Continue to do this for 1-2 minutes without stopping.
    Repeat the exercise moving your head and the card up and down in opposite directions.
    Repeat the exercises using a large pattern such as a checkerboard (full-field stimulus).

These exercises can be performed actively or passively; they can be performed while seated or standing; they can be performed with the target near or far.

---

[a] From Herdman (1990a), reprinted with permission of the American Physical Therapy Association.

[b] X1 = times one; X2 = times two. These numbers indicate the relationship between eye and head movement. If the eye and head were moving in the same direction at the same velocity (as in VOR cancellation), it would be X0 viewing.

Exercises for Postural Stability

The purpose of the exercises noted in Table 13-4 is to force the client to develop strategies of performing daily activities even when deprived of visual, proprioceptive, or normal vestibular inputs. The exercises are supposed to help the client develop confidence and establish functional limits. There is nothing magical about these exercises; you should be able to develop some of your own.

As you may note, the exercises suggested here progress from easy to more difficult (Tab 13-4). Basically, they make maintaining balance more difficult by doing the following:

1. Decreasing the client's base of support (eg, having the client move his feet from wide apart to together to a heel-to-toe position).

2. Limiting the client's ability to use arm movement to assist with maintaining balance.

3. Decreasing the number of sensory cues available to the client, at first intermittently and then continuously.

4. Changing the task from a static task (eg, quiet standing) to a more dynamic task (eg, walking).

5. Increasing the difficulty of the dynamic task (eg, walking a straight line to turning around).

6. Combining all of the above factors.

Specific Unilateral Lesions

Symptoms:

Spontaneous nystagmus

Decreased gain

Decreased time constant

Prolonged vertigo

Disorders of the labyrinth or vestibular nerve that result in decreased function or in loss of function unilaterally include viral inflammation (vestibular neuronitis and labyrinthitis), infection, slowly evolving disorders such as acoustic neuroma, surgical procedures for acoustic neuroma and Meniere's disease, and vascular diseases affecting the basilar or internal auditory arteries. Clients with these disorders may all benefit from exercises to enhance the adaptation of the vestibular system, but management of these problems differs somewhat. You may want to review the material on vestibular function tests and on the clinical examination of the vestibular system before reading this section so that you are familiar with the terminology.

Table 13-4

Exercises to Improve Postural Stability[a]

On all of these exercises you should take extra precautions so you do not fall.

1._____ Stand with your feet as close together as possible, with both hands helping you maintain your balance by touching a wall. Take your hand, or hands, off the wall for longer and longer periods of timewhile maintaining your balance. Try moving your feet even closer together. Repeat this for 10 minutes twice each day.

2._____ Stand with your feet shoulder-width apart, with eyes open looking straight ahead at a target on the wall.   Progressively narrow your base of support from
    feet apart to
    feet together to
    a semi--heel-to-toe position to
    heel-to-toe (one foot in front of the other) to
    standing on one foot.
Do the exercise first
    with arms outstretched and then
    with arms close to your body and then
    with arms folded across your chest.

Hold each position for 15 seconds and then move on to the next most difficult exercise .

3._____ Repeat exercise #2 with head bent forward 30 degrees and then back 30 degrees.

4._____ Repeat exercise #1 with eyes closed, at first intermittently and then continuously, all the while making a special effort to mentally visualize your surroundings.

5._____ Repeat exercise #2 with eyes closed, at first intermittently and then continuously, all the while making a special effort to mentally visualize your surroundings.

6._____Repeat # ___ above but while standing on a foam pillow.

7._____Walk close to a wall with your hand braced available for balancing. Walk with a more narrow base of support.   Finally, walk heel to toe. Do this with eyes _____ (open/closed). Practice for 5 minutes.

8._____Walk close to a wall and turn you head to the right and to the left as you walk. Try to focus on different objects as you walk. Gradually turn your head more often and faster. Practice for 2 minutes.

9._____Walk in a large circle clockwise, gradually make the circle smaller. Repeat in a counter-clockwise direction.

10._____Practice turning around while you walk. At first, make a large circle while you turn but gradually make smaller and smaller turns. Be sure to turn in both directions.

---

[a] From Herdman (1990*a*), reprinted with permission of the American Physical Therapy Association.

Unilateral Paresis

Clients with vestibular neuronitis, vestibular neuritis, or labyrinthitis usually have a paresis of the vestibular system. That is, there is some remaining function in the affected labyrinth or nerve. In vestibular neuronitis or neuritis, clients have an abrupt onset of mild to severe vertigo, with nausea and vomiting. An upper respiratory tract infection either precedes or accompanies the attack 36% to 50% of the time. Clients are usually 30 to 60 years old, and there is no difference in rate of occurrence between men and women. In vestibular neuronitis there are no auditory changes and no other neurological problems; in labyrinthitis there is decreased hearing on the involved side.

| With paresis, function is not completely lost. |

During the acute stage, the client will have a spontaneous nystagmus, usually with the fast phase toward the intact ear. You should review the mechanism behind spontaneous nystagmus to be sure that you understand why the fast phase is directed toward the intact ear. On testing, the caloric response is decreased or absent on the involved side. Rotational tests show both decreased gain and a slightly shortened time constant (Tc). Occasionally, there can be bilateral involvement.

The attack of vertigo is prolonged, lasting from days to weeks (usually about a week). Recovery occurs gradually over many weeks, but by 6 months, essentially all clients are normal although they may still have a sense of imbalance or unsteadiness when they move their heads quickly. If you retest them, the VOR gain will be normal, but the Tc does not recover. Some clients have only one attack, but others may have episodic attacks and may also have generalized disequilibrium between attacks.

Treatment

Acute management of the client with vestibular neuronitis or with labyrinthitis includes the use of vestibular suppressant medication and hospitalization for rehydration if the client has been vomiting excessively (Tab 13-5). The client will want to stay in bed with head still, eyes closed. Exercises are not appropriate at this stage because head movement will induce vomiting.

| Movement should be encouraged when it no longer induces vomiting. |

Within a few days, the vestibular suppressant medication usually is discontinued, and the client should be encouraged to move his head and to walk around. At this point clients can begin adaptation exercises, but physical therapists do not usually see them in the acute or even subacute stage because they tend to recover by themselves. What you will see are those clients who after many weeks or months have not recovered. These clients may really benefit from adaptation exercises. The trick is to get these clients to move their heads.

Clients who have not compensated for vestibular neuronitis usually do not move their heads much and certainly not at higher velocities because they are afraid of the vertigo that it produces. They walk slowly, with decreased rotation through the trunk and neck, and they turn en bloc. They also become excessively reliant on visual cues to maintain balance, even though they have useful vestibular and proprioceptive information available. In these clients, vestibular adaptation would be incomplete because the required error signal produced by a combination of eye and head movement is missing. The exercise program, therefore, should emphasize combined eye and head movements, first with the client sitting, then standing, and finally walking.

It is important to encourage these clients to be consistent about doing the exercises and to reenforce the notion that they should continue to make the head movement even if they feel dizzy or even a little nauseated. They may, in fact, feel worse before they feel better because they will have more vertigo and more imbalance until adaptation finally occurs.

> Clients need to understand that they must practice certain movements even it makes them feel worse.

Table 13-5

Vestibular Suppressants

Meclizine (antivert)
Scopolamine
Promethazine (Phenergan®)
Prochlorperazine (Compazine®)
Diazepam (Valium®)

Unilateral Loss From Surgical Procedures

A number of different surgical procedures result in the complete loss of vestibular function unilaterally. These include removal of acoustic (Cranial nerve VIII) neuromas and the surgical management of Meniere's disease in which the vestibular nerve is cut. This section first will describe the surgical procedures and then will present the physical therapy management of these two problems.

Acoustic Neuromas

Growth of a tumor on the eighth cranial nerve does not result in vertigo, because the normal mechanisms of adaptation will mask the deficit. The central nervous system simply keeps adjusting to the slow loss of vestibular function. Acoustic neuromas are the third most common intracranial tumor. This tumor usually grows from the Schwann cell of the vestibular nerve in the internal auditory canal. The tumors grow from 2 to 10 mm/year. As it becomes larger, it will extend medially into the cerebellar-pontine angle and, if they are not treated, will compress the brain stem and cerebellum.

Most clients with acoustic neuromas are seen initially because they have complaints of hearing loss or tinnitus (ringing or other sounds in the ears). Typically, there is a progressive, high frequency hearing loss and also decreased speech discrimination (difficulty identifying the spoken word). Acoustic neuromas are most prevalent in people 35 to 40 years old and are found in women twice as often as in men.

Usually when the acoustic neuroma is resected, the vestibular nerve is cut. Only rarely is any branch or portion of the vestibular nerve left intact. Resection of the tumor results in a sudden loss of the remaining vestibular input on that side and creates an imbalance between the vestibular nuclei on the lesioned and intact sides. The brain interprets the difference between the two sides as a signal that the head is moving. Visual and proprioceptive cues, however, signal that the head is stationary. This sensory conflict results in vertigo, nausea, and vomiting. The severity of the signs and symptoms of vestibular loss is in part related to how much loss of vestibular function occurred with the growth of the tumor.

The most common complication of resection of an acoustic neuroma is hearing loss. Other complications include facial paresis, cerebrospinal fluid (CSF) leak, and headache. Hearing loss probably occurs because of disruption of the blood supply to the cochlea. It is unusual for hearing loss that occurred before surgery to recover with resection of the tumor. Some degree of facial paresis is common after surgery, but in most cases, the facial nerve is preserved and the facial paresis is temporary. Clients may have the facial paresis as they come out of anesthesia or may develop it gradually over the week after surgery.

If the facial involvement is incomplete, recovery is fairly prompt and is usually complete. A complete facial palsy, when it is known that the nerve was not cut or removed during surgery, may take 4 to 6 months to begin to recover. The recovery course itself may extend for more than a year. Recovery may never be complete, although function is usually very good. Clients with complete loss may develop some synkinesis with recovery of function.

The third complication is one of CSF leakage. The risk of CSF leak varies with the type of approach used. With all approaches, the client is advised to avoid blowing the nose, sneezing, coughing, and bending over. One sign of a CSF leak is rhinorrhea (CSF dripping from the nose), which should be documented in the chart.

Slowly growing tumors do not produce vertigo.

Surgery for the tumor usually involves the vestibular nerve.

Complications of surgery:

Hearing loss

Facial paresis

CSF leakage

Headache

Cerebellar involvement

The fourth sequelae of acoustic neuroma surgery is headache. Headache may result from air trapped in the posterior fossa, from tight muscles as the clients "splints" to prevent head movement, from postsurgical migraine, or from more serious problems such as CSF leak or meningitis. Headache may occur immediately after surgery or may first appear many weeks later.

Finally, some clients with acoustic neuromas may have involvement of the cerebellum. Many acoustic neuromas compress the cerebellum without any cerebellar dysfunction, however, and permanent cerebellar problems are unusual after acoustic neuroma resection.

Meniere's Disease

Meniere's disease is believed to be caused by an increase in the volume of endolymph in the inner ear. Clients have episodic tinnitus, fluctuating hearing loss, vertigo, and a fullness or pressure in the ears. These attacks are severely disabling and may last for hours.

During the acute stage of an attack, the client is usually confined to bed because of the severity of the vertigo and nausea, and the client takes a vestibular suppressant medication. Between attacks, the client is normal. The only exception to this is in clients with long-term, chronic Meniere's disease who may have a paretic labyrinth.

> Exercise is not effective with Meniere's disease.

Exercises will not work with Meniere's disease because it is essentially a mechanical problem and because the condition changes too rapidly for central adaptation to be effective. Medical treatment of Meniere's disease may consist of diuretics, sedatives, and decreased sodium intake. If conservative treatment fails to control the attacks, and if the attacks are frequent enough and are disruptive enough, surgical control may be attempted.

One surgical intervention is directed at decreasing the pressure by shunting the endolymph. Endolymphatic shunts provide complete control of vertigo in only 50% of clients. Of those, some will eventually have a labyrinthectomy or a vestibular nerve section.

Labyrinthectomy is performed on those clients in whom hearing is not a consideration because when the labyrinth is opened, hearing will be lost. It has a smaller risk of facial paresis and of CSF leak than does a vestibular nerve section.

Vestibular nerve section is performed on those clients in whom an effort is being made to preserve hearing. As with resection of acoustic neuroma, hearing may be lost or diminished if the there is damage to the auditory nerve itself or to its blood supply. Facial paresis is another possible risk, but when it occurs, the probability of recovery is excellent. Risk of cerebellar damage is negligible. Failure of this procedure to control vertigo occurs if some of the vestibular nerve is missed. Clients can still have attacks of vertigo if this happens and will require a second procedure. The other symptoms of Meniere's disease--fullness and tinnitus--may not change after retrolabyrinthine vestibular nerve section.

Unfortunately, cutting the vestibular nerve means that the client will have a problem because of the surgically induced vestibular imbalance. Vestibular nerve section is only performed when everything else fails and when the client is disabled by the attacks of vertigo.

Treatment After Surgery

During the acute postoperative stage, whether after resection of an acoustic neuroma or a labyrinthectomy or vestibular nerve section for Meniere's, the client usually remains in bed because of the severity of the vertigo and nausea. Head movement causes an increase in these symptoms, and the client may be medicated to control the vertigo and nausea. After a few days, the medications are usually stopped because it is believed that drugs may suppress the remaining vestibular function and may prevent central compensation.

Recovery from most of the vertigo and nausea will occur within 2 to 4 days. Clients with vestibular nerve section for Meniere's disease or with small acoustic neuromas are more likely to have severe vertigo and nausea because the surgery has been performed on a relatively normal vestibular nerve. Other clients, especially those with large acoustic neuromas, will have less nausea and vertigo. Clients will also have a spontaneous nystagmus in the light when the eyes are in the middle of the orbit (center of gaze). In some clients, when the client looks toward the intact side, the amplitude of the nystagmus will increase. If the client is asked to look toward the side of the lesion, the fast phase of the nystagmus will decrease or the direction may reverse. This is called direction-changing nystagmus, and it suggests that the brain stem has been affected by the removal of vestibular function.

Spontaneous nystagmus usually will decrease over the course of a week, in part because of the subject's ability to visually suppress the nystagmus and in part, because of the rebalancing of the firing rates of the vestibular nuclei. Anatomical and physiological mechanisms that may contribute to this rebalancing include denervation supersensitivity and collateral sprouting. It is possible to observe nystagmus in some clients for many years after surgery by removing visual suppression (eg, viewing the eyes through Frenzel lenses).

The client's first attempts to stand are marked by a widened base of support. Surprisingly, most clients will have a normal Romberg test result within a few days after surgery. This may be because the Romberg tests static balance and these clients have a greater deficit of dynamic balance. Even though the Romberg test results may be normal, it is important to remember that these clients have poor balance and that all tests of balance must be done carefully. During walking, these clients will have a wide base of support, decreased trunk and head rotation, and an ataxic gait. Head movement and turning around will increase the ataxia. At this stage, the client may be at risk for falls when attempting to walk without assistance. The degree of gait instability varies considerably among different clients. Most clients will be able to walk without assistance within a few days, although they will still have an ataxic, wide-based gait.

At this time, it is not known whether physical therapy is necessary for all clients after surgery. Some clients, however, continue to avoid head movement after surgery and may benefit from an exercise program that encourages head movement. Initially, the client should keep his eyes open and the room lights on in order to get the visual input needed for vestibular adaptation. Within 2 to 3 days after surgery, most clients can begin an exercise program. The goals of the exercises are to improve gaze stability during head movements and to improve static and dynamic postural stability (Tab 13-4). These exercises frequently involve head movement. Initially, the velocity of the head movement should be relatively slow, at the lower range of head velocities. The head movements should be continuous even though at this time moving the head will probably cause an increase in vertigo and nausea.

Exercises to improve balance consists of ambulating with assistance and standing with eyes open, gradually decreasing the base of support (moving feet together). As compensation begins, clients should be encouraged to begin head and eye movements while standing and then while walking in order to facilitate vestibular adaptation. In clients after surgery for removal of acoustic neuromas, disequilibrium improves slowly over several weeks and may take up to 2 to 6 months or longer, for full recovery, depending on the age and activity level of the individual. In clients with vestibular nerve section only, the recovery is usually faster. In some cases, compensation is delayed or does not occur. This is more likely to happen in older clients, in clients with other sensory problems, or in clients in whom there is cerebellar or brain stem damage.

> **Fatigue may cause the biggest problems with returning to work.**

Some clients return to work as early as 2 to 3 months after resection of the acoustic neuroma, but many of them require longer to recover. Again, clients with vestibular nerve section tend to recover more quickly and may return to work as early as 3 to 4 weeks after surgery. We think fatigue is the biggest detriment to returning to work. The final level of recovery in both groups is usually excellent. Most clients recover with little residual problems except for complaints of slight instability with rapid head movements. This is because the remaining vestibular system responds to head movement toward the side of the lesion by decreasing its firing rate, but the firing rate of a neuron can only be decreased to zero. (If the effect of head movement on the firing rate of the vestibular system is not clear to you, go back and review the push-pull relationship of the vestibular inputs.) With faster head movements, the signal to the brain becomes less accurate, and the compensatory postural response will slightly be inadequate.

The perception of disequilibrium that many clients have may result in some limitation of activity in some of these clients; however, for most clients the changes are minimal. For instance, clients who play racquetball may have to switch where they stand in the court because turning the head rapidly toward the side of the lesion may make them feel slightly off-balance, although they will not actually lose their balance.

> It is very difficult to compensate for rapid head movements.

Study Questions:

1. List the mechanisms that will have an impact on or play a role in recovery from unilateral vestibular lesions.

2. What relationship does activity have to recovery?

3. How do exercises help to improve adaptation and recovery of function?

4. What are the physiological effects of a unilateral lesion of the vestibular system?

5. Explain why a client with a unilateral paresis will have a spontaneous nystagmus with the fast phase toward the intact ear.

6. Describe some principles that should be considered when designing treatment programs for clients with vestibular lesions.

7. How does treatment of clients with acoustic neuroma differ from treatments for clients with Meniere's disease?

Complete Bilateral Vestibular Loss

Signs and Symptoms

Oscillopsia

| Oscillopsia is the illusion that everything in the environment is moving. |

Clients with bilateral vestibular loss are often primarily concerned about their difficulties with balance. They come to the clinic because they are stumbling or falling, especially when they try to walk in the dark. On questioning, they will describe difficulty seeing clearly while walking or when driving in a car. This symptom, *oscillopsia*, is the illusionary movement of the world and occurs because there is no VOR to stabilize the eyes during head movement. In the article "Living with a Balance Problem" (J.C. 1952), a physician who was treated with streptomycin describes what happened to his visual function as he lost his vestibular function. At the worst point, his eyes moved every time his heart beat. He ended up wedging his head between the bars of his hospital bed to keep his head stable so he could see. After he had undergone some central compensation, he found that if he were stationary he could see clearly but that if he were walking he could not identify the faces of people walking toward him. He also could not read and walk at the same time, he had to stand still.

Oculomotor Disturbance

| Bilateral lesions do not affect a client who is standing still. |

Clients with bilateral vestibular deficits generally do not show signs of static disturbances in VOR. When the vestibular deficit is symmetrical, there will be no asymmetry in the tonic firing rate of the vestibular nuclei. These clients have neither spontaneous nystagmus nor a skew deviation (one eyeball riding higher in the orbit than the other). The exception to this would be the client in whom the bilateral deficit occurred in two stages, such as a sequential bilateral vestibular deficit, or in whom the degree of dysfunction was not the same in the two sides.

| Bilateral lesions result in severe dynamic disturbances of vestibular reflexes. |

Clients with bilateral loss do have a severe dynamic disturbance of the vestibular reflexes. They have no VOR to stabilize the eyes in space when turning the head horizontally or vertically. Initially, it is difficult for them to keep their eyes stable under any conditions. As mentioned before, these clients complain of oscillopsia, or the perception that the world is moving or jumping, and they complain of slip; that is, with movement of the head, images seem to be running across the retina. These clients usually have greater retinal slip than normal because the vestibular system is not generating the appropriate eye movement to compensate for the head movement. The effect of the loss of the VOR can be quite dramatic. If the VOR is not working, the eyes are not stable, and images will move across the retina. The degradation of visual acuity cannot be compensated for and these clients do not see clearly during head movements. The retinal slip is still an error signal but no increase in VOR gain occurs because the vestibular system is not functioning. Even small amounts of retinal slip can degrade vision significantly.

Postural Disturbance

Bilateral lesions severely disturb gait and other movements.

Clients with bilateral vestibular deficits also have a severe dynamic disturbance of postural stability during ambulation. In the acute stage, clients may be unable to stand unless they widen their base of support and keep their eyes open. In the chronic stage, they may be able to stand with feet together and eyes closed (normal Romberg) because they have learned to use proprioceptive cues more effectively, but they usually are unable to walk with eyes closed. Their gait tends to be wide based, and they can have a markedly ataxic gait pattern. Frequently, they are unable to turn around or turn their head when walking without a loss of balance. Even when fully compensated, their gait remains wide based and ataxic.

Treatment

Mechanisms of Recovery

When the VOR is lost, the COR will compensate to some extent.

Recovery of gaze stability is dependent on the substitution of alternative strategies for the lost vestibular function. These strategies have been well studied in human beings. One strategy used is the potentiation (increase) of the COR. During low-frequency, brief, head movements, sensory inputs from neck muscles and joint facets act to produce a slow phase eye movement that complements the VOR, although in normal subjects it contributes, at most, 15% of the compensatory eye movement. In clients with complete bilateral vestibular loss, the COR operates at higher frequencies than in normal and contributes up to 25% of the compensatory eye movement. The potentiation of the COR helps keep the image of the target on the fovea during head movements, although it cannot substitute for the lost VOR through the full frequency range of normal head movement.

Saccades are an impractical substitution for the VOR because you cannot see during a saccade.

Another strategy clients may use is to modify saccade amplitude and use corrective saccades to maintain fixation during combined eye and head movements. You cannot see during saccadic eye movements, however, so this strategy would not be a useful substitute during head movements for the lost VOR. Another strategy the client might adopt would be to restrict head movements or to decrease head velocity. These latter strategies are impractical and would result in limitations of daily activities.

343

In clients with bilateral vestibular loss, improvements in postural stability must also come about through the substitution of visual and somatosensory cues. The use of visual cues to maintain postural stability during most activities would not seem to be a completely successful strategy because without the VOR, the eyes are not stable during head movements and visual acuity is degraded. Even at a visual acuity of 20/40, postural stability is decreased. Studies suggest, however, that visual cues contribute useful information to help maintain balance even in these clients.

Bles et al (1984) have shown that during the course of recovery, clients with complete bilateral vestibular loss change how they rely on sensory cues. Initially, they rely on visual cues as a substitute for the loss of vestibular cues, but over a 2-year period, they increase their reliance on proprioceptive cues to maintain balance. Although there is evidence that proprioceptive responses increase after bilateral vestibular lesions in humans, the use of proprioceptive cues would also not be completely successful as a substitute for the lost vestibular responses. When postural stability is perturbed by viewing a sinusoidal lateral tilt of the visual surround, body sway recovers to within normal limits at lower frequencies but not at higher frequencies. Bles et al (1984) suggest that this is because visual cues cannot substitute for vestibular cues at higher frequencies. Proprioceptive input also cannot substitute for vestibular cues at higher frequencies.

> During fast body movements or sway, neither vision nor proprioception can substitute for vestibular cues.

The contribution of proprioceptive inputs, from the cervical region, to postural stability in clients with complete vestibular loss is not clearly understood. Bles et al (1984) found that changes in neck position did not affect postural stability in clients with complete bilateral vestibular loss. They concluded that proprioceptive signals from the neck do not contribute to balance. It is not known, however, if or how kinesthetic signals from the neck, which would occur during head movement, would affect postural stability. Certainly, clients with bilateral vestibular dysfunction become less stable if they turn their heads while walking. This instability may indicate either that kinesthetic cues do not contribute significantly to dynamic postural stability or that these clients are more reliant on visual cues than on proprioceptive cues to maintain postural stability. With head movement, however, the eyes move because there is no VOR, and these visual cues are degraded.

Improvement Through Activity

> Exercise may help with the recovery of postural stability in clients with bilateral lesions, but gait will never be normal.

There is some evidence that exercises facilitate recovery after bilateral ablation of the labyrinth in monkeys. Igarashi et al (1988) found that an exercise group reached the criterion of eight consecutive trials in which they could keep their balance at preoperative levels a number of days earlier (118 days) than did the control group (one animal 126 days, another 168 days, and one animal had not achieved criterion at 300 days). They concluded that the final level of function may be better when exercises are given after bilateral lesions. Improved postural stability after exercises in clients with bilateral vestibular loss have also been reported by Takemori et al (1985), but no control group was studied. These results suggest that the course of recovery of postural stability can be altered in clients after bilateral vestibular loss.

Exercises for Bilateral Loss

The treatment approach for clients with complete loss of vestibular function involves the use of exercises that foster the substitution of visual and somatosensory information to improve gaze and postural stability (Tab 13-6). The strategies used by clients to maintain gaze stability in the absence of a vestibular system have been well studied. The COR and the modification of saccades can be promoted through the use of specific exercieses to diminish oscillopsia and improve gaze stability during low-frequency head movements and during combined eye-head movements. The mechanisms involved in maintaining postural stability are somewhat less well understood, although significant research is being done in that area.

There are several factors to remember when working with these clients:

1. Recovery after bilateral deficits is slower than for unilateral lesions and can continue to occur over a 2-year period.

2. Recovery is easily upset by other medical problems, such as having a cold or receiving chemotherapy.

3. To maintain recovered function, clients may always need to be doing some exercises, at least intermittently.

4. Postural stability will never be completely normal. The client may have a negative result on the Romberg test and may be able to maintain the sharpened Romberg position with eyes open but not with eyes closed.

5. Initially, ambulation will be wide based and ataxic, with shortened stride length and side-stepping to the right and left. The client will turn en bloc, and turning the head will cause increased instability. Ambulation will improve, but again, it will not be normal.

6. Clients will be at increased risk for falls when walking in low-vision situations, over uneven surfaces, or when fatigued.

7. Many clients, especially older clients, need to use a cane at least some of the time.

Table 13-6

Exercises for Bilateral Vestibular Loss[a]

---

1. Horizontal targets: Active eye-head movements between two targets

Look directly at one target, being sure that your head is also lined up with the target;
Look at the other target with your eyes and then turn your head to the target
    (saccades should precede head movement). Be sure to keep the target in focus
    during the head movement.
Repeat in the opposite direction.
Vary the speed of the head movement but always keep the targets in focus.

Note: Place the two targets close enough together so that when you are looking directly at
    one, you can see the other with your peripheral vision. Practice for 5 minutes, resting
    if necessary. This exercise can also be performed with two vertically placed targets.

2. Imaginary targets

Look at a target directly in front of you.
Close your eyes and turn your head slightly, imagining that you are still looking directly at the
    target. Open your eyes and check to see if you have been able to keep your eyes on
    the target.
Repeat in the opposite direction. Be as accurate as possible.
Vary the speed on the head movement.
Practice for up to 5 minutes, resting if necessary.

Note: This exercise can be performed actively or passively; it can be performed while looking
    at a near target or a distant target; it can also be performed vertically.

3. Potentiation of the COR

Look at a target placed directly in front of you.
While keeping the target in focus, turn your head back and forth horizontally.
Keep your head movement slow enough that the target stays in focus.
Practice for 5 minutes, resting if necessary.

Note: This exercise can be performed in sitting or in standing.

---

[a] From Herdman (1990a), reprinted with permission of the American Physical Therapy
Association.

Specific Bilateral Lesions

Ototoxicity

A common cause of bilateral paretic labyrinthine dysfunction is the administration of systemic antibiotics, such as gentamicin or streptomycin, or of neoplastic drugs, such as cisplatin. With bilateral dysfunction from treatment with an ototoxic drug (Tab 13-7), the symptoms of oscillopsia, disequilibrium, and vertigo develop over time and may not appear until after the drug treatment is finished. Once the symptoms appear, they may continue to become worse for about 2 to 3 weeks. With some clients there may be a partial reversal of the symptoms with time. Often, the vestibular symptoms are accompanied by hearing loss.

Table 13-7
Ototoxic Drugs

---

aminoglycosides:
    gentamicin   streptomycin
    kanamycin   tobramycin
    neomycin   mikacin
neoplastic
    cisplatin
loop diuretics
    ethnacrynic acid
    furosemide (Lasix®)
quinine
organic solvents
    xylene
    toluene
    trochloroethylene
    methylchloroform

Bilateral Sequential Loss

Bilateral loss of vestibular function may also occur as a result of sequential attacks of neuronitis. Clients have an initial episode that is similar to any unilateral vestibular neuronitis. This is followed years later by a second episode of nausea, vertigo, ataxia, and oscillopsia, again without auditory symptoms. The acute care typically consists of vestibular suppressants for the vertigo and the vomiting, but the disequilibrium does not get better, and the client seeks further help. Clients frequently are given a battery of tests before anyone looks at vestibular function. The vertical axis rotational test would show

347

decreased gain and an extremely short Tc. Figures 13-5 and 13-6 show the rotatory tests with the gain and the Tc calculations for a unilateral lesion and a bilateral lesion.

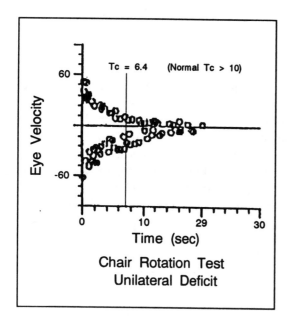

Figure 13-5 Vertical axis rotary-chair test results for a subject with a unilateral deficit. Note that the gain is normal but the Tc remains less than normal. See Figure 13-2 for comparison.

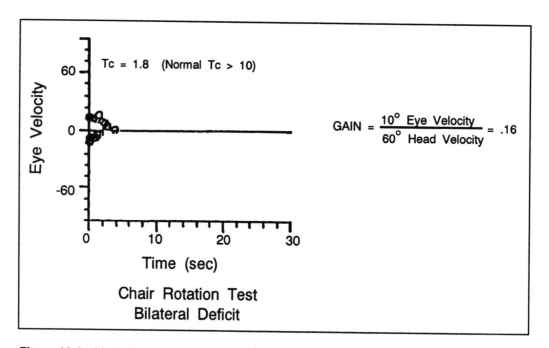

Figure 13-6 Vertical axis rotary-chair test results for a subject with a bilateral deficit. Notice that the gain and the Tc are severely decreased. See Figure 13-2 for comparison.

348

Idiopathic Bilateral Loss

A third cause of bilateral dysfunction is idiopathic bilateral vestibulopathy. This involves a slowly developing disequilibrium, with visual problems but without auditory problems and vertigo. Baloh et al (1989) describe it as relatively silent; that is, other systems mask the slowly developing vestibular problem. There is no history of ototoxic drugs, and the onset is not sudden as in neuronitis but rather is insidious. Clients complain of balance problems, mostly at night when visual cues are not available. It may be that the actual vestibular loss occurred many years ago but was well compensated. With changes in the compensatory mechanisms with age (such as decreased visual acuity), the vestibular loss becomes more evident.

Bilateral vestibular loss can also occur following trauma. For instance, skull-base fractures through the temporal bone bilaterally could result in a decrease or complete loss of vestibular function. There have also been reported cases of bilateral loss in clients with immune disorders.

Positional Vertigo

Signs and Symptoms

> In positional vertigo, it is the position and not the movement that causes the problem.

The term positional vertigo implies that the vertigo occurs when the head is placed in a certain position as opposed to vertigo occurring during movement of the head. There are many different etiologies, but only one, benign paroxysmal positional vertigo (BPPV), is particularly amenable to treatment with exercises.

Benign paroxysmal positional vertigo is a very different problem than vestibular hypofunction or vestibular loss because in this situation you are dealing with an overactive vestibular system rather than one in which vestibular function is suppressed. Remember the relationship of the utricle to the ampulla of the posterior canal. Imagine that some debris from the utricle (possibly fragments of otoconia) breaks free and, when the head is tilted back, floats into the ampulla of the posterior canal. The canal, on one side only, would become sensitive to gravity and would become excited inappropriately. One theory, cupulolithiesis, suggests that the debris adheres to the cupula of the posterior semicircular canal itself. The second theory, which might be called canalithiesis, suggests that the degenerative debris, rather than adhering to the cupula of the posterior canal, is free floating in the endolymph. When the head is in certain positions, the endolymph, moved by the falling otoconia, would push on the cupula and would excite the vestibular neurons.

> With BPPV, the vestibular system is overactive.

Benign paroxysmal positional vertigo has very characteristic clinical findings. Clients typically will experience vertigo when they lie down or when they roll over onto one side. Some clients have vertigo when they look up or when they straighten up after leaning forward. Exactly which positions produce the vertigo often is not clear, because clients move out of the provoking position as soon as the vertigo begins.

Careful testing is important to confirm the diagnosis and to develop the proper treatment approach. The onset of the vertigo is delayed for a few seconds after the client moves into the provoking position. The vertigo then increases in intensity and then decreases, usually lasting less than 30 seconds. Often, the vertigo is accompanied by a nystagmus that reflects the stimulation of the posterior canal. This nystagmus is torsional (fast phase toward the affected ear) when the eyes are directed toward the affected side and vertical when the eyes are directed away from the affected side. The change in the direction of the fast phase of the nystagmus with changes in eye position is because of the biomechanics of the eye ball and on how the extraocular muscles are attached.

Evaluation

> Positions of the head that bring on BPPV should carefully be documented.

In clients with suspected or documented BPPV, tests to determine the provoking positions are important in order to develop the appropriate treatment protocol and to monitor the progress of the client. The classical test is to move the client into a head-hanging position in the plane of the posterior canal (Fig 13-7). Measurement of the latency and the duration of the vertigo as well as the intensity (scaled 1-5 or 1-10) should be kept for each of the position changes.

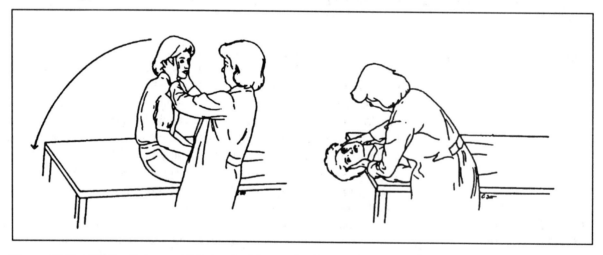

Figure 13-7 Hallpike maneuver. Moving the client rapidly from a sitting to a supine position with the head turned so that the affected ear is 30 to 45 degrees below the horizontal plane will stimulate the posterior canal and produce vertigo and nystagmus. From Herdman (1990*b*), reprinted with permission from the American Physical Therapy Association.

During assessment, it is important to perform the positional changes quickly in order to provoke a response. The severity of the vertigo will be related directly to how rapidly the client moves into the provoking position. Testing must be performed consistently because a decreased response, obtained when the positional change is made too slowly, may imitate improvement. Nystagmus is observed using Frenzel glasses, which magnify the clients eyes for the observer. These glasses prevent the client from using visual fixation to suppress the nystagmus. The direction and duration of the nystagmus should be noted.

Treatment

Brandt's procedure requires that clients move into the provoking position several times a day.

Several exercise approaches have been developed to treat clients with BPPV. These exercises seem to work equally well in clients with BPPV, but different exercises may be appropriate for different clients. One treatment approach, proposed by Brandt and Daroff (1980), requires the client to move into the provoking position repeatedly, several times a day. The client then stays in that position until the vertigo stops and then sits up. Some clients experience vertigo again when they sit up; if so, they should wait until the vertigo ceases. Then the client quickly moves into the opposite side-lying position and remains there for 30 seconds. This whole procedure is repeated 10 times or more, 3 times during the day.

Moving repeatedly into a side-lying position may aggravate neck or back pain. Although Brandt's exercises may be modified somewhat to reduce or avoid discomfort, some clients may not tolerate this approach. Clients may also have difficulty deliberately making themselves dizzy--they may move into the provoking position too slowly or they may move out of the position as soon as the vertigo begins. In these clients, the alternative treatment approach--the Liberatory maneuver--may be appropriate.

In the Liberatory maneuver, the affected side must be identified first. The client is then quickly moved from the sitting into the provoking side-lying position and kept in that position for 2 to 3 minutes. She is then turned rapidly to the opposite ear down position, with the therapist maintaining the alignment of the neck and head on the body. The client stays in this position for 5 minutes. Typically, nystagmus and vertigo reappear in this second position. The client is then slowly taken into a seated position. She must remain in a vertical position for 48 hours (including while sleeping) and must avoid the provoking positions for 1 week after the treatment. Unlike the exercises suggested by Brandt and Daroff (1980), the Liberatory maneuver usually requires only a single treatment. It supposedly works by floating the debris out of the posterior canal. Some clients may not be able to stay in an upright position for 48 hours as is required in this approach. For clients who cannot or do not want to stay upright, Brandt's exercises would be the more

351

appropriate choice. Brandt's exercises would also be the appropriate choice in clients with bilateral BPPV.

> The Liberatory maneuver is done only once but requires the client to be upright for 2 days.

In our center, we have used a maneuver that might be considered a modification of the Liberatory maneuver (Fig 13-8). The client is moved through a series of head positions to move the debris out of the posterior canal. The client is first sitting and is then quickly moved into the Hallpike position toward the side that produces the symptoms. The client is held in that position for 3 minutes, and then her head is slowly turned to the opposite Hallpike position. That position is held for 4 to 5 minutes, and then the client slowly sits up. As with the Liberatory maneuver, the client must remain in an upright position for 48 hours and must sleep sitting up. The client is advised to avoid lying on the provoking side, if possible, for the next 5 days.

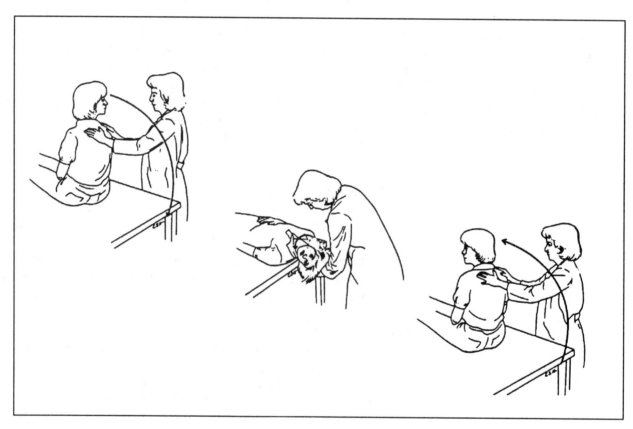

Figure 13-8 Modified Liberatory maneuver. The client is first moved quickly from a sitting position to the position that provokes the vertigo and is then kept in that position for 2 to 3 minutes. The head is then turned to the opposite ear-down position, with the therapist maintaining the alignment of the neck and head on the body. The client stays in this position for 5 minutes. The client is then slowly returned to a seated position. She must remain in a vertical position for 48 hours and must avoid the provoking position for 1 week. From Herdman (1990*b*), reprinted with permission from the American Physical Therapy Association.

From 30% to 50% of clients with BPPV also have hypofunction of the horizontal canal. They should be evaluated carefully for this (caloric test, rotational test, clinical exam), and an exercise program, which includes vestibular adaptation exercises, should be developed. Treatment may also include balance exercises for those clients with postural instability.

It is not clear why these exercises result in a decrease in the vertigo and nystagmus. One explanation is that the debris becomes dislodged from the cupula of the posterior canal and moves to a location no longer affecting the cupula during head movement. A second possibility is that central adaptation occurs, reducing the nervous system response to the signal from the posterior canal. Brandt argues against central adaptation as a mechanism for recovery because many clients recover abruptly.

It is important to remember that there are many other causes of positional vertigo. Positional vertigo occurs with lesions of both the central and the peripheral nervous systems. The characteristics of central positional vertigo and BPPV are different, however. In central positional vertigo, the vertigo begins as soon as the client is put into the provoking position, the response persists as long as the position is maintained, and it does not habituate with repeated positional changes. Central positional vertigo may occur in a variety of disorders affecting the brain stem, such as infarcts, tumors, or multiple sclerosis. Unfortunately, central positional vertigo does not respond to the treatments that can be used so effectively in BPPV. Positional vertigo may also occur in perilymph fistula, an abnormal communication between the middle and inner ears. The fistula can have the same characteristic nystagmus as BPPV, but perilymph fistula is usually treated with bed rest or with surgery.

Conclusions

In this chapter, we have discussed three different vestibular disorders: those with remaining vestibular function, those with complete bilateral vestibular loss, and one type with vestibular hyperexcitability--BPPV. The use of exercises as a treatment for these disorders is based on our knowledge of vestibular system anatomy and function and on how the vestibular system responds to injury. The treatment for each of these disorders is different. Development of a successful treatment plan must be based on the results of a thorough assessment of the client.

Study Questions:

1. Define oscillopia and explain its cause.

2. Explain the difference in static and dynamic disturbances in the VOR and postural stability in clients with bilateral and unilateral lesions.

3. Explain why visual and somatosensory inputs may not completely substitute for the vestibular cues in the presence of bilateral lesions.

4. Can clients with bilateral lesions expect to completely recover postural stability?

5. List the causes of bilateral vestibular loss.

6. Describe the different conditions that are associated with vertigo.

7. How does BPPV differ from other vestibular disorders?

8. Describe treatment procedures for clients with BPPV.

Bibliography - Section III

Baloh RW. *The Essentials of Neurotology*. Philadelphia, Pa: F A Davis Co; 1984.

Baloh RW, Honrubia V. *Clinical Neurophysiology of the Vestibular System*. Philadelphia, Pa: F A Davis Co; 1979.

Baloh RW, Jacobson K, Honrubia V. Idiopathic bilateral vestibulopathy. *Neurology*. 1989;39:272-275.

Bohannon RW, Larkin PA, Cook AC, et al. Decrease in timed balance test scores with aging. *Phys Ther*. 1984;64:1067-1070.

Black FO, Shupert CL, Peterka RJ. Effects of unilateral loss of vestibular function on the vestibulo-ocular reflex and postural control. *Ann Otol Rhinol Laryngol*. 1989;98:884-889.

Bles W, Vianney de Jong JMB, Rasmussens JJ. Postural and oculomotor signs in labyrinthine-defective subjects. *Acta Otolaryngol (Stockh)*. 1984;406:101-104.

Brandt T, Daroff RB. Physical therapy for benign paroxysmal positional vertigo. *Arch Otolaryngol*. 1980;106:484-485.

Brandt T, Buchele W, Arnold F. Arthrokinetic nystagmus and ego-motion sensation. *Exp Brain Res*. 1977;30:331-338.

Brandt T, Paulus WM, Straube A. Visual acuity, visual field and visual scene characteristics affect postural balance. In: Igarashi M, Black FO. eds. *Vestibular and Visual Control on Posture and Locomotor Equilibrium*. New York, NY: S Karger : 1985;93-98.

Dichgans J, Diener HC. The contribution of vestibulo-spinal mechanisms to the maintenance of human upright posture. *Acta Otolaryngol (Stockh)*. 1989;107:338-345.

Diener HC, Dichgans J, Guschlbauer B. The significance of proprioception on postural stabilization as assessed by ischemia. *Brain Res*. 1984;296:103-109.

Fetter M, Zee DS, Proctor LR. Effect of lack of vision and of occipital lobectomy upon recovery from unilateral labyrinthectomy in rhesus monkey. *J Neurophysiol*. 1988;59:394-407.

Fregly AR, Graybiel A, Smith MJ. Walk on floor eyes closed (WOFEC): a new addition to an ataxia test battery. *Aerospace Medicine*. 1972;4:395-399.

Fregly AR, Smith MJ, Graybiel A. Revised normative standards of performance of men on a quantitative ataxia test battery. *Acta Otolaryngol (Stockh)*. 1973;75:10-16.

Herdman SJ. Assessment and treatment of balance disorders in the vestibular-deficient patient. In: Duncan PW. ed. *Balance* Alexandria, Va: American Physical Therapy Association; 1990*a*.

Herdman, SJ: Treatment of benign paroxysmal positional vertigo. *Phys Ther*. 1990*b*;70:381-388.

Horak FB, Esselman P, Anderson ME, et al. The effects of movement velocity, mass displaced, and task certainty on associated postural adjustments made by normal and hemiplegic individuals. *J Neurol Neurosurg and Psychiatry*. 1984;47:1020-1028.

Horstmann GA, Dietz V. The contribution of vestibular input to the stabilization of human posture: a new experimental approach. *Neurosci Lett*. 1988;95:179-184.

House EL, Pansky B. *A Functional Approach to Neuroanatomy*. 2nd ed. New York, NY: McGraw-Hill Book Co; 1967.

Hudspeth AJ. The hair cells of the inner ear. *Sci Am*. January 1983:54-63.

Igarashi M, Levy JK, O-Uchi T. Further study of physical exercise and locomotor balance compensation after unilateral labyrinthectomy in squirrel monkeys. *Acta Otolaryngol (Stockh)*. 1981;92:101-105.

Igarashi M, Ishikawa K, Ishii M. Physical exercise and balance compensation after total ablation of vestibular organs. In: Pompeiano O. Allum JHJ, eds. *Progress in Brain Research*. New York, NY: Elsevier Science Publishing Co Inc; 1988:395-401.

Ito M: The vestibulo-cerebellar relationships: vestibulo-ocular reflex arc and flocculus. In: Naunton R, ed. *The Vestibular System*, San Diego, Calif: Academic Press Inc; 1975.

J.C. Living without a balance mechanism. *N Engl J Med.* 1952;246:458-460.

Jongkees LBW. On the physiology and the examination of the vestibular labyrinths. In: Naunton R, ed. *The Vestibular System.* San Diego, Calif: Academic Press Inc; 1975.

Kobayashi Y, Yagi T, Kamio T. The role of cervical inputs in compensation of unilateral labyrinthectomized patients. *Adv Otorhinolaryngol.* 1988;42:185-189.

Lacour M, Roll JP, Appaix M. Modifications and development of spinal reflexes in the alert baboon (papio papio) following an unilateral vestibular neurectomy. *Brain Res.* 1976;113:255-269.

Lowenstein O. The peripheral neuron. In: Naunton R, ed. *The Vestibular System.* San Diego, Calif: Academic Press Inc; 1975.

Maoli C, Precht W. On the role of vestibulo-ocular reflex plasticity in recovery after unilateral peripheral vestibular lesions. *Exp Brain Res.* 1985;59:67-272.

Mathog RH, Peppard SB. Exercise and recovery from vestibular injury. *Am J. Otolaryngol.* 1982;3:387-407.

Nyberg-Hansen R. Anatomical aspects of the functional organization of the vestibulospinal pathways. In: Naunton R. ed. *The Vestibular System.* San Diego, Calif: Academic Press Inc; 1975.

Parker D. The vestibular apparatus. *Sci Am.* November, 1980:118-135.

Segal BN, Katsarkas A. Long-term deficits of goal-directed vestibulo-ocular function following total unilateral loss of peripheral vestibular function. *Acta Otolaryngol (Stockh).* 1988;106:102-110.

Takemori S, Ida M, Umezu H. Vestibular training after sudden loss of vestibular functions. *ORL J Otorhrinolaryngol Relat Spec.* 1985;47:76-83.

Watanabe T, Hattori Y, Fukuda T. Automated graphical analysis of Fukuda's stepping test. In: Igarashi M, Black FO, eds. *Vestibular and Visual Control on Posture and Locomotor Equilibrium.* New York, NY: S Karger; 1985, p 80- 88.

Section IV

Evaluation and Treatment of Clients With Disorders of Motor Control

Chapter 14 - Principles of Motor Learning

It is interesting that candidates for physical therapy programs often assert that they do not wish to be teachers; however, when the duties of a physical therapist are carefully analyzed it becomes apparent that a considerable portion of what a therapist does is to teach. Among other things, therapists teach clients about movement, and many assumptions are made about the best way to accomplish this task. The job of teaching clients is often complicated by the presence of pain, abnormalities of the nervous system, musculoskeletal difficulties, and cognitive deficits; in many respects teaching is an almost overwhelming task.

A large body of knowledge exists concerning both learning theories and motor learning theories. Classroom teachers and physical educators are taught teaching methodologies grounded in these theories, but unfortunately, therapy students usually are not. It would seem valuable to explore the knowledge from the behavioral sciences relative to the teaching and learning of motor skills and to apply principles derived from them in the clinic.

Motor learning particularly addresses goal-directed behaviors. These are the purposeful, functional, intentional movement behaviors that dominate our everyday life. These movements stem from goals we establish that require action. We set goals to get from one place to another, to bake a cake, to wash the car, to change the baby's diaper, to put on clothes. It is through these movements that we cope with the environment, including the people and objects around us.

As you learned in Chapters 1 and 2, movement emerges as a consequence of a dynamic interplay between the individual and the environment or context. Movements are guided by feedback from both internal and external sources that tell us how far we are from accomplishing the functional ends toward which we are striving. Not all actions or movements are successful. Motor learning is a process by which successful movements may be developed and maintained.

Nature of Skill

Skill is a term that we often use loosely to refer to movements in general. Skill may be defined as consistency in achieving a particular goal with some economy of effort (Gentile 1992). As we all know, newly learned movements are not likely to be skillful. There is clearly a process involved through which movements become skilled. It does not mean using one specific movement pattern or organizing muscular contractions in one set way. Skill involves developing flexible solutions to motor problems.

How do I hit this ball with a bat and get a hit? This cannot effectively be achieved by one motor pattern or one solution. The ball may come to the hitter many different ways and at different speeds. The skilled hitter is able to solve those problems consistently and efficiently. Individuals with motor deficits also will need to be as flexible in solving problems. After all, we seldom walk down a tiled corridor devoid of objects or people. In real life, we must walk on carpets, grass, sand, and ice and negotiate objects in the environment and other people moving with and around us. One movement solution is not enough. For the ballplayer to acquire skill at hitting the ball, he had to expend much effort at motor learning. Clients with neuromotor problems also will have to spend this effort, and the therapist will have to be a partner in that process.

Motor learning occurs in stages. The learner first needs to explore various solutions to solving the problems presented by the conditions and demands of the environment and the movement that will accomplish the goal. As you learned in Chapter 2, the first stage involves getting the general movement form. Both the infant and the adult do this by first controlling the degrees of freedom through cocontraction. Thus early movements are stiff and lack smoothness and refinement.

In the later stages of motor learning, the individual will be able to incorporate and exploit contact forces, gravitational effects, and motion-dependent forces that occur because joints are linked together. (See Chapter 2). Only later will they be able to use these external field effects efficiently and to anticipate that they are going to occur. So the therapist must be aware of these stages in motor learning and devise ways of assisting the client appropriately at each stage. It is not possible to label the motor acts in the first stage as stiff and abnormal and attempt to jump to the second stage of skill development by discouraging such movement solutions. Thus motor learning is multifaceted and multidimensional. The effective therapist will master the principles involved and devise methods of applying them to the clinical setting.

Motor learning theories are usually related to certain theories of motor control. Some theorists who have made major contributions to motor learning theory have also proposed or espoused models of motor control. Much of current motor learning theory rests heavily on open and closed models of motor control and schema theory (Schmidt 1988).

In this chapter, we will present the principles of motor learning that may have significant influence on the practical application of the care given in the clinical setting. These principles of motor learning have been derived from laboratory experiments and are based on scientifically controlled research. They provide potentially powerful guidelines for the regaining of lost skills through clinical intervention and the development of motor skills in children with developmental delays and motor abnormalities.

It must be understood, however, that the movement researched is ordinarily oversimplified and artificial. Normal everyday activities or athletic endeavors are very complex, and it is not possible to control all the variables associated with them in a laboratory. Because a novel task is necessary for learning to take place, ordinary movements are eliminated because they have already been learned by the older children or young adults who most often make up the subject pools. Both the laboratory experiments and the practical applications have involved normal individuals.

Practical applications of motor learning theories have been done mostly in physical education settings, involving the teaching of athletic skills to young normal individuals but few include people with cognitive or motor deficits. These athletic skills are not about how to feed oneself or walk with a cane but rather how to put an arrow in the heart of the target or to play basketball. Thus how to modify and apply these principles effectively to a population with impairments, disabilities, and handicaps remain to be determined. This will be our task as clinical therapists!

> Clinical application of motor learning principles may require some modifications from those derived from normals.

Organization of This Chapter

Factors such as arousal, attention, motivation and memory that affect motor learning will be presented in this chapter before we explore motor learning itself. Considerable space is devoted to the classification of movements because the type of movement and the environment in which it occurs have a profound effect on motor learning. Classification of movements, then, will first be necessary before deciding what activities will be effective for a particular client in the clinical setting.

One of the most important variables in motor learning is the practice session itself. Numerous principles are involved in designing and implementing the practice session. Conveying the idea of the task to the client, or performer, through verbal instruction, demonstration, and verbal pretraining are important considerations. There are many components to the practice session, including scheduling practice activities and rest periods. The type of practice session can vary from presenting a part of the task to be learned to engaging in learning the task as a whole. This is a critical issue in therapy because breaking the task into parts is almost universally accepted as a necessary component of effective treatment programs.

> Classification of movement permits therapists to decide what types of training will be most effective.

Important practice issues include the necessity for providing variability in practice and determining whether practice should be blocked so that the learner knows exactly what is coming next or whether it should be presented randomly. The effects of mental practice on learning is an interesting topic to explore. The usefulness of guidance techniques such as those used clinically during "handling" will be examined as to their effectiveness. The remainder of this chapter will be devoted to the principles of feedback and the importance of the types of feedback and how they are effectively used in attaining motor skills. Clinical perspectives of these approaches are discussed.

Factors Affecting Motor Learning

Learning may be defined as a process that results in a relatively permanent change in behavior and is associated with practice or past experience. *Performance* is a temporary occurrence that fluctuates from time to time. It is necessary to differentiate between performance and learning because, although they are intimately related, they represent very different aspects of the process. A motor skill is any muscular activity that is directed to a specific objective. Motor skills can comprise almost any kind of movement, from playing the piano, executing a ballet step, walking, or creeping to breathing or smiling. Motor learning, then, is the process that results in a relatively permanent change in the ability to produce a motor skill resulting from practice or past experience. Before the particular nature of skill tasks themselves are studied, other aspects of behavior that affect motor learning should be explored. These are arousal, attention, motivation, and memory.

Learning is a process that results in a relatively permanent change in behavior.

Arousal

It is difficult to separate the concepts of attention, arousal, and motivation and their effect on motor learning. Many definitions of these terms exist, and they are used in a variety of ways, in some cases interchangeably.

Arousal may be defined as a state of being stirred into action or awakened from sleep. Some may consider arousal as the expenditure of mental effort. As was discussed in Chapters 2 and 3, the concept of state in infants relates to how the state of the nervous system is reflected in the level of arousal in the infant. Increasing levels of arousal in infants is reflected in increased activity in their muscles. The reciprocal kick of an infant shifts to a stiff two-legged extension pattern when the child is highly aroused and crying with gusto. The infant's ability to control his movements ultimately rests first on the ability to control his state. Self-calming measures as well as support from the care givers help to develop this control.

Movements are modified by state, or the level of arousal.

In adults and older children, more directed mental effort can be revealed in various physiological measures, such as pupil diameter, heart rate, and skin resistance, when mental tasks are performed. These measures reflect the level of excitation of the sympathetic nervous system.

362

Increased levels of arousal will result in increased effort, both mental and physical, producing stronger contractions of muscles and coactivation of agonists and antagonists. Although coactivation is not always abnormal or undesirable, coactivation can result in patterns that are more stiff and may interfere with the smoothness of the movement desired.

> High arousal levels are likely to result in stronger muscular contractions and cocontractions.

The inverted-U hypothesis shown in Figure 14-1 was proposed 80 years ago when scientists were studying responses of mice. The mice were given electric shocks to increase their learning by increasing their arousal. It was discovered that this worked only up to a certain point, and then it became detrimental to the performance of the task. The resulting pattern of responses shows an inverted-U relationship between arousal and performance.

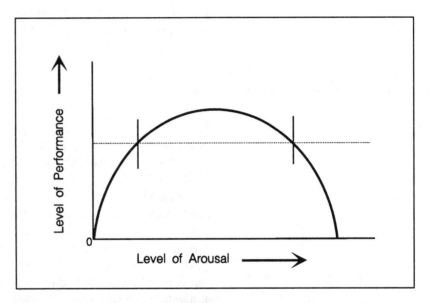

Figure 14-1 The inverted-U relationship between performance and arousal. Note that it is possible to achieve the same performance level at two levels of arousal, one high and one low.

Many other experiments, including those on humans, bear out this pattern. If subjects are motivated or subjected to stress, their performance will improve to a certain level and then fall as arousal level increases. Because increased arousal and motivation likely lead to increased effort, both mental and physical, the output of the neuromuscular system will increase. When too much muscle force is produced for effective task management, excessive coactivation of agonists and antagonists results, producing stiff and less effective and efficient movement.

> There is a limit as to just how much arousal is beneficial to performance.

Individuals have different ways of dealing with arousal, be they performer or coach, patient or therapist. Some individuals may not become highly aroused whatever the circumstances. Others are chronic worriers and appear to be under constant stress. Thus motivational and arousal techniques must take into account both the motivator and the person to be motivated when considering how each responds to the conditions present and how they interact with each other.

Attention

Attention may be defined in terms of arousal and effort. It also may be defined as focalization, or concentration, of thought. In this context, it may be seen that our ability for attention is limited, because we can think only one thought at a time. Regarding motor behavior, it also appears that we are somewhat limited, although there is a greater capacity to attend to more than one task at a time. Attention also has a serial nature in that it is possible to attend to, or perform, one task at a time and then another in serial order, but there are limitations to how many tasks can be performed at once (Schmidt 1988).

Motivation

Motivation may be defined as an inner urge that prompts a person to action with a sense of purpose. Infants may be motivated to pick up a toy. Parents can often increase that motivation, or interest, by rattling the toy and by increasing the tone and tempo of their voices. Adults, of course, are likely to require more complex forms of motivating activity. Motivation may extend from within as a desire to perform, acquire, or accomplish something. Motivation may be provided or augmented externally, as when a coach urges a team to an inspiring performance or when a therapist encourages a child to perform a task or a client to sit up appropriately. Certainly, there is a relationship between arousal and motivation that we exploit clinically.

Skinner (1971) proposed a learning theory called operant conditioning. He defined *operant behavior* as that behavior displayed by the individual without reference to any particular stimulus. His theory was that actions that are reinforced will be repeated and strengthened and those that are not will be diminished. Some authorities believe that this is not a learning theory but rather a system of motivation. Regardless of its position in the halls of learning theory, operant conditioning can provide powerful effects in changing or developing behavior. Stallings (1982) lists several principles, or guidelines, for the practitioner who wishes to engage in operant programming. Some of those principles include specifying the desired terminal behavior in specific and measurable terms and determining the current capacity of the individual to achieve the appropriate terminal behaviors.

> Selection of reinforcers is critical to effective motivation.

It is then necessary to select the appropriate motivating reinforcer. Some of the greatest misuses of the system relate to the use of reinforcers. People can be trained through the offering of extrinsic rewards, such as candy or praise, but the best reinforcers are internal ones. That is, the client may change a behavior because it fulfills some desire of his own. Therefore, practitioners must be careful to avoid contrived reinforcers. Reinforcement for poor performance as a method of encouragement should not be used because the poor performance will thus be reinforced. Additionally, a problem with weaning the individual from extrinsic rewards may develop when subjects learn to withhold desired behavior in order to extract promises of certain rewards. Reinforcers must be applied immediately after the desired behavior is obvious and before some other behavior is demonstrated; however, the rewards should be given intermittently rather than after every occurrence. The desired behavior can be shaped; that is, one might reward actions that approach the desired one if the complete task cannot be demonstrated. Shaping could be important when treating clients who cannot immediately master the activity. The therapist must reward approximate behavior as is seen rather than waiting for a polished performance. Operant conditioning may be most useful with children, particularly those with mental handicaps. It requires careful and knowledgeable use of the principles, but it does have great potential as a method of motivation,

All of these terms--arousal, attention and motivation--generally imply a highly elevated and energized condition with many physiological manifestations of alertness. These physiologic responses such as increased heart rate, dilated pupils, and increased skin resistance can be measured.

Memory

We should not leave a discussion of motor learning without making some consideration of memory because the importance of memory to performance and learning is obvious. It is the process that we know the least about, which probably explains why there are so many theories about it (Stallings 1982). Theories of movement memory abound, and the question still remains, What is stored in memory? We will not attempt to review all these theories and suppositions. It is obvious, however, that the individual must have sufficient mental processes and memory to learn. To be able to recognize the movements or tasks and to recall whatever aspects are required to repeat the activity are also vitally necessary aspects of movement learning. There are different kinds of memory, such as short term and long term memory, and they are stored in different parts of the brain.

In any event, we humans have limited attentional resources. Normally, we can only store in immediate memory a few pieces of information. This is clear when someone gives you explicit detailed verbal instructions on finding a address or producing a new motion. You quickly become lost in the number of right and left turns, gas stations, signs, and trees you are supposed to encounter. Think about individuals with impaired memory and neural processing. Problems with memory are likely to have a significant effect on the success of treatment.

Consideration for such deficits will have to be made, and approaches will have to be modified as needed. For instance, the pace may be slowed, instructions simplified, and nonverbal cues developed. The therapist will probably need to use a trial-and-error approach in finding effective interventions. Methods of training and improving memory and cognitive processes might be helpful. It is beyond the scope of this text to explore these possibilities, but materials directed to this purpose are available.

Arousal, attention, and motivation are often manipulated either consciously or unconsciously in the treatment of clients. The therapist may wish to decrease stress levels by gently rocking the child or by comforting the adult through assurance that the treatment will be effective and will not hurt. Indeed, the success of therapy often rests on the ability to motivate our clients, to direct their attention productively, and to decrease unwanted anxiety or increase a particular response. Because these interactions are so prevalent, it is necessary to understand some of the possible effects of arousal on motor performance. To be an effective therapist, one must evaluate the state of arousal, attention, motivation, and memory of each client and design a treatment program that will have a positive effect on these states relative to motor learning.

Study Questions:

1. Compare and contrast arousal, attention, and motivation.

2. What are the roles of reinforcers in motivation and how should they be chosen?

3. What is the relationship between arousal and performance?

4. Describe the relationship between arousal, attention, and motor learning.

5. What might you do for clients with problems in each of these areas?

Classification of Movements

A number of researchers and theorists have produced systems for classifying motor skills. Such systems are called taxonomies. A taxonomy is useful because it may provide insight into some of the components of motor skills. When these components are understood, they should produce a guide for evaluating skills and selecting appropriate activities for developing or enhancing the functions desired. The fact that movements or skills might be classified into categories suggests the possibility that the different types of movement may require different methods of learning to optimize their acquisition. And, individuals may perform one type of movement better than another.

Fitts (1962) proposed a one-dimensional classification based on the continuity characteristics of movements. Movements may be on a continuum from discrete to continuous, with *discrete movements* being those that have a recognizable beginning and end, such as getting up from a chair. *Continuous movements*, on the other hand, have no recognizable beginning or end. This construct is a little difficult to grasp because it would seem that at some point all movements begin or end. Continuous tasks, however, involve a repetitive series of movements that begin and end when the performer chooses to start and stop them. Walking, for example, is a continuous repetition of the gait cycle. There is no clear beginning or end to the task that can be identified other than that the walker moves toward a desired point, and the point could be 10 feet or 10 miles distant. Other examples of continuous movements would be jogging, driving a car, or swimming. (See Update! pg. 412b).

Serial movements are constructed from discrete movements pieced together to make a complete movement task. An example of a serial task would be typing a letter, because it is composed of several distinct movements: putting a piece of paper in the typewriter, typing each letter or word, returning the carriage at the end of each line, and removing the paper when the letter is complete. Starting a car is composed similarly of discrete series of steps, while driving the car is mostly a continuous task (Fig 14-2).

Continuous tasks usually take longer to complete than discrete tasks, and serial tasks would logically require an intermediate amount of time. It is generally accepted that continuous skills are retained better than discrete skills during a period when no practice occurs. This retention is probably the result of the repetitive nature of the performance.

> Discrete movements have a recognizable beginning and end.

> Continuous tasks are repetitive movements.
>
> Serial movements are discrete movements strung together to make a complete task.

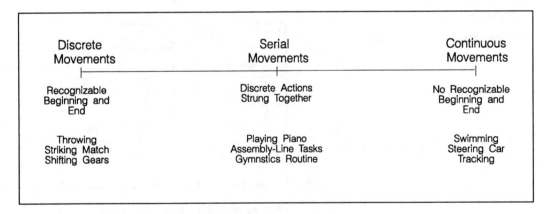

Figure 14-2   A classification scheme for motor behavior. Movements may be classified along a continuum from discrete to continuous. From Schmidt (1988), reprinted with permission.

Movements may also be classified in another one-dimensional scheme along a continuum based on the characteristics of the performance environment. *Closed skills* occur in a predictable environment, such as a

367

bowling alley or the physical therapy department. These environments are stable and can become very familiar and predictable to those who interact with them. *Open skills* occur in environments that are not predictable and may be changing constantly. Fielding a punt in football is a good example of an activity for which the performer cannot effectively plan a course of action beyond having a general response scheme, because the movement of the player on the field and the football in space are subject to constantly changing conditions (Fig 14-3).

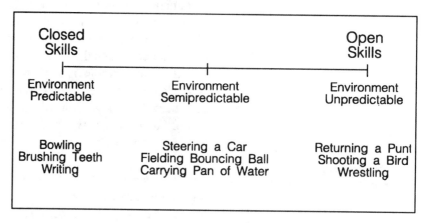

Figure 14-3 A classification scheme for environmental conditions as they affect motor skills. Closed skills incorporate action within a stable and unchanging environment. Open skills occur within unstable, moving, and changing environments. From Schmidt (1988), reprinted with permission.

> Movements can be classified both according to the motion of the body of the performer and the characteristics of the environment.

Fitts (1962) also proposed a two-dimensional taxonomy for classifying movements according to both the environment and the performer. In this scheme, the environment is either fixed or moving, and the performer is either at rest or in motion (Fig 14-4).

ENVIRONMENT	BODY	EXAMPLE
fixed or stable	at rest	driving a golf ball
stable or moving	in motion or at rest or "set"	bowling baseball batting
moving	in motion	football roll-out pass

Figure 14-4 Fitts' taxonomy of motor tasks.

Gentile et al (1975) devised what has been called a composite taxonomy of motor skills. As in Fitts' two-dimensional taxonomy, Gentile's classification of motor skills is also based on a consideration of both the

368

Environments can be unpredictable while the body is moving and at the same time objects are being manipulated.

performer and the performance environment, but another dimension is added as well: the role of the limbs in movement.

Gentile first begins with dividing the spectrum of movement into two broad categories of response: reflex and instrumental (Fig 14-5). Reflex movements will not be considered further in this classification. *Instrumental movements* are goal directed and involve forethought on the part of the performer. They embody the discovery of means-end relationships. The performer attempts to find a movement pattern (means) that will be successful in terms of the goal (end). Instrumental movement can be further divided into orienting and adaptive movements. *Orienting movements* occur to adjust the sensory apparatus in order to facilitate reception from the external environment. Turning the head and eyes to help judge the flight of a ball in space before catching it and adjusting the body to receive it are examples of orienting movements.

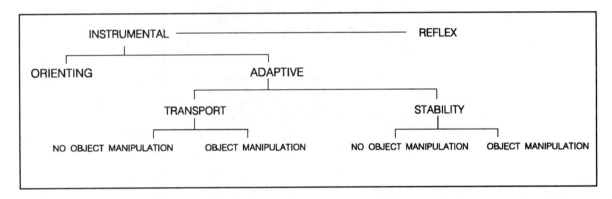

Figure 14-5 Gentile's taxonomy of human movement.

Adaptive movements are what we use to interact with our environment to achieve functional goals. They are used to maintain or change the position of the body in space or to maintain or change the position of objects in space or both at the same time. Responses for maintaining the body in space involve body stability, that is, the body is not moving as when standing or sitting. When the goal is to change the body position, it involves body transport with the body in motion, as when walking or running. Some types of motor tasks may have a secondary goal of object manipulation by the extremities in addition to the task of maintaining the body stability or changing the position of the body. Figure 14-6 shows the two dimensions of stability and object manipulation.

When the third dimension (environment) of the taxonomy is added, movements can be classified on the basis of both the movement and object manipulation and the environment (Gentile 1987). The performance context is evaluated along a continuum from closed to open. The movement response must be organized in such a way that the characteristics of movement match the regulatory characteristics or constraints of the environment. Movement emerges as the result of interaction of the structure of the performer and the structure of the environment. For example, to catch a ball the performer must be at the right place at the right time. The performer must modify his body structure to conform to what is necessary to catch a ball in his hands.

The structure of a closed environment is such that the conditions do not vary from trial to trial. This might be like walking up the steps in your own house. The steps usually do not vary between or during the time you are performing movements with them. Of course, someone could put toys or objects on the steps, or move the furniture in your living room and that stable environment would then vary from one time to another, thus from trial to trial.

Body Stability		Body Transport	
No object manipulation	Object manipulation	No object manipulation	Object manipulation
stand	throw at target	walk	walk with pan of water

Figure 14-6 A two-dimensional taxonomy incorporating the body, the limbs as involved in body transport, and manipulation of objects. Drawn from Gentile (1987).

Environments can be either moving but reliable or moving and unreliable.

A closed environment is relatively invariable and stable. The environment either can be stationary and predictable, such as those with which you are most familiar, or it can be stationary but unpredictable because it is unfamiliar, such as someone else's home or an unfamiliar store. The environment can also be moving but be consistent and reliable with no variation from trial to trial. Examples of this would be environments with escalators, elevators, and airline luggage conveyors. The whole environment could be structurally stable but moving and somewhat variable, such as that encountered when walking down the aisle in a moving train or on a boat.

Environments that are moving and unpredictable require the most complex interactions of all. These are present in the open end of the continuum. Running across a field to catch a ball requires maximal interaction of the body with the environment. People and objects are part of the environment and thus if they are moving it is considered a moving environment and in most situations varies from trial to trial. Driving a car is an example in which the environment is moving rapidly and the body is interacting but relatively stable. Manipulation of the steering wheel by the upper extremities also is present. In open tasks, therefore, objects or people are in motion and conditions change. The playing field may be stationary, but the person trying to catch a ball is in motion, the

370

ball is in motion and the point of contact with the field is actually changing because the player is running across its lumps and bumps, and the visual field is changing. All this is not even considering other players who are in motion. Thus the situation could hardly be considered stable or without variability.

With a closed environment, the environment dictates only the spatial elements of the motion. Movements can be self-paced, and the performer can initiate them when he wishes. With practice, the performer becomes less dependent on picking up information from that environment. He can relegate this to a memory sort of task and rely on a reproductive mode in which the movements produced are very similar to the previous ones. All the information necessary to produce an effective movement is available (Gentile 1987).

Open environments control both the spatial and the temporal aspects of the movement. The movements are externally paced as the events in the environment determine when you start and stop. When you are trying to catch a ball, you must calculate its trajectory and speed and react accordingly. You cannot wait until the ball arrives to make your move because the intrinsic delays in your neuromotor system keep you from reacting in time to catch it. These intrinsic time delays are not important in self-paced actions occurring in stationary environments. But when the environment is in motion you must compensate for the delay. All the information necessary to produce the movement is not present.

With open tasks, you have to pick up advanced cues and use that information to predict what is going to happen sometime in the future, and you organize the movement based on that prediction. You must be in a predictive mode rather than a reproductive mode. You have to learn to compose a movement on the spot that fits the environmental circumstances that prevail on each attempt. You cannot stop monitoring the environment visually and with other sensory systems. And you have to learn efficient search patterns to pick up useful information in time to generate an effective movement (Gentile 1992).

Clients who have had strokes or children with cerebral palsy may have difficulty performing those complex interactions like running or moving and manipulating objects at the same time. For them, the simpler classifications of movement and conditions may represent the maximum interaction of the body and the environment that is possible. They are likely to have difficulty with reproductive modes of action and certainly with predictive ones. A classification system should be very useful for determining the types of movements the individual can perform at the present and how the client might be progressed.

Most movements can be classified to some degree with Gentile's (1987) taxonomy. Experience in all or most of these levels of movement is important for normal everyday life. If clients are only given experience in the heavily structured, or closed, therapy department, it is no wonder it is difficult for them to perform outside the department in a more open environment.

Figure 14-7 is a representation of this three-dimensional taxonomy of movements. This diagram includes just a few samples of movements. But observe that the upper left box, which represents the simplest movements and environmental conditions, contains many of the daily activities encountered in therapy. Movements increase in complexity as you move down and to the right of the chart. In the clinic, these types of movement experiences may be only rarely encountered.

Environment	Body Stability		Body Transport	
	No object manipulation	Object manipulation	No object manipulation	Object manipulation

Stationary
 	
No intertrial variability
	sit on Rx table
	kneel on floor
	stand on a step
	stand on balance
	  beam
		sit on table and
		  catch ball
		throw at a target
		pedal stationary bike
		propel wheelchair
			basic locomotor
			  skills-walk in
			  empty hallway
				walk in empty
				  hallway with walker

Stationary
 	
Intertrial variability
	balance on one leg
	stand barefoot &
	  then with shoes
		feed self
		hit punching bag
		dress self
		pick up different
		  types of cups
			walk in park (no
			  people)
			stop and walk on
			  command
				run and bounce ball
				  in empty hallway
				therapist bats ball
				  over net to client

Motion
 	
No intertrial variability
	stand in Hubbard
	  tank
	ride escalator
	stand on foam
	  rubber
		shoot at steady
		  moving target
		stand in Hubbard
		  tank and catch ball
			walk on a treadmill
			walk on escalator
			catch elevator
			walk on foam rubber
				carry a cup of fluid
				  while on treadmill
				get on elevator with
				  crutches

Motion
 	
Intertrial variability
	sit on waterbed
	sit on gymnastics
	  ball with therapist
	  manipulating it
	stand on BAPS®*
	  board
		hold a cup of fluid
		  while standing on
		  BAPS®* board
		sit on gymnastics
		  ball and catch ball
		drive a car
			walk in busy mall
			walk on sand
				push cart in busy
				  store
				play team sport
				ride bicycle

Figure 14-7 A three-dimensional taxonomy of conditions of human movement. (1) Body stability or transport; (2) object manipulation; and (3) environmental variability with motion and without motion. *BAPS®=Biomechanical Ankle Platform System. Grid drawn from Gentile (1987).

Figure 14-8 is an identical form with blank spaces for movement examples. Use this grid to fill in movements you think clients with various conditions, such as traumatic head injury or hemiplegia, will lack or need to improve. Decide which category each of the movements should be listed in. Make more copies of the grid as necessary. Classifying movements will be very helpful when evaluating clients and designing programs.

Although you might not expect to fill out such a grid for every client you will encounter, the more you attempt to classify movements, particularly those encountered clinically, the better you will understand the concepts. Absolute accuracy in charting probably is not possible because individuals may see the movements differently. Remember that these open and closed tasks are on a continuum so they cannot be completely divided. Certain movements may actually be combinations of areas of classification. Nonetheless, an honest attempt to gain insight into such a process should be beneficial and absolute accuracy or agreement are not necessary.

Environment	Body Stability		Body Transport	
	No object manipulation	Object manipulation	No object manipulation	Object manipulation
Stationary No intertrial variability				
Stationary Intertrial variability				
Motion No intertrial variability				
Motion Intertrial variability				

Figure 14-8 Chart for classifying movements. Try to fill out each box with clinical and nonclinical examples. Drawn from Gentile (1987).

Once the classifications are established so that you know what needs improvement and what environmental conditions are required, other aspects of motor learning principles will be useful in proceeding to teach the client those skills. Undoubtedly, you can think of a number of ways to use the taxonomy in the clinic. Just knowing that there are at least 16 types of movements involving the environment, the body, the limbs, and objects may be enlightening in itself. The existence of the taxonomy suggests variety in movement of which we might not ordinarily be aware.

You might make an evaluation scheme of different movements that the client will perform in the environments that can be made available. An evaluation scheme might include different tasks for clients at various levels of ability. Even though the boxes can be filled with a variety of movements, any box could contain a range of difficulty that becomes even more complex when the client's deficits are incorporated. The tasks will also be different for children and for adults. It is likely that no evaluation scheme, or set of boxes, will be useful universally for all your clients. However, developing one will give you a framework that will guide your treatment and evaluation. Any such scheme could then be modified as needed for individual clients. To function more fully in real life, the client must be able to perform tasks in most, if not all, categories.

Study Questions:

1. List and define the three types of movement in Fitt's one-dimensional scheme and describe their relationship to each other.

2. What are open and closed skills? Describe a stable environment and give several examples.

3. Compare orienting and adaptive movements, as described by Gentile.

4. Describe the most open and variable environment that you can imagine.

5. How is a taxonomy of movement helpful when considering evaluating clients with deficits in movement?

6. Classify the following movements:

  a) getting up from a wheelchair
  b) getting luggage from a luggage conveyor
  c) using a swing-through crutch gait
  d) balancing on a tilt board

7. Develop an evaluation scheme using the taxonomy for an adult or child that would allow you to determine what skills the client can and cannot perform. Use a blank chart.

Principles of Practice

Remember that the definition of motor learning included the clause "associated with practice or past experience." Again, practice is one of the most important aspects of motor learning. This point should come as no surprise to therapists. Repetition has always been considered to be a fundamental element in a successful treatment program. However, practice often consists of simply repeating the same activity over and over. Studies have shown that if practice consists solely of repetition, the old adage "practice makes perfect" does not always hold true (Stallings 1982). Studies in motor learning have shown that there are many possible components to the conditions of practice and different practice modes have been described. These conditions and modes of practice have profound effects on motor learning.

> **Practice is more than just repetition of a task.**

Some of the prepractice considerations have already been mentioned. For example, the level of arousal will be important. And certainly it is important for the client to be motivated, with part of that motivation seeing that the client considers the task desirable and worth learning. Goals must be set. They help not only with motivation but also with analyzing tasks and determining whether the program was successful. It is most important that the client participate in the goal setting and that the goals become the client's goals as well as the therapist's. Goals must be challenging but realistic. Always set goals at a level to assure some achievement, because without it both you and the client, or learner, will become frustrated and defeated.

> **Mutual goals must be determined!**

Conveying the Idea of the Task

It would seem obvious that the client will require some idea of the task to be performed. The client might be given verbal instructions or a demonstration of the movement. The therapist might guide the client either passively or in an active-assistive manner through the movement or might provide some other form of sensory stimulation to elicit the movement.

Verbal Instructions

Instructions can provide useful and important information. It is probably best to simplify instructions as much as possible so they can be processed or comprehended adequately. This is particularly true for clients with cognitive deficits. *Verbal instructions* can convey the overall idea of the movement and some idea of how to recognize one's own errors. "Check to make sure your arm is sufficiently forward and your head is turned to follow your hand" would be such an instruction.

> **The client must be able to process verbal instructions.**

375

Some form of instruction is critical to the task. Suppose you simply tell a client to begin. It will take some time and perhaps a game of "20 questions" for him to get the idea of what it is he is supposed to do. However, as important as these instructions are, they are generally thought to be overly used in learning situations (Schmidt 1988). Only so many ideas can be conveyed at a time, and only so many can be retained, or remembered, by the client. This aspect of learning is particularly critical for clients with cognitive deficits and for children who normally have short attention spans. Probably, it is best to try getting across only the critical aspects of the task and then practicing a run or two to get across other points.

> Verbal instructions can be too vague and incomplete or too detailed and confusing.
>
> The goal of the task must be conveyed!

Conversely, the instructions sometimes given to a client are too incomplete. If the client is supposed to stand up from a chair, it is likely that the command "stand up" will not produce the desired action. If the client pushes on his thighs with his arms, fails to shift the center of gravity forward, or produces movements out of a desired sequence, it will be necessary to convey exactly what task is to be performed. It is critical that the goal of the task be conveyed to the client. Depending on the client and the type of task, it may be necessary to approach the task in steps rather than to try to attend to everything at the beginning. Conveying the exact nature of the task is certainly important and is too often overlooked. In fact, inadequate understanding of the tasks may be a significant cause of client nonadherence with treatment programs, especially home programs.

Demonstration

Demonstration is an important method for teaching motor skills, as noted by the following study. A research project was performed in which all subjects were given an audiotape of instructions on how to climb a special ladder. A third of the subjects were also shown how to climb the ladder before the task began. A third were given the demonstration half way through the series of trials, and the final third were given demonstrations both at the beginning and halfway through the task. The results show that the group with the initial demonstration did better at the beginning than those who started with only verbal instructions. Most importantly, those who were given a demonstration again in the middle ultimately performed the best (Fig 14-9).

> Showing the client what to do is a powerful way to convey the nature of the task.

Therefore, repeating demonstrations within the practice setting may be useful. Remember that none of these studies have involved clients with physical or cognitive deficits. Logically, it would seem that such techniques would be reasonably effective with patient populations, but whether this is true remains to be proven.

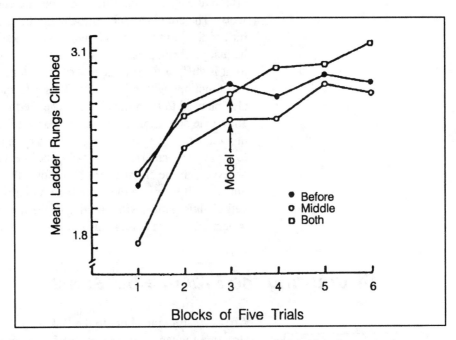

Figure 14-9 Performance on a ladder climbing task in which demonstrations were given to groups before or in the middle of the task. One group received information both before and in the middle of learning the task. From Landers (1975), reprinted with permission.

An interesting possibility is to have the client demonstrate the task for other clients.

As Schmidt (1988) points out, children learn a considerable amount of motor skill through observing and mimicking adults and other children without any formal practice at all. Some research has shown that low performers do better when the demonstrator is a peer and that high performers do better when the demonstrator is a teacher (Landers and Landers 1973). Although the area of observational learning is not well studied even among the normally functioning population, the idea of having other clients demonstrate for the learner may provide an important and effective aspect of motor learning for some clients.

Verbal Pretraining and Verbalization of Body Awareness

Verbal pretraining occurs in situations that are set up for the learner to run through the task to be accomplished. For example, runners may walk the track or visualize it and report about how best to get around a turn and so forth. This can be an effective tool with clients. Try having them explain what considerations will be necessary for them to walk down the hall or through an obstacle course. They might describe how they plan to approach the steps and with which foot it is best to lead.

377

It is necessary for the client to be responsible for the treatment. One effective way of doing this is to have the client explain how something feels. The client can tell you whether he is sitting up straight, whether he moved the joint far enough, what he thinks is wrong with the movement he just performed, how well the movement was performed, whether the joint is stiff, or what he senses of the internal awareness of the conditions and functions within his body. This information and verbalization can also be used to train the client to use feedforward information (to learn to anticipate conditions), so that the posture can be changed to enhance the movement. For example, it is necessary in a sit-to-stand movement first to perform an anterior weight-shift before attempting to stand up. If you observe that the client does not perform this preparatory step, then have him verbally explore the requirements for the movement. Then integrate verbal anticipation with practice of the movement until the weight-shift is performed as a natural early part of the movement.

Structuring the Practice Sessions

How practice is structured determines the effectiveness of the outcome.

After orienting the client to the task to be learned, it will be necessary to structure the learning session itself. The most important variable in motor learning is practice. It would seem obvious that the more practice the person engages in the more likely it will be that learning will take place. Therefore, anyone being given a motor learning task should have sufficient trials at that task in order to maximize the results. Watch an infant learn to perform some task. She will practice and practice and practice. It is unlikely that enough practice attempts are always provided in therapy.

There are a number of other considerations about practice that are important. How should the practice be structured? Should the client practice only a part of a skill? Will the schedule of practice sessions have an effect? Is there a difference in structuring practice sessions for tasks that are continuous in nature and those that are discrete? Should practice sessions incorporate variability? Should the client do something different on consecutive trials or should the same task be repeated? Could the client benefit from practicing the task mentally when not working at it physically? Should we provide hands-on guidance for the client's movements?

Performance and learning are two different behaviors.

Questions of this nature have been investigated in controlled laboratory experiments with normal subjects. Again, the literature does not address these questions in relation to abnormal populations that may have motor or cognitive deficits or both. The findings do, however, suggest some different approaches to teaching motor skills in the clinic. Truthfully, there is little scientifically verified bases for much of current clinical practice. Usually, some authority has proposed the treatment, basic science literature seems to suggest it, or intuition and common sense lead us to certain approaches. As you will see in the following section, some of the findings in experiments concerning the learning of motor tasks are

378

not what might have been expected. It well could be that constructing clients' practice sessions on an intuitive or logical basis is counterproductive.

Before continuing on the topic of motor learning research, it is necessary to distinguish between performance and learning. *Performance* scores are given as each trial is completed. The early trials that occur when the individual is developing the skill comprise the acquisition, or original learning, period. Many early experiments in motor learning stopped at this point. Thus only acquisition performance and not learning was scored. *Learning* is a relatively permanent condition and, therefore, some delayed form of testing must be done to evaluate it. These trials are also sometimes referred to as retention trials or transfer trials. In this case, the latter term does not mean transfer to a different skill. Figure 14-10 shows possible outcomes in learning experiments with transfer trials. Those who score high in the original learning trials may either produce high, medium, or low scores on the retention trials. The same is true for those who score low on the original learning trials.

Performance is the level of skill displayed at each trial.

Learning is demonstrated by a change in behavior that is stable over time.

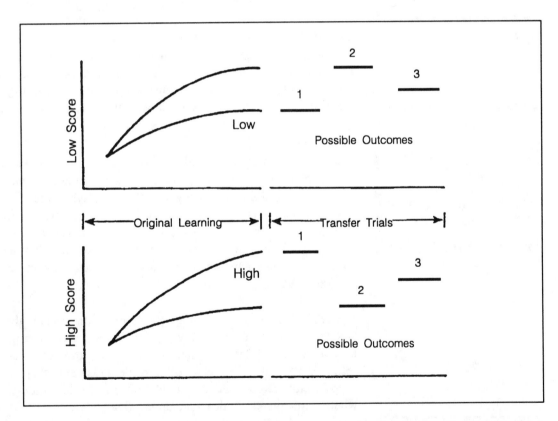

Figure 14-10 Possible outcomes in learning experiments using transfer designs. (In original learning, increasing the independent variable increases the task score [top] or decreases it [bottom]; Cases 1, 2, and 3 in the transfer trials are some possible outcomes of transferring to the low value of the independent variable.) Modified from Schmidt (1988), reprinted with permission.

Scheduling Practice and Rest Periods

In massed practice, the time between trials is less than the time needed to complete the each trial.

Investigators have divided the practice session into practice trials and rest periods. In one situation, the amount of time consumed by the practice trial is greater than the time permitted for rest between trials. In the opposite condition, the time for rest equals or exceeds the time required for the practice trial itself. The former condition is called *massed practice* and the latter *distributed practice*. Under certain conditions, massed practice will eventually lead to fatigue. If the task requires running, for instance, the subject will most likely fatigue faster than during less strenuous tasks. According to Schmidt (1988), most of the massed and distributed practice effects have been examined during performance of continuous tasks.

During massed practice, performance declined with successive trials but learning did not decline.

Massed practice could also consist of a pattern such as practicing Monday through Friday as compared with a distributed practice with sessions on Monday, Wednesday, and Friday. A study involving subjects who were working on skills with billiards had four practice groups: (1) massed practice for 9 consecutive days; (2) distributed practice 3 times a week for 3 weeks; (3) distributed practice once a week for 9 weeks; and (4) an additive program with massed practice for 3 days with additional sessions on the 5th, 8th, 13th, 21st, 34th, and 55th days. This study suggests that a practice schedule that has a relative massing of practice at the beginning of learning with subsequent spacing of practice in later stages is generally the most effective (Harmon and Miller 1950).

There are many forms of massed practice schedules, but more practice at the beginning seems to work best.

A study on the performance of archery and badminton showed that massed practice was better for archery and distributed practice was better for badminton. Kerr (1982) suggests that for physical education students, archery is likely to be a novel skill and badminton is related to other racquet sports with which subject may be familiar. Novel skills may require more intensive massed type practice opportunities, while familiar skills are maintained and improved better through less intensive programs (Stallings 1982).

It is difficult to relate these findings to therapeutic tasks in the clinical and home setting. We do not really know whether relearning is a novel task or a relatively familiar one. Adults and children may very likely respond differently, regardless of task. Perhaps the best approach is to keep careful records on client populations in an effort to determine whether treatments are designed appropriately.

The best schedule to choose may depend on the type of activity to be practiced.

Many of the conclusions about the type of practice come from psychological research that may not be related directly to learning in either physical education or physical therapy. Basically, research has shown that massed practice within a single practice session has a more detrimental effect on performance than does distributed practice.

Subjects were less and less able to perform as the task repetition progressed. This problem did not seem to affect learning the same way. Remember that performance and learning are two different conditions. The subjects still made gains in learning, despite the loss in performance during massed practice sessions.

What causes the decline in performance is not always known. In many cases, it is the result of fatigue. In the psychological tasks, the fatigue is likely to be mental. In tasks performed during physical therapy and physical education sessions or experiments, the fatigue is most likely to be physical, although the effort of concentrating very hard may also contribute to the fatigue. It is important for the performer or the client to have sufficient stamina to perform tasks in a massed mode, at least to some extent. It has been suggested that the most useful approach may be to use massed practice with rest intervals introduced when progress is lacking or fatigue is apparent and is sufficient to warrant a longer rest period (Schmidt 1988). Sometimes in therapy the rest periods total more than the activity periods during a treatment session. Possibly, therapists are overly concerned about the clients' state of fatigue and rest them to the detriment of their programs. If learning is not affected and health is not impaired, it would seem efficacious to continue practice in a more massed mode.

> If fatigue is a major factor, rest intervals may be introduced during massed practice.

Fatigue and Recuperative Motion

For the client, taking up much of the treatment period with rest periods is a waste in terms of the time the client has available to spend in therapy and the money that must be spent for the privilege of resting. Time spent by clients in resting may be deleterious in that it fragments the client's motor learning sessions. Excessive rest periods break the continuity of the therapist's efforts if she has to move back and forth between those clients who are resting to those who are active. Because rest seems to be detrimental except when necessary as a period of recovery or revitalization for the body systems, perhaps a visit with the notion of recuperative motion is in order.

> Do not automatically assume that the client is fatigued.

In the early part of the 20th century, a Russian scientist named Setchenov conducted a series of experiments to determine the optimal length of rest periods following exhaustive work. Much to his surprise he noticed that the amount of work he could perform with his right arm after a pause in which he worked with his nonfatigued left arm was considerably greater than if he had rested his entire body between exercise bouts. During the same period, Weber, a German researcher, made a similar observation. He discovered that work with a nonfatigued muscle group during the period that a fatigued muscle group was recuperating enhanced the recuperation of the fatigued muscle group (Asmussen and Mazin 1978a).

As a result of the findings of Setchenov, Weber, and others, the concepts of what came to be called active pauses and diverting activity were introduced in some industrial jobs and in sports. An *active pause* meant that activity was taking place somewhere in the body other than with the fatigued muscles. *Diverting activity* was defined as any physical or mental activity performed between or simultaneously with bouts of exhaustive work. Asmussen and Mazin (1978*b*) agreed that more work can be performed after active pauses than after passive pauses. They found this to be true both with small muscle groups, such as finger intrinsics, and with larger muscle groups, such as the elbow flexors. These two researchers also looked at activities ranging from heavy dynamic work, such as weight lifting, to light static work, such as pinching the fingers together.

Diverting activity performed simultaneously with test work was found to have the effect of increasing the amount of work that could be done in a particular bout. And mental activity performed as an active pause had the same positive effect on recuperation of fatigued muscles as did physical activity used as an active pause. An intriguing study by these same two Danish researchers resulted in finding that the amount of work that can be performed before exhaustion is larger when subjects work with their eyes open as opposed to working with the eyes closed. Further, when complete exhaustion has been reached with the eyes closed, opening the eyes results in an immediate return of a working capacity amounting to 20% to 30% of that already performed. Finally, these two men demonstrated that patellar reflexes are more brisk when the eyes are open than when they are closed, and the same thing is true when different forms of diverting activities are used (Asmussen and Mazin 1978*a;* 1978*b*).

Any student with an inquiring mind would be led to wonder what is the mechanism that generates the recuperative effects of active pauses and diverting activities. Before attempting to answer that question, a quick review of the physiologic causes of muscle fatigue may be in order.

It is generally agreed that muscle fatigue may have a central or a peripheral origin or both. Fatigue of a peripheral nature may originate at the neuromuscular junction, or transmission site, or it may be induced by changes in the muscle filaments or contractile mechanism or both. The cause of fatigue at either of these sites may be biochemical. Depletion of glycogen, high energy phosphates in muscle fibers, and acetylcholine in the nerve endings may be responsible. Instead of biochemical depletion, the accumulation of catabolites or other substances liberated from muscles during activity may be responsible for fatigue (Asmussen 1979).

Fatigue of central nervous system origin has been attributed to mood and motivation or behavioral state of the individual, and there is certainly evidence to support that concept. Feedback from fatigued muscles has been thought to stimulate the inhibitory part of the reticular formation, causing a diminution of voluntary muscle activity. Asmussen (1979) posits that central fatigue is caused by an inhibition elicited by nervous impulses from some kind of chemoreceptors in fatigued muscles.

Whatever its cause, we do know that the onset of fatigue must be considered in the designing of treatment programs and must be dealt with by therapists. There is good reason to believe that by properly motivating the client we may delay fatigue and make frequent rest stops unnecessary. Eliciting everything from volitional control to vision or to peripheral inputs may negate or help delay the onset of fatigue. Certainly, research has shown that diverting activities, which may produce an increased flow of nerve impulses from nonfatigued muscles in the body to the reticular activating system, help to nullify the effects of fatigue. When other forms of motivation seem to be ineffective, the use of active pauses and diverting activities may provide the solution to problems caused by muscle fatigue. When the diverting activities are also activities that are consistent with meeting the goals of the treatment, we have doubly enriched the client's treatment opportunities.

Use techniques to alter fatigue that are more effective and less wasteful than rest.

With a client, this might mean that we would move from attention to functional parts to functional wholes; that is, we might move from attending to dorsiflexion of the ankle to ankle and hip action in the swing phase of gait. As the leg appears to fatigue in gait training, attention to extension at the elbow joint leading to weight bearing support on the arm could be added to the gait cycle. Or we could move from attending to functional wholes to functional parts, move back to functional wholes on the right lower extremity and then to the same activities on the left lower extremity, and then move back to the right extremity or to functional use of patterns in both extremities simultaneously. Keeping a sharp eye on the clients autonomic responses such as breathing patterns, sweating, skin color, and temperature will enable the therapist to provide a margin of safety relative to fatigue and the necessity for rest.

Study Questions:

1. **What is the purpose of verbal instructions or demonstration and why is it important?**

2. **Explain how verbal pretraining can be used in a clinical setting.**

3. **Differentiate between performance and learning.**

4. **Compare massed and distributed practice, including the effects each has on learning.**

5. **Describe the effects of fatigue and how it can be countered.**

Type of Practice--Practice Content

Whole-Part Task Issues

Should the desired skills be taught as whole movements or should the skill be broken down into component parts and taught in those parts? A part of a skill in physical education might be teaching the arm action that is part of the sidestroke in swimming. The sidestroke itself comprises the whole skill. In the clinic, therapists are often concerned with this dilemma. Does the client practice dorsiflexion in the supine position and then in standing before achieving it in a gait pattern? Should weight shift be practiced over and over again before working on weight shift as it occurs in the actual gait cycle?

Is it possible that whether the task can be separated into parts depends on the type of task?

There are at least four possible ways practice can be divided (Kerr 1982): (1) whole learning in which the entire task is practiced, (2) pure part in which all the component parts of the skill are practiced independently and then put together later, (3) progressive part in which the components of the skill are combined additively in sequence, and (4) whole-part in which there is alternating practice between each part and the whole skill.

As might be expected, research into whole-part issues has produced some conflicting results. Certain tasks showed better results with whole learning and others with part learning. A task that involved basketball skills showed that simple skills such as passing the ball were best learned as whole learning. In this case, the whole learning task was playing the game. Whole-part learning was best for more complex skills, such as practicing a lay-up, and progressive-part practice was best for intermediate skills, such as finding a space where the player could safely receive a pass (Stallings 1982).

The nature of the learner and the task determine the best type of practice.

Some of the conflicting results are explained when the complexity of the task is considered as the key variable. Task complexity relates to the demands it places on the memory and the information processing capacity of the individual. Another important variable is task organization. Task organization refers to the number of separate components in the task and the timing and sequencing of the components. Thus a task could be low in complexity and high in organization, such as playing a new piano piece if one already knows how to play the piano. In this case, some type of whole-part practice should be best.

All tasks may be both highly complex and highly organized to a beginner. In addition, the organizational nature of certain tasks may indicate that either the whole or part learning procedure may be counterproductive. As noted earlier, there are three main types of movement: discrete, serial, and continuous. Splitting a discrete task may hinder learning. If sit-to-stand is a discrete task, then having the client practice part of it may not provide the best learning situation. Serial tasks are those in which a set of movements is performed in sequence and thus either part or progressive-part learning is likely to be best suited. Feeding oneself is probably a serial task, thus, it seems logical that cutting food, putting food on the spoon or fork, and bringing it to the mouth could all be practiced separately. Continuous tasks that usually involve the repetition of some short sequence such as riding an exercycle or using a rowing machine are most likely to be learned best with a whole method.

A model has been proposed for relating the nature of the task with the type of learning (Kerr 1982). In Figure 14-11, the horizontal axes on the top and the bottom of the box reflect the nature of task organization from low (left) to high (right). The vertical axes on both the left and right sides of the box represent task complexity from high (top) to low (bottom). Inside the box, in each corner, is one of the four basic combinations of whole and part practice.

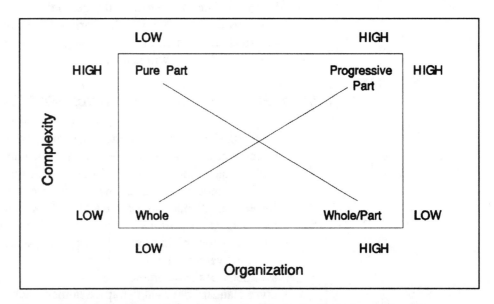

Figure 14-11 A model for relating the nature of the task with the type of learning necessary to best accomplish the task. Tasks may be of high or low complexity and high or low organization. Match the type of learning that should be most effective with each combination of conditions. For example, a task that is high in complexity and low in organization will probably be learned best when the task is broken into parts. Drawn from Kerr (1982).

Matching the tasks and learning methods together suggest possible alternatives in deciding which approach to take with a given learner. Very little specific task analysis has actually been completed even for sports skills. Deciding which category is most appropriate for a given task is somewhat judgmental. In therapy, of course, it becomes an even greater problem because the task may look very simple on the surface and yet it may represent one of great complexity or organization, given the particular deficits of the client. Nonetheless, it would seem helpful to attempt such classifications and to apply learning modes accordingly.

385

Careful analysis of the results and conditions will most likely provide ideas for practice approaches and how to change them if further effort is required.

Should continuous movements be broken into component parts?

Whether training of part of the task ever transfers to the whole task is a question that has haunted some practitioners. The assumption is usually made that movements must be broken down into component parts and mastered accordingly. One of the most important and fundamental questions that must eventually be answered scientifically, however, is the whole task-part task training dichotomy, if clinical treatment is to be validated successfully.

We also need some insight into the question as to whether we should break down tasks when they are continuous because it does not seem likely that continuous movements are learned effectively when decomposed. Gait, for example, is a continuous movement or task, and breaking gait into weight shifts and isolated muscle contractions may not be appropriate. If we can finally get the client to perform isolated dorsiflexion, either nonweight bearing or weight bearing, will there then be proper active dorsiflexion during gait? No evidence has yet surfaced to suggest that this will happen.

Clinical Evidence Concerning Whole-Part Task Transfer

Winstein (1990) addressed the issues of transfer of motor skills and the effectiveness of part-to-whole training procedures through a research project concerning the effect of standing balance training on locomotion in hemiparetic adults. Standing balance measures were taken with a forceplate, and both total-force and center-of-pressure measures were included. Body posture was assessed to determine whether the subjects were aligned upright or were listing to one side or the other. For gait, the averaged velocity, stride length, gait cycle duration, cadence, and symmetry of the locomotor pattern were recorded. Control subjects were given standard physical therapy treatment including sitting balance activities, coordination training, motor control facilitation, muscle strengthening, and routine standing balance and weight-shifting training. In addition to these activities, the experimental subjects also participated in specialized balance training with a standing visual-feedback trainer.

The results of this research project showed that all subjects improved in their standing balance skills, but those who received specialized balance training improved the most. At the very least this research proved the effectiveness of this particular form of feedback for this balance task. Some of the gait measures improved for both groups, but those who improved the most in standing balance failed to show any significant difference in improvement of the gait measures when compared with the control group.

Will work on standing balance change the balance in gait?

From this study, we can infer several points. First, it suggested that standing balance does not have a clear relationship to the balance

386

required during gait. The data also suggest, as do other studies in the literature, that these are different tasks. Transfer between motor tasks is apparently quite small and depends on how similar the tasks are (Schmidt 1988). Therefore, these tasks that would appear to be quite similar must have dissimilarities that are not always obvious. Thus we can work on standing balance for the sake of standing balance, but we should not expect that it will produce great changes in other functions such as gait.

Shumway-Cook et al (1988) showed the same type of results when training with a center-of-pressure biofeedback device. They found that the asymmetrical standing posture of their subjects was improved, but no change in total sway area was obtained.

Perhaps the first problem that needs to be solved is just how to categorize the movements in question. If gait is a continuous movement, the balance component that is required is likely to be a part of that movement and therefore cannot be separated or distinguished from it. In that case, any balance training for gait should most likely be incorporated in the practice of gait and should not be trained exclusively as a separate movement.

| Will the speed of gait affect the ability to perform the gait? |

In therapy, there are many lead up activities that are practiced for gait. These may include supine, sitting, and kneeling activities before any standing practice is begun. Initial gait training often begins in the parallel bars. The speed of the gait may be curtailed drastically as resisted gait patterns and other such activities are used to lead up to real practice on gait. Movements in positions other than standing are most likely to be completely different motor acts. It also seems quite likely that slowing the gait and using parallel bars have completely different requirements than regular gait and, thus, are functionally unrelated movement patterns or skills.

| In complex treatments, discovering the most effective element is difficult. |

Winstein's study also showed something else that may go unnoticed in the report of her research. She found that all clients engaging in what appeared to be a thorough therapy program improved in the measurements of gait. That certainly means something relative to the effectiveness of treatment intervention. Therapy in general is lacking this type of evidence as to its efficacy, so this study provides a positive statement for intervention. However, it is not possible to determine which of all the treatment components applied to these clients was the most effective element in improving the gait. Was it the muscle strengthening? Was it the coordination training, the facilitation of motor control, or some other specific activity within these programs?

Motor learning research has shown that discrete, serial, and continuous movements are best trained in different modes. Neither discrete nor continuous movements are likely to be learned effectively by breaking them down into parts. Because the discrete skill is already a small whole, splintering it does not seem to be helpful. Serial movements that are chains of discrete tasks or perhaps of discrete and continuous tasks may effectively be trained by breaking them down. If a swimming task involves three components--a racing dive, the swimming stroke, and performing turns at the end of the pool--it would seem from the evidence that for the best practice the coach should have the athlete practice the dive and the turn as discrete tasks but practice the swimming stroke as a whole continuous task. Thus the entire set of skills required for a swimming race can be broken down into certain components that are amenable to different approaches.

The key issue here again is the ability to identify the type of movement and whether there are identifiable components of serial tasks that could be practiced separately. For instance, a client learning wheelchair skills could certainly practice locking and unlocking the brakes and performing wheelies separately from practicing wheelchair propulsion and wheelchair transfers. A complete wheelchair activity may be to approach the mat, lock the wheels, position the body, and perform the transfer. This complete task is obviously serial in nature. It is not likely that practicing unlocking a door will help the client in learning to unlock the brakes. Therefore, the components of the serial task must be identified accurately.

> Categorizing some movements is difficult, but many common tasks appear to be continuous and thus may not be broken into parts effectively.

A major problem in therapy is that categorizing movements is difficult. This is particularly true of normal and natural movements such as walking, eating, combing the hair, and speaking. These are not skills that have easily identifiable components. Indeed, it would appear that many of the skills clients lack are of a continuous nature. If this is the case, clients are not likely to be trained effectively through too much persistence with any type of part practice. Many of the components of movement tasks that we have identified are probably artificial, so that practicing them, at least practicing them extensively, may result in less than optimal treatment programs.

Let us suppose the task before the client is to rise from the chair, walk across the room, turn around, walk back, and sit down. We might say this is a serial-type task. But closer analysis suggests that it is probably composed of continuous movements. Sit-to-stand, turning, and walking probably cannot effectively be broken down into more discrete tasks such as forward weight shift, raising up, isolated dorsiflexion, standing weight shifts, and picking up a leg and placing it forward and then backward. If we do not know how to subdivide tasks accurately, it may be best not to attempt to do so. At the very least, we should minimize the time spent in such activities. (See Update! page 412b).

Research has shown some important aspects of movement that are often deficient or defective in clients. Some of these are strength, accessibility of particular patterns (synergies), and timing and sequencing of muscular contractions. It may be more effective to figure out ways of working on these elements within the context of continuous movements.

Variability in Practice

Should the practice session be composed of the same task repeated without variation and under constant conditions? Some therapy programs are limited by the nature of the clinic itself. The clinic offers a relatively bare and fixed environment, lacking conditions that provide external variability to the practice sessions. In addition, skill acquisition is often considered accomplished best when the client masters one task before going on to another task. Therefore, the treatment session is often structured so that the same task is repeated a number of times consecutively, but is this the best approach?

It is obvious that some tasks contain considerable variability. These tasks are usually open tasks in which the person and an object or the environment are also moving. It would seem best to practice fielding ground balls by fielding many different ground balls. It is not clear whether relatively closed skills, such as archery, are best learned when practice is rigidly constant from trial to trial or when the session is varied. According to Schmidt (1988), variable practice increases the applicability or generalizability for achieving novel tasks with similar elements, but in some cases, variability has not proven to produce strong effects. Most of the evidence, however, suggests that increased variability is beneficial, and there is no evidence that it is detrimental (Schmidt 1988).

Figure 14-12 shows the results of one experiment structured to examine variability in practice. Those for whom the task was constant produced less error in the acquisition phase of the experiment. At the immediate posttest, the group receiving variable practice conditions produced less error and continued to be superior in this regard at the delayed transfer test.

In the clinical setting, therefore, clients will be needing to practice both open and closed skills in a variety of environments. Practice in the department on a tile floor with minimal distractions, plain walls, and uniform lighting may bear little resemblance to the individual's home, a store where they may wish to shop, or the outside terrain they must traverse. In reality, it is not always possible to go to the client's home or have him practice under supervision in a shopping mall or elsewhere. These conditions should be provided as much as is possible and practical. The client may be able to practice outside the facility to encounter different terrain, sunlight, people, and vehicles. In the department, walls can be decorated to provide visual distractions and experiences. Lighting conditions also can be altered. The amount and type of distraction and motion present in the surroundings can be varied by isolating the client or having several people milling about. Elevators and escalators in the facility may be used to help clients make decisions, initiate movement quickly, and control timing, all in a functional context. It is quite likely that the treatment will succeed to the point that the

> Is it best to repeat the same task over and over until it is done well?

> Variability in practice may result in poor performance initially but may be most effective for learning.

389

therapist is able to provide situations that help the client generalize learning and apply it to situations outside the department.

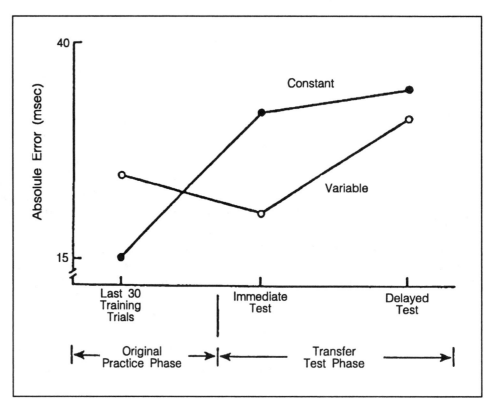

Figure 14-12 Performance in a particular task as a function of variability in practice conditions. From McCracken and Stelmach (1977), reprinted with permission.

Blocked and Random Practice

> Is it better to practice the same task repeatedly or to alternate between tasks?

In *blocked practice* the subject knows exactly what the task will be each time. If the task is to throw a ball at a stack of bottles every time, one certainly knows what is coming up next. In *random practice* the subject will engage in something different during each trial and will therefore not know exactly what is coming next. When these two types of practice are compared, some unexpected results occur. Subjects engaged in blocked practice perform better than those who do random practice during the acquisition phase of learning. They acquire the skill faster and easier. However, when these two groups are tested later for retention of the skill, the subjects who were given blocked practice did not do as well as those who practiced in random modes. Those who practiced in blocked trials did much more poorly on random type retention tests. No matter what type of transfer or retention test is performed, those who practiced under random conditions did better than those who did not do so (Fig 14-13).

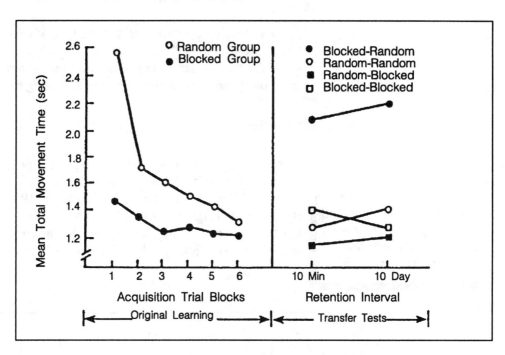

Figure 14-13 Performance on complex movement speed tasks under random and blocked presentations. From Shea and Morgan (1979, p 183), reprinted with permission of the American Psychological Association.

It has been speculated that this unexpected result occurs because random practice forces the learner deeper into conceptual processing, and this additional processing must occur when the tasks change each time. Another hypothesis is that one forgets the solution to a task if it is not repeated immediately and therefore has to generate it over, and generating solutions over and over helps the person produce a better retention of the skill (Schmidt 1988). Even though the theoretic explanations are not clear, these effects are present both in the laboratory and in practical situations and should have important practical implications for designing learning tasks and environments.

Quite possibly, real life activities are encountered more in random sequences than blocked ones, yet the client may be provided with only blocked types of learning situations. Most importantly, it does not appear that it is always possible to predict how the client will functionally perform based on the performance in the clinic during acquisition of the skills. The modes that are best for immediate learning are not always the ones best suited for later retention. Functionally, retention is the most important consideration; therefore, clinical practice modes should probably be altered for better retention. The client and everyone else involved probably has to expect poorer performance initially. This early performance, however, should not be the gauge for program success. This may require some convincing on the part of both

391

the therapist and the client because it flies in the face of the immediate gratification that we Americans are particularly prone to expect.

These research projects had neither the type of subjects nor the tasks like those encountered in clinical practice. Once again, however, it seems worth the effort to structure practice differently; remember logic and intuition are not necessarily helpful in designing treatment programs.

Mental Practice

Will mentally reviewing and practicing a task improve the actual performance and learning of the task?

Studies have shown that mentally going over a practice session can improve skill performance. A physical therapist completed a study on normal subjects learning a novel skill (Maring 1990). Physical therapy students were taught to throw a Ping Pong ball by flexing the elbow. A wrist splint prevented any participation by the wrist in the movement, and it held a cup from which the balls were flung (Fig 14-14).

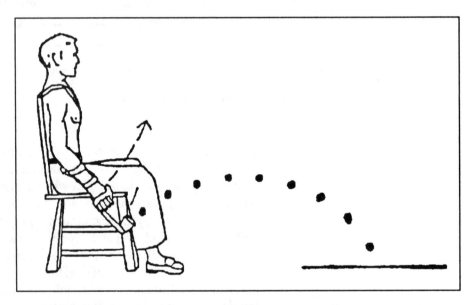

Figure 14-14 Subject executing ball toss with forearm splint. From Maring (1990, p 169), reprinted with permission of the American Physical Therapy Association.

The control group was given a poem to memorize during the rest periods; the experimental group was told to mentally practice the movement, to think about how it felt, and to visualize the arm moving the ball to the target. The results showed significant acceleration in learning the skill by the experimental group. It seems quite possible that the same tactics would be beneficial in clinical practice, but as Maring suggests, the individual must be cognitively capable of forming kinesthetic images and of rehearsing them. Figure 14-15 shows the results for target accuracy with succeeding trials.

392

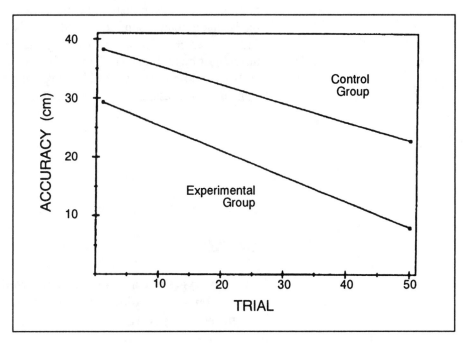

Figure 14-15 Group mean linear regressions of ball toss accuracy by trial. From Maring (1990, p 170), reprinted with permission of the American Physical Therapy Association.

Guidance

All therapists are familiar with guidance training during which the client is physically guided through the task that is to be learned. Subjects may be talked through the task as a form of guidance. The purpose of guidance is to prevent or minimize errors. It has been argued often that it is important for the client to avoid making errors so that unwanted forms of movement are not experienced and then incorporated in the movement repertoire as normal.

> Errors seem to be necessary for learning!!

The concept that errors are detrimental should be explored. Much evidence suggests that it is necessary for a learner to make errors in order to know what exactly must be corrected. Automatic error correction and an internal sense of what the correct movement feels like may depend on experiencing errors. Thus errors may be good and helpful rather than harmful, depending on how movements are learned.

Research shows that learning under guidance conditions is superior during acquisition. As with the random practice design, however, guidance was found to be inferior for the retention of tasks. Again, the therapist's observations made during clinical hands-on when the client is performing the task with guidance may not coincide with later forms of task retention, treatment carry over, and motor learning. Guidance may

393

be useful very early on to give the client the idea of the task. In some cases, for safety purposes, the client may be handled if he is about to fall or make some such potentially dangerous error. Otherwise, it seems likely that guidance should be used initially and applied minimally. Trial-and-error, or discovery learning, may be more effective because as the subject makes mistakes he will learn how to correct them. Errors in early acquisition phases should be expected by everyone involved. Immediate success, then, may come at the cost of true progress.

Study Questions:

1. What types of learning experience could be used to practice rhythmical coordination with a rowing machine? Use the model proposed by Kerr.

2. Describe task complexity.

3. Using Kerr's model, categorize the four-point crutch gait and determine the best learning mode for it.

4. Explain the pros and cons of practicing part tasks instead of or before practicing whole tasks, and cite the clinical evidence that supports or refutes those points.

5. Should gait training begin with weight-shifts? Why or why not?

6. Explain how variability in the environment affects the treatment procedure.

7. Compare blocked and random practice. Describe the effects each has on learning.

8. Describe how mental practice may be effective in learning novel skills.

9. What are the detrimental effects of guidance?

10. Describe a sit-to-stand movement in terms of type of complexity and organization

Feedback and Knowledge of Results

KP--knowledge of the quality of patterns of movement produced.

KR--knowledge of the extent to which the goal was achieved.

Perhaps the second most important variable in motor learning after practice itself is the information the learner receives about the performance of the task (Kerr 1982). In most learning situations, the learner receives both intrinsic and extrinsic feedback either during the movement or after the movement or both.

Intrinsic feedback is that received by the learner from all the sensory receptors and systems involved in the movement. Intrinsic feedback results as a direct consequence of performing the movement. Feedback also can be supplied from external sources and is then called augmented feedback. In this category are found the two most common types of augmented feedback: knowledge of performance (KP) and knowledge of results (KR). *Knowledge of performance* is concerned with the quality or efficiency of the pattern of movement produced. For example, a client is informed that he did not get enough hip extension in the stance phase of his gait. *Knowledge of results* is concerned with the extent to which some external goal was achieved (Kerr 1982). An example of such goal achievement or lack thereof would occur when the client is informed that, as he took steps, he did not keep his feet on a pattern of footsteps painted on the floor. The various types of feedback and their relationships to one another are illustrated in Figure 14-16.

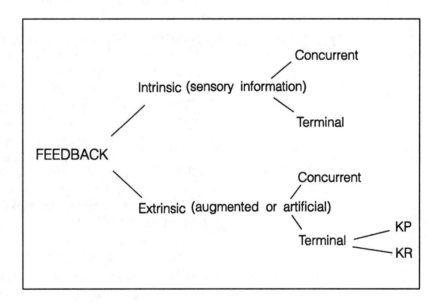

Figure 14-16 Different types of feedback.

Feedback can be differentiated further by whether it is evident during the movement or shortly afterward. The feedback that is available during the movement is called concurrent and that which occurs at the end of the movement is called terminal feedback. Probably the most common forms of KR and KP are provided by the teacher or therapist and for all practical purposes, are provided at the end of the movement. Concurrent feedback usually requires some technologic device such as an electromyographic (EMG) biofeedback machine or a computer that relays information constantly about certain responses or results.

Studying feedback in real situations is difficult because of all the variables that must be controlled. Thus many feedback projects involve artificial situations and tasks. Most of the tasks are simple and restricted. However, it is possible to glean a basic understanding of feedback processes and principles from these experiments.

> The principles derived for KP should be applicable for KR.

The biggest focus of research has probably been on knowledge of movement outcome, although the knowledge of movement pattern is likely to be the most useful for practical application (Schmidt 1988). It is much easier to measure the movement result, provide information for future correction, and record the result on subsequent trials than to do the same for movement patterns or components. The assumption is made that the mechanics of both KR and KP are basically the same; therefore, principles discovered for KR will be useful for practical situations when KP would be provided (Schmidt 1988).

Several questions that arise are relative to the use of KR: (1) Is it possible to learn without knowledge of results? (2) How often should feedback be given? (3) When should feedback be given? (4) Is the type or precision of feedback important?

(1) Is it possible to learn without knowledge of results?

Many studies have shown the necessity for KR in learning motor tasks. Bilodeau et al (1959) experimented with a lever-positioning task in which the correct response was a 33 degree displacement of a hidden lever. Success was measured as a drop in error by degrees. The experimental groups were given different schedules of withdrawing KR, and the control group was given no feedback. Their research showed that no learning took place without feedback. As KR was withdrawn, no further learning took place. Errors reached their lowest level when KR was given on all trials. From this study and others like it, many have concluded that learning does not take place without augmented feedback.

It is necessary to realize, however, that for most normal and practical tasks there is some form of feedback inherent in the task. We pick up clues from the environment with vision and hearing. It is not always necessary for someone to provide a score for us to know the result. When you hit the grass empty handed in football, you know that the tackle was missed. Thus, for all practical purposes, motor acts are not performed devoid of all modes of feedback. It is difficult, therefore, to conclude that in practical settings augmented feedback is required for learning to take place.

396

Although it may not be required for some learning to take place, KR is likely to be a very important element for enhancing motor learning and is perhaps more important in some tasks than others. Intrinsic feedback about movements may be sufficient for some learning to take place, perhaps even quite effective learning in some situations. With augmented feedback, however, a potential for greatly enhancing learning is available.

> KR may not be required for learning, but it usually enhances it.

It is interesting to wonder what the results of feedback would be if there is a problem with intrinsic feedback processing in individuals with central nervous system dysfunction. The effects and value of feedback in such circumstances would have to be carefully monitored and evaluated.

(2) How often should feedback be given?

> Absolute frequency is the total number of frequencies.
>
> Relative frequency is the number of trials before feedback is given.

Bilodeau and Bilodeau (1958) conducted an experiment in which they provided feedback on every trial or on every 3rd or 10th trial, depending on the group. This study showed that errors were reduced only after trials that included feedback (Fig 14-17). Thus it appears that the total number of trials with feedback (*absolute frequency*) is more important than the number of trials between feedback (*relative frequency*). From this information, one could infer that feedback improves performance and that the more frequently it is provided the greater the improvement is likely to be.

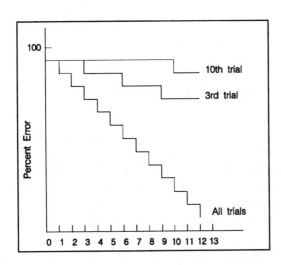

Figure 14-17 Percent of error when feedback is given after every trial, after every 3rd trial, and after every 10th trial. Drawn from Bilodeau and Bilodeau (1958).

One problem with such conclusions is that only the acquisition phase was examined when the skills were trained. Again, what is really important is the performance in the later retention phase. This retention represents real learning, that is, retention of the ability to perform the task. Other studies were designed with similar tasks, but the subjects were also tested in a delayed mode to evaluate transfer of learning and permanence of task proficiency. In these experiments, the groups that performed the best at retention were those who completed the greatest number of trials before feedback was given (Ho and Shea 1978). Thus increasing the number of trials before KR is given produced the greatest increases in learning. Once again, performance during the learning process, or acquisition phase, appears to be unreliable for estimating learning effects.

According to Schmidt (1988), the most effective feedback schedule for learning was a faded schedule in which there were fewer trials without KR early in the learning process and more and more trials between feedback as practice proceeded. Salmoni et al (1984) suggest that the reason feedback on every trial is effective for performance is that it provides motivation and guidance for the task. Unfortunately, the subject comes to rely on this feedback and does not need to process the information necessary to learn the task. One of the most important aspects of learning a motor skill is the ability to recognize one's errors and correct them. If the performer or client is not allowed to make mistakes, then there is every possibility that he will not be able to correct them later when augmented feedback about errors is not presented.

> **Constant feedback with normal subjects does not result in as much learning as other schedules of providing feedback.**

Clinically, therapists tend to provide feedback information almost constantly. Although EMG biofeedback has been used the most in clinical research projects, verbal forms of feedback are the most common in clinical practice. It would appear from research on normal subjects that feedback in this mode is good for performance during acquisition but detrimental to motor learning, as shown in the poorer performance on later retention tests. No current evidence suggests that clients should fare any differently. It would seem to be the best approach to consider using feedback in a more limited mode, particularly decreasing the amount as practice progresses so that the client does not come to rely on it too heavily. (See Update!, page 412a).

(3) When should feedback be given?

Besides structuring the amount of feedback, it is possible to alter the feedback schedule to give feedback concurrently, to give it immediately after task completion, or to delay it for varying amounts of time. Again, intuitively it would appear that feedback presented immediately or concurrently would be more effective than delayed KR. By now you are probably becoming suspicious of these conclusions. Good for you!

> **Delay in feedback does not appear to be detrimental to learning.**

There is little evidence to support the idea that delaying feedback after the trial is detrimental to learning. If the individual is required to do unrelated tasks during the delay interval, however, some confusion results. It appears that periods of delay should not be filled with other tasks (Schmidt 1988). Figure 14-18 shows these effects.

It is also possible to provide a delay schedule that puts the delay after the feedback and before the next trial of the task. Figure 14-19 shows the types of delays that can be presented. Apparently, a delay before the next trial involves different processes than a delay before the feedback is presented in that the learner is actively changing her approach to develop a better response. It does not appear that this delay is very important to learning, although there are studies that show mixed results.

There are other types of delay patterns that may be used. For example, it is possible to deliver feedback after two or more trials so that the subject may perform the task for several times before feedback is provided. ost research shows that during the acquisition trials those who were provided with feedback after every trial produced the least error. Again, this follows intuitive understanding of how learning takes place. Projects that included retention or learning trials, however, once again show the unexpected.

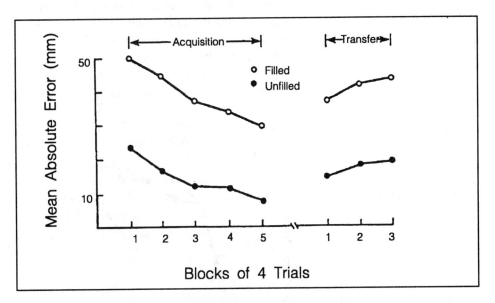

Figure 14-18 Absolute errors in positioning when KR-delay is filled with unrelated tasks or without other activity. From Shea and Upton (1976, p 280), reprinted with permission.

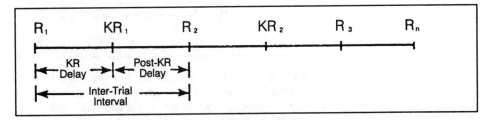

Figure 14-19 Temporal placement of feedback schedules in relation to practice trials. From Schmidt (1988), reprinted with permission.

Subjects were given either immediate feedback or summary feedback, that is, feedback following a complete set of trials. Others were given both immediate feedback and summary feedback about the blocks of trials as well. Figure 14-20 shows that those given immediate feedback

were the best during the acquisition phase of the experiment. When
retention and, therefore, learning was tested, however, those who
received only summary KR had learned the most. It is possible that
immediate feedback provides too much information, and the subjects
come to rely on it and fail to engage in whatever processes are required
for more permanent learning to take place.

Schmidt (1988) attempted to discover what the optimal length of the
summary KR might be. That is, one could provide summary information
after 1 trial or after 5, 10, and 20 trials and so forth. If applied after 1 or
2 trials, it would be effectively the same as immediate feedback. In
providing feedback after 1, 5, 10, and 15 trials, Schmidt found that those
receiving the least amount of summary information retained the skill the
best. In fact, no optimum interval was found, because each group
performed better as the interval was increased. Thus those tested after
summary information was provided after 15 trials did better than those
after 10, and they did better than those who received feedback after 5
trials, and so on (Fig 14-21). However, on a more complex task,
Schmidt found that 5 trials was optimum.

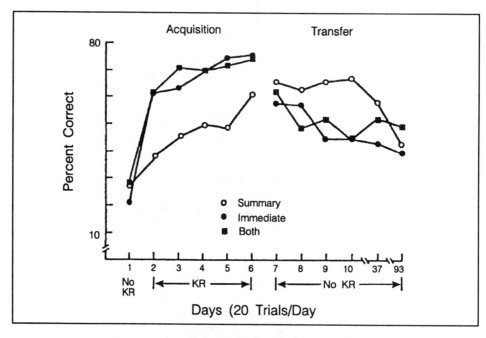

Figure 14-20 Percent correct responses for various schedules of summary-KR. Some
subjects were given KR feedback immediately after each trial. The summary
group received information about each trial after a block of 20 trials. One group
had both forms. From Lavery (1962, p 305), copyright 1962, reprinted with
permission of the Canadian Psychological Association.

Apparently, there is no fixed interval that is the most appropriate for all
motor learning tasks. Again, a schedule with summary information
given more often early in task learning and followed by increasing trials
between feedback later might be the most effective. Nonetheless, even

with normal individuals and very simple tasks it is difficult and dangerous to generalize.

Most of these research studies involve discrete tasks, that is, those with definite beginning and ending points. In addition, the tasks are usually relatively simple but unusual. That is, the task is not likely to be one that is performed every day. Many tasks involve manipulating a lever in response to a sequence of lights or other such activities that are not likely to be engaged in normally. Obviously, this is necessary because most everyday tasks are too complex for analysis, are usually already achieved, or are rarely forgotten once acquired.

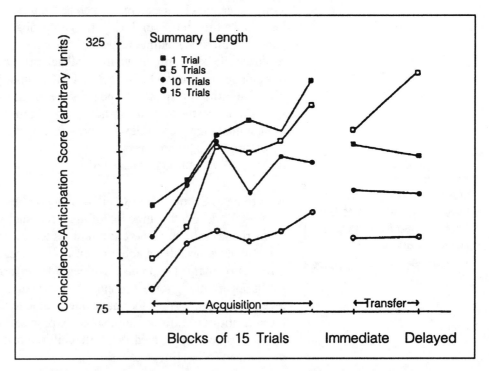

Figure 14-21 A combination error score as a function of the number of trials before summary feedback was given. Immediate and delayed transfer of learning is graphed on the right. From Schmidt (1988), reprinted with permission.

Feedback requirements for learning continuous tasks may not be the same as for learning discrete tasks. It appears that delay in concurrent feedback during some continuous tasks results in problems. For example, speaking into a public address system generates echoes that produce confusion as the speaker tries to continue speaking. With a delay in sound, the echo returns to the speaker just as she is ready to speak the next word, and the echo thus interferes with her ability to produce the next sound (Schmidt 1988). With continuous tasks, continuous feedback without delay is probably most effective--at least early on. If, when you are driving a car, what you see out of the windows is delayed even a couple of seconds from your maneuvers to steer the car, an accident would be a most likely result. Verbal feedback about performance during driving, however, could be delayed and still be

Feedback requirements
may not be the same
for all types of tasks.

effective. So the type of task and the type of feedback presented probably have great influence on whether the feedback presented in a particular mode is useful or detrimental to the learning of the task.

(4) Is the type or precision of feedback important?

How accurate must the feedback be? The therapist may give general information, such as "that's good." More specific information about accuracy could be conveyed with something like "you missed that by a half of an inch." Both accuracy and direction of error would be communicated with a statement such as "you were about an inch too long" or "a foot too far to the right." Biofeedback machines, on the other hand, can provide continuous data of extreme accuracy. Is verbal feedback the best form, or would feedback provided in pictures or through demonstration be better? Is EMG output from active muscles an effective form of feedback? The possible forms of feedback are actually limited only by the technology necessary to provide them. It is possible, though, that high technology feedback is not any more effective than verbal feedback given appropriately. Obviously, many questions relative to feedback remain to be answered.

Optimal levels of precision
feedback will have to be
determined for the types
of tasks and clients.

According to Schmidt (1988), adults respond best to feedback about both the magnitude and the direction of the error, such as "you were a foot off to the right." Although there is a limit as to how small an error can be and still have the subject able to control it, it does not appear that information that is too precise will degrade performance. This is because adults apparently ignore or round off precise information to a meaningful level. Children, on the other hand, are unable to make meaningful interpretations of information that is too precise. Thus there are optimal levels of precision for feedback with children that would have to be determined for each type of task.

Knowledge of Performance

Videotape replays of performance provide a potentially powerful feedback device for KP. Research results on videotapes are mixed, however. The most effective use of video replay is when the teacher directs the learners attention to the important aspects of the performance that need correction. Just watching the tape without direction may in fact impair performance (Schmidt 1988).

Other Methods of Supplying Feedback

Other types of feedback range from kinematic feedback, which can be very general (eg, "you bent your arm too far") to very precise feedback provided by sophisticated devices. Electromyographic and other types of biofeedback have proven to be useful for training certain movements and responses, but they are less effective with others. Feedback about the forces used in performing movements has tremendous potential for improving timing and effort in movements. Unfortunately, the technology for this approach is not readily available, and research into this area needs to be done.

In a relevant experiment, investigators studied the effect of feedback on learning joint mobilization skills by therapy students (Lee et al 1990). A forceplate was placed under the instructor, who was acting as a client (Fig 14-22).

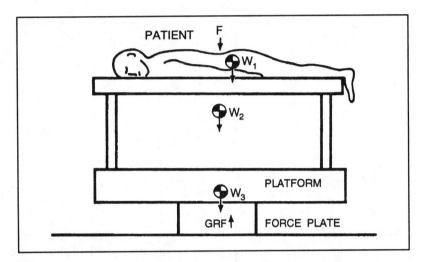

Figure 14-22 Arrangement for providing concurrent feedback during a spinal mobilization learning task. (F= mobilizing force applied to patient; GRF= ground reaction force; W_1 = weight of patient; W_2 = weight of plinth; W_3= weight of platform). From Lee et al (1990, p 99), reprinted with permission of the American Physical Therapy Association.

The students were given concurrent feedback about the forces they were using while performing a Grade II anterior-posterior mobilization of the third lumbar vertebra. The control group was taught mobilization in the traditional manner. Both groups of students received delayed qualitative feedback during classroom teaching. At the immediate posttest, the group receiving the force feedback produced a significantly better consistency and accuracy in generating the desired forces. A delayed test given 1 week later continued to show significantly less error from the experimental group, although the difference was less than on the immediate posttest (Fig 14-23). These results are consistent with other findings on the acquisition of simple motor skills. The authors admit that the general mobilization skills had been taught to all the students in prior classroom sessions. Thus the students in the experiment might have been more able to concentrate on the forces used than if the whole complex motor act was being learned for the first time.

This study is of interest for several reasons. It involves an everyday skill in the life of a therapist, even though it might not be a common skill for the average person. The anterior-posterior movement itself could be a serial movement, but arguments could be made that it is continuous in nature because it ends only when the therapist chooses to stop the movement. The results are consistent with earlier suppositions about the use of feedback in continuous skills; that is, concurrent feedback is best for the ongoing movement or skill. It is quite likely that a delay in the force-feedback method would confuse the learner to the point of interference with the learning process. In the traditional manner, delayed feedback was verbal in nature. It would have been interesting to see the effects of various types of feedback schedules for both the traditional verbal method and the forceplate method.

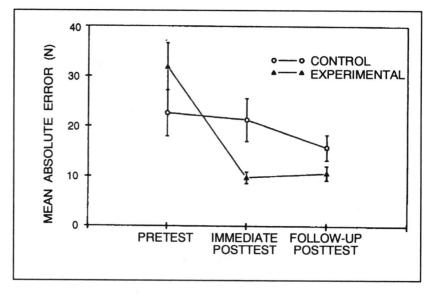

Figure 14-23 Mean absolute error at each test for experimental and control groups at pretest, immediate posttest and delayed posttest. From Lee et al (1990, p 101), reprinted with permission of the American Physical Therapy Association.

Clinical Perspectives

Although few if any studies have been done that address the schedules and components of practice, a number of clinical studies using feedback have been reported. Approximately 40 articles on feedback have been published in *Physical Therapy*, the Journal of the American Physical Therapy Association, over the past 13 years. In the vast majority of these projects, the form of feedback used was EMG biofeedback in which electrical activity of active muscles was displayed. Biofeedback was coined as a term in 1969 (Wolf 1983), and it refers specifically to the ability to make physiologic functions that usually cannot be seen or felt perceptible to the individual by using appropriate instruments. Some such responses are electrical muscle activity, blood pressure, and

404

skin resistance. The EMG activity is usually presented as a form of concurrent feedback to give the client information about the ongoing status of muscular contractions. This form of feedback has been used to produce isolated muscle control in normals and in clients with orthopedic injuries, but the largest portion of studies has been devoted to clients with neurologic dysfunction, particularly adult hemiplegics and children with cerebral palsy.

> **In physical therapy, the most common form of feedback used in research has been biofeedback.**

A study on normal female undergraduates showed that EMG biofeedback coupled with isometric exercise to the knee extensor muscles produced greater peak torque gains than isometric exercise alone or no exercise (Lucca and Recchiuti 1983.) Subjects were trained 5 days a week for 19 days, and the posttest was administered on the 20th day. No conditions were present to evaluate the different schedules, the forms of feedback, or the retention of gain through delayed tests. This problem is generally true of such studies.

Research involving neurologic clients almost universally shows that clients given EMG biofeedback gain significant improvement in peak EMG activity, movement torques, manual muscle test scores, and range of motion. It should be easy, therefore, to draw very nice graphs about the efficacy of biofeedback training in neurologic clients. Unfortunately, there are other points to consider.

Most studies failed to include a control group. Without a control group, it is difficult to assign the changes noted to the treatment itself. None of these studies provided for long-term retention by administering delayed tests, although there are some long-term studies in other literature that suggest some gains can be maintained. Different modes and schedules of feedback have not been performed to discover whether the principles derived from the studies described earlier are as applicable to the client population as they appear to be to normals.

> **Statistical significance of the measurement may not reflect an ideal relationship with function.**

Perhaps the biggest problem in most studies was that the measures taken may have lent themselves to statistical analysis, but they appeared to have less than ideal relationships with function, the issue of greatest concern to therapists and clients. Most of the studies failed to deal with functional transfer at all. The few studies that addressed changes in function failed to show any significant change in the function, although significant changes in such measures as EMG output were present (Wolf and Binder-MacLeod 1983*a*; 1983*b*). The greatest concern in performing research on neurologic clients is the same as the concern for demonstrating client progress to third party payers: there is a lack of adequate measures of function. When the function is broken down for research or treatment purposes, either the part-whole issue becomes a factor or the appropriateness of the measure for having any relationship to the function itself is questionable.

For instance, manual muscles testing scores have never been correlated with function. One possible reason for this lack of relationship is that natural functional movements are not the same movements as those tested in manual muscle testing. So the question arises once again, does an increase in active ankle dorsiflexion range of motion after feedback training mean that the hemiplegic walks better? (Wolf 1983). Such relationships have not been determined. Improvement in isolated muscular activity has not been correlated with evidence of changes in function on the few studies in which this was investigated (Wolf and Binder-MacLeod 1983a; 1983b). It is possible that the wrong components of useful movement have been focused on when such isolated activities are used.

Another likely possibility for functional correlation problems is that the activities measured are discrete movements while the assumption is made that those movements are components of a functional movement. For this assumption to be true, the functional movement would have to be a serial movement. It is quite possible that the movement in question is a continuous one. Isolated dorsiflexion is a discrete movement, but gait is a continuous movement; therefore, one movement may not provide transfer of function to the other. Perhaps the concurrent feedback provided by EMG would be more useful if the muscles were monitored during the full continuous movement rather than during an isolated muscle contraction that is not actually part of the task.

Some forms of feedback other than EMG have been used, but to a much lesser extent. Therapists have developed switches and other devices that produce tones, turn on music, or provide some other form of reinforcement when the client correctly performs a task. A classic single-subject case study was performed using a switch attached to a headband worn by a child with poor head control (Hallum 1984). The switch activated a radio when the child's head was held upright for an appropriate amount of time (Fig 14-24).

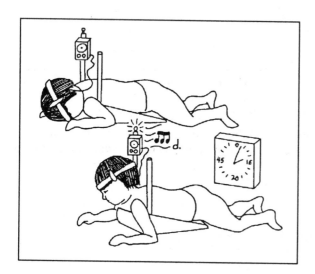

Figure 14-24 Positioning apparatus with mercury switch attached to a head band and connected to a radio and light. Second and minute interval timer is in the background. From Hallum (1984, p 139), reprinted with permission of the American Physical Therapy Association.

The treatment responses were considerably above the baseline observations. Responses decreased when feedback was withdrawn.

406

Additional treatment conditions with the music reinforcement continued to produce noticeable changes that became more stable over the 6 day trial period. This study did provide a delayed test at 1 week to measure how much time the child held her head properly without music reinforcement. A visual inspection of the graphs suggests an excellent result (Fig 14-25). What is particularly important about this study is that the desired function itself was measured and enhanced rather than some suspected component of it. The movement in this experiment is probably best classified as a discrete movement even though it could be sustained for periods longer than the duration of most discrete movements. If this supposition is true, the movement tested and the function are the same.

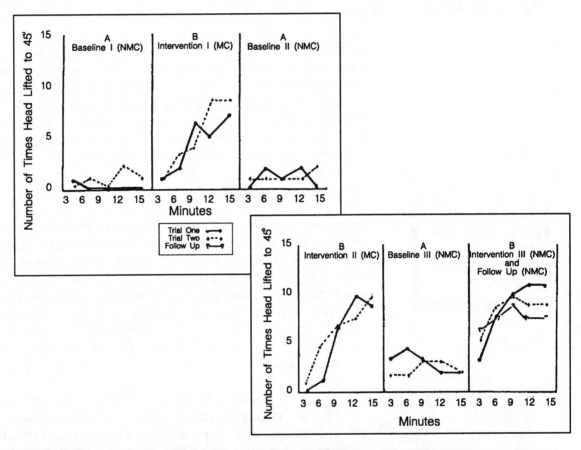

Figure 14-25 Elevation of the head to 45 degrees in nonmusic contingent (NMC) and music contingent (MC) and 1-week follow-up session. From Hallum (1984, p 1391), reprinted with permission of the American Physical Therapy Association.

From a clinical perspective, it appears that many possible avenues exist in which a practical knowledge of motor learning principles could provide useful guidance for client treatment. Although various forms of feedback have been used with appropriate instrumentation, the most common form of feedback used in the clinic is verbal. Therapists possibly use this feedback without recognizing the potential power of the tool or its great potential for misuse. And possibly, the usual clinical approach provides the wrong type of feedback or an ineffective feedback schedule.

Because guidance is so prevalent in clinical practice, it deserves closer scrutiny. Lessening the guidance given clients will probably produce greater learning, but it will be necessary to accept less error-free or error-diminished performance early in the learning process. This is something for which neither therapists, clients, supervisors, nor third party payers are apt to be prepared.

Client Adherence

Physical therapists, occupational therapists, exercise specialists, physicians, nurses, and athletic trainers--all of us--have at our disposal a vast, highly technical, sophisticated set of tools with which to wage war on pain, illness, injury, and disease. From statistical data, we may infer, however, that fully one half the time we attempt to do battle on behalf of our clients we lose. These battles are not lost, however, because of a lack of knowledge, skill, technology, or effort. They are lost because of a failure to enlist the client's cooperation in his own treatment program.

> The degree to which a client cooperates determines the effectiveness of the program.

The success that you as a therapist have in designing and implementing treatment programs for your clients will depend to a high degree on what has been termed patient adherence, patient compliance, or patient cooperation. Unfortunately, adherence is a problem that is not well understood, recognized, or studied by health professionals, including physical or occupational therapists. Because we therapists know so little about the problem of adherence, we contribute to it in ways that virtually guarantee that our treatment of clients will be modestly successful at best in many instances.

When we speak of *client adherence,* we mean the degree to which a client follows a treatment regimen designed for him and, hopefully, with him to ameliorate an existing health problem or to prevent a potential problem. As beginning practitioners, we all believe that clients will comply with any program designed for them; perhaps clients also believe that they will be religious in following their regimens to the letter. Unfortunately, however, such attention to a treatment program does not occur with the frequency or thoroughness that we expect.

Client adherence figures for physicians are plentiful and not very good. Adherence figures for physical or occupational therapists and other health professionals are not readily available, but there is no reason to suspect that they would be any better than those for physicians.

A fairly clear picture of the magnitude of the problem can be gleaned from the literature relative to medications and the clients adherence to the

408

physicians prescription (Sackett and Snow 1979; Hulka et al 1976; Dunbar and Argas 1980; Jette 1982; Kazis and Friedman 1988). Figures vary depending on the nature of the studies, but results generally fall within the ranges found in Table 14-1.

Table 14-1

Patient Adherence to Regimen of Medications

Activity	Cooperation
Take medications accurately	50%-60%
Keep appointments for preventive regimens	40%-60%
Keep appointments for curative regimens	60%-70%
Take medicine for relief of symptom	70%-80%
Take medication for prevention	60%-70%

In the case of clients on lifelong medication or restrictions, such as those for high blood pressure or diet, there is a 50% initial adherence to the program, but adherence decreases significantly over time (Marston 1970). Some preventive measures for cancer, heart disease, and stroke are well known, yet people fail to adopt nutritious eating habits, continue to smoke, drink too much, and avoid exercise.

The above representative figures are by themselves bad enough, but when one considers the already high but escalating cost of health care and the inability of so many people to obtain good care, the compliance-adherence figures help us paint a graphic picture of alarming waste.

Talcot Parsons, in his book published in 1951, may have inadvertently contributed to the problem of noncooperation of clients with physicians while at the same time suggesting a solution to it. Parsons describes the physician role in health care by saying that the physician is:

> The expert with an immense body of knowledge;
> The gate keeper who legitimizes the sick role. He gives life, battles death, and decides whether someone is really sick;
> The dispenser of privileges. He decides who gets what drugs, goes to the hospital, and even whose face gets lifted.
> The authority to whom patients must submit and comply.
> The superordinate. All other care givers are subordinate to him.

In the era in which Parsons' book was written, patients were seldom told the name of the medication they were taking, the expected result, or any of its side affects. In fact, patients were not allowed to see their own records or charts and were seldom told what was in that chart. If hospitalized, even the patient's temperature was a secret held for the physicians eyes only.

In the society in which we now live, things have changed greatly with respect to authority figures, access to information, and decision making in all walks and levels of life. The physician remains an expert with an immense body of knowledge, but we tend to hold her or him responsible for using that knowledge openly and appropriately and for our benefit. All the other roles that Parsons assigned to the physician no longer belong solely to him or her. There are, however, many physicians and other health care professionals who were trained during the Parson's period and who have not totally cast off the authoritarian mantle once worn by those in medical fields.

The words *patient compliance* are still used. *Compliance* by definition means the act of conforming or acquiescing; a tendency to yield readily. Because we know that it is not the major lifetime goal of most people in our society to conform, acquiesce, or yield readily, particularly in matters of their own health care, we would do well to drop the notion that the patients need to comply with the desires of the care givers. We need to think of adherence as defining a cooperative role for both the professional and the patient in developing the regimen to be adhered to.

There are some solutions to the problem of poor adherence, but before suggesting some, it would seem appropriate to take a more definitive look at causes relative to the undesirable behaviors of professionals and the less than desirable behaviors of the clients, or patients.

Some suggestions of inappropriate behaviors gleaned from studies of health care professionals are as follows: (1) in conversations, clients are identified by practitioner by class status, that is, that rich woman, that business man, or that migrant worker; (2) physically attractive clients are described as good patients; (3) practitioners tend to reject patients who do not comply and submit; (4) patients are frequently assumed to have a comprehension level that is lower than it really is; (5) practitioners spend far too little time informing patients about the treatment and often do not consult with them about the program; (6) decisions on heroic measures to save lives are often based on class or position or gender; and (7) physicians change dosage of drugs, and other practitioners do the same to other aspects of the treatment regimen, without writing down the changes. In fact, many times practitioners write down the regimen in the client's record but do not give the client a copy of the record or anything in writing.

Gajdosik and Campbell (1991) investigated the effects of socioeconomic status on mothers' compliance with the home exercise programs for their disabled children. While the study showed socioeconomic status of the family had no effect on adherence by the parent, the status did have an

410

influence on the therapist's estimates of compliance. Practitioners should be very careful about making unwarranted assumptions about the client's cooperation based on factors other than performance.

Some behaviors of clients that create problems with adherence are as follows: (1) clients forget much of what they are told, with estimates ranging from 30% to 60%; (2) the more clients are told, the more they will forget; (3) instructions and advice are most readily forgotten, but clients can recount other things about their conversations with professionals; (4) intelligent clients do not remember more than less intelligent ones; the same applies to educational level; (5) age has little to do with how much a client remembers; (6) anxiety plays a role; that is, the moderately anxious client remembers more than a highly anxious client or one who is not interested; (7) some medical knowledge helps clients to remember; (8) clients often want the health practitioner to assume the full responsibility for the treatment regimen; and (9) clients will rarely inform the practitioner that they do not understand what has been said or written.

After having read these short paragraphs on inappropriate client and professional behaviors, any notion that all we need to do is to tell the client that he needs to comply with the goals and treatment regimen we have designed for him should be easy to dismiss. Then the question immediately arises as to just what we do need to do to assure better client adherence. Following are some suggestions that are not meant to be all inclusive but which should enable you to greatly improve the chances that your clients will adhere much more strongly to their regimens.

As soon as the initial evaluation process is completed, conversation should turn immediately to the clients goals--what she wants to do with what she has. As soon as client goals are established you, the therapist, should establish your goals and then make an attempt to bring both sets of goals into close approximation. This should be done in a cooperating, negotiating session and not one where orders are passed down from a being of superior knowledge and station to a lesser being.

Once goals are clearly established, the roles of both the therapist and the client in attaining the goals must be established. It is the responsibility of both parties to design a regimen that can be carried out in the client's home and place of work. It is the therapist's responsibility to commit the regimen to paper and to go over it with the client to make certain the client understands it and can do it. It is the client's responsibility to inform the therapist if and when the program is not understood. It is the therapist's responsibility for seeing that the client talks freely about what she can and cannot do and what she does and does not understand. It is the therapist's responsibility to make clear to the client the limited role the therapist may play in helping the client attain the goals of treatment. It is the therapist's responsibility to remind the client constantly that it is the ultimate responsibility of the client, in most cases, for seeing that the treatment regimen is carried out to the fullest benefit of that client.

Capitalize on what is right and good about clients--on what they do well. Indicate that the client has a good foundation on which to build, and then plan for some early successes.

Enlist the support of significant others. Statistics show that when a spouse is interested in the client's behavior, the adherence to the regimen more than doubles. And when two or more family members understand and appreciate the necessity of the regimen, the figures are even better.

Finally, it may be a good idea for therapists to read and reread this chapter on motor learning until all those points on how learning best takes place become ingrained. Anything that enhances learning is quite likely to provide motivation for engaging in treatment programs and appreciation for the methods of improving function.

Study Questions:

1. What are intrinsic, concurrent, and terminal feedback?

2. Explain the differences between knowledge of performance (KP) and knowledge of results (KR).

3. Is it possible to learn without knowledge of results? Defend your answer.

4. What is generally the most effective feedback schedule?

5. Discuss concurrent and delayed feedback.

6. Summary feedback produces the best results during which phase? What may happen if the client has poor memory and the inability to attend to the task? What are your concerns and suggestions? What effect might summary feedback have in such situations?

7. Differentiate between the feedback requirements for learning continuous tasks and those required for learning discrete tasks.

8. Why is it possible to have information that is too detailed or precise for useful feedback?

9. Discuss the acquiescence or compliance of clients with their therapy programs by describing the elements that interfere with acquisition and ways that it might be enhanced.

UPDATE! Recent clinical investigations of motor learning principles

Practice and Feedback

Are motor learning principles appropriate for clients with neurologic deficits?

In this chapter we have often made the observation that motor learning principles have been derived from research on normal populations. It has also been noted that there is no evidence to suggest we that should not apply these principles to individuals with problems of motor control. However, relatively little evidence exists in the literature that proves such applications are appropriate. Studies are beginning to surface that address these issues.

Merians et al (1995) devised an experiment using augmented (extrinsic) feedback with individuals who had suffered a stroke. The project had two purposes. One was to determine the effects of practice with feedback during a motor task comparing those individuals poststroke with age-matched controls. The second objective was to compare the effectiveness of two different augmented feedback schedules.

Both the individuals who had suffered CVA's and the age-matched controls performed with increasing accuracy and consistency on the task with feedback. Both the 100 per cent and 67 per cent feedback schedules were effective during the acquisition phase. The improvements also remained during the retention phase. There was a remarkable similarity in the performance curves of the two groups. The result indicates the processes of skill acquisition may be similar between healthy subjects and those with CVA. As would be expected, although the effects were beneficial to the subjects with CVA, their performance was less accurate and consistent than that of the normal subjects. Thus motor control deficits persist even in the less affected limb.

Clients with CVA's show the same response to learning principles as normals!

When comparing the two feedback schedules the practice with reduced frequency (67%) was beneficial for performance consistency but not accuracy. This result was found for both the normal controls and those with neurologic deficits. The investigators have also begun to investigate the effects of different feedback modes. More studies should help us understand which of the many possible feedback conditions may best augment motor learning in particular situations. They should also provide further evidence of the validity of motor learning principles when applied to the rehabilitation of individuals with motor deficits.

Age related modes of learning have been investigated. Caffrey et al (1995) conducted an experiment with full-term infants as they were learning to sit. To determine whether adult motor learning strategies were relevant for this group, the infants were given support and verbal cues within blocked or variable practice trials. The results demonstrated that infants were capable of learning a motor skill while engaged in a directed motor learning activity. The EMG and video recordings revealed that among the infants a variety of strategies were used to accomplish the task. The results of this study indicate that initially

Adult modes of learning may not be appropriate for infants.

412a

blocked practice may be more effective than variable practice for infants, and possibly young children, when learning a new motor skill.

Classification of Movements; Whole-Task--Part-Task

Earlier we described the difficulty in classifying movements as discrete, serial, or continuous based on observation alone. Recent studies are beginning to show us that the outward appearance of a movement is not necessarily congruent with the less easily observed aspects or inner components of movement such as the trajectory of body parts and the force production involved in the movement. The **intention** of the movement appears to have considerable influence on these aspects of the movement. In studies of reach and grasp, the reach components vary in force and timing depending on whether the intention is to throw or to place the object. The brain plans or scales these parameters in advance (Winstein, 1995).

Earlier (see page 388) we discussed classifying the movement of sit-to-stand and then walking as possibly a combination task in which the sit-to-stand might be considered a discrete movement and walking a continuous movement. Fisher (Yakura and Fisher, 1994; Fisher et al, 1995) recorded sit-to-stand and sit-to-walk activities on videotape for kinematic analysis and used a force plate to describe kinetic profiles of these movements. The results show that the intention to walk has great influence on the movement component of rising from a chair. The power generation in the sit-to-walk was at the ankle which is required to propel the body forward for progression directly into gait. This progression is not required in the sit-to-stand in which the power generation was at the knee and hip.

These experiments remind us that classifying movements requires more than simple observation and logical thought. To classify movements accurately we will most likely have to wait until all of the movements of interest have been researched under appropriate conditions. However, if we simply consider the next step (intention) in the movement series we will be better able to decide on a certain movement's place in the scheme.

On page 388 we also noted the problems in practicing part-task vs whole task, and task transfer. These studies clearly show that practicing a sit-to-stand movement when the client is ultimately supposed to get up out of the chair and walk is not likely to be as effective as practicing the complete functional task. It appears that certain components of the movement, force and trajectory to name only two, cannot be mimicked or supplied in the part-task practice.

The *intention* of two similar movements changes the components within the movements even if they outwardly appear to be the same.

A movement may appear to have discrete parts when in fact it is programmed as a whole functional task.

412b

Chapter 15 - Evaluation of General Disorders of Motor Control

NOTE: Portions of this section are from Crutchfield et al (1989), reprinted with permission.

General Considerations of Postural Analysis

Clients who do not have specific vestibular lesions or disorders as previously described may have disordered postural control from other problems including vestibular system involvement that affects their ability to remain stable and move effectively. Such clients may have direct damage to the vestibular system, as might happen in head trauma. Clients may also have problems either with integration of vestibular and other sensory signals or with motor control mechanisms with which they are linked. Thus clients with diverse diagnoses such as cerebral palsy, Down syndrome, stroke, multiple sclerosis, head injury, Parkinson's disease, and many other neurologic conditions may have these disturbances. These clients are more likely to have altered postural control than they are to have vertigo and other such signs of vestibular dysfunction, although such signs may be present.

Clinical tests often currently used to differentiate between the various causes of imbalance and postural dysfunction have many flaws (Horak 1987). As noted earlier, the Romberg test of standing with eyes open and eyes closed on one or both legs often fails to detect disequilibrium in subjects who have vestibular dysfunction; thus it is not a sensitive test for vestibular dysfunction. If a subject is asked to walk a balance beam with heel-to-toe patterns, the ankle synergy is effectively diminished because there are biomechanical limitations at the ankle and loss of medial-lateral stability. The same situation occurs when the sharpened Romberg test is used in static conditions. The resulting use of the hip strategy by the subject may be graded as a failure because the movements are rather large and may be considered ungainly, even though it is an appropriate movement pattern in this circumstance. Nonetheless, these tests do provide a general test of balance functions. Norms are available for comparison. Most of the balance test results are measured by recording the time a particular position can be held or whether a task is completed within a certain time.

> The limits of stability are usually within only a few degrees of sway in a given position.

Although the body may assume an unlimited number of positions and still remain in equilibrium, in most positions only a few degrees of sway are possible if the subject is to remain in equilibrium and not fall or change to another position. This limitation in postural range of motion

413

makes it difficult to detect, with simple observation alone, critical postural adjustments. This area of stability is often referred to as the cone of stability because the limits represent an ever-widening area radiating from the base of support to the head and can be depicted as a conal shape surrounding the person (Fig 15-1). This cone represents the sway from side to side and back and forth that the person will use to attempt to maintain equilibrium within the limits of stability.

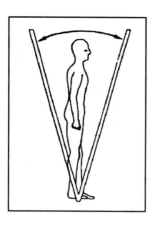

Figure 15-1 The cone of stability in standing. From Nashner (1990, p 6), reprinted with permission of the American Physical Therapy Association.

In normal standing, the center of gravity is in the center of the cone of stability. If the person sways forward, however, he may reach the limit of his stability and must step forward to make a new stability position or else fall. It is also possible that he can correct this position by using the ankle strategy or the hip strategy if the center of gravity has not been displaced too far forward. In walking, there is a constant movement through each cone of stability emanating from the stance foot. At heel strike, the center of gravity is at the rear of the cone; at heel-off, it is at the front of the cone, as seen in Figure 15-2 (Nashner 1990). According to Nashner, if the center of gravity is in the center of the cone, there may be as much as 12 degrees of sway that can be permitted without destabiliztion. Of course, any alteration in circumstances, such as a decreased range of motion in the ankle, will result in a smaller cone of stability, and fewer degrees of sway will be tolerated.

The cone of stability is dynamic and the limits change with the circumstances, although the biomechanical limits remain the same.

The cone of stability represents the individual's range of dynamic balance and if you are willing to sway to the edge of stability you probably have good balance control mechanisms. The cone of stability is dynamic and changes even when there is no motor problem. Try having a friend stand and notice his sway. Does he sway as far backward as forward or sideward? Have him close his eyes and note the sensory impact on voluntary sway. Then have him stand on a balance beam or on a chair or something high. Note the sway. Have him close his eyes and note the sway. Height, or the perception of height, influences the sway. The biomechanical limits are the same but the sway has been influenced by other factors. Now have your friend reach as far forward as possible. Next try a goal-directed reach, that is, ask him to reach for an object that you hold farther away than he was able to achieve with a self-directed reach. Note that he will be able to reach farther in a goal-directed activity, a task other than just initiated by himself.

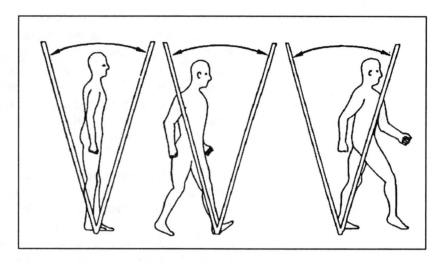

Figure 15-2   Moving cone of stability. From Nashner (1990, p 6), reprinted with permission of the American Physical Therapy Association.

Many factors can affect the limits of stability.

During the examination of the client who has postural dysfunction, finding the limits of stability will be important. Often an attempt is made to perturb the client and destabilize him, but this is done without a systematic view of what we are looking for. During commonly used balance tests, sensory conditions are not systematically changed or eliminated by altering either the visual surroundings or the nature of the supporting surface. Such systematic variations are necessary to determine which senses the subject can rely on for postural orientation. Further, these tests do not evaluate conditions that require different synergies or strategies for postural movement (Shumway-Cook and Horak 1986).

Often, evaluation of balance is attempted by using a tilt board or a ball to disturb the client's center of gravity. Other types of balance disturbances used include perturbing the subject by pushing against his trunk with the command, "Don't let me push you over." Most often large perturbations are given. The result we expect is not always clear. If we cannot knock over the client did he pass? What is his score if he falls over but catches himself with a protective reaction?

Useful and practical equipment for the clinical assessment of postural control has not been available. Expensive and highly complex computerized force platforms and motion analysis machines can provide accurate center-of-mass positions and kinematic analyses of motion, but the relationship between these measures and the clinical assessment of balance function is unclear. A new functionally oriented balance measure has been developed (Duncan el al 1990) and will be described later in this chapter.

Further compounding the problems of assessment is the requirement for as objective a measure as possible. Simple descriptions of movements and postures often are not sufficiently reliable for baseline or treatment progression measures. Neither do these descriptions provide a separation, or division, of the posture into basic functional components. Knowledge of the parts, or components, of a posture is necessary to break down the analysis and determine the problems that produce a dysfunctional movement or posture.

Horak (1987) has proposed some methods for clinical assessment of balance. Tools and devices used in this assessment are quite familiar to all physical therapists and these include postural grids and plumb lines. Scales can be developed to measure results. Stop watches provide accurate time recordings. Video recorders and Polaroid photographs produce hard copy for more accurate analysis and permanent recording of results.

These and other such tools used in combination with a systematic analysis should yield measurable results. Most importantly, the results should be of clinical relevance. In addition there are other important components of postural control that require assessment and they will now be discussed.

Evaluation of Biomechanical and Musculoskeletal Components

The integrity of the musculoskeletal system should be evaluated first, in a client with balance disorders, in order to determine the effect of musculoskeletal limitations on postural control. The presence of pain, alterations in joint range of motion, or alterations in muscle strength or length may produce dysfunction in balance. The therapist must differentiate among problems caused by a normal central nervous system acting on an abnormal biomechanical structure, problems caused by an abnormal central nervous system acting on a normal biomechanical structure, or problems caused by combinations of the two.

If the range of motion of a joint is not normal, posture and movements involving that joint will be altered.

Evaluation of joint range of motion is essential. If the joints involved in the posture or movement of interest are restricted or lack accessory motions, the posture itself will be altered. Postures and movements that occur in the presence of muscle weakness may be similar to those that result when joint motion is limited.

The presence of pain will affect the quantity and quality of movement, because normal movement cannot be superimposed over pain. Movement altered by pain may become habitual and persist even after

416

> Normal movement cannot be superimposed over pain.

the pain has disappeared. The therapist should attempt to gather sufficient client history concerning pain to judge whether such conditions could have existed that may explain or have contributed to the present circumstances.

Muscle weaknesses, muscle imbalances in length or strength, and lack of muscular endurance will affect the quality of movement and the type and maintenance of posture. Remember, however, that manual muscle tests may not provide a functional measure of strength. This is particularly true of postural weight-bearing patterns. It may be more useful to devise a measure for the muscle in a functional mode. For example, the gluteus medius muscle may be better evaluated by standing on one leg and attempting to raise the pelvis on the opposite side than by side lying in a nonweight bearing position. Quadriceps femoris muscles may be better evaluated during semisquats or other such functionally related activities than they are with certain devices that test or exercise the muscle while sitting.

> Muscle strength, or control of force, is critically important, but our methods of measuring it often lack specificity and functional relevance.

Sensory abnormalities may contribute to postural dysfunction. Decreased proprioception or faulty vision, in particular, will affect stability. Of course, as already noted, it is possible that the peripheral vestibular mechanism itself has been affected from a blow to the head or other such injury. It is necessary to determine whether the client has good sensory information available to him. It appears that loss of one of the sensory modalities will have a minimal effect but that loss of more than one or derangement of one or more systems may have a profound effect on balance and coordination. Often, the malfunctions demonstrated by neurologically involved clients are not the result of direct peripheral injury to the receptors themselves but to the central mechanisms that integrate these inputs.

Evaluation of Motor Components of Postural Control

Evaluation of Movement Strategies--Anterior-Posterior Perturbations

Undoubtedly, many strategies are used by clients to maintain postural stability, depending on the context in which stability must be maintained. Some basic strategies used when anterior-posterior perturbations are encountered by subjects standing on a moving platform are the ankle and hip synergies described earlier. It is possible to evaluate such synergies without expensive equipment. For example, muscles may be palpated during perturbations to determine whether they have been activated. Additionally, as one becomes familiar with the appearance of the synergies it becomes possible to see the substitution of one synergy for another or alterations in the synergies.

417

Grids drawn on the wall or produced on see-through plastic can provide background for visual or photographic measurements.

The type of synergy that will be elicited by perturbation will depend on the context, such as the initial position of the body, the type of support surface on which the client is standing, and the intensity of the perturbation. In standing, a small anterior-posterior perturbation will not move the center of mass very far and can be countered with an ankle synergy if the support surface is firm and wide enough to provide counter forces to ankle rotation.

How the perturbation is presented is of critical importance. If you say to the subject "Don't let me move you," the subject will set, or coactivate, most of the involved musculature to prevent being moved. This rigid response is not usually helpful when one is attempting to assess the subject's ability to recover from a perturbation. It is better to instruct the subject as follows: "Let me move you but try not to fall." With these instructions the therapist will more likely elicit an ankle synergy (Fig 15-3 A, B), if one is present, with a relatively small perturbation. This approach also allows the therapist to determine more effectively the limits of stability.

Larger and more rapid perturbations usually result in eliciting a hip synergy (Fig 15-3 C, D). In addition, if the supporting surface does not resist ankle rotational forces sufficiently to shift the center of mass, a hip synergy will result. To test whether the hip synergy is present, the client may stand crosswise on a narrow balance beam and a perturbation may be provided, if necessary, to disturb the center of gravity. Positions that do not allow both ankles to produce an ankle synergy may also be used. Examples of such positions include having the subject use a heel-to-toe stance or stand on one foot. This activity can be done lengthwise on a balance beam or simply on the floor. The largest and fastest perturbations may result in a stepping strategy.

It is important to change systematically the speed and intensity of the perturbations in conjunction with altering the support surface. Both expected and unexpected perturbations should be experienced and evaluated. A routine, or protocol, should be developed for your clinic that makes it easy to evaluate the movements and record the results as objectively as possible and that requires a minimum of time.

When abnormalities are present, the therapist should attempt to determine whether the following occur:

1. Do abnormalities lie within the synergies themselves? If the client has disorders of timing, sequencing, or the amount of muscular activity, you will want to pinpoint them so proper treatment can be applied after evaluation.

> Context involves the environmental conditions and the demands of the task to be completed.

> Strategies are used to keep the center of gravity over the base of support.

418

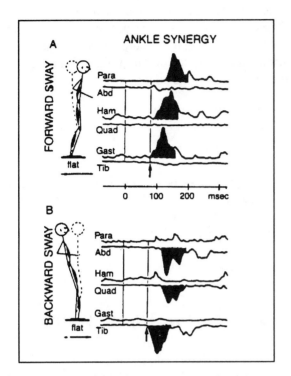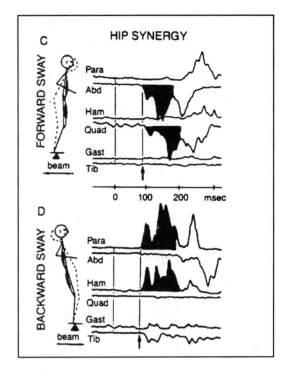

Figure 15-3 The ankle synergy and the hip synergy as described by Nashner. From Nashner (1990, p 9), reprinted with permission of the American Physical Therapy Association.

2. Does the client have a limited number of strategies that can be elicited?

3. Does the client have a full repertoire of strategies available but use or access them inappropriately? For example, a subject may have a hip synergy that can be elicited, but he consistently falls from the beam because the hip synergy is not elicited in that instance.

It is also important to understand that the ankle, hip, and stepping strategies have been observed as responses to a particular type of perturbation: the anterior-posterior disturbance provided by the movement of the supporting surface on which the subject is standing. The strategies also appear as automatic responses to other external perturbations, such as shoving the person, and are present during perturbed walking.

If the perturbations are supplied in a different manner, such as through the pelvis, some modifications of the strategies appear. In their development of the Postural Stress Test, Whipple and Wolfson (1990) devised a method of perturbation in which the subjects wore belts that were attached through cables and pulleys to weights. When the weights were dropped, the pelvis was sharply pulled backward. In these circumstances, the best and most efficient response was strong dorsiflexion, trunk flexion, and shoulder flexion (Fig 15-4). If these

419

movements were unavailable or insufficient, the subjects would take one or more steps backward. It would appear that these synergies are similar but different than those assembled for the platform perturbations. Because balance is such a complex process and because the context or environmental conditions under which balance responses are elicited are varied, the therapist must vary these conditions during testing and carefully record the response and the condition.

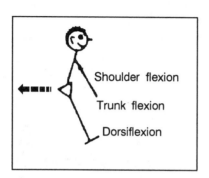

Shoulder flexion

Trunk flexion

Dorsiflexion

Figure 15-4   Muscular responses to perturbations at the pelvis.

Evaluation of Anticipatory Postural Adjustments

As noted in Chapter 11, every movement has a corresponding postural set that precedes the observable movement. Both the postural adjustment and the movement may be programmed, or assembled, as a single synergy. Preparatory postural adjustments may be analyzed through careful observation of movements that will potentially disturb balance.

> Every movement is associated with a preparatory postural set.

It is preferable first to observe preparatory activity associated with movement in normal individuals. Palpate muscles to confirm activity if an EMG machine is not available. In some cases, as when a load is added, the postural adjustment may be observable as a weight shift. Then compare these results with your client when he or she is asked to perform the movement. Does the weight shift occur? Are the correct muscles activated? If the correct muscles are activated but the preparatory motion is ineffective, most likely the onset of muscle activation is delayed or the muscle is weak.

Evaluation of Weight Shifts and Active Movement

The ability to perform active weight shifts in standing, sitting, and other positions may be assessed by having the client shift weight in all directions, such as forward, backward, and side to side. The quality of these movements should be noted. What are the limits, or boundaries, of stability? These boundaries are described by determining how large the active sway in each direction may be and still have stability maintained. These weight shifts may be measured with a grid or a plumb line. Most likely, some observations of normal individuals will help you in learning to determine the extent of abnormality in a client.

Weight shifts in a variety of positions can be imposed on the client by using a tilt board. The tilt imposed should be varied and not usually large and rapid. Each postural position is stable within only a few degrees. A protective reaction is only elicited when the client's center of mass exceeds the base of support, forcing the client to use his arms to prevent a fall. A scale may be developed to measure how many degrees of tilt can be imposed in which the subject maintains equilibrium (Fig 15-5).

Most important is that also during functional movement there are weight shifts. These are incorporated into the movement as an anticipatory set. For instance, when performing a sit-to-stand movement, there is not only an active shift of the weight forward over the feet but also a pelvic tilt that occurs as part of the weight shift. Again, it requires close observation or use of other processes such as video recordings to see how and when these weight shifts occur.

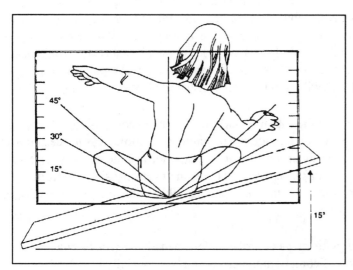

Figure 15-5 An example of a grid that can be made for measuring degrees of tilt. From Crutchfield et al (1989), reprinted with permission from J B Lippincott Co.

As you learned in Chapter 14 on motor learning, it is quite likely that there is little functional transfer between activities in one circumstance and another. For instance, weight shifts done while standing do not necessarily transfer to weight shifts needed during gait or in a sit-to-stand movement. Thus, if the sit-to-stand movement is the functional movement that you wish the client to accomplish, it should be practiced as a specific movement and the weight shift must be incorporated into the movement sequence. Isolated practice in standing will probably have a minimal effect on walking. Of course, weight shift in standing may be practiced for its own sake. The ability to stand is certainly a functional necessity.

Movements are goal-directed and task specific.

421

Evaluation of Sensory Organization

Shumway-Cook and Horak (1986) have described a clinical approach to assessing the effect of sensory interaction on balance. The test helps to identify which sense an individual relies on for postural orientation. Additionally, it is possible to test a client's ability to solve intersensory conflicts without the dependence on very sophisticated and expensive machinery. It should also be noted that no validity or reliability data have been presented for this test. In addition, no possible differences in performance by different age groups have been addressed.

The clients may be tested using the six sensory conditions described previously. The visual box used to present inaccurate visual information may be fabricated from a Japanese paper lantern, following instructions in the article by the above authors. The basic principle is to devise a box or globe that can be placed over the client's head and suspended in such a manner that the hood or globe moves when the head moves. The inside of the device should contain lines, or patterns, for visual stimulation and fixation. The globe must be large enough to place the visual stimulation a reasonable distance from the eyes so that focusing may occur. A helmet with adjustable straps, a dental headband, or simply the top ring of the lantern or any similar mechanism may be used to suspend the device from the head. If such a device cannot be fabricated, just placing a paper bag over the client's head may provide a change in visual conditions that will help with differential evaluation.

The principle of the rotating platform may be accomplished by having the subject stand on a relatively unstable, or compliant, surface, such as a piece of dense rubber foam. This material allows the ankle joint to at least begin rotating and prevents the somatosensory systems from relaying accurate information from the ankle joints and the skin (Fig 15-6).

A standing platform as described above can also be made of a combination of compliant materials and be especially effective for clinical purposes. The bottom layer should consist of dense foam rubber, the middle layer of a less dense foam, and the top layer of a very compliant foam, such as Pudgy foam. With these combinations, the foot will sink rapidly and the ankle will actually rotate farther before counterforces can occur. This situation will produce more inaccurate somatosensory feedback than will a single layer of dense less compliant foam. Experiment and see what works best for you.

To measure the amount of sway that occurs from the various conditions, use a grid or plumb line. Remember that video recording or Polaroid photographs are useful methods for obtaining permanent recordings for accurate analysis. A stop watch may be used to measure the time the subject can maintain the position without movement of the feet or arms or deviation from the erect position. Subjects should be able to maintain the position for 60 seconds in each of three trials. Instructions to the client must be clear and standardized so that they are the same for all clients.

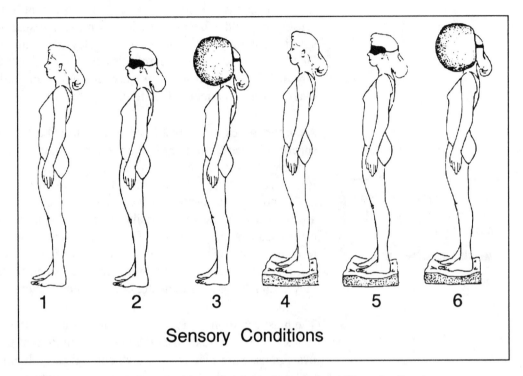

Figure 15-6 A clinical method for testing body sway and stability under the six sensory conditions.

It is important to compare responses to expected and unexpected displacements. Different synergies may be used in different circumstances. Also record any instances of vertigo, dizziness, nystagmus, or other such symptoms or complaints.

Interpreting the information gathered is extremely important. Even though the client may fall when under altered visual conditions, it may be that he is attending to inappropriate visual information rather than failing to rely on more appropriate somatosensory or vestibular inputs. Do not forget that the client may not be able to access the appropriate synergy or produce an appropriate motor response. All of these problems could produce destabilization, so be careful about interpreting the response solely as a failure to solve intersensory conflicts resulting from integrative dysfunction of the vestibular system (Newton 1990).

423

Considerations for Using VOR and Other Tests for Postural Control

Before the sophisticated studies of vestibular function were available, it was believed that vestibular dysfunction was a contributing factor in sensory-motor dysfunction of clients with such disparate diagnoses as spastic cerebral palsy, developmental delays, learning disabilities, and Down syndrome. As a result of this belief, considerable resources within physical or occupational therapy are directed specifically toward the diagnosis and treatment of vestibular dysfunction.

A number of tests exist that have been assumed to be valid for specifically identifying vestibular dysfunction, including the VOR, the Romberg tests, and the ability to assume a prone extended posture. Recent research suggests that these tests often do not measure what they are purported to measure. As mentioned previously, the Romberg tests are not sensitive tests of vestibular function. In addition, motor skills often used to assess vestibular function, such as the prone extension tests, do not correlate with the presence or absence of vestibular function. Because many sensory and motor components contribute to motor skills, they cannot be used as indicators of vestibular function alone.

| Many motor and sensory processes contribute to motor skills. |

The most common clinical approach to evaluating the vestibular-ocular reflex (VOR) is visual observation of the duration of postrotatory nystagmus. However, several methodological problems are associated with this approach. Visual observation is often inaccurate, and equipment such as Frenzel glasses is necessary. Electronastagmography can be used for more objective recording of eye movement responses to rotation as described previously. Additionally, VOR testing should be performed in the dark with the head restrained to rule out both visual-vestibular and cervical-vestibular interactions.

Finally, VOR tests measure the integrity of the semicircular canals. Correlation between VOR testing and posturography tests is poor. It has been suggested that posturography assesses primarily otolithic function, but it is not known whether it really does assess such a differential function. Current evidence suggests that VOR function is relatively independent of vestibulospinal function underlying postural control. Hence, one cannot necessarily infer vestibular-based postural dysfunction from VOR testing.

| Learning disabled children have normal VORs and abnormal motor performance. |

Horak et al (1988) evaluated the vestibular function in hearing impaired children and learning disabled children, 7 to 12 years of age. Balance and coordination problems have been reported previously in both groups. A common assumption by many therapists has been that vestibular dysfunction underlies all balance and coordination problems. However, evidence for peripheral vestibular abnormalities as a cause for coordination problems is poor.

These researchers found that while many children who had hearing impairments had abnormal VOR function, based on postrotatory electronystagmography, most children failed to show deficiencies in motor performance other than balance, as measured by the Bruininks-Oseretsky Test of Motor Proficiency. In contrast, the majority of children with learning disorders had normal VOR function yet showed significant deficiencies in motor performance.

> Hearing disabled children have abnormal VORs and no deficiencies in motor performance.

This study casts doubt on any assumed relationship between peripheral vestibular dysfunction, as measured by VOR tests, and motor deficiencies. Disorders of balance and coordination may result from problems with other peripheral sensory systems or motor systems as well as from the vestibular dysfunction. Clients with central nervous system lesions who do not have peripheral sensory abnormalities may still have marked movement dysfunction in balance and coordination. The central nervous system lesions may affect the integration of information from a variety of sensory inputs. Thus movement dysfunction may result from inadequate central integrating functions rather than from disease or disorders of the receptors themselves.

> Learning disabled children have normal VORs and abnormal postural tests.
>
> Normal children have normal VORs and normal postural tests.

In another study, Shumway-Cook et al (1987) examined the VOR and the postural responses to a moving platform in 15 children with learning disabilities and 54 normal children. Most of the children with learning disabilities had normal VOR tests, but all had abnormal scores on the postural balance tests. Ninety-three percent of the normal children had normal scores on both tests. Thus, again the balance and coordination problems demonstrated by the children with learning disabilities could not be attributed to abnormal sensory inputs from the vestibular system because the learning disabled children had normal VORs. The deficits were attributed to their inability to coordinate normal vestibular signals with other appropriate sensory inputs for postural orientation.

Study Questions:

1. **What is a cone of stability? Why is it important?**

2. **Describe how you would evaluate the client's limits of stability.**

3. **List some biomechanical-musculoskeletal components of balance and explain how they contribute to balance.**

4. **What are some strategies subjects demonstrate in response to anterior-posterior platform perturbations?**

5. **How might you evaluate the strategies clients may use to sustain balance?**

6. **Describe how you can determine that the client can or cannot solve intersensory conflicts.**

Objective Assessment of Functional Balance

In this and the preceding chapters, you have encountered a variety of procedures and instruments purported to measure balance. Although some tests have sensitive measures, they do not necessarily provide us with information that relates to clinical balance problems. Many tests, such as platform perturbations and center of pressure excursions, assess postural responses to artificially induced external stimuli rather than from movements generated from within through voluntary activity. Clearly, they may be useful in differential diagnosis for vestibular involvement and the like, but they do not always produce a measure that correlates with the functional difficulties exhibited by the client. Most individuals with balance problems are not concerned so much with the ability just to stand erect, to stand very still, or to stand on one foot as they are with their inability to move within their environment. They need to execute the postural changes that produce the stability necessary for performing functional activities.

Duncan et al (1990) have developed a simple, useful, inexpensive and functional measure of balance. It has been called the Functional Reach Test. It is designed to measure the margin of stability such as is done by the center of pressure excursion tests. However, rather than measure how still the subject can stand it involves determining the limits of a functional self-initiated movement. Many tests of instability require the individual to simply lean forward as far as possible, while this test requires the use of the arm and simulates a much more functional movement that constantly imposes a stress to one's balance. The subject is asked to reach along a yardstick attached to the wall to produce the measure. The test is easily performed and produces continuous data.

The initial study was performed with 137 normal male and female subjects ranging in age from 20 to 87 years. With this group, age was the most significant factor influencing functional reach. This measure was found to be precise, stable, reliable, and age-sensitive as a clinical assessment of instability.

A second sample of 217 elderly, community dwelling male veterans (aged 70-104 years) were given baseline screenings using the functional reach measure and were followed for 6 months to monitor falls (Duncan et al 1992). It was determined that those men who were able to stand but unable to reach forward any measurable distance were eight times more likely to fall than those who could reach forward 10 inches or more. If the subject's reach was less than or equal to 6 inches, he was four times more likely to fall, and if the reach was greater than 6 but less than 10 inches, he was 2 times more likely to fall. Thus this clinical test was proven to have predictive validity in identifying individuals likely to have recurrent falls.

Balance impairment is certainly one aspect of physical frailty in the elderly. In a third study, these investigators wanted to determine whether the functional reach test was an accurate marker of such frailty (Weiner et al 1992). The functional reach measure was analyzed along with measures of activities of daily living, social mobility, hierarchical mobility skills, walking speed, one-footed standing, and tandem walking. The functional reach measure was strongly associated with the other measures especially when corrected for age. The authors concluded that functional reach correlates with physical frailty even more closely than it does with age. For example, no one with a functional reach of less than 7 inches could maintain one-footed standing longer than 1 second, perform tandem walking, or leave their neighborhood without help.

In their latest study, Weiner et al (in press) investigated the changes in functional reach in persons undergoing rehabilitation compared with controls who were not in rehabilitation. Performance in functional reach, walking time (10 feet), and mobility skills changed significantly in the group receiving rehabilitation compared with the controls. The functional reach measures did not correlate strongly with the other measures, which may reflect the different aspects of physical performance that the tests measure.

The authors believe that mobility skills, walking time, and functional reach all rely on the integrity of postural control mechanisms. Functional reach appears to be a more pure measure of balance than the other activities, however, because it is less influenced by strength and endurance than are walking specified distances and other mobility skills. Functional reach may be used for following progress in balance skills as individuals undergo rehabilitation. Because it is a balance measure, clients may improve in areas that are less involved with balance and produce only a modest change in reach.

This test demonstrates that simple, objective measures can be developed to investigate relevant questions in our client populations. It is important to realize that although many different tests, which can and

The Functional Reach Test: A new, simple, accurate, and inexpensive measure of balance.

have been used to measure balance, may produce exquisite or complex measurements, we cannot be certain what they are actually measuring. In addition, we are not always aware of the demonstrated reliability and validity of the measures we do use. Table 15-1 shows that of the numerous tests designed to measure balance only for the Functional Reach Test have the investigators established all the statistical elements of reliability, validity, and sensitivity to change. It is easy to be misled or make global assumptions about test results that will produce inaccurate or ineffectual diagnoses or treatment regimens. The functional balance measure represents the ideal in establishing reliable and valid data. The sensitivity to change is reliable enough to require only 21 subjects for engaging in statistically meaningful clinical trials (Weiner et al in press).

> Only 21 subjects are required for statistically meaningful clinical trials.

In a recent study (Rose et al 1993), investigators used this measure in an attempt to differentiate among clients with dizziness problems related to either vestibular, vascular, or multisensory, deficits. Those clients with multisensory deficits had the shortest reach; however, their mean reach of 11.33 in was very close to the group that had vestibular deficits and the largest mean reach of 12.6 in. Normal subjects in this study had a mean reach of 13 in. The test was thus unable to differentiate between any except the normal and multisensory deficit categories, and only then if a low level of significance had been used ($P > .10$). In their first study, Duncan et al (1990) demonstrated very significant differences between age groups in which the mean differences among groups were generally greater than 1.5 in. Although the functional reach measure has yet to be fully assessed for true clinical utility, it would appear that it has great promise. Any therapist in a clinical situation may acquire the equipment and perform clinical experiments on balance with ease. Try it!

Functional Reach Test

Using Velcro® strips and a level, attach a yardstick to the wall at the level of the client's acromion process. (The Velcro® strips enable the examiner to adjust the yardstick readily to accommodate various heights.) Mark the foot position on the floor where the subject is to stand. Instruct the individual to keep his body perpendicular to the stick (Fig 15-7).

Have the subject make a fist and lift his arm to 90 degrees of forward flexion, keeping it parallel to the stick. Measure where the third metacarpal reaches on the ruler. Now ask the subject reach as far forward as possible without losing his balance or taking a step (Figure 15-8) then take the second measure. The functional reach measure is the difference between the two distances.

Table 15-1

Established Test Characteristics of Measures of Balance

Tests	Reliability		Validity		Sensitivity to Change
	Intraobserver	Test-Retest	Criterion	Construct	
Laboratory Measures					
Postural Sway[1]	NA	No	Yes	Concurrent -- not well established	No
Center of Pressure Excursion[2]	NA	Yes, (but marginal)	No	Concurrent -- Yes Predictive -- No	No
EMG analysis of Platform Perturbation[3]	NA	EMG latency -- Yes EMG patterns -- No	No	Concurrent -- not well established Predictive -- No	No
Maki-Pseude Random Perturbation[4]	NA	No	No	Concurrent -- No Predictive -- No	No
Anticipatory Postural Adjustments[5]	NA	No	No	Concurrent -- not well established Predictive -- No	No
Sensory -Organization Test[6]	NA	No	No	Concurrent -- not well established Predictive -- No	No
Clinical Measures					
Romberg[7]	Not tested	No -- in the elderly	No	Concurrent -- No Predictive -- No	No
One-leg stance[8]	No	No	No	Concurrent -- No Predictive -- No	No
Postural Stress Test[9]	Yes	Yes	Yes	Concurrent -- Yes Predictive -- No	No
Sternal Push[10]	No	No	No	Concurrent -- No Predictive -- No	No
Lee Maximal Load Test[11]	No	No	No	Concurrent -- poor association with other measures of balance--but discriminated individuals with pathology Predictive -- No	No
Tinetti--Performance Oriented Mobility Assessment[12]	Yes	No	No	Concurrent -- No Predictive -- Yes	No
Mathias Get Up & Go Test[13]	Yes	No	No	Concurrent -- Yes Predictive -- No	No
Functional Reach[14]	Yes	Yes	Yes	Concurrent -- Yes Predictive -- Yes	Yes

From Duncan et al (1990), reprinted with permission.

1 Standing postural sway (Brocklehurst el al 1982)
2 Device measures the limits of pressure in standing (Dettman et al 1987)
3 Platform moves and destabilizes subject (Nashner 1977; Woollacott et al 1988; Woollacott et al 1982)
4 Platform produces small random perturbations (Maki et al 1987)
5 Subject displaces his own center of gravity during a task such as raising an arm (Stelmach et al 1989)
6 Test stability under six sensory conditions (Shumway-Cook and Horak 1986; Whipple and Wolfson 1990)
7 Standing feet-together or heel-to-toe with eyes open and eyes closed (Black et al 1982)
8 Time an individual can balance on one leg (Bohannon 1984)
9 Weights are dropped that are attached to subjects belt, at waist, pulling him backward (Wolfson et al 1986)
10 Pushing subjects on the sternum (Weiner el al 1984)
11 Static loads applied at waist until subject can no longer maintain position (Lee et al 1988)
12 Fifteen performance activities (Tinetti 1986)
13 Subject stands up from chair, walks short distance, turns around, returns, and sits down (Mathias et al 1986)
14 Reaching as far forward as possible (Duncan et al 1990)

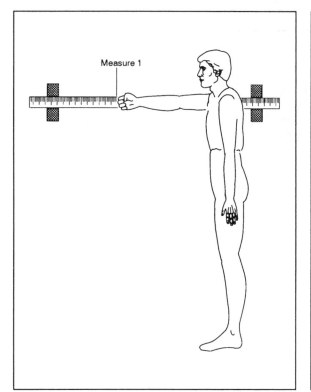

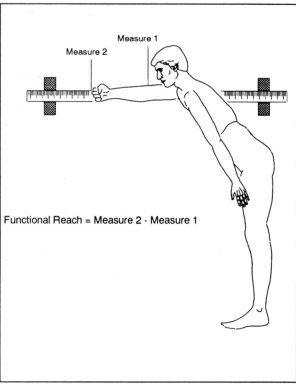

Figure 15-7 Functional Reach Test. beginning position. Measure the point on the yardstick where the client's fist rests.

Figure 15-8 Functional Reach Test ending position. As the client reaches as far forward as possible, measure where his fist comes on the yardstick.

Epidemiological Studies of Balance

Duncan and Chandler (1992) also have completed important epidemiological studies involving balance. Because falls are a major cause of morbidity and mortality in those over 65 years, studies were designed to investigate the reasons for falls in the elderly. The studies involved professionals from many disciplines and examined many factors that influence balance and motor control besides the integrity of the particular sensory-motor systems involved. Being aware of these factors should give us a broader insight into evaluation, treatment and prognostication of clients with a variety of conditions.

Environmental, behavioral, social, and functional factors regulate balance and motor control as significantly as physiological factors.

A possible functional outcome·of a loss in balance control is a fall. The investigators recognized, however, that falls result from more than just postural instability; therefore they broadened their areas of concern to incorporate other elements such as environmental, behavioral, social, and functional factors (Chandler and Duncan 1993).

430

Environmental conditions that might affect walking could be icy surfaces, gravel paths, steps, hilly terrain, carpets, waxed floors, and environmental obstacles such as chairs, tables, and cords. Children and pets who may share the individual's living space may affect his ability to stay upright through their unpredictable activity. Any of these environmental factors are likely to have different effects on children and adults depending on their ability to accommodate to these factors. Attempts to manage such obstacles or decisions to avoid them will influence the client's functional outcomes. Cognitive and behavioral factors, such as risk identification and risk-taking behaviors, also will affect the ultimate outcome of whether the individual will fall.

Movements are the result of the integrated functions of the postural control system. Observing and identifying important reactions and movements a person can perform or has difficulty with allows us to determine whether impairments can effectively be compensated so that functional movements are available (Chandler and Duncan 1993).

Relationship Between Impaired Mobility and Falls

Poor balance control obviously would affect an individual's ability to move from place to place and to interact with the environment. It would seem logical that the most likely candidates for falling would be those who do not have good mobility. Subjects were rated as having impaired mobility and as being at high risk for falls if they were unable to descend steps unsupported or sit unsupported (Chandler and Duncan 1993). Subjects in the highly mobile, low risk category were either independent or able to descend steps foot-over-foot without assistance. Data analysis showed that impaired mobility was significant in determining risks for falls.

Duncan and her group wanted to know, however, whether impaired mobility by itself is a sufficient reason for falls (Duncan and Chandler 1992). Would there be an association with impairments in behavioral, social, and environmental domains as well as impaired mobility that would more fully predict who will fall?

The investigators performed an environmental assessment by going into the subjects' homes and developing a scale based on the number of hazards present and the frequency with which the subject encountered the hazards. Because risk-taking behaviors influence an individual's history of falling, the investigators examined risk-avoidance behavior to assess the behavioral domain. Obviously, a subject's cognitive abilities will affect his behavioral responses and modify risk-taking behavior. Social support gained by having friends or family to provide emotional support or needed assistance was rated. After the study was controlled for mobility skill level, age, and cognition, the elements that significantly influenced fall status in high risk subjects were the environmental conditions and whether the subjects engaged in risk-avoiding behavior.

431

So clearly, poor mobility skills are not the only reason an individual might fall, and it is very important that the therapist be aware of other domains that influence a client's possible instability and include these factors in evaluation and treatment plans.

Physiological Measures of Balance and Their Relationship to Falls

The investigators also studied the physiological components of balance: central processing time, muscular firing patterns, muscle strength, and range of motion (Duncan and Chandler 1992; Chandler and Duncan 1993). Central processing time was investigated by measuring the latency of onset for muscular contractions in the ankle synergy as a response to perturbation. There was a significant delay in tibialis anterior response time during backward sway but not in gastrocnemius response time during forward sway when comparing those who fell often with those who did not.

> Muscular strength is an important component in maintaining balance.

The muscular firing patterns were difficult to interpret. The investigators wanted to know whether an activation sequence of distal to proximal (ankle strategy) or proximal to distal (hip strategy) would differentiate those who fell from those who did not. There was too much resting activity in the ankle muscles which resulted in too many uninterpretable trials for the investigators to be certain about pattern sequencing, but of the trials that could be interpreted there was no difference in those who used hip strategies instead of ankle strategies when evaluating their history of falls.

There was a significant difference in strength around the ankles and at the knee when comparing those subjects with a history of falls with those who did not. Once again, investigators have uncovered evidence that muscular weakness is critical in determining movement effectiveness. The investigators concluded that clients with unexplained falls did appear to have more profound impairment in strength than in central processing.

Evaluating Effects Across Multiple Domains

Chandler and Duncan (1993) believe that interactive effects and cumulative effects may be more important than single problems. That is, an individual could have one problem, such as visual impairment, or he might have involvement in several domains, such as vision, muscle strength, and range of motion. The investigators looked at the relationship between multiple levels of impairment and deficits in different functional categories.

Subjects were tested for impairments in vision, somatosensory and vestibular-ocular function (saccades), central processing time, muscular strength, and joint range of motion. Subjects were also classified as having high, intermediate, and low mobility skills. Those subjects categorized as having high mobility skills could tandem walk and negotiate steps; those with intermediate skills could negotiate steps but could not tandem walk; those in the low category either required support for ambulation or could not negotiate steps. Subjects were timed for how long it took them to walk 10 meters, and the distance they could walk in 6 minutes was measured.

The test results were analyzed for impairments in the different domains tested, such as sensory, central processing time, or strength. Those with the greatest functional impairments had deficits in multiple domains. The results also suggest that mobility difficulties in clients without significant pathology may be better explained by defects across domains rather than by any specific impairment in one domain, such as vision. When you evaluate clients for impaired functional performance of activities of daily living you will need to consider accumulation of deficits as a reason for decline even if specific deficits seem minor. It is also possible that correction or improvement in at least one domain might be sufficient to compensate for other impaired domains. For instance, it may not be possible to correct sensory deficits, but if strength is improved, the change may be just enough to make a significant difference in function despite other deficits.

> It may not be possible to correct deficits in all domains, however, improvement in one domain may improve function in spite of other deficits.

Currently, these investigators are conducting clinical trials asking whether changes in strength improve balance and function in elderly, such as improved distance in a 6 minute walk, decrease in the time to perform a 10 meter walk, or increases other mobility test scores. Will gains in strength improve such measures as functional reach distance or postural response times? While we often make assumptions about such possibilities, research documenting the efficacy of such an approach is required before we can truthfully make such claims.

Judge et al (1993) showed that a vigorous program of lower-extremity strengthening, walking, and postural control exercises improved single-leg stance measures in women 62 to 75 years of age. The authors note that although static single stance measures may not be the best measure of balance, most falls occur in activities that involve single stance such as turning or climbing steps and that 80% of the gait cycle involves single stance balance. It seems such a measure has some relevance to balance functions. Few functionally impaired persons are able to stand on one leg for more than a few seconds. In this case muscle strengthening appeared to improve the subjects' ability to perform this balance measure.

It is important to recognize that multiple domain influence is not limited to the elderly population. For instance, Cintas (1992) found that risk-taking by toddlers during exploration was significantly related to achieving the erect position and bipedal ambulation. That author suggests that it may be important to incorporate risk-taking behaviors systematically in therapy programming.

433

Vision

As you have learned throughout this text, vision is an extremely important sense that we rely on for motor control more than might have been expected. Vision is a key sense in the development of motor control and we know that children rely more heavily on vision for maintaining posture than do adults. However, vision remains important in that role throughout life. As therapists, we have often overlooked the sense of vision as having major importance in how humans move about and often have failed to incorporate it in treatment and evaluation procedures. Therefore, it is necessary to explore vision from both evaluation and treatment perspectives.

Vision is important in regulating movements. Earlier in Chapters 1 and 2 you read that vision seems to be a dominant source of information for movement and thus has both a proprioceptive and an exteroceptive role. Vision provides information about the environment in relation to the observer. Vision resulting from actively moving in the environment provides a far richer source of information than simply passively observing one's surroundings. The movement produces an optical flow of information past the retina, providing exteroceptive input for movement control. Vision is used often in a feed forward manner (ie, we use that information to change a response in anticipation of some forthcoming condition).

The integration of vision, somatosensory, and vestibular stimuli are critical to maintaining functional balance and movement skills. We have considered the integration of these senses when using the platform or "foam and dome" procedures (Fig 15-6) as methods of clinical evaluation. It appears, however, that vision should be evaluated separately to help determine whether visual deficits, particularly correctable ones, are contributing to postural instability, motor control difficulties, or the lack of appropriate integration.

Visual disturbances may impair balance and mobility.

Our eyes are quite well protected in sockets of hard bone. They are self-cleansing, self-lubricating, shuttered, and self-adjusting. But the eyes may reflect ill health elsewhere in the body, and they are subject to defects, accidents, and disorders of their own. These disorders may cause blindness, great discomfort, or minor or major handicaps of defective vision that often are correctable or preventable if treated properly. Visual disturbances may occur from injury or disease to the brain, the vestibular system, and the muscles of the head and neck. Therapists must recognize the possibility of visual deficits and the role they may play in movement. Although the lack of corrective lenses may cause problems, certain types of lenses themselves may contribute to instability. Thus therapists should be knowledgeable about the more common visual problems and be able to screen clients for visual difficulties.

434

Visual acuity

Some common visual problems that affect visual acuity are classified as refractive disorders and are identified as nearsightedness, farsightedness, and astigmatism. A wall or pocket chart of letters or symbols usually is used to determine visual acuity. Normal vision is described as 20/20. Vision of 20/30 means that a person can identify objects at 20 feet or less that a person with normal vision can identify at 30 feet or less. The card in Figure 15-9 is designed to be held at a specific distance and if you can read the bottom line of the chart, the visual measurement is 20/20. If you can read only down to the fourth (or 14 point) line, you see at 20 feet what a normal individual sees at 100 feet, or a 20/100 measure.

You can use such a chart with your clients to screen visual acuity if you have concerns. In most states, driving is prohibited with a visual acuity rating of 20/50 or worse. Serious problems with recognition of objects and people occurs at 20/70 and beyond. An acuity rating of 20/100 or greater may cause difficulty with balance and motor control, particularly if other senses are also involved (Chandler and Duncan 1993). Charts with pictures and symbols that children recognize are useful for screening children for visual problems. Many different types of charts are available and can be purchased from any ophthalmic supply company.

Astigmatism results from irregular curvature of the cornea and produces a blurred image because one part of a light ray is focused when another is not. This is similar to the distortion produced by a wavy pane of glass. A series of perpendicular lines are used to evaluate this disorder. The subject usually sees lines in one direction more clearly than in the other.

Corrective lenses should be worn by the client when they have been prescribed. Lenses themselves, however, may contribute to perceptual difficulties.

Refractive problems are usually corrected with glasses or contact lenses. If you have a client over 35 or 40 years of age in your clinic who is not wearing glasses, you might wish to inquire whether she has ever been fitted with them. If so, find the glasses, clean them, and place them properly on her face. If a client has corrective lenses, it is vital that they be worn during therapy. Any visual difficulties that may be corrected or improved with these lenses will manifest themselves during therapeutic activities.

As we age, the lens of the eye looses its ability to accommodate to near and far objects. By the age of 40 it is often necessary to correct both near and farsightedness with bifocal, trifocal, or progressive lenses. Such lenses produce distortions at the edges, between near and far corrections, and may cause perceptual difficulties. Because of the distortions, looking down when climbing steps or curbs can be very disorienting when wearing such lenses. The individual must be able to accommodate to these aberrations to prevent perceptual problems when looking through them. Therefore, the glasses themselves should be examined so that the therapist is aware of the type of lenses the client is wearing and the possible consequences during movement. Incorrect prescriptions may blur vision, make the eyes feel irritated, or cause headaches and nausea.

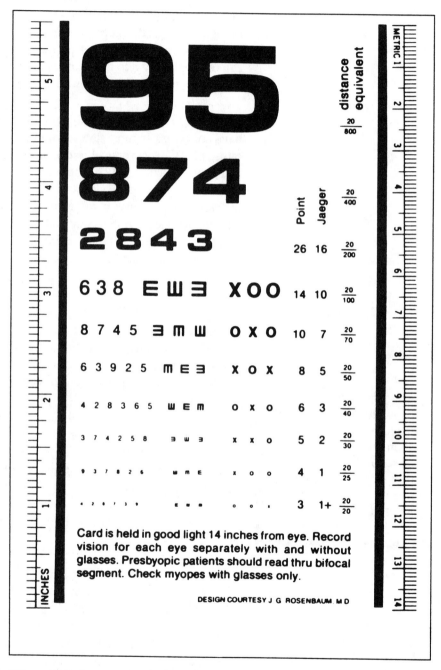

Figure 15-9 An example of a Snellen-type chart for evaluating visual acuity. From Weber (1988), reprinted with permission.

Visual Field

Many kinds of eye disorders affect the peripheral visual field,s such as glaucoma, cataracts, detached retina, and homonymous hemianopsia experienced by individuals suffering strokes. Because visual field defects may affect motor skills, it would seem reasonable that therapists should be able to screen for such defects and take them into account during therapy.

There are numerous ways to measure visual field defects. One of these, called a tangent screen, is a sheet of black felt marked with a central fixation target surrounded by concentric circles corresponding to segments of the retina. The client sits with one eye covered and fixates on the target while the examiner moves a small white ball centrally until the client first sees it. Any area of the field blind to this small object is tested with progressively larger objects to determine the extent of the loss.

A confrontation field is another simple measure that therapists can use to help screen for visual field defects. The client is seated 1 m from the examiner. The client closes his right eye and the examiner closes her left eye, and each fixates on the other's nose. The examiner moves an object or his finger in from the periphery. It should be seen simultaneously by both individuals. This is a gross screening process that reveals only large defects.

And another technique is to bring your fingers from behind the client's head as the client stares straight ahead. Keep moving your fingers forward beside his head until he indicates that he sees them. Again, large defects can be noted with this technique. You will have to practice with some individuals who have normal visual fields to determine when a field has been reduced.

Stereoscopic Vision

Collectively, a half-dozen muscles rotate the eyes, turn them up and down or sideways, and hold them straight. In addition, both eyes must work together in a stereoscopic fashion. This cooperation produces three-dimensional vision. Close one eye and discover how flat two-dimensional vision is. The central visual fields of both eyes overlap and must fuse to produce a clear image in three dimensions. The depth of field and positional relationships of objects are compromised with only one eye or when the eyes are not cooperating (eg, because of muscle imbalances) and visual fusion is not accomplished.

Eye muscle imbalances are relatively common. Cross-eye, wall-eye (divergent eyes), and strabismus are examples of conditions caused by

437

muscular imbalance. Many people have muscle imbalances of which they are unaware. Although unnoticed, eye muscle imbalances may produce significant problems. Blurred vision and diplopia, or double vision, are common defects associated with this problem. Eye fatigue also is likely to result from attempts to maintain fusion of the right and left visual fields.

To evaluate eye muscle function, have the client fixate on a small object and follow it as you move it in what is referred to as the six cardinal fields of gaze (Leitman el al 1981). Each position tests one muscle of each eye for a total of 12 muscles (Fig 15-10). Note any underaction or overaction of the muscles and ask the client if he see double images in any of the six fields.

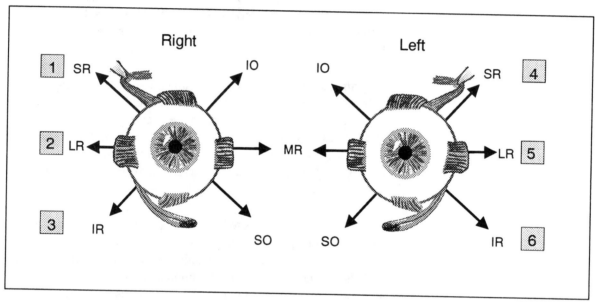

Figure 15-10 The six cardinal movements of the eyes. SR-superior rectus; IR-inferior rectus; MR-medial rectus; LR-lateral rectus; SO-superior oblique; IO-inferior oblique muscles. Each movement involves a muscle from each eye. For example, a movement in direction 1 involves the right superior rectus and the left inferior oblique muscles. Note that the muscles themselves are not labeled on this diagram; the abbreviations refer to the directional movement that particular muscle produces.

Depth of Field

Adequate depth perception is also vitally important to motor control. The ability to judge the relative distance of objects either to ourselves or to each other determines how well we are able to move about in the environment. Lights and shadows complicate depth of field. Elderly persons with reduced vision require increased lighting that does not increase glare; they will see better in natural, full spectrum light than in white light sources such as fluorescent lighting (Hughes and Neer 1981). In older clients, the ability to discern relationships in bright light or shadow will not be as effective as it is in younger individuals. Older individuals also find it particularly difficult to see during a rapid change in light and shadow as when entering the sun or shade while negotiating steps, curbs, or obstacles.

Depth of field can be screened by standing in front of the client and holding your index fingers parallel at eye level. Move one finger forward and one back separating the fingers. The client indicates when the fingers are brought back to parallel. If he is off by more than 3 inches, he may have difficulty with depth perception to a level significant to contribute to imbalance and perceptual dysfunction (Chandler and Duncan 1993).

Evaluation of Clients with Problems of Motor Control

There are many theories of motor control. Even the theories, such as systems theory, are subdivided into many elements. We have attempted to provide you with a working knowledge of some theories either for their historical relevance, or their current favor, or because elements of the theories resurface in other theories. We believe the self-organizing systems theories hold the most promise for a functional understanding of motor control. We have chosen to emphasize the dynamic action theory as developed by Esther Thelen and her colleagues to represent self-organizing systems theory because it is the easiest to comprehend (for us at least) and because we are able to derive many practical insights for therapeutic intervention from it.

You will want to develop plans and attitudes for evaluation and treatment using this information. We will suggest some guidelines and ideas that are based on systems perspectives and on motor learning principles.

According to a systems perspective, movement outcome is the result of the dynamic interaction of the components of the system within the current context of action. The assumption underlying the various component evaluations is that the outcome of movement is the result of the interaction of all components. To evaluate and treat movement dysfunction, then, we must address three areas: 1) the various systems or subsystems involved, such as biomechanical, motor, sensory, muscular, cardiovascular, nutritional, and behavioral; 2) the physical and social environment; and 3) the task.

Multiple Components of Movement

Because this newer systems way of looking at clients has an underlying assumption that no one system is fully responsible for movement, it means that we must evaluate all of the subsystems that participate or should participate in the movement in question. No longer can we afford the notion that we can evaluate the status of the central nervous system, for example, and from that evaluation design an effective treatment program. We must look at the bones and joints, the circulatory system, and even what has been introduced into the gastrointestinal system by way of medications or nutrition. We should be evaluating the skin, the respiratory system, and body weight and size--all systems--as they relate to the task in order to have reasonable information on which to build a treatment program. It is necessary to evaluate how muscles are working together as well as their relationship to the biomechanical components.

Some might argue that we have always looked at many or most of the body systems in evaluating clients, and that is true. The difference is that we have copied the medical model and used it in a multisystem approach to evaluation, which meant that we obtained as much information as we could relative to the functioning of each system. Using a systems approach, we should look at how and to what extent the systems and subsystems are interacting and interrelating in movement. This interrelationship cannot be overemphasized.

If we wanted to establish goals for enabling a client with hemiplegia to walk, for example, under the traditional approach to evaluation and treatment we might look at specific isolated elements such as the status of muscle activity (hypoactivity or hyperactivity), and we might do manual muscle testing, joint range of motion testing, reflex testing, and so on. Treatment would revolve around correcting these specifics. A therapist using a systems approach to evaluation might add looking for delayed muscle activity, inability to cease unwanted muscle contractions, inadequate gain or disorders of timing, inflexibility in changing context, incorrect strategies, or inadequate velocity and acceleration of the movements available. The traditional therapist might limit muscle function evaluation to a manual muscle test of particular groups of muscles, such as the hamstring group or the quadriceps femoris; a dynamic action therapist would be much more inclined to evaluate the muscle strength in functional modes and look at the interaction of a whole muscle synergy, that is, if the appropriate muscles in the synergy came in on time, too soon, not at all. A client's cognitive domain is as important as his behavioral patterns, such as risk-taking behaviors.

> All systems contributing to movement must be considered in evaluation and treatment.

Initial Evaluation

Performing initial evaluations, particularly of clients with neurological problems, is usually a daunting task for student therapists. What should be evaluated? What should be evaluated first? These are questions that come immediately to mind. We will present some suggestions for organizing your approach to evaluating clients. Remember that every therapist will not approach the client in the same way. As you gain experience, skill, and knowledge, other tests or measures might be added to your repertoire.

Most of your evaluation can and should be done in a functional manner. You should gain as much information as possible by carefully observing the client during functional activities. A wealth of information can be gathered just by observing how a client comes to the department (eg, walking, in a wheelchair, on a stretcher), what posture he assumes (eg, head droops, sits asymmetrically, does not seem to know when his body is upright), and how he responds to your interaction with him (eg, Can he hear, speak, understand simple commands? Is he aware of time and place?). An excellent way to view client evaluation is that it is an organized observation; therefore, your observational skills must be finely honed.

There are any number of published types of evaluation procedures for all categories of clients. You encountered a series of developmental evaluation procedures in Appendix A. Besides those, there are the Bailey, the Peabody, the Denver Developmental, and others. There are scales for evaluating skills of daily living such as the Barthel Index, the Tufts Assessment of Motor Performance, and the Katz index. Tests for coordination include the Purdue Pegboard Test and the Bruininks-Oseretsky Test of Motor Proficiency. Spasticity has been measured with the Ackworth Scale and by the Pendulum test. Balance tests abound, and you saw a list of them earlier in this chapter. For evaluating clients with specific disorders, specific instruments have been developed, such as the Fugl-Meyer Assessment, the Brunnstrom evaluations, and other tests designed for those who have had a stroke. This is only a partial listing to give you some insight into what is available. Your instructor or clinical center may use some of these tests or you may have to do some detective work to find out what is available and how to acquire the information.

You must keep the following questions in mind when selecting such instruments: 1) Is the instrument reliable and valid? and 2) What skill is involved in performing and interpreting the test? Many tests require the individual using them to have accomplished certification through supervised educational experiences. At the very least, the evaluator must be thoroughly familiar with the test and how to apply it.

More importantly, the evaluator must be able to interpret the findings. To do this it is necessary to know under what circumstances the test is reliable and valid. What assumptions have been made? These points are not made to justify or disparage any particular test but to point out that just because it is published or well-known does not make it suit your purposes or provide unblemished data.

A test may be perfectly valid for one type of application but completely invalid for another although it might seem to be appropriate. For instance, manual muscle testing appears to be quite valid and reliable for determining the level of lesion in clients with spinal cord injury, but there has been limited success in predicting functional outcomes based on normal manual muscle test scores. Yet, in our notes and for reports to insurance companies we often use these scores as if they were indicative of functional progress.

> Often there are published evaluation tools that may be helpful. The mere fact of publication does not assure reliability or appropriateness.

Objectivity

Your evaluation needs to be as objective as possible. Thus we often look to the published instruments to provide this objectivity. In some cases the objectivity is more an illusion than a reality. It is also important to understand that the evaluations you perform can be made more objective by your attention to detail and care in attempting to produce some type of measures. Very simple and useful tools for measuring are goniometers, rulers and tape measures, grids painted on the wall or poster board, stopwatches, and video cameras. You will have to be creative in using these tools to measure what you wish to measure. Quite possibly a clearly described observation may be the most appropriately objective finding that you may uncover.

Be sure to define operationally any terms that you use, such as normal, good, fair, weak, moderate, maximal, or independent. For instance, you might define independent as follows: client can safely transfer from chair to bed without assistance. Another category might refer to needing supervision in case there is a need for assistance. Minimal assistance might be defined as able to complete 75% of the task without assistance; another definition might be some specific notation such as requires slight assistance to initiate the sit-to-stand. Obviously, the 75% sounds more objective but do not be fooled. You will have to decide what is 75% of the task; the next therapist might not agree with you and actually may not know by your statement just what portion of the task can be completed independently and what requires assistance.

One Evaluation Model

It is not our intent that the following list and suggestions be taken either as the only approach to evaluation or as an all inclusive list of items to evaluate. It is offered as a guide to developing your own approach. Then, if your list is committed to memory you will always have some idea about where to begin when you are confronted with a new client.

A. Review chart.

B. Determine the client's goals and expectations.

C. Determine the client's habits and lifestyle (eg, what type of activities she engaged in before this problem arose, what problems were present before the current episode).

D. Determine the client's functional status in relation to the client's goals.

E. Determine what is hampering function.

Areas that might require more specific evaluation are as follows:

1. Pain
2. Range of motion and flexibility
3. Muscle strength
4. Endurance
5. Sensation
6. Vision
7. Hearing
8. Balance and Posture
9. Movement patterns-synergies
10. Physical and social environment
11. Cognition
12. Motivation and behavioral considerations

Evaluation Methods

Pain

Pain is a very complex subject. The psychological aspects of pain add to the complexity. You will find many texts and articles on evaluating and treating pain. Most simply, you need to have the client describe the type of pain, explain the circumstances of its appearance, and indicate the areas of the body involved. These might be noted on a front or back diagram of a body. Sometimes it is useful to use intensity scales in which the client rates his pain on a scale from 1 to 10. You will have to define the scales. Zero would likely be no pain and 10 might be the worst pain ever felt. There is considerable research on pain scales if you wish to look into them further.

Range of Motion and Flexibility

Standard goniometry can be used for both active and passive joint ranges. "Eyeball" estimations can almost be as accurate as goniometric measurements to the practiced eye and are certainly acceptable for most evaluations or reevaluations that do not require extremely specific data. Do not forget, however, that accessory motions are an important part of this range. Use your joint mobilization techniques to evaluate and restore any loss of these motions. Joint range and flexibility under functional demands should be assessed as noted below.

Muscle Strength and Endurance

There are several methods of measuring strength. Actually, strength is not easily defined, and different therapists may be referring to different definitions. A physiologist might define strength as the maximum force a muscle can exert along its longitudinal axis. An athlete might be more interested in defining strength as that force a muscle can exert on an external object. Strength might be defined dynamically as the maximum load that can be moved throughout the total range of motion. Bandy and Lovelace-Chandler (1992) define strength as "simply the ability of the muscle to develop force against an unyielding resistance in a single maximal contraction of unrestricted duration." Although such definitions are useful for clarity in research and professional discussions, they do not always relate to what is required to perform a daily activity. Power (performance of work per unit of time) and endurance (ability to repeat a given movement) are concepts related to strength and muscle function.

This information is presented just to keep you from getting too comfortable in your concepts of strength. In therapy, strength may be assessed through manual muscle testing or with dynamometers that give a readout in pounds. Either way, the resistance is applied to freely moving levers and might not be completely relevant to the functional task the client can or cannot perform. Cybex® and other such isokinetic devices will evaluate strength from the perspective of speed and provide a measure of the client's ability to generate torque under different conditions by changing the speed. This aspect of strength may be more relevant to the client's problem than static strength as measured by manual muscle testing.

Functional Measures of Flexibility, Strength, and Endurance

According to Bohannon (1992), muscle strength is known to correlate with a number of specific activities, especially gait. The relationship is the strongest between strength and the gait variables of walking speed,

444

distance, and cadence. Strength has also been shown to correlate with transfers, bed mobility, stair climbing, and wheelchair propulsion in clients with neurologic involvement.

It is important to note that all movements do not occur under the same circumstances. For instance, during gait the lower extremities function differently in stance than in swing phases. During stance the extremity is fixed to the surface and is bearing body weight as the muscles work through reversal of origin-to-insertion contraction. This is in contrast to the freely moving extremity functioning in swing. In these weight bearing activities, strength is more difficult to measure and even, perhaps, to define. These types of movements cannot be ignored because they are likely to be the most important measure for a given client in light of his ability to function.

Normal movement results from the interaction of forces produced at multiple joints. If we attempt to analyze complex motor behavior by assessing the range of motion, sensation, or strength available at each individual joint or segment, we are not likely to determine how that client will perform when presented with a multisegmental movement. Do not forget that pushing someone beyond her base of support is not equivalent to the subtle segmental changes required when stepping over an obstacle or reaching for a heavy book (Keshner 1990).

A functional way to evaluate strength might be to observe the client's attempt at functional activities. While evaluating her ability to perform activities such as rolling over, bed mobility, supine-to-sit, sit-to-stand, squat, gait, reaching, and lifting look for ways of quantifying what you observe. Describe the reactions and abilities carefully. Consider the following:

1. Ability to perform and control a squat-to-stand or a sit-to-stand (uses both concentric and eccentric contractions).

2. Ability to ascend 2- 4- 6- or 8 inch steps with control (concentric) and descend (eccentric). Can this be done step-over-step?

3. Ability to initiate quadriceps activity in a sit-to-stand.

4. Ability to reach for an object overhead and sustain a toe raise.

5. Ability to ambulate up an incline (dorsiflexor muscle strength.

6. Ability to perform a heel-sit to tall-kneeling (hip extensor muscle strength).

7. Ability to negotiate obstacles.

As far as grading is concerned, make up your own scale, but be sure that you define your categories. For instance:

Poor = 1/4 range or inability to move well against gravity.

Fair = 3/5 range or moves against gravity in most planes without difficulty throughout most activities.

445

Good = 4/5 range or can withstand some resistance and hold positions well against gravity.

Activities such as those listed will provide observations through which you can evaluate not only the functional strength of a particular muscle group, such as the quadriceps femoris, but also how many muscles cooperate and interact with others necessary for the task, such as the hip extensors and ankle plantar flexors. The functional requirements of eccentric and concentric contractions under weight or nonweight bearing conditions can be evaluated. The grades have been defined operationally so that everyone knows just what the evaluator means. It is certainly possible for you to define these measures in other ways and to name measures differently than poor, good, and so forth.

These activities can provide insight not only about muscle strength as you have chosen to define it but also about functional range of motion and flexibility, balance, movement patterns, cognitive abilities (eg, Can the client follow your requests and commands?), posture, endurance, and motivation.

Endurance can be evaluated with such activities as measuring how far the client can walk in so many minutes. Measure your hallway and note how many times the client walks it. How fast the client can walk a particular distance such as 10 m provides some additional functional insights.

Sensation

Somatosensory tests are undoubtedly familiar to you. You can test light touch with a cotton tuft, sharp-dull with a safety pin, hot and cold with tubes of water or something similar, proprioception by performing subtle movements of the joints, deep tendon reflexes with a reflex hammer, and vibration with a tuning fork. More complex interactions, such as two-point discrimination, can also be checked.

It is important to understand that you do not need a detailed, full body analysis of sensory abilities. Focus on the areas that are the most relevant, such as the lower extremities for gait and balance, and the hands and upper extremities for object manipulation. Quickly get an overall idea and do a few very specific area tests if needed. If sensation is intact distally, usually proximal tests do not need to be performed. Students often get overly involved in these particular sensory tests that may produce relatively little useful information for determining complex movement problems or what treatment they will be applying. The tests are, of course, primarily of diagnostic value.

Vision

Many components of vision can be investigated. Obviously, a therapist need not perform an evaluation best done by an optometrist or

446

ophthalmologist. Nonetheless, a few aspects can be screened quickly and will provide insight into whether vision may be contributing to the client's difficulty.

First note whether the client has glasses and is wearing them. Many times glasses are put in the hospital night stand and the client's inability to function relates directly to their absence. Certain types of lenses such a bifocals can contribute to difficulty especially with distance relationships, such as with stairs or curbs or objects in the path.

Some visual screenings that you can perform are visual acuity, visual field, and depth perception. Refer to the section on vision for suggestions about performing these evaluations.

Hearing

Try the whisper test. Can the individual understand if you whisper in such a manner that he cannot read your lips? The client may have hearing aids that are not turned on properly or that have been left in his room. You can also test the client's air and bone conduction with a tuning fork. Generally, you can make functional observations about the client's ability to hear and comprehend conversation as you interact with him.

Balance and Posture

You have now read enough to know that are a number of these tests and that they may be related but not as strongly as you might have thought. Chapter 13 and this chapter have provided many insights into balance and vestibular function. We know that some activities tell us about balance but not necessarily about the vestibular function associated with it and vice versa.

Vestibular function is often evaluated by observing the vestibular-ocular responses because few good clinical tests of vestibulospinal function exist (Chandler and Duncan 1993). Note whether or not the client can fix his eyes on a stationary target and maintain his gaze as he rotates his head rapidly. If he is not able to maintain gaxe, he will make corrective saccades to regain gaze fixation. Can the client walk and look from side to side and up or down and maintain balance? Can he read a book and walk at the same time? What is the difference in ability to perform activities with the eyes open and the eyes closed? Static posture may be evaluated with plumb lines and grids in addition to functional posture required for balance and movement.

The platform test findings described in Chapter 13 can be simulated in the clinic by using the sensory integration test ("foam and dome," Figure 15-6). This will provide some idea of the client's ability to solve intersensory conflicts between vision and the somatosensory input by the vestibular system.

Many tests of balance have been noted. A new and well-documented test is the Functional Reach Test, which is a measure of the cone of stability (Duncan et al 1990). This test has been validated and found to be reliable and sensitive to changes and levels of function. It is very inexpensive, easy to perform, and provides a most objective measure. This test should become a very important and basic part of your testing repertoire. The Functional Reach Test provides insight into the client's ability to use information in a feedforward mode as he makes the necessary adjustments to challenge the limits of his cone of stability during self-generated, potentially destabilizing movements.

You will want to evaluate the client's response to unexpected external perturbations as well. You may apply forces at the shoulder, sternum, or pelvis and observe the response. Do not forget that the client should be told to "let me move you, but don't fall" rather than have him rigidly set all his muscles by telling him "don't let me move you". Ankle, hip, or stepping strategies should appear in association with certain perturbations, depending on the intensity with which you apply the force.

Movement Patterns-Synergies

Functional movement patterns as discussed earlier provide insight into how the client constructs movements. The evaluation of hip and ankle strategies as appropriate responses to destabilizing stimuli has been discussed. In addition, you might use proprioceptive neuromuscular facilitation extremity and trunk patterns as a basis for determining the ability to sequence muscle activity appropriately, the strength of components of the movement, the response to facilitatory input (eg, quick stretch, traction, or approximation), the client's response to and comprehension of verbal commands, and the changes that occur in response to touch.

Handling techniques, such as those used in neurodevelopmental treatment approaches, may produce similar insights. In addition, it is possible to evaluate responses against gravity, effects of manual contacts, responses to demand, and other types of responses.

Physical and Social Environment

Using a systems, or dynamic systems, model to guide evaluation and treatment means that we would evaluate the client relative to the physical environment in which that person would be expected to perform certain movements. With babies, that may mean one thing; with adults, it may mean quite another. We watch a baby walking on carpet quite successfully, but it is not successful with the same gait strategy on a highly polished hardwood floor; moreover, the baby will not change its walking strategy to accommodate the slick floor. Watch an adult move from an ice-free environment to one in which the walking surface is ice coated. You will immediately recognize that a change in gait strategy has taken place. Different surfaces require different strategies for locomotion. You will also note that the adult client with a closed head injury may not change strategies in moving from one type surface to another.

How people interact with the client (social context) will greatly affect the motor learning that takes place. Therefore, the therapist also must be concerned with the client's psychosocial milieu. Are the parents of the baby going to be willing to let the baby learn, or will they insist on pulling him to stand and then moving his feet when they are ready for the baby to stand upright and walk? Will the caretakers of an adult wait while the adult learns to adapt to different environments, different strategies, or different tasks, or will they insist that the client cannot learn unless he is properly led to move correctly? Will both the young and the old be so protected from danger that neither has a social environment in which motor learning can effectively take place?

Cognition

Cognitive evaluation can be as simple as determining whether the individual is aware of person, place, and time. Ask him what day it is and where he is. Be certain you take care to understand his interpretation of your questions? He may have been through so many places in the hospital that he is not sure he is in therapy. But if he knows he is in a hospital, he is certainly somewhat oriented. For clients with head injury, the Rancho Los Amigos Levels of Cognitive Functioning exam can be used (Hagen et al 1979; Malkmus 1983).

Motivation and Behavioral Considerations

Complete behavioral assessment should be performed by appropriate professionals; however, the therapist needs to be aware of the impact of that behavior on their therapy. Some notation can be made of the subject's risk-taking behaviors and attitudes and his perceived level of motivation. For pediatric clients, the attitudes and behaviors of the family will be as important as those of the child.

Other Considerations

While this list may appear daunting, you most likely will not perform all those detailed exams on every client. Sometimes you will just want a quick idea about the area. Many pieces of information can be gleaned from one activity. Your targeting the most likely areas of concern will decease the time you will have to spend evaluating specific areas. It does

449

not have to be a long and involved process, but it should be an on-going process.

Evaluation is a process and not a series of tests. Evaluation should focus on the client's abilities, not deficits. It is the abilities that will provide the foundation from which to build a successful treatment program. Furthermore, focusing on what the client has will help with motivation and behavioral considerations. It is always nice to hear that you have something good and it can be enhanced rather than that you do not have this or cannot do that.

An excellent technique is to approach evaluation by asking and answering a series of questions. You can generate questions from your knowledge of motor control as well as from traditional approaches. For instance, answer the following:

What can the client do without assistance, with minimal assistance, and with moderate assistance?
Does the client initiate movement spontaneously?
How smooth are the movements?
How well can the client maintain alignment when he moves, is perturbed, is on a moving surface, or is on a compliant surface?
Is the client confused by movement or clutter in his environment?
How does the client compensate for his deficits?
Does he rely on particular sensory cues for movement?
Is the client aligned symmetrically at rest or in required movements?
Does he have the ability to shift weight while sitting and standing?
Can the client assume a position? Can he maintain it?
Does the client consider his own safety?
How much effort does the client expend in the activity?
Is there limitation of motion?
Is his strength adequate for the task?

Try putting your evaluation process into questions such as those above. That practice should automatically help you generate additional questions and give you a better insight into what and why you are evaluating and how you might approach treatment.

Study Questions:

1. Prepare an evaluation outline that you believe will work for you and then list some of the procedures you will want to remember to perform under each part of the outline. What questions will you ask?

2. Determine some objective measures you may use and operationally define them so they may be communicated to other professionals.

450

Chapter 16 - Treatment Suggestions for General Disorders of Motor Control

NOTE: Portions of this section are from Crutchfield et al (1989), reprinted with permission.

It should be clear by now that motor control appears to involve a complex interaction of many systems and subsystems of which the nervous system is only one. The environment, or context, in which the movement occurs shares equally with the elaboration of neuromuscular responses in determining the movement that will be generated. By now, it is probably also clear that balance underlies most movement and that postural control, muscular strength, pattern timing, and so forth have direct impact on balance. Most of the following suggestions for activities or approaches are useful, in whole or in part, for all aspects of motor control whether it be termed balance, coordination, or simply the ability to move.

> Our new understanding of motor control reflects a rethinking of the mechanisms underlying therapeutic practice, and it provides relevant guidelines for applying our present techniques.

Using a systems approach to assess components of abnormal postural control enhances the breadth of treatment techniques that may be used to resolve balance problems. A rich array of treatment procedures and possibilities reside in the evaluation procedures themselves. Most, if not all, of the methods and mechanisms used for evaluation of movement, balance, and coordination can be repeated and practiced for treatment effects. If, for example, your client has difficulty with the portion of the balance examination in which sensory conflicts are tested by standing on a foam pad, practice standing on the foam pad itself would certainly constitute a reasonable treatment procedure.

Disorders of motor control involving balance and coordination are present in clients with many kinds of diagnoses, including upper motor neuron lesions. The reasons for such dysfunction in movements and postures are multiple and varied. If clients are evaluated systematically and if the underlying neurophysiologic mechanisms are understood, appropriate treatment procedures will be developed.

The activities presented here under general exercises provide a graded series of exercises for balance and movement, using various methods for changing the sensory conditions. One begins with the very simplest postures and movements and progresses to more complex balance and movement skills. Practice of simple, active weight shifts in gradually increasing ranges is appropriate for clients beginning remediation of balance deficits. As clients improve, availability of sensory cues during practice of balance should be systematically altered. As the client gains mastery of relatively simple postures and movements, the same sensory conditions can be used for such complex movements as walking and complex balance activities. For instance, once a client can stand, perform weight shifts, and do spiral, diagonal trunk movements on a foam pad, have her walk on a foam mattress or floor mat.

All of these activities should be useful for achieving control of problems of muscular gain, timing, and sequencing which may manifest themselves in dysfunctional movement or inadequate balance skills or both. After the section on general exercises, some ideas concerning specific problems that were evaluated in the assessment section will be presented. These include specifically addressing disorders of the following: movement strategies, anticipatory postural adjustments, and sensory organization.

> Variety in experiences is a critical part of rehabilitation.

A very important concept in treating clients with movement dysfunction is that a wide variety of experiences should be provided. Aspects of the treatment program, such as amplitude, duration, direction, intensity, and speed, should be varied. Clients must experience different kinds of supporting surfaces. The client who can function on a tile floor in your clinic most likely will continue to have difficulty at home on carpet or gravel. These conditions must be a part of the client's experience during his training regimen.

General Exercises for Balance and Postural Control

Exercises described in Chapter 13 (Tabs 13-3 and 13-4) may be used in conjunction with these exercises, and some are quite similar. The exercises may begin with the very simplest and progress onward. Every exercise described can be modified further by altering the visual cues the client has available. This alteration may be done by diminishing visual input (by using dark glasses), by limiting peripheral vision (with goggles), or by removing vision (by closing the eyes or blindfolding the client). Visual inaccuracies may be presented with the visual hood or globe.

At any point, the therapist may provide perturbations to increase the difficulty level and change conditions. Perturbations should be graded in intensity and presented in a variety of directions and to different parts of the body. Other activities that stress the system by adding more input are to move the head by nodding, rotating it from side to side, or moving it diagonally while sitting, standing, or walking. The eyes can be moved in the same patterns by themselves or with head movements.

Remember that most of the evaluation procedures for balance that have been researched involve only the anterior-posterior planes. Obviously, everyone needs to move in all planes, and although specific research findings may not address different planes, exercises should address movement in general. For effective training the client will need to be challenged rather than to practice by simply repeating exercises.

452

Professionals should be supervising on the spot so that when balance is compromised or lost the client will be protected.

Sitting

It may be necessary to begin treatment under very stable conditions by using the sitting position. The client should sit on the edge of a chair, maintain good alignment, and do simple weight shifts from right to left and forward and backward. These should be done while attempting to enlarge the area of the weight shift and continuing to maintain stability. Change the visual cues and add perturbations.

More complex balance activities require sufficient postural control to perform movements that have a much greater range than the weight shifts performed in simpler activities. Again, it will be useful to do these activities by varying the visual cues and providing perturbations as described previously.

In sitting, more complex activities may begin with trunk rotations. Proprioceptive neuromuscular facilitation activities in diagonal rotational patterns can be used. Include the head in the movements. Add the arms so that reaching up and back to the left occurs with reversal of motion down and forward to the right. These proprioceptive neuromuscular facilitation activities are commonly called lifts and chops. If the client has difficulty keeping the arms together, have him hold a medium sized ball or some such object in the hands.

More complicated routines may be developed. Also, the client may sit on a Swiss gymnastics ball rather than on a rigid chair. This change in supporting surface requires new and additional postural adjustments to perform the activities. In addition, the therapist may impart a wide range of postural demands by simply manipulating the ball. An infinite variety of activities may be devised for use with the gymnastics ball not only for sitting but also for prone and supine trunk-supported activities. These exercises may incorporate various alterations in the visual feedback that the client experiences.

Standing

Activities that were used to evaluate standing balance make very useful treatment programs. For beginning balance activities, the goal is to keep the body in good alignment while systematically changing the conditions of the exercises. Activities should be performed while changing visual cues and providing perturbations.

The first level of difficulty includes weight shifts performed in standing. These may be voluntary postural sway type movements. The client should weight shift forward and backward and side to side, attempting to

453

enlarge the area of the sway and still maintain stability so that the vertical can be reassumed appropriately.

Shifting the body mass should be practiced while maintaining vertical alignment, with changes in the support surface. Have the client stand on his toes and on his heels. Another variation would be to stand first on one foot and then the other. Standing on the foam rubber platform that was made for sensory conflict testing will provide another challenge for postural adjustments. This condition may be varied by having the client stand on the platform first with one foot and then the other. Standing on the heels and then on the toes while on the foam platform should be tried. The client can stand on a tilt board to provide an unstable base of support. The therapist may shift the tilt board laterally and forward and backward, or the client may impart the tilt to the board by voluntarily shifting body weight in the desired direction.

Put the visual globe or hood, used during testing, on the client's head. All of the weight shifts and perturbations can then be repeated under these conditions. The foam rubber platform and the visual globe or hood should be combined to provide a very challenging and complex condition for these activities.

The above material provides an adequate list of suggestions and examples of methods for varying the sensory conditions and postural requirements to develop standing balance and postural set. With a knowledge of the postural mechanism and a little imagination and practice, an infinite variety of activities that expand on these presented may be developed.

To gain control of larger movements and more complex activities some clients must begin with simple rocking of the weight forward and backward as if to take a step. The client progresses to forward and backward stepping and then to walking. More complicated activities include movements of the head and neck. The upper extremities may be added, as in forward and upward reaching.

Spiral diagonal proprioceptive neuromuscular facilitation patterns may be used to incorporate rotation in the trunk. The client should lift both arms up and back to the left, following with his eyes and head, and rotate them down and forward to the right side. The knees are bent, and the movement is followed with the head.

Clients who do not have vertigo or great disequilibrium may also begin in this manner, but you will want to minimize the breakup of continuous movement such as walking by limiting work such as weight shifts.

More Complex Movement Activities

Many familiar developmental movements and activities are useful in working with individuals who have movement dysfunction. These movements provide a variety of experiences and a range in difficulty relative to the number of weight-bearing joints and to the demands on particular muscular patterns of activity. Rolling over, moving from prone or supine into sitting, kneeling, creeping, walking, and cross-over walking--or braiding--are good examples of complex activities. Obstacle courses, balance beam walking, marching, and walking on the commands of "start" and "stop" provide other avenues of variety and difficulty for practice and improvement.

Activities that demand and develop total body coordination and balance include swimming, skipping, jumping, hopping, hopscotch, and jumping rope. Dancing and activities with music and rhythm are useful.

At the highest level of demand, for those clients who are ready, are organized games, which may be modified for particular purposes as necessary. Wallyball, volleyball, hopscotch, dodge ball, croquet, miniature golf, roller-skating, and bicycling are but a few examples of pleasurable recreational activities that provide social interaction and require balance, agility, and coordination of all body parts. Obviously, clients must have the necessary postural control to perform in these activities. Practicing inappropriate movements under the stressful demands of such recreational activities could hinder progress and produce frustration. Appropriate modification of the activity will minimize such hindrances.

Activities for Selected Problems

Biomechanical Factors

Any abnormalities in joint range of motion, muscle strength, and other nonneural components of balance must first be corrected. As mentioned earlier, these conditions may be the sole cause or may contribute to abnormalities in equilibrium, lack of postural control, or abnormal movement. At least one individual (G. Cummings, personal communication, February, 1993) has related particular clinical incidents concerning peripheral biomechanical effects. The talus was subluxed in children who had plantar flexion postures and contractures. Mobilizing the joint and bringing the talus forward decreased the plantar flexion and improved the gait and balance.

Cusick and Stuberg (1992) indicate that at least 13 biomechanical factors can contribute to lower extremity malalignment in the transverse plane.

Children with neuromotor dysfunction commonly exhibit these problems in malalignment, which impose forces that affect normal skeletal structure and joint alignment. The authors cite a number of tests for assessing these problems. Although many of these procedures lack reliability and validity data or have other limitations, they provide a rich array of tools for clinical use. These authors clearly understand the relationship of biomechanical factors to motor function and dysfunction and the necessity for the clinician to be aware of the developmental and maturational changes that occur in these tissues.

Various types of platform systems, such as the BAPS® (biomechanical ankle platform system) and KATBB (kinesthetic ability training balance board) have been designed to develop strength, endurance, and range of motion at the ankle. Studies show that working on these devices may be useful in enhancing static balance and coordination. One study (France et al 1992) showed that subjects using the KATBB improved in static balance compared with a control group. Thus muscular and biomechanical elements appear to be components of balance; changing these elements may affect balance control.

Improper Motor Strategies

Certain clients may not be able to access certain synergies. For example, clients may not exhibit a hip synergy when that should be the most effective pattern. The ankle synergy is often not an available choice for clients who have diminished or absent somatosensory input. Methods that might be used to facilitate an ankle synergy include using many of the standing weight-shift activities listed in the general exercises. In the beginning, it may be necessary to keep the range of sway very small and controlled. Graded perturbations should begin with very slight amplitudes and slow speeds.

Certainly, more stable surfaces that are broad and noncompliant will be required initially. Begin on a wood, tile, or concrete floor. Progressions would include less compliant surfaces such as carpet and then perhaps floor mats. The objective of this progression would be to elicit the ankle synergy under progressively more difficult conditions. When the supporting surface becomes so noncompliant that an ankle synergy could not be effective, the limits for eliciting this synergy have been exceeded.

One clue, of course, that the client has no ankle synergy is that he responds to all postural demands, including slight perturbations, with a hip synergy. If this response occurs, the therapist may stabilize the hips manually with compression and resistance. Such techniques should decrease the movements at the hip. If these movements are suppressed, the client may respond favorably to smaller arcs of sway and begin to gain some control of movement at the ankle. Squatting is another position in which it is biomechanically difficult to use the hip synergy.

456

Rocking back and forth in a squat position should require ankle activity. Standing on an incline may also help to force activity at the ankle.

Progression may include varying visual cues, as described in the general exercise section. Although the client may not have difficulty resolving intersensory conflicts, the increased demand required when vision is altered should provide a further progression of difficulty for eliciting an ankle synergy.

Sensory stimuli may be offered under a number of circumstances. Specific muscles in the synergy can be facilitated with vibration or other sensory stimuli. Approximation of the ankle may be useful to enhance sensory feedback, through the joints and bottoms of the feet, to aid the client in awareness. Somatosensory input through the skin may be increased by having the client barefooted.

For clients who lack a hip synergy, activities that limit the effectiveness of ankle rotation are likely to be the best choices because they would force a hip synergy to be used. Standing on a balance beam either forward or sideways will minimize the usefulness of the ankle synergy and should be helpful in developing the hip synergy. Tandem walking with a heel-toe alignment, walking on a rail, and standing on one foot require the hip synergy to maintain equilibrium. Any position or activity that favors the hip synergy may be used to try to elicit it.

> Clients may not be able to construct proper patterns, or synergies, to accomplish the task. Hip and ankle strategies are examples of such patterns.

The client must know what the objectives of the exercises are and what the expected result will be. With this knowledge and the cognitive awareness of the body and its movements, it should be easier for the client to learn the correct responses. With repetition and variation in demand, the automatic nature of the responses should develop. Practice and experience in many different contexts will help in developing adaptability to the environment. (See motor learning case study in Chapter 17).

Some clients will have disorders within a synergy. Some clients with spastic hemiplegia have been shown to have a reversal of muscle activation within a synergy. Such disorders within synergies will be more difficult problems to treat than problems with accessing synergies. Although palpation can confirm muscle contraction, it is not likely to be sensitive enough to determine a few milliseconds difference in the onset of contractions. Instead, you must rely on your knowledge of the correct order of muscle activity in the synergy that you wish to facilitate. Using this knowledge, try to facilitate the correct order of the muscles using vibration, tapping, and other facilitatory input while eliciting weight shifts, performing perturbations, and so forth.

If the equipment is available, a biofeedback machine and an electrical stimulator can be rigged to produce stimulation to the desired muscle when some other muscle or a switch has been activated. This immediate feedback with a stimulus strong enough to cause a muscle contraction may be very effective in eventually changing the sequence.

Remember that most research involving such synergies often addresses only the hip, ankle, and stepping strategies in the anterior-posterior plane. Keep this limitation in mind when you develop programs and evaluation procedures for your clients. Undoubtedly, other strategies exist, particularly in other planes of movement or under different conditions, such as when perturbations are provided at the waist, pelvis, or shoulders rather than through a platform moving under the feet. Keshner (1990) discovered that response patterns do not always occur in a distal to proximal sequence. Individuals have distinct response patterns, but they vary among individuals. She suggests that muscles are activated from a variety of sensory inputs and that the central nervous system should provide multiple alternatives for achieving postural stability. Normal postural control mechanisms are more complex than described by Nashner's model.

Lack of Anticipatory Adjustments

Your client may not be capable of rapid movements or may become unstable when reaching for an object. As discussed in the assessment section, the prerequisites to these movements are the anticipatory adjustments. If the preparatory activities are missing or delayed, you must attempt to facilitate them.

One step might be to identify any weight shifts involved, then simplify the movements and restrict the client to using the desired ones. Many of the activities listed in the general exercises may be useful. Hand weights, ankle weights, medicine balls, and other such devices may be useful in accentuating body shifts in preparation for a movement. Try activities such as raising an arm to the side or holding or throwing a medicine ball.

Anticipatory adjustments may be lacking because the timing of muscular onset in the pattern is affected, particularly by muscles that are delayed in onset. Proprioceptive neuromuscular facilitation patterns may be helpful in developing proper timing. A technique that may prove particularly useful is timing for emphasis.

Use your hands to provide feedback for the desired movement. Mirrors and grids may help the client get a feeling for what is necessary. Do weight shifts first in sitting and then move to standing. Practice and repetition with a variety of conditions are required. Vary the visual and somatosensory feedback as well by leaving the eyes closed or doing the shifts on different surfaces. The client needs to understand what should occur; for instance, he should know to shift his weight backward automatically if he is to lift a weight forward. Stimulate required muscles, if desired, by using vibration, touch, ice, electrical stimulation, or biofeedback.

Sensory Organization Problems

Subjects with balance and coordination disorders may be dependent on one particular sensory system for stability. In many cases they do not have the ability to resolve intersensory conflicts. When incorrect or confusing visual or somatosensory information is present, staggering, falling, or moving abnormally may occur.

For clients who heavily depend on visual information, it will be necessary to increase their reliance on somatosensory and vestibular input. These clients will need experience and practice with most of the activities listed in the general exercises. Most likely it will be necessary to begin with weight shifts after vision has been eliminated by closing the client's eyes or blindfolding the client. If that makes it too difficult for the client, visual cues should be diminished, such as with dark glasses, rather than be eliminated. Fabricating blinders or using goggles might help to decrease the input from peripheral vision to narrow the scope of visual information. Clients can be progressed to more and more complex positions and movements with visual alterations.

Visual stimuli can be used to assist stability. Clients may visually fixate on an object to aid their balance. One experiment concerning the effect of eye movements on dynamic equilibrium showed, however, that having normal subjects track a moving visual stimulus had a negative effect on balance (Schulmann et al 1987). It is thus likely that the type of visual stimulus and the manner of its presentation will have a significant effect on the rehabilitation program.

> Some individuals cannot solve intersensory conflicts when they arise, which destabilizes them and impairs their balance.

Other clients may not be able to resolve intersensory conflicts. The same movements and positions just referred to can be used with conditions of inaccurate visual and somatosensory input. The client can stand, do weight shifts, produce dynamic movements, and walk on uneven surfaces, such as in sand and on foam rubber, carpet, floor mats, or other surfaces. All of these should be done with alterations in visual cueing by using a blindfold, goggles, sunglasses, and the visual hood or globe that was made for assessing responses to visual conflicts (Fig 15-6).

The principles of motor learning presented in Chapter 14 should be considered when devising treatment programs. The type and schedule of feedback and guidance and the structure of the treatment session will most likely have powerful effects on the true learning that takes place and the ultimate functional outcome of the experience.

Remember also that carry over from one type of balance to another may not be great. We are not certain as to the components or prerequisites of particular movements. Always keep your program in perspective. While working on weight shift or static balance, which are necessary for their own intrinsic value, remember that they are not likely to transfer automatically to increased balance control during gait, which also will have to be incorporated into the program as soon as posible.

Study Questions:

1. Describe a sequence of exercises you might prescribe for a client who has vestibular involvement and poor balance.

2. Explain the difference in approach for biomechanical problems and lack of anticipatory action.

3. Describe how to approach treatment when there is difficulty within a synergy.

Visual Problems

Remember that the client may have visual impairments he cannot overcome and that these deficits must be considered and compensated for as much as possible during movement. To the extent that properly prescribed and fitting lenses are available, they should worn by the client during therapy and should be accessible whenever they might be needed. Also visual distortions caused by bifocals and such lenses must be taken into account when engaging in motor activities.

Although your role may be to suggest a full eye examination to a client or to indicate that you believe the lenses he wears may need reevaluation, you may also consider prescribing some visual-motor exercises. These are often most useful for helping the client compensate for vestibular dysfunction by enhancing visual skills. Ocular muscle exercises, or orthoptics, can be useful in enhancing the fusion of the image of one eye with that of the other to produce stereoscopic vision. You already encountered numerous eye-head exercises that may be practiced for this purpose (Tab 13-3; Tab 13-6). In addition, other activities are described in the vestibular case studies in Chapter 17.

The therapist needs to become familiar with visual screening and treatment approaches that can be incorporated in the clinic. Vision is extremely important part of motor control and motor learning, and we have often failed to realize its value.

Additional eye exercises:

Table 16-1

Eye Exercises

Sitting with head still, move eyes up, down, and side to side as far as possible.

Focus on finger moving toward nose. Start at arms length and work to begin closer.

Without moving head, slowly roll eyes in both clockwise and counterclockwise directions, making a complete circle. Repeat counterclockwise. Start with small circles and expand.

Trace a line from the upper left corner of a wall to the lower right. Repeat from the upper right to lower left, lower right to upper left, and lower left to upper right.

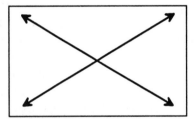

Visually trace a figure-of-eight horizontally and then vertically on the wall.

If eyes fatigue, stop and rest them. Exercise for 4 or 5 minutes and then rest with eyes closed for 1 minute.

Summary of Treatment Considerations

The treatment approach to a neurological client is often an extension or repetition of the conditions and activities set up and performed in the evaluation. If the client cannot walk on compliant surfaces, for instance, practice in that activity may be the most appropriate treatment. Some of the treatment considerations that have been discussed in this text are summarized on the following pages.

Tasks

Therapists must think in terms of functional tasks as opposed to specific activities that may or may not lead to efficient and effective movement.

When presented with a client whose goal is to walk, at some point, preferably early, we will evaluate that client in an upright, moving mode. We will not wait until we have strengthened her; worked on her range of motion; built up motor unit activity in the bridging position; and then advanced to sit-to-stand motions, to standing, and then to walking. Although some of all of these elements may be necessary, they must be put in perspective. For instance, bridging may be a necessary task for many clients, but it certainly does not provide all the prerequisites for walking. The biomechanics of moving upright are not the same as those required for upright standing, and the requirements for kneeling are quite different from those for bridging. Likewise, the preparatory muscle activity, the choice of a strategy, the muscle synergies and timing, and the muscle strength requirements are not the same from one task to another.

> All motor activities are task-specific. Therapists must consider functional activities.

Although some elements gained in one task may be helpful in another, they do not directly transfer and are not developmentally linked. The systems therapist will think in terms of specific functional tasks as opposed to considering activities that build on one another to accomplish some future goal and will evaluate clients relative to those specific goal-achieving tasks. It is important to use immediately any element gained in one task by following it with the desired task. Thus if we work on dorsiflexion in the supine posture and then bridging but wish to have dorsiflexion come in during gait, immediately follow the supine work with dorsiflexion while upright. Then quickly try to use the full gait cycle because gait is a continuous task.

If the client is not entirely successful in moving efficiently in the middle of a task, such as walking, it may be necessary to break the task into parts to detect correctly the component that is causing the dysfunction. It may be that a muscle group is not strong enough to participate in movement when it is appropriate for that group to do so. Perhaps the range of motion is not available, which could be a neurologic or an orthopedic problem. Perhaps the onset of muscular contraction is delayed. Whatever the cause, we may need to treat it separately to enhance that element before it will function appropriately within the task. Again, the key to success is that therapists should immediately attempt to use any improved isolated components within a functional movement.

It seems clear that if lack of strength is the problem in the stance phase of gait, then sufficient strength to overcome the problem might be best gained by using strengthening measures in an upright, weight-bearing position because to do so will place the muscles in the position specific to the task.

Malouin et al (1992) used a task-oriented gait training program with clients who had acute cerebrovascular accidents. By using a suspension harness mechanism they were able to initiate treadmill walking in the first 2 weeks after their strokes. Although this particular case study is fraught with procedural errors, it suggests an interesting possibility for early gait training. Vanderlinden et al (1993) report that individuals with hemiparesis exhibit weight bearing asymmetries when performing the sit-to-stand movement and that the movement time is prolonged. Most likely these deviations make the movement more difficult. The investigators suggest that it might be appropriate to train symmetrical weight bearing in dynamic tasks as well as static tasks. Additionally, increasing the speed of the movement may make the task easier and more effective. In fact, if the problem seems to be the timing in an activity such as gait, simply speeding up the gait pattern may change the timing pattern, which alters the gait. We often require movments to be practiced too slowly for functional requirements.

One way to measure functional activity would be to record the amount of time required to complete the task. Light and Rehm (1993) suggest that timing activities, such as lie-to-sit, sit-to-stand, ambulating forward 20 feet, side stepping 10 feet, climbing 5 stairs, and the reversal of these movements, may provide a desirable clinical tool for objectively measuring functional motility.

To assess and facilitate functional activities, good functional assessment tools will be necessary. Most published functional analyses or motor performance evaluations sample global functional skills and either are judgment based or require limited standardization for administration. They also are not applicable for motor assessment across the life span. Haley and Ludlow (1992) have provided evidence that the Tufts Assessment of Motor Performance can be used to describe the motor performance of adults and school-aged children with physical disabilities. This assessment includes activities such as writing, typing, cutting, placing objects, putting on clothes, manipulating fasteners, mat mobility, wheelchair function, transfers, and balance.

We have already noted that tasks may be categorized along a continuum from closed to open. Some tasks are simple and easy to perform because they do not change from one attempt to another and the environment in which they occur is stable and relatively unchanging. However, most everyday tasks do involve variation; the conditions change from one attempt to another. Even if we are simply reaching forward to grasp a beverage container, these objects vary in shapefrom glasses to cups or mugs, in size from large to small, and in texture from glass to plastic or polystyrene. Each requires that the movement change to grasp and manipulate it effectively. If the client is to practice drinking from a cup, a cup must be present. If drinking or the movements that are preparatory for drinking are the skills involved, the container must have fluid in it.

Goal setting is extremely important. But it is critical that therapists understand that they are not the ones in sole charge of setting the goals. If treatment is to be successful, it must address the clients' goals.

Other Systems

It is imperative that therapists remember that the inability to achieve certain functional goals may be caused by a malfunctioning subsystem that is not in the neuromusculoskeletal triad. Because vision, for example, can certainly alter gait and other activities, it is a serious waste of time to consider that system only when all else has failed. Sometimes simply finding a client's glasses and encouraging the client to wear them will correct dysfunctional gait, habit, and errors. Vision is a vital sense for motor control as you have learned. Unfortunately, we have often ignored it and failed to evaluate vision or use, train, and incorporate it into the treatment program. This failing needs to be corrected.

There may not be one specific deficit that accounts for the client's problems. Balance and motor control are complex and involve multiple systems. It is important to realize that small changes or deficits across multiple domains often combine to cause difficulties that are not apparent when concentrating on one system or domain. It is possible that one system is the greatest contributor to a problem. It is also possible that changes in one domain, such as muscular strength, may compensate for losses in systems that cannot be corrected.

An enormously important justification can be made for the therapist's need to attend to the dietary and water intake of clients, particularly older adults. For example, if there is not sufficient calcium available for the neuromusculoskeletal system, you can attempt to strengthen muscles for an eternity to no avail. And if water, with all it trace elements, is not available in sufficient qualities, neither the circulatory nor the neuromusculoskeletal systems will function appropriately, and functional tasks will be difficult to accomplish. Indeed, it is difficult to think of any one of any of the body's systems that a therapist can justifiably ignore without sacrifice to the client.

Pain

> Normal movement cannot be superimposed over pain.

Pain is certainly a paramount consideration if for no other reason than that normal movement cannot be superimposed over pain. Normal movement is defined as movement that allows us to accomplish a task without doing danger to other functional tasks that are also desirable. Normal movement for our purposes is not always that beautifully coordinated motion that the ballet artist achieves; it need not be smooth and pretty, but it allows the individual to accomplish functional tasks. Thus it becomes normal for that particular client. Pain, therefore, must be diminished to a point where this normal-for-the-client movement can result in the accomplishment of tasks.

Development Continues Across the Life Span

With infants and children, we need first to identify age-appropriate tasks and then to determine whether the child has the appropriate strength, range of motion, and transitory skills to perform the tasks. Age-appropriate tasks do not dictate that we follow the developmental sequence in the promotion of function. For example, creeping is not a prerequisite for standing and walking. In our culture the majority of children creep before they walk, but in cultures in which creeping is devalued or disallowed, children learn to walk perfectly well without it.

As a society and as a profession, we often consider aging to be a series of losses; that we "develop" no longer. This should be rethought to include normal changes or expected developments throughout the life span. Many of our attitudes are based on expectations of what will occur as we age. Researchers are just beginning to find out what actually happens with aging and whether changes can be made. Current research is showing that much of our capacities can remain, some can be expanded, and even some losses can be regained.

Balance abilities change across the life span. Body sway increases with age. Anacker and Di Fabio (1992) studied the influence of sensory inputs on standing balance in community-dwelling elders with a recent history of falling. They discovered that orientation input from the ankle appears to have a greater influence on preventing falls than visual references do. Thus it would seem prudent to emphasize the development of somatosensory orientation for elder clients.

Although balance capacity diminishes with increasing age, Era (1988) showed that balance is trainable. Three groups of elderly men were trained for 8 weeks. The first group received isometric and dynamic exercises for increasing limb and trunk strength, the second received gymnastics such as weight bearing, flexibility, and rhythmic exercises. The results showed that both of the training groups had less body sway than the control group that had no training. Johansson and Jarnlo (1991) tested healthy 70-year-old women in standing on one leg with various visual situations, walking along a beam, walking in a figure-of-eight, and walking as fast as possible. The balance training consisted of walking in different directions at different speeds, often combined with movements of the arms, neck, and trunk. Many dancing steps and weight transfer exercises while sitting, standing, and rising were used. The experimental group improved in most of the tests, including the ability to stand on one leg. The control group did not. Again these studies show that the elderly can improve their movement and balance abilities and that a variety of functional, goal-directed movements produce the most effective outcomes. Additionally, these studies suggest a direct link between muscular strength or level of activity and some balance measures.

In a research project involving high-intensity training, significant improvements were obtained despite of preexisting problems with hypertension, osteoporotic fractures, coronary artery disease, and other less than desirable conditions. Additionally, the subjects were on gastrointestinal, cardiovascular, neuropsychiatric, analgesic, and other medications. And the "not well" subjects of this research were all over 90 years of age (Fiatarone et al 1990). It would appear that we can help to keep people up and moving until very near the end of life.

> Preferred patterns of activity change across the life span. Important changes can be accomplished at any age.

The concept that motor development continues across the life span is a critical one that we are just beginning to gather data to support. As you noted in the chapter on rolling, there are developmental sequences that are age-related in that they continue throughout life, and it will be necessary for us to begin to identify them. Variation is the norm, and this understanding of the normal provides us with many more possibilities for training. There is no right way, for example, to roll or get up from the floor. There are many ways to do this, and the way chosen often is dictated by the environment in which the task occurs. The strength and activity level of the individual also influences the types of patterns that will emerge.

There are some basic assumptions that you should be able to make regarding the evaluation and treatment of infants, children, young adults and older adults, from the information you now have on just how motor learning takes place, what constitutes effective motor control, and how such control is developed. Additionally, you now have a working relationship with just how the visual, somatosensory, and vestibular systems interact to promote, adjust, and control movement.

From a reflex perspective, in the traditional past we might have been interested in inhibiting certain reflexes and facilitating others. In a systems approach, functional goals would not include the inhibition of primitive reflexes and the facilitation of postural reactions. However, a functional goal may be the promotion of hands to midline in the sitting position on a beach ball, achieved by having the child reach for objects while moving in various planes. The dominant motor synergies will become modified and others preferred, with practice. You might note that this approach seems to have the same effect as inhibiting the reflex pattern. In some respects, this is true; however, the active participation of the child in a functional outcome is drastically different than the passive positioning and handling for modifying the client's patterns.

Applying Motor Learning Principles to Treatment

Motor Learning Versus Performance

Therapists are interested in the motor learning that takes place on the part of the client as opposed to the client being able perform a motor task for the therapist. An example of motor performance might be that the client can dorsiflex his foot very nicely in the clinic, but when he tries to walk in a home environment or in the theater, will the foot dorsiflex at the appropriate time, in the appropriate order (or synergy), and with sufficient strength to enable him to negotiate the carpeted inclines and stairs? Will he have the correct strategy? Can he solve any intersensory conflict? Will he be flexible in changing context? In other words, did learning really take place or did the client merely perform for the therapist? Motor learning is the key to successful movement.

> Motor learning principles are the keys to developing successful movement.

Remember that skill development occurs in two stages (Gentile 1987). In the initial stages, the performer is trying out movements and patterns to find what works. Movements are stiff and lack smoothness because the individual must first control the degrees of freedom through cocontraction of opposing muscle groups. Give the client an opportunity to be stiff and uncoordinated. If learning is to be successful, the client must be an active problem solver. Thus his less-than-perfect early performances are required as part of the progression toward skill. Skill cannot be imposed by the therapist. We will have to learn to accept and prepare the client for the fact that early in treatment he may not appear to be mastering the movements or progressing as rapidly in that session as we might wish. The client needs to be his own error detector so he can learn by exploring and making mistakes. Therapists, clients, and third party payers need to understand that there is much to learn on bad days from poor performances.

In the early stages, the therapist can be most helpful in selecting a task with which the client can be somewhat successful. Certainly, the goal of the movement should be clear. Use the movement taxonomy described in Chapter 14 (Fig 14-7) to help determine the demands various movements place on the client. Rather than immediately describing to the client what he is to do, describe the task and let him decide how he might attempt it. If necessary, suggest general ideas about the movement form, but let the client work out the details. There must be concern for the environment in which the action will take place and an opportunity for the client to pick up information from that environment to solve the movement problem. Some individuals are efficient learners and will not repeat unsuccessful movements. Others are not so efficient and will persist in repeating such patterns. Therapists should discourage the latter tendencies.

> Structuring the environment is critical to successful motor learning.

467

An important task for the therapist to use to facilitate learning is to set up the environment so that all the conditions that regulate the desired movement are present. If you want the client to walk at home, then ambulation in an empty hallway will not provide the conditions necessary for him to achieve that functional outcome. You will want to discourage compensatory strategies, such as leaning away from the affected side or using asymmetrical weight bearing patterns. Set up the environment so that he has to reach for something that makes him bear weight evenly.

Practice and Feedback

It has been shown that the single most important predictor of how the individual will perform a task is how much time has been spent in practice. Skill is developed only through practice. Realizing that practice is more than simple repetition of the same pattern is crucial to effective health care. Carefully structure your client's practice sessions and consider the research that suggests some forms of practice may enhance performance while others will result in more permanent learning.

Practice will not be useful and result in achieving the desired goals if the movements practiced are not those that are desired. You do not want the client to develop one fixed habitual mode of movement and thus stop far short of achieving skill. The individual must be challenged to construct movements that are appropriate for different conditions. During everyday life we experience a wide variety of conditions. The gym of the therapy department must be modified and augmented if skill building in functional tasks is to occur.

As therapists, we often engage in guidance and feedback activities with our clients. Remember that constant and immediate feedback often results in good performance but poor learning. To be productive, we need to examine the feedback schedules we use and the type of feedback we give to alter them to obtain a maximal result. Remember that you will want to use augmented feedback but not redundant feedback. The client has already gained information from attempting the movement. The type of feedback you give should be in addition to that and bring in information to which he does not have immediate access. Trial and error are not foul words. Do your best to determine the most likely course of action and try it. If it does not work, try something else. The only unprofessional behavior a therapist can exhibit is *persisting* in activities that do not result in some desired outcome.

Feedforward processes must be addressed during the practice sessions that are structured for the client.

Further, it is important to remember that many, if not most, of our daily activities involve *feedforward* processes. Most movements involve predictive elements and conditions. Information gained through feedback is used to refine these processes and produce more effective and skillful movements in the future. It is absolutely necessary to include feedforward experiences in therapeutic practice.

Functional Activity Versus Discrete Task Activity

Practice and experience should be developed within functional activities. While flexing the elbow with a weight in hand, the client learns only to flex the elbow with a weight in her hand. That discrete task may enable the client to strengthen her elbow flexors, but it does nothing to suggest to the client which biomechanical elements, type of force control, errors in strategy or timing, or preparatory activities are necessary for her to learn in order for her to comb her hair. The functional activity is the goal, and if at all possible, the muscle should be strengthened within the goal activity. Most functional movements are not likely to be discrete tasks, so execssive time should not be spent on such activities.

Traditionally, our evaluation and treatment regimens have been geared toward accomplishing one thing at a time. We had to have adequate range of motion before we were interested in muscle strength. First we were interested in movement at the hip joint and then we worked on the ankle joint. We sought reflex control before incorporating voluntary control, and so on. But therapists need to be looking at how all of the systems are interacting as the client attempts to accomplish some functional goal. A client could have adequate muscle strength and range of motion, appropriate strategies, and necessary abilities to detect error in what she is doing, but an environmental distraction related to hearing problems could cause her to fall. All systems interact to provide adequate motor control for functional activity.

Carr et al (1987) strongly indicate that rehabilitation should be based on a framework of motor learning. The task should be analyzed, goals identified, and practice at the task instituted. In one analysis a client showed a tendency to slump in her chair. Because she used a flexed sitting posture before her stroke, she was undoubtedly predisposed to poor sitting skills. The simple provision of a lumbar support to tilt the spine made it easier for her to move and also to practice active extension of the spine more effectively. As a result, she could move more easily and began to take more notice of her surroundings. Clearly, the therapist must be able to identify the elements in movement and posture that interfere with the client's progress. This is no small task, and it requires a constant sharpening of observational skills and a willingness to approach the situation from a trial and error perspective. It also requires the therapist to be knowledgeable about movement and motor control in order to have a framework for directing observations and determining trials.

Figure 16-1 provides some insight into the differences in approach to the same problem from a traditional perspective, or facilitation model, and a newer motor control model. Traditionally, we might break prerequisites

469

into specific entities that are not clearly interrelated. In the newer model, of course, the systems interactions are emphasized. The traditional model depends on sequences, assuming that one develops from another, rather than on emphasis of the task itself. Remember that guidance and constant feedback do not seem to produce long-term learning, at least in the normal individual. The client must be allowed to make mistakes and learn how to solve the motor problems and correct them.

Goal: Weight Shift to the involved leg

Facilitation Model

- prerequisites: normal tone, inhibit reflexes or stereotypical synergies, facilitate equilibrium

- sequence of activities: bridging, sit-to-stand, stand, walk

- use facilitation cues to get weight shift: hands on, compression, resistance

- normal movement -- therapist corrects client if she is wrong

Motor Control Model

- prerequisites: range of motion, biomechanical alignment, force control, ability to detect error

- task specificity: improve weight shift in standing, then practice standing; if the goal is to improve weight shift in walking, then practice walking

- goal-directed tasks that require client to order and sequence tasks (eg, reaching)

- can make mistakes, the client develops error detection and is permitted to self-correct

Figure 16-1 Comparison of a traditional model and a contemporary motor control model in relation to one treatment goal. From Duncan (1991), reprinted with permission.

It is clear that the tools available to therapists and the techniques to be used will not undergo drastic change at this time. The major differences occur in how the techniques might be applied and for what reason. Much of this approach has been implemented almost intuitively by the master clinicians who recognized the need to alter the treatment methods as they proceeded. Now we have more clear scientific bases for making such alterations and a framework that will guide everyone for providing more effective care. Use your proprioceptive neuromuscular facilitation techniques and your neurodevelopmental handing skills to their best advantage, within a proper framework, to promote appropriate motor learning within functional contexts.

This chapter is meant to bring the various topics in this text together, particularly as they relate to evaluation and treatment of the client with neurological problems. There are many more specific guidelines and suggestions for client treatment and evaluation within the text. Appendix B provides more detailed information concerning the predictive studies using reflexes as indicators and the tests incorporating reflex evaluation. The case studies in Chapter 17 provide various applications of motor learning to clinical practice. In addition, the vestibular case studies address the involvement of the vestibular system and balance mechanisms in a variety of neurological problems, and illustrate evaluation and treatment approaches for these conditions.

The main thrust of this text, however, is to provide current information concerning motor control theories and their relationship to clinical practice in the past, the present, and the future. Armed with this knowledge, you should be able to develop many innovative approaches to the evaluation and treatment of clients, particularly those with nervous system deficits.

Remember that postural control is normally goal-directed and task specific; therefore, it is important to focus on the functional tasks you want the client to achieve and to provide practice for every task. Tasks involve both reproductive and predictive processes, but mostly predictive, using feedback and feedforward modes. Postural control is dynamic and adaptive. It is influenced by many variables, and these variables must be considered during treatment and evaluation sessions. Movements are constructed on the spot from a basic pattern to achieve a goal and involve most of the body by combining postural sets and movement patterns. The old idea, for instance, that gait is a gross motor skill and that manipulation of objects is a fine motor skill needs to be reconsidered, especially when realizing the incredible coordination of multiple joints and the exploitation of gravitational, inertial, and contact forces. All normal motor activities represent fine motor control.

| What is the value of basic theoretical research in the movement sciences? |

There is concern among some therapists that newer insights into motor control represent purely theoretical information. It is true that these research studies do not provide obvious, direct, and immediate applications nor do they result in new tools for treatment. It is, however, a very narrow view to suggest that only clinical research is of use in professional practice. Integration and application of new knowledge may not be easy or straightforward, but it is the therapist, not the research scientist, who is best suited to take such research, refine it for proper integration, and apply it to clinical practice (Winstein and Knecht 1990). Although we have made some suggestions in this text, we are more concerned that each learner create a fresh approach to clinical evaluation and treatment that is based on these scientific observations and principles. You can do it!

Study Questions: (not limited to this chapter)

1. Compare the various views of motor development. Include basic assumptions of the theorists in the comparisons.

2. Interpret several "developmental rules" and explain their relevance to therapeutic intervention.

3. What have we learned from fetal studies? Make a case for reflexes not being reflexes. What does it mean to say that even movements such as sucking and grasping are responsive to context?

4. What are the strengths and weakness of the various theories of motor control?

5. Relate the concepts of a self-organizing system of motor control to therapeutic evaluation and treatment. Include such concepts as degrees of freedom, coordinative structures, biomechanical elements, and thermodynamics.

6. Relate the various theories of motor control with the theories of motor development. Do they conflict? Can they be complimentary?

7. Relate the information concerning practice conditions, feedback, guidance, fatigue, feedforward processes, and whole-part task transfer to performance and learning in clients with motor, sensory, or memory deficits.

8. Describe how the approach to therapeutic practice should differ between that developed on a reflex-based, facilitation system and that based on knowledge of motor control and motor learning principles.

9. Discuss the concept of movement as an emergent, softly assembled, on-the-spot construction.

10. How would you define strength? Of what relevance is it to motor control? By what methods could you evaluate it. Describe as many techniques as you can for developing strength and methods of incorporating it in your treatment programs.

Chapter 17 - Case Studies

The following case studies are designed to give you some insight and ideas for treating clients. The first case study emphasizes the use of motor learning principles in the clinical setting. The next four case studies are of clients with various vestibular and balance problems. These histories together provide a powerful story of quality client care and address the complexity of issues in balance and motor control functions.

Motor Learning Case Study

Contributed by **Lois Deming Hedman, MS, PT,** Instructor in Clinical Physical Therapy, Programs in Physical Therapy, Northwestern University Medical School, Chicago, Ill.

Introduction

Many students, clinicians, and educators may initially have difficulty seeing how some of the theoretical ideas presented in the chapter on motor learning can be applied in the clinic. The purpose of this case study is to provide a clinical example of how principles of motor learning can be applied to the rehabilitation of an individual with central nervous system dysfunction. Specifically, I illustrate the process of applying the information processing model of human performance and one associated motor learning theory to a client with balance dysfunction resulting from cerebellar tumor removal.

Motor learning principles were derived from specific motor learning theories. In this case study I chose to apply the ideas of information processing stages and Schmidt's schema theory because they provided me with a useful conceptual framework for understanding this client's clinical presentation and devising a treatment program. It is important to keep in mind that the schema theory is only one of several rival motor learning theories. The clinical applicability of this theory, like any other theory, can only be determined through a process of trial and error with many clinicians applying its ideas to a variety of clinical situations.

Presenting History

The client, Amos Bradley, a 61-year-old business man, worked 18 hours a day up to the point of his illness. He was highly successful in his business, traveled extensively for his work, and was driven to succeed. He was referred to me for a consultation about 18 months after he had undergone brain surgery for the removal of a cerebellar tumor. Mr. Bradley had been receiving physical therapy up to the point of the referral, but his therapist thought he had reached a plateau. His major goal was independent ambulation, and fortunately, he had the resources and the will to pursue physical therapy toward that goal.

Evaluation

Functional Abilities - Mr. Bradley was functioning at home with the assistance of his wife and a private duty nurse. He could roll independently, but he required minimal assistance for supine-to-sit activities and moderate assistance for sit-to-stand activities. During ambulation he required minimal to moderate assistance while using a large based quad cane or a walker. He required minimal to moderate assistance for dressing, eating, and hygiene needs, depending on the task. Those tasks involving bilateral upper extremity use or upright balance control required more assistance.

Cognition - Mr. Bradley was alert; oriented as to time, place, date; and able to respond to multistep commands (instructions that require a series of responses). For example, when asked to do so, Mr. Bradley could wheel his wheelchair over to the exercise mat, take off his jacket, and prepare to transfer to the mat.

Passive Motion - He demonstrated minimal range of motion limitations at the end ranges of shoulder flexion, abduction, and external rotation and also in neck and trunk rotation. Muscle tone was slightly decreased in his trunk.

Active Motion - Mr. Bradley demonstrated isolated movements in all four of his limbs. Severe ataxia and intention tremor were evident in movements of his right arm, and moderate ataxia was present during movement of his right leg. In addition, he demonstrated truncal tremor. His muscle strength was within normal limits.

Sensation - Light touch and proprioception were within normal limits. He reported problems with diplopia, but he did not wear an eye patch because someone told him that wearing it would weaken his eyes. According to his physician, vestibular function test results were normal.

Balance - Mr. Bradley was able to sit unsupported for at least 30 seconds with eyes open, eyes closed, against manual resistance, and after active neck rotation and unilateral arm elevation. When his center of mass was manually displaced, he did not demonstrate any equilibrium responses but did show beginning upper extremity protective extension responses.

In standing, Mr. Bradley adopted a wide lateral base of support. His posture was characterized by forward bending at his hips, increased thoracic kyphosis, forward head and neck, and a shift of his body over his left leg. He demonstrated difficulty redistributing his weight in a controlled manner. He was able to stand for 30 seconds but exhibited excessive anterior-posterior postural sway. Closing his eyes or receiving external manual resistance did not significantly alter his sway.

Postural sway did increase after neck rotation or left arm elevation, causing him to lose his balance within a few seconds. He was unable to assume or maintain any upright position that decreased the width of his base of support (eg, tandem, Romberg, or single limb stance). He did not demonstrate any equilibrium responses when his center of mass was manually displaced.

His loss of balance in standing occurred most frequently in a posterior lateral direction on the left side. When he lost his balance he resembled a falling log (ie, no automatic protective reactions were seen). He stated he was unaware that he was falling until he felt himself being caught.

Gait - His gait was extremely slow and choppy, whether he was using the walker or the quad cane. The walker appeared to augment the forward bending at his hips and the quad cane accentuated his tendency to bear more weight on the left side. With either assistive device his gait was characterized by a large right step followed by a quick "step to" left step, after which he would pause briefly before initiating the next step. At times, because of the ataxia, his right foot would shoot out in an uncontrolled manner, interfering with his foot placement and his equilibrium. He tended to hold either assistive device with an extremely tight, rigid grip. When not in therapy, he typically walked with his private duty nurse and held onto both of her arms as she walked backward in front of him. While walking with her, his gait was significantly smoother, more symmetrical, and performed at a more reasonable speed than when he was using an assistive device.

Assessment

Although Mr. Bradley demonstrated many debilitating cerebellar signs, such as limb ataxia, intention tremors, and a wide-based uncontrolled gait, I thought that his lack of spatial orientation, which is not a typical cerebellar sign, was his most functionally limiting impairment. This could have been the sequela of additional brain damage from the postoperative hemorrhage Mr. Bradley experienced. Although I believed that spatial orientation would have to be the focus of treatment to improve his functional capabilities, I had to wonder about the potential for improvement given the length of time since onset of the problem and the functional level at which the client was currently operating. It occurred to me that Mr.

474

Bradley's history might provide evidence of an additional contributing factor to his disorientation.

Rationale for Developing the Treatment Approach

Mr. Bradley was fortunate to have a supportive wife and private duty nurse who assisted him in every phase of his daily activities, from the point of surgery onward. Although the level of assistance they provided was necessary and appropriate, especially at first, I thought it may have contributed inadvertently to the passive role his "system" had adopted in relation to the functional goal of maintaining equilibrium. Mr. Bradley had not experienced the need to control his equilibrium because the control was being provided for him. I thought that his spatial disorientation might have been in part a result of a lack of opportunity to relearn how to process sensory information and produce equilibrium responses.

My thinking was based on a theory of motor learning proposed by Schmidt (1988). According to Schmidt, we learn motor skills by learning rules (schema) about the relationship between the movement we intended to make, the expected sensory consequences, and what actually happened. Movements are assumed to be generated using generalized motor programs. After a movement, an individual stores information about the initial conditions, movement variables assigned to the generalized motor program (duration, force, muscle selection), outcome of the movement, and certain sensory consequences of the movement. These pieces of information are stored long enough for the individual to abstract some relationship between them. In other words, the individual learns to associate certain motor program variables with a particular movement outcome and sensory consequences. The schema is updated and strengthened with new information after each subsequent attempt. Therefore, according to this theory, optimal conditions for motor learning occur when an individual actively generates movements and experiences or receives some information about the movement outcome and sensory consequences.

Up to this point, my client's experiences did not meet these criteria. He had been cut off from participating in the active processes that would have enabled him to learn to recognize and maintain a state of equilibrium. Therefore, I thought he might be able to learn equilibrium control if he were placed in situations where he was responsible for his equilibrium control, making active responses, experiencing the consequences of his actions, and receiving feedback about his responses.

To clarify further this individual's clinical picture and plan a treatment approach, I tried to apply the information processing model of human performance discussed by Schmidt (1988) (Fig 17-1). This model has three major stages by which an individual generates active movements. These stages are stimulus identification, response selection, and response programming. It appeared to me that although Mr. Bradley had a problem in response programming as evidenced by his ataxic movement, it was not his primary problem. I came to this conclusion because he was clearly able to demonstrate a variety of goal-directed motor responses on command. For example, he could perform an equilibrium response on command even though it was delayed and not optimally smooth. He was unable, however, to generate this response spontaneously when his balance was disturbed. To me, his problem appeared to be more one of selecting as opposed to constructing the appropriate response. I interpreted this as a problem in the response selection stage. However, in my estimation his *main problem*, which likely interfered with response selection, was his apparent inability to identify sensory stimuli relevant to upright equilibrium. This was illustrated dramatically in his lack of awareness of falling, in spite of having relatively intact sensory systems. Therefore, I thought that treatment would first have to address stimulus identification in order to address his lack of equilibrium responses.

Treatment Program

The primary objective of my treatment plan was to make Mr. Bradley responsible for his own equilibrium control as much as possible. A second aim of treatment was to help him identify relevant sensory information in relation to equilibrium in

475

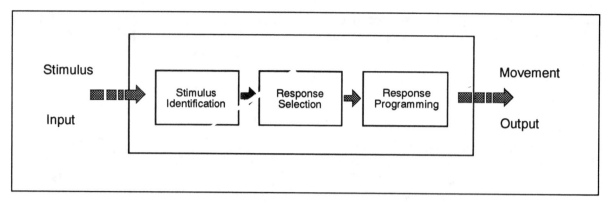

Figure 17-1 Schmidt's information processing model illustrating three proposed stages between the presentation of a stimulus and a movement response (adapted from Schmidt 1988, reprinted with permission).

order that he could perceive the orientation of his body in space. After working on the stimulus identification stage, a third goal was to work on response selection (Fig 17-1) by helping him generate appropriate equilibrium responses.

The two primary tasks I chose for him to work on were standing and walking. Because Mr. Bradley was unable to grade the support he received from an assistive device or an assistant and thus was unaware how much or little he relied on them, I decided that we would have to eliminate completely any external support and practice these tasks without assistive devices or physical assistance. Although I expected this change would present a major challenge for Mr. Bradley, I thought it was the only way to make him take an active role once again. My decision to have him work on walking even while he was having difficulty standing was based on two assumptions. One was that he would be more motivated if he could see that we were working on his primary goal, walking. Second, although I thought that spatial awareness in stance was a prerequisite for walking, I wasn't sure how much carry over I could expect in a dynamic activity, such as ambulation, from working in quiet stance (Winstein et al 1989) and decided it was important to work within the functional task concurrently.

Preparing the Client

I discussed the rationale behind this approach with Mr. Bradley and pointed out that his walking

would probably deteriorate in the beginning as we turned over control of equilibrium to him. Deterioration in performance was to be expected because we would be making his walking more difficult. I emphasized that because this approach would give him the opportunity to learn equilibrium control, he should eventually be more in control of his walking and less dependent on others for support. Additionally, I told him that he should consider "bad" days as being valuable practice rather than as a waste of time or a regression. Motor learning theory assumes that movement errors, rather than being disruptive to learning, are necessary and can be as useful as error free movements in strengthening the schema. In other words, his system could learn just as much from a poor performance as a good one.

Because of the uniqueness of his situation, I explained to Mr. Bradley that I was unable to make firm predictions about the long-term outcome of treatment. I suggested that we start with a trial period, two sessions a week, to see how he responded. Mr. Bradley was willing to try because he was frustrated with his current lack of progress and was convinced that he would walk independently someday and was highly motivated to do so. In addition, he was fortunate to have the resources that enabled him to commit to long-term physical therapy.

Minimizing the Fear

To ensure his safety during these activities I stood behind him with my arms encircling his body at

476

chest height but not contacting him. Using this method, I was able to prevent him from falling in any direction without disturbing his visual field. This obviously was a frightening prospect for him, especially because he could not see me as I was guarding him. Initially, I kept my arms in close to his body so he would be caught soon after he leaned too far in any one direction. Gradually, as he experienced consistency in being "saved" when he lost his balance, we were able to minimize (but not eliminate) his fear and work on these tasks for significant periods of time.

Learning to Identify and Use Sensory Information for Orientation

Under normal circumstances, visual, vestibular, and somatosensory information is used both in feedback and feedforward modes to maintain equilibrium (Ghez 1991). Mr. Bradley's inability to automatically use these available sensory cues left him unable to derive any information about his state of (dis)equilibrium and thus respond appropriately. I decided to try to see if he would be able to process sensory cues consciously in a simple feedback loop I could monitor. I directed him to pay attention to specific sensory cues. The initial goal was for him to identify the sensory cue and associate it with a specific direction of loss of balance. I was hoping that through this process Mr. Bradley would gain awareness of his position in space both when he was in equilibrium and when he was losing his balance. In addition, I was hoping that eventually he would be able to process these sensory cues more automatically.

The first form of sensory information I directed him to attend to was the pressure information he felt on his chest as he was being caught when he lost his balance. I directed him to match the sensation of pressure on a particular surface of his body with a loss of balance in that same direction (eg, pressure on the anterior aspect of his chest meant he was losing his balance in the forward direction). Initially, it was necessary to tell him where the pressure was and, therefore, in which direction he was falling. Gradually, he was encouraged to detect the location of the pressure sensation and match it with the direction of loss of

balance. I then provided him with knowledge of results (correct or incorrect) on his response.

Mr. Bradley himself supplied the idea for another form of sensory information we were able to use to generate orientation information. He had been complaining about his toes hurting him after standing or walking for long periods. I assumed this was a result of his weight being so far forward, putting excessive pressure on his toes. It occurred to me that pressure information from the soles of his feet could be used as feedback about his posture, which was the bellwether of his state of equilibrium. I instructed him that the sensation of an even pressure on the soles of his feet meant he was in an upright, stable position. For him to perceive disturbances, he was directed to match the location of greatest pressure on the soles of his feet with leaning too far or losing balance in the same direction. The same training procedures were used as with the chest pressure information. Although I could not validate the pressure he was feeling on the soles of his feet, I based my feedback to him on my observation of his posture.

As his diplopia resolved, I also directed Mr. Bradley to use vision to help him maintain an upright posture by visually fixating on an object in front of him at eye level. He was instructed to equate perceived movement of the object in one direction with sway or loss of balance in the opposite direction. This was most useful for frontal plane postural sway. This was one form of feedback that he had to monitor on his own because it was not possible for me to validate his visual information.

The three strategies described above provided an opportunity for Mr. Bradley to begin to be involved actively in feedback control of his equilibrium. The chest pressure sensations provided information about movement outcome (direction of loss of balance) that potentially could help him modify his responses in subsequent attempts. The information derived from foot pressure sensations and visual cues, on the other hand, provided ongoing feedback about his orientation (prior to actual loss of balance) and thus could potentially help him modify his responses in order to prevent a loss of balance. Thus, foot pressure and visual cues would likely be more useful functionally. In fact, these sensory cues are used normally for equilibrium, although not usually at a conscious level. At this point, all he was able to do was to identify the direction of loss of balance. This, however, was a major step for him. The functional carry over was that he reported he was beginning to gain some awareness of where he was in space. This indicated to me that he was beginning to process sensory information more automatically in relation to his equilibrium.

Learning to Select Appropriate Equilibrium Responses

His new spatial awareness, however, did not automatically lead to spontaneous equilibrium responses as I had hoped. Even though I had been trying to give his system maximal opportunity to respond by gradually moving my arms farther away from his body as I was guarding him, he was not demonstrating any equilibrium responses. In other words, his system was not completing the feedback loop by using the sensory information to modify his motor output. Considering Schmidt's model (Fig 17-1), it seemed as if response selection was a continuing problem.

I decided to address this problem by making the response selection for him, directing him how and when to respond. In doing so I was in effect using a feedforward mechanism to predict what the response should be to an upcoming disturbance (Lee 1989). For example, if he was losing his balance in the forward direction, I instructed him to perform a "jackknife" maneuver that approximates a normal equilibrium response to a large disturbance in this direction. Initially, he was instructed to do it "now," just before or as I caught him. The goal was simply that he respond to verbal cueing with appropriate equilibrium responses when a large disturbance of his center of mass occurred while he was standing or walking. Although his responses were too delayed to be effective initially, his timing gradually improved. In time, I eliminated my verbal cue to initiate the response and gave him the opportunity to self-initiate, directing him to use appropriate sensory information (foot pressure information or visual information) as his cue. Gradually, he was

able to respond well enough so that he was losing his balance much less frequently.

As his postural awareness improved, a secondary problem arose. He began to use these equilibrium responses when his balance was only minimally disturbed, resulting in further disequilibrium. I directed him to try more subtle postural adjustments in these circumstances (dorsiflexing his ankles when he perceived that his weight on the soles of his feet was slightly back toward his heels). Because equilibrium responses are graded along a continuum according to the amount of perceived center of mass disturbance, it was impractical for me to teach him every possible response. The ability to adapt postural responses has been shown to be affected in individuals with cerebellar deficits (Nashner 1976, Horak et al 1986, Horak 1990), and it was very difficult for Mr. Bradley to learn how to grade equilibrium responses appropriately.

Gait Training

Initially, the goal for Mr. Bradley was for him to be able to walk without loss of balance. Thus I did not attempt to alter his gait by cueing him or providing feedback about specific aspects of his gait. Rather, I attempted to provide knowledge of results about two functional outcomes of his gait. I asked him to walk as fast as possible and under as much control as possible for 25 feet while I timed him and counted how many times I had to "save" him to preserve his equilibrium. Figures 17-2 and 17-3 illustrate how the counts of "saves" and time were used to track his performance. As can be seen from the contrast in his performance during the three initial months as compared with three later months (total time in therapy spanned 20 months), Mr. Bradley not only reduced the number of saves required and the time to walk 25 feet but also significantly reduced the variability of his performance.

These counts provided a concrete measure of Mr. Bradley's progress for both of us. This was helpful because his performance was particularly difficult to track because its initial variability was high. I was always careful to keep each session's results in the long-term perspective, especially on bad

478

performance days, because poor performance discouraged him. I tried to remind him that he could learn from poor performances.

Later on as his balance improved I began to focus a little more on the quality of his gait; however, I still avoided breaking down gait into specific phases. As discussed earlier, it may not be appropriate to break down a continuous task such as gait into its component parts. In Mr. Bradley's case I felt it would serve only to disrupt his gait pattern that was basically sound. Rather, I tried to provide knowledge of performance on more global characteristics of his gait such as posture, width of his base of support, symmetry, rhythm, and speed. In addition to providing knowledge of performance, I also used music and rhythmic counting to help cue him to improve gait rhythm and speed.

Real Life Environment

One of the later goals of treatment was to have Mr. Bradley walk for short distances in his home, in the course of his daily activities, without the usual support from his private duty nurse. Despite his improvement in equilibrium control and gait in the clinic and his successful walking with his private duty nurse in the clinic, he continued to feel very uncomfortable walking at home and reportedly was not very successful. When I had the opportunity to treat him in his home, I saw for myself this limited ability to generalize walking to his home environment. It appeared as if he had been trained to walk in the clinic but nowhere else. To become a functional ambulator, he needed to develop the capacity to adapt to a variety of environments.

Up to this point, the conditions under which he was practicing in the clinic were relatively bland. Our clinic, not atypical of a physical therapy gym, had white tile floors; neutral colored, relatively undecorated walls; overhead fluorescent lighting; a wall of windows at one end; and lots of open space. In contrast, his home was filled with relatively ornate furnishings and wall decorations, several different carpets and rugs, variable lighting in each room, and very little space in which to walk. For him, walking at home was a completely different experience for which he was not prepared; his practice at the clinic to this point had been designed to get him walking but had not offered

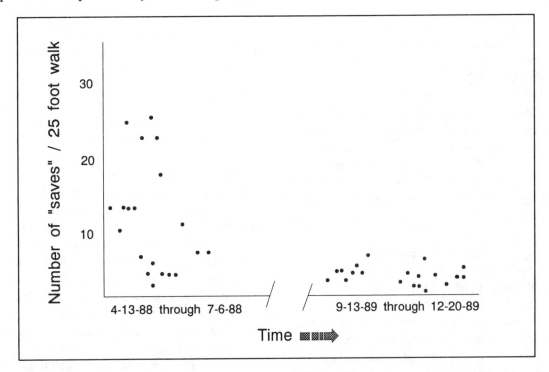

Figure 17-2 A clinical record of the number of "saves" required during a walk of 25 feet. Note the reduction in magnitude as well as variability of these measures from the initial to the final treatment periods. Total treatment time was 20 months.

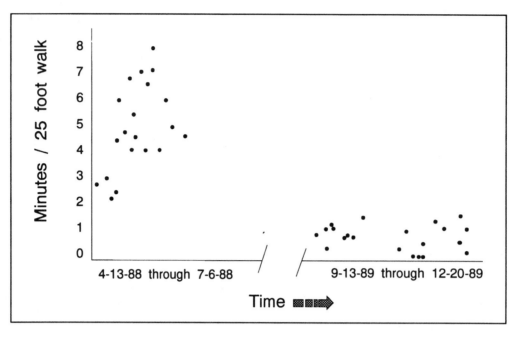

Figure 17-3 A clinical record of the time to walk 25 feet. Note the reduction in magnitude as well as variability of these measures from the initial to the final treatment periods. Total treatment time was 20 months.

opportunities to learn to generalize his walking skills.

According to Schmidt (1988), one key to being able to generalize skills is variability in practice. This means practicing the same task in a variety of ways while changing certain components of the task or alternating the practice of one task with other tasks. Variability of practice is thought to enhance motor learning during practice by forcing the individual to recreate the solution to the movement problem each time rather than just repeat the last successful response, thus reinforcing learning to solve the problem rather than memorize the answer.

Altering the clinic environment to simulate an individual's real life environment is not a new clinical concept. Most physical therapy departments and clinics have activity-of-daily-living rooms, and some now have simulated community settings (eg, stores, streets). What motor learning principles suggest is that *variety* rather than realism is the goal for practice. Providing individuals with a variety of experiences (realistic or not) in practicing motor tasks will

prepare them to deal with conditions in their real environment that we may not have been able to predict, much less simulate. In this particular clinic setting I was able to vary the lighting by adjusting the blinds or lights. We began intermittently using the carpeted hallway or walking on exercise mats to vary the terrain. I also encouraged Mr. Bradley to wear a variety of shoes. As we began to vary his practice in the clinic, he began to show improvements in his ability to walk at home.

In addition to environmental concerns, other behavioral factors, both predictable and unpredictable, can alter the conditions under which an individual has to perform motor tasks in real life. These factors need to be taken into consideration during rehabilitation. An example of a predictable behavioral condition for Mr. Bradley was his fear of knocking over valuable, fragile items in his home while he was walking. These objects were always in the same place and thus presented a predictable dilemma for him. In contrast, the movements of his small dog, who liked to follow him around, were unpredictable, and he was afraid he might step on his dog or that the dog might trip him. In both cases, Mr. Bradley chose to try to learn to deal with the conditions rather than remove them.

In an attempt to address these behavioral issues while practicing in the clinic, I tried to create a variety of situations that forced him to create a solution to a problem. For example, I had him practice walking as close as possible to various objects in the clinic with the goal of not touching them with any part of his body. To simulate the unexpected conditions he faced, I asked other therapists and staff members to walk in front of Mr. Bradley without warning as he was walking. I also disturbed his balance unexpectedly. Other examples of conditions that I began to weave into practice were walking to the bathroom when he had an immediate urgency and trying to get on an elevator before the door closed on him. Both these situations created stresses that required walking faster to achieve success.

Treatment Results and Conclusions

Mr. Bradley continued to improve in his ability to walk without falling in the clinic but also began to show improvement in his home situation, although the frequency of his loss of balance at home was considerably greater than in the clinic. In time, he became consistently willing to walk for short distances in his home. Although he continued to require physical assistance to prevent some falls, he demonstrated improved recognition of his orientation in space and ability to respond appropriately.

Although he was making significant progress, I was not sure that his walking without an assistive device was a realistic goal for him; he might become independent faster using an assistive device. Initially, I had him try walking with a quad cane or a walker to see how he was using them. Although he still required verbal cueing to decrease his grip and the amount of pressure he applied to the devices and to eliminate a pause in his gait every time he advanced the device, he was able to use them with supervision and occasional physical assistance. This was a big improvement from his original status, and practice with the cane and walker was routinely interspersed within his treatment sessions. Mr. Bradley continued to

improve beyond the 20 month time span of this case study. He progressed to being able to assume standing from sitting with supervision and can stand for up to 5 minutes independently with minimal postural sway. He also is able to ambulate in his home using a walker with occasional minimal assistance to prevent falls.

The particular type of therapy described in this case study was very cognitively oriented. Intense concentration was required, making it stressful and energy consuming. Thus a therapy program of this nature may not be appropriate for every client, especially those with significant cognitive deficits. Even those clients with adequate cognitive skills may not be able to tolerate an entire program of this nature. Additionally, it is unlikely that such a program would be sufficient to address all the

needs of most individuals. However, elements of this type of approach could be useful with a wide variety of clients within their total treatment program. Another factor with Mr. Bradley's therapy program was its length. Many clients cannot afford such a program. As with many therapeutic approaches, this one can be adapted for implementation by the client and his caregivers outside of a clinic setting.

Motor learning theories and the principles derived from them have been tested primarily on young healthy individuals. The clinical applicability of these ideas, especially for those individuals with central nervous system dysfunction, is unknown. It is the responsibility of clinicians, through a process of trial and error, to apply these ideas to specific clinical problems to determine their usefulness. I believe this case study demonstrates that it is clinically feasible to translate principles of motor learning into a meaningful treatment program for clients. The effectiveness of this type of approach, like that of most physical therapy interventions, remains to be demonstrated. In this case, it appears that this intervention might have had a positive effect because Mr. Bradley began to improve after its implementation following a plateau in his progress.

Acknowledgments

I thank Dr. Wynne A. Lee for introducing motor learning theories and principles to me and sharing her insights about their potential clinical applications. A version of this case study was presented as part of a presentation entitled "Motor Learning Principles at Work in the Clinic" at the Fegruary 1990 Combined Sections Meeting of the American Physical Therapy Association, New Orleans, La.

Vestibular Case Studies

The following four cases studies are contributed by **Mary M. Castiglione, PT**, Coordinator of Physical Therapy at Meadowbrook of Atlanta Community Reentry Rehabilitation Program, Atlanta, Ga.

Case Presentation #1

Medical History

Martha, a 34-year-old client, was involved in an automobile accident. She attempted to avoid hitting a cat when the car she was driving flipped over an embankment. She lost consciousness for about 10 minutes and was hospitalized overnight for observation. She was released the next day with no recommendations for further evaluation or rehabilitation.

At the time of the accident, Martha, a registered nurse, was director of health education for a community hospital. Before that she had been a critical care nurse in intensive care unit. She was a self-confessed workaholic who was involved in community programs that required meeting with the public, making public speeches, and participating in other demanding activities. She was an avid reader. She was separated from her husband and had a 10-year-old child. Her prior medical history included asthma and a bout with hepatitis 12 years before the accident.

Upon returning home after her release, she became "lost in my own house." Her daughter was the only companion at this time and the child managed to get to the grocery store by bus and thus manage some of the day to day activities necessary for their survival. Martha remained at home, in her night gown, and would sleep in the fetal position much of the time. She was aware that something was amiss, so she contacted her neurologist who failed to recognize the nature or the seriousness of her problem.

One day she decided she had to go to work, but she realized that she should not drive and wisely arranged to be taken to the building. Once there she could not find her office. When she finally arrived she sat down at her desk and thought "now what is it I used to do here?" She went around and asked her colleagues what she was supposed to do in her job. Friends and colleagues realized that something drastic had happened to Martha and were instrumental in arranging further evaluation and rehabilitation efforts. Martha was finally admitted to a resident rehabilitation facility 11 months after the injury. Her diagnosis at this time was traumatic brain injury (cerebral contusion with postconcussion syndrome).

General Evaluation

Physical examination showed a mild right hemiparesis (right extremities were graded about one-half of a muscle strength grade weaker than the left extremities). There were nonintentional tremors of the right upper extremity. Fine and gross motor coordination were impaired, and sensation and proprioception were intact. There was a deficit in depth perception, and her endurance was poor. After walking three fourths of a mile she would complain of moderate fatigue. Hemodynamic responses were normal, (ie, appropriate blood pressure changes occurred during the activity). The same responses occurred while riding a stationary bicycle at 40 rpm for 20 minutes. Her gait pattern showed a decreased right reciprocal arm swing, and after ambulating for approximately one-half mile, she would demonstrate a mild foot slap.

Cognitive Evaluation

Martha demonstrated numerous cognitive deficits. She had decreased attention and concentration and was often "flooded" with incoming information. She had diminished recall of new information, decreased problem solving and motor planning, and loss of an organizational approach to tasks.

Language problems included increased processing time required to construct verbal expressions. There was difficulty with word retrieval, decrease in auditory sequential memory, and impairment in reading comprehension.

Vestibular Evaluation

Her physical therapist began to suspect vestibular involvement and arranged for an examination by an otoneurologist. Martha was then diagnosed as having a labyrinthine concussion with positional vertigo.

Subjectively she complained of dizziness, lightheadedness, nausea, a spinning sensation, and imbalance. Symptoms increased with rapid head movements or quick turns, closed in spaces, crowds, ascending or descending stairs, or riding an elevator. Thus both angular and linear accelerations produced symptoms. Various positions of her head also produced these symptoms.

Martha was often asked to rate the intensity of her symptoms by using a scale in which 0 is a complete lack of symptoms and 10 is the worst level she had ever experienced. She complained of moderate to severe levels of vertigo with the latter being rated at 8 to 9 in response to angular head movement of 8 to 15 seconds duration. There was mild to moderate nystagmus. The intensity of all responses and reactions increased when her eyes were closed. Rapid rolling produced mild to moderate dizziness, and a supine-to-sit maneuver resulted in moderate dizziness.

Eye-Head Coordination

Visual blurring and moderate dizziness occurred during saccadic eye movement, smooth pursuit, and visual tracking tasks. There was decreased eye convergence and coordination, and nystagmus was noted.

Postural Control

During a "foam and dome" testing protocol (Fig 15-6) that eliminated visual and somatosensory cues, Martha was unable to stand without assistance when using only vestibular input for orientation. She exhibited moderate to severe postural sway measuring 30 to 40 degrees. She was relatively stable when standing on the floor with her eyes open, but when closing her eyes she demonstrated a marked increase in sway. She also had marked sway while standing on the foam rubber and required considerable support when her eyes were closed or when she was wearing the dome.

Sitting

During lateral weight shifts, with her eyes open, Martha demonstrated moderate disequilibrium and rated her dizziness a 6 on the 0 to 10 scale. With her eyes, closed she experienced severe disequilibrium and nausea, and she rated her dizziness as a 9 or 10. After performing anterior weight shifts with her eyes open, she complained of mild disequilibrium and rated her dizziness at 3 to 4; with her eyes closed, disequilibrium increased to moderate and the dizziness rating to 6.

Standing

Weight shifts in anterior-posterior or lateral directions while standing produced moderate disequilibrium and the resulting dizziness was rated an 8. She demonstrated moderate postural sway and used ankle, hip, and stepping strategies during this activity.

Gait

Martha used a wide base of support during ambulation and during horizontal and vertical head

483

movements; she also abducted her arms and often demonstrated stepping strategies. When ambulating indoors she would maintain contact with the walls or objects with her fingertip, thus "trailing" her route and maintaining somatic sensory input to help maintain equilibrium.

Rehabilitation Program

Treatment goals in physical therapy were limited to strengthening, endurance training, and vestibular rehabilitation. Problems with gross and fine motor coordination were addressed in occupational therapy.

Eye-head coordination exercises, including pursuit activities during which Martha was asked to follow a moving target with her eyes, were initiated. Saccades, produced by placing a target to the left and the right and then looking at one target and then the other, were used. Targets were also placed above and below the head and in diagonal planes. Angular head movements were practiced horizontally, vertically, and diagonally, and the rate of acceleration was altered while her eyes were both open and closed.

Basic proprioceptive neuromuscular facilitation diagonal patterns were performed in sitting and standing by having Martha bend over and pick up a ball by her left foot, lift it across her body and up over her right shoulder, and then return it to its original position beside her left foot. She was instructed to keep her eyes on the ball through the entire movement. She repeated the diagonal movements on the opposite side, again following the ball with her eyes, which effectively caused appropriate head movement. Functional activities that produced distress were repeated with emphasis on safety awareness. Thus these became both habituation exercises (repetitive positional changes designed to help the client adapt, accommodate, or habituate to the stress invoking positions) and activities that enhanced compensation of vestibular problems by other systems.

Eye convergence exercises were used during which Martha was asked to hold one of her arms in front of her body, at eye level with the thumb up, and then to pull the thumb toward her nose to the point

where she first saw double thumbs. At that double vision point she was instructed to extend her arm outward to a point where one thumb was visible. The object was to facilitate equal convergence of both eyes and decrease dizziness during convergence activities.

Ambulation activities included making angular head movements, quick stops, and turns while walking. Martha ultimately worked on a balance beam, stepping both sideways and forward. She practiced tandem gait and unilateral stance. She also marched on foam rubber with her eyes open and closed. Indoors, walking began in a hallway; visual targets were hung on the walls so that she would have to walk while turning her head and focusing on written signs. At the beginning of this activity she literally bounced along the walls using them for support. Later on we progressed to wider ambulation areas in larger rooms.

During the latter stages of the rehabilitation process, Martha was taken out into the community. Initially, she had poor tolerance for visual motion stimuli that were present in crowds and on escalators. Her environment was gradually increased in complexity and activity by having her visit malls during different business times, such as when they were nearly deserted or when they had a one day sale.

The ultimate test was negotiating the crowded narrow isles of the local farmers market. We also went to a local park and practiced walking on a wide variety of terrain, from grass to gravel and with flat to hilly changes in elevation.

Martha was instructed in using Nautilus® strengthening equipment, and she quickly became independent in performing her general fitness program at the YMCA. For aerobics, she used the swimming pool, beginning with her head and arms forward while grasping a float and limiting her motion to kicking. Ultimately, she was able to perform free-style swimming.

Treatment Results and Conclusions

Martha achieved full independence in all activities of daily living and was discharged from therapy 8 months after beginning vestibular rehabilitation. She stayed in the rehabilitation residential apartment for an additional 2 months for continued treatment for cognitive problems. She was discontinued from physical therapy having partially compensated for her vestibular problems (other systems made up for vestibular loss). In my experience, clients with only peripheral vestibular damage respond well to habituation exercises and activities for compensation. Clients with involvement of central vestibular connections and mechanisms usually do not completely clear or compensate. Because she never fully compensated for all of her vestibular problems, she probably had some central involvement. Thus Martha still experiences very mild dizziness or a feeling of being lightheaded or "spacey" when fully challenged.

This client showed tremendous deficits from what appeared to be a relatively minor head trauma. It is amazing that these deficits were not identified by her health care practitioners for a relatively long time. She clearly demonstrates the problems that may be associated with vestibular damage that may not be picked up in clients with head trauma or other neurological conditions. Her vestibular damage most likely involved both central and peripheral components.

Martha has discovered that she must remain active to stay habituated to positional stimuli and compensated for vestibular dysfunction. She does not find it necessary to do the specific habituation exercises or balance activities that she originally practiced, but rather, she follows her general fitness program at home to maintain the gains she was able to achieve.

Case Presentation #2

Medical History

Joan, a 58-year-old client, was the sole survivor of an airplane crash. She was treated acutely for intracranial hematoma and cranial lacerations. She had a grand mal seizure in the emergency room and was treated with intravenous Dilantin® to which she had an allergic reaction. Her computerized tomography scans showed intracerebral hemorrhage, subdural and subarachnoid space hemorrhage, and a small hemorrhage in the right thalamus. Her course was complicated by severe vestibular problems, hearing loss, visual difficulty, urinary tract infection, sinusitis, anemia, and hypothyroidism. She had a medical history of anterior and posterior fusion of the lumbosacral spine and a history of hypertension for which she received antihypertensive medication. She was admitted to a transitional residential rehabilitation center for the head injured 3 months after the accident.

Motor Control

Joan had a mild right hemiparesis with weakness greater proximally than distally. Gross and fine motor coordination were mildly reduced for both speed and quality of movement in her right extremities. She had full active and passive range of motion in the upper extremities except for an inability to fully oppose the right thumb. Pinch strength was reduced. Passive and active range of motion was normal in the lower extremities. Endurance was not normal in that she could walk for 30 minutes but then complained of moderate fatigue. She also showed a mildly hypoadaptive, hemodynamic response (blood pressure change during activity).

Gait and Functional Activities

Initially, Joan used a rolling walker to maintain balance for ambulation. After 1 month at the rehabilitation center she walked with a cane while under the supervision of a therapist. After the rolling walker was eliminated during gait she showed considerable abduction of the arms with wrist extension. In addition, during double stance she would produce a "dip" by flexing her hips and knees to lower her center of gravity. Any angular head movement or directional changes during gait resulted in considerable loss of balance.

Joan was unable to tandem walk either forward or backward. After she began to improve, quick stops always resulted in a relatively large slow hip strategy, flipping between forward and backward responses. She would often put a hand to her head and indicate that she was trying to hold it on because "it felt as though the top of it was spinning away."

In a grocery store she ambulated with a cart and supervision. She was able to reach both low and high shelved items but with some complaint of positional dizziness. Joan also complained of dizziness when scanning the shelves for a certain item. Where escalators in one store were lined with mirrors, the combination of her own bodily motion and visual motion stimuli from the mirrors caused significant destabilization.

Vestibular Status

A vestibular examination confirmed a reduced right vestibular response of 93% on electronystagmography. In the physical therapy clinic she was put through Hallpike maneuvers (Fig 13-7). A right Hallpike maneuver produced severe vertigo and nystagmus after a 3 to 4 second latency period. A left maneuver produced mild vertigo and nystagmus after a 3 to 4 second latency period. This response habituated, or fatigued, bilaterally after 5 to 6 repetitions. Although the client was not diagnosed as having benign paroxysmal positional vertigo, her symptoms clearly suggested this condition might be involved.

Other symptoms included vertigo and nausea when rolling over in bed, poor tolerance of visual motion stimuli, and decreased postural control during dynamic stance activities and ambulation. The client relied heavily on visual input to maintain balance by fixing her gaze on stationary objects. She was unable to stand on foam rubber with her eyes closed or with a visual dome over her head (Fig 15-6). There was much splinting of the head, neck, and upper trunk muscles, resulting in very little movement of these areas when walking or performing functional activities.

Treatment Goals

Goals for rehabilitation included achieving a decrease in the intensity and duration of vertigo and nausea during activities; independent ambulation with a cane over moderately varied terrain; and independent stair, curb, and escalator negotiation. Additional program goals were attaining good postural control while performing dynamic standing activities requiring head and upper trunk movements and increasing lower extremity timing and coordination to increase safety and independence during performance of functional activities. Joan was also working on cognitive and behavioral problems that had limited her return to the community. The treatment program had to be intensive and selective because her insurance would only support 90 days of rehabilitation.

Treatment Program

Joan performed positional exercises twice a day to produce adaptation or habituation to such positional stimuli. (See Chapter 13) With her we used a modified Hallpike position, usually referred to as Brandt's exercise (Fig 17-4). She was asked to rate the intensity of her symptoms on a scale of 0 to 10 in which 0 was no vertigo and 10 was the worst she had ever experienced. The intensity of her symptoms would decrease after each repetition, and by 5 or 6 repetitions, her intensity had decreased from 7 to 1. The next day the same process was repeated. Over time the intensity approached 0, and within 5 weeks she was at 0 from day to day. Thus at this point she was symptom-free during Brandt's positional changes.

Joan also practiced balance activities with her eyes open and eyes closed. These included weight shifts during stance, tandem gait, and standing and shifting on foam rubber. Emphasis was on functional balance while ambulating. She performed angular head movements with visual tracking while ambulating. Quick stops and directional changes also were practiced. Gait training progressed from ambulation with a cane over even terrain to ambulation over rough, varied terrain in the community, without assistive devices.

The client was gradually introduced to progressively more visual stimuli in the community by visiting malls and shops at different times, which provided an environment of changing

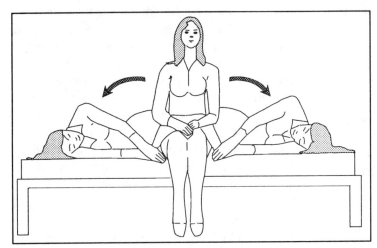

Figure 17-4 The Brandt's exercise. The client drops rapidly to the involved side and remains until symptoms subside, then sits up and drops rapidly to the opposite side.

complexity and motion depending on how big and how busy the mall or store was. She also engaged in a progressive walking program, when the cane was no longer needed, and in stationary bike pedaling and swimming for endurance.

Treatment Results and Conclusions

At discharge in July, Joan was ambulating independently, over all terrain without assistive devices. She was performing all activities of daily living independently, including shopping and driving. She was independent with an aerobic program that included walking 2 miles in the neighborhood 3 to 4 times a week. She continued swimming and resumed her interest in golf. She appeared to have successfully habituated to vestibular dysfunction because positional changes no longer resulted in dizziness. She also appeared to be completely compensated, that is, other systems made up for any vestibular loss. Her vestibular home program consisted solely of performing Brandt's exercise every other day.

About a year later, Joan decided that it was not necessary to continue the home program. Ultimately, she called to tell me that the dizziness had come back. Her Brandt's exercises were reinstated and within 2 weeks she was once again symptom free. Obviously, this client is able to remain habituated and compensated on a minimal program (daily for 10 minutes). It is clear, however, that the program is necessary to maintain her status. It also appears that she had primary, if not total, peripheral involvement and that the Brandt's exercises for habituation to positional stimuli were most effective in clearing her

symptoms and maintaining her equilibrium, further suggesting benign paroxysmal positional vertigo as the likely problem.

Case Presentation #3

Medical History

Heather, a 56-year-old client, was shopping for groceries when she fell on a wet floor and sustained a mild head injury. She was not taken to a hospital but later went to a neurologist complaining of severe dizziness, nausea, and problems with balance. She found it nearly impossible to walk without holding on to someone. At this time she was diagnosed as having benign paroxysmal positional vertigo and was given exercises, by the physician, for vestibular adaptation (habituation), particularly exercises emphasizing repetitive movements and positional changes that are designed to lessen the vertigo by accommodating to these activities.

By the time she was referred to physical therapy, she had quit practicing the habituation exercises on her own because they made her sick, and she was experiencing frequent falls. At this time, Heather was confined to her house because she could not walk anywhere else, even her own yard, without holding on to her husband. She had intense nystagmus, severe vertigo, and nausea with any angular head movements, positional changes, or eye movements. Her proprioception was intact. She did not go out in public often because she could not tolerate visual motion stimuli, and the bustling activity in stores and malls produced severe balance and orientation problems.

Treatment

With succeeding evaluations I became concerned that the vestibular damage might not be limited to the peripheral system and referred the client for an electronystagmography. These test results indicated that the problem was entirely central in nature with no demonstrable peripheral involvement. In my experience, clients with central vestibular problems do not always respond to habituation exercises by eventually "clearing" or experiencing a decrease in symptoms as do those with peripheral problems. Actually, habituation exercises only seem to stir them up and aggravate their discomfort, more than likely because there is no peripheral problem that is amenable to an habituation approach.

For this individual, I decided to work on postural balance activities and oculomotor control. There was not much change with oculomotor activities. She did obtain a copy of an Eyerobics video tape and followed the program. She was then able to perform repetitive smooth pursuit and saccadic eye movements without as much dizziness and nausea as she had originally experienced. We asked Heather to try to stop or control her nystagmus with visual fixation activities. When nystagmus is elicited in normal individuals, it can be stopped by fixing on a particular visual target. She was not able to gain control of her nystagmus through this technique.

Heather continued to work on balance activities such as weight shifts in standing and sitting on a mat in anterior-posterior directions and in sidesitting, unilateral stance with eyes open and closed, tandem walking, and walking on different surfaces and terrain. She was not sure of her center and would often overshoot with her responses producing huge postural corrections. She worked a little on the balance beam but was very apprehensive while using it. She was generally very anxious and exhibited apprehension throughout her program. She did learn to ambulate alone with a cane, even in her yard. Her balance activities were complicated by worsening osteoarthritis in her left knee. She would not consent to having surgical procedures performed on the knee. Because her knee was hampering any further progress, she was discontinued from therapy with the understanding that balance activities might be resumed if this problem could be alleviated. Before discharge the major emphasis in her program was safety. These included suggestions for installing night lights, removing any throw rugs, and being very careful when walking on compliant surfaces such as soft carpeting.

Heather, like Martha in Case #1, is another example of a client who experienced severe functional problems from an apparently minor head trauma. These cases suggest that there may be many unidentified candidates for therapy, particularly vestibular and balance therapy, who may be residing in the community. The rehabilitation of clients with balance difficulties or dizziness is complex and involves more than following a single protocol. Diagnosis of the problem may be inaccurate or incomplete if certain diagnostic procedures have not been performed. Even when such procedures are performed, variations in interpretation may occur. Additionally, we may discover that some clients score well on tests purported to evaluate balance, such as standing on one foot, and continue to manifest functional balance problems. Conversely, some clients may not score well on these tests but are able to negotiate varied terrain and perform other tasks quite well. The therapist must decide on a program that may be based as much on experience, logic, and trial-and-error as it is on specific protocols that have been developed for particular problems. The therapist must monitor the results and modify or discontinue the program as necessary.

Case Presentation #4

Medical History

Mary, a 55-year-old client, was admitted to an acute care hospital with altered mental status, nausea and vomiting. She had a history of hypertension and had been taking HydroDiuril®. The computerized axial tomography scan showed a large amount of subarachnoid hemorrhage bilaterally. The next day she underwent a left craniotomy for clipping of an aneurysm. Follow-up scans within 2 weeks showed a decrease in the amount of hemorrhage. She was admitted to a residential rehabilitation center 1 1/2 months after her stroke.

General Evaluation

Mary complained daily of headaches. Her sensation and proprioception were intact. She had a mild right hemiparesis with strength grades generally one-half grade weaker on the right. Her endurance was only fair. She could ambulate for 1 mile but occasionally experienced a hypoadaptive blood pressure response and reported moderate fatigue. She had full, active range of motion. Her fine and gross motor coordination were minimally decreased for speed and control of high level tasks.

Her visual acuity screening was within normal limits. Mary was able to warm her hand voluntarily during biofeedback sessions, indicating she would likely be successful in training to help achieve relaxation and gain control of her headaches. Audiological screening at 20 dB revealed decreased acuity at higher frequencies.

Overall communication skills were within normal limits. Mild defects were noted for understanding long complex material; however, repetitions frequently improved responses. Her ability was good to define words, recite a short paragraph, give correct biographical data, express ideas, and describe pictures. Mild word retrieval difficulties were observed with more difficult information; however, Mary appeared to compensate well for these problems. Reading skills were generally normal, although she occasionally reread items to assure herself of responses. She had some problems with mathematic abilities such as percentages, measurements, fractions, equations, and higher level tasks.

Functional Skills

Mary was independent in all aspects of grooming and dressing. She was able to plan a weekly menu and follow a low-salt diet with minimal assistance. She required minimal assistance to organize her shopping list into appropriate groups. She also required moderate assistance to use environmental cues and locate all items in an aisle in one trip. She required minimal assistance in reading labels, choosing an appropriate check-out aisle, and using her calculator. Mary was independent with simple familiar meal preparation. However, she experienced mild difficulty following unfamiliar and lengthy recipes, and she had moderate difficulty with divided attention when preparing more than one dish. That is keeping track of two separate preparations such as boiling rice and frying meat presented some problems. She had similar difficulties with divided attention when monitoring her own physiologic responses during endurance training. That is, she could either watch the clock or palpate her pulse but could not do both simultaneously. She required minor assistance for organization while writing checks to pay her bills.

Vestibular Status

Motor strategies were present for maintenance of postural control, but balance was mildly decreased for performance of higher level motor tasks such as jumping, unilateral stance, and tandem gait. Mary experienced mild blurred vision, dizziness, and occasional nausea with angular head movement and rapid changes of position. She had difficulty maintaining smooth pursuit in vertical, horizontal, and diagonal planes, and her saccadic eye movements required concentration and resulted in a mild "spacey" sensation when she would occasionally loose track of what she was looking at.

Postural control was mildly reduced in the presence of visual motion stimuli and in the absence of a firm supporting surface. She ambulated over moderately varied terrain in the community with an assistant standing by in case assistance was required. She varied speed and direction of ambulation correctly around environmental objects.

When she made a sharp turn, she would often overly rotate her upper trunk. She would complain on occasion that she "walked like a crab," and indeed, she would sometimes list or rotate sideways. A sudden stop would result in this axial rotation so that she twisted away from a vertical alignment. She exhibited extreme hip strategies when on the balance beam, expressing her determination to stay on it.

An examination by an otoneurologist showed that Mary had a positional vertigo with 50% hypofunctioning on the left. She also showed electronystagmographic changes, suggesting some central abnormalities.

Rehabilitation Program

In addition to cognitive, behavioral, communicative, and functional living skills programs, physical therapy was instituted for vestibular rehabilitation and general strengthening. She also engaged in low impact aerobic activities, such as stationary bike riding, to increase cardiopulmonary status and endurance.

Mary was given habituation exercises to try to diminish the intensity of her vertigo in provoking positions. She was also instructed in oculomotor exercises to gain more control of her eye movements and to minimize the disequilibrium aggravated by eye movements. At the beginning, visual tracking with horizontal and vertical eye movements produced sore eyes and increased her headaches. On a scale of 0 to 10 (0 no dizziness; 10 the worst dizziness she could experience) she would rate her dizziness as a 7 or 8, and the symptoms would continue for over 2 minutes. Head movements with her eyes open produced dizziness rated at 2 or 3, which persisted for about 1 minute. She also used an Eyerobics exercise tape in the evenings and on weekends to enhance her oculomotor function.

Mary participated in balance activities to gain compensation for lost vestibular functions. Some of these activities were standing on one leg, standing weight shifts on the floor and on foam rubber, all with eyes open and then with eyes closed, and tandem gait. In addition, she walked over varied terrain and performed quick stops, directional changes, angular head movements, and visual tracking of moving objects in her environment.

Treatment Results and Conclusions

Mary was discharged from the rehabilitation center 5 months later. At the time of her discharge, her symptoms resulting from oculomotor activities had diminished in that eye movements now produced dizziness rated between 1 and 5; however, most activities produced vertigo rated between 2 and 3. The duration of symptoms was usually about 30 seconds. She described some headache or pressure in her eyes and continued to demonstrate poor control of some eye movements. Over this time she experienced a decrease in intensity and duration of dizziness with angular head movements and rapid positional changes.

Mary was reasonably independent in all functions at discharge. She was receiving vocational counseling and was working in a voluntary position in the Veteran's Administration hospital, assisting a doctor in organizing a backlog of charts. A permanent position had not been found. She was becoming less anxious about her deficit areas and was learning techniques to reduce anxiety and to help her and her family deal with episodes of impatience or short temper that developed after her aneurysm. Her functional living skills were acceptable, and she concentrated on recreational therapy and on alternative forms of transportation such as the rapid transit system.

By the end of her vestibular rehabilitation program, Mary was able to perform the oculomotor activities that included moving her eyes up and down, horizontally, clockwise, and counterclockwise, and performing saccadic and convergence exercises. I also constructed a tray with lipped edges and drew a cross on it to be used as a visual target. Then marbles were put on the tray, and it was tilted so that the marbles moved while she was attempting to attend to the visual target. Again, we were trying to find exercises to help her cope with movement in her visual field. At this time, she reported a dizziness rating of 1 and a duration of symptoms ranging from 10 to 14 seconds, both of which were significant decreases from her beginning levels. No nausea or headaches were noted, although eye control remained somewhat poor.

This client demonstrates the vestibular involvement that may occur with insults to the brain, such as from a stroke or perhaps a brain tumor. The problems were both peripheral and central in nature. Habituation activities produced some decrease in the intensity of her positional vertigo but reached a certain level without further improvement. Thus it became important for me to judge when to discontinue these activities before the gains might be compromised by the aggravation produced with continued practice. I find that clients with central involvement usually are not as responsive to such activities as are those with peripheral involvement and, indeed, often are aggravated by them. Visual-vestibular exercises and balance therapy for her resulted in a significant decrease in symptoms but did not produce complete compensation, most likely because of her central involvement. Her functional capacity improved through balance activities, as I find is often the case with clients who have central vestibular problems. Much of vestibular rehabilitation in these situations thus becomes a judgment call on the part of the therapist. I must determine what is likely to be the optimum outcome and decide when to change or stop the program.

Study Questions:

The following cases are offered for you to see what you can do with them. Given what you now know about motor control and motor learning, what approaches might you take with these clients? What else do you need to know? Be sure to consider all the aspects of treatment and evaluation that have been presented in this text.

Case Study #1

History

Jozelle is a 6-year-old girl who was born at full term to a 36-year-old mother by cesarean section after 24 hours of unfruitful labor. The girl went into respiratory arrest shortly after birth, followed by seizure. By 5 months of age, she demonstrated some stiffness and posturing of her right arm, with a general decrease in movement of the right side. She continued to have seizures occasionally. At 7 months of age she was diagnosed as having a right spastic hemiplegia. She was put on seizure control medication, which has been effective.

Jozelle is currently enrolled in an urban public school with special education classrooms. She has an IQ score of 68 and is mildly mentally retarded. She receives speech therapy and physical therapy at the school.

Evaluation

Jozelle is a cooperative, happy child. On the left side, joint range of motion is within normal limits, and the muscles are relatively extensible and flexible. On the right side there is a flexion contracture at the elbow (10°) and a plantar flexion contracture at the ankle (5°). There is mild restriction between the scapula and the humerus. Resistance to passive range of motion can be demonstrated in both the right arm and leg. The trunk appears mildly hypotonic. Jozelle has normal muscle strength on the left. Movement patterns using the right side are diminished, and some posturing occurs. The right arm is held in some flexion and internal rotation at the shoulder and in slight flexion at the elbow. The wrist may be flexed and the thumb is occasionally held in the palm of the hand. Thus either pattern abnormalities or muscular weakness or both affect the movements on the right.

Protective extension reactions are present on the left and absent on the right. Equilibrium reactions are slow and incomplete in both the trunk and the extremities, particularly on the right. Righting responses are adequate. Jozelle shows marked asymmetry when standing and bears most of her weight on the left leg. She is not able to maintain standing balance on soft and compliant surfaces, and she has decreased limits of stability especially to the left. Even gentle external perturbations produce a hip strategy or a stepping strategy. Sitting posture is adequate. Jozelle is independently ambulatory and on the right demonstrates typical gait deviations of toe contact or flat-foot placement, lack of complete hip extension at terminal stance, and decreased stance time.

Jozelle demonstrates gross motor skills of 18 to 20 months of age on the Peabody Developmental Motor Scales. She can balance on the right leg for less than 3 seconds and cannot perform jumping and other bilateral skills. She can walk backward and can kick or throw a ball 3 feet. Her fine motor skills are at a more advanced level of about 28 months. She can copy a circle and a cross on paper and remove the cap from a bottle. Bilateral activities such as cutting with scissors and stringing beads cannot be completed properly. The right hand lacks full functional grasp but can be used as a helping hand. She demonstrates tactile hypersensitivity, particularly about the face. She can self-feed and has mild speech problems, especially in breath control and articulation.

Case Study #2

History

Arron is an 11-month-old boy born at full term to a 24-year-old mother who had experienced a normal pregnancy, although she noted that the developing baby seemed to lack the usual amount of movement. This was her second child. He weighed 5 lb 9 oz at birth. His APGAR scores were 8 and 9 at 1 and 5 minutes.

Evaluation

Arron's joint range of motion is fairly normal, although he demonstrates some hyperextensibility particularly at the hips. He appears to have a less than normal amount of muscle bulk, and his muscle strength is generally mildly decreased. Sometimes the extremities are held stiffly, and a very mild

increased resistance to passive stretch occurs at the ankles. Muscle activity in the trunk is low.

Protective reactions are absent. Righting reactions are slow and incomplete. Arron has a repertoire of normal or near normal movement patterns, such as prone on elbows and prone extension, although these patterns are lacking in strength, and he does not demonstrate a full range of the activity. This is particularly true of cervical and thoracic extension. He can lift his legs to play with his feet but does not use a good abdominal muscle pattern to do this. He also demonstrates abnormal patterns such as holding the right arm in flexion and internal rotation with a fisted hand. Generally, at rest he assumes a "frog-legged" posture in the lower extremities, with abduction and external rotation of the hips, flexion of the knees, and excessive eversion at the ankle. When kicking, eversion is noted at the ankles. In performing a pull-to-sit maneuver he provides minimal assistance and demonstrates moderate head lag when the sacrum is at 60 degrees or less from the surface. When highly agitated he stiffens his whole body and demonstrates excessive extension.

Functionally, he is able to roll from side to side and with some assistance will roll all the way to prone. He shows minimal reach and grasp for toys or other objects of interest. He will hold objects placed in his hands. He cannot assume sitting and can sit only by flexing the trunk and resting on his hands or when supported externally. He tends to retract his neck and stiffen the upper musculature to provide more background support. His thoracic spine become kyphotic. If supported, Arron will take some weight on his lower extremities, but his knees hyperextend. Any stepping movements he may attempt are poorly coordinated. The general hypotonia of the trunk and extremities is apparent.

He is a "lazy" feeder and does not demonstrate strong bottle-sucking patterns, requiring extra time for feeding. He does not have an adequate gag reflex. Milk often pools in his mouth and then spills out because appropriate coordination is lacking for sucking and swallowing. Soft or pureed foods appear to be managed best. Munching or chewing movements are weak and incomplete.

Arron was evaluated with the Bayley Scales of Infant Development and had an age equivalence of 5 months. The Mental scales scores also suggested a cognitive functioning of 5 months.

Case Study #3

History

Joyce Sarnoff is a 42-year-old woman who experienced a right cerebrovascular accident as a result of a ruptured aneurysm 2 months ago. She suddenly experienced left-sided weakness and was transferred to an acute care center. Twenty-three days later she was transferred to this rehabilitation center. She received physical, occupational, and speech therapy in the acute care center. Initially, her paralysis was flaccid, and the physical therapy notes indicate that she was oriented and cooperative. She was able to come to standing without assistance and walk with a quad cane at the time of transfer to our center.

Evaluation

At this time, Joyce is alert and oriented. She shows some aphasia but communicates effectively with words and gestures. Her affect is somewhat flat. She is cooperative but impulsive. She can follow two-step commands 80% of the time but is not adequately able to follow three-step commands. She has deficits in decision making and short-term memory.

Her passive range of motion is limited on the left at the ankle (comes only to neutral) and at the wrist (5° of wrist extension). The left arm is in Brunnstrom Stage IV, the hand is in Stage III, and the lower extremity is in Stage IV. Thus she can begin to move out of synergy with simple combinations such as putting her hand behind her back and flexing the knee when sitting. The hand shows mass grasp without voluntary release. She shows increased resistance to passive stretch in most muscles on the left and hyperactive deep tendon reflexes. Effort produces associated reactions. She demonstrates influences from tonic reflexes such as the asymmetric tonic neck reflex. Protective extension is absent on the left. Weakness is apparent in the trunk and the extremities. She has poor reciprocal movements and is not able to perform movements at any speed other than slow.

Joyce can manage her wheelchair, has bed mobility, and can transfer with minimal assistance. She can walk 50 feet on level surfaces with her quad cane. Her left pelvis is retracted, she has active hip flexion but shows some circumduction because her hip and knee motion is decreased during swing. Foot placement is poor; the initial contact is with the toes. At terminal stance, she has genu recurvatum and incomplete hip extension. She needs moderate assistance for dressing and toileting. The sequencing of such activities needs direction.

The appreciation of tactile and position sense is generally poor in the left extremities, particularly the arm. Light touch is mildly impaired in the left face and trunk. She demonstrates a moderate amount of left-sided neglect. She has a left visual field defect. Perception of auditory stimuli is intact. Her balance during standing, walking, and transfers is impaired, particularly during transfers. Her limits of stability are narrow, and she cannot regain her balance if perturbed. She demonstrates a hip strategy when lightly perturbed. She cannot stand on a compliant surface for more than 30 seconds, even with eyes open. If her vision is stabilized (by putting on a visual dome), she cannot stand at all on a compliant surface and has difficulty on a firm surface. She tends to list to the left side when sitting and is unaware that such a posture is not appropriate.

Case Study #4

History

Jon Jones is a 19-year-old male college student who sustained a closed head injury as the result of a motorcycle accident. At the time he was admitted to the hospital he was comatose but demonstrated intact brain stem reflexes, such as reacting pupils. His Glasgow Coma Scale Score was 9. At the time of transfer 3 months later, he had spasticity in all extremities, particularly the lower. Range of motion was limited in some joints, and he had very little trunk and head control, requiring considerable support when sitting. He is now at a specialized center for spinal cord and brain injury. He has a well-educated and supportive family.

Evaluation

Jon is now 8 months posttrauma. Although he is sometimes combative in therapy, he is best classified as level V: confused appropriate (Rancho Las Amigos Level of Cognitive Functioning). He is able to follow simple instructions but degenerates quickly when more complex interaction is attempted. He has difficulty concentrating on tasks and is easily distracted. He has moderately severe deficits in memory, and his most obvious problems are with his short-term memory. He shows inappropriate use of objects and is often unable to identify common objects. He responds to sensory input but it is difficult to evaluate his perception and integration of such input. His family members indicate that he is a totally different person than before the accident. They indicate that he was a friendly, soft-spoken, cooperative individual with greater than average intelligence.

He has several joint contractures: plantar flexion contractures 10 degrees on the right and 7 degrees on the left; he lacks 10 degrees of knee extension on the left, and 5 degrees of hip extension on the left. There is increased resistance to passive stretch throughout his extremities, particularly on the left side. Functionally it appears that muscle strength is decreased somewhat throughout the body but perhaps more so in the lower extremities, particularly on the left.

Jon shows disturbances in balance processing. Any deviations are greatly increased when his eyes are closed. When sitting, he lists to the left, and his head control is intermittent. He sits unevenly, bearing more weight on the right ischial tuberosity. He can stand with maximal assistance and move some in the parallel bars with constant guidance and assistance. He must be reminded to put weight more evenly on both sides, to advance the leg, or to assume an appropriate posture for his trunk. He also shows considerable tremulousness and instability when sitting, standing, or walking. His movements are very slow, and if he moves his head too rapidly, he complains of dizziness and vertigo. He has nystagmus that is positionally related.

Functionally, Jon is able to manage his wheelchair. The family wishes to provide an electric wheelchair but have been discouraged from doing this both for the exercise and coordination benefits of a regular chair and for the cognitive and behavioral problems that may render the chair dangerous. He can roll and come to sitting with minimal guidance and can perform standing pivot transfers with moderate assistance. His movement patterns are uncoordinated and lacking in strength, but they would not be described as a particular synergy pattern or resulting from obligatory reflex dominance.

Bibliography - Section IV

Anacker SL, Di Fabio RP. Influence of sensory inputs on standing balance in community-dwelling elders with a recent history of falling. *Phys Ther*. 1992;72:575-584.

Asmussen E. Muscle fatigue. *Med Sci Sports Exerc*. 1979;11:313-321.

Asmussen E, Mazin B. A central nervous component in local muscular fatigue. *Eur J Appl Physiol*. 1978a;38:9-15.

Asmussen E, Mazin B. Recuperation after muscular fatigue by diverting activities. *Eur J Appl Physiol*. 1978b;38:1-7.

Bandy WD, Lovelace-Chandler. Determinants of muscle strength. *Physical Therapy Practice*. 1992;2:1-10.

Bilodeau EA, Bilodeau IM. Variable frequency knowledge of results and the learning of a simple skill. *J Exp Psychol[Learn Mem Cogn]*. 1958;55:379-383.

Bilodeau EA, Bilodeau I, Schumsky DA. Some effects of introducing and withdrawing knowledge of results early and late in practice. *J Exp Psychol[Learn Mem Cogn]*. 1959;58:142-144.

Black FO, Wall C, Rocketter HE, et al. Normal subject postural sway during the Romberg test. *Am J Otolaryngol*. 1982;3:309-318.

Bohannon RW. Nature, Implications, and measurement of limbs and muscle strength in patients with orthopedic and neurological disorders. *Physical Therapy Practice*. 1992;2:22-31.

Bohannon RW, Larkin P. Decrease in timed balance test scores with aging. *Phys Ther*. 1984;64:1067-1070.

Brocklehurst JC, Robertson D, James-Groom P. Clinical correlates of sway in old age--sensory modalities: *Age Aging*. 1982;11:1-10.

Caffrey S, Hendricks T, Hickey M, et al. Comparison of Kinematic and electromyographic analysis of sitting balance in infants using blocked and variable practice. Presented at the 12th International Congress of the World Confederation for Physical Therapy, June, 1995, Washington DC.

Carr JH, Shepherd RB, Gordon J, et al. *Movement Science: Foundations for Physical Therapy in Rehabilitation*. Rockville, Md: Aspen Publishers Inc; 1987

Chandler JM, Duncan PW. Balance and falls in the elderly: issues in evaluation and treatment. In Guccione AA, ed. *Geriatric Physical Therapy*. St Louis, Mo: Mosby Co; 1993:237-251.

Cusick BD, Stuberg WA. Assessment of lower-extremity alignment in the transverse plane: implications for management of children with neuromotor dysfunction. *Phys Ther*. 1992;72:3-15.

Cintas HM. The relationship of motor skill level and risk-taking during exploration in toddlers. *Pediatric Physical Therapy*. 1992;4:165-170.

Crutchfield C, Shumway-Cook A, Horak FB. Balance and coordination training. In: Scully R, Barnes M, eds. *Physical Therapy*. Philadelphia, Pa: J B Lippincott Co; 1989.

Cummings GS. Personal communication, February, 1993.

Dettman MA, Linder MT, Sepic S. Relationships among walking performance, postural stability, and functional assessments of the hemiplegic patient. *Am J Phys Med*. 1987;66:77-90.

Dunbar JM, Agras WS. Compliance with medical instructions. In: Ferguson J, ed. *The Comprehensive Handbook of Behavioral Medicine, III*. New York, NY: Spectrum Publications; 1980.

Duncan PW. Stroke: physical therapy assessment. In: *Contemporary Management of Motor Control Problems: Proceedings of the II Step Conference*. Alexandria, Va: Foundation for Physical Therapy; 1991:209-217.

Duncan PW, Chandler JM. Strategies for assessment in falls in the elderly. Presented at the 67th Annual Conference of the American Physical Therapy Association; June 1992; Denver, Colo.

Duncan PW, Weiner DK, Chandler JM et al. Functional reach: a new clinical measure of balance. *Journal of Gerontology (Medical Sciences)*. 1990;45:192-197.

Duncan PW, Studenski SA, Chandler JM, et al. Functional reach: predictive validity in a sample of elderly male veterans. *Journal of Gerontology*, Medical Sciences. 1992; 47:93-98.

Duncan PW, Chandler JM, Prescott BL, et al. How do physiologic components of balance affect function in elders?1993, (Unpublished data).

Era P. Posture control in the elderly. *International Journal of Technology and Aging*. 1988;1:166-179.

Fisher BE, Sullivan KJ, Powers CM. The effect of imposed mobility restrictions on movement patterns of a healthy individual. Presented at the 12th International Congress of the World Confederation for Physical Therapy, June, 1995, Washington DC.

Fiatarone MA, Marks EC, Ryan ND, et al. High-intensity strength training in nonagenarians. *JAMA*. 1990;263:3029-3034.

Fitts PM. Factors in complex skill training. In: Glaser R, ed. *Training Research and Education*. Pittsburgh, Pa: University of Pittsburgh Press; 1962.

France DP, Derscheid G, Irragang J, et al. Preliminary clinical evaluation of the Breg K.A.T. effects of training in normals. *Isokenetic & Exer Sci*. 1992;2:133-138.

Gajdosik VG, Campbell SK. Effects of weekly review, socioeconomic status, and maternal belief on mother's compliance with their disabled children's home exercise program. *Physical and Occupational Therapy in Pediatrics*. 1991;11:47-65.

Gentile AM, Higgins JR, Miller EA, Rosen BM. Structure of motor tasks. *Movement, Actes du 7 Symposium en Apprentissage Psycho-motor du Sport, Quebec. Professionalle de L'Activite Physique du Quebec;* 1975;11-28.

Gentile AM. Skill acquisition: action, movement, and neuromotor processes. In: Carr JH, Shepherd RB, Gordon J, Gentile AM, Held JM. *Movement Science: Foundations for Physical Therapy in Rehabilitation*. Rockville, MD: Aspen Publishers Inc; 1987

Gentile AM. *Nature of Skill Acquisition*. Presented at the 67th Annual Conference of the American Physical Therapy Association; June 1992; Denver, Colo.

Ghez C. Posture. In: Kandel ER, Schwartz JH, Jessell TM, eds. *Principles of Neural Science*. 3rd ed. New York, NY: Elsevier Science Publishing Co Inc; 1991:596-607.

Hagen C, Malkmus D, Durham P. Levels of cognitive functioning. In *Rehabilitation of the Head Injured Adult: Comprehensive Physical Management*. Downey, Calif: Professional Staff Association of Rancho Los Amigos Hospital, Inc; 1979.

Hallum A. Subject induced reinforcement of head lifting in the prone position: a case report. *Phys Ther*. 1984;64:1390-1392.

Haley SM, Ludlow LH. Applicability of the hierarchical scales of the Tufts Assessment of Motor Performance for school-aged children and adults with disabilities. Phys Ther. 1992;72:191-206.

Harmon JM, Miller AG. Time patterns in motor learning. *Research Quarterly*. 1950;21:182-187.

Ho L, Shea JB. Effects of relative frequency of knowledge of results on retention of a motor skill. *Percept Mot Skills*. 1978;46:859-866.

Horak FB. Clinical measurement of postural control in adults. *Phys Ther*. 1987;67:1881.

Horak FB. Comparison of cerebellar and vestibular loss on scaling of postural responses. In: Brandt T, et al, eds. *Disorders of Posture and Gait: Xth International Symposium of the Society of Postural Gait Research*. New York, NY: Thieme Medical Publishers Inc; 1990.

Horak FB, Esselman P, Anderson ME, Lynch MK. The effects of movement velocity, mass displaced and task certainty on associated postural adjustments made by normal and hemiplegic individuals. *J Neurol Neurosurg Psychiatry*. 1984;47:1020-1028.

Horak FB, Nashner LM, Diener HC. Abnormal scaling of postural responses in cerebellar patients. *Neuroscience Abstracts*. 1986;12:1419.

Horak FB, Shumway-Cook A, Crowe TK, Black FO. Vestibular function and motor proficiency in hearing impaired and learning-disabled children. *Dev Med Child Neurol*. 1988;30:64-79.

Hughes P, Neer R. Lighting for the elderly: a psychological approach to lighting. *Hum Factors*. 1981:23:65-85.

Hulka S, Casses JC, Kupper LL. Disparities between medications prescribed and consumed among chronic disease patients. In: Lasagna L, ed. *Patient Compliance.* Mount Kisco, NY: Futura Publishing Company; 1976.

Jette AM. Improving patient cooperation with arthritis treatment regimens. *Arthritis Rheum.* 1982;25:447-453.

Johansson G, Jarnlo G. Balance training in 70-year-old women. *Physiotherapy Theory and Practice.* 1991;7:121-125.

Judge JO, Lindsey C, Underwood M, Winsemius D. Balance improvements in older women: effects of exercise training. *Phys Ther.* 1993;73:254-265.

Kazis LE, Friedman RH. Improving medication compliance in the elderly: strategies for the health care provider. *J Am Geriatr Soc.* 1988;36:1161-1162.

Keshner EA. Controlling stability of a complex movement system. *Phys Ther.* 1990;70:844-854.

Keshner EA. Reflex, voluntary, and mechanical processes in postural stabilization. In: Duncan PW, ed. *Balance.* Alexandria, Va: American Physical Therapy Association; 1990.

Kerr R. *Psychomotor Learning.* New York, NY: CBS College Publishing; 1982.

Landers DM. Observational learning of a motor skill: temporal spacing of demonstrations and audience presence. *Journal of Motor Behavior.* 1975;7:285-290.

Landers DM, Landers DM. Teacher versus peer models: effect of model's presence and performance level on motor behavior. *Journal of Motor Behavior.* 1973;5:129-139.

Lavery JJ. Retention of simple motor skills as a function of type of knowledge of results. *Can J Psychol.* 1962;16:305.

Lee M, Mosley A, Refshauge K. Effect of feedback on learning a vertebral joint mobilization skill. *Phys Ther.* 1990;70:97-104.

Lee WA. A control systems framework for understanding normal and abnormal posture. *Am J Occup Ther.* 1989;43:291-301.

Lee WA, Deming L, Sahgal V. Quantitative and clinical measures of static standing balance in hemiparetic and normal subjects. *Phys Ther.* 1988;68:970-976.

Leitman MW, Gartner S, Henkind P. *Manual for Eye Examination and Diagnosis.* Oradell, NJ: Medical Economics Co; 1981.

Light KE, Rehm S. Timed functional movements in elderly clients with balance or dizziness disorders. Presented at the Combined Sections Meeting of the American Physical Therapy Association; February 1993; San Antonio, Tex.

Lucca JA, Recchiuti SJ. Effects of electromyographic biofeedback on an isometric strengthening program. *Phys Ther.* 1983;63:200-203.

Maki BE, Holliday PJ, Fernie G. A posture control model and balance test for the prediction of relative postural stability. *IEEE Trans Biomed Eng.* 1987;10:797-809.

Maki BE, Holliday PJ, Fernie G. A posture control model and balance test for the prediction of relative postural stability. *IEEE Trans Biomed 'Eng.* 1987;10:797-809.

Malkmus D. Integrating cognitive strategies into the physical therapy setting. *Phys Ther.* 1983:63:10-17.

Malouin F, Potvin M, Prevost J, et al. Use of an intensive task-oriented gait training program in a series of patients with acute cerebrovascular accidents. *Phys Ther.* 1992;72:781-793.

Maring JR. Effects of mental practice on rate of skill acquisition. *Phys Ther.* 1990;70:165-172.

Marston M. Compliance with medical regimens. *Nurs Res.* 1970 19:312-323.

Mathias S, Nayak USL, Issacs B. Balance in elderly patients: the get up and go test. *Arch Phys Med Rehabil.* 1986;67:387-389.

McCracken HD, Steimach GE. A test of schema theory of discrete motor learning. *Journal of Motor Behavior.* 1977;9:197.

Merians A, Winstein C, Sullivan K, et al. Effects of feedback for motor skill learning in older healthy subjects and individuals post-stroke. *Neurology Report.* June, 1995.

Nashner LM. Adapting reflexes controlling the human posture. *Exp Brain Res.* 1976;26:59-72.

Nashner LM. Fixed patterns of postural responses among leg muscles during stance. *Exp Brain Res.* 1977;30:13-34.

Nashner LM. Adaptation of human movement to altered environments. *Trends in Neuroscience.* 1982;5:351-361.

Nashner LM. Sensory, neuromuscular, and biomechanical contributions to human balance. In: Duncan PW, ed. *Balance.* Alexandria, Va: American Physical Therapy Association; 1990:5-12.

Newton R. Recovery of balance abilities in individuals with traumatic brain injuries. In: Duncan PW. ed. *Balance.* Alexandria, Va: American Physical Therapy Association; 1990:69-72.

Parsons T. *The Social System.* Glencoe, Ill: Free Press; 1951.

Rose DK, Light KE, Cedar J. Use of the Functional Reach Test in a balance and dizziness clinic for older adults. Presented at the Combined Sections Meeting of the American Physical Therapy Association; February 1993; San Antonio, Tex.

Sakett DL, Snow JC. The magnitude of compliance and noncompliance. In: Haynes RB, Taylor CW, Sackett DL, eds. *Compliance in Health Care.* Baltimore, Md: The Johns Hopkins University Press; 1979.

Salmoni AW, Schmidt RA, Walter CB. Knowledge of results and motor learning: a review and critical appraisal. *Psychol Bull.* 1984;95:355-386.

Schmidt RA. *Motor Control and Learning: A Behavioral Emphasis.* 2nd ed. Champaign, Ill: Human Kinetics Publishers Inc; 1988.

Schulmann DL, Godfrey B, Fisher AG. Effect of eye movements on dynamic equilibrium. *Phys Ther.* 1987;67:1054-1059.

Shea JB, Morgan RL. Contextual interference effects on acquisition, retention, and transfer of motor skill. *J Exp Psychol [Learn Mem Cogn].* 1979;5:183.

Shea JB, Upton G. The effects of skill acquisition of an interpolated motor short-term memory task during the KR-Delay interval. *Journal of Motor Behavior.* 1976;8:280.

Shumway-Cook A, Anson D, Haller S. Postural sway biofeedback: its effect on reestablishing stance stability in hemiplegic patients. *Arch Phys Med Rehabil.* 1988;69:395-400.

Shumway-Cook A, Horak FB. Assessing the influence of sensory interaction on balance. *Phys Ther.* 1986;66:1548-1550.

Shumway-Cook A, Horak FB, Black FO. A critical examination of vestibular function in motor-impaired learning-disabled children. *Int J Pediatr Otorhinolaryngol.* 1987;14:21-20.

Skinner BF. *Beyond Freedom and Dignity.* New York, NY: Knopf; 1971.

Stallings LM. *Motor learning From Theory to Practice.* St Louis, Mo: C V Mosby Co; 1982.

Stelmach GE, Phillips J, DiFabio RP, et al. Age, functional postural reflexes, and voluntary sway. *Journal of Gerontolgy and Biological Science.* 1989;44:100-106.

Studenski SA, Duncan PW, Weiner DK, Chandler JM. The role of instability in falls among older persons. In Duncan PW, ed. *Balance.* Alexandria, Va: American Physical Therapy Association; 1990:57-60.

Tinetti ME. Performance oriented assessment of mobility problems in elderly patients. *J Am Geriatr Soc.* 1986;34:119-126.

Vanderlinden DW, Brunt D, Behrman AL. Weight-bearing asymmetries during sit-to-stand in persons with hemiplegia from cerebral vascular accident. Presented at the Combined Sections Meeting of the American Physical Therapy Association; February 1993; San Antonio, Tex.

Weiner DK, Bongiorni DR, Studenski SA, Duncan PW. Functional reach and rehabilitation. *Arch Phys Med Rehabil.* In press.

Weiner DK, Duncan PW, Chandler JM, Studenski S. Functional reach: a marker of physical frailty. *J Am Geriatr Soc.* 1992; 40:203-207.

Weiner WJ, Nora LM, Glantz RH. Elderly inpatients: postural reflex impairment. *Neurology.* 1984;34:945-947.

Whipple R, Wolfson LI. Abnormalities of balance, gait, and sensorimotor function in the elderly population. In: Duncan PW, ed. *Balance.* Alexandria, Va: American Physical Therapy Association; 1990:61-68.

Winstein CJ. Balance retraining: does it transfer? In: Duncan PW, ed. *Balance.* Alexandria, Va: American Physical Therapy Association; 1990:95-103.

Winstein CJ, Gardner ER, McNeal DR, et al. Standing balance training: effect on balance and locomotion in hemiparetic adults. Arch Phys Med Rehabil. 1989;70:755-762.

Winstein CJ, Knecht HG. Movement science and its relevance to physical therapy. *Phys Ther*. 1990;70:759-762.

Winstein CJ. Motor Learning and Motor Control. Presented at the 12th International Congress of the World Confederation for Physical Therapy, June, 1995, Washington DC.

Weber J. *Nurses' Handbook of Health Assessment*. Philadelphia, Pa: J B Lippincott Co; 1988.

Wolf SL. Electromyographic biofeedback applications to stroke patients: a critical review. *Phys Ther*. 1983;63:1448-1461.

Wolf SL, Binder-MacLeod SA. Electromyographic biofeedback applications to the hemiplegic patient: changes in upper extremity neuromuscular and functional status. *Phys Ther*. 1983a;63:1393-1403.

Wolf SL, Binder-Macleod SA. Electromyographic biofeedback applications to the hemiplegic patient: changes in lower extremity neuromuscular and functional status. *Phys Ther*. 1983b;63:1404-1413.

Wolfson LI, Whipple R, Amerman P, et al. Stressing the postural response: a qualitative method for testing balance. *J Am Geriatr Soc*. 1986;34:845-850.

Woollacott MH, Shumway-Cook A, Nashner LM. Postural reflexes and aging. In: Mortemar J, Pirolzzolo F, Maletta G, eds. *The Aging Nervous System*. New York, NY: Praeger Publishers; 1982;108-119.

Woollacott MH, Inglin B, Manchester D. Response preparation in neuromuscular and postural control: neuromuscular changes in older adults. *Ann NY Acad Sci*. 1988;575:42-53.

Yakura J, Fisher B. How to analyze movement: a model for physical therapy. Presented at the 2nd Joint Congress of the American Physical Therapy Association/Canadian Physiotherapy Association, June, 1994, Toronto, Canada.

Appendix A - Screening and Evaluation Tools*

Assessment of Preterm Infant Behavior (APIB) (Als et al 1982).

This behavioral test assesses the preterm infant's behavioral organization along five dimensions: physiologic, motor, state, interactional, and self-regulatory. The test, composed of increasingly demanding environmental inputs, or packages, includes eight reflexes on the low tactile package; six on the medium tactile-vestibular package; and two on the high tactile-vestibular package. The elicitation of reflexes is not used in the traditional neurological sense but provides systematic elicitations of specific movements (SEMs) to bring out the range of various postures, movements, and tonus capacities of infants and to document their developmental course. Additionally, how these SEMs affect the organization of the autonomic, motor, state, and regulatory systems are also identified. The administration and scoring of the SEMs are from Prechtl (1977), when appropriate. Scoring is on an ordinal scale from 0 (not elicitable) to 3 (very strong hyperactive or obligatory response).

Chandler Movement Assessment of Infants-Screening Test (CMAI-ST) (Chandler 1986).

This criterion-referenced test that screens children from 2 to 8 months of age is constructed along the lines of its parent test, Movement Assessment in Infants. The four sections of the test include: muscle tone, primitive reflexes, automatic reactions, and volitional movements. Three possible scores are used for each item: 1) mature--normal response pattern, 2) developing pattern and 3) least mature--abnormal pattern. The test is normed; interrater reliabilities, established by two examiners on infants, average 87.1%. Test-retest reliability is currently being conducted. This test is waiting final publication.

Milani-Comparetti Motor Development Screening Test (Milani-Comparetti and Giodioni 1967a).

This criterion-referenced screening tool, designed for infants from birth through the first 2 years of life, is composed of reflexes and reactions and of voluntary activities. Five primitive reflexes and 13 postural reactions encompassing righting, parachute, and tilting reactions are included on the evaluation. The original publication (1967a) provides minimal instructions on how to elicit or score motor responses. In 1977, the original test form was modified, and specific criteria for elicitation and scoring of the reflexes were developed (Tremblath et al 1977). In 1987, the manual was revised to provide additional clarification of testing and scoring procedures (Stuberg et al 1987).

Four scoring systems have been published. The original publication (1967a) and the second (1977) are identical in content but represent different ordering of the items. The responses are on a nominal scale: present or absent. The third scoring system scores responses on an ordinal scale of 1-5, with 5 indicating normal movement and 1-2, abnormal function (Stuberg et al 1987). Vanderlinden (1985) developed another way to score it. No data are available on the reliability or validity of the test. Standardization studies have not been conducted.

Movement Assessment of Infants (MAI) (Chandler et al 1980).

This test, developed for infants up to the age of 12 months, is composed of four sections: 1) muscle tone (readiness of muscles to respond to gravity), 2) primitive reflexes, 3) automatic reactions, and 4) volitional movement. The primitive reflexes and automatic reactions of righting, protection, and equilibrium are scored on a unidirectional 4-point ordinal scale, where 1 represents the most mature or optimal response and 4 represents the least mature or most aberrant response. Specific testing procedures are indicated for each reflex and automatic reaction, with specific scoring criteria identified for each.

These items do not stand alone but are part of the more comprehensive test of movement of infants. Administration of the entire test results in a risk score for motor dysfunction. Data on predictability of this test for later functional dysfunction is available for 4 month olds (Chandler et al 1980) and 8 month olds (Swanson 1990). There is limited normative data for the 4- and 8-month-olds' profiles. The overall reliability of the test for the 4 month olds is acceptable (Harris et al 1984a), and there is some measure of concurrent and predictive validity (Harris et al 1984b). In a recent study, inter-rater and test-testest reliabilities were considered excellent (Brander et al 1993).

Neonatal Behavioral Assessment Scale (NBAS) (Brazelton 1984).

This behavioral test was developed to be used with full-term infants through 1 month postterm age. It can also be used with the preterm infant from a corrected age of 38 weeks. A modified version of the test (BNBAS-K) has been used with full-term infants through 3 months postterm. In addition to 26 behavioral items, the test also includes 20 reflex items. Each test is scored on a ordinal scale from 0 (absent) to 3 (high). The techniques of elicitation of the reflexes are according to Prechtl (1977). The test is not normed. Reliability has been reported from .85 to 1 (Brazelton 1984).

Neonatal Neurobehavioral Examination (NNE) (Morgan et al 1988).

This test, similar to the NAPI (see next test), has three sections: muscle tension and motor patterns, primitive reflexes, and behavioral responses. The evaluation is primarily intended for use with the preterm infant at a corrected age between 37 and 44 weeks. Nine items are included on the reflex section. Scoring is ordinal, 1-3, with a score of 1 being indicative of responses of preterm infants of 32 weeks GA; 2, of 32 to 36 weeks GA; and 3, 37 to 42 weeks GA. Abnormal responses are included in a separate column and are scored a 1, 2, or 3. A numerical quotient is obtained for each of the three section and for the test as a whole. The test

was standardized in full-term and at-risk infants. Intertester agreement was 95%, by total score in each section. Validity studies are currently being conducted.

Neurological Assessment of the Preterm and Full-Term Newborn Infant (NAPI) (Dubowitz and Dubowitz 1981).

This test combines both neurological and behavioral items and was developed to evaluate the preterm and full-term infant, in serial format. The test is divided into four sections, providing information on habituation, posture: passive and active motor activity, reflexes, and interactional behavior. Six reflexes are included on the test and are scored on a 5 point ordinal scale, with 0 for absent and 5 for obligatory.

Neurological Examination of the Full-Term Newborn Infant (Prechtl 1977).

This standardized neurologic test, appropriate for the full-term infant of 38 to 42 weeks GA and the preterm infant to 38 weeks GA, is composed of primitive reflexes. Specific directions for elicitation of the reflexes are present. Scoring criteria are variable for each reflex, and no total score is obtained. Intertester reliability is high (.890-.96).

Primitive Reflex Profile (PRP) (Capute et al 1978b).

This profile consists of scoring eight primitive reflexes: (ATNR, STNR, positive support, TLR-prone, TLR-supine, derotational righting (head and body), Galant, and Moro. These reflexes were chosen because their maximal developmental velocities centered around 6 months of age and thus could be used to predict cerebral palsy prior to 1 year. In addition, the authors stated that these eight reflexes had the greatest predictive value for later motor function. There are specific directions for eliciting each reflex, accompanied with specific scoring criteria of an ordinal nature: 0-4, with 0 being absent and 4 being obligatory. Each reflex is scored separately; there is no composite score for the

502

total profile. Data on standardization and validity are lacking. Minimal interrater reliability is available.

Reflex Profile (Barnes et al 1978).

This test, composed of reflexes and postural reactions, was developed to be used with individuals throughout their life span. Directions for elicitation of each reflex and automatic reaction are provided, and response scores are given as present or absent, with a coding system denoting incipient or obligatory. No standardization, reliability, or validity studies are available.

_____

*See Section II Bibliography for references cited in this section.

Appendix B - Predictive Studies Involving the Presence of Reflex Patterns*

This section may seem tedious to you, but it contains the results of studies designed to determine whether certain activities, or patterns, ,or tests are predictive of later function. This information is vitally important for helping clinicians decide what to use in the evaluation of patients. As with much research, the answers are not completely clear. Some studies support a relationship between a particular observed item and later function, and others may not. The research conditions will vary, as will the approach of the investigators; thus you, the consumer of such information, must make the final judgements as to the relevance of any such study to your own practice.

Early coordinated patterns (primitive reflexes) can be used as early developmental markers, that is, an index of the state or stage of development. The earliest indication of the presence of a significant motor disability may be the delay in the disappearance of an early reflex pattern or the presence of such a coordinated pattern to an abnormal degree. Obligatory early reflexes, or those that control the posture and movement of an infant or child, may signify the presence of a severe motor disability. Such dominant patterns are always considered pathologic, and one might suspect that the child who has such reflexes also has cerebral palsy (Capute 1979; Capute et al 1984). The obligatory responses of the ATNR, STNR, TLR-prone, and TLR-supine should always be a cause for concern. Persistence of obligating reflexes as the child grows is a definite sign of absent motor control (Badell-Ribera 1985). If the normal timetable for the appearance or disappearance of early reflexes is significantly delayed, cerebral palsy is predicted (Paine et al 1964; Stern 1971). Thus changes in the evolution of such reflex patterns may be one of the earliest indicators of motor dysfunction.

It is important to keep in mind that rarely do findings appear as single isolated entities, and if they do, no significant conclusions can usually be drawn from them. Try to keep in mind that these studies are ultimately designed to determine if the presence of findings at a particular early age will predict the diagnosis or status of the child at a later point in time. In some cases, the resarch was done retrospectively, that is, after the diagnosis was made, the subject's files were studied to determine what evidence existed earlier that might have led to the diagnosis being made earlier. Keep these overall goals in mind and do not let the various methods of investigating them confuse you.

Infants with low birth weight have routinely been followed since 1975 in the Neonatal Intensive Care Unit Follow-up Clinic at the University of Washington in Washington state. Generally, as part of their high-risk condition, these infants demonstrated retention of early reflexes, abnormal muscle activity--often referred to as tone--delayed postural reactions, and some delay in development at 4 months. In an early normative study of the Movement Assessment of Infancy (MAI), the high-risk score obtained at 4 months corrected age was compared with the handicapping condition of the infant at 12 months. Of 35 infants originally demonstrating the abnormalities listed, 27 proved to have normal movement at 1 year, and 8 were diagnosed with cerebral palsy. The significant early reflexes present were the TLR in prone and supine, the ATNR, and an exaggerated neonatal positive support. The postural reactions that were not present were trunk rotations (neck-on-body and body-on-body righting reactions) (Chandler et al 1980). Thus, in this study, the presence of certain reflexes would have been predictive for 8 of the 35 infants.

A retrospective study, also conducted at the University of Washington, included 18 infants who had been diagnosed with spastic diplegia at or before 1 year corrected age. These infants were matched with 28 control infants. At 4 months of age, 12 (67%) of the infants who would eventually be identified as having spastic diplegia remained undiagnosed. Of these 12, 6

505

infants were believed to have had some neurologic abnormality but were not diagnosed as having cerebral palsy at this age. The signs present that were signifcant for distinguishing abnormal infants from controls included the persistence of early reflexes (specifically the TLR prone and supine and the exaggerated support reflex), high muscle tension in different postures, and the inability to bring the hands together. None of the matched controls exhibited this triad. The presence of the Moro response and an ankle clonus were not helpful in early identification and did not distinguish infants with spastic diplegia from control infants (Bennett et al1981).

Harris and colleagues, in two studies, examined the predictive validity of the MAI for identifying infants at risk for neuromotor dysfunction in a sample of 246 high-risk infants. High risk infants were defined as those having one or more of the following: 1) low birth weight of less than 1500 g, 2) idiopathic respiratory distress syndrome, 3) history of CNS infection or insult, or 4) other high-risk conditions. In the first study (Harris et al 1984a), the relationship of MAI scores at 4 months to developmental outcome at 1 or 2 years of age was addressed (Harris et al 1984b). In the second study, the relationship of MAI scores at 4 months to developmental outcome at 3 to 8 years of age was examined (Harris 1987).

In the first study, the four sections of the MAI had highly significant correlations with the MAI total-risk scores in early infancy and the 1 and 2 year developmental outcome. The developmental outcome was measured by the Bayley Scales of Infant Development (Tab 1) and by the pediatrician's ratings of motor development, muscle activity or tone, and handicap (Tab 2).

Although the correlations of the MAI scores were significant with the Bayley scales, the strength of the relationships was poor, with the early, or primitive, reflex section being the poorest. The relationship of the MAI to the pediatrician's ratings showed similar results. The authors concluded that as a group, the early reflexes were the least valid of the observations

made for predicting later motor handicaps at 1 or 2 years of age (Harris et al 1984b).

TABLE 1 Pearson Product-Moment Correlations: MAI and Bayley Scales of Infant Development

MAI at 4 months	Bayley Motor Scale		Bayley Mental Scale	
	1 year (N=216)	2 years (N=121)	1 year (N=217)	2 years (N=122)
Total risk score	-0.36[a]	-0.37[a]	-0.42[a]	-0.32[a]
Categorical risk scores				
Tone	-0.23[a]	-0.27[a]	-0.31[a]	-0.21[c]
Primitive reflexes	-0.20[a]	-0.25[a]	-0.31[b]	-0.23[b]
Automatic reactions	-0.33[a]	-0.31[a]	-0.30[a]	-0.30[b]
Volitional movement	-0.42[a]	-0.42[a]	-0.44[a]	-0.31[a]

[a] $P < 0.001$.
[b] $P < 0.001$.
[c] $P < 0.05$.

From Harris et al (1984a), reprinted with permission.

In the second study, which used the same infants as in study one, individual items of the MAI were delineated with respect to which items at 4 months of age were predictive of a later diagnosis of cerebral palsy between 3 and 8 years of age. With respect to early reflexes, those present at 4 months and found to be predictive were TLR supine and prone, spontaneous ATNR, plantar grasp, spontaneous stepping, and Galant's reflex. Those not predictive of cerebral palsy were evoked ATNR, Moro response, palmar grasp, and neonatal positive support. The presence of automatic reactions that were not found to be predictive were the head righting in flexion and the placing of the hands and feet. Head righting in the lateral position, head righting in extension, Landau reaction, rotation of the trunk, and equilibrium reactions prone were found to be significant for the prediction of cerebral palsy when the diagnosis was made between 3 and 8 years of age (Harris 1987).

Dietz et al (1987) followed 77 of the children who had been in the Washington study and compared these children's 4 month evaluation

TABLE 2 Kendall Correlation Coefficients: MAI and Pediatricians' Ratings of Motor Development, Muscle Tone, and Handicapp

MAI Scores at 4 months	Motor Development		Muscle Tone		Degree of Handicapp
	1 year (N=212)	2 years (N=109)	1 year (N=218)	2 years (N=121)	2 years (N=101)
Total risk sccore	0.23[a]	0.36[a]	0.23[a]	0.23[a]	0.32[a]
Categorical risk scores					
Tone	0.22[a]	0.32[a]	0.26[a]	0.24[a]	0.26[a]
Primitive reflexes	0.07	0.22[a]	0.10[c]	0.09	0.20[b]
Automatic reactions	0.24[a]	0.32[a]	0.14[b]	0.21[a]	0.30[a]
Volitional Movement	0.33[a]	0.36[a]	0.26[a]	0.27[a]	0.37[a]

[a] $P < 0.001$.
[b] $P < 0.01$.
[c] $P < 0.05$.

From Harris (1987), reprinted with permission

results with the Peabody Gross Motor Scale and the Frostig Eye-Motor Coordination subtest. The primitive reflex and automatic reaction sections were significantly related, although the relationship was not strong with the Frostig test (Tab 3). No other significant relationships were demonstrated. The authors concluded that the 4 month profile of the MAI is not a good predictor of the motor performance that will occur during the preschool years. One factor that may have influenced the results between these two ages was the presence of transient dystonia, which is an accepted feature of low-birth-weight infants. Because some of the subjects were of low birth weight and may have exhibited the transient dystonia at 4 months, the presence of this finding may have led to the failure to reach significance in the study.

Piper et al (1989) also used the MAI at 4 months of age to demonstrate that preterm infants born at less than 32 weeks GA accrued more risk points in the primitive, or early, reflex section than preterm infants born on or after 32 weeks of age. These same infants did not differ with respect to more risk points acquired on the automatic reaction section. The authors concluded that early reflexes and automatic reactions in the preterm infant may be influenced both by

biological maturation, as might be expected, and by environmental experience that may be present early when the infant is born before 32 weeks.

TABLE 3
Spearman's Correlation Coeffients Between 4-month MAI Scores and Motor Performance at 4.5 Years (N=77)

Test Item	Peabody Gross Motor Scale	Frostig Eye-Motor Coordination Subtest
MAI-total risk	-.12	-.23[a]
Muscle tone	-.01	-.13
Primitive reflexes	-.15	-.25[a]
Automatic reactions	-.12	-.20[a]
Volitional movement	-.09	-.01

[a] $P < .05$.

From Dietz et al (1987), reprinted with permission.

Campbell and Wilhelm (1982; 1985) followed a small sample (15) of extremely high-risk infants from the neonatal period through the first 1 to 3 years of life. Of these infants, 9 were preterm, 5 were full-term, and 1 was a postterm, large for GA infant. At 3 years the following diagnoses

507

had been made: severe cerebral palsy and severe mental retardation (2 children); mild cerebral palsy and mild mental retardation (2 children); mild cerebral palsy (2 children); mild mental retardation (2 children); minor neurologic symptoms and moderate mental retardation (3 children); moderate mental retardation (1 child); normal both neurologically and cognitively (3 children).

These researchers found that the 3 month scores on the motor portion of the Bayley Scales of Infant Development were predictive of later motor outcome at 6 and 9 months and at 1, 2, and 3 years. All correlations were significant. The Brazelton test was administered when these infants were medically stable and taking nourishment orally. The number of abnormal reflexes on the Brazelton test was predictive for motor outcomes at 3 months through 3 years of age. At 3 months of age, the correlation was significant, indicating that the large number of deviant reflexes demonstrated during the newborn period were related to low motor scores at 3 months. After omitting those children with severe cerebral palsy, the correlation at 3 months was only slightly lower but was no longer significant. Apparently, the presence of these reflexes is most predictive when the child has severe problems. The correlations for subsequent time periods were similar.

With these same children, numbers of aberrant reflexes on the Milani-Comparetti test were used to depict the developmental course of the infants at various assessment points, ranging from 3 months to 3 years. At 3 months of age all children ultimately diagnosed as having severe or mild cerebral palsy had a low number of aberrant reflexes. By 6 months, the two children diagnosed as having severe cerebral palsy were clearly deviant, with seven aberrant responses. The children who were later categorized as having mild cerebral palsy had three deviant reflexes at 6 months and four at 9 months; these children at 12 months of age became indistinguishable from children who had no cerebral palsy.

The pattern of development reveals that the children with severe cerebral palsy demonstrated the expected pattern of severely delayed motor milestones and postural reactions; abnormal muscle tone; and retention of primitive, or early, reflexes. Those children with mild cerebral palsy had a few retained early reflexes and an occasional delay in postural reaction development. The authors concluded that at some points in time, the assessment of motor milestones may better delineate poorly functioning infants than reflex assessment alone.

In an earlier study, the reflex performance of the first seven children in the above study was described in detail by Campbell and Wilhelm (1982). At 6 months of age, all the children showed the head righting and the body-on-body righting reactions, with the exception of one infant who was diagnosed as having cerebral palsy. In contrast, the early reflexes were present beyond the usual time of disappearance or integration in many of the infants, even those with normal outcome. The authors concluded that delayed righting reactions may be more predictive of later outcome than the retention of primitive reflexes. However, the presence of persistent obligatory reflex responses may be significant for differentiating children with cerebral palsy from children with either developmental delay or mental retardation.

Relationship of Retained Reflex Patterns to Locomotor Development

Whether reflexes will remain and thus influence later development is questionable. Only through serial evaluation will you be able to obtain a clear understanding of the developmental profile of an infant. A number of researchers have investigated the value of selected clinical signs in children with cerebral palsy, including the relationship of retention of early reflexes to later ambulation (Tab 4).

Bleck (1975) studied locomotor prognosis based on the presence or absence of seven early reflexes in 73 nonambulatory children with diagnoses of cerebral palsy, suspected cerebral palsy, or delayed motor development. These children, aged 10 to 54 months, were examined longitudinally over a period of 15 years. There

TABLE 4	Primitive Reflexes in Cerebral Palsy and Locomotor Prognosis	
Author	Positive Correlation with Nonambulation	No Correlation with Ambulation
Bleck 1975	Asymmetric tonic neck reflex	Foot placement
	Extensor thrust (positive supporting- exaggerated)	proprioceptive placing, lower extremities
	Moro	
	Neck righting (neonatal)	Symmetric tonic neck reflex
	Parachute[a]	
Molnar and Gordon 1976	Asymmetric tonic neck reflex	
	Positive supporting (exaggerated)	
	Moro	
	Symmetric tonic neck reflex	
	Tonic labyrinthine reflex	
	Extensor positioning	
Capute et al 1978b	Asymmetric tonic neck reflex	Derotational neck righting[a]
	Positive supporting (exaggerated)	Galant reflex
	Symetric tonic neck reflex	Moro
	Tonic labyrinthine reflex	
Effgen 1982	Plantar grasp	

[a] Postural reactions.

From Cambell and Wilheim (1985), reprinted with permission.

was a 95% prediction of nonambulation for children over 1 year of age on the basis of reflexes present. The five most frequently appearing prognostic signs were presence of extensor thrust, absent parachute, and persistent asymmetric tonic neck reflex, Moro reaction, and neonatal neck on body righting reaction.

Molnar and Gordon (1976) conducted a longitudinal study to correlate reflex development with later ambulatory status in children with cerebral palsy. A total of 164 children with known cerebral palsy were first seen at or before 12 months of age and were followed from 2.5 to 10 years. At the time of data analysis, 117 children were walking, 47 were not. Six primitive movement patterns were studied in the nonsitters at 12, 18, and 24 months of age. All six were present and obligatory at 12 months of age in 20 out of 21 children who never became ambulatory and in 21 out of 26 children

at 18 months of age. At 24 months, these six primitive reflexes were still present in 26 of 33 children.

Capute et al (1978b) studied seven primitive reflexes in 53 children with cerebral palsy to correlate their presence with functional levels of ambulation. The children ranged in age from 18 months to 21.5 years. Four of the reflexes were positively correlated with nonambulation.

Effgen (1982) investigated the relationship of a persistent plantar grasp, as tested in the standing position, to the presence of independent ambulation. She saw 26 developmentally disabled children initially at a mean age of 6.1 months, and she tested them either monthly until they walked independently or from 3 to 5 years later if independent walking was not achieved. Of the 13 children who did not demonstrate

509

integration of the plantar grasp, 12 failed to achieve ambulation.

With the exception of the Effgen study, a *cluster* of primitive reflexes was important in the prognostication of ambulation or nonambulation in children with cerebral palsy. With this exception, the presence of the tonic reflexes (ATNR, STNR, TLR) and exaggerated positive supporting reactions were the reflexes most predictive of future ambulatory status.

Relationship to Retained Reflexes and Development of Postural Reactions

A number of studies have shown a delayed integration of primitive reflexes and a delayed emergence of postural reactions in children with Down syndrome and those with mental retardation. Molnar (1978; 1979) studied the relationship of four early reflexes and 10 postural reactions with the attainment of motor milestones in 53 infants and young children with mental retardation and delayed motor development. These children were evaluated on two to six occasions, starting at 10 to 23 months of age until 20 to 46 months old. Results indicated that early reflexes were integrated at the expected age, but that the presence of postural reactions was significantly delayed from 5 to 27 months. Once the postural reactions became present, the attainment of related motor milestones appeared within 1 month.

Cowie (1970), in a longitudinal study of 79 infants with Down Syndrome, found a delay in the integration of primitive reflexes and a delayed emergence of righting and equilibrium reactions. Rast and Harris (1985) investigated four postural reactions in 15 infants with Down syndrome and 15 nonimpaired infants between ages 3 months 15 days and 4 months 15 days. The postural reactions studied were the head righting in lateral position, head righting in extension, head righting in flexion, and active use of the hips. There were significant differences between these two groups of infants. The infants with Down syndrome showed difficulty in adjusting their heads in space against the pull of gravity, and they demonstrated less antigravity control of the lower extremities.

In another study, 20 infants with Down syndrome, from 2 to 24 months of age, were compared with 40 nonhandicapped infants, ages 2 to 10 months (Haley 1986*b*). The study showed that infants with Down syndrome had slower development of postural reactions than did the nonhandicapped. In addition, there was less variability in equilibrium reactions in infants with Down syndrome than in nonhandicapped infants, indicating that infants with Down syndrome develop only those postural reactions that were necessary for the attainment of motor milestones.

---

* See Section II Bibliography for references cited in this section.

Index

511

Index

Index

Index

Index

Index

Index